TERRORISM

Documents of International and Local Control

VOLUME 96

TERRORISM

Documents of International and Local Control

VOLUME 96

CYBERTERRORISM: EVOLVING PERCEPTIONS OF THE THREAT

Douglas C. Lovelace Jr., Esquire
Senior National Security Strategist

Oceana®
NEW YORK

OXFORD
UNIVERSITY PRESS

Oxford University Press, Inc., publishes works that further Oxford University's objective of excellence in research, scholarship, and education.

Published by Oxford University Press, Inc.
198 Madison Avenue, New York, New York 10016

Cataloging-in-Publication information is available from the Library of Congress.

ISSN 1062-4007
Terrorism: Documents of International and Local Control

ISBN: 978-0-19-538298-3 (v. 96)

Note to Readers:

This publication is designed to provide accurate and authoritative information in regard to the subject matter covered. It is based upon sources believed to be accurate and reliable and is intended to be current as of the time it was written. It is sold with the understanding that the publisher is not engaged in rendering legal, accounting, or other professional services. If legal advice or other expert assistance is required, the services of a competent professional person should be sought. Also, to confirm that the information has not been affected or changed by recent developments, traditional legal research techniques should be used, including checking primary sources where appropriate.

(Based on the Declaration of Principles jointly adopted by a Committee of the American Bar Association and a Committee of Publishers and Associations.)

TABLE OF CONTENTS

VOLUME 96

CYBERTERRORISM: EVOLVING PERCEPTIONS OF THE THREAT

DOCUMENTS

PREFACE

CYBERTERRORISM

We devote this volume of *Terrorism: Documents of International and Local Control* to an assessment of perceptions of the cyber-terrorist threat to U.S. national security. We note that such perceptions have evolved significantly over the past decade and continue to change, as the passage of time and availability of information prove or disprove beliefs about the vulnerability of U.S. information systems to terrorist attack and the relative severity of the consequences of such attacks. This in-stride assessment is both timely and useful, given how perception of the cyber-terror threat has waxed and waned over the years, the apparent renewed concern over it, and the extraordinary difficulty and expense involved in defending against a genuine and significant cyber-terror threat.

Some analysts postulated a cyber terrorist threat in the 1980s, as astute information technology specialists began discerning the contours of the emerging "information age." The terrorists' attacks of September 11, 2001 made the terrorist threat to the United States palpable for every American. Perceptions of the threat posed by terrorists are multidimensional, and the possibility of cyber-terrorism seemed much more likely in the immediate aftermath of the "9/11 attacks." Although several definitions of cyber-terrorism have been offered, Kevin G. Coleman's is as useful as any. He defines cyber-terrorism as the premeditated use of disruptive activities, or the threat thereof, against computers and/or networks, with the intention to intimidate or cause harm or further social, ideological, religious, political or similar objectives.

The internet and the world-wide web it created are both blessings and curses. They have facilitated the formation of a global community that connects individuals, groups, organizations, functions, systems and ideologies, with unforeseen speed, effectiveness, and consequences. While many positive results have obtained, many dangers also are posed. A sizeable number of national security strategists argue that terrorists have learned to use the internet for nefarious purposes and continue to hone their diabolical cyber-skills. As a result, every node of the internet, ranging from personal computers, to systems that control national infrastructure and major national security systems, to major financial networks are subject to terrorist attack and disruption. Many have argued that that as the internet continues to expand, so will the cyber-terrorist threat, and that it is virtually impossible to defend a system the development of which defies control. They explain the lack of a major cyber-terror attack to date as just luck or because terrorists are waiting until they can deliver a debilitating blow.

There are those, however, who assess the cyber terrorist threat to be exaggerated or overblown, if it even exists in any real sense. They see the postulated threat as being nothing more than that posed by unorganized and uncoordinated hackers who lack a common, much less terroristic purpose, and whose impact is limited and largely negated by effective cyber-defenses. Rather than being cyber-terrorists, those cyber-vandals and cyber-criminals, it is argued, seek self-aggrandizement in terms of prestige, wealth, or both. Although their cyber attacks, ranging from embarrassments, to disruptions, to identity and other thefts increase internet transactions costs and offend private, commercial, and governmental segments of society, they are not considered terroristic in purpose or nature.

One of the first strategists to question the viability of a major cyber-terror threat was Gabriel Weimann. In his 2004 book, *Terror on the Internet*, he assessed the reality of the cyber-terror threat. He concluded that many security strategists, political figures, and the news media have created unwarranted alarm over the danger of cyber-terrorism that could invade and cripple government and private computer systems, including the military, financial, and service sectors. He noted that in spite of all the hype, there has been a conspicuous absence of cyber-terrorism of any consequence, an observation that apparently remains valid today.

Weimann posited that several psychological, political, economic and technological factors combined to exaggerate the threat of cyber-terrorism. He does not dismiss the fact that cyber-attacks could inflict massive damage and have devastating psychological impact, due to widespread media coverage. He notes, however, that successfully mounting such attacks is no easy task because of the protections afforded to federal, state and local government information systems and private commercial systems are relatively well defended, as well. He seals his argument with the fact, as mentioned above, that no large-scale, effective cyber-terror attack has been executed. He makes a familiar caveat, however: that "paradoxically, success in the 'war on terror' is likely to make terrorists turn increasingly to unconventional weapons, such as cyber-terrorism. And as a new, more computer-savvy generation of terrorists comes of age, the danger seems set to increase."

Weimann's assessment apparently represented the view of the national security community circa 2004, since it was at about that point that interest in developing defensive (and some offensive) strategies for countering the threat seemed to wane. Very few strategic assessments of the cyber-terrorist threat were conducted from 2004 to 2007. As we carry Weiman's paradoxical warning forward to today, we encounter renewed concern over the cyber-terrorist threat, but also that many strategists continue to believe the threat is exaggerated. The national security community appears split over the viability of a significant cyber-terror threat perception.

One contemporary argument is that while there is a cyber-terror threat, it should not be exaggerated. Certainly, terrorists could use the internet to damage national security by attacking economic and government communication networks. But mounting such attacks requires comprehensive technical knowledge that is not readily available or quickly and easily acquired. Also, the attacks that have occurred are believed to have been mounted by hackers, have caused some loss of data and economic damage, but have not caused any physical damage. There have been no instances of cyber-terrorists attacking critical infrastructure such as gaining control of the air traffic management system, major electrical grids, dam controls, or any other system the disruption of which could lead to catastrophic damage.

Those who make this minimal threat argument note that failures of portions of the nation's infrastructure occur daily and are dealt with relatively successfully. They argue further that the preventive measures in place that preclude failures significantly protect the systems from cyber-terror attacks. The minimalists argue that the possibility of physical disruption is not the most worrisome use of the internet by terrorists. They worry more about terrorist using the internet to disseminate information, spread propaganda and recruit more terrorists. Physical damage and disruption are more easily and economically achieved the old fashioned way—explosives—than through the internet. The more important cyber-terror threat is use of the internet to plan, facilitate, coordinate, and direct kinetic terror attacks.

On the other side of the debate are the cyber-terror hawks. They point out that the May 2007 cyber-attack against the Estonian government networks and banking systems were examples of how crippling and costly cyber-terror attacks can be, although in that case, the putative terrorist was a major power: Russia. The attack actually was a number of distributed denial of service attacks that forced selected sites to shut down. The results attracted world attention. Most Estonian government ministry networks were rendered inoperable, major banking systems were disrupted, and the ruling government's political party website was exploited for propaganda purposes. The Russian government denied responsibility for the attacks. Interestingly, a Russian nationalist youth group, the Eurasian Youth Movement, claimed responsibility for the October 2007 cyber-attack on the President of Ukraine's website, a political figure opposed by the Russian government.

Over the past four years, the hawks seem to have been gaining the upper hand over the minimalists. As a result, beginning in 2005 and 2006, the U.S. government has shown renewed interest in the cyber-terrorist threat. As a result, greater attention has been directed toward the U.S. Strategic Command, the organization within the U.S. Department of Defense responsible for countering and combating cyber-terrorism. U.S. Strategic Command employs its Joint Task Force-Global Network Operations to defend DoD's Global Information Grid. Additionally, on November 2, 2006, the U.S. Air Force announced the creation of a new major command, the Air Force Cyber Command, to defend America in cyberspace. However, since then, the Air Force has scaled back its organizational innovation, a move some attribute to the firing of the Secretary of the Air Force and its Chief of Staff over an unrelated nuclear surety issue.

International perceptions of the cyber-terror threat also have varied widely. For example, during an international conference at London's Royal United Services Institute in April, an Estonian defense ministry official explained that the 2007 cyber-attacks were mounted by hackers and sophisticated cyber-terrorists who remotely manipulated "zombie computers known as botnets." He went on to say that the world has entered an era of cyber-terror and perhaps even cyber-war. His assertion was challenged by a top British security official who stated cyber-terrorism was a myth. The Director of the United Kingdom's Centre for the Protection of National Infrastructure said there was no evidence to support perceptions of a genuine cyber-terrorist threat. He stated that the most dangerous terrorist threats remained physical in nature.

Nonetheless, in March of this year, the head of head of NATO's Computer Incident Response Capability Co-ordination Centre stated that the cyber-terrorist threat should be viewed with the same alarm as the threat of a missile attack. He went on to say that a well-conducted cyber-attack would be almost impossible to stop. Consequently, he called for nations to increase their abilities to mitigate the effects of cyber-attacks and to improve their abilities to recover from such attacks.

Two months later, the United Nations issued a cyber-terrorist threat warning. It stated that cyber-terrorism could threaten facilities such as nuclear power plants and countering it must be an international effort. Hamadoun Toure, Secretary General of the International Telecommunication Union, the UN's leading information technology agency, stated that "Cybersecurity must become a cornerstone of every aspect of keeping ourselves, our countries and our world safe." Thus, it seems that the international community, consistent with American strategic assessments, has evolved from the minimalist school of thought regarding the threat of cyber-terrorism, to a position in which it perceives the threat to be real and significant.

Given the resurgence in concern over the cyber-terrorist threat, presentation of the documents in this volume is both timely and relevant. We begin with a Congressional Research Service (CRS) report to Congress that helps the reader understand the possible significance of a cyber-terrorist attack by assessing the potential economic consequences. We next present a Government Accountability Office report that assesses technology for cyber-security of U.S. critical infrastructure. As an exemplar of how accessible computer databases could be to cyber-terrorists, we offer a CRS report to Congress that addresses the many compromises of personal data security we have witnessed over the past several years.

Having provided a context for understanding the feasibility, scope, and nature of the cyber-terrorist threat, we complete this volume with a number of up-to-date documents that provide a contemporary assessment of the perceived cyber-terrorist threat. Taken together, the documents show clearly renewed appreciation of the threat and suggest actions the United States must take to counter it. Length constraints preclude an exhaustive presentation of such documents; however, what is provided gives the reader sufficient background, contemporary data, and analysis to gain an informed appreciation of the cyber-terrorist threat.

CYBERTERRORISM: THE CONTEXT

Commentary

By
Douglas C. Lovelace, Jr.

The Economic Impact of Cyber-Attacks

We lead-off this volume with a presentation of one of the serious effects of cyberterrorism. Successful cyberterrorism can levy several costs on the American public ranging from fear and personal insecurity to economic loss. Economic loss is arguably the most significant cost, but it is very difficult to measure, let alone predict. Nonetheless, virtually every successful act of cyberterrorism will have economic consequences. *The Economic Impact of Cyber-Attacks* poses several questions: What are the costs, both historical and potential, of security breaches? How frequently can attacks be expected? Can these factors be quantified precisely, so that organizations can determine the optimal amount to spend on information security and measure the effectiveness of that spending for achieving the desired results? The Congressional Research Service (CRS) report does not actually answer these questions adequately, but it does shed considerable light on them and provide useful context.

The U.S. government's ability to measure the economic cost of a cyber-attack, even after it has occurred, is severely limited, at both the microeconomic and macroeconomic levels. The CRS report correctly observes that there are two fundamental reasons for this shortcoming. First, a comprehensive, valid, and reliable methodology for measuring the economic costs of cyber-attacks has yet to be developed. Second, commercial enterprises victimized by cyber-attacks normally will not make their losses known for fear of revealing vulnerabilities to investors, customers, and competitors. For these two reasons the CRS report accurately assesses that there is a dearth of empirical data on cyber-attack costs. Nevertheless, the report provides two useful analyses: it synthesizes and summarizes the extant, albeit paltry, empirical data while supplementing that limited analysis with observations of theoretical approaches to assessing and estimating the costs.

The report examines the insurance industry's response to rising perceptions of the cyber-terror threat and notes that most insurance companies do not offer insurance against cyber-attacks, neither to commercial entities nor to private individuals. However, the report correctly notes that the reason may not be that the risk is considered too high, but that the risk cannot be quantified adequately to allow for development of actuarial tables. Even if the risk were high, insurance companies could quote a commensurate price, if the underlying data were available. Since it is not, the cyber-attack insurance market has not grown appreciably, even though some companies offer limited and specialized cyber-risk policies.

In explaining that macroeconomic costs of cyber-attacks are equally difficult to determine and predict, the report astutely states that the ability to recover quickly from a cyber-attack is just as important as efforts to prevent such attacks, since the shorter the recovery time the less the economic damages. This is a key point suggested in the preface to this volume. It also comports with one of the basic tenets of counter-terrorism—that a key to defeating terrorism is to deny terrorists the terror they seek to instill; that can be accomplished by mitigating the effects of terrorist attacks.

Unfortunately, the conclusions and recommendations the report draws and makes may not result in actions to reduce the economic impact of cyberterrorism. Any attempt to require commercial enterprises to accurately report losses due to cyber-attacks would certainly meet resistance for the reasons stated above. Even if the government were able to overcome such resistance, satisfying the reporting requirement with useful data may be beyond the capability of many businesses, because of the difficulty in identifying and measuring second and third order effects. The report concludes by accurately pointing out that the situation is not hopeless. It observes that three important market forces will lead to improvements in cyber-attack risk management: competition, liability, and insurance.

Technology Assessment of Cyber-security for Critical Infrastructure Protection

The next document offered to provide context to the cyber-terrorist threat is a Government Accountability Office report entitled *Technology Assessment: Cybersecurity for Critical Infrastructure Protection*. It examines, in some depth, the technologies that may be applied to provide security of the nation's critical infrastructure. Published in 2004, the report is somewhat dated but still provides relevant information and important insights into the extent to which extant and emerging technologies can be applied to secure the nation's critical infrastructure from the threat of cyberterrorism. The assessment is quite appropriately organized around three questions: What are the key cyber-security requirements in each of the critical infrastructure sectors? What cyber-security technologies can be applied? What are the implementation issues associated with using cyber-security technologies for critical infrastructure protection, including policy issues such as privacy and information sharing?

For the sake of brevity, we omit the report's appendixes. The main body of the report presents some eighteen technologies that can be brought to bear to defend against the cyber-terrorist threat. But, the report laments that experts assess that many of the technologies are not being purchased or implemented to realize the full extent of their effectiveness. Of course, the extent to which businesses invest in cyber-security will be a result of cost/benefit analyses. The report introduces but does not provide much detail on several categories of technologies that may be used to thwart or mitigate the effects of cyberterrorism. Some of the technologies are mature while others require further development. The categories include access control technologies, system integrity technologies, cryptography, audit and monitoring tools, and configuration management and assurance technologies.

The report offers a cyber-security framework to assist selection of technologies for protecting critical infrastructure. The framework includes determining the business requirements for security; performing risk assessments; establishing a security policy; implementing a cyber-security solution that includes people, processes, and technologies to mitigate identified security risks; and continuously monitoring and managing security. The report's authors correctly acknowledge that cyber-security investments compete with other investments designed to increase the economic health and profitability of commercial enterprises. As the report puts it, investments in cyber-security must make business sense. The problem is how do businesses determine what makes business sense when they may be unable to assess the potential economic costs of cyber-attacks.

This report's assessment of cyber-security technologies points to the pervasive American predilection for technological solutions for all manner of problems. The report's authors understand this and observe that technology alone is insufficient for meeting the cyber-terrorist challenge. The authors astutely state that cyber-security technologies "do not work in isolation; they must work within an overall security process and be used by trained personnel." Without explicitly saying so, the authors suggest that there must be a cyber-security strategy that identifies objectives and provides resources to enable implementation of strategic concepts designed to achieve cyber-security. Technology will make some strategic concepts feasible and enhance others, but technology itself is not the solution.

The final area of analysis the report provides concerns actions that the federal government can take to promote technological approaches to cyber-security.

They include assisting the owners of critical infrastructure in determining their cyber-security needs, set the example by providing cyber-security for its own systems, and pursue strategic initiatives to promote development of more advanced an effective cyber-security technologies. Since the report's publication in 2004, the federal government has pursued all three tracks and has made significant progress. What is needed now is for the Government Accountability Office or the Congressional Research Service to perform the research and analysis necessary to update this report and point the way forward for the next five to ten years.

Data Security Breaches: Context and Incident Summaries

We complete setting the context for this volume by presenting a Congressional research Service report entitled, *Data Security Breaches: Context and Incident Summaries.* The document provides the reader an appreciation for the vulnerability of U.S. information systems to cyberterrorism. The report correctly notes that personal data security breaches are being reported with increasing regularity. The report's observation that over half the states have considered security breach notice and security freeze legislation is dated. In fact, as of September 18, 2008, at least 44 states, the District of Columbia and Puerto Rico had enacted legislation requiring notification of security breaches involving personal information. While, to date, there is little evidence to suggest cyber-terrorists are responsible for personal security data breaches, they can be assumed to be aware of the vulnerability of personal data systems to hacking and could exploit them for various purposes, to include fund raising.

The report estimates that ten million consumers are affected annually by lost or stolen data at a cost to the economy of $53 billion. The report also estimates that victims spend almost $300 million hours a year trying to clear their names and re-establish good credit ratings. Those data suggest that personal data compromise could become an important objective for cyber-terrorists. However, the report also correctly notes that personal data compromise and subsequent exploitation on a scale that would interest cyber-terrorists would require considerable technical knowhow and resources. The reason there has not been a significant cyber-terrorist attack that compromised and exploited personal information on a large enough scale to inflict terror in businesses and consumers could well be due to unfavorable cost/benefit analyses by cyber-terrorists or simple resource inadequacy.

DOCUMENT NO. 1

THE ECONOMIC IMPACT OF CYBER-ATTACKS

CRS Report
RL32331

April 1, 2004

Brian Cashell, William D. Jackson, Mark Jickling, and Baird Webel
Government and Finance Division

Summary

Information security—the safeguarding of computer systems and the integrity, confidentiality, and availability of the data they contain—has long been recognized as a critical national policy issue. Its importance is growing as the integration of computers into more and more aspects of modern life continues. In addition, cyber-attacks, or breaches of information security, appear to be increasing in frequency, and few are willing to ignore the possibility that the severity of future attacks could be much greater than what has been observed to date.

A central issue, in both public and private sectors, is whether we are devoting enough resources to information security. Part of the answer must come from economic analysis. What are the costs, both historical and potential, of security breaches? How frequently can attacks be expected? Can these factors be quantified precisely, so that organizations can determine the optimal amount to spend on information security and measure the effectiveness of that spending?

No one in the field is satisfied with our present ability to measure the costs and probabilities of cyber-attacks. There are no standard methodologies for cost measurement, and study of the frequency of attacks is hindered by the reluctance of organizations to make public their experiences with security breaches. This report summarizes the limited empirical data on attack costs, and surveys recent theoretical work that seeks to overcome the absence of reliable and comprehensive statistics.

Investigations into the stock price impact of cyber-attacks show that identified target firms suffer losses of 1%–5% in the days after an attack. For the average New York Stock Exchange corporation, price drops of these magnitudes translate into shareholder losses of between $50 million and $200 million.

Several computer security consulting firms produce estimates of total worldwide losses attributable to virus and worm attacks and to hostile digital acts in general. The 2003 loss estimates by these firms range from $13 billion (worms and viruses only) to $226 billion (for all forms of overt attacks). The reliability of these estimates is often challenged; the underlying methodology is basically anecdotal.

The insurance industry's response to rising perceptions of cyber-risk has been twofold. Initially, most companies excluded, and continue to exclude, cyber-attacks from standard business insurance coverage. After this initial exclusion, several insurers then began selling specialized cyber-risk policies. Growth of the market has been slow; lacking the empirical data to construct actuarial tables, insurers are unable to price risk with the degree of confidence they enjoy in traditional insurance lines.

Estimates of the macroeconomic costs of cyber-attacks are speculative. As long as any cyber-attack is limited in scope and short-lived it is likely that macroeconomic consequences will be small. But the ability to recover quickly is important, since the length of time computers are affected is an important determinant of the costs. It may be almost as important for firms to address their abilities to restore operations as to insulate themselves from potential attacks.

This report will not be updated.

The Economic Impact of Cyber-Attacks

The importance of electronic information systems is obvious to all participants in the modern economy. When information fails to circulate, whole sectors of the economy are vulnerable. Finance, wholesale and retail trade, transportation, much of manufacturing, and many service industries would slow to a crawl without computers. Vital public services—utilities, national defense, and medicine—are equally dependent.

Information security—the safeguarding of computer systems and the integrity, confidentiality, and availability of the data they contain—has long been recognized as a critical national policy issue. Two current trends indicate that its importance is growing. First, the integration of computers into more and more aspects of modern life continues. Second, cyber-attacks, or breaches of information security, appear to be increasing in frequency, and few observers are willing to ignore the possibility that future attacks could have much more severe consequences than what has been observed to date.

The core issue, in both public and private sectors, is whether we are devoting enough resources to information security. Part of the answer must come from economic analysis. What are the costs, both historical and potential, of security breaches? How frequently can attacks be expected? Can these factors be quantified precisely, so that business firms and other organizations can determine the optimal amount to spend on information security and measure the effectiveness of that spending?

This report surveys the state of knowledge on the cost of cyber-attacks and the economics of information security. First, we summarize several studies that use stock market capitalization as a measure of the cost of cyber-attacks to victim firms. The studies find substantial short-term drops in the prices of shares of firms following the announcement of an information security breach: between 1% and 5% of market capitalization, with greater losses (up to 15%) recorded by some financial institutions where attackers had gained access to confidential customer records.

Second, we present summaries of the existing empirical data on costs attributable to cyber-crime and computer worms and viruses. What is available is a limited amount of survey data, which is frankly described by its compilers as anecdotal, but is nonetheless widely reported in the press.

Third, we analyze the reasons for the lack of statistical data: firms and organizations have strong incentives to conceal information about cyber-attacks, and there are significant uncertainties and measurement difficulties that limit our ability to specify the dollar amount at risk from information security breaches. Theoretical models that describe the returns to spending on information security shed some light on the size of potential losses, but—in the absence of better statistical data—assigning an overall figure to the cost of cyber-attacks remains highly speculative.

Fourth, we examine the efforts of the insurance industry to develop policies that cover cyber-risk. These initiatives are in their infancy; the chief obstacle has been a lack of data with which to construct actuarial tables on the costs and frequency of attacks.

Finally, we consider cyber-attacks as macroeconomic events.

Appendices to this report include a summary of information risk assessment practices in a Fortune 500 manufacturing company and an overview of efforts by financial institutions and regulators to manage cyber-risk in that industry.

Studies of the Effect of Cyber-Attacks on Stock Prices

Thus far, reported cyber-attacks have been relatively limited in scope, and have not yet been on a scale that would have significant macroeconomic consequences. Individual firms, however, may have suffered significant losses as a result of past attacks. An examination of the effects of those attacks might be illuminating. Most estimates of the cost to companies of cyber-attacks are based on surveys. Survey responses are often expressed in such a wide range as to indicate considerable subjectivity and thus they may be of limited use. There may, however, be a more objective measure of the effect of cyber-attacks on individual firms.

In theory, the price of a company's stock is primarily determined by the present discounted value of the cash flows expected to result from that firm's output. That cash flow is what contributes to the wealth of the stockholders, either in the form of dividends or in the expansion of the firm's stock of productive capital. Any event that changes investors' expectations about that future stream of income is likely to affect the price of the stock.

Four recent studies have examined a number of actual cyber-attacks in an effort to see if any of those attacks could be linked to a change in the stock prices of the affected companies. In some cases, the studies attempted to measure if any stock-price effect depended on the different characteristics of either the firm or the attacks.

It seems at least intuitively obvious that some firms are more exposed to cyber-attacks than are others. It is conceivable that firm size may affect vulnerability to attack, but more to the point some firms are more dependent on computer networks than others to conduct business.[1] Conventional firms, which have been referred to in this context as "brick and mortar" firms, might be expected to be the least vulnerable to cyber-attacks as they are the least dependent on the Internet to conduct business. Some firms, characterized as "click and mortar," conduct business both off-line and over the Internet. These firms face an increased vulnerability because of the risk that the business they conduct via the Internet might be interrupted. Finally, there are firms whose business is conducted almost exclusively over the Internet. These firms would seem to be most at risk.

The extent to which a business is affected might reasonably be expected to depend on the type of attack. Most attacks have fallen into one of two categories. The first is a "denial-of-service" attack (DoS). A DoS attack renders a firm's Internet portal inaccessible and interferes with its ability to conduct on-line business. For the most part, this kind of attack causes no lasting harm. The more serious category of attacks are those that involve the theft or destruction of secure information. This kind of security breach is more likely to have lasting effects on the targeted firm.

[1] This discussion draws on: Huseyin Cavusoglu, Birendra Mishra, and Srinivasan Raghunathan, "The Effect of Internet Security Breach Announcements on Market Value: Capital Market Reactions for Breached Firms and Internet Security Developers," *International Journal of E-Commerce*, forthcoming, p. 57.

Table 1. Potential Financial Consequences of a Cyber-Attack

Type of Firm	Type of Attack	
	DoS	Security Breach
Conventional Brick and Mortar (e.g., Coca-Cola)	Lowest	
Click and Mortar (e.g., Borders)		
Internet Firms (e.g., Amazon, E-bay)		Highest

Other things being equal, the more dependent a firm is on the Internet, and the more intrusive an attack is, the more likely it is that any attack will have significant consequences for the financial health of that firm. Table 1 summarizes these considerations.

It might be expected in a study of the effects of past attacks that a pure Internet company whose network security is breached would suffer more than would a conventional firm that is affected by a DoS attack. But, it might also be presumed that those firms are fully aware of their respective vulnerabilities and so they allocate resources to computer security to differing degrees.

In contrast, firms that provide computer security might be expected to benefit from cyber-attacks (unless their products were publicly blamed for an attack's success). An increase in the apparent vulnerability of computer networks could be expected to raise future earnings of those companies and thus boost their stock price.

Cavusoglu, et. al., examined five specified hypotheses regarding the consequences of cyber-attacks.[2] To do so, they identified 66 distinct security breaches that occurred between 1996 and 2001. Of those 66 events, 34 were availability (DoS) attacks. Of the 66 events, 31 affected firms whose business was conducted almost entirely over the Internet.

First, the study found, using the entire set of observations, that firm value was negatively affected by Internet security breaches. Firms affected by the attack experienced a 2.1% decline in value, relative to unaffected firms.

Second, the authors also found that firms that rely on the Internet for conducting business were more affected than were more conventional firms. Internet firms affected by an attack experienced a 2.8% decline in value relative to the other firms that were studied.

Third, the study found that smaller firms tended to lose more than did larger firms as the result of an attack.

[2] Ibid.

Fourth, the kind of attack seemed to make no significant difference. A DoS attack was not found to be any less costly than an attack where there was a more severe breach in security.

Finally, the authors found that following the announcement of an attack, computer security firms experienced a 1.4% increase in market value, relative to other firms.

Campbell, et al., examined 43 attacks, affecting 38 firms, which occurred between 1995 and 2000.[3] Looking at stock prices over a three-day period centered on the attack, they found that there was a significant, if modest, decline in the market values of affected firms as a result of the attack. The authors separately examined those attacks that did not involve unauthorized access to confidential data and those that did. They found that there was a significantly larger response in the latter type of attack. Those instances accounted for the significance of the overall effects. The stock price reaction to attacks which did not involve unauthorized access to confidential information was insignificant. The study concluded that investors, apparently, do not consider DoS attacks to be important, with respect to the long-run profitability of firms.

Ettredge and Richardson examined the effects of DoS attacks against Internet firms that occurred in February 2002.[4] This study examined the behavior of the stock prices of over 100 Internet-only firms, during a three-day window centered on the day of the DoS attack. Specifically, the authors wanted to know if the costs of an attack were greater for those firms that had a greater dependence on the Internet. They found that, on average, as a result of the February 2002 attack Internet firms lost 5% more in market value than did non-Internet firms, immediately following the attack.

Ettredge and Richardson also looked to see if there were differences among Internet firms. Using sample data describing different firms' own assessment of the risks they face due to conducting "e-commerce," the authors examined if those assessments were correlated with the loss following the February 2002 attack. The authors found that variations in perceived exposure to risk were correlated with variations in the loss of market value. The authors suggest that is evidence investors are able to distinguish among Internet firms based on their vulnerability to a cyber-attack.

---

[3] Katherine Campbell, Lawrence A. Gordon, Martin P. Loeb, and Lei Zhou, "The Economic Cost of Publicly Announced Information Security Breaches: Empirical Evidence From the Stock Market," *Journal of Computer Security*, vol. 11, issue 3, 2003, pp. 431–448.

[4] Michael Ettredge, and Vernon J. Richardson, "Assessing the Risk in E-Commerce," *Proceedings of the 35th Hawaii International Conference on System Sciences—2002*, p. 11.

Garg, et al., studied 22 events that occurred between 1996 and 2002.[5] The authors determined that as a result of those attacks, the affected firms experienced a 2.7% decline in their stock price relative to the overall market on the day following the attack. Three days after the attack the stock prices of the affected firms had dropped 4.5%, relative to the rest of the market.

The attacks were divided into four distinct types: simple web site defacing; DoS; theft of credit card information; and theft of other customer information. In the case of web site defacing, the average loss in stock value was 2% on the second day, which rebounded somewhat to a 1.1% loss on the third day. DoS attacks resulted in a 2.9% drop on the second day, and a 3.6% decline on the third day. For attacks that compromise non-financial information, there was an average drop in stock value of 0.5% on the day of the attack, and a total decline of 1.5% on the third day. Attacks which compromised financial information, chiefly credit card data, caused the largest declines. On the day of the attack, stock prices of affected firms fell a average of 9.3% and by the third day the decline reached 15%. The authors also found that there was a correlation between the number of credit cards that were compromised and the magnitude of the stock price hit.

All the studies found that there was a significant decline in stock prices of affected firms in the days immediately following a cyber-attack. The time frame is necessarily restricted in an effort to isolate the effects of the attack. To extend the time horizon would increase the likelihood that any variation in stock prices was due to other events. Therefore, the studies do not attempt to determine if there is any persistent change in stock prices, or if the drop in stock prices is temporary.[6]

Two of the studies determined that the drop in stock price was related to the type of attack, with DoS attacks generally having a smaller effect than attacks which compromised confidential information. One of the studies found that there was no significant correlation between the kind of attack and the magnitude of the effect on stock prices. The fourth study found that the magnitude of the drop in price of stock was correlated with managers' assessments of the firm's exposure to the risk of cyber-attacks. Table 2 summarizes the findings.

How significant are these percentage drops in dollar terms? At the end of 2003, the average market capitalization (stock price times number of shares outstanding) for a company listed on the New York Stock Exchange (NYSE) was about $4.4 billion; for a company traded on Nasdaq, it was $870 million. A 2% drop in market capitalization is equivalent to an average dollar loss

[5] Ashish Garg, Jeffrey Curtis, and Hilary Halper, "Quantifying the Financial Impact of IT Security Breaches," *Information Management & Computer Security*, vol. 11, no. 2., pp. 74–83.

[6] Neither do any of the studies address differences among firms in how much they spend on computer security.

Table 2. Summary Findings of Stock Market Studies

	Does Attack Cause Drop in Stock Price?	Does Type of Attack Matter?
Cavusoglu, et al.	-2.1% overall	no
Campbell, et al.	significant modest decline	yes
Ettredge & Richardson	-5% (DoS only)	N.A.
Garg, et al.	web site defacing: -1.1% DoS: -3.6% non financial info: -1.5% financial info: -15%	yes

Source: Studies cited in text.

of about $88 million for an NYSE firm and about $17 million for a Nasdaq company.[7]

Survey Data on Cyber-Attack Costs

CSI[8]/FBI Computer Crime and Security Survey

In 2003, the Computer Security Institute (CSI) and the Federal Bureau of Investigation (FBI) published their eighth annual survey on computer crime and security. Computer security practitioners in 530 U.S. corporations, financial institutions, government agencies (federal, state, and local), medical institutions, and universities provided information about their organizations' experience with computer crime over the previous year.[9]

In 2003, 56% of respondents reported some unauthorized use of computer systems within the last 12 months. No such unauthorized use was reported by 29%, and 15% did not know. Figure 1 below shows the 2003 data on the percentage of respondents reporting various types of misuse and attacks, and the expected dollar value of losses by type attack. (Not all respondents provided dollar figures, as is discussed below.)

Figure 1 shows that the types of attacks most frequently reported are not the ones that cause the greatest losses. Theft of proprietary information (reported by 21% of respondents) and denial of service (reported by 42%)

[7] It must be remembered that these are not out-of-pocket losses to the target firms, but paper losses spread over thousands of investors. Market capitalization is simply the stock market's implicit estimate of a company's total value at any point in time.

[8] The Computer Security Institute (CSI) is a membership organization for computer security professionals. CSI's activities include educational and advocacy programs.

[9] The 2003 survey is available online at [http://www.gocsi.com].

Figure 1: Types of Attacks Reported, and the Dollar Value of Related Losses, in the 2003 CSI/FBI Survey

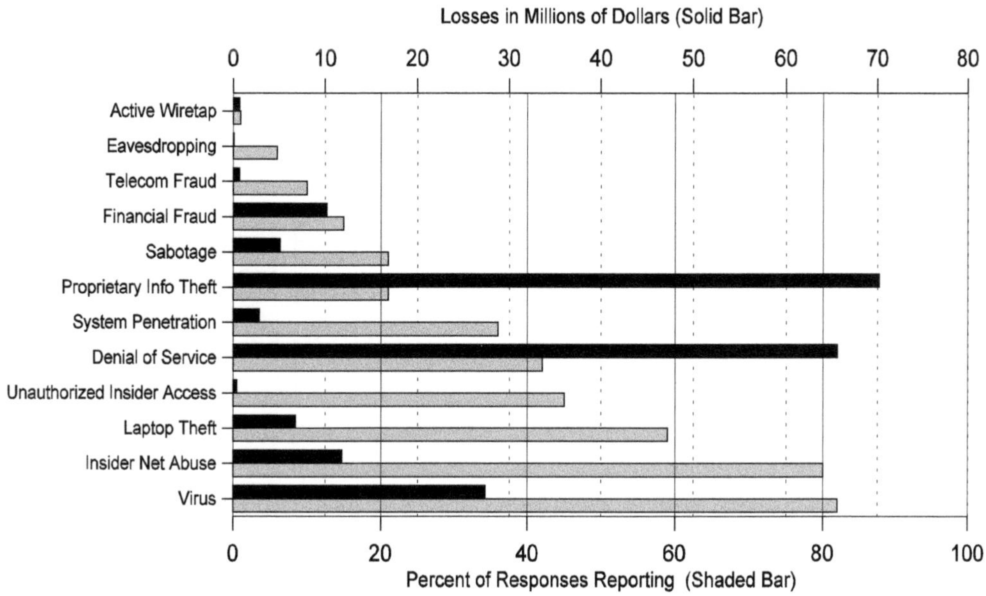

accounted for 67.3% of total reported money losses ($135.8 million out of $201.8 million).

The distribution of losses by type of attack has not been consistent over the years that the survey has been conducted. In the 2000 survey, for example, theft of proprietary information was the most expensive type of attack, as it was in 2003. However, financial fraud accounted for 21.1% of all losses reported in 2000, as opposed to only 5.0% in 2003.[10]

There is no consistent trend in total reported financial losses to computer crime, as Figure 2 shows. It is likely that the results are skewed from year to year by a small number of relatively large loss reports. In addition, the number of respondents varies from year to year.

The survey also presents data on the reported costs of individual attacks, with highest, lowest, and average values, by type of incident. For 2003, the lowest cost reports drop into the hundreds of dollars; the highest values range up to $35 million (theft of proprietary information) and $60 million (denial of service).

Besides the cost and frequency of attack data summarized here, the CSI/FBI surveys include information on incidents related to web sites, computer security practices, and the sources and methods of attacks.

[10] *2003 CSI/FBI Computer Crime and Security Survey*, p. 20.

Figure 2: Cost of Computer Crime As Reported in the CSI/FBI Surveys, 1997–2003

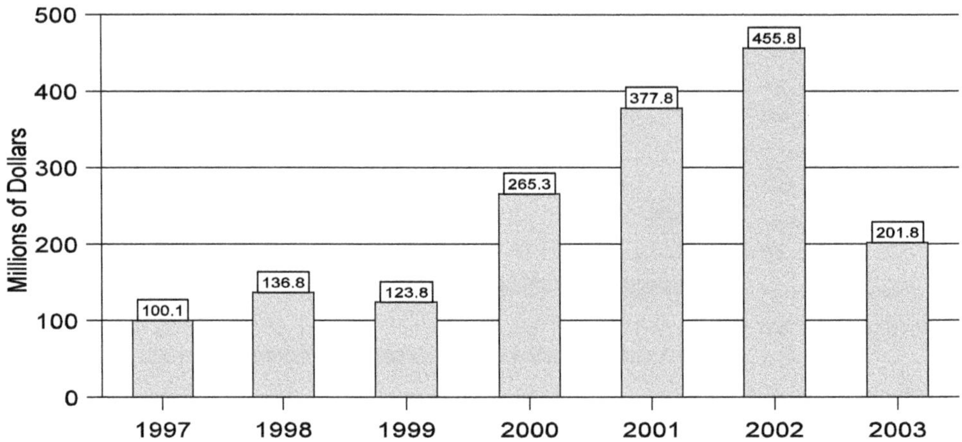

What do the CSI/FBI survey results have to tell us about the overall costs of cyber-attacks in the United States? Unfortunately, not much. The survey's authors do not claim that their respondents are a representative sample of the businesses, organizations, and other entities that are exposed to cyber-risk.[11] Survey recipients are not randomly chosen, but are self-selected from among security professionals. As a result, there is no rigorous, statistically sound method for extrapolating the loss reports of the 530 respondents to the national level.

Secondly, the cost data reported are incomplete even for the sample. As noted above, 15% of respondents to the 2003 survey did not know whether there had been unauthorized use of their systems. More significantly, while 75% of respondents reported financial losses, only 47% could quantify the losses.[12] Thus, the figures in the charts above represent only measurable losses, and substantially understate total losses, though no one can specify the degree of understatement. Furthermore, if less than half of respondents reporting losses can put a dollar figure on those losses, the clear inference is that there is no standard technique for quantifying the amount of loss.

The survey does provide numerical support for a number of propositions that are generally accepted in the computer security literature: that insiders are the source of a substantial percentage of attacks;[13] that many attacks are unreported;[14] and that there is no simple, standardized method for quantifying the costs of cyber-attacks. Although limited as a statistical tool, the

[11] Ibid., p. 18–19.
[12] Ibid., p. 20.
[13] Ibid., p. 7 and 9.
[14] Only 30% of organizations that experienced computer intrusions reported them to the police, and only 21% reported intrusions to legal counsel. Ibid., p. 18.

surveys usefully provide, in the authors' own words, "a series of snapshots of how the people in the trenches viewed their situation at a given time."[15]

Figures on Worldwide Costs of Viruses, Worms, and Other Attacks

The cyber-attack cost figures most often reported in the media come from two computer security consulting firms, Computer Economics Inc. and Mi2g.[16] These firms are not primarily research organizations; their data are not published freely, but are available only to subscribers and clients. The figures presented below are derived from press accounts and from a limited amount of material made available to CRS on a courtesy basis.

Computer Economics Inc.

Computer Economics (CEI), based in Carlsbad, California, has for several years published estimates of the financial costs of malicious code attacks—viruses, worms, and the like. The table below presents CEI estimates for the worldwide costs of major virus attacks between 1995 and 2003.

How does CEI calculate these figures? Its basic data sources, as described in a Cisco Systems study,[17] include the following: data collected from its own clients and other organizations around the world, review of statistical reports and studies, surveys of security practices and spending, and the activity reports of security companies. The firm has developed benchmarks to measure the costs of recovery and cleanup after attacks, lost productivity, and lost revenue from downtime. These benchmarks underpin a model

Table 3. Annual Financial Impact of Major Virus Attacks, 1995–2003

Year	Cost ($ billions)	Year	Cost ($ billions)
1995	0.5	2000	17.1
1996	1.8	2001	13.2
1997	3.3	2002	11.1
1998	6.1	2003	12.5
1999	12.1		

Source: Computer Economics Inc. *Security Issues: Virus Costs Are Rising Again.* September 2003, p. 3. (Note: 2003 figure is an estimate based on January through August data.).

[15] Ibid., p. 20.

[16] For overviews of these companies, see: [http://www.computereconomics.com] and [http://www.mi2g.co.uk], respectively.

[17] *Economic Impact of Network Security Threats*, Cisco Systems, Inc. White Paper, 2002, p. 16.

that permits extrapolation from the data CEI collects to an estimate of the worldwide costs of malicious code attacks.

Mi2g

Mi2g, a British firm, publishes estimates of the costs of worm, virus, and other malicious software (which it calls "malware") attacks. In addition, the firm publishes figures on the incidence and costs of a broader category of cyber-attack, which it calls "overt digital attacks."[18] The number of such attacks reported has gone from near zero in the mid-1990s (4 attacks reported in 1995) to about 200,000 in 2003.[19] Cost estimates for digital attacks, including hacking, malware, and spam, are shown in table 4 below. The estimated costs include business interruption, denial of service, data theft or deletion, loss of sensitive intelligence or intellectual property, loss of reputation, and share price declines.

For the full year 2004, Mi2g has projected that worldwide economic damage from digital attacks will exceed $250 billion.[20] This figure may be out of date: the firm has reported that February 2004 was the most costly month in history, with economic damage estimated at $83 billion.[21]

Table 4. Worldwide Economic Damage Estimates for All Forms of Digital Attacks, 1996–2004

Year	Cost ($ billions)		Year	Cost ($ billions)	
	Lower	Upper		Lower	Upper
1996	0.8	1.0	2001	33	40
1997	1.7	2.9	2002	110	130
1998	3.8	4.7	2003	185	226
1999	19	23	2004	46	56
2000	25	30			

Source: Mi2g, *Frequently Asked Questions: SIPS and EVEDA, v1.00*, updated February 6, 2004. (2004 data are on a "so far" basis.).

[18] Mi2g defines an overt digital attack as one in which a hacker group gains unauthorized access to a computer network and modifies any of its publicly visible components. Overt attacks may include either data attacks, where the confidentiality, authenticity, or integrity of data is violated, or control attacks, where network control or administrative systems are compromised. Overt attacks are those that become public knowledge, as opposed to covert attacks, which are known only to the attacker and the victim.

[19] Mi2g, *SIPS Report*, November 2003, p. 8.

[20] Bien Perez, "Defence Key as Digital Hazards Accelerate," *South China Morning Post*, Jan. 6, 2004, p. 3.

[21] Tim Lemke, "Computer Viruses, Worms Set Costly Internet Record," *Washington Times*, March 1, 2004.

A document on the company's website[22] lists the following sources of data: personal relationships with banks, insurers, and reinsurers; monitoring hacker bulletin boards and hacker activity; and anonymous channels to "black hat" hacker groups. Economic information is collected from a variety of open sources and extrapolated to the global level using a proprietary set of algorithms. These algorithms, like CEI's benchmarks, are the key to the economic cost estimates. Since these models are proprietary, and based in large part on the consulting firms' contacts and experience in the IT security field, outside researchers cannot evaluate the models and their underlying assumptions.

These published figures are characterized as the firms' best estimates. Both firms are vendors of security services. The acceleration of costs since the mid-1990s, as reported by both CEI and Mi2g, is considerably more pronounced than the results of the CSI/FBI survey would suggest. Between 1997 and 2003, attack or crime costs either doubled (according to CSI/FBI data), quadrupled (according to CEI), or went up a hundredfold (Mi2g). Of course, the surveys are not measuring identical sets of phenomena, but the variation suggests how far we are from a standard method of quantification of these costs.

Table 5 below presents cost data for specific worm and virus attacks from both CEI and Mi2g. For some attacks, the estimates are very close; for others, they diverge sharply. The differences may reflect either differences in cost estimation models, or the two firms may define the episodes differently. (For example, one may break out cost figures for a number of separate attacks which the other regards as a single episode and produces a larger, consolidated cost estimate.)

Other IT firms and organizations, including TrendMicro, Jupiter Media Matrix, and Britain's IT Corporate Forum, produce estimates of the cost of virus and other attacks. While they do not publish time series or descriptions of their methodologies, their estimates are likely similarly derived—by extrapolation from a relatively small sample of cases based on their best judgement of how computer users worldwide are affected. Essentially, these estimates constitute anecdotal rather than statistical evidence.

Why Empirical Data Are Scarce

Accurate and statistically comprehensive data on the incidence and costs of cyber-attacks are critical to the analysis of information security. Nevertheless, as a 2002 World Bank study found, "the existing base of information that supports projections about the extent of the electronic

[22] Mi2g, *Frequently Asked Questions: SIPS and EVEDA, v1.00*, updated Mar. 17 2004, see [http://www.mi2g.com/cgi/mi2g/press/faq.pdf] visited Mar. 31, 2004.

Table 5. Estimated Costs of Selected Virus and Worm Attacks, 1999–2003 (in billions of dollars)

Attack	Year	Mi2g	CEI
SoBig	2003	30.91	1.10
Slammer	2003	1.05	1.25
Klez	2002	14.89	0.75
BadTrans	2002	0.68	0.40
Bugbear	2002	2.70	0.50
Nimda	2001	0.68	1.50
Code Red	2001	2.62	2.75
Sir Cam	2001	2.27	1.25
Love Bug	2000	8.75	8.75
Melissa	1999	1.11	1.10

Sources: Mi2g figures: Richard Waters, "When Will They Ever Stop Bugging Us?" *Financial Times*, September 17, 2003, special report, p. 2 (The figures in this table average Mi2g's upper and lower estimates.); CEI figures: Computer Economics Inc. *Security Issues: Virus Costs Are Rising Again*. September 2003, p. 2.

security problem is substantially flawed."[23] If information gathering has the potential to reduce costs and risks, why does the data shortfall persist?

There are two chief obstacles. First, there are strong incentives that discourage the reporting of breaches of information security. Second, organizations are often unable to quantify the risks of cyber-attacks they face, or even to set a dollar value on the cost of attacks that have already taken place. Thus, even if all the confidential and proprietary information that victims have about cyber-attacks were disclosed and collected in a central database, measurement of the economic impact would still be problematical.

Incentives to Not Reveal Information

Comprehensive data on information security breaches are lacking not because the value of such data is not generally recognized. The problem is

[23] Thomas Glaessner, Tom Kellerman, and Valerie McNevin, *Electronic Security: Risk Mitigation in Financial Transactions*, World Bank, June 2002, p. 16.

that organizations have real economic incentives not to reveal such information. The costs of public disclosure may take several forms:

- *Financial market impacts.* The stock and credit markets and bond rating firms may react to security breach announcements. Negative reactions raise the cost of capital to reporting firms. Even firms that are privately held, and not active in public securities markets, may be adversely affected if banks and other lenders judge them to be more risky than previously thought.
- *Reputation or confidence effects.* Negative publicity may damage a reporting firm's reputation or brand, or cause customers to lose confidence. These effects may give commercial rivals a competitive advantage.
- *Litigation concerns.* If an organization reports a security breach, investors, customers, or other stakeholders may use the courts to seek recovery of damages. If the organization has been open in the past about previous incidents, plaintiffs may allege a pattern of negligence.
- *Liability concerns.* Officials of a firm or organization may face sanctions under federal laws such as the Health Insurance Portability and Accountability Act of 1996 (HIPAA), the Gramm-Leach-Bliley Act of 1999 (GLBA), or the Sarbanes-Oxley Act of 2003, which require institutions to meet various standards for safeguarding customer and patient records.
- *Signal to attackers.* A public announcement may alert hackers that an organization's cyber-defenses are weak, and inspire further attacks.
- *Job security.* IT personnel may fear for their jobs after an incident and seek to conceal the breach from senior management.

Any of these disclosure costs can be significant. They may swiftly follow a public announcement and are borne by single firms or individuals within those firms. On the other hand, the presumed benefits of improved disclosure—improved efficacy and cost savings in data security—are likely to be slow to arrive and to be diffused among many firms (including competitors). The imbalance between costs and benefits results in a market failure: individuals and organizations acting rationally in their own self-interest are unwilling to support an activity that would be beneficial to all if undertaken collectively. Gal-Or and Ghose construct a game theory model to show that information sharing would yield direct and indirect benefits to firms and industries and increase social welfare.[24]

[24] Esther Gal-Or and Anindya Ghose, *The Economic Incentives for Sharing Security Information,* Paper presented to the 2nd Annual Workshop on Economics and Information Security, University of Maryland, May 29–30, 2003.

In standard economic theory, a market failure represents an equilibrium state. Market participants following their individual interests will not change behavior that yields suboptimal outcomes unless some outside stimulus is applied. The government has for several years tried to encourage information sharing. In 1998, Information Sharing and Analysis Centers (ISACs) were established in several critical infrastructure industries by executive order.[25] The CSI/FBI surveys represent another public/private initiative. In 2004, the Bureau of Justice Statistics and the Department of Homeland Security are planning a full-scale survey of 36,000 businesses nationwide to map computer attacks, with critical infrastructure as a focus. To date, such programs have had limited success in overcoming what has been called "the tremendous power of suppressive forces [that] prevent information sharing."[26]

The Census Bureau recently completed a pilot test of a computer security survey, and reports that fewer than half of the surveyed companies responded, despite the bureau's strong track record in protecting confidential information. More than three fourths of the companies willing to provide reasons for non-response listed the voluntary nature of the survey as the reason for not filing. Census draws the following conclusion:

> The Bureau of Justice Statistics and the Bureau of the Census are now rethinking their options. It may be possible to redesign the collection instrument in ways that improve response. But, there are serious doubts about the potential success of such efforts without mandatory collection authority. The future of this collection effort is unknown.[27]

Measuring Costs

While organizations may have good reasons not to make public disclosures regarding security breaches, one would expect their incentives to measure the costs of such incidents internally to be strong. Without accurate cost data, how would organizations assess the cyber-risks they face, make rational decisions about how much to spend on information security, or evaluate the effectiveness of security efforts? In fact, there are no standard methods for measuring the costs of cyber-attacks. Attacks produce many kinds of costs, some of which cannot be quantified easily, if at all. As a result, there is a presumed gap in private, internal data that mirrors the absence of public data on cyber-attack costs.

---

[25] Presidential Decision Directive 63.

[26] Kevin Soo Hoo, *How Much Is Enough? A Risk-Management Approach to Computer Security*, Stanford University Consortium for Research on Information Security and Policy (CRISP) Working Paper, June 2000, p. 30.

[27] See:[http://www.census.gov/eos/www/css/css.html], visited Mar. 31, 2004.

The costs associated with cyber-attacks can be divided into direct and indirect costs. Direct costs include the expenses incurred in restoring a computer system to its original, pre-attack state. Recovery from an attack will typically require extra spending on labor and materials; these are the easiest costs to measure. But even at this basic level of cost accounting, complexities may arise. If an attack leads to increased spending on IT security, to what extent are those costs attributable to the attack? If a planned upgrade in hardware or software is accelerated after an attack, should the upgrade be classified as a security cost?

Another set of direct costs arises from business interruption. These costs may include lost revenue and loss of worker productivity during the disruption. Lost revenues may be easily measured by reference to a pre-attack period, but this may not tell the whole story. Lost sales may be a transitory phenomenon, limited to the attack period (and possibly made up afterwards), or they may be long-term, if, for example, some customers switch permanently to competing firms.

Measurement of productivity loss is not always straightforward or uniform. Generally, this is not an added dollar cost: the workers are paid what they would have been paid anyway. Assigning a value to lost time depends on each individual organization's estimates of its own costs related to business opportunities forgone (during the disruption) or diversion of resources (during the recovery effort).

Another direct cost may involve the loss of value in information assets that are stolen, compromised, or otherwise degraded during an attack. Soo Hoo summarizes the difficulties in measurement that may arise here:

> [T]he value of an information asset is highly dependent upon who possesses the information. Sensitive commercial R&D information in the hands of a competitor is significantly more problematic than if it were in the hands of a Netherlands teenager. Time sensitivity can also complicate the valuation problem. For example, a password that expires in ten seconds is worthless after it has expired, but it is quite valuable during the ten seconds that it could be used to gain system access. Add to these difficulties the quantification challenges posed by intangible values, such as reputation, trust, embarrassment, etc., and the task of valuation quickly becomes a highly uncertain and potentially contentious enterprise.[28]

Attacks also have indirect costs, which may continue to accrue after the immediate damage has been repaired. Many indirect costs flow from loss of reputation, or damage to a firm's brand. Customers may defect to competitors, financial markets may raise the firm's cost of capital, insurance costs may rise, and lawsuits may be filed. Some of these cost factors are

[28] Ibid., p. 40.

readily quantifiable, but other aspects of loss of trust or confidence are intangible and difficult to measure.

Some analysts regard these indirect, intangible costs as more significant than direct costs. Cavusoglu, Cavusoglu, and Raghunathan conclude that the inability to measure intangible costs leads many firms to grossly underestimate the costs of security breaches, and that this explains why estimates of incident costs reported in the CSI/FBI survey are much lower than the price of an attack on a major company would be in terms of stock market capitalization.[29]

Indirect costs of cyber-attacks may also include economic harm to individuals and institutions other than the immediate target of an attack. An attack on one firm's computer networks may affect other firms up and down the supply chain. When credit card data is hacked, or an internet service provider goes down, consumers suffer costs. From an accounting perspective, these do not count as costs to the target firm, but from a policy perspective they can be significant. The possibility of cascade effects—disruption spreading from computer to interlinked computer—is well-known, but we are far from being able to quantify the economic impact of an event of this type.

To a profit-seeking business, measurement of costs already incurred is useful primarily to the extent that it facilitates prevention or mitigation of future losses. In the cyber-security field, as elsewhere, risk assessment is primarily a forward-looking activity. It is no less important or necessary because certain costs cannot be quantified. The next section of this report discusses the cost models that firms and organizations use for cyber-risk.

Cyber-Risk Cost Models

It is normal for businesses to make decisions on the basis of incomplete information. In cyber-risk management, these decisions involve the amount to spend on information security and how to allocate that budget. Despite the gaps in data and measurement capabilities, businesses, government, and other organizations have strong incentives—both economic and legal—to develop risk management programs that are as robust as possible.

Early attempts to measure cyber-risk led to the annual loss expectancy (ALE) model, developed in the late-1970s at the National Institute for

[29] Hasan Cavusoglu, Huseyin Cavusoglu, and Srinivasan Raghunathan, "Economics of IT Security Management: Four Improvements to Current Security Practices," unpublished paper, p. 5.

Standards and Technology (NIST).[30] ALE is a dollar figure, produced by multiplying the cost, or impact, of an incident (in dollars) by the frequency (or probability) of that incident. In other words, ALE considers security breaches from two perspectives: how much would such a breach cost, and how likely is it to occur? ALE combines probability and severity of attacks into a single number, which represents the amount a firm actually expects to lose in a given year.

ALE has become a standard unit of measure for talking about the cost of cyber-attacks, but the model is not universally used to assess cyber-risk. The reasons why not are apparent: the ALE model assumes that cost impact and frequency of attack are known variables, when in fact they both resist quantification. The difficulties in cost measurement have been set out above, and similar uncertainties apply to efforts to specify the likelihood of an attack.[31] Attempts to calculate a value for ALE run afoul of "the unrealistic and time-wasting assumption of numerically precise information."[32]

If a precise calculation of amounts at risk is not feasible, what are the alternatives? Numerous methodologies that measure risk qualitatively, rather than quantitatively, are in use. A common practice is to rank information assets according to (a) how valuable they are and (b) how vulnerable they are to attack. The results, which can be displayed in a matrix with high-risk, high-value assets in one corner and low-risk, low-value assets in the opposite corner, may guide a firm's allocation of its IT security spending. Appendix A to this report, an overview of the risk assessment policies of a Fortune 500 manufacturing company, provides an illustration of such a qualitative ranking system.

A comprehensive survey of risk assessment methods is beyond the scope of this report. Worth noting, however, is one theme that emerges from a review of the information security literature: a drive to develop new methodologies that allow for the quantification of risk. Although the data needed to perform traditional business calculations, such as return on investment or cost/benefit analyses of security spending may be unavailable, "the urge to measure is everywhere."[33] The only alternative to developing new and better quantitative methods—expressed in a mordant acronym that

---

[30] For historical accounts of how the ALE and subsequent models evolved, see: Howard E. Glavin, "A Risk Modeling Methodology," *Computer Security Journal*, v. 19, no. 3 (Summer 2003), pp. 1–2; and Soo Hoo, *How Much Is Enough?* pp. 4–12.

[31] The CERT Coordination Center and others publish raw data on the number of attacks, but these figures (which have been growing rapidly in recent years) do not distinguish between major and minor incidents. The data sharing problem discussed above hampers efforts to collect reliable figures on the frequency of attacks in the past, but such figures, even if available, might be of limited use if cyber-attacks are becoming more common, as the CERT data suggest.

[32] Love Ekenberg, Subhash Oberoi, and Istvan Orci, "A Cost Model for Managing Information Security Hazards," *Computers and Security*, v. 14, no. 8 (1995), p. 715.

[33] Dan Geer, "Risk Management Is Still Where the Money Is," *Computer Security*, Dec. 2003, p. 131.

occurs again and again—is said to be FUD, or "fear, uncertainty, and doubt." It has been proposed that IT security can borrow from models in use in other fields, such as industrial quality control, public health reporting, financial market portfolio management, accelerated failure testing in manufacturing, and insurance.[34] It remains to be seen whether avenues like these will lead to better measurement of cyber-risk.

IT Security Spending

For businesses facing cyber-risk, the "bottom line" question is how much to spend on information security. The difficulties in measuring risk set forth above translate into similar uncertainties regarding security spending. Security budgets cannot be justified through the basic financial tests—return on investment (ROI) and cost/benefit analysis—that are applied to most other corporate investments. It is hard to overstate the starkness with which this inability to quantify appears in the information security literature. As one observer stated:

> It's fairly easy to find out how many people die from smoking cigarettes in the United States each year. It's impossible to find out how many hours of computer downtime result from computer virus outbreaks in a year.
>
> It's fairly easy to find out how much physical money is stolen from banks in the United States each year. It's impossible to find out how much money is stolen from banks through electronic attacks.
>
> It's easy to find out how likely you are to be injured in a head-on accident in a particular kind of vehicle in the United States. It's impossible to find out how likely your server is to be taken offline by a virus attack.
>
> It's easy to find out how long a gun safe will resist the attentions of a thief armed with an acetylene torch. It's impossible to find out how long your server will resist the attentions of a thief armed with hacking tools publicly available on the Internet.
>
> A core problem of the information security industry is that, as an industry, we do not have a unit which measures product effectiveness. We are selling something which is intangible and unquantifiable; we are basically selling fashion rather than function.[35]

Of 1,400 organizations surveyed by Ernst & Young in 2003, 59% reported that they rarely or never made an ROI calculation for information security

---

[34] Daniel Geer, Jr., Kevin Soo Hoo, and Andrew Jaquith, "Information Security: Why the Future Belongs to the Quants," *IEEE Security and Privacy*, v.1, July/Aug. 2003, pp. 26–28.

[35] Bob Blakely, "The Measure of Internet Security Is Dollars", Paper presented at the Workshop on Economics and Computer Security, University of California, Berkeley, May 16–17, 2002.

spending.[36] Nevertheless, all organizations must decide how much to spend.

Survey evidence shows that many organizations are spending increasing amounts on IT security. International Data Corp. (IDC) found that nearly 40% of organizations polled in 2003 reported that security spending was growing faster than general IT spending. For very large organizations, the proportion was 51%. Only about 10% reported that IT security spending was growing at a slower rate than IT spending.[37]

Rising security spending suggests that organizations perceive either an increase in risk or that past expenditures were inadequate to manage current risk. Does the level of IT security spending provide clues to the dollar amounts at risk from cyber-attacks?

Given the uncertainties in measuring costs, risks, and the effectiveness of security efforts, we cannot make simple statements like the following: a company that expects to lose *x* dollars per year to cyber-attacks will generally spend *y* dollars to mitigate those losses. Until better empirical cost data become available, such calculations will remain speculative.

However, theoretical models have been developed that attempt to shed some light on the returns to security spending. These models are fairly rudimentary, but as they are refined, or even in their present state, they may help put security spending decisions on a more rational and rigorous basis.[38]

The Smokestack Curve

The first observation from these theoretical models is that there are diminishing returns to security spending. A little spending can bring a substantial reduction in expected losses (ALE). At higher levels of spending, the reduction per dollar spent will be less. At very high levels, the extra amount of loss reduction purchased may be very low, or even approach zero. In graphic terms, this pattern is called a smokestack curve, resembling a plume of smoke rising vertically at first, then flattening out as it cools and drifts away on the wind.

Diminishing returns are observed in many business situations; Moitra and Konda provide evidence for them in security spending. They conduct a simulation of malicious attacks against network systems, and measure survivability—the degree to which a system is able to withstand attack and

[36] Ernst & Young LLP, *Global Information Security Survey 2003*, p. 8. (The survey is available online at: </www.ey.com/global/Content.nsf/International/Press_Release_-_2003_Global_Information_Security_Survey>.

[37] Brian E. Burke, et al., *IDC's Enterprise Security Survey, 2003*, Nov. 2003, p. 14.

[38] Scott Berinato, "Finally, a Real Return on Security Spending," *CIO*, v. 15, Feb. 15, 2002, p. 43.

still function at a certain level—when different levels of defense mechanisms are deployed. Their results show survivability at various levels of security expenditure. They summarize their findings as follows:

> As cost increases, survivability increases rapidly at first, and then more slowly. Such a plot can provide a systems manager with the ability to make an informed decision about the level of defense that is most appropriate for his or her organization since it shows the tradeoff involved between cost and expected survivability.[39]

In Moitra and Konda's analysis, firms' security spending decisions will depend upon how risk averse they are. If a particular security breach will cause intolerable losses, firms may continue to spend on security even when the marginal return is low. Gordon and Loeb[40] introduce the assumption of risk neutrality, which means that the firm is indifferent to investments that have the same expected return, even though the investments may have varying amounts of risk.[41] Under risk neutrality, a profit-maximizing firm would increase spending on IT security as long as the return (in terms of reduction in ALE, or expected loss) exceeded the marginal expenditure. The firm would stop spending when one additional dollar spent on security reduced ALE by less than a dollar.

By assuming risk neutrality, Gordon and Loeb identify an optimum level of security spending, found at the point on the smokestack curve where marginal security spending equals marginal loss reduction. This is shown in figure 3 below. The horizontal axis represents IT security spending (S); the vertical axis shows the amount by which ALE is reduced (L). The dotted line from the origin is a 45 degree line, along which an increase in S produces an equal increase in L. Optimal security spending (S^1) is determined by the point at which the slope of the flattening curve is 1 (where the change in L divided by the change in S equals one), or where the tangent of the curve is parallel to the 45-degree line. This point on the curve is also where the difference between benefits and costs is maximized.

Loeb and Gordon push this analysis further. By making several assumptions about the shape of the cost/loss reduction curve, they reach some numerical conclusions about the optimal level of security spending as a percentage of ALE:

> Our analysis shows that for two broad classes of security breach probability functions, the optimal amount to spend on information security never

[39] Soumyo D. Moitra and Suresh L. Konda, *The Survivability of Network Systems: An Empirical Analysis*, Carnegie Mellon Software Engineering Institute (CMU/SEI-2000-TR-021), Dec. 2000, p. 27.

[40] Lawrence A. Gordon and Martin P. Loeb, *ACM Transactions on Information and System Security*, Nov. 2002, p. 438.

[41] In IT security terms, risk neutrality would mean that the firm did not differentiate between a high-cost, low-probability event and a low-cost, high-risk attack. Clearly, this is a simplifying assumption that will not always hold true in the real world.

Figure 3: Returns to IT Security Spending

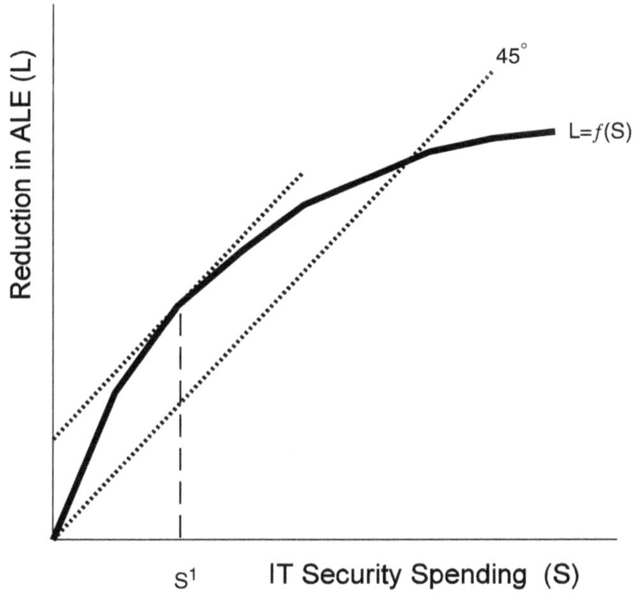

Source: Chart by CRS, based on Gordon and Loeb, "The Economics of Information Security Investment."

> exceeds 37% of the expected loss resulting from a security breach (and is typically much less than that 37%). Hence, the optimal amount to spend on information security would typically be far less than the expected loss from a security breach.[42]

Since Loeb and Gordon's model is theoretical and not based on empirical data, the nature of their assumptions determines their results. Without evaluating the robustness of their assumptions (or the completeness of the mathematical proofs of the propositions that flow from the assumptions), it may be interesting to see what their estimate of optimal IT security spending suggests for the value of ALE.

We can roughly estimate the amount spent on IT security, even though there is no standard definition of what constitutes security spending (as opposed to, for example, normal upgrades of hardware and software), and even though statistics based on direct measurement or reporting are not available. A common rule of thumb is that organizations devote roughly 5% of their total IT spending to IT security.[43] Forrester Research,

[42] Ibid., p. 453.

[43] Evidence for this comes mainly from surveys. See, e.g., George V. Hulme, "Companies Not Spending More on Security, Even With Increased Threats," *CMP TechWeb*, July 28, 2003 (companies spent 5.4% of their IT budget on security in 2003, according to Gartner Associates); Bob Violino, "Survey Report—The Security Team—IT Organizations Are Making Security a Primary Job Function,"

Inc. projects that total IT spending by business and governments in the United States in 2004 will be $743 billion.[44] With these two assumptions, we can estimate that IT security spending by U.S. businesses and governments in 2004 will be about $37 billion.

Gordon and Loeb's model suggests that this figure does not exceed (and is probably considerably less than) 37% of ALE, or the amount organizations expect to lose as a result of cyber-attacks. Thus, a figure of $100 billion represents a lower bound estimate for the annual expected loss in the United States. To the extent that firms spend less than 37% of their expected loss on security, the estimated figure for ALE rises.

Is IT Security Spending Too High or Too Low?

Gordon and Loeb's model estimates an optimal level of security spending. There are arguments, however, that organizations do not now spend an optimal amount on security—that current spending is either too high or too low.

Why would firms spend too much on security? One reason that is cited repeatedly is that some security spending is driven by legal and regulatory, rather than economic, considerations. Over 40% of respondents to IDC's 2003 security survey reported that "compliance with industry regulations" was the most important factor contributing to growth in IT security spending. Only about 25% cited "risk-level concern at executive level" as the most important factor.[45]

Another argument is that since many firms cannot perform a satisfactory return-on-investment calculation for security spending, they adopt a "best practices" approach and simply make the same kind of investments they see other firms making. Critics of this approach claim that the result is a herd mentality, leading to expenditure on security features that may be of little value to the buyer's specific needs. For example:

> Think about why firewalls succeeded in the marketplace. It's not because they're effective; most firewalls are installed so poorly as not to be effective, and there are many more effective security products that have never seen

Network Computing, Sept. 25, 2003 (Secure Enterprise survey finds that 5% is the median security expenditure); Robert D. Austin and Christopher A.R. Darby, "The Myth of Secure Computing," *Harvard Business Review*, June 2003, p. 121 (the average company spends 5% to 10% of its IT budget on security); and Computer Economics Inc., *2003 Information Systems Spending*, p. 11-1 (security software and hardware alone account for 2.8% of total IT budgets).

[44] This figure includes hardware, software, consulting and services, outsourcing, and IT salary and benefits. Tom Pohlmann, et al., "CIOs Still Have Cautious Outlook for 2004 IT Budgets," *Business Technographics Brief Series*, Nov. 7, 2003, Figure 4.

[45] *IDC's Enterprise Security Survey, 2003*, p. 15.

widespread deployment. Firewalls are ubiquitous because auditors started demanding firewalls.[46]

On the other hand, some companies regard existing security products and services as useful and desirable but not affordable. Many executives view security as an underfunded area. "Insufficient budget" was cited as the primary obstacle to effective information security by 56% of respondents to the Ernst & Young survey.[47] Similarly, "lack of resources" was most often named as the biggest challenge to security infrastructure management in the IDC security survey.[48]

Some analysts tend to discount these views: "Individuals who self-select into security professions may be those biased toward greater risk avoidance than are members of the general population, and thus might be prone to overestimate potential losses or willing to authorize greater prevention expenses than actually necessary."[49]

Given the lack of empirical data about cyber-attack costs and the measurement difficulties that have been discussed in this report, it is not surprising that there are different views on the appropriate level of security spending. A single dramatic security breach could produce a significant shift in risk perceptions. Nevertheless, there is no strong reason to think that firms consistently spend too much or not enough: over time, a competitive market ought to punish both those that overspend (and divert resources from more productive uses) and those that spend too little and suffer larger losses as a result. The amount of scarce resources actually allocated to security is a market judgement on the severity of cyber-risk, and it is hard to assume that arguments from theory or abstract principles can improve on that judgement.

Cyber-Attacks and the Insurance Industry

As an industry dedicated to accepting risks that people and businesses want or need to shed, the insurance industry is unsurprisingly interested in the increasing risk of cyber-attack. As these risks became larger and more evident with the growth of the Internet, the insurance industry's reaction was essentially two-fold. The initial reaction was largely to make it clear that existing business insurance did not include coverage of cyber-risks. The premiums charged for existing types of business insurance essentially did not account for the risk from some form of cyber-attack and thus to

46 Bruce Schneier, "Computer Security: It's the Economics, Stupid," Paper presented at the Workshop on Economics and Computer Security, University of California, Berkeley, May 16–17, 2002.

47 *Global Information Security Survey 2003*, p. 9.

48 *IDC's Enterprise Security Survey, 2003*, p. 16.

49 Rebecca T. Mercuri, "Analyzing Security Costs," *Communications of the ACM*, v. 46, June 2003, p. 18.

cover these risks at the existing lower premium rate would have been economically damaging to the insurance company. In general, the reaction of excluding a new risk once it becomes known is quite common in the insurance industry. One can see it, for example, in the reaction to the 9/11 attacks and in the industry's reaction to the increase of homeowners' claims for mold damage, particularly in Texas. In both cases, these risks were presumed to be included in policies when they were low frequency and low cost risks. Once it became clear that they were not such low frequency and low cost risks, insurance contracts began to specifically exclude them.

The second reaction to this new cyber-risk was to introduce specific policies to cover those risks that had been excluded from traditional business insurance coverage. This largely began occurring in 1999 although some coverage was offered as far back as 1997. The market leader in cyber-risk policies, AIG, is estimated to have approximately 70% of the market for cyber-risk insurance with approximately 2,500 policies issued.[50] Other companies writing policies include Chubb, St. Paul, Zurich American, Hartford, and Ace Ltd. The total premium for such policies has been estimated to be between $60 million and $120 million in 2002.[51] These numbers are, however, quite different compared to those found in other types of commercial insurance. For example, general business liability insurance premiums totaled more than $30 billion in 2002,[52] and AIG is able to lead the market for commercial lines with only 9% of the total commercial market in 2002.[53] Estimates for growth in cyber-insurance coverage are substantial, with the Insurance Information Institute seeing $2 billion in premiums by 2007 or 2008,[54] while Conning and Co. projects a 100% annual growth rate and a total premium volume as high as $6 billion by 2006.[55]

The policies offered by the companies in this area vary greatly as to the terms and coverages. There is no standard cyber-insurance policy. Policies can include both first party and third party risks with most companies apparently showing a preference for covering third party risks before covering first party risks. This seems to be due to a faith that the computer systems under a company's direct control are sufficiently secured to prevent direct loss of company data or the like. Risks that can be covered include: network security (damage due to direct attack on a network/transmission of a virus/unauthorized access), web content (copyright infringement/libel or slander claims from material posted on a website), business interruption (lost income due to loss of computer function after

[50] Ron Panko, "Under Separate Cover," *Best's Review*, July 1, 2003, pg. 96-8.
[51] Ibid, p. 95.
[52] Insurance Information Institute, "Fact Book 2004," pp. 73–74
[53] Ibid, p. 71.
[54] See [http://www.iii.org/media/hottopics/insurance/computer], visited Mar. 11, 2004.
[55] See [http://www.conning.com/irpstore/PressReleases/020318.asp], visited Mar. 11, 2004.

an attack), cyber-extortion (settlement of an extortion attempt against a network), and public relations (cost of repairing a company's image after a cyber-attack).

The principal challenge facing the insurance industry in this realm is a lack of data. Insurance pricing rests critically on an understanding of the risks that are being transferred, particularly the frequency of the risk and the possible damages that could result. With enough experience and data, the insurance industry can be extremely accurate in its predictions and very efficient at dealing with risk, even with risks that might be very rare or very damaging. The risks to be covered by cyber-insurance, however, were not only unexpected, but also are to a large degree qualitatively different from what has been seen in the past. This leads to a situation where insurers are writing policies without the type of information that they prefer, particularly when compared to lines like fire or auto where insurers have long historical experience. AIG might estimate, as it has, that computer viruses caused $13 billion in damage in 2001. However, this would only be the beginning of the questions that might need to be answered. What is the likely frequency of such attacks? Is this number a high number or low number compared to what the costs might be in the future? What steps has a particular company taken to mitigate the damage from a future attack and will these steps be successful in doing so? Successfully pricing insurance in the long run demands answers to such questions. The experience that a few years have given the companies is important and the estimates now are more accurate than they were five years ago, but more experience is certainly needed before insurers will as comfortably write cyber-risk polices as they write other lines today.

Macroeconomic Consequences of the Cyber-terror Threat

In order to assess the macroeconomic effects of a cyber-attack on computers it may first be useful to examine how computers contribute to economic activity. It is that contribution that is presumed to be at some risk.

Robert Solow, a major contributor to the theory of economic growth, is often quoted for his remark that the effect of computers can be seen everywhere but in the productivity statistics.[56] Through the 1980s and early 1990s, there seemed to be no big payoff from the growing stock of computers. That presented a puzzle to those who expected significant returns. But it is now believed that computers have had much to do with an acceleration in productivity growth that began in the mid-1990s.

[56] Robert Solow, "We'd Better Watch Out," *New York Times Book Review*, July 12, 1987, p. 36.

Consumers have come to expect a rapid rate of innovation in the manufacture of computers. It is also widely expected that the speed and memory capacity of those computers will continue to improve rapidly. Such a rapid rate of technological advance in the development and manufacture of computers was predicted in 1965 by Gordon E. Moore, one of the co-founders of Intel Corporation.[57] Specifically "Moore's Law" predicted that the number of transistors that could be put on a computer chip would double every 18 months. Whether or not that prediction was a self-fulfilling prophecy may be open to question, but the fact is that the pace of technological advance in the manufacture of computers has vindicated Moore's Law over time.

Because of the rapid innovation in the production of computer chips, the prices of computers, as well as other goods related to information processing and communications, sometimes referred to collectively as information technology (IT), have been falling steadily for some time. Between 1959 and 1995, computer prices fell at an average annual rate of nearly 16.9%, and between 1995 and 2002 prices fell at an annual rate of 20.1%.

These price declines reflect substantial improvements in the quality of computers. The Bureau of Labor Statistics (BLS) has developed a procedure for estimating price indexes for goods whose characteristics are changing rapidly. These are referred to as "hedonic" price indexes. Hedonic price indexes attempt to estimate a statistical relationship between prices and a set of characteristics, such as memory and processor speed.

These price indexes are important to the measurement of productivity, because estimating price change is necessary to estimating change in real output and thus productivity. If the rate of price decline in computers is overestimated, then measures of productivity will be overstated. Most studies estimate that, in the late 1990s, prices for personal computers alone fell at an annual rate of somewhere between 30% and 40%.[58]

Rapid declines in computer prices have, not surprisingly, stimulated a surge in investment. Although there are data back to 1959, production of computers was negligible until the 1980s. Thus, even though real output of IT equipment was increasing rapidly, it did not account for a very large share of total output until recently.

Computers have affected growth in productivity in at least two ways. First, there has been rapid productivity growth in the production of computers which, as computers accounted for an increasing share of total production,

[57] Gordon E. Moore, Cramming more components onto integrated circuits, *Electronics*, Volume 38, Number 8, April 19, 1965. See also the Intel web site: [http://www.intel.com/research/silicon/mooreslaw.htm].

[58] J. Steven Landefeld and Bruce T. Grimm, "A Note on the Impact of Hedonics and Computers on Real GDP," *Survey of Current Business*, Dec. 2000, pp. 17–22.

tended to raise the overall measure of productivity growth. Second, the sharp drop in computer prices has stimulated increased investment in computers, which has contributed to an increase in the overall amount of capital available to the workforce. This is often referred to as "capital deepening." Increases in the capital stock generally tend to raise worker productivity.

In part because of increased spending on IT equipment, the overall rate of investment spending rose significantly in the 1990s. Prior to the recent acceleration in productivity growth, most analyses found that computers yielded little benefit. One reason is that, until recently, computers accounted for a relatively small share of the total capital stock.[59]

But, that view has now changed. Economists are encouraged that the acceleration in productivity growth of the late 1990s may mean that the economy is on a higher growth path and many believe that computers have had a lot to do with it.

Two recent studies found considerable evidence that the computer, or more generally IT equipment, is behind most of the recent acceleration in productivity growth. There is also evidence of a modest "spillover" into other sectors of the economy. In other words, investment in computers can raise the productivity of the workers who use them, but it may also lead firms to change the way they operate leading to further productivity gains.

The first study, by Oliner and Sichel at the Federal Reserve Board, found that of a 0.9 percentage point increase in the growth rate of total factor productivity from the first half of the 1990s to the second half, all could be accounted for by advances in the production of computers themselves and the also by the use of those computers.[60] Table 6 presents a breakdown of Oliner and Sichel's accounting for productivity growth for selected periods since 1974.

Oliner and Sichel found that of an 0.89 percentage point increase in average labor productivity between the early and late 1990s, 0.56 was due to increased investment in IT related capital (an increase from 0.46 to 1.02), and 0.35 was due to increased productivity in the production of IT equipment (an increase from 0.26 to 0.61 in the combined computer and semiconductor sectors). Thus, the contribution of IT equipment to the increase in productivity was greater than the overall increase. Oliner and Sichel also found that labor quality's contribution to productivity growth declined during the 1990s. That is likely related to cyclical factors as the unemployment rate fell and the available pool of skilled workers shrank.

[59] Stephen D. Oliner and Daniel E. Sichel, "Computers and Output Growth Revisited: How Big is the Puzzle?" *Brookings Papers on Economic Activity*, 2:1994, pp. 273–334.

[60] Stephen D. Oliner and Daniel E. Sichel, *Information Technology and Productivity: Where Are We Now and Where Are We Going?* Board of Governors of the Federal Reserve System, May 2002, 78 pp.

Table 6. Contributions to Productivity Growth

	1974–1990 (1)	1991–1995 (2)	1996–2001 (3)	change (3) - (2)
Growth rate of labor productivity	**1.36**	**1.54**	**2.43**	**0.89**
Contributions from:				
Capital Deepening	**0.77**	**0.52**	**1.19**	**0.67**
Information technology capital	0.41	0.46	1.02	0.56
Other capital	0.37	0.06	0.17	0.11
Labor quality	**0.22**	**0.45**	**0.25**	**–0.20**
Multi-factor productivity	**0.37**	**0.58**	**0.99**	**0.41**
Semiconductors	0.08	0.13	0.42	0.29
Computer hardware	0.11	0.13	0.19	0.06
Software	0.04	0.09	0.11	0.02
Communication equipment	0.04	0.06	0.05	–0.01
Other nonfarm business	0.11	0.17	0.23	0.06

Source: Oliner and Sichel, op. cit.

Oliner and Sichel, using an economic model, attempted to assess the implications of recent developments in the technology sector for prospects for continued rapid productivity growth. They conclude that productivity growth is likely to fall somewhere in the range of 2–2¾% over the next 10 years.

A second study, by Jorgenson, Ho, and Stiroh, came to similar conclusions.[61] Table 7 presents the results of their analysis.

According to Jorgenson, Ho, and Stiroh's estimates, of a 0.69 percentage point rise in average labor productivity growth during the 1990s, increased investment (capital deepening) accounted for 0.59 percentage point, and improved productivity in the IT sector itself contributed another 0.20 percentage point of the acceleration.

The evidence suggests that increased productivity in the sector producing IT equipment has had a modest direct effect on total factor productivity. By far the more important factor has been the declining price of IT equipment stimulating a surge in investment and increasing the size of the capital stock.

[61] Dale W. Jorgenson, Mun S. Ho, and Kevin J. Stiroh, *Lessons From the U.S. Growth Resurgence*, paper prepared for the First International Conference on the Economic and Social Implications of Information Technology, held at the U.S. Department of Commerce, Washington, D.C., on Jan. 27–28, 2003, 28 pp.

Table 7. Sources of Productivity Growth

	1959–1973 (1)	1973–1995 (2)	1995–2001 (3)	change (3) - (2)
Growth rate of labor productivity	2.63	1.33	2.02	0.69
Contributions from:				
Capital Deepening	1.13	0.80	1.39	0.59
IT Capital Deepening	0.19	0.37	0.85	0.48
Other Capital Deepening	0.95	0.43	0.54	0.11
Labor Quality	0.33	0.27	0.22	–0.05
Total Factor Productivity	1.16	0.26	0.40	0.14
Information Technology	0.09	0.21	0.41	0.20
Non-information Technology	1.07	0.05	–0.01	–0.06

Source: Jorgenson, Ho, and Stiroh.

Remember that total factor productivity measures changes in output that are not accounted for by changes in economic inputs such as labor and capital. There is no doubt that computers are raising productivity of many firms, but, as long as economic statistics measure them correctly, the increased share of work that computers do will not show up in increased multi-factor productivity because that measure of productivity tracks the increase in output not associated with the increase in investment in computers.[62] It is unclear whether or not computers have had any "spillover" effects on multi-factor productivity beyond their direct contribution to growth in output.

There is some evidence to suggest that those spillover effects—of computers on total factor productivity—are fairly small. In 2000, Jorgenson and Stiroh found that those sectors of the economy that invest most heavily in computers and IT equipment, such as financial services, had among the lowest rates of productivity growth measured.[63]

Jorgenson, Ho, and Stiroh also estimated projections of growth in average labor productivity. They projected in 2003 that productivity growth would

[62] Barry P. Bosworth and Jack E. Triplett, *What's New About the New Economy? IT, Economic Growth and Productivity*, Brookings Institution, December, 2000, 35 pp.

[63] Dale W. Jorgenson and Kevin J. Stiroh, "Raising the Speed Limit: U.S. Economic Growth in the Information Age," *Brookings Papers on Economic Activity*, 2000(1), volume 2, pp. 125–212.

range between 1.14% and 2.38% over the following decade, with a base case of 1.78%, just below the 1995–2001 rate of growth.

In another study, Robert Gordon found that most of the acceleration in labor productivity was attributable to capital deepening and faster productivity growth in the production of computers and IT equipment.[64] Of the roughly 0.2 percentage point increase in total factor productivity, most was accounted for by faster productivity growth in the manufacture of durable goods. That suggests that any spillover effects of computers on the overall economy were limited.

It seems evident that, at least in the recent past, computers and other IT equipment have made a significant contribution to the production of goods and services. But those investments may also have introduced new vulnerabilities. Because many of the computer systems are interconnected they may be subject to attacks designed to interfere with their operations.

In the face of uncertainty about the risk and the potential cost of threats to computer operations and security, firms must allocate some resources to the protection of their computer networks and databases. The result is a one-time reduction in the productivity for those firms. Because of the increased need for computer security, there is an increase in the inputs to the production of goods and services without any corresponding increase in the output of those firms. Productivity is a ratio of the output of a firm to the inputs used in the goods produced by that firm. Any increase in inputs that do not contribute to output will reduce measured productivity. In the case of a one-time increase in the cost of computer security there will be a one-time drop in the level of productivity. Firms may also direct IT employees to spend more time on computer security problems and less time enhancing and developing new customer services. Whether or not the increased need for computer security has any long-term effects on productivity growth may depend on improving productivity in the provision of computer security. Unless there is some increase in risk, or unless firms reassess their perception of the potential threat, much of the effect of increased computer security costs on productivity has already happened.

Estimates of the magnitude of the effect on productivity of the increased cost of computer security are hard to come by. There are estimates, however, of the overall effect on productivity of the increased spending on homeland security following the September 11 terror attacks. Increasing physical security is likely to be more expensive than increasing computer security because much of the provision of physical security is labor intensive. In an analysis published by the New York Federal Reserve Bank,

---

64 Robert J. Gordon, *Technology and Economic Performance in the American Economy*, Working Paper 8771, National Bureau of Economic Research, Feb. 2002, 58 pp.

Hobijn estimated that increased homeland security spending would have only a modest effect on productivity.[65] Hobijn calculated that if homeland security spending were to double, the one-time total drop in the level of productivity would be 1.1%.

If somehow, a cyber-attack were able to disable some or all of the nation's network of computers, what might the macroeconomic effects be? It might help to put things into perspective by examining previous events that have been labeled "disasters," and looking at estimates of the economic costs associated with them.

The Bureau of Economic Analysis (BEA) is the agency responsible for publishing estimates both of national income and also of the capital stock. In order to do that it must also estimate how much of the capital stock is lost due to some catastrophic event above and beyond the depreciation that occurs over the lifetime of any physical asset. Table 8 presents selected BEA estimates of the value of structures and equipment destroyed as the result of various significant events. The value of the loss is expressed as a percentage of gross domestic product (GDP). Also shown is the rate of economic growth in the quarter preceding the event and for the quarter in which the event occurred as well.

It might be unwise to read too much into the differences in economic growth between the quarter prior to and the quarter of the event. However, it may be worth noting that economic growth declined in less than half of the cases shown. It appears that whatever effect these disasters had on the macroeconomy was not significant relative to other factors that influence economic growth.

There is a fundamental difference between a cyber-attack and a conventional physical attack in that a cyber-attack generally disables—rather than destroys—the target of the attack. Because of that difference, direct comparison with previous large-scale disasters may be of limited use. There have been two other events in the recent past that may also serve as bases for comparison. The first was the requirement to upgrade many computers and their software to avoid what was a potentially serious problem related to recognition of the date in the last year of the 20th century. This was generally known as the "Y2K problem." The second recent event was the electrical blackout that affected much of the northeastern United States in August 2003.

The problems associated with Y2K were different from the potential costs of a cyber-attack in that it was known with some degree of certainty that there was a problem and there was a known deadline by which the problem

[65] Bart Hobijn, "What Will Homeland Security Cost?," Federal Reserve Bank of New York *Policy Review*, Nov. 2002, pp. 21–33.

Table 8. Value of Physical Capital Destroyed by Natural Disasters

Event	Location	Year and Quarter	Value as a Percent of GDP	Annual Rate of Change in GDP in:	
				Previous Quarter	Event Quarter
Earthquake	California	1971:I	0.04	–1.9	–0.7
Hurricane Agnes	Middle Atlantic	1972:II	0.55	7.3	9.8
Flood	Mississippi	1973:II	0.16	10.6	4.7
Tornadoes	Alabama, Indiana, Kentucky, Ohio, Tennessee	1974:II	0.05	–3.4	1.2
Flood dam collapse	Idaho	1976:II	0.03	9.3	3.0
Windstorms, flood	Kentucky, Virginia, West Virginia	1977:II	0.07	4.9	8.1
Floods, Tornadoes	Alabama, Mississippi, North Dakota, Arkansas, Texas	1979:II	0.06	0.8	0.4
Hurricanes David and Frederick	Alabama, Mississippi	1979:III	0.10	0.4	2.9
Mudslides	California	1980:I	0.03	1.2	1.3
Riots, Mount St. Helens eruption	Miami (Florida),Oregon, Washington	1980:II	0.04	1.3	–7.8
Hurricane Iwa, Floods	Hawaii, Arkansas, Missouri	1982:IV	0.10	–1.5	0.4
Hurricane Alicia	Texas	1983:III	0.12	9.3	8.1
Hurricanes Elena and Gloria	Atlantic and Gulf Coasts	1985:III	0.08	3.5	6.4
Tropical Storm Juan, Hurricane Kate, Floods	Atlantic and Gulf Coasts	1985:IV	0.08	6.4	3.1
Hurricane Hugo	North and South Carolina	1989:III	0.29	2.6	2.9
Earthquake	Loma Prieta (California)	1989:IV	0.26	2.9	1.0

Event	Location	Year and Quarter	Value as a Percent of GDP	Annual Rate of Change in GDP in:	
				Previous Quarter	Event Quarter
Fire	Oakland (California)	1991:IV	0.10	1.9	1.9
Hurricane Andrew	Florida, Louisiana	1992:III	1.02	3.9	4.0
Hurricane Iniki	Hawaii	1992:III	0.13	3.9	4.0
Winter Storm	24 Eastern States	1993:I	0.12	4.5	0.5
Floods	9 Midwestern States	1993:III	0.13	2.0	2.1
Earthquake	Northridge (California)	1994:I	1.15	5.5	4.1
Hurricane Opal	10 Southern States	1995:IV	0.13	3.3	3.0

Source: Department of Commerce, Bureau of Economic Analysis.

had to be solved. It was similar in the sense that firms had to divert resources in order to fix a problem in the same way that firms must divert resources to protect their computer networks from attack.

There was some uncertainty regarding the possible economic effects of not fixing the Y2K glitch, but because the problem was widely recognized well in advance and there were clear incentives (including regulatory mandates for some) to fix it ahead of time, the year change in fact presented no indication of difficulty.

Total spending, private and public, to upgrade computers and software to avoid the Y2K problem has been estimated at about $100 billion.[66] In some cases, software upgrades that solved the problem might have taken place anyway, since the useful lifetime of software tends to be much shorter than the useful lifetime of most physical assets. There also may have been a slight offsetting boost to productivity because of Y2K preparations. Some software and hardware upgrades that had not been scheduled to take place prior to the date change were sped up along with any addition to productivity they may have contributed.

[66] U.S. Department of Commerce, Economics and Statistics Administration, "The Economics of Y2K and the Impact on the United States," Nov. 1999, 25 pp.

The electrical blackout of August 2003, may also serve as a case for comparison. Estimates of the cost of the blackout range from $6 to $10 billion for the entire U.S. economy.[67] That accounted for 0.1% of GDP. The power failure imposed costs on both households and businesses. Production was disrupted, affecting earnings and profits, food stocks spoiled because of lack of refrigeration, and government costs rose because of the increased demand for police and other emergency services. In some cases production may have simply been delayed in which case losses may not have been permanent; but in other cases businesses may not have been able to make up the loss by shifting production.

The determinants of the cost of the power outage were principally the size of the area affected and the duration of the blackout. Costs may have been less than they otherwise would have been because power was lost late in the afternoon and began to be restored the following morning.

Of all the cases cited, the northeast power failure may be the most relevant to a consideration of the potential costs of a cyber-attack. In the case of the power failure, there was little, if any, destruction of physical capital. The cost of the outage was primarily determined by its size and duration. Those two factors would likely also determine the economic cost of a cyber-attack.[68]

Any estimate of the potential economic cost of a cyber-attack must ultimately be speculative. Computers and other information processing equipment that might be vulnerable to attack make a direct contribution to the production of goods and services. But it is unclear how much other factors of production, both labor and capital, are dependent on computers. It seems within the realm of possibility that the effect of an attack on computers and their networks could have an effect on output much larger than that amount that is accounted for by their direct contribution. Electric power supplies might be affected. Banks might be unable to transfer funds. Electronic payment for goods and services might be interrupted. Market transactions might be limited to whatever currency is in circulation. A significant proportion, if not all, of total production might be interrupted. For all of these things to occur simultaneously would presumably require an extremely sophisticated attack that was completely successful. While the probability of such an event may be extremely low, it still gives a basis for an upper limit to any estimate of the economic damage that might be done.

---

[67] See, for example: Anderson Economic Group, "Northeast Blackout Likely to Reduce US Earnings by $6.4 Billion," Aug. 19, 2003, 8 pp.; The Brattle Group, "Economic Cost of the August 14th 2003 Northeast Power Outage: Preliminary Estimate," Aug. 18, 2003, 4 pp.; ICF Consulting, "The Economic Cost of the Blackout," 3 pp.

[68] This presumes that any data and software have been backed up and stored in such a way that they can not be corrupted, and that they can be restored once the attack has subsided.

If all economic activity were to be temporarily interrupted by a cyber-attack, the only consideration in estimating the cost would be the duration of the event. The share of GDP produced on a given day is about 0.3% of the total for the entire year. Some of the production that might be interrupted is unlikely to be a permanent loss, but would simply be deferred until the effects of the attack dissipated. Since a considerable, if unknown, share of output is not dependent on computers, the final cost would be less than that.

Historically, total annual production of goods and services has averaged roughly one-third of the value of the total stock of physical capital. As of 2001, computer equipment and software accounted for roughly 18% of the total capital stock. If equipment and software are assumed to contribute to output in the same way as other forms of capital, their direct contribution would account for about 18% of total annual production.[69] If that share of output were interrupted for a single day it would amount to about 0.05% of total annual GDP.

As long as any cyber-attack is less than comprehensive and short-lived it is likely that any macroeconomic consequences will be fairly small. But, whatever the scope of the attack, the ability to recover quickly is important, since the length of time computers are affected is an important determinant of the costs. It may be almost as important for firms to address their abilities to restore operations as it is to work to insulate themselves from any potential attack.

Conclusion and Policy Options

This report has described the difficulties that attend the measurement and quantification of cyber-risk. There is no question that our present level of knowledge is below what we would like it to be. By briefly setting out the chief obstacles to progress, and the market forces that are driving efforts to improve cyber-risk management, some conclusions about the avenues available to policy makers can be drawn.

The first major obstacle is the lack of data on the frequency and severity of cyber-attacks. Organizations—particularly private businesses—have strong incentives not to share information about attacks. Several government agencies are planning or conducting survey research on a much greater scale than has been done before; the results, together with other government-sponsored efforts to increase information sharing, may in time lead to significant improvements in our ability to assess cyber-risk. If incentives to conceal information remain strong,[70] however, some form of mandatory

[69] Their indirect contribution is higher to the extent that other sectors, such as communication and transportation, rely upon them. Setting a figure on this indirect contribution is impossible.

[70] And the recent experience of the Bureau of the Census suggests that they do (see p. 14).

reporting regime might be considered. A model could be the public health system, where the benefits of a central data base on cases of certain illnesses outweigh an individual's right to privacy.

The other chief obstacle is the inherent difficulty in measuring costs that may be intangible and subject to innumerable contingencies. Current research focuses on how to improve quantification of risk and costs in the face of this complexity. "[I]t is too hard to solve the fully general security problem. Therefore, we must simplify, we must model."[71] Modeling involves a trade-off: the simpler the model, the easier to use, but if a model is too simple, it may fail to capture cyber-risk in its entirety. On the other hand, if a model is elaborated to take into account more and more possible attack scenarios, it may become so complex that the cost of measurement itself becomes material to the risk management calculation, particularly for small firms and organizations. At the present stage of knowledge, we cannot identify any one best cyber-risk model that all firms and organizations could usefully adopt. There may never be such a one-size-fits-all procedure.

There are three major market forces at work that will lead to improvements in cyber-risk management: competition, liability, and insurance. What might policy do to encourage these forces, or at least not to interfere with them?

Firms that best manage cyber-risk will be rewarded by a competitive market. This simple statement implies that it may be premature for policy makers to attempt to move forward with a general standard for risk management. In addition to the information on security research published in journals and conferences, we can be sure that much of the cutting-edge work in the field is being done out of the public eye, behind the corporate proprietary veil. It may be useful for public and private groups to put forward sets of guidelines and best practices, but only to the extent that these are seen as minimum requirements, not complete and sufficient responses to cyber-risk. Deciding that today's methods are good enough may discourage future research.

The second market force is liability. The prospect of being sued for damages when confidential information is stolen or destroyed is a major incentive for firms to improve information security. It is also, however, a major disincentive for sharing information about cyber-attacks. Some may suggest that limits or caps on liability related to cyber-security breaches would make firms less reluctant to disclose incidents. In theory, lower liability would also reduce the incentive to invest in security, but, in practice, since

[71] Daniel Geer, Jr., "Making Choices to Show ROI," *Secure Business Quarterly*, v.1, 4th quarter 2001, p. 3.

liability is only one of many costs that influence risk management decisions, this effect might be very slight.

Finally, market forces—in the form of profit opportunities—are driving the development of cyber-risk insurance. A thriving insurance market would greatly reduce the costs associated with the inability to quantify risk. With insurance, firms would not have to measure potential risks of cyber-attacks themselves, any more than homeowners have to calculate the exact probability that their houses will burn down. Significant economic efficiencies will be obtained as the risk assessment function is shifted from millions of individual organizations and firms to insurers, who specialize in pricing risk. Growth of cyber-risk insurance is hindered primarily by a lack of reliable actuarial data related to the incidence and costs of information security breaches; enhanced collection of such figures would probably be the most important contribution that policy can make.

Appendix A: An Overview of Cyber-Risk Management in a Fortune 500 Manufacturing Company

Information Protection Management Guidelines

Background

The Information Protection Management Guidelines (IPMG) were developed by a non-profit organization in collaboration with IT managers from all divisions, and approved by the IT Leadership Team in 2001. The IPMG provides standards and guidance for all business units to utilize good information protection practices to ensure the company's confidential and proprietary information, in all of its forms, is protected.

Highlights of the IPMG

Risk-based Approach to Information Security

The IPMG's underlying principle is to require business units to assess the risk to information from the perspective of impact to the company and the likelihood of an attack against that information. The areas of exposure are unauthorized disclosure, modification, and loss of availability of information. By classifying information into risk levels, business units will ensure that cost of protection is justified by the severity and likelihood of exposure.

Risk Levels

The IPMG sets risk levels at four levels:

Level 3	Irreparable Harm to the Company, Very likely target
Level 2	Significant Harm, Possible target
Level 1	Moderate Harm, Unlikely target
Level 0	No Harm, Not a target

Most of the company's information falls into Level 0 and Level 1. Only a small percentage of information falls into the highest risk level of 3.

Information Security Officers (ISOs)

The IPMG requires that business units appoint ISOs to implement the information protection guidelines. Corporate Security provides a training class on information protection, including the methodology for determining risk levels and developing a cost effective Information Protection Plan (IPP). Currently, there are approximately 400 trained ISOs throughout the Company.

Information Protection Control Objectives (Controls Matrix)

The IPMG contains a detailed matrix of approximately 200 information security controls, based on Risk Level, which provides specific guidance to ISOs and IT professionals for proper information protection. These controls are consistent with best practice and internationally recognized information security standards (ISO standard 17799). The controls include detailed standards in areas of password policy, auditing and logging, authentication, confidentiality, network security, third party and remote access, standards for vendors, temps, and consultants, and other relevant areas.

Information Protection Plans

ISOs are responsible for developing IPPs for their business units, and implementation of the applicable controls. Global Security has developed a web based software utility to assist ISOs in plan development, including the automated selection of applicable controls.

Compliance

Corporate Internal Audit (CIT) is responsible for auditing business unit compliance to the IPMG.

CIT and IT Groups

CIT is responsible for providing the technical infrastructure and IT security services to secure the enterprise and assist divisional IT groups in meeting the control objectives. Thus, IT groups are able to select which security services are required to meet the requirements of their IPP.

Appendix B: Cyber-Risk Management in the Financial Services Sector

Recovery modes to mitigate financial market disasters, including such special cases as cyber-attacks, have been developed and tested from within and without the financial providers' networks. Financial responsibility requires the financial institutions so important in supporting and maintaining domestic and international commerce to take steps to safeguard their ability to carry out basic functions. The backbone of the financial economy—the payment system—comes through banks, only two of which form the entire and vital U.S. government securities clearing and settlement market. Other crucial intermediation functions come through a variety of other financial companies, including brokers, exchanges, other secondary market facilities, and insurance companies. Thus, many regulators and trade associations are involved. The combinations of public and private initiatives have largely resulted in qualitative prescriptions to date; no government regulation numerically dictates how much information security spending a financial institution, or indeed any company, must undertake.

Financial institutions, not only banks and other depositories, but also securities dealers, insurers, and investment companies, are collectively considered a critical infrastructure element for the U.S. economy.[72] They also rely heavily on information technology, both making them particularly vulnerable to cyberattack and amplifying the danger from such an attack. Long before 9/11/01, analysts identified financial sector system vulnerabilities as elements of national economic security in the work of the President's Commission on Critical Infrastructure Protection in 1996 and 1997.[73] America has grown far beyond a bank-centered financial economy started with bank notes; financial value has largely become resident on computers as data rather than physical means of payment.

Financial institutions face two categories of emergencies that could impair their functioning. The first is directly financial: danger of a sudden drop in the value of financial assets, whether originating domestically or elsewhere in the world, such that a global financial crisis might follow. The second is operational: failure of physical support structures that underlie the financial system. Either, whether from natural causes or human malice, could disrupt the nation's ability to supply goods and services and alter the behavior of individuals in fear of the disruption (or fear of greater disruption). This could reduce the pace of economic activity, or at an extreme, cause an actual contraction of economic activity. Financial regulators generally address the former set of problems through deposit insurance and other sources of liquidity to distressed institutions, safety and soundness regulation, and direct intervention. They address the latter set of problems through remediation (as with the Y2K problem), redundancy, and other physical security protocols.

Financial firms' regulators, separately and collectively, have issued regulations for redundancy and security in physical systems and financial systems. They have long required banking institutions to consider operating (security) risks such as embezzlement, fire, flood, robbery, etc., to which they have added physical-and cyber-terrorism in specific terms during recent years. Many of the protocols address problems arising from any

[72] See, for example, Homeland Security Presidential Directive 7, issued December 17, 2003, at [http://www.whitehouse.gov/news/releases/2003/12/20031217-5.html], visited Mar. 17, 2003.

[73] "The President's Commission on Critical Infrastructure Protection," on web site [http://www.ciao.gov/resource/commission.html]; and, "Banking and Finance," on web site [http://www.ciao.gov/resource/pccip/ac_bank.pdf], visited Apr. 15, 2003.

kind of computer/electrical shutdown, while others necessarily address only one adversity such as denial-of-service attacks. By necessity, many protocols remain confidential, as both public-sector and private-sector participants realize that concealed defenses, or even the suggestion of such defenses, act to deter cyberattacks.

Regulators, especially the Fed, have set out best practice guidelines. These steps include business information technology protocols, physical security protocols, and plans for continuity of markets and participants considered critical for the nation's transactions. The "Interagency Paper on Sound Practices to Strengthen the Resilience of the U.S. Financial System,"[74] issued by the Fed, the OCC, and the SEC, is aimed at assuring the survivability of financial businesses. Controversies have arisen; e.g., some insurers believe that federal regulators have no authority to require them to take such steps, and some in New York are concerned that the area will lose jobs as facilities are necessarily dispersed. Costs of undertaking security measures also remain of concern. Further governmental and public-private initiatives have sought to strengthen the resiliency of the financial system's computers in view of increasing cyberattacks.

Role of Department of Homeland Security

The Department of Homeland Security (DHS) has jurisdiction over functions previously assigned to many agencies with respect to certain communications, transportation, and computer ("cyber") security. These are essential parts of the physical infrastructure upon which the financial system relies as a user. They are also parts of the electronic infrastructure of information storage, retrieval, and transmission. The heart of financial services is information that providers transform into useful forms, such as account balances at banks, securities price quotations, executions of purchase and sales of financial assets, and payments on contractual obligations such as loans.

Although networks of communication are vital to their work, financial services companies do not generally maintain communications and transportation networks, nor design software or manufacture hardware and carriage devices such as airplanes and trucks. Security of communication thus resides with sectors covered by DHS.[75] Financial institutions and their regulators operate in a different environment than nonfinancial ones: they have been developing appropriate (sometimes different) security protocols within existing frameworks. DHS interacts with the Treasury Department, which has taken the lead role for the overall defense of finance against

---

[74] *Federal Register*, vol. 68, no. 70, April 11, 2003, pp. 17809–17814.

[75] See "Administering the New Department of Homeland Security," on web site [http://www.congress.gov/erp/legissues/html/isdhs2.html], visited April 15, 2003.

cyberattacks. The Treasury has recently reached agreement with DHS to assign an expert in financial services matters from Treasury to Homeland Security. Eventually, experts from other financial regulators will be rotated into that new position.[76]

Safety and Continuity in Recent Experience

Y2K Threat. The widely anticipated Y2K "millennium bug" was a software programming problem that could have caused failures in the infrastructure upon which the system relies. Public and private groups spent much effort to prevent widely feared collapse of financial capabilities on January 1, 2000; they succeeded. Y2K came and went without serious incident in 2000, but the systematic backups and safeguards provided against it proved invaluable when the unthinkable happened the next year.

2001. With the September 2001 destruction of the World Trade Center, both potential problems—financial loss of asset values, and operational interruption—occurred simultaneously.

The financial side of the response worked well, as the Fed provided the necessary liquidity to prevent panic.[77] The SEC issued emergency rules encouraging buying in the stock market once it reopened. Trading recommenced rapidly, as the U.S. Treasury security market opened on September 13, and the equities market was in full operation by September 17.

Physical infrastructure recoveries took a few days of heroic efforts (e.g., running new connections into Manhattan). Off-site record keeping and backup facilities, sharing of working space with displaced competitors, and increasing reliance on electronic tracing and communications systems by institutions outside the attack area allowed for resumption of near-normal operations quickly. Much of the off-site infrastructure and response plans had already been developed in the aftermath of the 1993 bombing at the World Trade Center. Physical and virtual destruction of the heart of the nation's financial markets did not stop their workings for more than a few days. Nonetheless, regulators and industry groups made it known that financial firms would need new contingency plans and stress tests to protect against extreme situations in the future.

Blackout of 2003. It seems emergency response measures helped reduce the financial market damages from the massive Aug. 14 power blackout in the northeastern United States and Canada. The Treasury Department received no reports of major disruptions or losses of financial data, in large

[76] "Treasury Introduces Upgrades Designed To Help Safeguard Financial Service System," *BNA's Banking Report*, Dec. 8, 2003, p. 836.
[77] "Economic Repercussions: Overview," by Gail Makinen. In the CRS *Electronic Briefing Book on Terrorism*, at web site [http://www.congress.gov/brbk/html/ebter110.html], visited April 15, 2003.

part because of steps taken to make systems resilient and redundant. Despite glitches, the major markets, in stocks, options, commodities, futures, and bonds, were soon open. Banks closed affected offices, but otherwise, the banking system stayed open. The Fed's payments and emergency lending to banks systems operated well. Banks borrowed $785 million from the Fed after the blackout, the most since $11.7 billion in the week after Sept. 11, 2001. When it was determined, contrary to initial fears, that terrorists had not caused the blackout the stress on the financial economy was greatly reduced.[78] Such initial fears may have been raised by recent press reports of the increasing frequency and severity of cyberattacks directed against financial institutions. A paging and alert system set up after 9/11 by the Financial Services Roundtable (a group of major financial providers) and its technology arm, called BITS, aided the rebound from the computer shutdown due to the blackout.[79]

[78] "Measures Prompted by Sept. 11 Helped Banks Weather Electrical Outage, Snow Says," *BNA's Banking Report*, August 25, 2003, p. 254; Todd Davenport, "In Brief: Outage Sparked $785M of Fed Lending," *American Banker Online*, Aug. 22, 2003; and Rob Blackwell, "Backup Site Questions, Utility Loan Prospects," *American Banker Online.*, Aug. 18, 2003.

[79] Blackwell, "Backup Site Questions."

DOCUMENT NO. 2

TECHNOLOGY ASSESSMENT: CYBERSECURITY FOR CRITICAL INFRASTRUCTURE PROTECTION

GAO Report
GAO-04-321

May 2004

What GAO Found

Many cybersecurity technologies that can be used to protect critical infrastructures from cyber attack are currently available, while other technologies are still being researched and developed. These technologies, including access control technologies, system integrity technologies, cryptography, audit and monitoring tools, and configuration management and assurance technologies, can help to protect information that is being processed, stored, and transmitted in the networked computer systems that are prevalent in critical infrastructures.

Although many cybersecurity technologies are available, experts feel that these technologies are not being purchased or implemented to the fullest extent. An overall cybersecurity framework can assist in the selection of technologies for CIP. Such a framework can include (1) determining the business requirements for security; (2) performing risk assessments; (3) establishing a security policy; (4) implementing a cybersecurity solution that includes people, processes, and technologies to mitigate identified security risks; and (5) continuously monitoring and managing security. Even with such a framework, other demands often compete with cybersecurity. For instance, investing in cybersecurity technologies often needs to make business sense. It is also important to understand the limitations of some cybersecurity technologies. Cybersecurity technologies do not work in isolation; they must work within an overall security process and be used by trained personnel. Despite the availability of current cybersecurity technologies, there is a demonstrated need for new technologies. Long-term efforts are needed, such as the development of standards, research into cybersecurity vulnerabilities and technological solutions, and the transition of research results into commercially available products.

There are three broad categories of actions that the federal government can undertake to increase the use of cybersecurity technologies. First, it can take steps to help critical infrastructures determine their cybersecurity needs, such as developing a national CIP plan, assisting with risk assessments, and enhancing cybersecurity awareness. Second, the federal government can take actions to protect its own systems, which could lead others to emulate it or could lead to the development and availability of more cybersecurity technology products. Third, it can undertake long-term activities to increase the quality and availability of cybersecurity technologies in the marketplace.

Ultimately, the responsibility for protecting critical infrastructures falls on the critical infrastructure owners. However, the federal government has several options at its disposal to manage and encourage the increased use of cybersecurity technologies, research and develop new cybersecurity technologies, and generally improve the cybersecurity posture of critical infrastructure sectors.

Abbreviations

ABA	American Bankers Association
AMS	Automated Manifest System
ANSI	American National Standards Institute
ASTM	American Society for Testing and Materials
CERT/CC	CERT Coordination Center
CIA	Central Intelligence Agency
CIAO	Critical Infrastructure Assurance Office
CIDX	Chemical Industry Data Exchange
CIP	critical infrastructure protection
CMVP	Cryptographic Module Validation Program
CPU	central processing unit
CVE	Common Vulnerabilities and Exposures
DARPA	Defense Advanced Research Projects Agency
DHCP	Dynamic Host Configuration Protocol
DHS	Department of Homeland Security
DISA	Defense Information Systems Agency
DoD	Department of Defense
ES-ISAC	Electricity Sector Information Sharing and Analysis Center
FAA	Federal Aviation Administration
FBI	Federal Bureau of Investigation
FBIIC	Financial and Banking Information Infrastructure Committee
FDIC	Federal Deposit Insurance Corporation

FIPS	Federal Information Processing Standards
FISMA	Federal Information Security Management Act of 2002
FOIA	Freedom of Information Act
FS-ISAC	Financial Services Information Sharing and Analysis Center
FSSCC	Financial Services Sector Coordinating Council
FTP	File Transfer Protocol
GPS	Global Positioning System
HIPAA	Health Insurance Portability and Accountability Act
HSPD-7	Homeland Security Presidential Directive 7
HTTP	Hyper Text Transfer Protocol
I3P	Institute for Information Infrastructure Protection
IP	Internet Protocol
IAIP	Information Analysis and Infrastructure Protection
IDS	intrusion detection system
IEEE	Institute of Electrical and Electronics Engineers
IPS	intrusion prevention system
ISAC	information sharing and analysis center
ISP	Internet service provider
IT	information technology
LAN	local area network
NAS	National Academy of Sciences
NERC	North American Electric Reliability Council
NFS	Network File System
NIAP	National Information Assurance Partnership
NIPC	National Infrastructure Protection Center
NIST	National Institute of Standards and Technology
NNTP	Network News Transfer Protocol
NSA	National Security Agency
NSF	National Science Foundation
OSTP	Office of Science and Technology Policy
PC	personal computer
PDD 63	Presidential Decision Directive 63
PIN	personal identification number
PKI	public key infrastructure
POP	Post Office Protocol
R&D	research and development
RADIUS	Remote Authentication Dial-In User Service
RAM	random access memory
RFC	Request for Comments
ROM	read-only memory
SCADA	Supervisory Control and Data Acquisition
SDLC	system development life cycle
SEMATECH	Semiconductor Manufacturing Technology
SMTP	Simple Mail Transfer Protocol

SNMP	Simple Network Management Protocol
SSL	secure sockets layer
ST-ISAC	Surface Transportation Information Sharing and Analysis Center
TACACS+	Terminal Access Controller Access System
TCP	Transmission Control Protocol
TCP/IP	Transmission Control Protocol/Internet Protocol
TTIC	Terrorist Threat Integration Center
UDP	User Datagram Protocol
VPN	virtual private network
WAN	wide area network

United States General Accounting Office
Washington, DC 20548

May 28, 2004

Congressional Requesters

Consistent with guidance provided by the Senate's Fiscal Year 2003 Legislative Branch Appropriations Report (Senate Report 107-209), you asked us to conduct a technology assessment on the use of cybersecurity technologies for critical infrastructure protection. This report discusses several current cybersecurity technologies and possible implementations of these technologies for the protection of critical infrastructure against cyber attacks. Potential actions to increase the availability and use of cybersecurity technologies are discussed. Key considerations for the implementation of these actions by infrastructure owners and the federal government are also discussed.

We are sending copies of this report to the Secretary of Homeland Security, the Director of the National Science Foundation, and interested congressional committees. We will provide copies to others on request. In addition, the report is available on GAO's Web site at http://www.gao.gov.

If you have questions concerning this report, please contact Keith Rhodes at (202) 512-6412, Joel Willemssen at (202) 512-6408, or Naba Barkakati, Senior Level Technologist, at (202) 512-4499. We can also be reached by e-mail at rhodesk@gao.gov, willemssenj@gao.gov, and barkakatin@gao.gov, respectively. Major contributors to this report are listed in appendix VI.

Keith A. Rhodes
Chief Technologist
Director, Center for Technology and Engineering

Joel Willemssen
Managing Director
Information Technology

List of Congressional Requesters

The Honorable Susan M. Collins
Chairman
The Honorable Joseph I. Lieberman
Ranking Minority Member
Committee on Governmental Affairs
United States Senate

The Honorable Ernest F. Hollings
Ranking Minority Member
Committee on Commerce, Science, and Transportation
United States Senate

The Honorable Adam H. Putnam
Chairman
Subcommittee on Technology, Information Policy,
Intergovernmental Relations and the Census
Committee on Government Reform
House of Representatives

Technology Assessment Overview

Our nation's critical infrastructures include those assets, systems, and functions vital to our national security, economic need, or national public health and safety. Critical infrastructures encompass a number of sectors, including many basic necessities of our daily lives, such as food, water, public health, emergency services, energy, transportation, information technology and telecommunications, banking and finance, and postal services and shipping. All of these critical infrastructures increasingly rely on computers and networks for their operations. Many of the infrastructures' networks are also connected to the public Internet. While the Internet has been beneficial to both public and private organizations, the critical infrastructures' increasing reliance on networked systems and the Internet has increased the risk of cyber attacks that could harm our nation's infrastructures.

Cybersecurity refers to the defense against attacks on our information technology infrastructure. Cybersecurity is a major concern of both the government and the private sector.[1] Technologies such as firewalls and antivirus software can be deployed to help secure critical infrastructures against cyber

[1] It is important to note that physical security and cybersecurity are interwined and both are necessary to achieve overall security. Physical security typically involves protecting and physical asset—from entire buildings to computer hardware—from physical attacks, whereas cybersecurity usually focuses on protecting software and data from attacks that are electronic in nature and that typically arrive over a data communication link.

attacks in the near term, but additional research can lead to more secure systems. While there are many challenges to improving cybersecurity for critical infrastructures, there are potential actions available to infrastructure owners and the federal government. Since 1997, we have designated information security as a government-wide high-risk issue. In January 2003, we expanded this high-risk issue to emphasize the increased importance of protecting the information systems that support critical infrastructures.[2]

This technology assessment focuses on the use of cybersecurity technologies for critical infrastructure protection (CIP). Consistent with guidance provided by the Senate's Fiscal Year 2003 Legislative Branch Appropriations Report (Senate Report 107-209), we began this assessment in response to a request from the chairman and ranking minority member of the Senate Committee on Governmental Affairs; the ranking minority member of the Senate Committee on Commerce, Science, and Transportation; and the chairman of the Subcommittee on Technology, Information Policy, Intergovernmental Relations and the Census, House Committee on Government Reform. The assessment addresses the following questions:

1. What are the key cybersecurity requirements in each of the critical infrastructure protection sectors?

2. What cybersecurity technologies can be applied to critical infrastructure protection? What technologies are currently deployed or currently available but not yet widely deployed for critical infrastructure protection? What technologies are currently being researched for cybersecurity? Are there any gaps in cybersecurity technology that should be better researched and developed to address critical infrastructure protection?

3. What are the implementation issues associated with using cybersecurity technologies for critical infrastructure protection, including policy issues such as privacy and information sharing?

To answer these questions, we began by reviewing previous studies on cybersecurity and critical infrastructure protection, including those from the National Research Council, the CERT® Coordination Center (CERT/CC), the Institute for Information Infrastructure Protection (I3P), the National Institute of Standards and Technology (NIST), and GAO. We used a data collection instrument to interview representatives of several critical infrastructure sectors, as identified in national strategy documents. We met with officials from the Department of Homeland Security's (DHS) Information Analysis and Infrastructure Protection (IAIP) directorate to discuss their

[2] U.S. General Accounting Office, *High-Risk Series: Protecting Information Systems Supporting the Federal Government and the Nation's Critical Infrastructures*, GAO-03-121 (Washington, D.C.: Jan. 2003). This report highlights our key prior findings and recommendations for federal information security and critical infrastructure protection.

efforts in organizing and coordinating critical infrastructure protection activities. In addition, we met with representatives of the National Science Foundation (NSF), NIST, the National Security Agency (NSA), the Advanced Research and Development Activity, the Infosec Research Council, and DHS's Science and Technology directorate to discuss current and planned federal cybersecurity research efforts. We also met with representatives from two Department of Energy national laboratories, Sandia National Laboratories and Lawrence Livermore National Laboratory, and from Software Engineering Institute's CERT/CC. We interviewed cybersecurity researchers from academic institutions (Carnegie Mellon University, Dartmouth College, and the University of California at Berkeley) and corporate research centers (AT&T Research Laboratories, SRI International, and HP Laboratories). Based on our initial analysis, we prepared a draft assessment outlining the cybersecurity challenges in critical infrastructure protection and actions that could be undertaken by key stakeholders. In October 2003, we convened a meeting, with the assistance of the National Academy of Sciences (NAS), to review the preliminary results of our work. Meeting attendees included representatives from academia, critical infrastructure sectors, and public policy organizations. We incorporated the feedback from the meeting attendees into the draft report. We provided our draft assessment report to DHS and NSF for their review. We also had the draft report reviewed by selected attendees of the meeting that NAS convened for this work, as well as by members of other interested organizations.

We conducted our work from May 2003 to February 2004 in the Washington, D.C., metropolitan area; the San Francisco, California, metropolitan area; Princeton, New Jersey; and Pittsburgh, Pennsylvania. We performed our work in accordance with generally accepted government auditing standards.

Our report describes the cybersecurity requirements of critical infrastructure sectors and their use of information technology. Currently available cybersecurity technologies and standards are organized by control categories. The report then covers cybersecurity implementation issues. We provide some guidance for infrastructure owners on using a risk-based framework to implement current cybersecurity technologies. We also identify specific actions that the federal government could initiate or continue, along with a policy analysis framework that could guide the implementation of these actions. Finally, in appendixes, we provide a summary of federal government's CIP policies and present technical details of current cybersecurity technologies.

Background

Since the early 1990s, increasing computer interconnectivity—most notably growth in the use of the Internet—has revolutionized the way that our government, our nation, and much of the world communicate and conduct business. While the benefits have been enormous, this widespread interconnectivity also poses significant risks to the government's and our nation's computer systems and, more important, to the critical operations and infrastructures they support. The speed and accessibility that create the enormous benefits of the computer age, if not properly controlled, allow unauthorized individuals and organizations to inexpensively eavesdrop on or interfere with these operations from remote locations, for mischievous or malicious purposes including fraud or sabotage.

CIP involves activities that enhance the security of our nation's cyber and physical public and private infrastructures that are critical to national security, national economic security, or national public health and safety. With about 85 percent of the nation's critical infrastructures owned and operated by the private sector, public-private partnership is crucial for successful critical infrastructure protection.

Recent terrorist attacks and threats have further underscored the need to manage and encourage CIP activities. Vulnerabilities are being identified on a more frequent basis, which, if exploited by identified threats, could disrupt or disable several of our nation's critical infrastructures.

Through a number of strategy and policy documents, including the recent Homeland Security Presidential Directive 7 (HSPD-7), the federal government has identified several critical infrastructure sectors (see table 1) and sector-specific agencies that are to work with the sectors to coordinate CIP activities. The critical infrastructure owners are ultimately responsible for addressing their own cybersecurity needs, but several other stakeholders play critical roles in enhancing cybersecurity for CIP. These include organizations representing sectors, such as sector coordinators and information sharing and analysis centers (ISAC), the federal government, and information technology (IT) vendors. Sector coordinators are individuals or organizations that help and encourage the entities within their sector to improve cybersecurity.

Results in Brief

All critical infrastructure owners rely on computers in a networked environment. Although all infrastructure sectors make use of similar computer and networking technologies, specific cybersecurity requirements in each sector depend on many factors, such as the sector's risk assessments, priorities, applicable government regulations, market forces, culture, and the state of its IT infrastructure. These factors, in combination with financial and other factors like costs and benefits, can affect an infrastructure entity's use of IT as well as its deployment of cybersecurity technologies.

Table 1. Critical Infrastructure Sectors Defined in Federal CIP Policy

Sector	Description
Agriculture	Includes supply chains for feed and crop production.
Banking and finance	Consists of commercial banks, insurance companies, mutual funds, government-sponsored enterprises, pension funds, and other financial institutions that carry out transactions, including clearing and settlement.
Chemicals and hazardous materials	Produces more than 70,000 products essential to automobiles, pharmaceuticals, food supply, electronics, water treatment, health, construction, and other necessities.
Defense industrial base	Supplies the military with the means to protect the nation by producing weapons, aircraft, and ships and providing essential services, including information technology and supply and maintenance.
Emergency services	Includes fire, rescue, emergency medical services, and law enforcement organizations.
Energy	Includes electric power and the refining, storage, and distribution of oil and natural gas.
Food	Covers the infrastructures involved in post-harvest handling of the food supply, including processing and retail sales.
Government	Ensures national security and freedom and administers key public functions.
Information technology and telecommunications	Provides information processing systems, processes, and communications systems to meet the needs of businesses and government.
Postal and shipping	Includes the U.S. Postal Service and other carriers that deliver private and commercial letters, packages, and bulk assets.
Public health and healthcare	Consists of health departments, clinics, and hospitals.
Transportation	Includes aviation, ships, rail, pipelines, highways, trucks, buses, and mass transit that are vital to our economy, mobility, and security.
Drinking water and water treatment Systems	Includes about 170,000 public water systems that rely on reservoirs, dams, wells, treatment facilities, pumping stations, and transmission lines.

Source: GAO analysis based on the President's national strategy documents and HSPD-7.

Cybersecurity Technologies

There are a number of cybersecurity technologies that can be used to better protect critical infrastructures from cyber attacks, including access control technologies, system integrity technologies, cryptography, audit and monitoring tools, and configuration management and assurance technologies. In each of these categories, many technologies are currently available, while other technologies are still being researched and developed. Table 2 summarizes some of the common cybersecurity technologies, categorized by the type of security control they help to implement.

Critical infrastructure sectors use all of these types of cybersecurity technologies to protect their systems. However, the level of use of technologies varies across sectors and across entities within sectors.

Table 2. Common Cybersecurity Technologies

Category	Technology	What it Does
Access control		
Boundary protection	Firewalls	Controls access to and from a network or computer.
	Content management	Monitors Web and messaging applications for inappropriate content, including spam, banned file types, and proprietary information.
Authentication	Biometrics	Uses human characteristics, such as fingerprints, irises, and voices to establish the identity of the user.
	Smart tokens	Establish identity of users through an integrated circuit chip in a portable device such as a smart card or time synchronized token.
Authorization	User rights and privileges	Allow or prevent access to data and systems and actions of users based on the established policies of an organization.
System integrity	Antivirus software	Provides protection against malicious code, such as viruses, worms, and Trojan horses.
	Integrity checkers	Monitor alterations to files on a system that are considered critical to the organization.
Cryptography	Digital signatures and certificates	Uses public key cryptography to provide (1) assurance that both the sender and the recipient of a message or transaction will be uniquely identified, (2) assurance that the data have not been accidentally or deliberately altered, and (3) verifiable proof of the integrity and origin of the data.

Category	Technology	What it Does
	Virtual private networks	Allow organizations or individuals in two or more physical locations to establish network connections over a shared or public network, such as the Internet, with functionality that is similar to that of a private network using cryptography.
Audit and monitoring	Intrusion detection systems	Detect inappropriate, incorrect, or anomalous activity on a network or computer system.
	Intrusion prevention systems	Build on intrusion detection systems to detect attacks on a network and take action to prevent them from being successful.
	Security event correlation tools	Monitor and document actions on network devices and analyze the actions to determine if an attack is ongoing or has occurred. Enable an organization to determine if ongoing system activities are operating according to its security policy.
	Computer forensics tools	Identify, preserve, extract, and document computer-based evidence.
Configuration management and assurance	Policy enforcement Applications	Enable system administrators to engage in centralized monitoring and enforcement of an organization's security policies.
	Network management	Allow for the control and monitoring of networks, including management of faults, configurations, performance, and security.
	Continuity of operations tools	Provide a complete backup infrastructure to maintain availability in the event of an emergency or during planned maintenance.
	Scanners	Analyze computers or networks for security vulnerabilities.
	Patch management	Acquires, tests, and applies multiple patches to one or more computer systems.

Source: GAO analysis.

Cybersecurity Research

Despite the availability of current cybersecurity technologies, there is a demonstrated need for new technologies. Long-term efforts are needed, such as the development of standards, research into cybersecurity vulnerabilities and technological solutions for these problems, and the transition of research results into commercially available products.

While several standards exist for cybersecurity technology in the areas of protocol security, product-level security, and operational guidelines, there is still a need to develop standards that could help guide the use of cybersecurity technologies and processes. There are several research areas being pursued by the federal government, academia, and the private sector to develop new or better cybersecurity technologies. We have identified some of the important cybersecurity research needs shown in table 3.

In addition to the need for cybersecurity research that addresses existing cybersecurity threats, there is a need for long-term research that anticipates the dramatic growth in the use of computing and networks in the coming years. Some of the possible long-term research areas include tools for ensuring privacy, embedding fault-tolerance in systems, self-managing and self-healing systems, and re-architecting the Internet. Prior information technology developments have shown that more than 10 years are often required to develop basic research concepts into commercially available products.

Cybersecurity Framework

The use of an overall cybersecurity framework can assist in the selection of technologies to protect critical infrastructure against cyber attacks.

Table 3. Cybersecurity Research That Needs Continuing Attention

Research Area	Description
Composing secure systems from insecure components	Building complex heterogeneous systems that maintain security while recovering from failures
Security for network embedded systems	Detect, understand, and respond to anomalies in large, distributed control networks that are prevalent in electricity, oil and natural gas, and water sectors.
Security metrics and evaluation	Metrics that express the costs, benefits, and impacts of security controls from multiple perspectives—economic, organizational, technical, and risk
Socioeconomic impact of security	Legal, policy, and economic implications of cybersecurity technologies and their possible uses, structure and dynamics of the cybersecurity marketplace, role of standards and best practices, implications of policies intended to direct responses to cyber attacks.
Vulnerability identification and analysis	Techniques and tools to analyze code, devices, and systems in dynamic and large-scale environments
Wireless security	Device- and protocol-level wireless security, monitoring wireless networks, and responding to distributed denial-of-service attacks in wireless networks

Source: GAO analysis.

An overall cybersecurity framework includes:

(1) determining the business requirements for security;

(2) performing risk assessments;

(3) establishing a security policy;

(4) implementing a cybersecurity solution that includes people, process, and technology to mitigate identified security risks; and

(5) continuously monitoring and managing security.

Risk assessments, which are central to this framework, help organizations to determine which assets are most at risk and to identify countermeasures to mitigate those risks. Risk assessment is based on a consideration of threats and vulnerabilities that could be exploited to inflict damage.

Even with such a framework, there often are competing demands for cybersecurity investments. For example, for some companies or infrastructures, mitigating physical risks may be more important than mitigating cyber risks. Further, investing in cybersecurity technologies needs to make business sense. For some critical infrastructure owners, national security and law enforcement needs do not always outweigh the business needs of the entity. Without legal requirements for cybersecurity, security officers often need to justify cybersecurity investments using either strategic or financial measures. Further, critical infrastructures and their component entities are often dependent on systems and business functions that are beyond their control, such as other critical infrastructures and federal and third-party systems.

Several of the currently available cybersecurity technologies could, if used properly, improve the cybersecurity posture of critical infrastructures. It is important to bear in mind the limitations of some cybersecurity technologies and to be aware that their capabilities should not be overstated. Technologies do not work in isolation. Cybersecurity solutions make use of people, process, and technology. Cybersecurity technology must work within an overall security process and be used by trained personnel. In our prior reviews of federal computer systems, we found numerous instances of cybersecurity technology being poorly implemented, which reduced the effectiveness of the technology to protect systems from attack. Best practices and guidelines are available from organizations such as NIST to assist infrastructure owners in selecting and implementing cybersecurity technologies. To increase the use of currently available cybersecurity technologies, various efforts can be undertaken. These efforts could include improving the cybersecurity awareness of computer users and administrators, considering security when developing systems, and enhancing information sharing mechanisms between the federal government and critical infrastructure sectors, state and local government, and the public.

Federal Government Actions to Improve Cybersecurity of Critical Infrastructures

Because about 85 percent of the nation's critical infrastructure is owned by the private sector, the federal government cannot by itself protect the critical infrastructures. There are three broad categories of actions that the federal government can undertake to increase the usage of cybersecurity technologies. First, the federal government can take steps to help critical infrastructures determine their cybersecurity needs, and hence their needs for cybersecurity technology. These actions include developing a national CIP plan, assisting infrastructure sectors with risk assessments, providing threat and vulnerability information to sector entities, enhancing information sharing by critical infrastructures, and promoting cybersecurity awareness. These activities can help infrastructure entities determine their needs for cybersecurity technology. This information can help the federal government to prioritize its actions and to assess the need to take further action to encourage the use of cybersecurity technology by critical infrastructure entities. Because the security needs of critical infrastructure could differ from the commercial enterprise needs of infrastructure entities, the federal government could assess the needs for grants, tax incentives, regulations, or other public policy tools to encourage nonfederal entities to acquire and implement appropriate cybersecurity technologies.

Second, the federal government can take actions to protect its own systems, including parts of the critical infrastructure. These actions could lead others to emulate the federal government or could lead to the development and availability of more cybersecurity technology products. Third, the federal government can take long-term actions to increase the quality and availability of cybersecurity technologies available in the marketplace. Table 4 highlights many of the federal policy options and some examples of the current or planned activities undertaken by the federal government that implement these options.

As table 4 shows, the federal government is already taking several actions to improve the cybersecurity posture of critical infrastructure sectors. For example, it has designated sector-specific agencies for each critical infrastructure sector that are to work with their counterparts in the private sector to assess sector vulnerabilities and to develop plans to eliminate those vulnerabilities. It has helped to fund risk assessment activities in both the water and the surface transportation sectors. Through agencies such as NIST, DISA, and NSA, the federal government has published a variety of best practices and guidelines that assist in the planning, selection, and implementation of cybersecurity technologies. These guidelines could also prove useful to private sector infrastructure entities. DHS provides vulnerability and threat information to critical infrastructures. Agencies, such as

Table 4. Policy Options and Examples of Current or Planned Federal Activities to Improve Critical Infrastructure Cybersecurity

Policy Option	Description	Examples of Federal Activities
Develop a national CIP plan	The plan could be used as a framework for federal CIP activities. The plan should clearly define the roles and responsibilities of federal and nonfederal CIP organizations, define objectives milestones, set time frames for achieving objectives, and establish performance measures.	According to HSPD-7, by December 2004, DHS is to produce a comprehensive and integrated plan for critical infrastructure protection that will outline national goals, objectives, milestones, and key initiatives.
Assist infrastructures with risk assessments	Provide funding to sectors and sector entities to conduct risk assessments so that vulnerabilities, threats, and mitigation strategies can be identified.	The Environmental Protection Agency (EPA) has provided funding to assist utilities for large drinking water systems in preparing vulnerability assessments. The Department of Transportation has performed a vulnerability assessment of the surface transportation sector and of the sector's reliance on the Global Positioning System. HSPD-7 directs sector-specific agencies to conduct or facilitate vulnerability assessments in each sector.
Provide threat and vulnerability information to critical infrastructures	Increase the private sector's awareness of cyber threats and the need for cybersecurity technologies by improving the federal government's capabilities to identify, analyze, and disseminate information about threats to and vulnerabilities of critical infrastructure sectors and their member entities.	DHS gathers and disseminates information on threats to critical infrastructures and issues warning products in response to increases in the threat condition.
Enhance information sharing by critical infrastructures	Increase the federal government's and the private sector's awareness of cyber threats and the effective implementation of technology by developing fully productive information sharing relationships within the federal government and between the federal government and state and local governments and the private sector.	The Department of the Treasury has contracted with the Financial Services ISAC to improve its capabilities so that it can better share information about threats and response strategies. The InfraGard program provides the Federal Bureau of Investigation with a means for sharing information securely with individual members. EPA issued a $2 million grant to the Association

Policy Option	Description	Examples of Federal Activities
		of Metropolitan Water Agencies to help support the on-going efforts of the Water Information Sharing and Analysis Center, a state-of-the-art, secure information system that shares up-to-date threat and incident information between the intelligence community and the water sector.
Promote cybersecurity awareness	Ensure that the private sector is aware of the cybersecurity services that are provided by the federal government and the critical infrastructure sectors.	The Federal Deposit Insurance Corporation has sponsored conferences with the financial services sector to make sector members aware of CIP-related services provided by the federal government and the private sector.
Promote the use of cybersecurity technologies and processes	Provide tax incentives or funding to sector entities to purchase cybersecurity technology to better protect, detect, or react to cyber attacks. The government could require the use of particular cybersecurity technologies or processes. This could also be accomplished through regulations. This option requires the development of minimum standards for cybersecurity technology.	HSPD-7 instructs sector-specific agencies to encourage risk management strategies to protect against and mitigate the effects of attacks against critical infrastructures.
Develop standards and guidelines	Develop protocol and product standards for cybersecurity technology and operational guidelines for the selection, implementation, and management of cybersecurity technologies. In addition, guidance could also be provided to critical infrastructure owners on how to perform risk assessments.	In response to the Federal Information Security Management Act (FISMA) of 2002, NIST is leading the development of key information system security standards and guidelines as part of its FISMA Implementation Project. NIST and NSA are using the Common Criteria to develop comprehensive security requirements and specifications for key technologies that will be used by the federal government. The Defense Information Systems Agency (DISA) and NSA have also prepared

Policy Option	Description	Examples of Federal Activities
		implementation guides to help system administrators to configure their systems in a secure manner.
Secure federal government systems	Implement appropriate management, operational, and technical controls to secure critical federal computer systems from cyber attacks. Critical infrastructure owners rely on federal computer systems to provide certain services.	FISMA requires federal agencies to provide risk-based information security protections for their computer systems. *The National Strategy to Secure Cyberspace* identifies the need to secure government's cyberspace as one of its five priorities.
Procure secure products and services for the federal government	Require sector entities to address cybersecurity needs prior to interacting with government computer systems. Impose security requirements in federal procurements of information technology.	*The National Strategy to Secure Cyberspace* states that the federal government is identifying ways to improve security in agency contracts and evaluating the overall procurement process as it relates to security.
Foster cooperation with foreign countries regarding cyber attacks	Because cyber attacks may not originate in the United States and could cross several geopolitical boundaries, the cooperation of foreign countries is important to facilitate the tracing of cyber attacks and the apprehension of attackers.	*The National Strategy to Secure Cyberspace* states that the United States will actively foster international cooperation in investigating and prosecuting cyber crime. HSPD-7 assigns the State Department this responsibility.
Develop cybersecurity education programs	Teach the importance of cybersecurity and how to use information technology securely. Increase the number of trained computer security professionals.	The Department of Justice has a Cyberethics for Kids program that teaches students in elementary and middle schools about the risks of some online behavior and ways to protect themselves from such behavior. NSF administers the Federal Cyber Service in universities to increase the number of cybersecurity professionals.
Fund the research and development of cybersecurity technology	Provide funding to research and develop new technologies	The Defense Advanced Research Projects Agency, DHS, NSF, NIST, and NSA have ongoing efforts to research and develop new cybersecurity technologies. CIP policy documents identify the further need to better prioritize and coordinate research efforts.

Source: GAO analysis.

the Department of Justice and NSF, have established educational programs designed to teach students about cybersecurity. The federal government has also let several grants to support cybersecurity technology research and development.

Policy Analysis Framework for Federal Actions

When deciding whether to continue or expand existing programs or to create new programs, it will be important for the federal government to consider the scope of the problem and the costs and benefits, the implementation issues, and the consequences of each option. Factual information is needed on the scope and scale of cyber vulnerabilities and the consequences of possible cyber attacks on critical infrastructures. The technology issues surrounding the problem and the structure of the security marketplace have to be determined. To help determine the proper approach for federal action, the government will require information from the private sector on the scope and size of the cybersecurity problem and the actions that the private sector is already taking to address the problem. Further, information on critical infrastructure assets, vulnerabilities, and priorities, which could be gleaned if private sector entities follow the risk-based framework for security that we have described, is needed from the private sector.

As with any federal program, it will be important to measure the results of any federal cybersecurity program. However, the lack of well-defined security standards or benchmarks makes it difficult to measure the benefit of such a program. Further, what may be appropriate for some sectors may not be appropriate for others. While all sectors place some value on protecting the confidentiality, integrity, and availability of their computer systems and data, the relative importance of these objectives varies among the sectors. Further, because of business or other demands, the emphasis on cybersecurity issues varies from entity to entity and from sector to sector.

It is also important to consider the proper role of the federal government. Sometimes, the best course of action may be to take no action at all. In some critical infrastructure sectors, private sector responses may adequately address a problem so that federal involvement is not required. For example, according to chemical infrastructure sector officials, during the second quarter of 2003, the Chemical Industry Data Exchange (CIDX) released its cybersecurity guidance for the Responsible Care Security Code, cybersecurity guidance for security vulnerability assessment methodology, and the results of baseline assessments against the ISO 17799 standard for security management practices. The railroad sector has conducted a risk assessment that identified and evaluated threats to and vulnerabilities of the rail system, quantified the risks, and devised appropriate countermeasures.

Because many organizations are involved in this nation's critical infrastructure protection, it is important for all levels of government—federal, state, and local—and the private sector to work cooperatively to ensure that the most critical cybersecurity issues are addressed. A national CIP plan that defines the roles and responsibilities of federal and nonfederal CIP organizations; identifies and prioritizes critical assets, systems, and functions; and establishes standards and benchmarks for infrastructure protection could help the federal government to apply its limited resources where they are most needed. Ultimately, the protection of critical infrastructures in this country falls on the critical infrastructure owners. However, as we have described, the federal government has several options at its disposal to manage and encourage the increased use of cybersecurity technologies, research and develop new cybersecurity technologies, and generally improve the cybersecurity posture of critical infrastructure sectors.

Agency Comments and External Reviewer Comments

We provided a draft of this report to the Department of Homeland Security and the National Science Foundation for their review. DHS generally concurred with the report and provided detailed comments, which we incorporated as appropriate. NSF said that this is an important and timely report that provides broad coverage of current and emerging cybersecurity and infrastructure technologies. We include DHS's and NSF's comments in appendixes IV and V, respectively, and summarize them in chapter 5.

We also provided a draft of this report to 26 organizations, representing government, industry, and academia, for their review. We received comments and suggestions from 15 reviewers. The comments included the clarification of issues and the highlighting of certain aspects of the assessment that reviewers considered important. We have incorporated these comments, where appropriate, in the report. We summarize these comments in chapter 5.

Chapter 1: Introduction

Computers have been crucial to the operations of government and business. In the early days of computing, computers calculated the designs of the first strategic weapons and projections of bombing effectiveness. Businesses used computers to automate business calculations. The role of computers evolved into record keeping and automating many tasks to the point that, by now, computers play a role in nearly everything. The advent of networking made it possible for computers to communicate and become even more pervasive. Nowadays, our water, food, fuel, lights, heat, home, work, and vehicles are all supported, if not directly run, by computers and networks. Essentially, computers and networks run our nation's critical infrastructures that are vital to national defense, economic security, and public health and safety.

Unfortunately, many computer systems and networks were not designed with security in mind. As a result, the core of our critical infrastructure is riddled with vulnerabilities that seem to require constant patches and fixes. These vulnerabilities could enable an attacker to disrupt the operations of or cause damage to critical infrastructures. The potential exists for causing physical damage to people and property by exploiting vulnerabilities in computers and networks. The problem is exacerbated by increasing computer interconnectivity, most notably growth in the use of the Internet since the 1990s. While the benefits of the Internet have been enormous, widespread interconnectivity also poses enormous risks to computer systems and to the critical operations and infrastructures they support. Reliance on the Internet has created a new avenue for attack on infrastructures. These attacks are called *cyber attacks* because they arrive over the network by means of information packets that traverse communication links and attack cyber assets—the software and data. We have seen these cyber attacks in the form of viruses and worms—malicious software that is designed to propagate from one system to another, either automatically or by some user action such as opening an e-mail attachment. Because of the increasing threats of cyber attacks, *cybersecurity*—the defense against cyber attacks—is a major concern of the government and the private sector.

There is a variety of technologies that can be used in support of cybersecurity. Some technologies, such as firewalls and biometrics, help to protect computers and networks against attacks, while others, such as intrusion detection systems and continuity of operations tools, help to detect and respond to cyber attacks in progress.

Critical infrastructure protection (CIP) involves activities that enhance the security of our nation's cyber and physical public and private infrastructure that are critical to national security, national economic security, or national public health and safety. Federal awareness of the importance of securing our nation's critical infrastructures has continued to evolve since the mid-1990s. Recent terrorist attacks and threats have further underscored the need to manage and encourage CIP activities. Numerous vulnerabilities are being identified more and more frequently which, if exploited by the increasing number of threats, could disrupt or disable several of our nation's critical infrastructures. However, with about 85 percent of the nation's critical infrastructures owned and operated by the private sector, CIP is not an endeavor that the federal government can undertake alone. Since 1997, we have designated information security as a government-wide high-risk issue.[3] In January 2003, we expanded this high-risk issue to

[3] This series identifies areas at high risk because of either their greater vulnerabilities to waste, fraud, abuse, and mismanagement or major challenges associated with their economy, efficiency, or effectiveness.

emphasize the increased importance of protecting the information systems that support critical infrastructures.[4]

Critical Infrastructure Protection Policy Has Evolved since the Mid-1990's

Since the mid-1990s, the federal government has articulated its approach to CIP through several reports, orders, directives, laws, and strategy documents. Appendix II describes the policies in more detail. Within the federal government, the Department of Homeland Security (DHS) has a number of responsibilities for critical infrastructure protection, including the responsibility to (1) develop a comprehensive national CIP plan; (2) recommend CIP measures in coordination with other federal agencies and in cooperation with state and local government agencies and authorities, the private sector, and other entities; and (3) disseminate, as appropriate, information analyzed by the department both within DHS and to other federal agencies, state and local government agencies, and private sector entities. Within DHS, the Information Analysis and Infrastructure Protection (IAIP) directorate serves as the primary point of contact for CIP activities. Most recently, Homeland Security Presidential Directive 7 (HSPD-7) established a national policy for federal departments and agencies to identify and prioritize critical infrastructure and key resources and to protect them from terrorist attack. To ensure the coverage of critical sectors, HSPD-7 designates sector-specific agencies for the critical infrastructure sectors identified in the *National Strategy for Homeland Security* (see table 5).

Sector-specific agencies are responsible for infrastructure protection activities in their assigned sectors and are to coordinate and collaborate with relevant federal agencies, state and local governments, and the private sector to accomplish these responsibilities. To facilitate private sector participation, federal CIP policy states that sector-specific agencies are to support sector-coordinating mechanisms. In addition, the federal government's CIP approach encourages the voluntary creation of information sharing and analysis centers (ISAC) that facilitate gathering, analyzing, and appropriately sanitizing and disseminating information to and from infrastructure sectors and the federal government through DHS.

Federal and Private Sector Computer Security Is Affected by Various Laws

Several laws affect the cybersecurity of federal and private sector entities and could drive the development of cybersecurity-related tools. These laws include requirements for federal agency information security programs, funding

[4] U.S. General Accounting Office, *High-Risk Series: Protecting Information Systems Supporting the Federal Government and the Nation's Critical Infrastructures*, GAO-03-121 (Washington, D.C.: Jan. 2003).

Table 5. Critical Infrastructure Sectors Identified by the Federal Government

Sector	Description	Sector-Specific Agencies
Agriculture	Provides for the fundamental need for food. The infrastructure includes supply chains for feed and crop production.	Department of Agriculture
Banking and finance	Provides the financial infrastructure of the nation. This sector consists of commercial banks, insurance companies, mutual funds, government-sponsored enterprises, pension funds, and other financial institutions that carry out transactions including clearing and settlement.	Department of the Treasury
Chemicals and hazardous materials	Transforms natural raw materials into commonly used products benefiting society's health, safety, and productivity. The chemical industry represents a $450 billion enterprise and produces more than 70,000 products that are essential to automobiles, pharmaceuticals, food supply, electronics, water treatment, health, construction and other necessities.	Department of Homeland Security
Defense industrial base	Supplies the military with the means to protect the nation by producing weapons, aircraft, and ships and providing essential services, including information technology and supply and maintenance.	Department of Defense
Emergency services	Saves lives and property from accidents and disaster. This sector includes fire, rescue, emergency medical services, and law enforcement organizations.	Department of Homeland Security
Energy	Provides the electric power used by all sectors, including critical infrastructures, and the refining, storage, and distribution of oil and natural gas. The sector is divided into electricity and oil and natural gas.	Department of Energy
Food	Carries out the post-harvesting of the food supply, including processing and retail sales.	Department of Agriculture and Department of Health and Human Services

Sector	Description	Sector-Specific Agencies
Government	Ensures national security and freedom and administers key public functions.	Department of Homeland Security
Information technology and telecommunications	Provides communications and processes to meet the needs of businesses and government.	Department of Homeland Security
Postal and shipping	Delivers private and commercial letters, packages, and bulk assets. The U.S. Postal Service and other carriers provide the services of this sector.	Department of Homeland Security
Public health and healthcare	Mitigates the risk of disasters and attacks and also provides recovery assistance if an attack occurs. The sector consists of health departments, clinics, and hospitals.	Department of Health and Human Services
Transportation	Enables movement of people and assets that are vital to our economy, mobility, and security with the use of aviation, ships, rail, pipelines, highways, trucks, buses, and mass transit.	Department of Homeland Security
Drinking water and water treatment systems	Sanitizes the water supply with the use of about 170,000 public water systems. These systems depend on reservoirs, dams, wells, treatment facilities, pumping stations, and transmission lines.	Environmental Protection Agency

Source: GAO analysis based on the President's national strategy documents and HSPD-7.

for security research and grant programs, and requirements for private sector entities to protect citizens' personal, financial, and medical information. For example, the Federal Information Security Management Act of 2002 (FISMA) requires federal agencies to provide risk-based information security protections for information collected or maintained by or on behalf of an agency, as well as information systems used or operated by an agency or by a contractor or other organization on behalf of an agency.[5] According to FISMA, agencies are to identify and provide information security protection commensurate with the risk and magnitude of the potential harm resulting from the unauthorized access, use, disclosure, disruption, modification, or destruction of information. The Health Insurance Portability and Accountability Act (HIPAA) of 1996 required the electronic exchange of information and mandated protections for the privacy and security of

[5] Federal Information Security Management Act of 2002, Title III, Public Law 107-347 (Dec. 17, 2002).

this information.[6] In 1999, the Gramm-Leach-Bliley Act established a new requirement for protecting the privacy of personal financial information.[7] In the area of research funding, the Cyber Security Research and Development Act authorized funding for computer and network security research and grant programs through NIST and the National Science Foundation (NSF).[8]

Report Overview

This technology assessment focuses on three key questions:

1. What are the key cybersecurity requirements in each of the critical infrastructure protection sectors?
2. What cybersecurity technologies can be applied to critical infrastructure protection? What technologies are currently deployed or currently available but not yet widely deployed for critical infrastructure protection? What technologies are currently being researched for cybersecurity? Are there any gaps in cybersecurity technology that should be better researched and developed to address critical infrastructure protection?
3. What are the implementation issues associated with using cybersecurity technologies for critical infrastructure protection, including policy issues such as privacy and information sharing?

To answer these questions, we describe the critical infrastructure sectors, the efforts currently being taken to improve their cybersecurity postures, and the challenges they face in implementing cybersecurity strategies. While critical infrastructure protection must guard against both physical and cyber threats, we focus our report on approaches to protect against cyber threats. We describe how several cybersecurity technologies work and how they can be applied to cybersecurity problems. We discuss the limitations to some of these technologies. We also describe ongoing cybersecurity research and some of the key areas that require further work. We identify challenges to improving cybersecurity and several options available to the federal government to improve the cybersecurity posture of critical infrastructure sectors.

Chapter 2: Cybersecurity Requirements of Critical Infrastructure Sectors

Protecting our nation's critical infrastructures is a formidable challenge. Numerous threats and vulnerabilities are being identified on a more frequent basis. If these vulnerabilities can be successfully exploited by threats, several

6 Health Insurance Portability and Accountability Act of 1996, Public Law 104-191 (Aug. 21, 1996).
7 Gramm-Leach-Bliley Act of 1999, Public Law 106-102 (Nov. 12, 1999).
8 The Cyber Security Research and Development Act of 2002, Public Law 107-305 (Nov. 27, 2002).

of our nation's critical infrastructures could be disrupted or disabled. To assess the need for cybersecurity technology, it is important to understand the cybersecurity needs of critical infrastructure sectors by examining the threats that they face as well as the vulnerabilities that could be exploited. Further, to determine the information technology (IT) assets that will need to be protected, it is important to examine the types of computer and networking technologies that are used in various sectors.

Threats, Vulnerabilities, Incidents, and the Consequences of Potential Attacks Are Increasing

Critical infrastructures can be threatened using both physical and cyber means. Several organizations and individuals are capable of conducting such attacks. Historically, attacks on our infrastructures could be conducted only by a relatively small number of entities. However, with critical infrastructures' increasing reliance on computers and networks, more organizations and individuals can cause harm using cyber attacks. Further, U.S. authorities are becoming increasingly concerned about the prospect of combined physical and cyber attacks that could have devastating consequences. Table 6 lists sources of threats that have been identified by the U.S. intelligence community.

Over the last decade, physical and cyber events, as well as related analyses by various organizations, have demonstrated the increasing threats faced by critical infrastructure sectors in the United States. For example, on February 11, 2003, the National Infrastructure Protection Center (NIPC)

Table 6. Threats to Critical Infrastructure

Threat	Description
Criminal groups	International corporate spies and organized crime organizations pose a threat to the United States through their ability to conduct industrial espionage and large-scale monetary theft and to hire or develop hacker talent.
Hackers	Hackers sometimes crack into networks for the thrill of the challenge or for bragging rights in the hacker community. While remote cracking once required a fair amount of skill or computer knowledge, hackers can now download attack scripts from the Internet and launch them against victim sites. Thus, while attack tools have become more sophisticated, they have also become easier to use. According to the Central Intelligence Agency (CIA), the large majority of hackers do not have the requisite tradecraft to threaten difficult targets such as critical U.S. networks. Nevertheless, the worldwide population of hackers poses a relatively high threat of an isolated or brief disruption causing serious damage.

Threat	Description
Hacktivists	Hacktivism refers to politically motivated attacks on publicly accessible Web pages or e-mail servers. These groups and individuals overload e-mail servers and hack into Web sites to send a political message. Most international hacktivist groups appear bent on propaganda rather than damage to critical infrastructures.
Insider threat	The disgruntled organization insider is a principal source of computer crimes. Insiders may not need a great deal of knowledge about computer intrusions because their knowledge of a victim system often allows them to gain unrestricted access to cause damage to the system or to steal system data. The insider threat also includes outsourcing vendors.
National governments and foreign intelligence services	Several nations are aggressively working to develop information warfare doctrine, programs, and capabilities. Such capabilities enable a single entity to have a significant and serious impact by disrupting the supply, communications, and economic infrastructures that support military power—impacts that could affect the daily lives of U.S. citizens across the country. The threat from national cyber warfare programs is unique because they pose a threat along the entire spectrum of objectives that might harm U.S. interests. According to the CIA, only government-sponsored programs are developing capabilities with the prospect of causing widespread, long-duration damage to U.S. critical infrastructures.
Terrorists	Terrorists seek to destroy, incapacitate, or exploit critical infrastructures to threaten national security, cause mass casualties, weaken the U.S. economy, and damage public morale and confidence. However, traditional terrorist adversaries of the United States are less developed in their computer network capabilities than other adversaries. Terrorists likely pose a limited cyber threat. The CIA believes terrorists will stay focused on traditional attack methods, but it anticipates growing cyber threats as a more technically competent generation enters the ranks.
Virus writers	Virus writers are posing an increasingly serious threat. Several destructive computer viruses and worms have harmed files and hard drives, including the Melissa Macro Virus, the Explore.Zip worm, the CIH (Chernobyl) Virus, Nimda, Code Red, Slammer, and Blaster.

Source: GAO analysis based on data from the FBI, CIA, and CERT/CC.

issued an advisory to heighten the awareness of an increase in global hacking activities as a result of the increasing tensions between the United States and Iraq. This advisory noted that during a time of increased international tension, illegal cyber activity often escalates, such as spamming, Web page defacements, and denial-of-service attacks. Further, this activity can originate within another country that is party to the tension, can be state sponsored

Table 7. Likely Sources of Cyber Attacks According to Respondents to the CSI/FBI 2003 Computer Crime and Security Survey

Potential Source	Percentage of Respondents
Independent hackers	82%
Disgruntled employees	77%
U.S. competitors	40%
Foreign governments	28%
Foreign corporations	25%

Source: 2003 CSI/FBI Computer Crime and Security Survey.

or encouraged, or can come from domestic organizations or individuals independently. The advisory also stated that attacks may have one of several objectives, including political activism targeting Iraq or those sympathetic to Iraq by self-described "patriot" hackers, political activism or disruptive attacks targeting U.S. systems by those opposed to any potential conflict with Iraq, or even criminal activity masquerading or using the current crisis to further personal goals.

Respondents to the 2003 Computer Security Institute (CSI) and Federal Bureau of Investigation (FBI) Computer Crime and Security Survey identified independent hackers as the most likely source of cyber attacks, as shown in table 7.[9]

It is important to consider the threat posed by insiders. According to the CSI/FBI survey, 45 percent of respondents reported unauthorized access by insiders, and 80 percent of respondents reported insider abuses of network access. As shown in table 7, disgruntled employees are believed to be a likely source of attack by 77 percent of respondents. According to a National Security Telecommunications and Information Systems Security Committee report, insiders include employees, contractors, service providers, and anyone else with legitimate access to a system.[10] Insiders may have a variety of motives for their actions. For example, insiders may have views that conflict with those of the organization they are employed by and may want to impose their beliefs on the organization. Another group of insiders may just be curious and attempt to access systems they are not authorized to use. Other insiders are employees who do not intend to cause any harm to the organization but who unwittingly can cause damage either through their ignorance, carelessness, or disregard for organizational policies.

[9] Computer Security Institute, *2003 CSI/FBI Computer Crime and Security Survey (2003).*

[10] National Security Telecommunications and Information Systems Security Committee, *The Insider Threat to U.S. Government Information Systems,* NSTISSAM INFOSEC/1-99 (Fort Meade, MD: July 1999). In 2001, this committee was redesignated the Committee on National Security Systems.

Actions such as disabling antivirus software, leaving passwords on workstations, and installing unauthorized software may open a large enough vulnerability for a hacker to gain access to a system.

As larger amounts of money are transferred through computer systems, as more sensitive economic and commercial information is exchanged electronically, and as the nation's defense and intelligence communities increasingly rely on commercially available IT, the likelihood increases that information attacks will threaten vital national interests.

Critical Infrastructure Sectors Face Various Physical Threats

With the coordinated terrorist attacks against the World Trade Center, in New York City, and the Pentagon, in Washington, D.C., on September 11, 2001, the threat of terrorism rose to the top of the country's national security and law enforcement agendas. Even before these catastrophic incidents, attacks against people, property, and infrastructures had increased concerns about terrorism. The terrorist bombings in 1993 of the World Trade Center in New York City and in 1995 of the Alfred P. Murrah Federal Building in Oklahoma City prompted increased emphasis on the need to strengthen and coordinate the federal government's ability to effectively combat terrorism domestically. The 1995 Aum Shinrikyo sarin nerve agent attack in the Tokyo subway system also raised new concerns about U.S. preparedness to combat terrorist incidents involving weapons of mass destruction.[11] However, as clearly demonstrated by the September 11, 2001 incidents, a terrorist attack would not have to fit the definition of weapons of mass destruction to result in mass casualties, destruction of critical infrastructures, economic losses, and disruption of daily life nationwide.

U.S. intelligence and law enforcement communities continuously assess both foreign and domestic terrorist threats to the United States. The U.S. foreign intelligence community—for example, the CIA, the Defense Intelligence Agency, the FBI, and the Department of State's Bureau of Intelligence and Research—monitors terrorist threats of foreign origin. In addition, the FBI gathers intelligence and assesses the threat posed by domestic sources. According to the U.S. intelligence community, conventional explosives and firearms continue to be terrorists' weapons of choice. The community also believes that terrorists are less likely to use weapons of mass destruction, although the possibility that they will use these weapons may increase over the next decade. Table 8 identifies weapons that can be used to physically attack critical infrastructure.

Nevertheless, in February 2004, the Director of Central Intelligence testified that in his view, terrorist organizations continue to pursue chemical,

[11] A weapon of mass destruction is a chemical, biological, radiological, or nuclear agent or weapon.

Table 8. Weapons for Physically Attacking Critical Infrastructures

Weapon	Description
Biological weapons	Biological weapons, which release large quantities of living, disease-causing microorganisms, have extraordinary lethal potential. Biological weapons are relatively easy to manufacture, requiring straightforward technical skills, basic equipment, and a seed stock of pathogenic microorganisms. Biological weapons are especially dangerous because we may not know immediately that we have been attacked, allowing an infectious agent time to spread. Moreover, biological agents can serve as a means of attack against humans as well as livestock and crops, inflicting casualties as well as economic damage.
Chemical weapons	Chemical weapons are extremely lethal and capable of producing tens of thousands of casualties. Like biological weapons, chemical weapons are relatively easy to manufacture, using basic equipment, trained personnel, and precursor materials that often have legitimate dual uses. As the 1995 Tokyo subway attack revealed, even sophisticated nerve agents are within the reach of terrorist groups.
Nuclear weapons	Nuclear weapons have enormous destructive potential. Terrorists who seek to develop a nuclear weapon must overcome two formidable challenges. First, acquiring or refining a sufficient quantity of fissile material is very difficult—though not impossible. Second, manufacturing a workable weapon requires a very high degree of technical capability—though terrorists could feasibly assemble the simplest type of nuclear device. To get around these significant though not insurmountable challenges, terrorists could seek to steal or purchase a nuclear weapon.
Radiological weapons	Radiological weapons, or "dirty bombs," combine radioactive material with conventional explosives. The individuals and groups engaged in terrorist activity can cause widespread disruption and fear, particularly in heavily populated areas.
Conventional means	Terrorists, both domestic and international, continue to use traditional methods of violence and destruction to inflict harm and spread fear. They have used knives, guns, and bombs to kill the innocent. They have taken hostages and spread propaganda. Given the low expense, ready availability of materials, and relatively high chance for successful execution, terrorists will continue to make use of conventional attacks.

Source: *National Strategy for Homeland Security.*

biological, radiological, and nuclear weapons.[12] He also stated that although the Al Qaeda leadership is seriously damaged, it, along with other groups supporting its views, continues to pose a threat to the United States. In addition, he stated that terrorism directed at U.S. interests goes beyond religious extremist groups, adding that the Revolutionary Armed Forces of Colombia and the Revolutionary People's Liberation Party/Front—a Turkish group—have shown a willingness to attack U.S. targets.

Critical Infrastructure Sectors Face Various Cyber Threats

In addition to posing these physical threats, terrorists and others with malicious intent, such as transnational criminals and foreign intelligence services, pose a threat to our nation's computer systems. Government officials are increasingly concerned about attacks from individuals and groups with malicious intent, such as crime, terrorism, foreign intelligence gathering, and acts of war. According to the National Security Agency (NSA), foreign governments already have or are developing computer attack capabilities, and potential adversaries are developing a body of knowledge about U.S. systems and methods to attack these systems. Since the terrorist attacks of September 11, 2001, warnings of the potential for terrorist cyber attacks against our critical infrastructures have also increased. For example, in February 2002, the threat to these infrastructures was highlighted by the Special Advisor to the President for Cyberspace Security, during a Senate hearing, when he stated that although to date none of the traditional terrorists groups, such as al Qaeda, had used the Internet to launch a known assault on an American infrastructure, information on water systems was discovered on computers found in al Qaeda camps in Afghanistan.[13] Also, in February 2002, the Director of Central Intelligence testified before the Senate Select Committee on Intelligence on the possibility of cyber warfare attacks by terrorists.[14] He stated that the September 11 attacks demonstrated the nation's dependence on critical infrastructure systems that rely on electronic and computer networks. Further, he noted that attacks of this nature would become an increasingly viable option for terrorists as they and other foreign adversaries become more familiar with these targets and the technologies required to attack them.

According to the FBI, terrorists, transnational criminals, and intelligence services are quickly becoming aware of and using tools such as computer viruses, Trojan horses, worms, logic bombs, and eavesdropping programs

---

[12] Testimony of George J. Tenet, Director of Central Intelligence, before the Senate Select Committee on Intelligence (Feb. 24, 2004).

[13] Testimony of Richard A. Clarke, Special Advisor to the President for Cyberspace Security and Chairman of the President's Critical Infrastructure Protection Board, before the Senate Committee on the Judiciary, Subcommittee on Administrative Oversight and the Courts (Feb. 13, 2002).

[14] Testimony of George J. Tenet, Director of Central Intelligence, before the Senate Select Committee on Intelligence (Feb. 6, 2002).

("sniffers") that can destroy, intercept, degrade the integrity of, or deny access to data (see table 9).

Viruses and worms are commonly used to launch denial-of-service attacks, which generally flood targeted networks and systems with so much transmission of data that regular traffic is either slowed or completely interrupted. Such attacks have been utilized ever since the groundbreaking Morris worm, which brought 10 percent of the systems connected to the Internet to a halt in November 1988. In 2001, the Code Red worm used a denial-of-service attack to affect millions of computer users by shutting down Web sites, slowing Internet service, and disrupting business and government operations.

In the case of insider attacks, the use of these tools may not even be necessary because of the unfettered access insiders often have to their computer systems. An example of an insider causing damage to a system occurred at the U.S. Coast Guard in July 1997. A former U.S. Coast Guard employee used her programming skills to access the service's nationwide personnel database and deleted crucial data that caused the computer system to crash. The crash wiped out almost two weeks' worth of personnel data used to determine promotions, transfers, assignments, and disability claim reviews. It took 115 Coast Guard employees working more than 1,800 hours to recover and re-enter the data, at a cost of more than $40,000.

The growing number of known vulnerabilities increases the number of potential attacks that can be created by the hacker community. As vulnerabilities are discovered, attackers may attempt to exploit them. Attacks can be launched against specific targets or widely distributed through viruses and worms. The risks posed by this increasing and evolving threat are demonstrated in reports of actual and potential attacks and disruptions. For example,

- On August 11, 2003, the Blaster worm was launched, and it infected more than 120,000 computers in its first 36 hours. When the worm was successfully executed, it could cause the operating system to crash. The worm affected a wide range of systems and caused slowness and disruptions in users' Internet services. The worm was programmed to launch a denial-of-service attack against Microsoft's Windows Update Web site. The Maryland Motor Vehicle Administration was forced to shut down its computer systems, and systems in both national and international areas were also affected.
- According to a preliminary study coordinated by the Cooperative Association for Internet Data Analysis, on January 25, 2003, the SQL Slammer worm (also known as "Sapphire") infected more than 90 percent of vulnerable computers worldwide within 10 minutes of its release on the Internet. As the study reports, exploiting a known

Table 9. Types of Cyber Attacks

Type of Attack	Description
Denial of service	A method of attack that denies system access to legitimate users without actually having to compromise the targeted system. From a single source, the attack overwhelms the target computer with messages and blocks legitimate traffic. It can prevent one system from being able to exchange data with other systems or prevent the system from using the Internet.
Distributed denial of service	A variant of the denial-of-service attack that uses a coordinated attack from a distributed system of computers rather than a single source. It often makes use of worms to spread to multiple computers that can then attack the target.
Exploit tools	Publicly available and sophisticated tools that intruders of various skill levels can use to determine vulnerabilities and gain entry into targeted systems.
Logic bombs	A form of sabotage in which a programmer inserts code that causes the program to perform a destructive action when some triggering event occurs, such as terminating the programmer's employment.
Sniffer	Synonymous with packet sniffer. A program that intercepts routed data and examines each packet in search of specified information, such as passwords transmitted in clear text.
Trojan horse	A computer program that conceals harmful code. A Trojan horse usually masquerades as a useful program that a user would wish to execute.
Virus	A program that "infects" computer files, usually executable programs, by inserting a copy of itself into the file. These copies are usually executed when the infected file is loaded into memory, allowing the virus to infect other files. Unlike the computer worm, a virus requires human involvement (usually unwitting) to propagate.
War-dialing	Simple programs that dial consecutive phone numbers looking for modems.
War-driving	A method of gaining entry into wireless computer networks using a laptop, antennas, and a wireless network adaptor that involves patrolling locations to gain unauthorized access.
Worms	An independent computer program that reproduces by copying itself from one system to another across a network. Unlike computer viruses, worms do not require human involvement to propagate.

Source: GAO analysis.

vulnerability for which a patch had been available since July 2002, Slammer doubled in size every 8.5 seconds and achieved its full scanning rate (55 million scans per second) after about 3 minutes. It caused considerable harm through network outages and such unforeseen consequences as canceled airline flights and automated teller machine failures. Further, the study emphasizes that the effects would likely have been more severe had Slammer carried a malicious payload, exploited a more widespread vulnerability, or targeted a more popular service.

- In November 2002, a British computer administrator was indicted on charges that he accessed and damaged 98 computers in 14 states between March 2001 and March 2002, causing some $900,000 in damage to the computers. These networks belonged to the Department of Defense (DoD), the National Aeronautics and Space Administration, and private companies. The indictment alleges that the attacker was able to gain administrative privileges on military computers and copy password files and delete critical system files. The attacks rendered the networks of the Earle Naval Weapons Station in New Jersey and the Military District of Washington inoperable.
- On October 21, 2002, NIPC reported that all 13 root-name servers that provide the primary road map for almost all Internet communications were targeted in a massive distributed denial-of-service attack. Seven of the servers failed to respond to legitimate network traffic, and two others failed intermittently during the attack. Because of safeguards, most Internet users experienced no slowdowns or outages.
- In August 2001, we reported to a subcommittee of the House Government Reform Committee that the attacks referred to as Code Red, Code Red II, and SirCam affected millions of computer users, shut down Web sites, slowed Internet service, and disrupted business and government operations.[15] Then, in September 2001, the Nimda worm appeared, using some of the most significant attack profile aspects of Code Red II and 1999's infamous Melissa virus, which allowed it to spread widely in a short amount of time. Security experts estimate that Code Red, Sircam, and Nimda have caused billions of dollars in damage.

As the number of individuals with computer skills has increased, more intrusion, or hacking, tools have become readily available and relatively easy to use. Frequently, skilled hackers develop exploitation tools and post them on Internet hacking sites. These tools are then readily available for others to download, allowing even inexperienced programmers to create a

[15] U.S. General Accounting Office, *Information Security: Code Red, Code Red II, and SirCam Attacks Highlight Need for Proactive Measures*; GAO-01-1073T (Washington, D.C.: Aug. 29, 2001).

computer virus or to literally point and click to launch an attack. According to the National Institute of Standards and Technology (NIST), 30 to 40 new attack tools are posted on the Internet every month.[16] Experts also agree that there has been a steady advance in the sophistication and effectiveness of attack technology. Intruders quickly develop attacks to exploit vulnerabilities that have been discovered in products, use these attacks to compromise computers, and share them with other attackers. In addition, they can combine these attacks with other forms of technology to develop programs that automatically scan the network for vulnerable systems, attack them, compromise them, and use them to spread the attack even further.

Because automated tools now exist, the CERT® Coordination Center (CERT/CC) has noted that attacks that once took weeks or months to propagate over the Internet now take just hours, or even minutes.[17] For instance, while in July 2001, Code Red achieved an infection rate of over 20,000 systems within 10 minutes, less than a year and a half later, in January 2003, the Slammer worm successfully attacked at least 75,000 systems, infecting more than 90 percent of vulnerable systems within 10 minutes.

The threat to systems connected to the Internet is illustrated by the increasing number of computer security incidents reported to CERT/CC. This number rose from just under 10,000 in 1999 to over 52,000 in 2001, to about 82,000 in 2002, and to 137,529 in 2003 (see figure 1). However, the Director of CERT Centers stated that he estimates that as much as 80 percent of actual security incidents go unreported, in most cases because (1) the organization was unable to recognize that its systems had been penetrated or there were no indications of penetration or attack, or (2) the organization was reluctant to report.

In addition, flaws in software code that could cause a program to malfunction generally result from programming errors that occur during software development. The increasing complexity and size of software programs contribute to the growth in software flaws. For example, Microsoft Windows 2000 reportedly contains about 35 million lines of code, compared with about 15 million lines for Windows 95. As reported by NIST, based on various studies of code inspections, most estimates suggest that there are as many as 20 flaws per thousand lines of software code. While most flaws do not create security vulnerabilities,[18] the potential for these errors reflects

[16] U.S. General Accounting Office, *Information Security: Weaknesses Place Commerce Data and Operations at Serious Risk*, GAO-01-751 (Washington D.C.: Aug. 13, 2001).

[17] The CERT/CC is a center of Internet security expertise at the Software Engineering Institute, a federally funded research and development center operated by Carnegie Mellon University. CERT and CERT Coordination Center are registered in the U.S. Patent and Trademark Office by Carnegie Mellon University.

[18] A vulnerability is the existence of a flaw or weakness in hardware or software that can be exploited resulting in a violation of an implicit or explicit security policy.

Figure 1: Information Security Incidents, 1995–2003

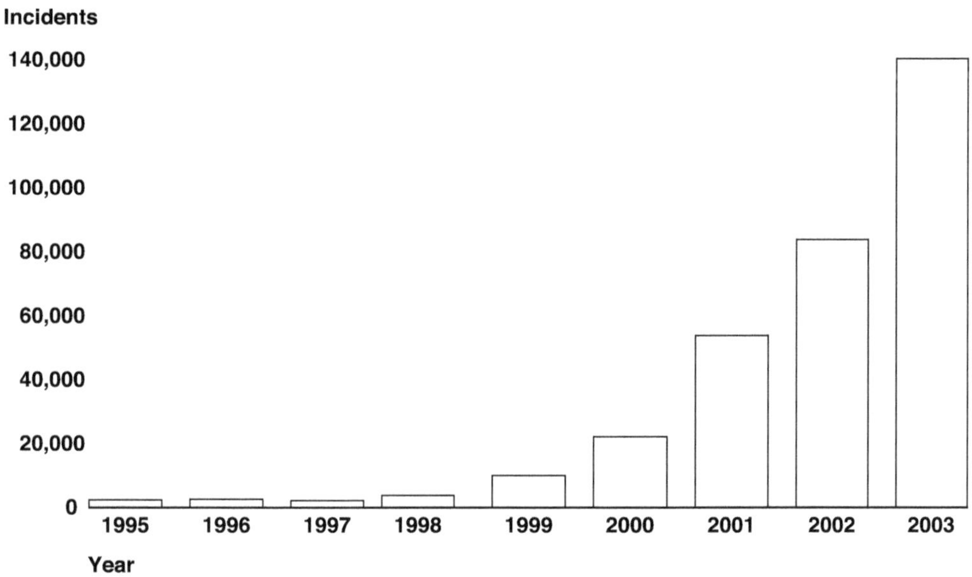

Source: GAO analysis based on CERT/CC data.

the difficulty and complexity involved in delivering trustworthy code.[19] By exploiting software vulnerabilities, hackers and others who spread malicious code can cause significant damage, ranging from Web site defacement to taking control of entire systems, and thereby being able to read, modify, or delete sensitive information, destroy systems, disrupt operations, or launch attacks against other organizations' systems.

Between 1995 and 2003, CERT/CC reported 12,946 security vulnerabilities that resulted from software flaws. Figure 2 illustrates the dramatic growth in security vulnerabilities over these years.

Poor Systems Management Can Be Costly and Disruptive

Despite the heightened national security and terrorism concerns occasioned by the September 11, 2001 attacks, it is important to recognize that up to the present, many of the most costly and disruptive cyber events have not been caused by malicious cyber attacks, but instead originated with mundane problems or routine systems mismanagement. For example, according to ICF Consulting, the cost to the U.S. economy of the August 14,

[19] National Institute for Standards and Technology, *Procedures for Handling Security Patches: Recommendations of the National Institute of Standards and Technology*, NIST Special Publication 800-40 (Gaithersburg, MD: August 2002).

Figure 2: Security Vulnerabilities, 1995–2003

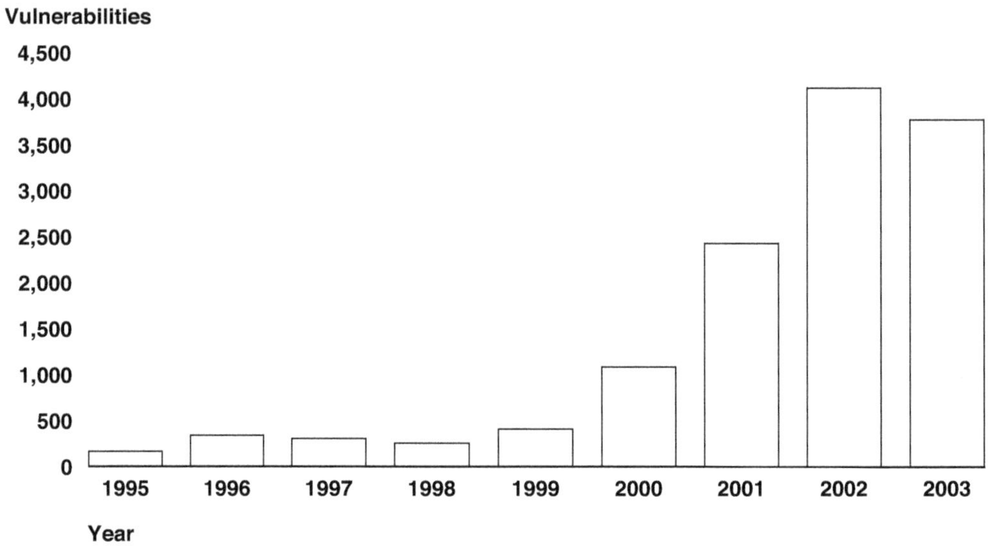

Source: GAO analysis based on CERT/CC data.

2003, blackout has been estimated at between $7 billion and $10 billion dollars. A joint U.S.-Canada Power System Outage Task Force investigated the causes of the blackout and issued a report in April 2004.[20] This report details a chain of mishaps, starting with a malfunctioning monitoring and control system that was deployed by power grid operators in Ohio. Environmental factors combined with a higher than normal demand for power caused a local overload of a type that might normally trigger a brownout or a brief local blackout. System designers had not anticipated such a contingency because it involved a series of seemingly unlikely events. But what is unlikely in small systems may not be so rare in large systems. In this case, interconnectedness of the power grid permitted the disruption to spread to other operators in Canada, New York, and elsewhere on the U.S. East Coast, who could not take remedial actions because of their inability to understand what was happening.

This single event illustrates many hallmarks of what could be called the mundane cybersecurity threat:

- inadequate system monitoring and control tools;
- unplanned growth of a large, complex, system with external interdependencies;

[20] U.S.-Canada Power System Outage Task Force, *Final Report on the August 14, 2003 Blackout in the United States and Canada: Causes and Recommendations* (Apr. 2004).

- a combination of seemingly unlikely external factors;
- lack of a well-defined stakeholder responsible for overall robustness; and
- operator confusion and mistakes.

Mundane cybersecurity threats receive little attention, and yet are emerging as a serious risk to national economic growth and to the success of several government and private sector initiatives. These activities place computer-operated systems into critical roles for the economy, the government, the military, or nationally important industry sectors. The systems are growing through an unplanned, organic process of accretion, without any sort of global plan, and without a well-defined entity with clear responsibility for security and reliability. The resulting systems are intrinsically hard to analyze or monitor, so that even if the nation were to mandate that they be controlled, the science for doing so would often be lacking.

To make matters worse, today's mundane cybersecurity threat may become tomorrow's terrorist target. In the wake of the August 2003 blackout, many experts pointed out that even if terrorism had no role in that particular incident, terrorists could easily target the power grid with similarly spectacular results at some future time. Actions taken over an extended period to harden nationally critical infrastructure sectors against mundane failures may thus be the best preventive measures against some future terrorist threat targeting those infrastructures. The August 2003 blackout occurred despite more than a decade of government concern about the growing risk of such instability and despite the existence of all sorts of power industry groups with responsibility for aspects of power security. The U.S.-Canada Power System Outage Task Force report reveals that while such organizations have a valuable role, with the emergence of an increasingly interconnected power grid, a need has emerged for a new kind of stakeholder with responsibility for large-scale stability of the grid.

Growing Concern over Connections between Cyber and Physical Worlds

Since September 11, 2001, the critical link between cyberspace and physical space has been increasingly recognized. As we have described, critical infrastructures face an increasing threat of cyber attacks in addition to physical attacks. In July 2002, NIPC reported that the potential for compound cyber and physical attacks, referred to as "swarming attacks," is an emerging threat to our critical infrastructures. As NIPC reported, the effects of a swarming attack include slowing or complicating the response to a physical attack. For instance, a cyber attack that disabled the water supply or the electrical system, in conjunction with a physical attack, could deny emergency services the necessary resources to manage the consequences of the physical attack—such as controlling fires, coordinating actions, and generating light.

Second, there is a general consensus—and increasing concern—among government officials and experts on control systems about potential cyber threats to the control systems that govern our critical infrastructures. In his November 2002 congressional testimony, the Director of the CERT Centers at Carnegie Mellon University noted that supervisory control and data acquisition (SCADA) systems and other forms of networked computer systems have been used for years to control power grids, gas and oil distribution pipelines, water treatment and distribution systems, hydroelectric and flood control dams, oil and chemical refineries, and other physical systems.[21] These control systems are increasingly being connected to communications links and networks to reduce operational costs by supporting remote maintenance, remote control, and remote update functions as well as to enhance performance. These computer-controlled and network-connected systems are potential targets for individuals intent on causing massive disruption and physical damage. The use of commercial off-the-shelf technologies for these systems without adequate security enhancements can significantly limit available approaches to protection and may increase the number of potential attackers. As components of control systems increasingly make critical decisions that were once made by humans, the potential effect of a cyber attack becomes more devastating.

According to NIST, cyber attacks on energy production and distribution systems—including electric, oil, gas, and water treatment systems, as well as on chemical plants containing potentially hazardous substances—could endanger public health and safety, damage the environment, and have serious financial implications, such as loss of production, generation, or distribution of public utilities; compromise of proprietary information; or liability issues. When backups for damaged components are not readily available (e.g., extra-high-voltage transformers for the electric power grid), such damage could have a long-lasting effect.

Additionally, control system researchers at the Department of Energy's national laboratories have developed systems that demonstrate the feasibility of a cyber attack on a control system at an electric power substation, where high-voltage electricity is transformed for local use. Using tools that are readily available on the Internet, the researchers are able to modify output data from field sensors and take control of programmable logic controllers directly in order to change settings and create new output.

[21] Testimony of Richard D. Pethia, Director, CERT Centers, Software Engineering Institute, Carnegie Mellon University, before the House Committee on Government Reform, Subcommittee on Government Efficiency, Financial Management and Intergovernmental Relations (Nov. 19, 2002).

These techniques could enable a hacker to cause an outage, thus incapacitating the substation.

Critical Infrastructures Rely on Information Technology to Operate

Entities within each of the critical infrastructure sectors rely on similar types of information technology to perform both critical and non-critical functions such as accounting, finance, personnel, manufacturing, engineering, and logistics that are essential to fulfilling their missions, such as generating and transmitting electric power, providing water, making chemicals, transporting goods and people, or supporting financial transactions.

Commercially Available Information Technologies Are Widely Deployed

Although some critical infrastructures use proprietary systems to fulfill their missions, commercially available off-the-shelf hardware and software are commonly used across all sectors. Infrastructure sectors use both dedicated, private communication links (for example, leased fiber optics) as well as shared, public communications (such as public switched networks and the Internet), as well as radio and satellite. These products are typically used in a networked environment to allow groups of individuals to share data, printers, communications systems, electronic mail, and other resources. These resources are provided by servers, which are computers that run specialized software to provide access to a resource or a part of the network. The network communication links between servers and devices such as printers and modems can be wired or wireless (using radio waves).

For the purposes of this assessment, we define a *network* as an interconnected collection of computers and networks. A network in a relatively small geographical area is known as a local area network (LAN). Most entities have one or more LANs at each of their offices; a LAN can be as small as two networked PCs, or it may support hundreds of users and multiple servers. Larger entities also have wide area networks (WAN) that connect the various LANs the organization has that are dispersed over a wide geographical location. Devices such as bridges, routers, and switches move *packets* (blocks of data packaged with the information necessary for their delivery) within and between networks, offering different levels of data-handling capability, depending on the origin and destination of the packets. Networks use predefined sets of rules known as *protocols* to communicate with each other. For example, the Transmission Control Protocol/Internet Protocol (TCP/IP) suite is the set of protocols used to communicate over the Internet.[22] In a TCP/IP network, each server or hardware device is assigned an IP address—a unique numeric location based on

[22] The Internet refers to the specific interconnected global network of TCP/IP-based systems that began with the Department of Defense's network known as ARPANET.

the IP addressing scheme. Every computer or device with an IP address is considered a connection point, or *node*, of the network. Each node can run network services such as the World Wide Web, electronic mail, and file transfer, storage, and retrieval. Each network service uses specific protocols and is identified by a port number that enables other nodes to locate and connect to the service. As seen in figure 3, computer servers and devices are interconnected into networks, which in turn are often connected to the Internet.

Internet services and their underlying network protocols are used in the operation of infrastructures such as electric power, transportation, banking, and many more. According to infrastructure sector representatives, entities within their infrastructures use IP- and non-IP-based networks, LANs, WANs, the Internet, and other information technology. Entities also utilize a variety of operating systems and off-the-shelf and proprietary applications. In addition, they use a variety of communications methods, including satellites, radio, the public switched network, leased lines, private fiber optics, and wireless networks. Sector representatives reported the following:

- The banking and finance sector entities use all forms of information technology—client/server, Internet and non-Internet connected, proprietary, and mainframe networks. The sector's communications are split between private (dedicated, leased, and private fiber optics) and public (public switched network, Internet). According to an industry

Figure 3: An Example of Typical Networked Systems

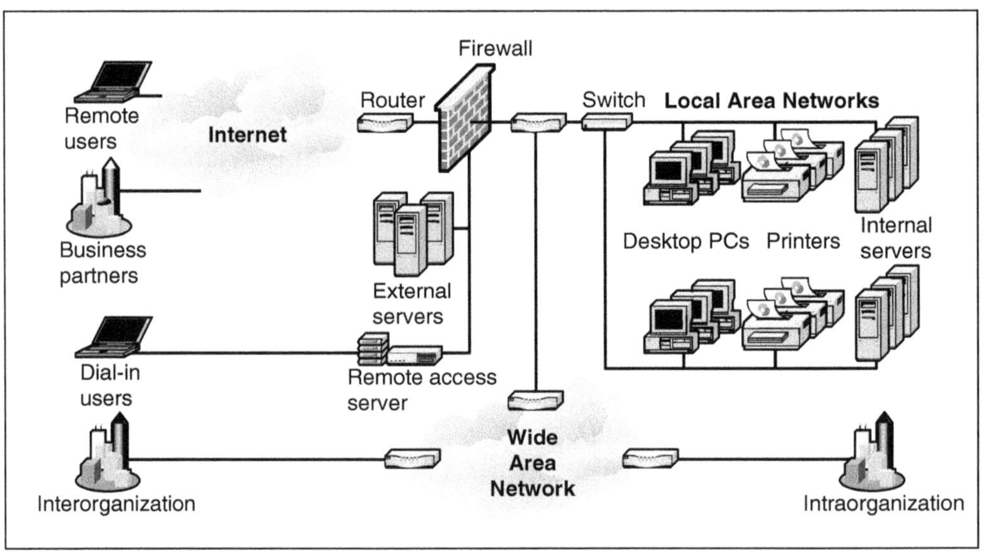

Source: GAO analysis and Microsoft Visio.

representative, the banking and finance infrastructure sector cannot operate in the absence of information technology. The criticality of a function depends on the business context—in one context, ATMs and online banking (bill payments) are critical to customers; in another, wholesale operations are important to support infrastructure operations such as payroll and personnel. As we discuss later, the most critical systems are not controlled by the individual financial institutions but are centrally controlled by government and other entities.

- The chemical sector entities use LANs, WANs, the Internet, other IP-based networks, wireless networks, and other (non-IP-based) proprietary networks. According to industry representatives, the business processes that are most critical to sector performance are manufacturing and engineering, environmental, health and safety, supply chain and logistics, financial, and personnel.
- The defense industrial base sector uses all types of information technology to perform business functions (accounting, finance, payroll) and operational functions that could instantly affect national security operations. Two critical areas that rely on information technology are the supply chain for manufacturing and the IT infrastructure that is owned and operated by the defense industrial base for DoD.
- Within the energy sector, the electricity industry uses a combination of information technologies, including LAN, WAN, Internet, wireless networks, satellite, and radio. According to industry representatives, information technology is used for a variety of business functions and operational processes, including control functions and marketing of power to consumers. Some of these processes, such as payroll, are important to the entities but not necessarily essential from a CIP perspective.
- Also within the energy sector, the oil and natural gas industry uses a combination of information technologies, including LAN, WAN, Internet, virtual private networks, wireless networks, satellite, and radio. In addition, representatives stated that in the pipeline environment, 80 to 90 percent of the applications purchased from vendors are TCP/IP, UNIX, or Windows NT-based. The remainder are based on older or proprietary protocols, such as SNA, DECnet, Appletalk, and IPX. The sector is also reliant on specialized control systems. The sector is highly dependent on technology for its communications and operations.
- Within the transportation sector, the rail segment relies on information technology and modern communications for rail operations and customer service. Business systems are isolated, physically separated from the control and dispatching centers. The control and dispatching

systems[23] are typically the responsibility of railroads' operations officers, not the chief information officer's staff. Control systems, i.e., signal systems located in the field (not central office based), are used to monitor train location. Signaling systems typically use both private and public networks, wired and wireless. These communications networks allow the dispatch system to set train routes and provide train location in return. Wayside sensors are used to monitor such things as wheel bearing condition and whether rock slides have impeded the track.

- Also within the transportation sector, the freight transportation industry, which includes trucking, air, rail, and waterborne transportation, uses general purpose business applications to manage internal processes and to link them with internal and external entities, mobile communications and tracking to maintain control over assets, and the Internet for electronic commerce and to link various systems.
- The telecommunications sector uses all forms of information technology, including some specialized systems, for business operations (pay/personnel), infrastructure (providing service to customers), and operational support (monitoring of telecommunications traffic). In addition, entities within this sector provide information technology and IT services to its customers.

Some Infrastructure Entities Utilize Specialized Systems and Technologies

Entities within certain critical infrastructures, such as banking and finance, transportation, chemical, telecommunications, and energy, use technologies that provide them with unique capabilities to perform critical functions. For example, there are centrally and federally controlled systems that allow entities to complete financial transactions, expedite transportation of goods, monitor the location of their assets and goods, and provide for safe travel.

Other information technologies provide entities with the means to monitor or control processes and to monitor the status of assets remotely and without human intervention. Referred to collectively as control systems, they are used by many infrastructures and industries (including electric power generation, transmission, and distribution; oil and gas refining and pipelines; water treatment and distribution; chemical production and processing; railroads and mass transit; and manufacturing) to monitor and control sensitive processes and physical functions. Control system functions vary

[23] Dispatching systems provide time slots for trains to enter the rail network. These systems are critical to the operation of the rail network. The dispatching process can no longer be performed manually because the level of operation needed to maintain the flow of the trains, and thus of the goods, is too high to perform without the computers. The first priority of dispatching operators is to maintain safety.

from simple to complex; they can be used simply to monitor processes—for example, the environmental conditions in a small office building—or to manage most activities in a municipal water system or even a nuclear power plant.

Sectors Have Similar Cybersecurity Requirements but the Specifics Vary

Because infrastructure sectors make use of similar computer and networking technologies, they have similar needs for cybersecurity. However, the level of importance placed on various aspects of cybersecurity varies. For instance, cybersecurity requirements are often described in terms of the confidentiality, integrity, or availability of data and systems. Confidentiality ensures the preservation of authorized restrictions on the access and disclosure of information, including means for protecting personal privacy and proprietary information. Integrity is defined as guarding against improper modification or destruction of information, and includes information nonrepudiation and authenticity. Availability means ensuring timely and reliable access to and use of information.

We found that sector entities generally share these basic cybersecurity objectives for their systems and networks, but they vary in the relative importance they place in these objectives based on the operational area or function involved. According to sector representatives, the importance placed on these objectives varies depending on the sector's risk assessment, priorities, current regulations, market forces, culture, and history. For example, water industry officials believe that integrity is the most important of the three requirements, while officials from the defense industrial base believe that availability is the most important. In contrast, sector representatives from the chemical industry stated that the importance of confidentiality, integrity, and availability is relative to the task being performed. Chemical sector officials stated that if manufacturing is the task, then integrity is paramount, but if personnel is the task, then confidentiality is the most important. According to electric power infrastructure representatives, the priority depends on the segment of the business that is referred to—generation, transmission, or distribution. These officials defined the priority order in the generation of power as (1) integrity, (2) availability, then (3) confidentiality. However, in the power-marketing segment of the business, confidentiality is a high priority because of the requirement to keep bids sealed prior to sales.

These factors, in combination with financial factors like costs and benefits, can affect an infrastructure entity's use of IT as well as its need for and deployment of cybersecurity technologies.

Chapter 3: Cybersecurity Technologies and Standards

Critical infrastructure owners use current cybersecurity technologies, such as firewalls and antivirus software, to help protect the information that is processed, stored, and transmitted in the network systems that are prevalent in the infrastructures.[24] To help infrastructure owners purchase cybersecurity technologies, standards are available that describe the operating characteristics and qualities of cybersecurity technology products. Standards that describe protocols and operating guidelines that describe how to use technology products are also available.

Cybersecurity Technologies

The following categories of cybersecurity technology products represent common control elements that help to secure IT systems and networks:

- **Access controls** restrict the ability of unknown or unauthorized users to view or use information, hosts, or networks. Access control technologies can help protect sensitive data and systems. Access controls include boundary protection, authentication, and authorization technologies.
- **System integrity controls** are used to ensure that a system and its data are not illicitly modified or corrupted by malicious code. Antivirus software and integrity checkers are two types of technologies that help to ensure system integrity.
- **Cryptography controls** include encryption of data during transmission and when it is stored on a system. Encryption is the process of transforming ordinary data into a code form so that the information is accessible only to those who are authorized to have access. Two applications of cryptography are virtual private networks and digital signatures and certificates.
- **Audit and monitoring controls** help administrators to perform investigations during and after an attack. We describe four types of audit and monitoring technologies: intrusion detection systems, intrusion prevention systems, security event correlation tools, and computer forensics.
- **Configuration management and assurance controls** help administrators to view and change the security settings on their hosts and networks, verify the correctness of security settings, and maintain operations in a secure fashion under duress conditions. We discuss five types of configuration management and assurance technologies: policy enforcement, network management, continuity of operations, scanners, and patch management.

[24] GAO has previously reported on cybersecurity technologies available to help secure federal computer systems. See U.S. General Accounting Office, *Information Security: Technologies to Secure Federal Systems*, GAO-04-467 (Washington, D.C.: March 9, 2004).

Table 10 lists some of the currently available cybersecurity technologies, organized according to these categories of security controls. Appendix III provides further details on these technologies.

Table 10. Common Types of Current Cybersecurity Technologies

Category	Technology	What it Does	Limitations
Access control			
Boundary protection	Firewalls	Control access to and from a network or computer.	Some types of firewalls are vulnerable to spoofing. More complex firewalls require more time to pass message traffic through.
	Content management	Monitors Web and messaging applications for inappropriate content, including spam, banned file types, and proprietary information.	Need to be able to accurately characterize inappropriate content for the filters to maximize matches and minimize false matches. For Web pages, filters may be difficult to keep up-to-date because of the growth of content on the Internet.
Authentication	Biometrics	Uses human characteristics, such as fingerprints, irises, and voices, to establish the identity of the user.	Effectiveness is based on the quality of the devices used. Human characteristics change over time and individuals may need to periodically update their information.
	Smart tokens	Establish identity of users using an integrated circuit chip in a portable device such as a smart card or time synchronized token.	Tokens can be lost or stolen and hence cannot reliably be bound to a specific identity when used in isolation from other methods of authentication.
Authorization	User rights and privileges	Allow or prevent access to data, systems, and actions of users based on the established policies of an organization.	Can be cumbersome to maintain in large organizations. Need to establish an effective balance between reducing unauthorized actions and granting access to resources to those that have a need for them.

Category	Technology	What it Does	Limitations
System integrity	Antivirus software	Provides protection against malicious code, such as viruses, worms, and Trojan horses.	Because new types of malicious code are discovered on a regular basis, virus signature updates are required on a regular basis. If not updated, antivirus software will not be able to detect new viruses.
	Integrity checkers	Monitor alterations to files on a system that are considered critical to the organization.	Does not prevent changes to the files, but can provide a record that changes did occur. Effectiveness depends on the accuracy of the baseline. Cannot always distinguish between authorized and unauthorized changes to the baseline.
Cryptography	Digital signatures and certificates	Uses public key cryptography to provide (1) assurance that both the sender and the recipient of a message or transaction will be uniquely identified, (2) assurance that the data have not been accidentally or deliberately altered, and (3) verifiable proof of the integrity and origin of the data.	Management processes such as ensuring the security of private keys and being able to establish trust in certificate authorities are instrumental to the success of this technology.
	Virtual private networks	Allow organizations or individuals in two or more physical locations to establish network connections over a shared or public network, such as the Internet, with functionality similar to that of a private network.	Does not ensure the security of the hosts on either end of the virtual private network. Implementation often requires specialized software or customization of applications.
Audit and monitoring	Intrusion detection systems	Detect inappropriate, incorrect, or anomalous activity on a network or computer system.	Effectiveness is limited by capture of accurate baselines or normal network or system activity.

Category	Technology	What it Does	Limitations
			Technology is prone to false positives and false negatives and is not as effective in protecting against unknown attacks. Cannot prevent attacks from damaging the network or host.
	Intrusion prevention systems	Build on intrusion detection systems to detect attacks on a network and take action to prevent them from being successful.	Effectiveness is limited by accuracy of the intrusion detection component. Technology results in reduced throughput through a network.
	Security event correlation tools	Monitor and document actions on network devices and analyze the actions to determine if an attack is ongoing or has occurred. Enable an organization to determine if ongoing system activities are operating according to its security policy.	These tools are limited by their ability to interface with numerous security products. Because of the reliance on logs, new attacks that are not reported on logs may go unseen. Proper access controls to log files are required to maintain their integrity.
	Computer forensics tools	Identity, preserve, extract, and document computer-based evidence.	Technology has no standards from which to judge the validity of results produced by these tools and their admissibility as evidence for law enforcement purposes.
Configuration management and assurance	Policy enforcement applications	Enable system administrators to engage in centralized monitoring and enforcement of an organization's security policies.	Effectiveness is based on security policies. Some applications do not work on all operating systems.
	Network management	Allow for the control and monitoring of networks, including management of faults, configurations, performance, and security.	Must often work with different vendor-specific elements to communicate with its network components.

Category	Technology	What it Does	Limitations
	Continuity of operations tools	Provide a complete backup infrastructure to maintain the availability of systems or networks in the event of an emergency or during planned maintenance.	Technologies may be complex to manage.
	Scanners	Analyze computers or networks for security vulnerabilities.	This technology can identify vulnerabilities but does not have the capability to fix them. Cannot identify unknown vulnerabilities.
	Patch management	Acquires, tests, and applies multiple patches to one or more computer systems.	Organization still needs to determine whether patches will negatively affect the operation of target systems. Automated distribution may create a potential security exposure.

Source: GAO analysis.

Access Controls

Boundary protection technologies protect a network or a node by controlling the network traffic at a network boundary—typically the point where an internal network or a node connects to an external network such as the Internet. Typical boundary protection technologies include firewalls and content management tools.

- Firewalls control the network packets that pass between two networks or a network and a node, and can keep unwanted external data out and sensitive internal data in. A firewall acts as a protective barrier because it is the single point through which both incoming and outgoing communications pass. There are many types of commercially available firewalls, including packet filters, stateful inspection firewalls, application proxy gateways, and dedicated proxy servers. Properly configured firewalls provide a level of protection for critical infrastructure systems that connect to the Internet and that are susceptible to cyber attacks from hackers anywhere in the world.
- Content management or filtering technologies can monitor Web, e-mail, and other messaging applications for inappropriate content, such as

spam, proprietary information, and banned files types. The technologies can also check for noncompliance with an organization's security policies. These technologies can help keep illegal material out of an organization's systems, reduce network traffic from spam,[25] and stop some forms of cyber attacks. In addition, these tools can track which users are browsing the Web, when they are doing so, which sites they are viewing, and the duration of time spent at those sites.

Authentication technologies help to establish the validity of a user's claimed identity, typically during access to a system or application (for example, login). Users can be authenticated using mechanisms such as requiring them to provide something they have (for example, a smart card); something they alone know (for example, a password or a personal identification number); or something they are (for example, a biometric). Cryptography is also often used to provide integrity to the authentication process.

- Biometrics cover a wide range of technologies that are used to verify identity by measuring and analyzing human characteristics. Identifying an individual's physiological characteristic is based on measuring a part of the body—such as fingertips and eye irises. Biometrics are theoretically very effective personal identifiers because the characteristics they measure are thought to be distinct to each person.
- Smart tokens are easily portable devices that contain an embedded integrated circuit chip capable of storing and processing data. Smart cards, a type of smart token, contain an embedded microprocessor and can exchange data with other systems. Other types of smart tokens include time-synchronized tokens that generate unique values at regular time intervals and challenge-response tokens that can produce a onetime password based on prompts from a central server.

Once a user is authenticated, **authorization technologies** are used to allow or prevent actions by that user based on predefined rules. Authorization technologies support the principles of legitimate use, least privilege, and separation of duties. These technologies help to define and maintain what actions an authenticated user can perform once granted access to a system. Operating systems have some built-in authorization features such as user rights and privileges, groups of users, and permissions for files and folders. Network devices, such as routers, may have access lists that can be used to authorize those who can access and perform certain actions on the device. Access rights and privileges can be used to implement security policies that determine what a user can do after being allowed into the system.

[25] Spam is electronic junk mail that is unsolicited and usually is advertising for some product.

System Integrity

Antivirus software can help to detect known viruses and worms and stop them before they cause damage to a system's software or data.

Antivirus software provides protection against viruses and malicious code such as worms and Trojan horses. Effective antivirus software should reliably detect and remove viruses and malicious code, in addition to preventing the unwanted effects and repairing the damage that could result. There are several different types of antivirus software, including signature scanning, where the software contains a database of virus signatures and scans files in a computer system for certain "signature strings" that are associated with known viruses. Other technologies scan for lines of computer code that are associated with virus-like behaviors, or check untrusted code for suspicious behavior before it is permitted to execute.

Integrity checking tools can detect whether any critical system files have been changed, thus enabling the system administrator to look for unauthorized alteration of the system. Integrity checkers examine stored files or network packets to determine if they have been altered or changed. These checkers are based on checksums—a simple mathematical operation that turns an entire file or a message into a number. More complex hash functions that result in a fixed string of encrypted data are also used. The integrity checking process begins with the creation of a baseline, where checksums or hashes for clean data are computed and saved. Each time the integrity checker is run, it again makes a checksum or hash computation and compares the result with the stored value.

Cryptography

Encryption technologies can be used on data to (1) hide their information content, (2) prevent their undetected modification, and (3) prevent their unauthorized use. When properly implemented, encryption technologies can provide assurance regarding the confidentiality, integrity, or origin of information that has been exchanged. It can also provide a method by which the authenticity of a document can be confirmed.

Several levels of cryptographic technology are currently in use. Cryptographic modules implement algorithms that form the building blocks of cryptographic applications. Using these modules, technologies are available that can be used to encrypt message transmissions so that eavesdroppers cannot determine the contents of the message. Digital signature technologies use cryptography to authenticate the sender of a message. Hash technologies use cryptography to provide assurance to a message recipient that the contents of the message have not been altered.

Several cryptographic technologies are used to ensure the confidentiality and integrity of data as it is being transmitted over the network.

These technologies include digital certificates, digital signatures, secure sockets layer (SSL), and virtual private networks (VPN). Many of these technologies are built into applications that are commonly available on many computer systems. For example, most Web browsers support SSL for secure communications between a computer and the Web server.

Digital signatures use public key cryptography to provide authentication, data integrity, and nonrepudiation for a message or transaction. Just as a physical signature helps to provide assurance that a letter has been written by a specific person, a digital signature helps provide assurance that a message was sent by a particular individual or machine. A digital certificate is an electronic credential that can help verify the association between a public key and a specific entity.

Virtual private networks allow organizations or individuals in two or more physical locations to establish network connections over a shared or public network, such as the Internet, with functionality similar to that of a private network. VPNs establish security procedures and protocols that encrypt communications between the two end points. VPNs encrypt not only the data but also the originating and receiving network addresses.

Audit and Monitoring

Intrusion detection systems (IDS) and **intrusion prevention systems (IPS)** monitor and analyze events occurring on a system or network and either alert appropriate personnel or prevent the attack in progress from continuing. Both technologies can use a pattern matching algorithm or an anomaly-based algorithm that identifies deviations from normal network or system behavior in order to detect attacks. While an IDS can only provide alerts to an administrator that an attack is occurring, an IPS can take steps to defend against the attack or mitigate its effects.

Security event correlation tools produce audit logs, or lists of actions, that have occurred from operating systems, firewalls, applications, and other devices. Depending on the configuration of the logging functions, critical activities, such as access to administrator functions, are logged and can be monitored for anomalous activity. During an investigation, the logs can be examined to determine the method of entry that was used by an attacker and to ascertain the level of damage that was caused by the attack. Because of the volume of data involved on some systems and networks, correlation tools are available to analyze the logs and identify key information using particular search terms or correlation analysis. These tools can provide a dynamic picture of ongoing system activities that can be used to confirm that the system is operating in accordance with the organization's security policies.

Computer forensics tools identify, preserve, extract, and document computer-based evidence. They can be used to recover files that have been deleted, encrypted, or damaged. Computer forensics tools are used during the investigation of a computer crime to determine the perpetrator and the methods that were used to conduct the attack. There are two main categories of computer forensics tools: (1) evidence preservation and collection tools, which prevent the accidental or deliberate modification of computer-related evidence, and (2) recovery and analysis tools.

Configuration Management and Assurance

Policy enforcement applications help administrators to define and perform centralized monitoring and enforcement of an organization's security policies. These tools examine desktop and server configurations that define authorized access to specified devices, and they compare these settings against a baseline policy. These applications provide a centralized way for administrators to use other security technologies, such as access control and security event and correlation technologies.

Network management provides system administrators with the ability to control and monitor a computer network from a central location. Network management systems obtain status data from network components, enable network managers to make configuration changes, and alert them of problems. Network management includes management of faults, configurations, performance, security, and accounting.

To provide **continuity of operations**, secure backup tools are available that can restore system data and functionality in the event of a disruption. Typically these products have been used to address naturally occurring problems, such as power outages. But these tools are now being applied to help recover from system problems resulting from malicious cyber attacks. Technologies are also available to help systems and networks continue to operate in spite of an ongoing cyber attack. To keep systems and networks up and running, many procedural and operational techniques, such as redundant systems and high-availability systems, are available.

Scanners are common testing and audit tools, used to identify vulnerabilities in networks and systems as a part of proactive security testing. A wide variety of scanners is available that can be used to probe modems, internet ports, databases, wireless access points, Web pages, and applications. These tools often incorporate the capability to monitor the security posture of the networks and systems by testing and auditing the security configurations of hosts and networks.

Patch management tools automate the otherwise manual process of acquiring, testing, and applying patches to a computer system. These tools can be used to identify missing patches on systems, deploy patches, and generate reports to track the status of a patch across various computers.

Cybersecurity Standards

Cybersecurity standards can help to provide the basis for the purchase and sale of security products by defining a set of rules, conditions, or requirements that must be met by the products. There are three broad categories of standards that govern cybersecurity technology: (1) protocol security standards, such as IPSEC and Secure BGP; (2) product security criteria, such as Common Criteria protection profiles; and (3) operational guidelines, such as those issued by NIST. Protocol security standards are interface standards that define points of connection between two devices. Product standards establish qualities or requirements for a product to ensure that it will serve its purpose effectively. Operational guidelines define a process to be followed in order for a security process or system to perform effectively.

Designers and builders of products can use protocol and product standards to create and test products to ensure that they meet the criteria set forth by the standards. Buyers can select standards-compliant technology with assurance that the technology meets the standards. There is considerable interest in cybersecurity standards on the part of governments, industry associations, and the Internet Engineering Task Force. However, precise definitions are needed to test whether standards have been met or not. Such precise definitions are often difficult to articulate for cybersecurity.

Nevertheless, the development and use of a standard can attract a scrutiny that helps to reduce design flaws and promote security. Additionally, the existence of standards promotes the availability of detailed technical information about a technology, which may serve as a basis for determining where vulnerabilities remain. At the same time, however, an attack against a specific standard-conforming technology can succeed against all systems that use the standard. On the other hand, a single countermeasure could protect all standards-compliant systems. Thus, standards can help as well as hurt cybersecurity. Overall, standards would be useful in promoting cybersecurity because they would make it possible for organizations, including the federal government, to purchase cybersecurity technologies that meet minimum standards.

Technology standards are developed and adopted in a number of ways. First, there are national and international standards bodies such as the American National Standards Institute (ANSI) and ISO that typically administer and coordinate voluntary standardization efforts. ANSI is a private, nonprofit organization that promotes and facilitates voluntary consensus standards and conformity assessment systems and safeguards their integrity. ISO is a network of national standards institutes from 148 countries that works in partnership with international organizations, governments, industry, and business and consumer representatives to develop technical standards.

Professional organizations such as the Institute of Electrical and Electronics Engineers (IEEE) and the American Society for Testing and Materials (ASTM) develop technical standards in their areas of expertise. For example, there are IEEE standards for networking technologies such as Ethernet over many different media, including wireless.

A different standards process drives the Internet standards that are related to protocols, procedures, and conventions that are used in or by the Internet. Internet standards begin life as a specification written in the form of a Request for Comments (RFC) document. The RFC undergoes a period of development, several iterations of review by the Internet community, and revision based on experience. Then it is adopted as a standard by the Internet Engineering Steering Group and is published. The detailed Internet standards process itself is documented as an RFC.[26]

Government agencies are also involved in developing and promoting standards. For example, in the federal government, NIST has the mission to develop and promote measurement, standards, and technology to enhance productivity, facilitate trade, and improve the quality of life. NIST is leading the development of key information system security standards and guidelines as part of its FISMA Implementation Project. This includes the development of Federal Information Processing Standards (FIPS) that apply to information systems built or acquired by the civilian agencies in the federal government. NIST also publishes many special publications on computer security that provide guidance to federal agencies on many aspects of computer security.

Table 11 lists examples of current cybersecurity standards, organized by high-level control categories.

A number of other security standards and guides cover more than one of the control categories shown in table 11. One good example is ISO 17799, which is a standard for information security management.[27] Some sectors, such as the health care sector, have their own guides, such as ASTM E1762, *Standard Guide for Electronic Authentication of Health Care Information*.[28]

[26] Bradner, Scott, *The Internet Standards Process—Revision 3*, RFC 2026 (Oct. 1996).

[27] International Organization for Standardization, *Information Technology—Code of Practice for Information Security Management*, ISO 17799 (2000). ISO 17799 is a widely recognized information security standard and is described as a "comprehensive set of controls comprising best practices in information security".

[28] ASTM International, *Standard Guide for Electronic Authentication of Health Care Information*, ASTM E1762 (2003).

Table 11. Examples of Cybersecurity Standards

Control Category	Standards
Access controls	Boundary Protection • Network Address Translation (RFC 3022) • SOCKS Protocol Version 5 (RFC 1928)
	Authentication • IP Security Protocol (IPSEC) • DNS Security Extensions (DNSSEC) (RFC 2535) • SNMPv3 Security (RFC 3414) • IEEE P1363 PKI standards • A One-Time Password System (RFC 2289) • ISO/IEC 7816: Smart Card Security • ISO 9798-1: Security Techniques—Entity Authentication Mechanism
	Authorization • CCITT X.500 directory standard
System integrity	Integrity • Federal Information Processing Standard (FIPS) 198: The Keyed-Hash Message Authentication Code (HMAC) March 2002 • FIPS 180-2: Secure Hash Standard (SHS), (SHA-1, SHA-256, SHA-384, and SHA-512) • ISO 10118-1: Security Techniques—Hash Functions Non-repudiation—digital signature • FIPS 186-2: Digital Signature Standard (DSS) • ANSI X9.31-1998: Digital Signatures Using Reversible Public Key Cryptography for the Financial Services Industry • ANSI X9.62-1998: Public Key Cryptography for the Financial Services Industry: The Elliptic Curve Digital Signature Algorithm • ISO 9796: Security Techniques—Digital Signature Scheme Giving Message Recovery • ISO 13888-1: Security Techniques—Non-repudiation • ASTM E2084-00: Standard Specification for Authentication of Healthcare Information Using Digital Signatures
Cryptography	Encryption algorithms • RSA Public Key Cryptography Standards (PKCS) • FIPS 197: Advanced Encryption Standard (AES) • FIPS 46-3: Data Encryption Standard (DES) • ANSI X9.52-1998: Triple Data Encryption Algorithm Modes of Operation • FIPS 185: Escrowed Encryption Standard (EES)-Skipjack
	Encrypted transmission • Secure Sockets Layer (SSL) v3.0 • Transport Layer Security (TLS) v.1 (RFC 2246) • IP Security Protocol (IPSEC) and IKE (Internet Key Exchange) (RFC 2409) • Secure Shell (SSH) • Layer Two Tunneling Protocol (L2TP) for VPN (RFC 2661) • IEEE 802.11 and 802.11i (in process) • Wi-Fi Protected Access (WPA) Encrypted storage • OpenPGP Message Format (RFC 2440) • MIME Security with OpenPGP (RFC 3156)

Control Category	Standards
Audit and monitoring	Intrusion detection • The Intrusion Detection Exchange Protocol (IDXP), Internet Draft
	System event correlation tools • ASTM E2147-01: Standard Specification for Audit and Disclosure Logs for Use in Health Information Systems
Configuration management and assurance	Network management • Simple Network Management Protocol (SNMP) (RFC 3416)

Source: GAO analysis.

Another well-known security standard is the Information Technology Security Evaluation Criteria, also known as the Common Criteria.[29] European and North American governments are moving toward Common Criteria as a unified set of security criteria. Version 2 of the Common Criteria attempts to reconcile a number of existing criteria, including the United States Trusted Computer System Evaluation Criteria, the so-called Orange Book criteria. Common Criteria has two underlying dimensions: (1) the protection profiles that capture the security functionality, and (2) the evaluation assurance level that specifies how much to trust the claims of the security profile.

Standards such as the Common Criteria are written in general terms because the criteria must cover a variety of products and technologies. When such criteria are applied to a specific product, the criteria must be interpreted, and it is the interpretation that sets the level of security that the product must meet.

NIST and NSA are undertaking a collaborative effort, the National Information Assurance Partnership (NIAP), to produce comprehensive security requirements and security specifications for key technologies that will be used to build more secure systems for federal agencies. These security requirements and security specifications will be developed with significant industry involvement and will employ the Common Criteria. Protection profiles in key technology areas such as operating systems, firewalls, smart cards, biometrics devices, database systems, public key infrastructure (PKI) components, network devices, virtual private networks, intrusion detection systems, and Web browsers will be the primary focus of this project.

[29] Common Criteria consists of three ISO standards: ISO 15408-1 *Information Technology— Security Techniques—Evaluation Criteria for IT Security—Part 1: Introduction and General Model (1999); ISO 15408-2 Information Technology—Security Techniques—Evaluation Criteria for IT Security—Part 2: Security Functional Requirements* (1999); and ISO 15408-3 *Information Technology— Security Techniques—Evaluation Criteria for IT Security—Part 3: Security Assurance Requirements* (1999).

The NIAP Common Criteria Evaluation and Validation Scheme Web site also provides information about Common Criteria-validated products, validated protection profiles, products that are in evaluation, and protection profiles that are in development.[30] For example, some of the validated product types include switches, routers, wireless local area networks, firewalls, virtual private networks, operating systems, antivirus software, biometrics, and intrusion detection systems. Validated U.S. government protection profiles exist for a number of security technologies such as firewalls, operating systems, smart card tokens, and intrusion detection systems.

In addition to supporting Common Criteria evaluations of products, NIST operates the Cryptographic Module Validation Program (CMVP), which uses independent, accredited, private sector laboratories, to perform security testing of cryptographic modules for conformance to FIPS 140-2, *Security Requirements for Cryptographic Modules*, and related federal cryptographic algorithm standards. A government body validates the results of the CMVP testing, and evaluation processes to ensure that the security standards are being applied correctly and consistently.

Unfortunately it takes time and money to evaluate products against the Common Criteria. There is a shortage of evaluated components, and there is little or no rigorous methodology for assessing the security of systems composed of components that have been evaluated using the Common Criteria. Further, with an ever increasing number of threats emerging, Common Criteria protection profiles would need to be regularly updated to ensure that products certified with the criteria remain secure.

Chapter 4: Cybersecurity Implementation Issues

Critical infrastructure owners are ultimately responsible for addressing their cybersecurity needs. However, as we have described, there are several other stakeholders involved with efforts to enhance cybersecurity. For some infrastructure sectors, sector coordinators—individuals or organizations—perform a collective role in helping the entities within their sector to improve cybersecurity. In addition, federal, state, and local governments have a stake in ensuring that the interests of national security and the public good are addressed, and they have a variety of policy tools that can be used to influence how the nation's critical infrastructures are protected, including regulations, grants, and partnerships. In some cases, the federal government plays an important role in the operations of a critical infrastructure sector. For example, the Federal Aviation Administration's (FAA) air traffic control system is essential to the operations of the aviation

[30] Validated product lists are available online at the Common Criteria Evaluation and Validation Scheme Web site at http://niap.nist.gov/cc-scheme/ValidatedProducts.html.

transportation sector. IT manufacturers, including cybersecurity technology companies, develop and market the tools used by critical infrastructure owners to conduct their business and protect their information technology infrastructure from security risks. All of these parties face various challenges in addressing the nation's cybersecurity needs. Such challenges range from identifying cybersecurity problems within an organization to creating business cases so that specific cybersecurity technologies can be deployed in or developed for it. Many of these challenges are common to all types of critical infrastructures while some challenges are unique to specific sectors. Concomitant with the challenges, there are opportunities for action by the federal government, critical infrastructure sectors, individual entities that own critical infrastructures, and technology manufacturers.

This chapter focuses on two major categories of potential actions for improving cybersecurity for CIP. First, the implementation of available cybersecurity technologies and processes could help address critical infrastructure owners' immediate cybersecurity needs. We present cybersecurity challenges that are faced by critical infrastructure owners and suggest approaches and actions that are available to help meet those challenges, including the use of cybersecurity technology.

Second, we discuss policy options available to the federal government that can make more cybersecurity technologies available and encourage their use by infrastructure owners. Several activities have already been undertaken by the federal government and by critical infrastructure sectors to improve critical infrastructure protection. To determine whether to continue or expand current programs or to develop new cybersecurity programs, it would be useful to examine the effectiveness of these current activities and assess whether further investment is required.

Further, an important common thread in all the opportunities for actions is the certainty of consequences—both intended and unintended—of any policy action. Before proposing or implementing any policy action, the federal government needs to consider these potential consequences, as well as the costs and benefits of the action.

A Risk-Based Framework for Infrastructure Owners to Implement Cybersecurity Technologies

A basic challenge facing critical infrastructure owners is that they have to address many different issues that affect their operations. Security issues, both physical and cyber, are only one element of what affects an entity's operations. Management's primary concern is the day-to-day operation, the investments needed for the future, and stakeholder, stockholder or owner satisfaction with its performance. An overall security framework can help an entity properly evaluate the importance of cybersecurity problems within the context of its operations. Security best practices recommend that a risk assessment methodology be used to make informed security investment decisions. If an entity has not conducted a risk assessment, it cannot know the extent of its cybersecurity problem. Even when it knows the extent of cybersecurity needs, it cannot protect everything. Further, an entity often needs a business case to invest in cybersecurity.

On the basis of the results of a risk assessment, infrastructure owners can implement available cybersecurity technologies to mitigate identified risks. There are several categories of cybersecurity technologies available that could be used to better secure critical infrastructure systems. However, infrastructure owners also need to bear in mind the limitations of these technologies, as well as the interactions of the technologies with the security processes and the people using the technologies.

Using an Overall Framework for Cybersecurity

It is important to think of cybersecurity in an overall framework (see figure 4) that includes the following processes: (1) determining the business requirements for security; (2) performing risk assessments; (3) establishing a security policy; (4) implementing a cybersecurity solution that includes people, process, and technology to mitigate identified security risks; and (5) monitoring and managing security continuously.

A cybersecurity framework starts with the development of a security policy based on business requirements and a risk analysis. The business requirements identify the needs of the enterprise, including cybersecurity requirements—the computer resources and information that have to be protected, including any requirements imposed by applicable laws, such as HIPAA, FISMA, and requirements to protect the privacy of some types of data. Some risks are external to the entity conducting the risk assessment and involve considerations beyond the risks that are within the entity's control.

On the basis of the risk analysis and the business requirements for cybersecurity, an entity can develop its security policy. Such a security policy typically addresses high-level objectives such as ensuring the confidentiality, integrity, and availability of data and systems. As we previously described, we found that sector entities generally share these basic cybersecurity objectives for their systems and networks, but they vary in the relative importance they place on these objectives based on the operational area or function involved.

These security objectives are achieved by implementing cybersecurity solutions that make use of people, process, and technology. Because of the variation in cybersecurity objectives among critical infrastructure sectors, while

Figure 4: An Overall Framework for Security

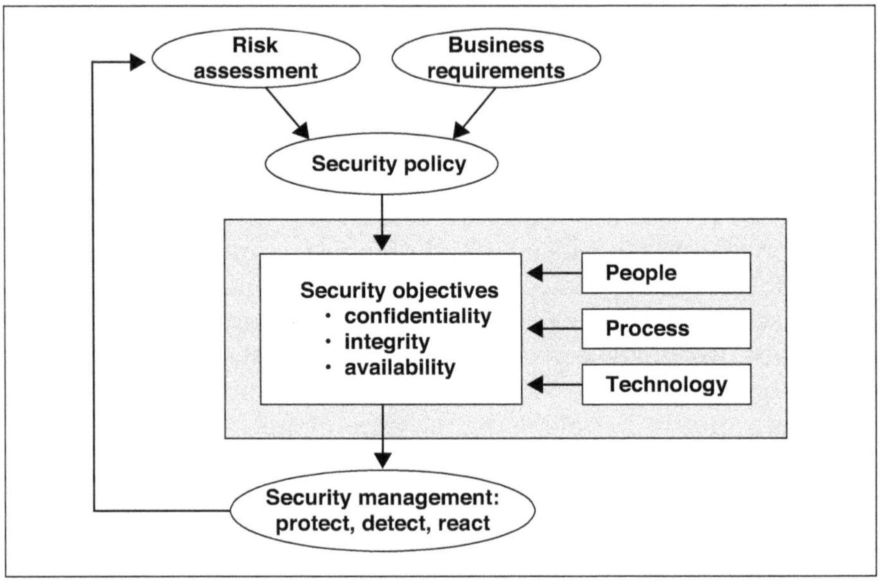

Source: GAO Analysis.

the types of IT and cybersecurity technologies are the same across all sector entities, the details of implementation and the level of their use differ from one sector to another. In addition to implementing security solutions, entities need security management that continuously protects against, detects, and reacts to any security incidents. The combination of risk analysis, security policy, security solutions, and security management provides the overall cybersecurity framework and represents a continuous process. Such an overall security framework can help an entity to establish a common level of understanding of its cybersecurity posture and a common basis for the design and implementation of cybersecurity solutions in it.

Risk Assessments Are Key to Cybersecurity Planning

Risk analysis or risk assessment is a key component within the overall framework for cybersecurity. The approach to good security is fundamentally similar, regardless of the assets being protected. As we have previously reported, applying risk management principles can provide a sound foundation for effective security whether the assets are information, operations, people, or federal facilities.[31] A risk management methodology can

[31] U.S. General Accounting Office, *National Preparedness: Technologies to Secure Federal Buildings*, GAO-02-687T (Washington, D.C.: Apr. 25, 2002).

provide the basic information that is required to make decisions on how to protect an entity's information systems. As seen in figure 5, these principles can be reduced to five basic steps that help to determine responses to five essential questions:

What Am I Protecting?

The first step in risk management is to identify the assets that must be protected and the impact of their potential loss.

Who Are My Adversaries?

The second step is to identify and characterize the threat to these assets. The intent and capability of an adversary are the principal criteria for establishing the degree of threat to the identified assets.

How Am I Vulnerable?

Step three involves identifying and characterizing vulnerabilities that would allow identified threats to be realized. In other words, what weaknesses would allow a security breach?

What Are My Priorities?

In the fourth step, risk must be assessed and priorities determined for protecting assets. Risk assessment examines the potential for the loss of or

Figure 5: Five Steps in the Risk Management Process

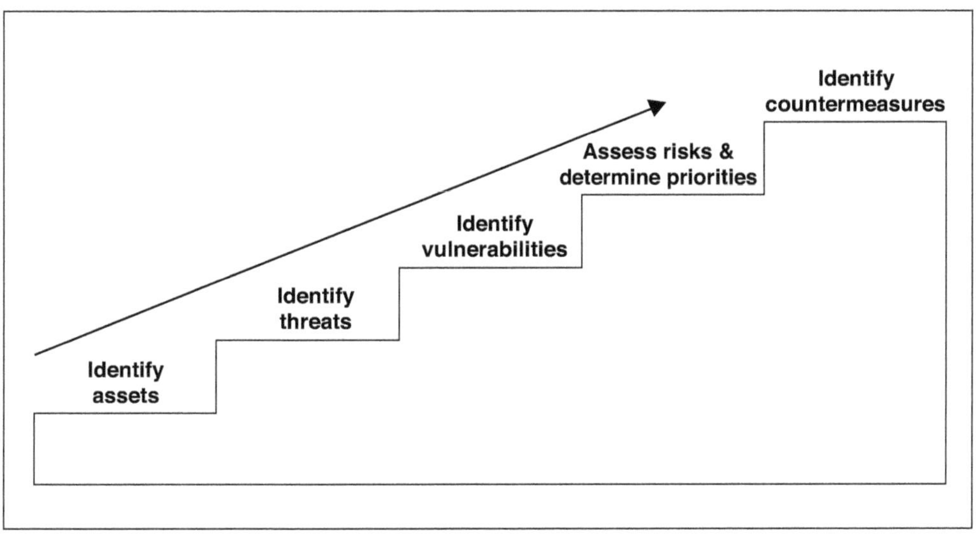

Source: GAO analysis.

damage to an asset. Risk levels are established by assessing the impact of loss or damage, threats to the asset, and vulnerabilities.

What Can I Do?

The final step is to identify countermeasures to reduce or eliminate risks. In doing so, the advantages and benefits of these countermeasures must also be weighed against their disadvantages and costs.

One of the roadblocks to understanding the importance of cybersecurity is the lack of solid information on the scope and scale of cyber vulnerabilities and the consequences of cyber attacks. Risk assessment is a key proactive step that can be used to help an entity decide what to do to protect its cyber assets from potential attacks. Risk assessment provides a framework for analyzing alternatives to mitigate risks and implement countermeasures. Instead of reacting to the latest news of vulnerabilities in software, critical infrastructure owners can use the results of risk assessments to proactively take steps to reduce the risks of cyber attacks. It is important to note that it is not practical or possible to eliminate all risks. There will always be some level of risk that cannot be mitigated without unacceptably large expenditures or the use of overly obtrusive controls.

Risk assessments can be conducted by both sector-wide organizations and critical infrastructure owners. A sector's risk assessment should be based on its knowledge of its exposure to various threats, and it should provide guidance to infrastructure owners on which risks may apply to them. Some infrastructure sectors have completed risk assessments for their sector. For example, the rail segment of the transportation infrastructure sector performed a terrorism risk analysis and related security management plan that provides recommended actions under various alert levels.

Critical infrastructure owners in each sector also conduct risk assessments for their own enterprise and develop mitigation approaches based on available countermeasures. For example, entities within the electric, banking and finance, and chemical sectors have performed risk assessments. These infrastructure owners periodically reassess threats and vulnerabilities after implementing the countermeasures. Thus, risk assessment is a continuing task for any entity that has responsibility for protecting critical infrastructures.

However, while risk assessment is a commonly accepted practice, not all sector entities employ it. Some entities do not even know which of their assets need to be protected, while others have not conducted a vulnerability assessment. Entities in some sectors seem more accustomed than others to using risk assessments for cybersecurity. For example, the banking and finance sector routinely performs risk assessments in the conduct of its business, so its culture seems better suited to taking a risk-based approach to cybersecurity. In addition, regulations require banks to be proactive about cybersecurity monitoring and response.

Risk is the combination of two probabilities: (1) the probability that a threat exists that will locate and exploit a vulnerability and (2) the probability that the threat will succeed in its attempt. A combination of the threat, the vulnerability being exploited by the threat, and the effect of a realized threat can guide entities to mitigate the greatest security risks. Because infrastructure entities have limited resources, a risk management approach can help them focus their efforts on those areas most at risk.

To conduct risk assessments, entities need information about threats and vulnerabilities. Vulnerability information is documented in a variety of publicly available sources. Some well-known online resources that identify and categorize cybersecurity vulnerabilities include the following:

- CERT/CC analyzes vulnerabilities and issues advisories on the most urgent of problems. For less critical problems, CERT/CC publishes incident notes and vulnerability notes.[32]
- Common Vulnerabilities and Exposures (CVE) is a list of standardized names of vulnerabilities.[33] It is common practice to use CVE names to describe vulnerabilities.
- The ICAT Metabase is a searchable index of information on computer vulnerabilities, published by NIST.[34] The ICAT vulnerability index lists over 6,200 vulnerabilities, and it provides links to vulnerability advisories and patch information for each vulnerability.
- The SANS Institute publishes the SANS/FBI Top 20 List—a list of the 20 most critical Internet security vulnerabilities that is updated periodically.[35]

Sector entities can identify relevant cyber vulnerabilities based on their understanding of the assets in their system environment. The President's *National Strategy for Homeland Security* states that comprehensive vulnerability assessments of all of our nation's critical infrastructures are important from a planning perspective because they can enable authorities to evaluate the potential effects of an attack on a given sector and then invest accordingly to protect it. Without a vulnerability assessment, sector entities will not have a comprehensive approach to determine what parts of their information technology infrastructure require security investments. While some vulnerabilities may be addressed in such an ad hoc manner, it will be difficult to know with any certainty that those vulnerabilities that could cause the greatest harm or are most likely to be exploited have been addressed.

[32] The CERT/CC vulnerability notes database can be accessed at http://www.kb.cert.org/vuls/.
[33] Common Vulnerabilities and Exposures is available online at http://cve.mitre.org/.
[34] The ICAT Metabase is available online at http://icat.nist.gov/.
[35] The SANS/FBI Top 20 List is available online at http://www.sans.org/top20/.

A more proactive testing approach can also be used to identify system vulnerabilities. Sector entities can use automated vulnerability scanning tools that scan a group of hosts or a network for known vulnerable services. Another approach is to conduct a security test and evaluation. Such an approach entails the development and execution of a plan to test the effectiveness of the security controls of IT systems. Penetration testing can also be employed to test for unknown problems. The objective of penetration testing is to test systems and networks from the viewpoint of a threat and identify potential failures in the security control environment.

Although the general threats to cybersecurity are well known, the specific threats to each critical infrastructure sector may not be readily apparent to the entities within the sector. While some sectors have their own threat assessment capability, other sectors rely on the government to provide them with information on threats. It is critical to ensure that appropriate intelligence and other threat information, both cyber and physical, is received from the intelligence and law enforcement communities. Since the 1990s, the national security community and the Congress have identified the need to establish analysis and warning capabilities to protect against strategic computer attacks on the nation's critical computer- dependent infrastructures. Such capabilities should address both cyber and physical threats and involve (1) gathering and analyzing information for the purpose of detecting and reporting otherwise potentially damaging actions or intentions and (2) implementing a process for warning policy makers and allowing them time to determine the magnitude of the related risks.

During a risk assessment, it is important to consider the threat that insiders pose to critical infrastructures. As we have described, because of the access that insiders have to an organization's computer systems, the damage that can be caused by them can be severe. Several steps can be taken to prevent insiders from causing damage to a system. Placing limits on access to sensitive systems and information and separating the duties of employees can minimize the damage that an insider can cause. In addition, organizations can maintain and review reliable logs that track user actions. Technologies can also be used that help to secure the sensitive systems and detect unauthorized access.

Risk assessment also requires an estimate of the consequences of a risk. This entails estimating what happens to an entity if a threat succeeds in exploiting a specific vulnerability in its networked information systems. However, it is difficult to estimate the effect of failures caused by cyber attacks. For example, attacks on Internet infrastructures such as the domain name servers can be varied. Corporations that manage their own internal networks may be totally unaffected by such an attack. Even widespread outages may not affect some users if they have access to cached information.

There have been many reports highlighting the monetary impact of cyber attacks, but the basis of those costs are not well understood. The inability to predict the consequences of cyber attacks complicates the process of assessing risks.

Protection, Detection, and Reaction Are Integral Security Concepts

Because it is impossible to protect computer systems from all attacks, countermeasures identified through the risk management process must support three integral concepts of a holistic security program: protection, detection, and reaction (see figure 6). Protection provides countermeasures such as policies, procedures, and technical controls to defend against attacks on the assets being protected. Detection monitors for potential breakdowns in the protective measures that could result in security breaches. Reaction, which often requires human involvement, responds to detected breaches to thwart attacks before damage can be done. Because absolute protection from attacks is impossible to achieve, a security program that does not incorporate detection and reaction is incomplete.

There is a variety of cybersecurity technologies available for addressing protection, detection, and reaction. For example, firewalls can protect a network

Figure 6: Protection, Detection and Reaction Are All Essential to Cybersecurity

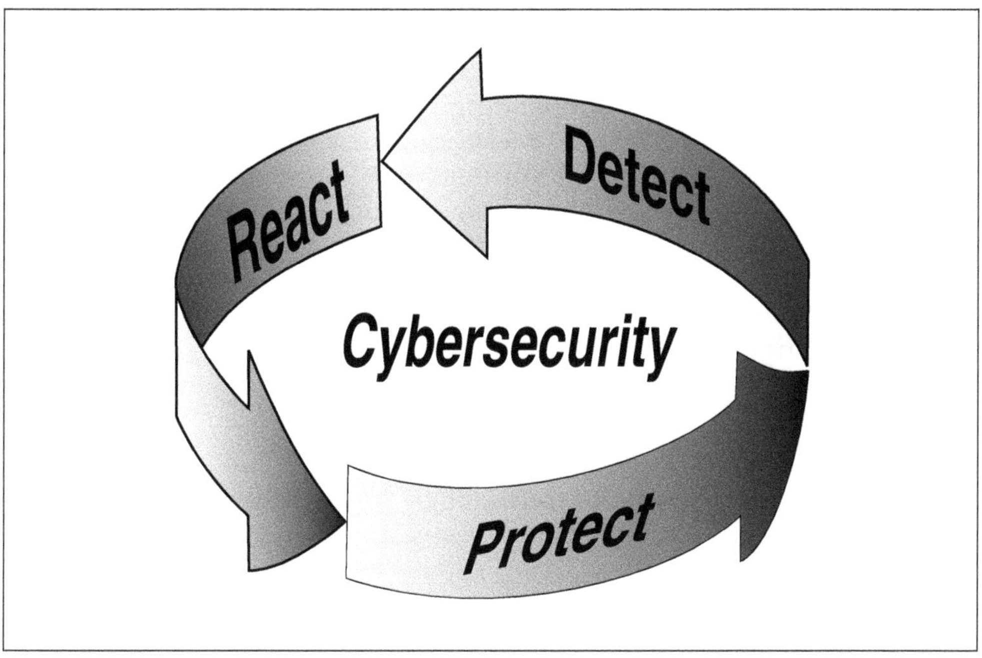

Source: GAO.

from some attacks as well as detect when those attacks are attempted. However, some aspects of the protection-detection-reaction triad are difficult to support with current technologies and practices. For example, because of limitations in the current Internet environment, the tracking and tracing of cyber attacks is a very difficult task. The ability to identify the source of an attack could allow for a better response and potentially contain the damage caused by the attack. Law enforcement needs this information in order to investigate, collect evidence, and potentially prosecute the perpetrators of the attack.

One key problem is the untrustworthiness of the source IP address in Internet data packets. The source IP address is supposed to be the IP address of the originator of the network message. However, because the Internet was originally designed to be used by trusted users, no authentication of the source of messages was built into internet protocols. It is possible for malicious users to forge the source address of IP packets to obscure the real source of the attack. Further, IP addresses may identify only a computer involved in the attack. Because of the prevalence of publicly available computers and of weak access controls and authorization policies on private computers, linking a computer to an attack does not necessarily link the attack to a specific person.

Another key problem is that the Internet crosses administrative and geopolitical boundaries. Different organizations administer different parts of the Internet. There is no central administrative authority of the Internet. While there are common technical standards and protocols that need to be followed by each administrative domain, there are different governing structures in each country. Depending on the configuration of routing tables and network traffic, an IP packet can cross multiple administrative and geopolitical boundaries as it journeys to its destination. The tracing of attacks could require cooperation from several administrative organizations of the Internet to obtain information about the packets in question. If an organization is uncooperative and law enforcement has no legal means to ensure its cooperation, it becomes extremely difficult to trace attacks back to their origin. One of the problems is that there are no universal laws or agreements as to what constitutes a cyber attack.

A Business Case Needs to Be Made for Cybersecurity

Best practices for information technology investment recommend that prior to making any significant project investment, information about the benefits and costs of the investment should be analyzed and assessed in detail. It is further recommended that a business case be developed that identifies the organizational needs for the system and provides a clear statement of the high-level system goals. The high-level goals address the system's expected outcomes, such as preventing unauthorized users from gaining access to a system or detecting and logging security breaches. Certain performance parameters, such as transaction times or maximum loads, are also usually specified.

Some critical infrastructure sector representatives told us that it is difficult for them to address cybersecurity unless it makes business sense to do so—that is, the investment is cost-beneficial. Typically this means that investments must generate revenue, save or avoid costs, or increase productivity. In some cases, IT investments are undertaken for non-quantitative reasons, such as strategic impact or because such investments are necessary to protect critical infrastructure important to national security. While most companies realize that information security breaches are bad for business, in some cases, information security managers find it difficult to justify investments in security based only on the fear of attacks.

However, security managers face challenges in providing this type of justification. According to the Institute for Information Infrastructure Protection (I3P), there are insufficient models and a lack of data to support effective decision making. I3P identified the need for additional research and development in the area of economic analysis in its cybersecurity research and development agenda. It states that sound models to assess the costs and benefits of cybersecurity alternatives need to be developed, and that methods are required to better predict the consequences of risk management choices.

Cost-benefit analyses and return-on-investment calculations are the normal methods used to justify investments. Security technology manufacturers and managed security service providers, as well as some researchers, have developed methodologies to perform this type of analysis for security.

Decision makers also lack baseline data on the costs, benefits, and effects of security controls from an economic and technical perspective. While it is possible to determine the costs of security, it is difficult to quantify the value from such investments because good and consistent security metrics are not available. Without metrics, it is difficult to assess the effectiveness of different security options. NIST has developed guidelines on developing security metrics that could be used to help justify security investments.[36] NIST is also developing guidelines for federal agencies to use to support successful integration of security into the capital investment planning process.

Other Needs Compete with Cybersecurity for Resources

Organizations have limited resources—people and money—and consequently, they typically focus on improving cybersecurity only to the extent that those security needs are necessary to continue their business operations

[36] National Institute of Standards and Technology, *Security Metrics Guide for Information Technology Systems*, NIST Special Publication 800-55 (Gaithersburg, MD: July, 2003).

or are demanded by their customers. As we have described, in order to maximize the return from these resources, an entity is best served by taking a risk-based view that considers all the risks that the entity faces. According to its own prioritization of these risks, the entity may determine the threat of cyber attacks to be a significant risk that it must mitigate. At this point, the entity can proceed to implement countermeasures to mitigate the risk of cyber attacks, based on its analysis of the cost-effectiveness of the countermeasures.

On the other hand, an entity may find that the threat of cyber attacks is not its most significant problem. As we have described, not all threats that an infrastructure faces are of the cyber variety—many threats are physical. By using a risk assessment approach, an entity may determine that the combination of threat, vulnerability, and consequences of physical risks outweigh those of cyber risks. The entity may then primarily implement countermeasures to address those risks and pay less attention to cyber risks.

As we have mentioned, most of the critical infrastructure is owned by the private sector. Similarly, most manufacturers of cybersecurity technology are also in the private sector. These organizations balance the competing needs of their own commercial enterprise, national security, and law enforcement.

- **Commercial enterprise needs**. As we have described, investing in cybersecurity has to make business sense. Typically, this means that companies need to see some type of value to the investment, through either increased sales or reduced costs. However, if a company's customers are not asking for security in its products, it is unlikely that the company will build security into its offerings. Even without an appreciable product or service benefit, a company may still be willing to invest in cybersecurity technologies if doing so will reduce its overall cost structure. However, without a noticeable benefit in either increased sales or a reduction in costs, it becomes very difficult for a company to justify an investment in cybersecurity technology.
- **National security needs**. The designation of critical infrastructure includes those systems and assets that are vital to national security, national economic security, or national public health and safety. However, because most of the critical infrastructure is owned and operated by the private sector, the federal government alone cannot ensure the security of these systems and assets. While it may provide assistance, cultivate partnerships, and establish regulations, the federal government relies on the private sector to carry out its critical infrastructure protection responsibilities.
- **Law enforcement needs**. As we have described, it is impossible to achieve 100 percent protection. Therefore, it is necessary to implement

detection and response capabilities into a security program. The needs of law enforcement are part of these capabilities. The ability to successfully prosecute and convict cyber criminals can also act as a deterrent to others. However, such cases require that companies cooperate with law enforcement and be able to provide evidence of criminal behavior. A working group of law enforcement and industry representatives has issued guidelines for evidence collection for computer crimes.[37]

The needs of these three distinct objectives sometimes conflict with one another. The national security needs could motivate a company to invest in protection technologies and strategies, such as firewalls and access control technologies. The law enforcement needs could cause a company to invest in detection technologies such as intrusion detection systems and audit and logging technologies. However, investment in cybersecurity technologies for national security or law enforcement purposes instead of business reasons can be a tough sell in many companies.

Further, to initiate law enforcement actions against the perpetrator of an attack, a company must report the attack. The reporting of an attack could have a negative business effect, and because of that companies may choose not to report attacks. According to a survey conducted by CSI and the FBI in 2003, only 30 percent of respondents reported computer security incidents to law enforcement.[38] Seventy percent of respondents reported that they did not report intrusions to law enforcement because of concerns about negative publicity. Sixty-one percent were concerned that competitors would use information about computer attacks to their advantage.

We found that entities within the different sectors have different motivations for implementing different levels of cybersecurity. In the absence of any specific guidance from government or the infrastructure sector, some infrastructure owners typically focus on what is best for their own business or mission. To help ensure that national security needs are met, it may be necessary for the federal government to reduce the difference between the commercial needs of an entity and the needs of national security and law enforcement by providing incentives such as funding for cybersecurity improvements. Some of the potential government investments for the public benefit include hardening the Internet, securing the public health network, and making the power grid resilient. Government resources, however, are limited, and these investments need to be prioritized based on the overall criticality of the infrastructures.

[37] International Association of Chiefs of Police Advisory Committee for Police Investigative Operations, Pricewaterhouse Coopers LLP, Technical Support Working Group, and the United States Secret Service, *Best Practices for Seizing Electronic Evidence, Version 2.0.*

[38] CSI. 2003 CSI/FBI *Computer Crime and Security Survey.*

Some Risks Are Beyond the Control of Critical Infrastructure Sectors

A vulnerability assessment may find that there are dependencies on systems or infrastructures beyond the control of an entity. For example, several sectors are dependent on the electrical grid and the telecommunications infrastructure. Some sectors are dependent on computer systems that are operated by other sectors or by the federal government. These interconnections could lead to the introduction of vulnerabilities, and they should be accounted for accordingly.

However, because many of these dependencies are beyond the control of the entity, the options for mitigating these potential vulnerabilities may be limited. To account for such a failure, one possible option for dependent entities is to develop a business continuity plan. As part of a risk management process, a business continuity plan can help an entity to identify its most critical business processes and the actions it can take before and during an outage to mitigate potential risks. Depending on the service provided by the external organization, the criticality of the business process, and the cost of the mitigation strategies, an entity could develop an action plan that would allow it to continue business as usual; operate at some degraded, but minimally acceptable, level; or cease operations until the outage is corrected.

Infrastructures Are Interdependent

Critical infrastructures rely on one another to successfully perform their primary functions. As discussed earlier, understanding these interdependent relationships is critical to protecting our nation's economy, security, and public health. *The National Strategy to Secure Cyberspace* discusses the risks posed by interdependent sectors. It states that unsecured sectors of the economy can be used to attack other sectors and that disruptions in one sector may have cascading effects that can disrupt multiple parts of the nation's critical infrastructure.

For example, the banking and finance infrastructure and the federal government have raised concerns about the financial services sector's interdependency with other critical infrastructures, including telecommunications and energy, and the potential negative impact that attacks in those sectors could have on its ability to operate. According to the financial services sector's national strategy, the industry must take into account the effect of damage from disruptions in other critical sectors, such as telecommunications, electrical power, and transportation. The attacks of September 11, 2001, demonstrated the dependence of the financial services industry on the stability of other sectors' infrastructures. For example, the industry was negatively affected by disrupted communications for its broker-dealers, clearing banks, and other core institutions.[39] In addition, other sectors are dependent on the banking and finance infrastructure. For example, the chemical industry relies on it for currency management and funding.

The August 2003 electricity blackout demonstrated the effect of the water infrastructure's dependency on the electric sector. Wastewater treatment plants in Cleveland, Detroit, New York, and other locations that lacked backup generation systems discharged millions of gallons of untreated sewage, and power failures at drinking water plants led to boil-water advisories in many communities.

According to industry representatives, the chemical sector is dependent on emergency services, information technology and telecommunications, energy, transportation, and banking and finance. For example, it is highly dependent on rail, trucking, and pipeline services for movement of its products. According to the industry, in 2001, more than 760 million tons of chemical products were shipped by domestic truck, rail, water, and other means. In addition, the industry has a strong relationship with emergency services in communities across the United States in order to enhance their ability to respond to emergencies. Entities within the chemical infrastructure are also dependent on each other as suppliers and customers of each other's products. While the chemical infrastructure is reliant on other infrastructures, industry representatives identified several sectors that are dependent on the chemical infrastructure, including

- agriculture for pesticides, insecticides, and fertilizers;
- emergency services for protective equipment and agents;
- food for packaging;
- information and telecommunications for products that protect memory chips;
- public health for devices that neutralize weapons of mass destruction; and
- water for water purifiers.

While these examples indicate that the critical infrastructures are interdependent, the full extent of all the interdependencies is hard to determine.

Infrastructures Rely on Federal and Third-Party Systems

Some officials stated that their infrastructures rely on the availability of centrally controlled or federal systems that are essential to critical operations. For example, according to an infrastructure representative, the banking

[39] Banking and Finance Sector, *Defending America's Cyberspace: Banking and Finance Sector: The National Strategy for Critical Infrastructure Assurance*, Version 1.0 (May 13, 2002).

and finance sector relies upon critical systems related to the clearance and settlement activities for open transactions in the wholesale financial market, which are performed by a combination of government-sponsored services, industry-owned organizations, and private sector firms. According to an interagency paper on strengthening the U.S. financial system, the failure of firms that play a significant role in critical financial markets (defined in the paper as federal funds, foreign exchange, and commercial paper; U.S. government and agency securities; and corporate debt and equity securities) to settle their own or their customers' pending material transactions by the end of the business day could threaten the stability of financial markets.[40]

In addition, according to a Transportation Research Board report, the freight industry has links to government agencies, including manifest filings, operating authorities and permits, and electronic funds transfer.[41] For example, ocean carriers must post information on imported cargo on a DHS Bureau of Customs and Border Protection (formerly the U.S. Customs Service) system—the Automated Manifest System (AMS). According a shipping industry representative, there is now a requirement to submit cargo manifests to this system 24 hours before loading in the foreign port for cargoes destined for the United States. He added that AMS and a related system are becoming the preeminent centralized government data management systems for security prescreening of imported cargoes. Recently, DHS proposed the mandatory electronic submission of advance import cargo information to AMS for all transportation modes. DHS also has proposed that advance information for all export cargoes from the United States be submitted, for all modes, to the agency's Automated Export System, to enhance cargo security. According to a shipping industry official, disabling one or more of these systems could have results at least as disastrous as those of a physical attack on the maritime infrastructure by stopping the flow of goods. The importance of the Global Positioning System (GPS) to the transportation sector has also been pointed out in multiple reports.[42] DoD maintains GPS, which includes 24 satellites and provides high levels of accuracy in determining Earth positions using triangulation principles and land-based receivers. GPS is used to track the locations of trailers, trucks, railcars, and other mobile assets and their contents.

---

[40] In April 2003, the Federal Reserve, the Office of the Comptroller of the Currency, and the Securities and Exchange Commission issued a study titled *Interagency Paper on Sound Practices to Strengthen the Resilience of the U.S. Financial System* to advise financial institutions on steps necessary to protect the financial system. The practices focus on the appropriate backup capacity necessary for recovery and resumption of clearance and settlement for material open transactions in the wholesale financial market.

[41] National Research Council, *Cybersecurity of Freight Information Systems: A Scoping Study* (Washington, D.C.: 2003).

[42] NRC, *Cybersecurity of Freight Information Systems* and the President's National Security Telecommunications Advisory Committee, *Information Infrastructure Group Report* (June 1999).

The aviation-related segments of the transportation infrastructure rely on the availability of the air traffic control system to safely and efficiently move people and goods. The U.S. civil aviation system comprises thousands of airports and aircraft and over 12 million flights each year that carry over 60 million passengers. To carry out its duties, the FAA has approximately 50,000 employees who oversee federal interests in the national airspace system, working at more than 5,000 public use airports. In addition, federal information systems are in use at over 38,000 facilities. These systems are relied on for both passenger and commercial air transportation. Air traffic control systems are responsible for overseeing and tracking most air traffic, including both departing and approaching aircraft. FAA systems provide information to aircraft regarding weather, routes, terrain, and flight plans. There would be detrimental effects on the national economy and possibly on passenger safety if these systems did not function properly.

Considerations for Implementing Current Cybersecurity Technologies

In the near term, critical infrastructure owners face the challenge, based on risk assessments, of developing and implementing strategies to mitigate identified risks. Risk mitigation strategies are a matter of trade-offs among different options, such as adding security to a large number of products, adding significant security features to a few selected products, or increasing the ability to identify and quarantine attackers.

As we have described, there are several cybersecurity technologies that can be used to improve the security posture of critical infrastructure owners. Organizations can select from and implement available cybersecurity technologies to mitigate the highest cybersecurity risks. Best practices recommend that technologies be selected and implemented in the context of an overall security management process that is designed to address the identified risk mitigation strategy. Individually, these technologies address specific cyber vulnerabilities, and in this sense, each technology is a point solution. The selection of multiple technologies should be in the context of the overall system and not aimed solely at specific components of the system.

When implementing cybersecurity technologies, it is important to consider the effects of the technologies and processes on the entity's business. The entity has to balance security against the level of service that the computers and network must provide in order to operate the critical infrastructure. In other words, a system that is not connected to any network is safe from cyber attacks, but it may not do anything useful for the critical infrastructure. If an authentication process takes too long, users may try to bypass the process or use different ways to conduct their business. For example, control systems have been cited as being difficult to secure because their limited computing resources cannot support security technologies such as encryption without hindering performance.

Further, when selecting and implementing these technologies, it is important to bear in mind that they are not cure-alls. There are limitations to some of these technologies. Technology is only part of the solution. Poorly trained personnel or ineffective security processes can limit the effectiveness of good technology.

Limitations of Cybersecurity Technologies

It is important to take into consideration the limitations of cybersecurity technologies. Security processes must account for these limitations, and the people responsible for using the technology and implementing the security process need to be aware of these issues.

Some technologies are sold as definitive solutions to cybersecurity problems. However, specific technologies can help to solve only a limited number of problems. For instance, firewalls can control the flow of traffic between networks. However, they cannot protect against threats from within the network. Antivirus software can help protect against viruses and worms but cannot protect the confidentiality of data on a system. A suite of technologies is required to adequately protect most computer systems.

Further, infrastructure owners need to determine how effective technologies really are. Because there is a lack of security standards and metrics, it is difficult for buyers to quantitatively determine the effectiveness and performance of cybersecurity technologies. For example, during our review of biometrics, we found instances in which the performance estimates that vendors provided were far more impressive than those obtained through independent testing.[43]

Also, some technologies, such as biometrics and intrusion detection systems, have to account for exception processing. False matches and false non-matches sometimes occur with these types of technologies, and procedures need to be developed to handle these situations. Exception processing that is not as good as primary processing could be exploited as a security hole. For example, for the use of smart card technologies, administrators would need to consider how to handle users whose cards are not being recognized. Under what conditions will an administrator allow access to such a user?

Further, the constraints that some IT environments face in using cybersecurity technologies need to be considered. For instance, according to industry experts, the use of existing security technologies, as well as strong user authentication and patch management practices, generally cannot be implemented in control systems because control systems operate in real time, typically are not designed with cybersecurity in mind, and usually

[43] GAO-02-687T and U.S. General Accounting Office, *Technology Assessment: Using Biometrics for Border Security*, GAO-03-174 (Washington, D.C.: Nov. 15, 2002).

have limited processing capabilities. Existing security technologies, such as authorization, authentication, encryption, intrusion detection, and filtering of network traffic and communications require more bandwidth, processing power, and memory than control system components typically have. Because controller stations are generally designed to do specific tasks, they use low-cost, resource-constrained microprocessors. In fact, some devices in the electrical industry still use the Intel 8088 processor, introduced in 1978. Consequently, it is difficult to install existing security technologies without seriously degrading the performance of the control system. Further, complex passwords and other strong password practices are not always used to prevent unauthorized access to control systems, in part because their use could hinder a rapid response to safety procedures during an emergency. As a result, according to industry officials, weak passwords that are easy to guess, shared, or infrequently changed are reportedly common in control systems. Sometimes a default password or even no password at all is used.

In addition, although modern control systems are based on standard operating systems, they are typically customized to support control system applications. Consequently, vendor-provided software patches are generally either incompatible or cannot be implemented without compromising service by shutting down "always-on" systems or affecting interdependent operations. Although technologies such as robust firewalls and strong authentication can be employed to better segment control systems from enterprise networks, research and development could help to address the application of security technologies to the control systems themselves. Information security organizations have noted that a gap exists between current security technologies and needed additional research and development to secure control systems.

Poor Implementations Can Reduce the Effectiveness of Cybersecurity Technologies

When implementing technologies, it is important to note that each element of the technology-people-process triad plays a role in the cybersecurity of critical infrastructures (see figure 7). Strong processes can often help to overcome potential vulnerabilities in a security product, while poor implementation can render good technologies ineffective. Often, human weaknesses can diminish the effectiveness of technology. A prime example is the millions of PCs that have unnecessary Internet and networking services running simply because users are unaware that these services are running by default and could contain vulnerabilities.

In our reviews of cybersecurity controls at federal agencies, we have found several instances where the effectiveness of technology was limited through improper configuration of the technology or through human errors. These types of failures can lead to the exploitation of vulnerabilities, resulting in compromised computers and networks.

Figure 7: Technology, People, and Process Are All Necessry for Cybersecurity

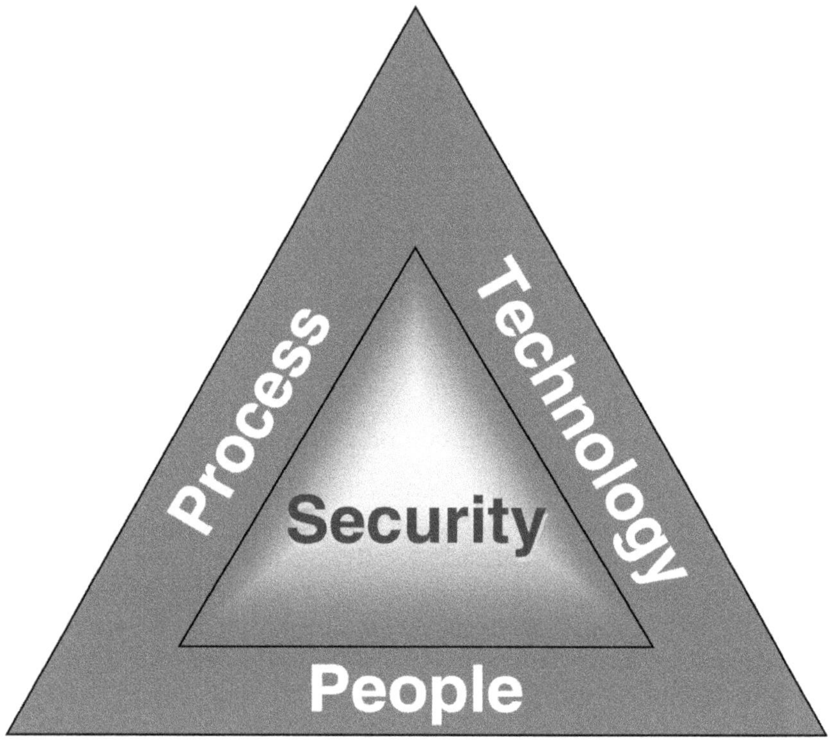

Source: GAO.

For example, the most common access control technology is the use of user names and passwords. We have found three common implementation problems in the use of passwords:

- Failure to disable or change default vendor accounts and passwords. In some cases, these accounts could provide a malicious user with administrative privileges.
- Easily guessable passwords, such as children's names or birthdays. Some accounts do not have a password.
- Storage or transmission of user accounts and passwords with weak or no encryption.

Another common issue is the failure of system administrators or security officers to follow procedures:

- Many operating systems and applications provide the capability to log events and transactions, including security-related items such as changes to critical files, network connections, and administrator actions.

However, in many cases, we found that logging was not enabled or was not adequately covering enough events. Once logs are created, someone must review them to scan for significant or anomalous activities. However, we have found that logs often are not adequately monitored.

- Patch management, a component of configuration management, is a process used to help mitigate vulnerabilities on computer systems. We have found that reported vulnerabilities on systems frequently remain unpatched. Unpatched systems could allow remote access through a variety of vulnerabilities. For example, we previously reported that almost a month before the Blaster worm attack in August 2003, a patch was made available by Microsoft to address a vulnerability in its Windows Distributed Component Object Model Remote Procedure Call interface.[44] System administrators face challenges in maintaining current technology inventories, identifying relevant vulnerabilities and corresponding patches, and testing and distributing the patches.

Problems also arise when computers and network components are poorly configured. Some examples include the following:

- Key network servers were not adequately configured to restrict access. As a result, anyone, including contractors, with connectivity into the agency network could copy or modify files containing sensitive network information that would allow an intruder to control critical network resources.
- Poorly configured firewalls and internal hosts allowed anyone on the Internet to connect and shadow internal user sessions.
- Poorly configured world-writable file permissions allowed Trojan horse programs to be installed using a low-level account to gain administrator privileges.

Poor configuration management has also led to the introduction of vulnerabilities. For example:

- Unbeknownst to the administrators, server configurations had unnecessary services running on them. Because the administrators did not know about these applications, they did not know that patches were required to address vulnerabilities in those applications.
- Dial-in modems did not require passwords to access the internal agency network, thereby circumventing the security controls provided by the firewalls.

[44] U.S. General Accounting Office, *Information Security: Effective Patch Management is Critical to Mitigating Software Vulnerabilities*, GAO-03-1138T (Washington, D.C.: Sept. 10, 2003).

- In some instances outdated software versions were exploitable from the Internet. These could be used by an attacker to bypass firewall controls and to launch attacks against other computers in the network.

Configuration management is particularly important for organizations that perform some form of security testing, including the certification and accreditation of systems. Configuration management involves the identification of all software and hardware components of a system at a given point in time and systematically controlling changes to that configuration. Effective security testing loses its value when there is no assurance that the system that is being used in the operational environment is the same system that was successfully tested.

Best Practices and Guidelines Are Available to Select and Implement Current Technologies

When implementing cybersecurity technologies and processes, organizations can avoid making common implementation mistakes by consulting best practices and guidance developed by various other organizations. While federal agencies are required to follow certain security guidelines issued by NIST, private sector organizations may also benefit from these guidelines.

Recently, NIST published a guide on selecting information technology security products.[45] The guide presents the types of products, product characteristics, and environment considerations for each of the following categories of products: identification and authentication, access control, intrusion detection, firewalls, PKI, malicious code protection, vulnerability scanners, forensics, and media sanitizing. NIST has also published a number of other guides on implementing security products.[46] For example, it has guides on electronic mail security and wireless network security, as well as on firewalls and intrusion detection systems.[47]

Other federal agencies, such as the Defense Information Systems Agency (DISA) and NSA have prepared implementation guides to help their administrators configure their systems in a secure manner.[48] Guides exist for the configuration of operating systems such as Windows, UNIX, and OS/390.

---

[45] National Institute of Standards and Technology, *Guide to Selecting Information Technology Security Products*, NIST Special Publication 800-36 (Gaithersburg, MD: Oct. 2003).

[46] For a list of NIST Special Publications, as these guides are called, see the NIST Web site at http://csrc.nist.gov/publications/nistpubs/.

[47] National Institute of Standards and Technology, *Guidelines on Electronic Mail Security*, NIST Special Publication 800-45 (Gaithersburg, MD: Sept. 2002); *Wireless Network Security: 802.11, Bluetooth and Handheld Devices*, NIST Special Publication 800-48 (Gaithersburg, MD: Nov. 2002); *Guidelines on Firewalls and Firewall Policy*, NIST Special Publication 800-41 (Gaithersburg, MD: Jan. 2002); and *Intrusion Detection Systems*, NIST Special Publication 800-31 (Gaithersburg, MD: Nov. 2001).

[48] For DISA's security technical implementation guides, see http://csrc.nist.gov/pcig/cig.html. For NSA's security recommendation guides, see http://www.nsa.gov/snac/index.html.

Some industry groups have also developed best practices and guidelines to help their member entities implement cybersecurity. For example, the Network Reliability and Interoperability Council (NRIC), a Federal Communications Commission advisory committee, has developed a number of best practices to enhance the reliability of the nation's public communications networks and services.[49] These best practices include homeland security best practices, which in turn include cybersecurity best practices for the telecommunications sector and Internet services. These cybersecurity best practices include a wide variety of specific practices, such as disabling unnecessary network-accessible services, using strong encryption algorithms and keys, and defining a security architecture.

In addition, some sectors have issued guidelines to assist entities within the sector in improving their security posture. For example, NERC, the sector coordinator for the electric sector, created *Security Guidelines for the Electricity Sector* as a collection of practices for protecting critical facilities against a range of physical and cyber threats.[50] Its topics include vulnerability and risk assessment, business continuity, physical and cyber security, and protection of sensitive information. The cybersecurity subcategories are risk management, access controls, information technology firewalls, and intrusion detection. In addition, one segment of the chemical industry has a mandatory security code to address security issues within the business of chemistry.[51] The code's purpose is to help protect people, property, products, processes, information, and information systems by enhancing security, including security against a potential terrorist attack, throughout a company's activities that are associated with the design, procurement, manufacturing, marketing, distribution, transportation, customer support, use, recycling, and disposal of products. This code is intended to help companies achieve continuous improvement in security performance using a risk-based approach to identify, assess, and address vulnerabilities; prevent or mitigate incidents; enhance training and response capabilities; and maintain and improve relationships with key stakeholders. It requires each company to implement a risk-based security management that includes the following 13 management practices:

1. **Leadership commitment**—senior leadership commitment to continuous improvement through published policies, provision of sufficient and qualified resources, and established accountability.

2. **Analysis of threats, vulnerabilities, and consequences**—prioritization and periodic analysis of potential security threats, vulnerabilities, and consequences, using accepted methodologies.

---

[49] The NRIC best practices are available online at http://www.nric.org/.

[50] North American Electric Reliability Council, *Security Guidelines for the Electricity Sector*, Version 1 (Princeton, NJ: June 14, 2002).

[51] American Chemistry Council, *Responsible Care Security Code of Management Practices* (July 1, 2002).

3. **Implementation of security measures**—development and implementation of security measures commensurate with risks, taking into account inherently safer approaches to process design, engineering and administrative controls, and prevention and mitigation measures.

4. **Information and cybersecurity**—recognition that protecting information and information systems is a critical component of a sound security management system.

5. **Documentation**—documentation of security management programs, processes, and procedures.

6. **Training, drills, and guidance**—enhancing awareness and capability of employees, contractors, service providers, value chain partners, and others, as appropriate.

7. **Communications, dialogue, and information exchange**—sharing information on appropriate security issues with stakeholders such as employees, contractors, communities, customers, suppliers, service providers, and government officials and agencies, balanced with safeguards for sensitive information.

8. **Response to security threats**—evaluation, response, reporting, and communication of security threats as appropriate.

9. **Response to security incidents**—evaluation, response, investigation, reporting, communication, and corrective action for security incidents.

10. **Audits**—assessing security programs and processes and the implementation of corrective actions.

11. **Third-party verification**—third-party verification that, at chemical operating facilities with potential off-site impacts, companies have implemented the physical site security measures to which they have committed.

12. **Management of change**—evaluation and management of security issues associated with changes involving people, property, products, processes, information, or information systems.

13. **Continuous improvement**—continuous performance improvement processes entailing planning, establishment of goals and objectives, monitoring of progress and performance, analysis of trends and development, and implementation of corrective actions.

Further, the oil and natural gas segment of the energy infrastructure sector has security guidelines available that include guidance on cybersecurity.[52] The guidance provides a means to improve the security of the oil and natural

[52] American Petroleum Institute, *Security Guidelines for the Petroleum Industry*, Second Edition (Washington, D.C.: Apr. 2003).

gas industry from cyber terrorism and to effectively allocate resources. It also endorses the use of ISO/IEC International Standard 17799 on information security management as a voluntary framework to protect the industry against cyber terrorism.

Considering Security when Developing Systems

To build security into a system, NIST recommends that security requirements for a system be considered as early as possible in the system development life cycle (SDLC).[53] According to NIST, security should be considered as early as the needs determination stage of an IT acquisition or development. A high-level description of the security controls of the proposed system should be included as a part of the preliminary requirements definition for the whole system, which will drive the scoping of the entire effort. If the system acquisition or development is approved, NIST describes several additional steps for considering security, including conducting a risk assessment to derive the security functional and assurance requirements, testing security controls, and certifying and accrediting the system security.

Defense in depth is a common design strategy for protecting computers and networks with a series of defensive mechanisms such that if one mechanism fails, another will already be in place to thwart an attack. Because there are so many potential attackers with such a wide variety of attack methods available, there is no single method for successfully protecting a computer network. Using a strategy of defense in depth can reduce the risk of suffering a successful cyber attack.

In addition, the director, CERT Centers, testified before Congress about the need for "higher quality information technology products with security mechanisms that are better matched to the knowledge, skills, and abilities of today's systems managers, administrators, and users."[54] He added that good software engineering practices can dramatically improve the ability to withstand attacks, and he suggested that the solutions required a combination of

- systems and software that constrain the execution of imported code, especially code that comes from unknown or untrusted sources;
- adoption of known, effective software engineering practices that dramatically reduce the number of flaws in software products; and

[53] National Institute of Standards and Technology. *Security Considerations in the Information System Development Life Cycle*, NIST Special Publication 800-64 (Gaithersburg, MD: Oct. 2003).

[54] Testimony of Richard D. Pethia, Director, CERT Centers, Software Engineering Institute, Carnegie Mellon University, before the House Select Committee on Homeland Security, Subcommittee on Cybersecurity, Science, and Research and Development (June 25, 2003).

- shipment of products with "out of the box" configurations that have security options turned on rather than configurations that require users to turn them on.

Critical Infrastructure Sectors Have Taken Actions to Address Threats to Their Sectors

Federal CIP policy calls for a range of actions intended to improve the nation's ability to detect and respond to serious computer-based and physical attacks and establish a partnership between the federal government and the private sector. It encourages the private sector to voluntarily take efforts to raise awareness, share information, and increase the security posture of their physical and cyber assets. Some infrastructure sectors have taken extensive steps to voluntarily achieve these suggested activities. Considering the current efforts of critical infrastructure sectors can help inform legislative decision making on the need for further government policy making to increase the use of cybersecurity technologies.

Coordination of Efforts and Increasing Participation in Sector Activities

As previously discussed, federal CIP policy states that sector-specific agencies are to continue to support sector-coordinating mechanisms. While some critical infrastructure sectors identified in federal policy have not formally designated a coordinator, including the postal and shipping, public health, food, and agriculture sectors, many other critical infrastructure sectors have established individuals or organizations to coordinate sector-wide activities and initiatives to improve the overall cybersecurity of their sectors. For example, banking and finance, telecommunications, information technology, transportation, and water infrastructure sectors and the electricity and oil and natural gas segments of the energy sector have established sector coordinators. In some cases, the sector coordinators are industry associations that represent a large part of the sector. For example, for the electricity segment of the energy infrastructure sector, the North American Electric Reliability Council (NERC) serves as the sector coordinator.[55] According to NERC officials, it represents 100 percent of the entities in the extended regional control area systems, which corresponds to the bulk of U.S. megawatt electricity generation. Also, in the chemical sector, the American Chemistry Council has taken the lead to improve security within the sector.

To ensure the appropriate level of sector participation and build a better consensus on the objectives of the sector-wide efforts, sector coordinators or other key organizations have also taken steps to broaden the involvement

[55] NERC was formed in 1968 and operates as a voluntary industry organization charged with ensuring that the bulk electric system in North America is reliable, adequate, and secure.

of sector entities and relevant trade or industry associations. For example, the financial services sector coordinator organized the Financial Services Sector Coordinating Council for Critical Infrastructure Protection/ Homeland Security (FSSCC) to "foster and facilitate the coordination of sector-wide voluntary activities and initiatives designed to improve Critical Infrastructure Protection and Homeland Security." It includes major sector associations, professional institutes, national exchanges, and other broad industry organizations that, according to the sector coordinator, provide a way to broaden its membership—potentially reaching more of the approximate 27,000 different financial services entities.[56] In addition, the Chemical Sector Cybersecurity Program was established to enhance cybersecurity throughout the chemical sector value chain in order to help protect people, property, products, processes, information and information systems. The Chemical Sector Cybersecurity Information Sharing Forum consists of senior-level company officials and staff representatives from trade associations and individual companies representing key industry segments within the sector, which serves a critical role in fostering involvement and commitment on the part of chemical companies across the sector.[57] Its objective is to serve as the communications channel for the more than 2,000 chemical companies that constitute the associations' collective membership. In addition, according to an infrastructure sector official, the existing sector coordinators from the various infrastructure sectors have formed a council as the Partnership for Critical Infrastructure Security to coordinate on strategic issues.

Collection and Analysis of Incident, Threat, and Vulnerability Information from Sector Entities

Federal policy recognizes the importance of sharing information about physical and cyber threats, vulnerabilities, and incidents, and continues to encourage the development of ISACs as a mechanism for sharing information. The ISACs recognized by DHS include the following: chemical

[56] Current members of the FSSCC include: the American Bankers Association; the American Council of Life Insurers; America's Community Bankers; ASIS International; the Bank Administration Institute; BITS and the Financial Services Roundtable; Credit Union National Association; the Consumer Bankers Association; the Depository Trust and Clearing Corporation; Fannie Mae; FS-ISAC, the Futures Industry Association; Independent Community Bankers of America; the Investment Company Institute; the Managed Funds Association; NASD, Inc.; the NASDAQ Stock Market, Inc.; the National Association of Federal Credit Unions; the National Automated Clearinghouse Association; the Securities Industry Association; the Securities Industry Automation Corporation/ New York Stock Exchange; the Bond Market Association; the Clearing House; the Options Clearing Corporation; and VISA USA, LLC.

[57] Ten chemical trade associations came together to form this forum, including: American Chemistry Council, Compressed Gas Association, Consumer Specialty Products Association, CropLife America, Dangerous Goods Advisory Council, Institute of Makers of Explosives, National Association of Chemical Distributors, Synthetic Organic Chemical Manufacturers Association, the Chlorine Institute, and the Fertilizer Institute.

industry, electric power, energy, financial services, information technology, telecommunications, surface transportation, and water. The ISACs are designed to facilitate information sharing among members by collecting, analyzing, and disseminating information on vulnerabilities, threats, intrusions, and anomalies reported by members, the government, or other sources, in order to avert or mitigate the impact of these factors. Some ISACs consider themselves clearinghouses for information within and among the various sectors. This includes disseminating information technology security information—such as incident reports and warnings, as well as ways to prevent or recover from them. Some ISAC operations are performed completely in-house, while others use contractors to provide warning and analysis functions or simply forward government-issued warnings and alerts. Several provide their members some level of watch services 24 hours a day, 7 days a week. In April 2004, we testified[58] about the management and operational structures used by the 15 ISACs, federal efforts to interact with and support the ISACs, and challenges to and successful practices for ISACs' establishment, operation, and partnership with the federal government.

For example, the Financial Services ISAC (FS-ISAC) was formed in October 1999 to, among other objectives, facilitate sharing of information and provide its members with early notification of computer vulnerabilities and attacks. In 2003, the FS-ISAC broadened its mission to serve all financial services sector participants. The goal of the FS-ISAC is to disseminate information on cyber and physical security risks to sector participants on a timely basis. In December 2003, the next generation FS-ISAC was implemented; it includes varying levels of participation, from being a free member to being a premier member ($10,000/year). Available resources to members include early notification of computer vulnerabilities and attacks and access to subject-matter expertise and other relevant information, such as trending analysis for all levels of management and for first responders to cyber incidents.

Another example is the chemical sector ISAC that the American Chemistry Council established in April 2002 to provide a secure facility that allows the sharing of information associated with incidents, threats, vulnerabilities, resolutions, and solutions. It is operated through the American Chemistry Council's 24-hour hazardous material emergency communications center and is linked with DHS's IAIP directorate. According to chemical infrastructure sector officials, the ISAC capability is still in its early development stage regarding cybersecurity.

Also, NERC operates the Electricity Sector ISAC (ES-ISAC), which works with DHS, the Department of Energy, and other entities to help protect the

[58] U.S. General Accounting Office, *Critical Infrastructure Protection: Establishing Effective Information Sharing with Infrastructure Sectors*, GAO-04-699T (Washington, D.C.: April 21, 2004).

North American electric system from cyber and physical attacks. It is NERC's responsibility to gather, disseminate, and interpret security-related information, operating between industry and the government and among all the sector entities. In addition, the ISAC posts advisories, alerts, warnings, and the current threat alert levels for the Homeland Security Advisory System, the Department of Energy, and the electricity sector.

Further, the railroad industry formed a Surface Transportation ISAC (ST-ISAC). The ST-ISAC operates a 24 × 7 center that collects, analyzes, and distributes critical security and threat information from worldwide resources to protect its members' vital information and IT systems from attack. ST-ISAC reporting includes daily information provided by government intelligence, law enforcement, and regulatory agencies. ST-ISAC services are specifically tailored to meet the security demands of each one of its members. Currently, the ST-ISAC supports almost 200 member entities. ST-ISAC membership consists of more than 90 percent of the North American freight railroad industry (including Mexico and Canada), AMTRAK and most public transit providers servicing the major population centers in the United States, key railroad customers (such as chemical companies and car manufacturers), and others.

Development of Strategies, Guidance, and Standards for Improving Security

As part of their efforts to improve the security posture of their respective sectors, sector representatives have developed strategies and other guidance to drive their sector-wide activities and assist individual entities. Several sectors, including financial services, electricity, oil and gas, the rail segment of the transportation sector, information and telecommunications, water, and chemical, have developed strategies that outline priorities and efforts for the sector that were part of the efforts to develop *The National Strategy to Secure Cyberspace*. These strategies address subjects, such as increasing the awareness of senior officials, encouraging greater participation in sector activities, and identifying and reducing vulnerabilities. For example, we reported in January 2003[59] that financial services industry representatives collaborated on a Treasury-sponsored working group to develop the sector's *National Strategy for Critical Infrastructure Assurance*, which was issued in May 2002.[60] In addition, one of the five key elements of the chemical sector's cybersecurity strategy involves the establishment of management practices, procedures, guidelines, and standards to support overall sector cybersecurity.

[59] U.S. General Accounting Office, *Critical Infrastructure Protection: Efforts of the Financial Services Sector to Address Cyber Threats*, GAO-03-173 (Washington, D.C.: Jan. 30, 2003).
[60] Banking and Finance Sector, *Defending America's Cyberspace.*

As we have previously described, there have also been efforts in the energy and chemical sectors to provide greater specificity with regard to the elements in the strategies and to provide guidance and standards. For example, in January 2003, the Chemical Industry Data Exchange (CIDX)[61] established the Chemical Sector Cybersecurity Practices, Standards, and Technology Initiative to address two elements of the chemical sector cybersecurity strategy: (1) establishing sector cybersecurity practices and standards by working with the American Chemistry Council's Responsible Care Security Code program,[62] and (2) accelerating development of improved security technology and solutions by bringing technology solution providers to the table with chemical sector information technology and process control system experts to improve technology security. According to chemical infrastructure sector officials, during the second quarter of 2003, CIDX released its first work products, including cybersecurity guidance for the Responsible Care Security Code, cybersecurity guidance for security vulnerability assessment methodology, and the results of baseline assessments against the ISO 17799 standard for security management practices.

The energy infrastructure sector has also taken steps to develop guidance and standards. For example, NERC has developed minimum security requirements to govern the exchange of electronic information needed to support grid reliability and market operations.[63] In addition, the oil and natural gas segment of the energy infrastructure sector has security guidelines available that include guidance on cybersecurity.[64] The guidance provides a means to improve the security of the oil and gas industry from cyber terrorism and to effectively allocate resources. It also endorses the use of ISO/IEC International Standard 17799 on information security management as a voluntary framework to protect the industry against cyber terrorism.

Providing Methods for the Independent Validation of Software and Hardware

Infrastructure sectors have recognized the need to improve the ability of individual entities to understand the level of security offered by the technology products they use and the risks of using those technologies.

[61] CIDX is a trade association and standards body focused on improving the ease, speed, and cost of transacting business electronically between chemical companies and their trading partners.

[62] The Responsible Care initiative, now in its 14th year, is a comprehensive management system developed by experts for use throughout the chemical sector to continuously improve safety performance and communications and to protect employees, communities, and the environment. Members of sector associations, such as the American Chemistry Council and the Synthetic Organic Chemical Manufacturers Association, along with other companies and associations involved in the sector's supply chain, participate in Responsible Care as partners. As a result, hundreds of companies are working together to further improve safety and performance throughout commerce and communities.

[63] The North American Electric Reliability Council, *The North American Electric Reliability Council's Urgent Action Standard 1200—Cyber Security*, adopted by NERC Board of Trustees August 13, 2003.

[64] American Petroleum Institute, *Security Guidelines for the Petroleum Industry*, Second Edition (Washington, D.C.: Apr. 2003).

For example, as we reported in January 2003, BITS provides for the financial services sector through the BITS Product Certification Program—designed to test products against baseline security criteria—a vehicle to significantly enhance safety and soundness by improving the security of technology products and reducing technology risk.[65] In addition, as one of its key elements, the chemical sector cybersecurity strategy included the acceleration of the development of cost-effective technology solutions by proactively working with service providers, government, and academia.

Raising Awareness about the Importance of Cybersecurity

An important aspect of improving the cybersecurity of an entity is raising the awareness of senior executives and others about the risks their entities face because of their reliance on IT and the importance of appropriately protecting those assets and the related information. For example, the financial services sector's efforts are designed to increase the awareness of officials within the sector about the importance of cybersecurity. In addition, the financial services sector's strategy addresses actions to educate industry executives and information security specialists.

Encouraging the Performance of Vulnerability Assessments

As discussed earlier, the most recent federal CIP policy, HSPD-7, requires sector-specific agencies to conduct or facilitate vulnerability assessments of their respective sectors, which is a continued emphasis on performing such assessments. To address the need for vulnerability assessments, some sectors have taken steps to perform sector-wide vulnerability assessments or encourage or require individual entities to perform vulnerability assessments for their facilities and operations. For example, following the September 11, 2001 terrorist attacks, the railroad industry established five critical action teams, including an information technology and communications team, to assess both short-term and long-term security needs. The teams, with assistance from outside experts, evaluated threats to the rail system, identified vulnerabilities, quantified risks, and devised appropriate countermeasures. As a result of the team's efforts, a railroad security plan was developed that identifies industry action and government support required to enhance the security of the freight rail industry, including the need to cooperate to meet the security and redundancy requirements for critical data communications and train control systems. Further, the chemical sector cybersecurity strategy has as one of its key elements

[65] BITS is the name of the Technology Group for The Financial Services Roundtable. As part of its mandate, BITS strives to sustain consumer confidence and trust by ensuring the safety and security of financial transactions, and it has several initiatives under way to promote improved information security within the financial services industry. BITS's and the Roundtable's membership represents 100 of the largest integrated financial services institutions providing banking, insurance, and investment products and services to American consumers and corporate customers.

identifying and reducing infrastructure vulnerabilities to guard against cyber attacks and speed recovery from incidents. Also, as one of its current focuses, CIDX has taken steps to develop a cybersecurity risk management process and framework, participate in the development of process control standards and technical reports that provide preliminary security recommendations, and develop requirements for manufacturing process controls. The financial services sector strategy also identifies a framework for sector actions that presents efforts necessary to identify, assess, and respond to sector-wide threats, including completion of a sector-wide vulnerability assessment.

Some infrastructure entities have also conducted vulnerability assessments. For example, entities in the chemical sector that are required to follow the Responsible Care Security Code perform security vulnerability assessments by prioritizing their sites. Entities are also to conduct assessments of their value chain and cyber networks. In addition, according to chemical sector representatives, there are efforts under way to partner with other institutions, including Sandia National Laboratories, to develop a more robust cybersecurity vulnerability assessment methodology. Together with Sandia Laboratories and the Center for Chemical Processing Safety, CIDX has submitted to DHS a request for funding to develop a combined cyber and physical vulnerability assessment methodology for use in site vulnerability assessments. Industry representatives at the time of our study also stated that 14 chemical companies had conducted an assessment of their company's performance against ISO 17799. Also, according to defense industrial base representatives, individual companies continually perform security assessments.

Sharing CIP-Related Activity Information across Sectors

Individual sectors share information with other sectors because they use the same technology and thus face the same security challenges and are interdependent on each other. For example, to encourage cross-sector coordination and information sharing, the ISAC Council was formed by several ISACs to advance the physical and cyber security of the critical infrastructures of North America by establishing and maintaining a framework for valuable interaction between and among the ISACs and with government. Currently, the participating ISACs include Chemical, Electricity, Energy, Financial Services, Highway, Information Technology, Public Transit, Surface Transportation, Telecommunications, and Water. In addition, the Multi-state and Research and Education Networking ISACs are participants.

The Council has met with DHS to discuss mutual expectations. According to one infrastructure sector official, the ISAC Council has resulted in better communications among the various ISACs, and they have begun to help each other to establish and maintain a policy for inter-ISAC coordination, a dialogue with governmental agencies that deal with ISACs, and a practical data and information-sharing protocol. In February 2004, the council issued eight white papers to reflect the collective analysis of its members and to cover a broad set of issues and challenges, including government/private sector relations, information sharing and analysis, ISAC analytical efforts, policy and framework for the ISAC community, and the reach of major ISACs.

Sharing Best Practices

As part of their efforts to share information, sectors have established methods for individual entities to share best practices across the sector. For example, NERC has created best practices for protecting critical facilities against physical and cyber threats. In addition, one of FSSCC's goals is to identify, develop, and share industry best practices to maximize sector resiliency. Also within the financial services sector, BITS actively seeks information security improvements, including issuing a framework of industry practices and regulatory requirements for managing technology risk for IT service provider relationships.

Leveraging Existing Efforts

To address CIP issues within their respective sectors, some sectors have attempted to use existing efforts to enhance the level of awareness and action and minimize the risk of duplicative efforts. For example, in the financial services sector, one of the main initiatives of the FSSCC is to share information on CIP activities that are already being performed by member associations across the entire sector. For example, the American Bankers Association (ABA) and BITS have a number of initiatives to improve the cybersecurity of the sector.[66] In addition, according to industry representatives, the Chemical Sector Cybersecurity Program is leveraging proven sector initiatives, including chemical trade associations (through the Chemical Sector Cybersecurity Information Sharing Forum), CIDX, and the Chemical Sector ISAC.

Federal Government Actions to Improve Cybersecurity for CIP

As we have described, the federal government has several ongoing activities designed to improve the cybersecurity posture of critical infrastructures. There is a variety of ways in which the federal government could encourage the use of cybersecurity technologies for critical infrastructure protection. Besides merely continuing the current programs, the federal government could choose to expand current programs or develop new programs to assist critical infrastructures. The design of federal policy will play

[66] ABA is an industry group whose membership includes community, savings, regional, and money center banks; savings associations; trust companies; and diversified financial holding companies.

a vital role in determining success and ensuring that national goals are met. Key to the national effort will be determining the appropriate level of funding, so that policies and tools can be designed and targeted to elicit a prompt, adequate, and sustainable response while also protecting against federal funds being used to substitute for spending that would occur anyway.

As with any policy decision, there are a number of factors that should be considered before selecting an approach. First, the problem needs to be identified. There is a need for factual information on the scope and scale of the cyber vulnerabilities and the consequences of possible cyber attacks on the critical infrastructure. The technology issues surrounding the problem and the structure of the security marketplace have to be determined. Although experts agree that cybersecurity is an important element of critical infrastructure protection, the scope and scale of the problem and the consequences of cyber attacks are not easily quantifiable.

As we have described, because about 85 percent of the critical infrastructure is owned by the private sector, the federal government cannot act alone to protect it. To help determine the proper approach for federal action, the government will require information from the private sector on the scope and size of the cybersecurity risks and the actions that they are already taking to address them. To make informed decisions on cybersecurity policy, federal policy makers need information on critical infrastructure assets, vulnerabilities, and priorities from the private sector, information that could be gleaned if the risk-based framework for security that we have described is followed.

After the parameters of the problem have been established, possible private and public responses can be proposed. To interact with the private sector, the federal government can use a variety of policy options to motivate or mandate private sector entities to take actions to address cybersecurity concerns. These options include grants, regulations, tax incentives, and coordination and partnerships.

Two key considerations in developing a grant program are targeting the funds to those with the greatest need and striking a balance between accountability and flexibility. Accountability can be established for measured results and outcomes that permit greater flexibility in how funds are used while at the same time ensuring some national oversight. An example of a grant program would be one where the federal government funds or subsidizes the purchase of security technology for specific critical infrastructure sectors or specific groups of vulnerable entities within a sector. There is precedent for this in the Help America Vote Act of 2002, which provides funding to states for buying new voting machines.[67]

[67] Help America Vote Act of 2002, Public Law 107-252 (Oct. 29, 2002).

Another example is the Environmental Protection Agency, which reported providing 449 grants to assist large drinking water utilities in developing vulnerability assessments, emergency response/operating plans, security enhancement plans and designs, or a combination of these efforts.

In designing regulations, key considerations include determining how to provide federal protections, guarantees, or benefits while preserving an appropriate balance between the federal government and state and local government and between the public and private sectors. In designing a regulatory approach, one of the challenges is determining who will set the standards and who will implement or enforce them.

Tax incentives are the result of special exclusions, exemptions, deductions, credits, deferrals, or tax rates in the federal tax laws. Unlike grants, tax incentives do not generally permit the same degree of federal oversight and targeting, and they generally are available to all potential beneficiaries who satisfy congressionally established criteria. However, according to some infrastructure sector officials, tax incentives will not provide adequate motivation to organizations that are already under financial strain or under bankruptcy protection.

Sometimes the federal government can make change happen in a sector by requiring that sector to work in a certain way when it interacts with government systems. An example is the Department of the Treasury directive that required electronic funds transfer transactions involving federal systems to use DES encryption. Similarly, to promote adoption of more secure products and practices, specific sector systems that connect to government systems could be required to meet specific cybersecurity provisions. The key is for government and the sector to decide what types of cybersecurity requirements to adopt and to understand why these requirements improve security.

The government owns approximately 15 percent of the critical infrastructure and is otherwise a major purchaser of information technology. Consequently, it could affect market behavior through its own purchases. For instance, government could promulgate procurement rules specifying that after a certain number of years it will no longer buy PCs without certain security features built into the hardware and operating system. For example, currently all cryptography products purchased by the federal government must be compliant with FIPS 140-2.

Critical infrastructure protection is a complex mission that requires high levels of interagency, interjurisdictional, and interorganizational cooperation. Different levels of government—federal, state, and local—as well as various public, private, and nongovernmental organizations are involved with CIP. Promoting partnerships among these different organizations facilitates the maximizing of resources and supports coordination.

Without appropriate consideration of public policy tools, private sector participation in sector-related information sharing and other CIP efforts may not reach its full potential. For example, in January 2003, we reported on the efforts of the financial services sector to address cyber threats, including industry efforts to share information and to better foster and facilitate sector-wide efforts.[68] We also reported on the efforts of federal agencies and regulators to partner with the financial services industry to protect critical infrastructures and to address information security. We found that although federal agencies had a number of efforts ongoing, the Treasury Department, in its role as sector liaison, had not undertaken a comprehensive assessment of the potential public policy tools that could be used to encourage the financial services sector in implementing information sharing and other CIP-related efforts. Since then, Treasury provided $2 million to help establish the next generation FS-ISAC and its new capabilities, including improving information sharing by upgrading the technology supporting the FS-ISAC and adding information about physical threats to the cyber threat information it disseminates.

In addition, in February 2003, we reported on the mixed progress that the telecommunications, electricity, information technology, energy, and water sectors had made in accomplishing the activities suggested by Presidential Decision Directive 63 (PDD 63).[69] We found that the responsible lead agencies needed to better assess the need for public policy tools to encourage increased private sector CIP activities and facilitate greater sharing of intelligence and incident information between the sectors and the federal government.

Considerations for Federal Action

For each possible policy option, it is necessary to analyze the costs and benefits, how the policy can be implemented, and the consequences of action and inaction. Because resources are scarce, decisions on spending must achieve two overarching goals: to devote the right amount of resources to cybersecurity and to spend those resources on the right activities. To achieve the first goal, the benefit of each endeavor must be carefully weighed, and resources should only be allocated where the benefit of reducing risk is worth the amount of additional cost.

One of the essential parts of any federal program is the ability to measure the results from the program. However, the lack of well-defined security standards or benchmarks makes it difficult to measure the benefit of a security program. Further, what may be appropriate for some sectors may not

[68] GAO-03-173.

[69] U.S. General Accounting Office, *Critical Infrastructure Protection: Challenges for Selected Agencies and Industry Sectors*, GAO-03-233 (Washington, D.C.: Feb. 28, 2003).

be appropriate for other sectors. For policy options such as grants, tax incentives, and regulations, there needs to be a way of defining the actions or the outcomes that are being sought by the federal government. Instead of requiring a set of actions, it is best to aim for specific outcomes. A problem with this approach is that sometimes it is not possible to specify a measurable outcome. In the absence of such criteria, it will be challenging to define and implement such a federal program.

For example, to use grants for the purchase of cybersecurity technology or to impose requirements for government purchases, the government needs to work with the sectors and the technology vendors to set standards for cybersecurity products or establish measurable outcomes to be achieved by the technology. Unfortunately, it is difficult to set product-level standards that can be evaluated efficiently and without incurring significant additional cost.

The federal government has several ongoing cybersecurity programs. For example, the federal government has previously assisted sectors with conducting risk assessments, provided threat and vulnerability information to sectors and their entities, and established education and awareness programs on cybersecurity. To assist with the costs and benefits determination of future programs, it would be useful to examine the effectiveness of existing programs.

One possibility is to measure the costs saved by preventing a cyber attack. According to *The National Strategy to Secure Cyberspace*, surveys have repeatedly shown that although the likelihood of suffering a severe cyber attack is difficult to measure, the costs associated with mitigating and reconstituting after a successful attack are likely to be greater than the investment in a cybersecurity program to prevent it. Financial losses resulting from worms and viruses have been significant. PricewaterhouseCoopers estimated that in 2001, hackers, worms, and viruses caused almost $1.6 trillion in downtime and recovery costs. Table 12 shows the estimated costs of recent notable computer attacks.

It is important to consider the proper role of the federal government. Sometimes, the best course of action may be to take no action at all. The federal government can take action because a particular activity is best performed at a national or sub-national level. For example, intelligence gathering and national defense are best accomplished by the federal government. On the other hand, while the costs of recovering from cyber attacks can be high, some have argued that the potential effect of cyber attacks on national security or public safety is relatively small. It is argued that many critical infrastructure sectors are more robust and resilient than generally believed. For example, during the October 2002 distributed denial-of-service attack on the Domain Name Server root servers, 8 of the 13 servers were forced

Table 12. Estimated Costs of Recent Worm and Virus Attacks

Incident	Date	Estimated Cost
Melissa	1999	$0.3 billion
I Love You	2000	$8.0 billion
Code Red	2001	$2.6 billion
Slammer	2003	$1.0 billion

Source: Canadian Office of Critical Infrastructure Protection and Emergency Preparedness.

off-line. However, the attack did not noticeably degrade Internet performance. Similarly, while thousands of networks were disabled during the August 2003 northeast blackout, there was no significant increase in end-to-end delays on the Internet.

In other situations, the federal government may need to take action because the market will not address the issue in a timely fashion. Ideally, private sector responses will adequately address a problem. In some sectors, market forces may be enough to improve cybersecurity throughout the sector. Some well-organized sectors could also develop their own rules requiring all member entities to achieve specific cybersecurity results. For example, the chemical infrastructure sector established mandatory requirements under its responsible care program. As previously discussed, the oil and natural gas industry also endorsed international standards for security management programs. In other cases, state and local government may be taking action to address the problem. Regardless of the specific actions taken by the federal government, it is important for all levels of government—federal, state, and local—and the private sector to work cooperatively to ensure that the most critical issues are addressed by the appropriate party.

The Federal Government Is Assisting with Risk Assessments

The federal government has a direct interest in ensuring that the private sector is adequately protecting critical infrastructures. To assist with the critical infrastructure risk assessment process, the federal government provides two primary functions: (1) it provides guidance and establishes relationships to help conduct risk assessments, and (2) it provides threat and vulnerability information to sectors and their member entities.

HSPD-7 and the *National Strategy for Homeland Security* identified lead federal agencies, referred to as sector-specific agencies, to work with their counterparts in the private sector, referred to as sector coordinators. HSPD-7 called for a range of activities intended to establish a partnership between the public and private sectors to ensure the security of our nation's critical infrastructures. The sector-specific agency and the sector coordinator are to work with each other to address problems related to CIP for their sector. In particular, HSPD-7 stated that they are to (1) conduct or facilitate vulnerability assessment of their sector, and (2) encourage risk management strategies to protect against and mitigate the effects of attacks against critical infrastructures and key resources. It also required federal agencies to establish a system for responding to a significant attack on an infrastructure while it is under way so that damages can be isolated and minimized and for rapidly reconstituting minimum required capabilities for varying levels of successful infrastructure attacks.

The National Strategy for Homeland Security and HSPD-7 identified 13 industry sectors, expanded from the 8 originally identified in PDD 63, and lead federal agencies, including the Department of Homeland Security. The lead agencies and their corresponding sectors are listed in table 13.

For example, as part of its responsibilities as the lead agency for the banking and finance infrastructure sector, the Department of the Treasury chairs the Financial and Banking Information Infrastructure Committee (FBIIC), which is responsible for coordinating federal and state regulatory efforts to improve the reliability and security of U.S. financial systems. Treasury has taken steps designed to establish better relationships and methods of communication among regulators, assess vulnerabilities, and improve communication within the financial services sector. In addition, federal regulators, such as the Federal Reserve System and the Securities and Exchange Com-mission, have taken several steps to address information security issues, including the consideration of information security risks in determining the scope of their examinations of financial institutions and the development of guidance for examining information security and for protecting against cyber threats.

Further, the federal government can also help fund risk assessment activities by sectors and their member entities. This support can be provided directly to infrastructure owners or through their ISACs or sector coordinators. There is already precedence for such support. For example, as mentioned earlier, the Environmental Protection Agency reportedly has provided funding for 449 grants totaling $51 million to assist utilities for large drinking water systems in preparing vulnerability assessments, emergency response/operating plans, and security enhancement plans and designs. In addition, the Department of Transportation has performed related studies, including a vulnerability assessment of surface transportation and of the transportation infrastructure's reliance on the global positioning system.[70] The Department of the Treasury provided $2 million for

[70] John A. Volpe National Transportation Systems Center, *Vulnerability Assessment of the Transportation Infrastructure Relying on the Global Positioning System*, Final Report (Cambridge, MA: Aug. 29, 2001).

Table 13. Critical Infrastructure Sector-Specific Agencies

Sector-specific Agency	Sectors
Department of Agriculture	• Agriculture • Food (meat and poultry)
Department of Defense	• Defense industrial base
Department of Energy	• Energy (electrical power, oil and gas production and storage)
Environmental Protection Agency	• Drinking water and water treatment systems
Department of Health and Human Services	• Public health (including prevention, surveillance, laboratory services, and personal health services) and health care • Food (all except meat and poultry)
Department of Homeland Security	• Chemicals and hazardous materials • Continuity of government • Emergency services • Information technology and telecommunications • Transportation (aviation; rail; mass transit; waterborne commerce; pipelines; and highways, including trucking and intelligent transportation systems) • Postal and shipping
Department of the Treasury	• Banking and finance

Source: *National Strategy for Homeland Security, The National Strategy to Secure Cyberspace,* and HSPD-7.

the next generation Financial Services ISAC to provide alerting services to a greater number of sector entities.

Additionally, the federal government could provide guidance to critical infrastructure owners on how to perform risk assessments. Such guidance could be in the form of risk assessment templates that cover key elements such as threat and vulnerability assessments.

The federal government also provides assistance by disseminating threat and vulnerability information to critical infrastructure sectors. DHS is responsible for analyzing terrorist threats to the homeland, mapping these threats to our vulnerabilities, and taking protective action. For example, DHS administers the Homeland Security Advisory System, including coordination with other federal agencies to provide specific warning information and advice to state and local agencies, the private sector, the public, and other entities about appropriate protective measures and countermeasures to homeland security threats.

In March 2003, DHS assumed many of the functions of NIPC from the FBI. DHS's IAIP directorate provides a focal point for gathering and disseminating information on threats to critical infrastructures and issues warning products in response to increases in threat condition. The Homeland Security Act gives DHS broad statutory authority to access intelligence information, as well as other information relevant to the terrorist threat, and to turn this information into useful warnings. For example, DHS is one of the partner organizations in the multi-agency Terrorist Threat Integration Center (TTIC), which began operations on May 1, 2003.[71] IAIP integrates all-source threat information and analysis that it receives from TTIC and other agencies with its own vulnerability assessments to provide tailored threat assessments.

The United States Computer Emergency Readiness Team, a partnership between DHS and the private sector, issues a variety of information products through its National Cyber Alert System. This system distributes three types of information products: (1) cybersecurity alerts, which are available for non-technical and technical audiences, provide real-time information about security issues, vulnerabilities, and exploits current occurring that could require rapid action; (2) cybersecurity bulletins are targeted at technical audiences and provide biweekly summaries of security issues, new vulnerabilities, potential effect, patches, and workarounds; and (3) cybersecurity tips are targeted at non-technical audiences and provide biweekly information on best computer security practices. According to IAIP officials, if it is necessary to relay classified material, secure communication links have been established with each of the 50 state homeland security offices and some of the ISACs. Once it is determined that information should be disseminated, it is sent out by multiple paths. The difficult task is determining the appropriate audience for the information. The interdependency among the infrastructures is one reason why it is difficult to determine the appropriate audience.

A National CIP Plan Can Help Prioritize Needs

The scope of any federal program must account for the wide breadth of critical infrastructure sectors. However, the assets, functions, and systems within each critical infrastructure sector are not equally important. For example, the transportation sector is vital, but not every bridge is critical to the nation as a whole. To ensure a comprehensive and well-coordinated approach to critical infrastructure protection across all organizations, we have previously reported on the need for a national CIP plan.[72] Such a plan

---

[71] The center was formed from elements of the FBI, the CIA, and the Departments of Defense, Homeland Security, and State.

[72] U.S. General Accounting Office, *Information Security: Serious Weaknesses Place Critical Federal Operations and Assets at Risk*, GAO/AIMD-98-92 (Washington, D.C.: Sept. 23, 1998); *Combating Terrorism: Selected Challenges and Related Recommendations*, GAO-01-822 (Washington, D.C.: Sept. 20, 2001); and *Critical Infrastructure Protection: Federal Efforts Require a More Coordinated and Comprehensive Approach for Protecting Information Systems*, GAO-02-474 (Washington, D.C.: July 15, 2002).

should clearly define the roles and responsibilities of federal and nonfederal CIP organizations, define objectives and milestones, set time frames for achieving objectives, and establish performance measures. The federal government could then use this plan as a framework to help it determine the appropriate amount and types of federal actions that would best protect critical infrastructures from attack.

The need for a coordinated plan results from the widely varying operations of the critical infrastructure sectors and the sheer number of organizations that are involved in CIP efforts. For example, in 2002, we reported that at least 50 federal organizations were involved in national or multinational cyber CIP efforts, including 5 advisory committees; 6 Executive Office of the President organizations; 38 executive branch organizations associated with departments, agencies, or intelligence organizations; and 3 other organizations.[73] In addition, there are many state and local government agencies involved in CIP efforts, such as state regulators, law enforcement agencies, and water authorities, as well as private sector organizations, such as trade associations, industry groups, corporations, and information sharing and analysis centers. While each sector can take a sector-wide look and entities can focus on the details of the infrastructure they own, the federal government is in a better position to look across all critical infrastructure sectors and conduct a risk-based identification of the truly critical infrastructures—assets whose destruction or incapacitation would have a debilitating impact on national security, the economy, or public health and safety. Because such a large number of organizations are involved in CIP efforts, it is necessary to clarify how these organizations coordinate their activities with each other.

As we have described, several federal CIP policy documents have identified the need for such a plan. *The National Strategy for Homeland Security* assigns the development of a national infrastructure protection plan to the Department of Homeland Security. The Homeland Security Act of 2002 further assigns this responsibility to the IAIP directorate.[74] Most recently, HSPD-7 requires that this plan be developed by December 2004 and states that it should include a strategy to identify, prioritize, and coordinate the protection of critical infrastructure. Nationwide critical infrastructure risk assessments could enable the federal government to develop and maintain a prioritized list of key infrastructures across sectors. Knowing which infrastructures are truly critical across all sectors can help the government apply limited resources where they are most needed. This plan is expected to inform DHS's annual process for planning, programming, and budgeting critical infrastructure protection activities, including research and development.

[73] GAO-02-474.

[74] Public Law 107-296, §201(d)(5).

However, the development of such a plan is not without its challenges. For instance, methodologies to prioritize efforts to enhance critical infrastructure protection are inconsistent. Further, in order to properly define roles and responsibilities for critical infrastructure organizations, it is necessary to overcome ineffective communication among the federal, state, and local governments, which has resulted in untimely, disparate, and at times conflicting communication.

Increasing the Use of Available Cybersecurity Technologies

While many cybersecurity technologies are available, experts believe that these technologies are not being purchased or implemented to their fullest extent. Besides providing funding for the purchase of technology by critical infrastructure owners, other methods have been suggested to increase the use of available cybersecurity technologies, including increasing the security awareness of system administrators and users and enhancing information sharing so that security vulnerabilities can be better understood.

Improving Cybersecurity Awareness

As computers are increasingly interconnected and achieve appliance status, they are no longer strictly the domain of technology-savvy workers. According to CERT/CC, the expertise of the average system administrator continues to decline. A larger number of systems that are connected to the Internet are administered and used by individuals with little or no security training or expertise. Many experts agree that there is a need to improve cybersecurity awareness at all user levels, even for business and home users, because any Internet-connected PC could be used as a launching pad for denial-of-service attacks. Users often are unaware that their computers have been compromised and are being used to launch attacks.

Even among those who are familiar with cybersecurity technologies such as firewalls, encryption, and antivirus software, users do not always implement these security-improving technologies to their fullest extent. Some say that users often are complacent about possible cyber threats or do not adequately maintain the security posture of their systems by implementing security patches on a timely basis. Others say that users simply cannot keep up with the constant stream of software patches that are needed to correct defects in software.

The federal government could take the lead in promoting cybersecurity awareness as it has done in other awareness campaigns such as the campaign to discourage illicit drug use and the Buckle Up America campaign, which promotes automobile seat belt use. The federal government can fund the development of education campaigns that teach the importance of cybersecurity and how to use information technology securely.

Educational institutions could incorporate cybersecurity and cyberethics education in primary and secondary school and in colleges. The Department of Justice has established a Cyberethics for Kids program that teaches students in elementary and middle schools about the risks of harmful and illegal behavior online and shows them how to protect themselves from such behavior. For university students, NSF funds the Federal Cyber Service program to increase the number of qualified students in the cybersecurity field and to increase the number of cybersecurity professionals. The Federal Cyber Service program has two tracks: a Scholarship Track and a Capacity Building Track. The Scholarship Track provides funding to colleges and universities to award scholarships in information assurance and computer security fields. Upon graduation, after their 2-year scholarships, the scholarship recipients are required to work for a federal agency for 2 years in fulfillment of their Federal Cyber Service commitment. The Capacity Building Track provides funds to colleges and universities for professional development of information assurance faculty and the development of academic programs.

Some experts also commented that all business managers should learn the basics of cybersecurity—why it is important to the business and how to include it in risk analyses. Even if a business does not deal with life-and-death systems, managers need to know that cybersecurity helps protect against industrial espionage that could be used to steal sensitive information such as business plans, creative ideas, and trade secrets.

Critical infrastructure sectors could conduct their own security awareness campaigns. For example, the Federal Deposit Insurance Corporation (FDIC) has sponsored regional information sessions for the FBIIC and FSSCC to inform financial services organizations about the importance of a public-private sector partnership and to raise awareness of the services available to those organizations that are provided by the federal government and by the financial services sector.

Some experts have stated that one of the causes of vulnerable computers is a lack of awareness by users and system administrators in keeping up with available security patches. To remedy this problem, various tools and services are available to assist them in identifying vulnerabilities and their respective patches.

Because it can be difficult to identify vulnerabilities, the use of multiple sources can help to provide a more comprehensive view. As we have described, there are several sources of vulnerability information, including CERT/CC and NIST's ICAT Metabase. ICAT links users to publicly available vulnerability databases and patch sites, thus enabling them to find and fix vulnerabilities on their systems. Other organizations, such as the Last Stage of Delirium Research Group, research security vulnerabilities and maintain databases of such vulnerabilities. In addition, mailing lists, such as BugTraq, provide forums for announcing and discussing vulnerabilities, including information on how to fix them. Security Focus monitors thousands of products in order to maintain a vulnerability database and provide security alerts. Finally, vendors such as Microsoft and Cisco provide software updates on their products, including notices of known vulnerabilities and their corresponding patches.

Several services and automated tools are available to assist organizations in performing their patch management function, including tools designed as stand-alone patch management systems. In addition, systems management tools can be used to deploy patches across an organization's network. Patch management vendors also offer central databases of the latest patches, incidents, and methods for mitigating risks before a patch can be deployed or before a patch has been released. Some vendors provide support for multiple software platforms, such as Microsoft, Solaris, Linux, and other platforms, while other vendors, such as Microsoft, focus on certain platforms exclusively.

Enhancing Information Sharing

Information sharing is a key element in developing comprehensive and practical approaches to defending against cyber attacks that could threaten critical infrastructures. Sharing of vulnerability or threat information with infrastructure owners facilitates the prevention or detection of cyber attacks. However, as we have reported in recent years, establishing the trusted relationships and protocols necessary to support information sharing can be difficult.[75] In addition, the private sector has expressed concerns about sharing information with the government and about the difficulty of obtaining security clearances.

Critical infrastructure sectors can benefit from sharing information about vulnerabilities, threats, and details of cyber attacks among the entities that make up the sector. Information on threats, vulnerabilities, and incidents experienced by others can help to identify trends, better understand the risks they faced, and determine what preventive measures should be implemented. However, for such information sharing to work, it is necessary to develop fully productive information-sharing relationships within the federal government and between the federal government and state and local governments and the private sector.

Shared information could be used for tactical purposes. Sharing information on incidents and solutions during an attack can lead to better responses

[75] U.S. General Accounting Office, *Information Sharing: Practices That Can Benefit Critical Infrastructure Protection*, GAO-02-24 (Washington, D.C.: Oct. 15, 2001).

by all involved in the information-sharing arrangement. Such a structure could be used to contain and minimize the damage caused by cyber attacks. Shared information can also have strategic uses. Computer security experts and researchers can use historical data about attacks to better understand threats and vulnerabilities and to develop better technologies that can defend against similar attacks. Further, analysis of such information can help intelligence and law enforcement organizations to identify trends in attacks and potentially to identify the perpetrators of attacks or sources of future attacks.

We have previously reported on federal information sharing practices that could benefit CIP.[76] These practices include:

- establishing trust relationships with a wide variety of federal and nonfederal entities that may be in a position to provide potentially useful information and advice on vulnerabilities and incidents;
- developing standards and agreements on how shared information will be used and protected;
- establishing effective and appropriately secure communications mechanisms; and
- taking steps to ensure that sensitive information is not inappropriately disseminated, steps that may require statutory changes.

A number of activities have been undertaken to build relationships between the federal government and the private sector, such as InfraGard, the Partnership for Critical Infrastructure Security, efforts by the former Critical Infrastructure Assurance Office, and efforts by lead agencies to establish ISACs. For example, the InfraGard Program, which provides the FBI with a means for sharing information securely with individual companies, has expanded substantially. Members include representatives from private industry, other government agencies, state and local law enforcement, and the academic community. As of March 30, 2004, InfraGard members totaled over 11,000.

PDD 63 encouraged the voluntary creation of ISACs and suggested some possible activities. However, their actual design and functions were left to the private sector, along with their relationships with the federal government. HSPD-7 continues to encourage the development of information-sharing mechanisms and does not suggest specific ISAC activities. As a result, the ISACs have been designed to perform their missions based on the unique characteristics and needs of their individual sectors, and although their overall missions are similar, they have different characteristics. They were created to provide an information-sharing and analysis

[76] GAO-02-24, 18.

capability for members of their respective infrastructure sectors in order to support efforts to mitigate risk and provide effective response to adverse events, including cyber, physical, and natural events.

As previously discussed, Treasury provided $2 million to establish the next generation FS-ISAC and its new capabilities, including upgrading the technology supporting it that would benefit Treasury, other financial regulators, and the private sector. In announcing this contract in December 2003, Treasury reported that it would:

- Transform FS-ISAC from a technology platform that serves approximately 80 financial institutions to one that serves the entire 30,000 institution financial sector including banks, credit unions, securities firms, insurance companies, commodity futures merchants, exchanges, and others.
- Provide a secure, confidential forum for financial institutions to share information among one another as they respond in real-time to particular threats.
- Add information about physical threats to the cyber threat information that FS-ISAC currently disseminates.
- Include an advance notification service that will notify member financial institutions of threats. The primary means of notification will be the Internet. If, however, Internet traffic is disrupted, the notification will be by other means, including telephone calls and faxes.
- Include over 16 quantitative measures of FS-ISAC's effectiveness that will enable the leadership of FS-ISAC and Treasury to assess both the FS-ISAC's performance and the aggregate state of information sharing within the industry in response to particular threats.

Laws recently enacted by Congress and the administration strengthen information sharing. For example, the USA PATRIOT Act promotes information sharing among federal agencies, and numerous terrorism task forces have been established to coordinate investigations and improve communications among federal and local law enforcement agencies.[77] Moreover, the Homeland Security Act of 2002 includes provisions that restrict federal, state, and local government use and disclosure of critical infrastructure information that has been voluntarily submitted to DHS.[78] These restrictions include exemption from disclosure under FOIA, a general limitation on use to CIP purposes, and limitations on use in civil actions and by state or local governments. The act also specifies penalties for any

[77] The Uniting and Strengthening America by Providing Appropriate Tools Required to Intercept and Obstruct Terrorism Act of 2001 (USA PATRIOT Act) (Public Law 107-56, Oct. 26, 2001).
[78] Public Law 107-296, §§211-215.

federal employee who improperly discloses any protected critical infrastructure information.

Nonetheless, some in the private sector have expressed concerns about voluntarily sharing information with one another and with the federal government. Specifically, concerns have been raised that sector members could face antitrust violations for sharing information with other industry partners, have their information subject to the Freedom of Information Act (FOIA),[79] or face potential liability concerns for information shared in good faith. For example, the information technology, energy, and water ISACs do not share their libraries with the federal government because of concerns that information could be released under FOIA. Officials of the energy ISAC stated that they had not reported incidents to NIPC because of FOIA and antitrust concerns.

Developing New Cybersecurity Technology

While there is clearly a short-term need for cybersecurity solutions, many researchers have described this approach as short-sighted. Because new vulnerabilities are being discovered on an increasingly frequent basis, many have argued that what is required is a re-engineering of security. Researchers have argued that there is a need to design secure systems from the bottom up, because it is difficult to deploy secure systems based on insecure components. Longer-term efforts, such as research into cybersecurity vulnerabilities and technological solutions for those problems and the transition of research results into commercially available products, are needed.

Continuing Cybersecurity Technology Research

Research in cybersecurity technology is needed to create a broader range of choices and more robust tools for building trustworthy networked computer systems. Research provides a science base and engineering expertise for building secure systems. Because research takes time to produce results, it is important to initiate research soon.

The federal government supports cybersecurity research, primarily through the Defense Advanced Research Projects Agency (DARPA) and NSA, but also through other Department of Defense and civilian agencies, such as NSF and DHS. There is also industry-funded research and development in the area of information security, but that work typically emphasizes development over research. It is difficult to enumerate all federally funded cybersecurity research because of problems in understanding how different projects are accounted for and also because many projects are classified.

[79] 5 U.S.C. §552.

Additionally, research in cybersecurity may include system development activities. For example, some recent research projects involve building network testbeds to develop and test defenses against cyber attacks. Two recent examples are the jointly NSF- and DHS-funded Cyber Defense Technology Experimental Research network, or DETER, at the University of California at Berkeley and the University of Southern California, and the Department of Justice-funded Internet-Scale Event and Attack Generation Environment at Iowa State University. Such test bed projects include the cost of the network itself in the project costs.

Because research is often geared toward producing short-term results and rapid transition to industry, high-risk theoretical and experimental investigations are not always encouraged. Many research problems are difficult, and the focus on short-term results can divert effort from critical areas.

A number of recent publications provide cybersecurity research agendas with varying degrees of detail.[80] These research agendas have similarities with one another. While several research agendas have been produced, some researchers have commented that insufficient action has been taken to implement them. Table 14 summarizes the typical research topics from a number of agendas.

Current research projects at universities and projects funded by several government agencies cover many of the research areas identified in the research agendas. Table 15 shows a sampling of some of the current research topics and is organized by the major control categories.

Some researchers commented that the research topics are too often narrowly defined and focus on topics that are most likely to get funded. For example, research on automating security-related system administration tasks such as configuring or patching software does not get enough attention in the funded projects. The push to show results in a relatively short time causes researchers to avoid taking broad, system-wide views. Instead research projects look at narrowly scoped parts of a system. This tends to balkanize research projects and detract from a system-wide look at security.

Some researchers pointed out that academic research and corporate research seem to be on different paths. Corporate research tends to focus on improving

[80] Some of these sources of research agendas include (1) Institute for Information Infrastructure Protection (I3P), *Cyber Security Research and Development Agenda* (Jan. 2003); (2) INFOSEC Research Council, *Information Assurance R&D Strategy: National Needs and Research Programs* (July 2, 2002); (3) NSF/OSTP, *New Vistas in CIP Research and Development: Secure Network Embedded Systems, Report of the NSF/OSTP Workshop on Innovative Information Technologies for Critical Infrastructure Protection* (Sept. 19-20, 2002); (4) National Security Telecommunications Advisory Committee (NSTAC), *Research and Development Exchange Proceedings: Research and Development Issues to Ensure Trustworthiness in Telecommunications and Information Systems That Directly or Indirectly Impact National Security and Emergency Preparedness* (Mar. 13-14, 2003); and (5) National Research Council, *Trust in Cyberspace* (Washington, D.C.: National Academy Press, 1999).

Table 14. Typical Research Areas Identified in Research Agendas

Research Area	Description
Building secure systems from insecure components	Biological metaphors (autonomic); Intelligent microsystems.
Correction of current vulnerabilities	Tools and techniques to help system administrators fix current vulnerabilities; Human factors in security.
Denial-of-service attacks	Identify and deter denial-of-service and distributed denial-of-service attacks.
Detection, recovery, and survivability	Prediction of events; Reconstitution of system of systems; Autonomic computing; Global network surveillance and warning (similar to public health surveillance).
Law, policy, and economic issues	Market issues; Standards; Tradeoffs
Security engineering tools and techniques	Tools and methods for building more secure systems; Architecture for improved security; Formal methods; Programming languages that enforce security policy; Generative programming.
Security metrics	Data to support analysis; Metrics and models for economic analysis, risk analysis, etc.; Technical metrics to measure strength of security.
Security of foreign and mobile code	Ability to confine and encapsulate code; Tamper-proof software.
Security of network embedded systems	Security of real-time control systems such as SCADA.
Security policy management	Maintain a defined risk posture; Protect a defined security perimeter.
Traceback, forensics, and attribution of attacks	Correct attribution and retribution; Automatic counterattack.
Trust models for data and distributed applications	Peer-to-Peer (P2P) security; Establishing trust in data.
Vulnerability identification and analysis	Automated discovery and analysis of vulnerabilities; Code scanning tools; Device scanning.
Wireless security	Device and protocol level wireless security; Monitoring wireless network; Addressing DDoS attacks in wireless networks.

Source: GAO analysis.

existing product lines in the near-term, whereas university research typically looks at ideas irrespective of their viability as products. The transition from university research into products can be time-consuming and there is no well-defined approach.

Table 15. Sampling of Current Research Topics

Control Category	Research Topics
Access controls	• Biometric access using facial recognition • Role-based access control
System integrity	• Storage devices that can detect changes to critical files • Network interfaces that can throttle worm/virus propagations • Software analysis for vulnerability detection • Code integrity verification • Proof-carrying code
Cryptography	• PKI for communications and computational security • Certification authority with defense against denial-of-service attacks • Quantum cryptography • Quantum key distribution
Audit and monitoring	• High-speed network monitoring for worm/virus detection • Emergent behavior detection • Honeynets to entice and deceive would-be attackers
Configuration management and assurance	• Survivable systems • Trusted computing • Evaluation and certification of systems

Source: GAO analysis.

Among some of the areas needing attention, researchers cited developing ways to measure security and assessing the economic effectiveness of proposed cybersecurity technologies. Such economic effectiveness studies can help make the case for specific cybersecurity technologies.

A long-term research objective is to develop systems that are inherently secure, with security engineered into the system from the start. Contrast this with current security technologies that are bolted on—added after the fact. A larger goal than security alone is to design and build survivable systems. Survivable systems have resiliency so that they can continue to perform, albeit at a degraded level, even when they are under attack. Such survivable systems require forethought in design, much as guardrails along dangerous curves are most effective only when they are built before anyone drives on the road. Survivability concepts can include the notion of defense-in-depth with defensive perimeters taken down to the level of system components such as storage devices and network interface cards and their associated software modules.

By comparing the identified research needs with the ongoing research, we arrive at the following research areas as a selection of some of the important areas that need continuing attention in cybersecurity research programs:

1. **Vulnerability identification and analysis**. There is a need for better methods to determine, throughout a product or system's life cycle (development, integration, update and maintenance, decommissioning, or replacement of components), whether exploitable defects have been introduced or unanticipated security problems have emerged. Research is needed into techniques and tools to analyze code, devices, and systems in dynamic and large-scale environments.

2. **Composing secure systems from insecure components**. Research is needed to develop approaches for composing complex heterogeneous systems that maintain security while recovering from failures. New approaches, such as the use of biological metaphors (autonomic) and intelligent microsystems, may be explored to create more secure systems.

3. **Security metrics and evaluation**. Research is needed to define metrics that express the costs, benefits, and impacts of security controls from multiple perspectives—economic, organizational, technical, and risk—so that the effect of security decisions can be better understood. Techniques are needed for modeling the security-related behavior of systems and predicting the consequences of risk mitigation approaches.

4. **Wireless security**. In principle, many of the security concerns for wireless networks mirror those for the wired world; in practice, solutions that have been developed for wired networks may not be viable in wireless environments. Research is needed to make security a fundamental component of wireless networks, develop the basic science of wireless security, develop security solutions that can be integrated into the wireless device itself, investigate the security implications of existing wireless protocols, integrate security mechanisms across all protocol layers, and integrate wireless security into larger systems and networks. In particular, research is needed into security situational awareness techniques for wireless networks and strategies to address distributed denial-of-service attacks.

5. **Socioeconomic impact of security**. Research is needed to determine the scope and size of the cybersecurity problem and the effect that forces, such as laws, policy, and technology, have on infrastructure protection. For any technology, it is necessary to determine the legal, policy, and economic implications of the technology and its possible uses. Research is needed to describe the structure and dynamics of the cybersecurity marketplace. There is a need for research into the role of standards and best practices in improving cybersecurity posture, the policy and legal considerations relating to collection and use of data about the information

infrastructures, and the implications of policies that are intended to direct responses to cyber attacks.

6. **Security for network embedded systems**. Research is needed on assessing the security of control systems that are prevalent in electricity, oil, gas, and water sectors. Security should be integrated into network embedded systems where previously it has not existed. Models of control networks can help in predicting the responses of control systems to changes and anomalies. Techniques are needed to detect, understand, and respond to anomalies in large, distributed control networks.

Some of these research areas are already receiving attention from the federal government. For example, NSF has recently announced a new program to foster cybersecurity research in areas such as trustworthy computing technology, evaluation and certification methods, efforts to prevent denial-of-service attacks, and long-term data-archiving technology. The NSF program also plans to support multidisciplinary research that covers the social, legal, ethical, and economic compromises that affect the design and operation of secure network systems. The DHS Science and Technology Directorate is planning or has under way programs in the following areas: prevention and protection against attacks; monitoring, attack detection and response; mitigation of effects, remediation of damage, and recovery; and forensics and attribution. Other DHS research programs include infrastructure security (network protocols and process control systems) and foundations for cyber security (economic assessment activities, large scale data sets for testing).

Universities are also proposing research efforts to develop new science and technology for improving the cybersecurity of critical infrastructures. For example, recently teams of researchers from the University of California at Berkeley, Carnegie Mellon University, Cornell University, Stanford University, and Vanderbilt University have proposed a research center called the Team for Research in Ubiquitous Secure Technologies (TRUST) that would focus on designing systems that continue to work despite attacks or errors. The TRUST proposal presents three broad research categories—security technology, systems science, and social science. These categories are further broken down into 11 specific research areas that include topics such as software and network security, secure network embedded systems, and economics, public policy, and societal challenges of security.

As the federal government's research programs consider funding these cybersecurity research areas, it is important to note that there are many R&D needs vying for a limited amount of R&D dollars. Federal R&D program managers face tough choices in deciding where the R&D money should go and how much is appropriate for critical infrastructure protection. Depending on the infrastructure sector, it may be better to focus on overall infrastructure survivability, instead of the cybersecurity aspects alone. Some experts have suggested that if cybersecurity is deemed important to national security, it may be appropriate to adopt the R&D model adopted by DoD, where postulated threat models drive R&D in a progression from basic research through exploratory development, ending in government-funded engineering development of products and systems.

Addressing Long-Term Cybersecurity Research Needs

In addition to cybersecurity research that addresses existing cybersecurity threats, there is need for long-term research that anticipates the dramatic growth in the use of computing and networks. Some indicators of an upcoming period of dramatic growth include the increasing use of broadband networking technologies such as cable modems, the emergence of new wireless communication options, and the emergence of Web Services that enable computers to communicate with one another directly using Web technologies.

High-speed networks and standards such as Web Services make it easy for an organization to connect its computers directly to the computers of its suppliers, but this surge in interconnections may bring a new wave of cybersecurity threats to a variety of critical business and government computing systems. Not enough is understood about security and reliability of these emerging complex systems. The rapid evolution of new styles of computing creates a pressing need for research into the fundamental options for securing Web Services and other complex, interconnected computing systems, and for ensuring that they will be reliable, highly available, self-managed, and self-repairing after disruption.

New options for connectivity and new wireless communication technologies also create new potential for undesired intrusion. Existing security research has focused more on establishing barriers against intrusion, with less attention to the preservation of personal privacy and the protection of intellectual property. New technical options are needed to protect privacy. Yet privacy is a two-edged sword because the same technologies that can protect private data may also help criminals and terrorists. Resolving such quandaries will require both technical advances as well as legal and social advances.

Recently, program managers at DARPA highlighted the Internet itself as perhaps the most serious security and reliability obstacle present in many sensitive military and intelligence systems. Increasing numbers of academic and commercial researchers echo these concerns. The Internet was created by a very cooperative, mutually trusting research community, and was designed with file transfers as its primary mission. This is simply not the appropriate model for applications such as broadband media transmission, highly available access to mission-critical services, or applications in which security and privacy are of primary importance. Although discarding the existing Internet does not make sense, researchers are suggesting an approach whereby the existing Internet hardware runs multiple side-by-side networks that might share the same hardware but have very different properties. However, like the development of the Internet itself, a substantial research investment would be required to achieve such new networks.

Table 16 lists some areas in which long-term research will be required. This research may occur in a diversity of settings, including academic institutions, government-funded small business innovation research programs, and classified research programs that address the needs of military and intelligence communities.

Developing Approaches to Transition Research into Commercial Products

As we have described, there are many promising cybersecurity research projects ongoing in universities and government laboratories. For such research to be useful in improving the security of critical infrastructures, the results of the research must make their way into commercial products and systems that can then be deployed in the infrastructures. This transition from research to actual products is not easy, and it takes time. The National Research Council has found that, for federal IT research, at least 10 years, and sometimes more than 15 years, elapse between initial research on a new idea and commercial success.[81] The council found that the relationship between government-funded research and industry research has been important in transitioning research results into commercial products.

Some have suggested the possibility of using a model based on SEMATECH—Semiconductor Manufacturing Technology—that was established by an act of Congress in 1987, when 14 U.S.-based semiconductor manufacturers and the U.S. government came together to strengthen the U.S. semiconductor industry. The consortium focused on solving common manufacturing problems by leveraging resources and sharing risks. By 1994, it had become clear that the U.S. semiconductor industry—both device makers and suppliers—had regained strength and market share; at that time, SEMATECH's board of directors voted to seek an end to matching federal funding after 1996, reasoning that the industry had returned to health and should no longer receive government support. Federal government may need to work with the computer security industry—the information technology sector—to develop options for migrating research results into IT products.

[81] National Research Council. *Innovation in Information Technology*, (Washington, D.C.: National Academy Press, 2003), 11.

Table 16. Sampling of Long-Term Research Areas

Research Area	Description
Privacy	Better tools are needed for ensuring the privacy of sensitive information such as individual health records and financial records. Research is needed on the legal basis of privacy in an era of computer networks, on the emergence of new social patterns disruptive of traditional property ownership rules, and on technologies to enforce privacy.
Fault-tolerance	Some of the most disruptive cyber attacks start by provoking some form of failure or overload, causing the targeted system to degrade or become unresponsive. Technologies for embedding fault-tolerance into the major commercial platforms, such as Web services, are needed to greatly reduce the threat of such disruptions.
Scalability	As computing systems grow in size, enterprises are beginning to encounter problems of scale. Research is needed into managing systems that may include thousands or tens of thousands of machines. Progress in this area would reduce the cost of operating large systems.
New monitoring capabilities	Whereas computing systems of the past were relatively easy to instrument and monitor, the trend toward Web-based systems has created a new world in which an application may reside partly within a data center and partly on client systems spread over the Internet. New techniques are needed for monitoring such configurations, for diagnosing problems such as denial-of-service attacks and for reacting when problems occur.
Self-management	Existing computing systems often require human managers in rough proportion to the size of the system. Technology for self-management could enable deployment of large numbers of machines without a great deal of management and control by humans.
Self-healing	Technology is lacking for diagnosing the problem and carrying out an automated repair of systems that are damaged because of mundane problems or cyber attacks. Technology for building self-healing systems would be tremendously beneficial in a great variety of settings. This is a hard problem, because problems build on one another to produce a large number of symptoms that may vary greatly despite their common root cause.
Rearchitecting the Internet	It is time to revisit the core architecture of the Internet, moving from a "single network for all uses" model to one in which network connections might be portals to a small number of side-by-side networks, sharing the same hardware infrastructure but offering different properties. Development of such a capability will require many years of research but could ultimately provide better options for cybersecurity and robustness.

Source: Kenneth Birman, Cornell University.

Chapter 5: Summary

In this report we described a variety of cybersecurity technologies that can be used to help secure critical infrastructures from cyber attacks. Some technologies, such as firewalls and biometrics, can help to better protect computers and networks against attacks, while others, such as intrusion detection and continuity of operations tools, help to detect and respond to cyber attacks while they are in progress. These technologies can help to protect information that is being processed, stored, and transmitted in the networked computer systems that are prevalent in critical infrastructures. Although many cybersecurity technologies are available, experts feel that these technologies are not being purchased or implemented to their fullest extent. In addition to the need for a short-term solution of properly implementing current cybersecurity technologies, there is also a longer-term need for cybersecurity research and for transitioning the research results into commercially available products. On the basis of a number of research agendas and ongoing cybersecurity research, we found that a number of research areas need continuing attention. These cybersecurity research areas include composition of secure systems, security of network embedded systems, security metrics, socio-economic impact of security, vulnerability identification and analysis, and wireless security. Federal cybersecurity research programs are already beginning to address these research areas.

There are many implementation issues associated with using cybersecurity technologies for critical infrastructure protection. The issues include using a holistic approach to security, augmenting technology with people and processes, building security into new information systems, and considering non-technical options that can improve cybersecurity.

For a holistic approach to security, entities can use an overall security framework that includes a combination of risk assessments, security policies, security solutions, and security management, representing a continuous security process. Even when an entity has conducted a risk assessment and knows the extent of its cybersecurity needs, it cannot protect everything. Often, a business case is required to invest in cybersecurity. The interaction of technology with security processes and the people using the technology and the limitations of certain cybersecurity technologies can influence the purchase of technology. When building new information systems, organizations such as NIST have recommended that security requirements be considered as early as possible in the system development life cycle. System designers can use defense in depth—a strategy that uses a sequence of defensive mechanisms to enhance security.

Because critical infrastructures are so important to national security and the public good, the federal government has a stake in ensuring that the nation's critical infrastructures are protected. IT vendors provide the products, including cybersecurity technologies that entities use in their infrastructures. There are a number of opportunities for potential action by all stakeholders—from the entities to the government—in the areas of risk assessment, cybersecurity awareness, cybersecurity technology adoption and implementation, information sharing, cybersecurity research and development, and cybersecurity standards development. The federal government and other stakeholders already have several ongoing activities in these areas, which could help improve the cybersecurity posture in critical infrastructures.

Because the private sector owns most of the critical infrastructures, the federal government needs to gain insight into the infrastructures' vulnerabilities and relative priorities. The use of a risk-based framework for security and the conduct of risk assessments by infrastructure owners could provide the federal government with the information necessary to make informed policy decisions.

All federal actions have consequences—both intended and unintended. It would be irresponsible to propose or implement any action without examining the potential consequences, including the cost and benefits of the action. In particular, when discussing any potential action, it is crucial to carefully consider the following elements of a policy analysis framework:

- scope and size of the problem,
- market forces at play and their timeliness,
- level of organization of the critical infrastructure sectors and their ability to set and implement cybersecurity goals,
- costs and benefits of federal action,
- the intended and unintended consequences of federal action, and
- consequences of inaction by the federal government.

Although we focus primarily on federal actions, all levels of government—federal, state, and local—and the private sector have to work cooperatively to improve the cybersecurity of our nation's critical computer-dependent infrastructures.

Critical infrastructure owners are ultimately responsible for the cybersecurity of the infrastructures. They can use a risk-based framework to select and implement available cybersecurity technologies. The federal government can consider a number of options to manage and encourage the increased use of cybersecurity technologies, support research and develop new cybersecurity technologies, and generally improve the level of cybersecurity of critical infrastructure sectors.

Agency Comments and Our Evaluation

We provided a draft of this report to the Department of Homeland Security and the National Science Foundation for their review.

We include DHS's comments in their entirety in appendix IV. We include NSF's comments in their entirety in appendix V.

Department of Homeland Security

In written comments on a draft of this report, the Department of Homeland Security stated that it generally concurred with the report. DHS said that the report effectively discusses many of the important cybersecurity issues and the report will be of great value to those entrusted with protecting critical systems and networks.

DHS provided technical comments on the draft, which we incorporated as appropriate. Specifically, DHS provided more details on its cybersecurity research and development programs and expressed concerns with our characterization of the breadth of cybersecurity research that is necessary. We agree that the cybersecurity research areas that we highlight in the report do not address all areas that require research funding. Our intent was to highlight some of the important research topics based on our review of cybersecurity research agendas and discussions with cybersecurity researchers. DHS suggested that we remove wireless security as a research area because funding is limited and there is a significant level of private sector activity and funding for wireless security. We consider wireless security an important area and wireless security appears in some well-known cybersecurity research agendas. Additionally, the list of research areas is meant to be for both government and private sector. We agree that federal R&D dollars are limited and not all research areas may be candidates for federal funding.

National Science Foundation

In written comments on a draft of this report, the National Science Foundation noted that this is an important and timely report that provides broad coverage of current and emerging cybersecurity and infrastructure technologies. NSF highlighted its engagement in the intertwined issues of critical infrastructure protection and computing. NSF went on to state that cybersecurity improvements may be made through the widespread deployment of architectures already recognized to be more resistant to attacks.

Citing new technology discoveries and major information technology shifts as drivers, NSF emphasized the critical ongoing role of long range research both for developing newly robust infrastructures and for achieving security as an inherent property of these infrastructures. Finally, NSF noted that an essential component of security is the use of credible deterrents. NSF believes that research in cyber forensics and its effective use by law enforcement may reduce the overall threat and serve as a deterrent to would-be attackers.

External Review Comments

We provided a draft of this report to 26 organizations, including representatives of six critical infrastructure sectors, for their review. Individuals from these organizations were selected because of their assistance during the data collection phase of our work or their attendance at our cybersecurity meeting, convened for us by the National Academy of Sciences. The reviewers represented government, industry, and academia. We received comments and suggestions from 15 reviewers. The comments ranged from clarifying issues to highlighting certain aspects of the assessment that the reviewers considered important. We have incorporated these comments, where appropriate, in the report.

Several reviewers commended us for putting together a good report. One reviewer congratulated us for pulling such challenging material into an exceptionally coherent and solid document. Another reviewer felt that the report is very thorough and manages to stay on task given the scope and complexity of the issues.

Among the detailed comments, one suggestion was to briefly discuss long-term research that takes into account an anticipated dramatic growth in the use of computing and networks. We added a section on long-term research that includes a table with a sampling of research areas. A reviewer noted that run-of-the-mill poor systems management can be as serious a threat as a deliberate cyber attack. The reviewer characterized such poor systems management as a mundane cybersecurity threat. On the basis of that reviewer's suggestion we included a discussion of the serious consequences of such routine mismanagement.

Another reviewer stated that the report is no longer relevant because waves of worm/virus attacks in recent months have made the Internet a far more dangerous place and that any risk management approach would be problematic. We disagree with this characterization and believe that the threats to both the Internet and other critical infrastructure networks continue to be relevant and that risk management remains a logical approach to addressing the cybersecurity needs of critical infrastructures.

Comments from the critical infrastructure sectors were generally favorable. One sector representative commented that the report strikes a reasonably good balance between analysis and recommendations, and that the three key questions that provide the overall structure for the report are relevant and timely. Some sector representatives also provided clarifying details about information related to their sector. For example, one sector representative cited a recent government grant to help support that sector's ISAC. Another sector representative clarified how a segment of that sector relies on information technology for its operations. We incorporated the sector-suggested clarifications and changes as appropriate.

Appendix I: Technology Assessment Methodology

This technology assessment focuses on three key questions:

1. What are the key cybersecurity requirements in each of the critical infrastructure protection sectors?

2. What cybersecurity technologies can be applied to critical infrastructure protection? What technologies are currently deployed or currently available but not yet widely deployed for critical infrastructure protection? What technologies are currently being researched for cybersecurity? Are there any gaps in cybersecurity technology that should be better researched and developed to address critical infrastructure protection?

3. What are the implementation issues associated with using cybersecurity technologies for critical infrastructure protection, including policy issues such as privacy and information sharing?

To identify cybersecurity technologies that can be used for critical infrastructure protection (CIP), we reviewed relevant cybersecurity reports and vendor literature. We met with representatives of the National Science Foundation (NSF), the National Institute of Standards and Technology (NIST), the National Security Agency (NSA), the Infosec Research Council, and the Department of Homeland Security's (DHS) Science and Technology directorate to discuss current and planned federal cybersecurity research efforts. We also met with representatives from two Department of Energy national labs, Sandia National Labs and Lawrence Livermore National Lab, and one Department of Defense center, the CERT Coordination Center (CERT/CC).[82] We interviewed cybersecurity researchers from academic institutions (Carnegie Mellon University, Dartmouth College, and the University of California at Berkeley) and corporate research centers (AT&T Research Labs, SRI International, and HP Labs).

To identify the key cybersecurity requirements in each critical infrastructure sector, we developed a data collection instrument and used it to interview sector representatives such as industry groups or companies within the sector. We used the critical infrastructure sectors defined in the Administration's national strategy documents.[83] We interviewed representatives from the Banking and Finance, Chemical Industry and Hazardous Materials,

[82] The CERT/CC is a center of Internet security expertise at the Software Engineering Institute, a federally funded research and development center operated by Carnegie Mellon University. CERT and CERT Coordination Center are registered in the U.S. Patent and Trademark Office by Carnegie Mellon University.

[83] The White House, Office of Homeland Security, *National Strategy for Homeland Security*, (Washington, D.C.: July 2002) and The White House, *The National Strategy for The Physical Protection of Critical Infrastructures and Key Assets*, (Washington, D.C.: Feb. 2003).

Defense Industrial Base, Energy, Information and Telecommunications, Transportation, and Water sectors. We met with officials from DHS's Information Analysis and Infrastructure Protection (IAIP) directorate to discuss their efforts in organizing and coordinating CIP activities. We also met with IAIP's National Communications System (NCS), which operates the information-sharing and analysis center (ISAC) for the telecommunications sector. We met with the Coast Guard to discuss its efforts in the maritime transportation sector.

To identify implementation issues, we reviewed previous studies on security and CIP, including those from the National Research Council, CERT/CC, the Institute for Information Infrastructure Protection (I3P), and NIST. We interviewed critical infrastructure sector representatives to identify the challenges they face in implementing cybersecurity technologies. We also relied on previous GAO reports on cybersecurity and CIP. To examine policy issues, we reviewed current federal statutes and regulations that govern the protection of computer systems. On the basis of information that we collected through literature reviews and interviews, we assessed the effects of several policy options that could be employed by the federal government.

In October 2003, we convened a meeting, with the assistance of the National Academy of Sciences (NAS), to review the preliminary results of our work.[84] Meeting attendees included representatives from academia, critical infrastructure sectors, and public policy organizations.

We provided a draft of this report to DHS and NSF for their review. We include their comments in appendixes IV and V, respectively. In addition, we provided a draft of this report to selected attendees of the meeting that we convened with NAS for this work and with other interested organizations.

We conducted our work from May 2003 to February 2004 in the Washington, D.C., metropolitan area; the San Francisco, California, metropolitan area; Princeton, New Jersey; and Pittsburgh, Pennsylvania. We performed our work in accordance with generally accepted government auditing standards.

Appendix II: Summary of Federal Critical Infrastructure Protection Policies

Over the years, several working groups have been formed, special reports written, federal policies issued, and organizations created to address CIP. Although these steps have raised awareness and spurred activity by many critical infrastructures and the federal government, the nation still faces

[84] We have a standing contract with NAS under which NAS provides assistance in convening groups of experts to provide information and expertise to our engagements. NAS uses its scientific network to identify participants and uses its facilities and processes to arrange the meetings. Recording and using the information in a report is our responsibility.

several challenges in CIP. To provide a historical perspective, table 17 summarizes the key developments in federal CIP policy since 1997. Four key actions that have shaped the development of the federal government's CIP policy are

- Presidential Decision Directive 63 (PDD 63)
- Homeland Security Act of 2002
- The National Strategy to Secure Cyberspace
- Homeland Security Presidential Directive 7 (HSPD-7)

Table 17. Federal Government Actions Taken to Develop CIP Policy

Policy Action	Date	Description
Critical Foundations: Protecting America's Infrastructures[a]	Oct. 1997	Described the potentially devastating effects of poor information security for the nation and recommended measures to achieve a higher level of CIP that included industry cooperation and information sharing, a national organizational structure, a revised program of research and development, a broad program of awareness and education, and a reconsideration of related laws.
Presidential Decision Directive 63	May 1998	Established CIP as a national goal and presented a strategy for cooperative efforts by government and the private sector to protect the physical and cyber-based systems essential to the minimum operations of the economy and the government. Established government agencies to coordinate and support CIP efforts. Identified lead federal agencies to work with coordinators in eight infrastructure sectors and five special functions. Encouraged the development of information-sharing and analysis centers.
National Plan for Information Systems Protection[b]	Jan. 2000	Provided a vision and framework for the federal government to prevent, detect, and respond to attacks on the nation's critical cyber-based infrastructure and to reduce existing vulnerabilities by complementing and focusing existing federal computer security and information technology requirements.
Executive Order 13228	Oct. 2001	Established the Office of Homeland Security within the Executive Office of the President to develop and coordinate the implementation of a comprehensive national strategy to secure the United States from terrorist threats or attacks.

Policy Action	Date	Description
		Established the Homeland Security Council to advise and assist the President with all aspects of homeland security and to ensure coordination among executive departments and agencies.
Executive Order 13231	Oct. 2001	Established the President's Critical Infrastructure Protection Board to coordinate cyber-related federal efforts and programs associated with protecting our nation's critical infrastructures and to recommend policies and coordinating programs for protecting CIP-related information systems.
National Strategy for Homeland Security[c]	July 2002	Identified the protection of critical infrastructures and key assets as a critical mission area for homeland security. Expanded the number of critical infrastructures to 13 from the 8 identified in PDD 63 and identified lead federal agencies for each.
Homeland Security Act of 2002[d]	Nov. 2002	Created the Department of Homeland Security and assigned it the following CIP responsibilities: (1) developing a comprehensive national plan for securing the key resources and critical infrastructures of the United States; (2) recommending measures to protect the key resources and critical infrastructures of the United States in coordination with other groups; and (3) disseminating, as appropriate, information to assist in the deterrence, prevention, preemption of, or response to terrorist attacks.
The National Strategy to Secure Cyberspace[e]	Feb. 2003	Provided the initial framework for both organizing and prioritizing efforts to protect our nation's cyberspace. Provided direction to federal departments and agencies that have roles in cyberspace security and identified steps that state and local governments, private companies and organizations, and individual Americans can take to improve our collective cybersecurity.
The National Strategy for the Physical Protection of Critical Infrastructures and Key Assets[f]	Feb. 2003	Provided a statement of national policy to remain committed to protecting critical infrastructures and key assets from physical attacks. Built on PDD 63 with its sector-based approach and called for expanding the capabilities of ISACs. Outlined three key objectives: (1) identifying and assuring the protection of the most critical assets, systems, and functions; (2) assuring the protection of infrastructures that face an imminent threat; and (3) pursuing collaborative measures and initiatives to assure the protection of other potential targets.

Policy Action	Date	Description
Executive Order 13286	Feb. 2003	Superseded Executive Order 13231 but maintained the same national policy statement regarding the protection against disruption of information systems for critical infrastructures. Dissolved the President's Critical Infrastructure Protection Board and eliminated the board's chair, the Special Advisor to the President for Cyberspace Security. Designated the National Infrastructure Advisory Council to continue to provide the President with advice on the security of information systems for critical infrastructures supporting other sectors of the economy through the Secretary of Homeland Security.
Homeland Security Presidential Directive 7	Dec. 2003	Superseded PDD 63 and established a national policy for federal departments and agencies to identify and prioritize U.S. critical infrastructure and key resources and to protect them from terrorist attack. Defined roles and responsibilities for the Department of Homeland Security and sector-specific agencies to work with sectors to coordinate CIP activities. Established a CIP Policy Coordinating Committee to advise the Homeland Security Council on interagency CIP issues.

Source: GAO analysis.

[a]President's Commission on Critical Infrastructure Protection, *Critical Foundations: Protecting America's Infrastructures* (Washington, D.C.: Oct. 1997).

[b]The White House, *Defending America's Cyberspace: National Plan for Information Systems Protection: Version 1.0: An Invitation to Dialogue* (Washington, D.C.: Jan. 2000).

[c]The White House, Office of Homeland Security, *National Strategy for Homeland Security.*

[d]Homeland Security Act of 2002, Public Law 107-296 (Nov. 25, 2002).

[e]The White House, *The National Strategy to Secure Cyberspace* (Washington, D.C.: Feb. 2003).

[f]The White House, *The National Strategy for the Physical Protection of Critical Infrastructures and Key Assets.*

Presidential Decision Directive 63 Established Initial CIP Strategy

In 1998, the President issued PDD 63, which described a strategy for cooperative efforts by government and the private sector to protect the physical and cyber-based systems essential to the minimum operations of the economy and the government. PDD 63 called for a range of actions that were intended to improve federal agency security programs, improve the nation's ability to detect and respond to serious computer-based and physical attacks, and establish a partnership between the government and the private sector. The directive called on the federal government to serve as a model of how infrastructure assurance is best achieved, and it designated lead agencies to work with private sector and government entities. Further, it established CIP as a national goal and stated that, by the close of 2000, the United States was to have achieved an initial operating capability to protect the nation's critical infrastructures from intentional destructive acts and, by 2003, have developed the ability to protect the nation's critical infrastructures from intentional destructive attacks.

To accomplish its goals, PDD 63 established and designated organizations to provide central coordination and support, including

- the Critical Infrastructure Assurance Office (CIAO), an interagency office housed in the Department of Commerce, which was established to develop a national plan for CIP based on infrastructure plans that had been developed by the private sector and federal agencies;
- the National Infrastructure Protection Center (NIPC), an organization within the FBI, which was expanded to address national-level threat assessment, warning, vulnerability, and law enforcement investigation and response; and
- the National Infrastructure Assurance Council, which was established to enhance the partnership of the public and private sectors in protecting our critical infrastructures.[85]

To ensure the coverage of critical sectors, PDD 63 identified eight infrastructures: (1) banking and finance; (2) information and communications; (3) water supply; (4) aviation, highway, mass transit, pipelines, rail, and waterborne commerce; (5) emergency law enforcement; (6) emergency fire services and continuity of government; (7) electric power and oil and gas production and storage; and (8) public health services. It also identified five special functions: (1) law enforcement and internal security, (2) intelligence, (3) foreign affairs, (4) national defense, and (5) research and development. For each of the infrastructures and functions, the directive designated lead federal agencies, referred to as sector liaisons, to work with their counterparts in the private sector, referred to as sector coordinators. To facilitate private sector participation, PDD 63 also encouraged the voluntary creation of ISACs to serve as mechanisms for gathering, analyzing, and appropriately sanitizing and disseminating information to and from infrastructure sectors and the federal government through NIPC.

[85] Executive Order 13231 replaced this council with the National Infrastructure Advisory Council.

PDD 63 called for a range of activities that were intended to establish a partnership between the public and private sectors to ensure the security of our nation's critical infrastructures. Sector liaisons and sector coordinators were to work together to address problems related to CIP for each sector. In particular, PDD 63 stated that they were to (1) develop and implement vulnerability awareness and education programs, and (2) contribute to a sector National Infrastructure Assurance Plan by

- assessing the vulnerabilities of the sector to cyber or physical attacks;
- recommending a plan to eliminate significant vulnerabilities;
- proposing a system for identifying and preventing major attacks; and
- developing a plan for alerting, containing, and rebuffing an attack in progress and then, in coordination with the Federal Emergency Management Agency, as appropriate, rapidly reconstituting minimum essential capabilities in the aftermath of an attack.

PDD 63 also required every federal department and agency to be responsible for protecting its own critical infrastructures, including both cyber-based and physical assets. To fulfill this responsibility, PDD 63 called for agencies' chief information officers to be responsible for information assurance, and it required every agency to appoint a chief infrastructure assurance officer to be responsible for the protection of all other aspects of an agency's critical infrastructure. Further, it required federal agencies to

- develop, implement, and periodically update a plan for protecting its critical infrastructure;
- determine its minimum essential infrastructure that might be a target of attack;
- conduct and periodically update vulnerability assessments of its minimum essential infrastructure;
- develop a recommended remedial plan, based on vulnerability assessments, that identifies time lines for implementation, responsibilities, and funding; and
- analyze intergovernmental dependencies and mitigate those dependencies.

Other PDD 63 requirements for federal agencies included providing vulnerability awareness and education to sensitize people regarding the importance of security and training them in security standards, particularly regarding computer systems; establishing a system for responding to significant ongoing infrastructure attacks to help isolate and minimize damage; and establishing a system for rapidly reconstituting minimum required capabilities for varying levels of successful infrastructure attacks.

The Homeland Security Act of 2002 Created the Department of Homeland Security

The Homeland Security Act of 2002, signed by the President on November 25, 2002, established the Department of Homeland Security. The act assigned the department a number of CIP responsibilities, including: (1) developing a comprehensive national plan for securing the key resources and critical infrastructure of the United States; (2) recommending measures to protect the key resources and critical infrastructure of the United States in coordination with other federal agencies and in cooperation with state and local government agencies and authorities, the private sector, and other entities; and (3) disseminating, as appropriate, information analyzed by the department both within the department and to other federal agencies, state and local government agencies, and private sector entities to assist in the deterrence, prevention, preemption of, or response to terrorist attacks.

To help accomplish these functions, the act created the Information Analysis and Infrastructure Protection Directorate within the department and transferred to it the functions, personnel, assets, and liabilities of several existing organizations with CIP responsibilities, including NIPC (not including the Computer Investigations and Operations Section) and CIAO.

The National Strategy to Secure Cyberspace Provided an Initial Cyber CIP Framework

The National Strategy to Secure Cyberspace is intended to provide an initial framework for both organizing and prioritizing efforts to protect our nation's cyberspace. It also provided direction to federal departments and agencies that have roles in cyberspace security and identified steps that state and local governments, private companies and organizations, and individual Americans can take to improve our collective cybersecurity. The strategy lists the critical infrastructure sectors and the related lead federal agencies that are identified in the *National Strategy for Homeland Security*, which expanded the number of critical infrastructures from the 8 defined in PDD 63 to 13. In addition, the strategy identifies DHS as the central coordinator for cyberspace efforts. As such, DHS is responsible for coordinating and working with other federal entities that are involved in cybersecurity.

The National Strategy to Secure Cyberspace is organized according to five national priorities, with major actions and initiatives identified for each.

1. Security Response System—provides a public/private architecture for analyzing, warning, and managing incidents of national significance, promoting continuity in government systems and private sector infrastructures, and increasing information sharing.

2. Threat and Vulnerability Reduction Program—reduces threats and deters malicious actions through effective programs to identify and punish violators, identifies and remediates existing vulnerabilities, develops new systems with fewer vulnerabilities, and assesses emerging technologies for vulnerabilities.

3. Awareness Training—emphasizes the promotion of a comprehensive national awareness program to empower all Americans to secure their own parts of cyberspace.

4. Securing Government's Cyberspace—protects, improves, and maintains the federal government's cybersecurity.

5. National Security and International Cyberspace Security Cooperation—identifies major actions and initiatives to strengthen the U.S. national security and international cooperation.

Homeland Security Presidential Directive 7 Defined Federal CIP Responsibilities

In December 2003, the President issued HSPD-7, which established a national policy for federal departments and agencies to identify and prioritize critical infrastructure and key resources and to protect them from terrorist attack and superseded PDD-63. HSPD-7 defines responsibilities for DHS, lead federal agencies, or sector-specific agencies, that are responsible for addressing specific critical infrastructure sectors, and other departments and agencies. It instructs federal departments and agencies to identify, prioritize, and coordinate the protection of critical infrastructure to prevent, deter, and mitigate the effects of attacks. To accomplish these tasks, the federal government is to work with state and local governments and the private sector.

The Secretary of Homeland Security is assigned several responsibilities, including:

- coordinating the national effort to enhance critical infrastructure protection;
- identifying, prioritizing, and coordinating the protection of critical infrastructure, emphasizing protection against catastrophic health effects or mass casualties;
- establishing uniform policies, approaches, guidelines, and methodologies for integrating federal infrastructure protection and risk management activities within and across sectors; and
- serving as the focal point for security of cyberspace, including analysis, warning, information sharing, vulnerability reduction, mitigation, and recovery efforts for critical infrastructure information systems.

To ensure the coverage of critical sectors, HSPD-7 designated sector-specific agencies for the critical infrastructure sectors identified in the *National*

Strategy for Homeland Security (see table 18). These agencies are responsible for infrastructure protection activities in their assigned sectors and are to coordinate and collaborate with relevant federal agencies, state and local governments, and the private sector to accomplish these responsibilities. Specifically, sector-specific agencies are to conduct or facilitate vulnerability assessments of the sector and encourage risk management strategies to protect against and mitigate the effects of attacks against critical infrastructures. In addition, they are to identify, prioritize, and coordinate the protection of critical infrastructures and facilitate the sharing of information about physical and cyber threats, vulnerabilities, incidents, potential protective measures, and best practices. Sector-specific agencies are to report to DHS on an annual basis on their activities to meet these responsibilities. Further, the sector-specific agencies are to continue to encourage the development of information-sharing and analysis mechanisms and to support sector-coordinating mechanisms.

Table 18. Critical Infrastructure Sectors Identified by the National Strategy for Homeland Security and HSPD-7

Sector	Description	Sector-Specific Agencies
Agriculture	Provides for the fundamental need for food. The infrastructure includes supply chains for feed and crop production.	Department of Agriculture
Banking and finance	Provides the financial infrastructure of the nation. This sector consists of commercial banks, insurance companies, mutual funds, government-sponsored enterprises, pension funds, and other financial institutions that carry out transactions including clearing and settlement.	Department of the Treasury
Chemicals and hazardous materials	Transforms natural raw materials into commonly used products benefiting society's health, safety, and productivity. The chemical industry represents a $450 billion enterprise and produces more than 70,000 products that are essential to automobiles, pharmaceuticals, food supply, electronics, water treatment, health, construction and other necessities.	Department of Homeland Security
Defense industrial base	Supplies the military with the means to protect the nation by producing weapons, aircraft, and ships and providing essential services, including information technology and supply and maintenance.	Department of Defense
Emergency services	Saves lives and property from accidents and disaster. This sector includes fire, rescue, emergency medical services, and law enforcement organizations.	Department of Homeland Security

Sector	Description	Sector-Specific Agencies
Energy	Provides the electric power used by all sectors, including critical infrastructures, and the refining, storage, and distribution of oil and gas. The sector is divided into electricity and oil and natural gas.	Department of Energy
Food	Carries out the post-harvesting of the food supply, including processing and retail sales.	Department of Agriculture and Department of Health and Human Services
Government	Ensures national security and freedom and administers key public functions.	Department of Homeland Security
Information technology and telecommunications	Provides communications and processes to meet the needs of businesses and government.	Department of Homeland Security
Postal and shipping	Delivers private and commercial letters, packages, and bulk assets. The U.S. Postal Service and other carriers provide the services of this sector.	Department of Homeland Security
Public health and healthcare	Mitigates the risk of disasters and attacks and also provides recovery assistance if an attack occurs. The sector consists of health departments, clinics, and hospitals.	Department of Health and Human Services
Transportation	Enables movement of people and assets that are vital to our economy, mobility, and security with the use of aviation, ships, rail, pipelines, highways, trucks, buses, and mass transit.	Department of Homeland Security
Drinking water and water treatment systems	Sanitizes the water supply with the use of about 170,000 public water systems. These systems depend on reservoirs, dams, wells, treatment facilities, pumping stations, and transmission lines.	Environmental Protection Agency

Source: GAO analysis based on the President's National Strategy documents and HSPD-7.

By December 2004, the Secretary of Homeland Security also is to produce a comprehensive and integrated national plan for critical infrastructure and key resources protection that will outline national goals, objectives, milestones, and key initiatives. If appropriate, the plan is also to include:

- a strategy to identify, prioritize, and coordinate the protection of critical infrastructures, including an approach for how DHS will coordinate with other federal agencies, state and local governments, the private sector, foreign countries, and international organizations;

- a summary of activities to define and prioritize, reduce the vulnerability of, and coordinate the protection of critical infrastructures;
- a summary of initiatives for sharing critical infrastructure information and for providing threat warning data to state and local governments and the private sector; and
- coordination and integration with other federal emergency management and preparedness activities, such as the National Response Plan.

To support information-sharing efforts, HSPD-7 instructs the Secretary of Homeland Security to establish appropriate systems, mechanisms, and procedures to share homeland security information on threats and vulnerabilities in critical infrastructures with other federal agencies, state and local governments, and the private sector in a timely manner.

HSPD-7 establishes a CIP Policy Coordinating Committee, which will advise the Homeland Security Council on interagency policy related to physical and cyber infrastructure protection. The Office of Science and Technology Policy (OSTP) will coordinate interagency research and development to enhance CIP activities. In coordination with OSTP, DHS is to prepare an annual federal research and development plan to support critical infrastructure protection activities. To better understand the potential effects of attacks on the critical infrastructure, DHS is to develop models on the potential implications of attacks on critical infrastructures, focusing on densely populated areas. Further, DHS is to develop a national indications and warnings architecture for infrastructure protection that will facilitate (1) an understanding of baseline infrastructure operations; (2) the identification of indicators and precursors to an attack; and (3) surge capacity for detecting and analyzing potential attack patterns.

Consistent with PDD 63, HSPD-7 requires all federal departments and agencies to be responsible for protecting their own internal critical infrastructure. These agencies are to develop plans for the protection of their physical and cyber critical infrastructures and to provide them to the Office of Management and Budget for approval by July 2004. These plans are to address identification, prioritization, protection, and contingency planning, including the recovery and reconstitution of essential capabilities.

Appendix III: Cybersecurity Technologies

Overview of Network Systems

Computer systems are most visible in the information technology (IT) that organizations use in their data, voice, and video centers and that workers use on their desks and for remote access. Computers, in many different forms, are also embedded in many systems that run infrastructures in sectors ranging from electric power systems to medical, police, fire, and rescue systems. Infrastructures use interconnected computer systems extensively. These networks of computer systems consist of host computers that are connected by communication links, which can be wired or wireless. We use the term *host* to refer to a computer of any form—a mainframe, a server, or a desktop personal computer (PC), as well as other, less obvious computers, such as a router or a real-time process-control computer. Hosts store information and run software, typically an operating system and one or more application programs. The term *network* refers to the data communication links and the network elements such as routers, hubs, and switches that enable the hosts to communicate with each other. The network systems infrastructure can be viewed as an interconnected collection of hosts and networks, as illustrated in figure 8.

As figure 8 shows, computer systems are interconnected by networks, which, in turn, are often connected to the Internet—the worldwide collection of networks, operated by some 10,000 Internet Service Providers (ISP). Most organizations have one or more local area networks (LANs) at each of their offices. Larger organizations also have wide area networks (WANs) that connect the organization's various offices in different geographical locations.

Figure 8: An Example of Typical Networked Systems

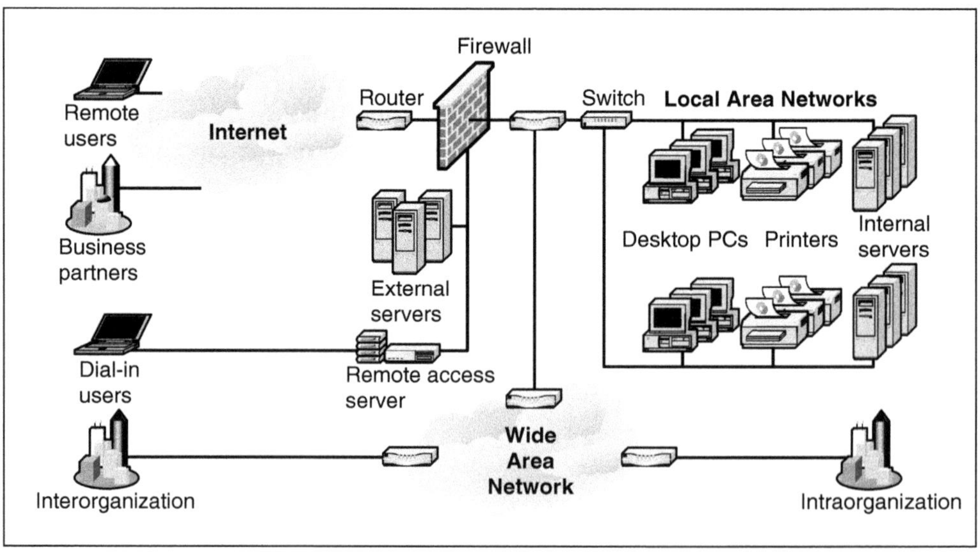

Source: GAO analysis and Microsoft Visio.

There Are Different Types of Hosts

The hosts in these network systems can be grouped into four main types according to their typical usage:

- **Mainframes** are large computers that are capable of supporting thousands of simultaneous users. Although historically they have been associated with centralized computing, today's mainframes can be used in networks to serve distributed users and smaller servers. Hitachi and IBM are examples of mainframe computer manufacturers.
- **Mid-range systems** are powerful computers that often are used in corporate settings as servers or single-user computers. Mid-range system manufacturers include Hewlett-Packard, IBM, and Sun Microsystems.
- **Personal computers** are small, relatively inexpensive computers that are designed for a single user. Although they vary in speed and performance, PCs use microprocessors and have self-contained data storage devices. PC manufacturers include Apple, Dell, Gateway, Hewlett-Packard, and IBM.
- **Embedded systems** are specialized computer systems that are part of a larger system or machine. Typically, an embedded system is housed on a single microprocessor board with the programs stored in read-only memory. Virtually all appliances that have a digital interface—for example, watches, microwaves, video cassette recorders (VCR), digital video disk (DVD) players, and cars—utilize embedded systems.

Whether it is a large mainframe computer or a desktop PC, each host has three basic components: (1) a central processing unit (CPU), which performs the instructions that are contained in a computer program; (2) random access memory (RAM), which stores computer programs and information while the CPU is processing them; and (3) permanent storage media, such as hard disk, read-only memory (ROM), or CD-ROM, which serves as the permanent storage space for computer programs and data. In addition to these basic components—CPU, memory, and permanent storage—a host typically has other devices attached to it. These devices can range from the network interface that connects the computer to the network to user input/output devices such as keyboards, monitors, and printers.

Hosts Run Operating Systems and Applications

Each host computer typically runs an *operating system*. The operating system is a special collection of computer programs that has two primary purposes. First, operating systems provide the interface between application programs and the CPU and other hardware components. Second, operating systems load and run other programs. All operating systems include one or more command processors that allow users to type commands and perform tasks like running a program or printing a file. Most operating systems also include a graphical user interface that enables the user to perform most tasks by clicking on-screen icons. Some examples of operating systems are Microsoft Windows, Unix, Linux, OS/390, z/OS, and Mac OS.

Some embedded systems include an operating system, but many are so specialized that the entire logic can be implemented as a single program. Embedded systems are widely used in many critical infrastructures.

Computer application programs make use of the capabilities that the operating system provides. For example, computer programs read and write files by using built-in capabilities of the operating system.

Operating systems include some built-in security features like user names, passwords, and permissions, to perform specific tasks, such as running certain applications or accessing specific information such as a file or a database.

Networks Use Protocols

Networks use a predefined set of rules known as protocols to communicate with each other. For example, the Transmission Control Protocol/Internet Protocol (TCP/IP) suite is the protocol of choice on the Internet. A *network protocol* refers to a detailed process the sender and receiver agree upon for exchanging data.

TCP/IP networking can best be explained and understood in terms of a model with four layers, where each layer is responsible for performing a particular task. The layered model describes the flow of data between the physical connection to the network and the end-user application. Figure 9 shows the four-layer network model for TCP/IP.

In this four-layer model, information always moves from one layer to the next. For example, when an application sends data to another application, the data go through the layers in this order: Application—>Transport—> Network—>Physical. At the receiving end, the data go up from Physical—> Network—>Transport—>Application.

Each layer has its own set of protocols for handling and formatting the data. The way in which data are sent on a network is similar to the way in which letters are sent through the postal service. For example, a typical protocol involved in sending a letter would be a preferred sequence of data for a task such as addressing an envelope (first the name; then the street address; and then city, state, and zip or other postal code). Similarly, a protocol in the network layer of TCP/IP might be to prepare a packet for transmission from one network to another. There would be some information in that packet identifying the network where the packet originated as well as

Figure 9: TCP/IP Four-layer Network Model

Application	**SMTP** (Simple Mail Transfer Protocol), **FTP** (File Transfer Protocol), **HTTP** (Hyper Text Transfer Protocol) (Web), **Telnet**, **DNS** (Domain Name System), and **RTP/RTCP** (Real-Time Transport Protocol/Real-Time Control Protocol) (audio and video streams)
Transport	**TCP** (Transmission Control Protocol), **UDP** (User Datagram Protocol)
Network	**IP** (Internet Protocol)
Physical	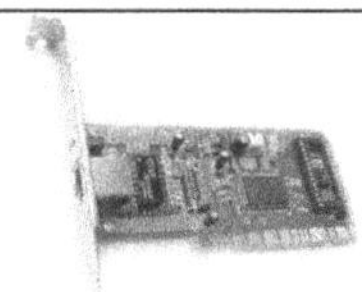

Source: GAO.

the destination network. Software that implements the TCP/IP protocols is typically included as part of the operating system.

Each of the four layers performs a specialized function:

- **Application layer**: Applications such as e-mail readers and Web browsers interface with the application layer to transmit data over TCP/IP networks. There are application-level protocols such as Simple Mail Transfer Protocol (SMTP) and Post Office Protocol (POP) for e-mail; Hyper Text Transfer Protocol (HTTP) for the Web; File Transfer Protocol (FTP) for file transfers; and Real-Time Transport Protocol/Real-Time Control Protocol (RTP/RTCP) for delivery of audio and video streams. Application-level protocols also have a port number that can be thought of as an identifier for a specific application. For example, port 80 is associated with HTTP or a Web server.
- **Transport layer**: This layer breaks large messages into data packets for transmission and reassembles them at the destination. The two most important protocols in this layer are Transmission Control Protocol (TCP) and User Datagram Protocol (UDP). TCP guarantees delivery of data; UDP just sends the data without ensuring that it actually reaches its destination.

- **Network layer**: This layer is responsible for getting data packets from one network to another. If the networks are far apart, the data packets are routed from one network to the next until they reach their destination. The primary protocol in this layer is the Internet Protocol (IP).
- **Physical layer**: This layer consists of the physical networking hardware (such as an Ethernet card or Token Ring card) that carries the data packets in a network.

The benefit of the layered model is that each layer takes care of only its specific task, leaving the rest to the other layers. The layers can mix and match—TCP/IP networks can work over any type of physical network medium, from Ethernet to radio waves (in a wireless network). In addition, each layer can be implemented in different modules. For example, typically the transport and network layers already exist as part of the operating system, and any application can make use of these layers.

TCP/IP Networks Use IP Addresses to Identify Networks and Hosts

TCP/IP networks such as the Internet comprise many networks as well as many hosts on each network. Each host in a TCP/IP network is identified by its IP address. Because TCP/IP deals with internetworking—interconnecting many networks—the IP address is a network address that identifies the network on which the host is located and a host address that identifies the specific computer on that network. The IP address is a 4-byte (32-bit) value. The convention is to write each byte as a decimal value and to put a dot (.) after each number. For example, a typical IP address might be 192.168.0.1. This way of writing IP addresses is known as dotted-decimal or dotted-quad notation. In decimal notation, a byte (which is made up of 8 bits) can have a value between 0 and 255. Thus a valid IP addresses can use only the numbers between 0 and 255 in the dotted-decimal notation. The numbers 0 and 255 in the network or host address part of the IP address have special meanings.

Internet Services Use Well-Known Port Numbers

The TCP/IP protocol suite has become the de facto communications standard of the Internet because many standard services are available on all systems that support TCP/IP. These services make the Internet useful by enabling the transfer of mail, news, and Web pages. A well-known port is associated with each of these services. A transport layer protocol, such as TCP, uses this port to locate a service on any system. A server process—a computer program running on a system—implements each service. These services include

- **DHCP (Dynamic Host Configuration Protocol)** is used to dynamically configure TCP/IP network parameters on a computer. DHCP is primarily used to assign dynamic IP addresses and other networking information such as name server, default gateway, and domain names that are needed to configure TCP/IP networks. The DHCP server listens on port 67.

- **FTP (File Transfer Protocol)** enables the transfer of files between computers over the Internet. FTP uses two ports—data is transferred on port 20, while control information is exchanged on port 21.
- **HTTP (Hypertext Transfer Protocol)** is a recent protocol for sending Hypertext Markup Language (HTML) documents from one system to another. HTTP is the underlying protocol of the Web. By default, the Web server and client communicate on port 80.
- **NFS (Network File System)** is for sharing files among computers. NFS uses Sun's Remote Procedure Call (RPC) facility, which exchanges information through port 111.
- **NNTP (Network News Transfer Protocol)** is for distribution of news articles in a store-and-forward fashion across the Internet. NNTP uses port 119.
- **SMTP (Simple Mail Transfer Protocol)** is for exchanging e-mail messages between systems. SMTP uses port 25 for information exchange.
- **Telnet** enables a user on one system to log into a remote system on the Internet (the user must provide a valid user ID and password to log into the remote system). Telnet uses port 23 by default.
- **SNMP (Simple Network Management Protocol)** is used to manage all types of network devices on the Internet. Like FTP, SNMP uses two ports: 161 and 162.

Current Cybersecurity Technologies

There are several technologies that can be used by critical infrastructure owners to enhance their cybersecurity postures.[86] While several classifications of cybersecurity technologies are available, we present a taxonomy based on controls. Security controls are the management, operational, and technical safeguards that are used to protect a system and its information. Table 19 lists the five control categories and control types that support these categories. Several different technologies are available that provide functionality in support of these control categories and types. Some technologies can support more than one control type. Some of these technologies

[86] GAO has previously reported on cybersecurity technologies available to help secure federal computer systems. See U.S. General Accounting Office, *Information Security: Technologies to Secure Federal Systems*, GAO-04-467 (Washington, D.C.: March 9, 2004).

Table 19. Cybersecurity Technology Control Categories and Types

Control Category	Control Type
Access controls • Boundary protection • Authentication • Authorization	 • Firewalls • Content management • Biometrics • Smart tokens • User rights and privileges
System integrity	• Antivirus software • File integrity checkers
Cryptography	• Digital signatures and certificates • Virtual private networks
Audit and monitoring	• Intrusion detection systems • Intrusion prevention systems • Security event correlation tools • Computer forensics tools
Configuration management and assurance	• Policy enforcement applications • Network management • Continuity of operations • Scanners • Patch management

Source: GAO analysis.

are implemented on hosts and network elements as "add-on" functionality. Other cybersecurity technologies are sold as integrated hardware and software platforms.

Access Controls

Access control technologies ensure that only authorized users or systems can access and use computers, networks, and the information stored on these systems and help to protect sensitive data and systems. Access control simplifies network security by reducing the number of paths that attackers might use to penetrate system or network defenses. Access control includes three different control types: boundary protection, authentication, and authorization.

Boundary protection technologies demark a logical or physical boundary between protected information and systems and unknown users. Boundary protection technologies can be used to protect a network (for example, firewalls) or a single computer (for example, personal firewalls). Generally, these technologies prevent access to the network or computer by external unauthorized users. Another type of boundary protection technology, content management, can also be used to restrict the ability of authorized system or network users to access systems or networks beyond the system or network boundary.

Authentication technologies associate a user with a particular identity. People are authenticated by three basic means: by something they know, something they have, or something they are. People and systems regularly use these means to identify people in everyday life. For example, members of a community routinely recognize one another by how they look or how their voices sound—by something they are. Automated teller machines recognize customers because they present a bank card—something they have—and they enter a personal identification number (PIN)—something they know. Using a key to enter a locked building is another example of using something you have. More secure systems may combine two of more of these approaches.

While the use of passwords is an example of authentication based on something users know, there are several technologies based on something users have. Security tokens can be used to authenticate a user. User information can be coded onto a token using magnetic media (for example, bank cards) or optical media (for example, compact disk-like media). Several smart token technologies containing an integrated circuit chip that can store and process data are also available. Biometric technologies automate the identification of people using one or more of their distinct physical or behavioral characteristics—authentication based on something that users are. The use of security tokens or biometrics requires the installation of the appropriate readers at network and computer access points.

Once a user is authenticated, authorization technologies are used to allow or prevent actions by that user according to predefined rules. Users could be granted access to data on the system or to perform certain actions on the system. Authorization technologies support the principles of legitimate use, least privilege, and separation of duties. Access control could be based on user identity, role, group membership, or other information known to the system.

Most operating systems and some applications provide some authentication and authorization functionality. For example, user identification (ID) codes and passwords are the most commonly used authentication technology. System administrators can assign users rights and privileges to applications and data files based on user IDs. Some operating systems allow for the grouping of users to simplify the administration of groups of users who require the same levels of access to files and applications.

Boundary Protection: Firewalls

What the technology does

Firewalls are network devices or systems running special software that control the flow of network traffic between networks or between a host and a network. A firewall is set up as the single point through which communications must pass. This enables the firewall to act as a protective barrier between the protected network and any external networks. Any information leaving the internal network can be forced to pass through a firewall as it leaves the network or host. Incoming data can enter only through the firewall.

Firewalls are typically deployed where a corporate network connects to the Internet. However, firewalls can also be used internally, to guard areas of an organization against unauthorized internal access. For example, many corporate networks use firewalls to restrict access to internal networks that perform sensitive functions, such as accounting or personnel.

Personal computer users can also use firewalls, called personal firewalls, to protect their computers from unauthorized access over a network. Such personal firewalls are relatively inexpensive software programs that can be installed on personal computers to filter all network traffic and allow only authorized communications. Essentially, a firewall can be likened to a protective fence that keeps unwanted external data out and sensitive internal data in (see figure 10).

How the technology works

Typically, a firewall is a network device or host with two or more network interfaces—one connected to the protected internal network and the other connected to unprotected networks, such as the Internet. The firewall runs

Figure 10: A Typical Firewall Protecting Hosts on a Private Network from the Public Network

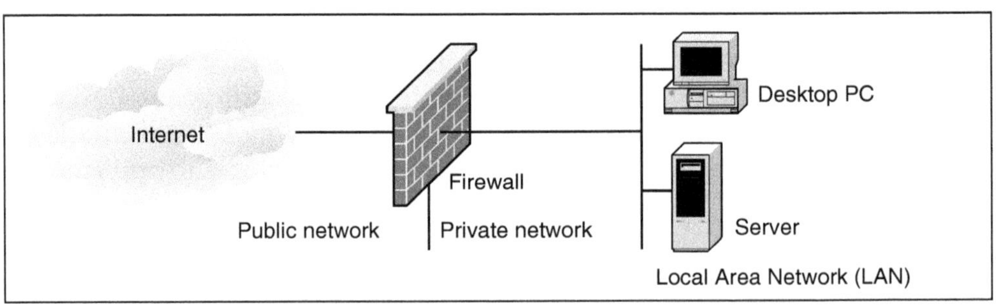

Source: GAO analysis and Microsoft Visio.

software that examines the network packets arriving at its network interfaces and takes appropriate action based on a set of rules. The idea is to define these rules so that they allow only authorized network traffic to flow between the two interfaces. Configuring the firewall involves setting up the rules properly. A configuration strategy is to reject all network traffic and then enable only a limited set of network packets to go through the firewall. The authorized network traffic would include the connections necessary to perform functions such as visiting Web sites and receiving electronic mail.

NIST describes eight kinds of firewall platforms: packet filter firewalls, stateful inspection firewalls, application proxy gateway firewalls, dedicated proxy firewalls, hybrid firewall technologies, network address translation, host-based firewalls, and personal firewalls/personal firewall appliances.[87]

Packet filter firewalls are routing devices that include access control functionality for system addresses and communication sessions. The access control functionality of a packet filter firewall is governed by a set of rules that allows or blocks network packets based on a number of their characteristics, including the source and destination addresses, the network protocol, and the source and destination port numbers. Packet filter firewalls are usually placed at the outermost boundary with an untrusted network, and they form the first line of defense. An example of a packet-filter firewall is a network router that employs filter rules to screen network traffic.

Stateful inspection firewalls keep track of network connections that are used by network applications to reliably transfer data. When an application uses a network connection to create a session with a remote host system, a port is also opened on the originating system. This port receives network traffic from the destination system. For successful connections, packet filter firewalls must permit inbound packets from the destination system. Opening up many ports to incoming traffic creates a risk of intrusion by unauthorized users, who may employ a variety of techniques to abuse the expected conventions of network protocols such as TCP. Stateful inspection firewalls solve this problem by creating a directory of outbound network connections, along with each session's corresponding client port. This "state table" is then used to validate any inbound traffic. The stateful inspection solution is more secure than a packet filter because it tracks client ports individually rather than opening all inbound ports for external access.

[87] National Institute of Standards and Technology, *Guidelines for Firewalls and Firewall Policy*, NIST Special Publication 800-41, (Gaithersburg, MD: Jan. 2002).

Application proxy gateway firewalls provide additional protection by inserting the firewall as an intermediary between internal applications that attempt to communicate with external servers such as a Web server. For example, a Web proxy receives requests for external Web pages from inside the firewall and relays them to the exterior Web server as though the firewall was the requesting Web client. The external Web server responds to the firewall and the firewall forwards the response to the inside client as though the firewall was the Web server. No direct network connection is ever made from the inside client host to the external Web server.

Dedicated proxy servers are typically deployed behind traditional firewall platforms. In typical use, a main firewall might accept inbound network traffic, determine which application is being targeted, and then hand off the traffic to the appropriate proxy server (for example, an e-mail proxy server). The proxy server typically would perform filtering or logging operations on the traffic and then forward it to internal systems. A proxy server could also accept outbound traffic directly from internal systems, filter or log the traffic, and then pass it to the firewall for outbound delivery. Many organizations enable the caching of frequently used Web pages on the proxy server, thereby reducing firewall traffic. In addition to authentication and logging functionality, dedicated proxy servers are useful for Web and electronic mail content scanning.

Hybrid firewall technologies are firewall products that incorporate functionality from several different types of firewall platforms. For example, many vendors of packet filter firewalls or stateful inspection packet filter firewalls have implemented basic application-proxy functionality to offset some of the weaknesses associated with their firewall platform. In most cases, these vendors implement application proxies to provide improved logging of network traffic and stronger user authentication. Nearly all major firewall vendors have introduced multiple firewall functions into their products in some manner; therefore it is not always a simple matter to decide which specific firewall product is the most suitable for a given application or enterprise infrastructure. Selection of a hybrid firewall product should be based on the supported feature sets that an enterprise needs.

Network address translation (NAT) technology is an effective tool for "hiding" the network addresses of an internal network behind a firewall environment. In essence, NAT allows an organization to deploy a network addressing plan of its choosing behind a firewall while still maintaining the ability to connect to external systems through the firewall. Network address translation is accomplished by one of three methods: static, hiding, and port. In static NAT, each internal system on the private network has a corresponding external, routable IP address associated with it. This particular technique is seldom used because unique IP addresses are in short supply. With hiding NAT, all systems behind a firewall share the same external, routable IP address, while the internal systems use private IP addresses. Thus, with a hiding NAT system, a number of systems behind a firewall will still appear to be a single system. With port address translation, it is possible to place hosts behind a firewall system and still make them selectively accessible to external users.

Host-based firewalls are firewall software components that are available in some operating systems or as add-ons. Because a network-based firewall cannot fully protect internal servers, host-based firewalls can be used to secure individual hosts.

Personal firewalls and personal firewall appliances are used to secure PCs at home or remote locations. These firewalls are important because many personnel telecommute or work at home and access sensitive data. Home users dialing an ISP may potentially have limited firewall protection available to them because the ISP has to accommodate many different security policies. Therefore, personal firewalls have been developed to provide protection for remote systems and to perform many of the same functions as larger firewalls. These products are typically implemented in one of two configurations. The first configuration is a personal firewall, which is installed on the system it is meant to protect; personal firewalls usually do not offer protection to other systems or resources. Likewise, personal firewalls do not typically provide controls over network traffic that is traversing a computer network—they protect only the computer system on which they are installed. The second configuration is a personal firewall appliance. In most cases, personal firewall appliances are designed to protect small networks such as networks that might be found in home offices. These appliances usually run on specialized hardware and integrate some other form of network infrastructure components in addition to the firewall itself, including the following: cable or digital subscriber line broadband modem with network routing, network hub, network switch, DHCP server, SNMP agent, and application-proxy agents. In terms of deployment strategies, personal firewalls and personal firewall appliances normally address connectivity concerns associated with telecommuters or branch offices. However, some organizations employ these devices on their organizational intranets, practicing a layered defense strategy.

Centrally managed distributed firewalls are centrally controlled but locally enforced. A security administrator—not the end users—defines and maintains security policies. This places the responsibility and capability of defining security policies in the hands of a security professional who can properly lock down the target systems. A centrally managed system is scalable because it is unnecessary to administer each system separately. A properly executed distributed firewall system includes exception logging. More advanced systems include the capability to enforce the appropriate policy, which is enforced depending on the location of the firewall. Centrally managed distributed firewalls can be either software- or hardware-based firewalls. Centrally managed distributed software firewalls are similar in function and features to host-based or personal firewalls, but the security policies are centrally defined and managed. Centrally managed distributed hardware firewalls combine the filtering capability of a firewall with the connectivity capability of a traditional connection.

Effectiveness of the technology

When properly configured, all firewalls can protect a network or a PC from unauthorized access through the network. Although firewalls afford protection of certain resources within an organization, there are some threats that firewalls cannot protect against: connections that bypass the firewall, new threats that have not yet been identified, and viruses that have been injected into the internal network. It is important to consider these shortcomings in addition to the firewall itself in order to counter these additional threats and provide a comprehensive security solution. Each type of firewall platform has its own strengths and weaknesses.

Packet filter firewalls have two main strengths: speed and flexibility. Packet filter firewalls can be used to secure nearly any type of network communication or protocol. This versatility allows packet filter firewalls to be deployed into nearly any enterprise network infrastructure. Packet filter firewalls have several weaknesses: They cannot prevent attacks that exploit application-specific vulnerabilities or functions; they can log only a minimal amount of information, such as source address, destination address, and traffic type; they do not support user authentication; and they are vulnerable to attacks and exploits that take advantage of flaws within the TCP/IP protocol, such as IP address spoofing.[88]

Stateful inspection firewalls share the strengths and weaknesses of packet filter firewalls, but because of the state table implementation, they are generally considered to be more secure than packet filter firewalls. Stateful inspection firewalls can accommodate other network protocols in the same manner as packet filters do, but stateful inspection technology is relevant only to the TCP/IP protocol.

Application-proxy gateway firewalls have numerous advantages over packet filter firewalls and stateful inspection firewalls. First, application-proxy gateway firewalls are able to examine the entire network packet rather than only the network addresses and ports. This enables these firewalls to provide more extensive logging capabilities than packet filters or

[88] IP address spoofing involves altering the address information in network packets in order to make packets appear to come from a trusted IP address.

stateful inspection firewalls. Another advantage is that application-proxy gateway firewalls can authenticate users directly, while packet filter firewalls and stateful inspection firewalls normally authenticate users based on the network address of the system (i.e., source, destination, and type). Given that network addresses can be easily spoofed, the authentication capabilities inherent in application-proxy gateway architecture are superior to those found in packet filter or stateful inspection firewalls. The advanced functionality of application-proxy gateway firewalls also results in several disadvantages when compared with packet filter or stateful inspection firewalls. First, because of the "full packet awareness" found in application-proxy gateways, the firewall is forced to spend significant time reading and interpreting each packet. Therefore, application proxy gateway firewalls are generally not well suited to high-bandwidth or real-time applications. To reduce the load on the firewall, a dedicated proxy server can be used to secure less time-sensitive services, such as e-mail and most Web traffic. Another disadvantage is that application proxy gateway firewalls are often limited in terms of support for new network applications and protocols. An individual, application-specific proxy agent is required for each type of network traffic that needs to go through the firewall. Most vendors of application-proxy gateways provide generic proxy agents to support undefined network protocols or applications. However, those generic agents tend to negate many of the strengths of the application-proxy gateway architecture, and they simply allow traffic to "tunnel" through the firewall.

Dedicated proxy servers allow an organization to enforce user authentication requirements and other filtering and logging of any traffic that goes through the proxy server. This means that an organization can restrict outbound traffic to certain locations, examine all outbound e-mail for viruses, or restrict internal users from writing to the organization's Web server. Because most security problems originate from within an organization, proxy servers can assist in foiling internally based attacks or malicious behavior.

In terms of strengths and weaknesses, each type of NAT—static, hiding, or port—is applicable in certain situations; the variable is the amount of design flexibility offered by each type. Static NAT offers the most flexibility, but it is not always practical because of the shortage of IP addresses. Hiding NAT technology is seldom used because port address translation offers additional features. Port address translation is often the most convenient and secure solution.

Host-based firewall packages typically provide access-control capability for restricting traffic to and from servers that run on the host, and logging is usually available. A disadvantage of host-based firewalls is that they must be administered separately, and maintaining security becomes more difficult as the number of configured devices increases.

Centrally managed distributed software firewalls have the benefit of unified corporate oversight of firewall implementation on individual machines. However, they remain vulnerable to attacks on the host operating system from the networks, as well as to intentional or unintentional tampering by users logging in to the system that is being protected. Centrally managed distributed hardware firewalls filter the data on the firewall hardware rather than the host system. This can make the distributed hardware firewall system less vulnerable than software-based distributed firewalls. Hardware distributed firewalls can be designed to be unaffected by local or network attacks via the host operating systems. Performance and throughput of a hardware firewall system are generally better than they are for software systems.

Boundary Protection: Content Management

What the technology does

Content filters monitor Web and messaging applications for inappropriate content, spam, intellectual property breach, non-compliance with an organization's security policies, and banned file types.[89] The filters can help to keep illegal material out of an organization's systems, reduce network traffic from spam, and stop various forms of cyber attacks. They can also keep track of which users are browsing the Web, when, where, and for how long.

There are three main types of content filters: (1) Web filters, which screen and exclude from access or availability Web pages that are deemed objectionable or non-business related; (2) messaging filters, which screen messaging applications such as e-mail, instant messaging, short message service, and peer-to-peer service for spam or other objectionable content;[90] and (3) Web integrity filters, which ensure the integrity of an entity's Web pages.

How the technology works

Web filters screen and block objectionable Web pages by (1) intercepting a user's request to view a Web page, (2) determining that the requested page contains objectionable content, and (3) prohibiting the user from accessing that Web page (see figure 11). Web filters can observe and respond to

[89] Spam is electronic junk mail that is unsolicited and usually is advertising for some product. An intellectual property breach can include client information, trade secrets, ongoing research, and other such information that has been released without authorization.

[90] Short message service is the transmission of short text messages to and from a mobile phone, fax machine or IP address. Messages must be no longer than 160 alphanumeric characters and contain no images or graphics. On the Internet, peer-to-peer (referred to as P2P) networks allow computer users to share files from one another's hard drives. Napster, Gnutella, and Kazaa are examples of this kind of peer-to-peer software.

Figure 11: How a Web Filter Works

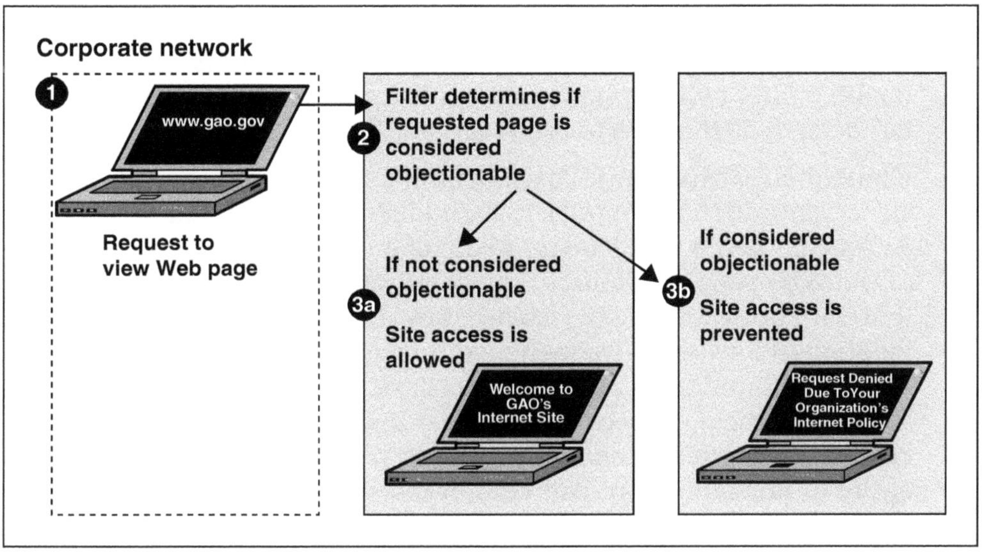

Source: GAO analysis and Microsoft Visio.

requests in two main ways. One method, pass-through technology, requires the Web filtration software to be integrated with other network devices such as proxies or gateways. This ensures that all requests pass through the Web filter to be accepted or denied. Another method of handling requests, known as pass-by technology, requires the Web filtration software to be installed on a stand-alone server and placed on the network of machines that it is to filter. The Web filter then receives all of the traffic that exists on the network, but it does not prevent the network traffic from reaching its intended destination. If a request is made for a restricted Web page, the Web filter will display an error message stating that the user's access to the Web page was denied. The user's connection with the Web site is then closed to prevent the Web server from sending additional information to the user's computer. Web filters also vary in their methods of determining if a requested Web page contains objectionable material:

- **Site classification** technology compares the requested Web site against a database of Web pages that are considered objectionable. Typically, vendors provide a basic database of objectionable Web pages as part of the Web filter software, which may then be modified by an administrator. Vendors often provide subscription services so customers' databases can be automatically updated with new sites that were found to be objectionable. The database consists primarily of a list of Web site addresses, typically categorized into groups such as gambling, adult material, and sports. An administrator can then decide which sites should be blocked, based on the category they fall into. If the requested Web site is on the list of objectionable Web sites, the Web filter will display a message informing the user that he or she has been denied access to the Web page.

- **Content classification** uses artificial intelligence in conjunction with site classification techniques to maintain an updated database. Before a user can view a Web site, the Web filter examines the textual content of the Web page, the source code, and metatags.[91] Questionable content is identified by the presence of key words or phrases or by a combination of key word frequency and level of obscenity of the words. Web sites found to be objectionable, based on the content, can then be added into the database of objectionable sites, and the user would not be allowed to view them. Web sites do not have to be blocked for an entire organization, but can be blocked based on IP address ranges, host names, or other criteria.

Messaging filters operate similarly to Web filters, and can examine the content of a message to filter out spam, offensive language, or recreational e-mails that lower the productivity of workers. Messaging filters also block messages based on the types of file attachments and the senders of e-mails, as determined by an organization's policy. Files are excluded based on their file extensions, or the last part of their name, which indicates the file type. The file might be excluded to limit the trafficking of illicit material, stop viruses from entering the network, limit intellectual property breaches, or carry out other such functions intended to increase the security of an organization. File extensions that are typically excluded are MP3 (music files), JPG (graphic files), MPEG (video files), and EXE (typically used for executable files), among others.

A Web integrity filter ensures the integrity of the content of a Web page. If a Web server is attacked or becomes inaccessible to users, the Web integrity filter attempts to keep unauthorized information from being released to the public, and only the original content would still go out. The content filter is a separate device on the network, located between the Web server and the router or firewall. The device contains a collection of digital signatures of authorized Web content that is known to be legitimate. When a request is made to the Web server, each object's[92] digital signature is compared with the digital signature that the device had previously collected. If the digital signatures do not match, the page is considered to be unauthorized

[91] The source code is the text of a program while it is still in its programming language. The Hypertext Markup Language (HTML) metatag is used to describe the contents of a Web page.

[92] An object can be an HTML page, a graphic file, a music file, and so forth.

and it is immediately replaced with a secure archived copy of the original pages, and the software notifies the appropriate personnel via phone, e-mail or pager.

Effectiveness of the technology

Content filters have significant rates of both erroneously accepting objectionable sites and of blocking sites that are not objectionable. If implemented correctly, filtering can reduce the volume of unsolicited and undesired e-mails. However, it is not completely accurate, and legitimate messages might get blocked. Also, some content filters do not work with all operating systems.

While pass-through technology can be effective at stopping specified traffic, there are several disadvantages to using it. First, because the requests for Web sites are actually stopped at the gateway while the filtering product analyzes the request against its rules, a certain amount of latency can result, especially during periods of high traffic volume.[93] Second, pass-through products might be considered a single point of failure: If the product fails, so might Internet connectivity. Third, because pass-through devices are dependent on another network device, if an entity changes firewalls or proxy servers, it might have to purchase a new content filter product as well. Pass-by technology can also be effective at stopping specified traffic. Because traffic does not have to be screened before it goes through, the pass-by technology does not cause latency. Also, because pass-by products do not require integration with other network devices, a change in a firewall or proxy would not result in a need to change the content filtering product. However, a disadvantage of the pass-by solution is that a separate server must be dedicated to performing the monitoring and filtering functions.

Site classification is effective at keeping users from accessing sites that have been determined to have objectionable content. However, because of the size and growth of the Internet, this technology faces difficulties in keeping a full and accurate list of objectionable sites, and the cost of subscriptions for updates can be very expensive. Content classification can assist in classifying new sites without the cost of subscribing to an update service, but this method has its drawbacks as well. First, Web sites that are predominantly graphical in nature may not contain enough key words for the program to categorize the site. Second, there are some topics that are so ambiguous that it is very difficult to classify them by their content. Third, users may circumvent the filtered lists by using proxy sites.

[93] Latency is the amount of time it takes a packet to travel from source to destination. Together, latency and bandwidth define the speed and capacity of a network.

Authentication: Biometrics

What the technology does

The term *biometrics* covers a wide range of technologies that are used to verify identity by measuring and analyzing human characteristics. Biometric technologies are authentication techniques that rely on measuring and analyzing physiological or behavioral characteristics. Identifying an individual's physiological characteristic involves measuring a part of the body, such as fingertips or eye irises; identifying behavioral characteristics involves data derived from actions, such as speech.

Biometrics are theoretically very effective personal identifiers because the characteristics they measure are thought to be distinct to each person. Unlike conventional identification methods that use something you have (for example, a smart card), or something you know (for example, a password), these characteristics are integral to something you are. Because they are tightly bound to an individual, they are more reliable, cannot be forgotten, and are less easily lost, stolen, or guessed.

How the technology works

Although biometric technologies vary in complexity, capabilities, and performance, they all share several elements. Biometric identification systems are essentially pattern recognition systems. They use acquisition devices such as cameras and scanning devices to capture images, recordings, or measurements of an individual's characteristics, and they use computer hardware and software to extract, encode, store, and compare these characteristics. Because the process is automated, biometric decision making is generally very fast, in most cases taking only a few seconds in real time. The different types of biometric technologies measure different characteristics. However, they all involve a similar process, which can be divided into two distinct stages: (1) enrollment and (2) verification or identification.

Enrollment stage. Acquisition devices such as cameras and scanners are used to capture images, recordings, or measurements of an individual's characteristics, and computer hardware and software are used to extract, encode, store, and compare these characteristics. In the enrollment stage, the captured samples are averaged and processed to generate a unique digital representation of the characteristic, called a reference template, which is stored for future comparisons. It is impossible to recreate the sample, such as a fingerprint, from the template. Templates can be stored centrally on a computer database, within the device itself, or on a smart card.

Verification or identification stage. Depending on the application, biometric technologies can be used in one of two modes: verification or identification. Verification is used to verify a person's identity, answering the question

"Is this person who she claims to be?" Identification is used to establish a person's identity, comparing the individual's biometric with all stored biometric records to answer the question "Who is this person?"

Current biometric technologies that are used to protect computer systems from unauthorized access include fingerprint recognition, iris recognition, and speaker recognition. These technologies are used by some entities to replace passwords as a way to authenticate individuals who are attempting to access computers and networks.

Fingerprint recognition technology extracts features from impressions that are made by the distinctive ridges on the fingertips. An image of the fingerprint is captured by a scanner, enhanced, and converted into a template. Various styles of fingerprint scanners are commercially available. The scanner can be built into the computer or into the mouse or the keyboard that are attached to the computer, or it can be a hardware device that is used only for capturing fingerprints (see figures 12 and 13).

Iris recognition technology is based on the distinctly colored ring surrounding the pupil of the eye. Made from elastic connective tissue, the iris is a very rich source of biometric data, having approximately 266 distinct characteristics. Iris recognition systems use a small, high-quality camera to capture a black-and-white, high-resolution image of the iris. The boundaries of the iris are defined and a coordinate system is established over the iris before visible characteristics are converted into a template (see figure 14).

Speaker recognition technology uses the distinctive characteristics in the sound of people's voices as a biometric identifier. These differences result from a combination of physiological differences in the shape of vocal tracts and learned speaking habits. Speaker recognition systems capture samples of a person's speech by having him or her speak into a microphone or telephone a number of times. Some systems require that a predefined phrase, such as a name or a sequence of numbers, be used for enrollment. This phrase is converted from analog to digital format, and the distinctive vocal characteristics, such as pitch, cadence, and tone, are extracted to create a template.

Figure 12: An Example of Fingerprint Recognition Technology Built into a Keyboard

Source: Key Tronic Corporation.

Figure 13: An Example of Fingerprint Recognition Technology Built into a Mouse

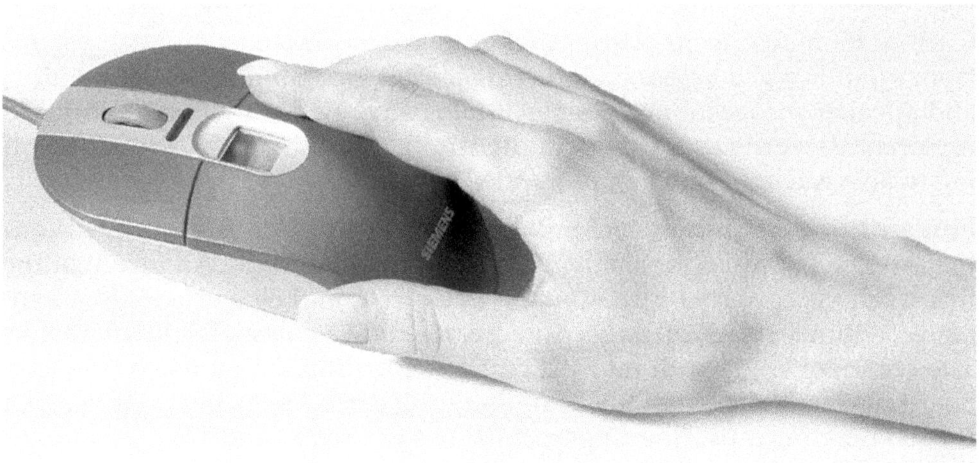

Source: Siemens PSE TechLab.

Figure 14: A Desktop Iris Recognition System

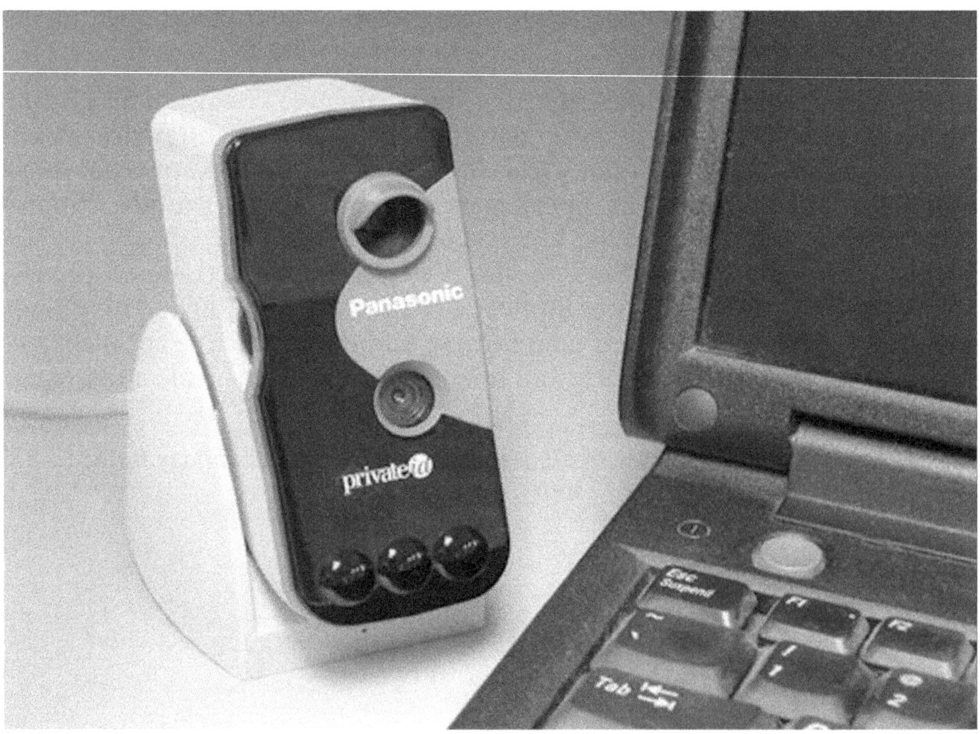

Source: Matsushita Electronic Corporation of America.

Effectiveness of the technology

The quality of templates is critical in the overall success of a biometric system. Minute changes in positioning, distance, pressure, environment, and other factors influence the generation of a template. For example, in a speaker recognition system, performance can be affected by background noise, the use of different capture devices for enrollment and verification, speaking softly, and poor placement of the capture device. In addition, because biometric features can change over time, people may have to re-enroll to update their reference templates.

Furthermore, not all people can use biometric technologies. For example, the capturing of fingerprints for about 2 to 5 percent of people is not possible because the fingerprints are dirty or have become dry or worn from age, extensive manual labor, or exposure to corrosive chemicals. People who are mute cannot use speaker recognition systems, and people lacking fingers or eyes from congenital disease, surgery, or injury cannot use fingerprint or iris recognition systems.

The effectiveness of biometric technologies is affected by the quality of the capture device. For example, some fingerprint recognition scanners can be prone to error if there is a buildup of dirt, grime, or oil—producing leftover fingerprints from previous users, which are known as latent prints. Severe latent prints can cause the superimposition of two sets of prints and degrade the capturing of the image. Similarly, the performance of speaker recognition systems improves with higher-quality input devices.

Tests have shown that certain capture devices can be tricked into accepting forgeries. Fingerprint scanners have been tricked into accepting latent prints that were reactivated by simply breathing on the sensor or by placing a water-filled plastic bag on the sensor's surface. It is possible to reconstruct and authenticate latent fingerprints by dusting the sensor's surface with commercially available graphite powder and lifting the fingerprint with adhesive tape. A vulnerability of speaker authentication is that the voice can be easily recorded and therefore duplicated. However, some speaker verification systems provide safeguards against the use of a recorded voice to trick the system. For these systems, the electronic properties of a recording device, particularly the playback speaker, will change the acoustics to such a degree that the recorded voice sample will not match a stored voiceprint of a live voice.

Authentication: Smart Tokens

What the technology does

A smart token is an easily portable device that contains an embedded integrated circuit chip that is capable of both storing and processing data. Most smart tokens are used instead of static user IDs and passwords to provide a stronger and more convenient means for users to identify and authenticate themselves to computers and networks. When it is used for this function, a smart token is an example of authentication based on something a user possesses (for example, the token itself). Although authentication to some computer systems is based solely on the possession of a token, typical smart token implementations also require a user to provide something he or she knows (for example, a password) in order to successfully utilize the smart token.

How the technology works

In general, smart tokens can be classified according to physical characteristics, interfaces, and protocols used. These classifications are not mutually exclusive.

1. **Physical characteristics**. Smart tokens can be divided into two physical groups: smart cards and other tokens. A smart card looks like a credit card but includes an embedded microprocessor. Smart tokens that are not smart cards can look like calculators, keys, or other small objects.

2. **Interfaces**. Smart tokens have either a human or an electronic interface. Smart tokens that look like calculators usually have a human interface, which allows humans to communicate with the device. Other smart tokens, including smart cards, have an electronic interface that can only be understood by special readers and writers. Two physical interfaces for smart cards have been standardized through the International Organization for Standardization, resulting in two types of smart cards. The first type, known as contact cards, works by inserting the card in a smart card reader, while the second type, known as contactless cards, uses radio frequency signals and the card needs only to be passed within close proximity to a card terminal to transmit information. Smart cards can be configured to include both contact and contactless capabilities, but because standards for the two technologies are very different, two separate interfaces would be needed.

3. **Protocols**. Smart tokens use three main methods for authentication, based on different protocols. The first method, static password exchange, requires users to first authenticate themselves to a token before the token can then authenticate the user to the computer. The other two methods are known as time-synchronized and challenge-response, and are based on cryptography. These methods generate a one-time password, which is a password or pass code that can be used only once, for a brief interval, and then is no longer valid. If it is intercepted in any way, the password has such a limited life span that it quickly becomes invalid. The next time the same user attempts to access a system, he or she must enter a new one-time password that is generated by the security token.

Time-synchronized tokens generate a unique value that changes at regular intervals (for example, once a minute). A central server keeps track of the token-generated passwords in order to compare the input against the expected value. To log onto a system, users enter a one-time password that consists of their personal PIN followed by the unique value generated by their token. The PIN helps the central server to identify the user and the password value that should be entered. If the number entered by the user and the one generated by the server are the same, the user will be granted access to the system. Figure 15 shows an example of a time-synchronized token.

Challenge-response tokens utilize a central server to generate a challenge (such as a random string of numbers), which a user would then enter into the token. The token then calculates a response that serves as a one-time numeric password that is entered into the system. If the response from the user is the same as the response expected by the server, the user will be granted access to the system. In some implementations, the user must enter a PIN before the server will generate a challenge. Figure 16 illustrates an example of a challenge-response token.

Universal Serial Bus (USB) tokens are slender tokens with USB connectors that plug into PCs' USB ports. The token has an integrated chip that offers the same storage and processing power as smart cards. USB tokens can be used to securely store a user's private keys and, optionally, to securely perform cryptographic processing. A USB token can also securely store many user names and passwords, with the benefit of portability and additional security of off-PC storage.

Effectiveness of the technology

If they are implemented correctly, smart tokens can help create a secure authentication environment. Onetime passwords eliminate the problem of electronic monitoring or "password sniffing" and tokens that require the use of a PIN help to reduce the risk of forgery.

Figure 15: Example of the Time-Synchronized Token

Source: RSA Security Inc.

Figure 16: Example of a Challenge-Response Token

Source: © 2004 Secure Computing Corporation.

However, smart tokens do not necessarily verify a person; they only confirm that a person has the token. Because tokens can be lost or stolen, an attacker could obtain a token and attempt to determine the user's PIN or password. If an older algorithm is used to formulate a onetime password, it is possible that modern computers could crack the algorithm used to formulate the random numbers generated by a token. For these reasons, these technologies are generally not considered acceptable as stand-alone systems to protect extremely sensitive data, and additional controls—such as biometric identification—may be required. As a result, smart token systems are considered more effective when combined with other methods of authentication.

In addition, at times the token could become unavailable to the user. For example, tokens can be broken, their batteries eventually discharge, and users could simply forget to bring tokens to work. For these reasons, organizations need to have an effective policy on how legitimate users can access systems without a token. If the policy is weak or poorly implemented, the security of the authentication system is weakened.

A problem that can arise with time-synchronized tokens is that the token and the central authentication server can get out of sync. If the token's clock drifts significantly ahead of or behind the server's clock, the authentication server may be vulnerable to a cryptographic attack.

Authorization: User Rights and Privileges

What the technology does

User rights and privileges grant or deny access to a protected resource, whether it is a network, system, an individual computer, a program, or a file. These technologies authorize appropriate actions for users and prevent unauthorized access to data and systems. Typically, user rights and privileges are capabilities that are built into an operating system. For example, most operating systems include the concept of read, write, or read-and-write privileges for files and the capability to assign these privileges to users or groups of users.

Mainframe-based access control software controls users' entry to the system, their access to data on the system, and the level of usage available to them with programs and other logical resources that are on the system. Administrators can use these software tools to perform many access control functions—including identifying system users and authorizing user access to protected resources—while also ensuring individual accountability and logging unauthorized attempts at gaining access to the system protected resources.

Additionally, some communication protocols can be used to control dial-up access into networks. Protocols that provide these services include Terminal Access Controller Access System (TACACS+), which centrally manages multiple connections to a single user, a network, or a subnetwork, and interconnected networks, and Remote Authentication Dial-In User Service (RADIUS), which provides central authentication, authorization, and logging.

How the technology works

Mainframe-based access control software uses algorithms to determine whether to grant a user access to specific files, programs, or other defined resources (such as a printer queue or disk space to run a program). These algorithms are typically customized by a security administrator and result in access rules that are either user- or resource-based. User-based rules can be created to specify access for individuals or for groups. When access is requested, the software first identifies and authenticates the user, then determines what resource the user is requesting access to, and then refers to the access rules before permitting the user to gain access to protected system resources. Access is denied to unauthorized users, and any authorized or unauthorized attempt to gain access can be logged.

Technologies that use resource-based rules assign a security classification to both users and data files in the form of security levels and categories. The levels and categories of a user and a resource are compared to determine whether the user has sufficient privileges to access a file or other resource.

The TACACS+ protocol allows a separate access server to independently provide the services of authentication, authorization, and accounting. The authentication service allows a user to use the same user name and password for multiple servers, which may employ different communication protocols: TACACS+ forwards the user's user name and password information to a centralized database that also has the TACACS+ protocol. This database then compares the login information to determine whether to grant or deny access to the user.

RADIUS is implemented in a client/server network architecture, where a centralized server using the RADIUS protocol maintains a database of all user authentication and network service access information for several client computers that also use the RADIUS protocol. When a user logs on to the network via a RADIUS client, the user's password is encrypted and sent to the RADIUS server along with the user name. If the user name and password are correct, the server sends an acknowledgement message that includes information on the user's network system and service requirements. If the login process conditions are met, the user is authenticated and is given access to the requested network services.

Effectiveness of the technology

An operating system's built-in user rights and privileges can be effective when used with a well-defined security policy that guides who can access which resources.

A key component to implementing adequate access controls is ensuring that appropriate user rights and privileges have been assigned. If any one user has too many rights or has rights to a few key functions, the organization can be susceptible to fraud. Limiting user rights and privileges ensures that users have only the access they need to perform their duties, that very sensitive resources are limited to a few individuals, and that employees are restricted from performing incompatible functions or functions that are beyond their responsibilities. Excluding roles and user rights reduce the possibility of fraudulent acts against the organization.

System Integrity

System integrity technologies are used to ensure that a system and its data are not illicitly modified or corrupted by malicious code. Malicious code includes viruses, Trojan horses, and worms. A virus is a program that infects computer files, usually executable programs, by inserting a copy of itself into the file. These copies are usually executed when a user takes some action, such as opening an infected e-mail attachment or executing a downloaded file that includes the virus. When executed, the virus can infect other files. Unlike a computer worm, a virus requires human involvement (usually unwitting) to propagate. A Trojan horse is a computer program that conceals harmful code. A Trojan horse usually masquerades as a useful program that a user would wish to execute. A worm is an independent computer program that reproduces by copying itself from one system to another. Unlike a computer virus, a worm does not require human involvement to propagate.

Antivirus software and integrity checkers are two types of technologies that help to protect against malicious code attacks. Antivirus software can be installed on computers to detect either incoming malicious code or malicious code that is already resident on the system and to repair files that have been damaged by the code. Integrity checkers are usually applied to critical files or groups of files on a computer system. These programs typically take a snapshot of the files of interest and periodically compare the files with the snapshot to ensure that no unauthorized changes have been made.

Antivirus Software

What the technology does

Antivirus software provides protection against viruses and malicious code, such as worms and Trojan horses, by detecting and removing the malicious code and by preventing unwanted effects and repairing damage that may have resulted. Antivirus software uses a variety of techniques—such as signature scanners, activity blockers, and heuristic scanners—to protect computer systems against potentially harmful viruses, worms, and Trojan horses.

How the technology works

Antivirus software products can use a combination of the following technologies:

Signature scanners can identify known malicious code. Scanners search for "signature strings" or use algorithmic detection methods to identify known code. They rely on a significant amount of prior knowledge about the malicious code. Therefore, it is critical that the signature information for scanners be current. Most scanners can be configured to automatically update their signature information from a designated source, typically on a weekly basis; scanners can also be forced to update their signatures on demand.

Activity (or behavior) blockers contain a list of rules that a legitimate program must follow. If the program breaks one of the rules, the activity blockers alert the users. The idea is that untrusted code is first checked for improper behavior. If none is found, the code can be run in a restricted environment, where dynamic checks are performed on each potentially dangerous action before it is permitted to take effect. By adding multiple layers of reviews and checks to the execution process, behavior blockers can prevent malicious code from performing undesirable actions.

Heuristic scanners work to protect against known viruses and are also able to detect unknown viruses. Heuristic scanners can be classified as either static or dynamic. Static heuristic scanners use virus signatures, much like standard signature scanners, but instead of scanning for specific viruses, they scan for lines of code that are associated with viruslike behaviors. These scanners are often supplemented by additional programs that search for more complex, viruslike behavior patterns. Dynamic heuristic scanners identify suspicious files and load them into a simulated computer system to emulate their execution. This allows the scanner to determine if the file is infected.

Effectiveness of the technology

Signature scanners require frequent updates to keep their databases of virus signatures current. This updating is necessary to safeguard computer systems against new strains of viruses. When they are properly updated, scanners effectively combat known viruses. However, they are less effective against viruses that change their code each time they infect another computer system.

Activity blockers are generally ineffective against many viruses, including macro viruses that make use of the programming features of common applications such as spreadsheets and word processors. Macro viruses constitute the majority of today's viruses and are encoded within a document as macros—sequences of commands or keyboard strokes that can be stored and then recalled with a single command or keystroke. The macro generally modifies a commonly used function (for example, opening or saving a file) to initiate the effect of the virus. Activity blockers are generally more successful against Trojan horses and worms than they are against viruses.

Heuristic scanners have the primary advantage of being able to detect unknown viruses. Static heuristic scanners, when supplemented with additional programs that can detect behaviors associated with more complex viruses. Dynamic heuristic scanners consume more time and system resources than static heuristic scanners.

File Integrity Checkers

What the technology does

File integrity checkers are software programs that monitor alterations to files that are considered critical to either the organization or the operation of the computer (including changes to the data in the file, permissions, last use, and deletion). Because both authorized and unauthorized activities alter files, file integrity checkers are designed for use with critical files that are not expected to change under normal operating conditions.

File integrity checkers are valuable tools with multiple uses, including

- **Intrusion detection.** File integrity checkers can help detect system compromises because successful intruders commonly modify system files to provide themselves with a way back into the system (backdoor), hide the attack, and hide their identity.

- **Administration.** Some file integrity checkers have the ability to collect and centralize information from multiple hosts, an ability that assists system administrators in large network environments.
- **Policy enforcement.** System administrators can use file integrity checkers as a policy enforcement tool to check whether users or other administrators have made changes that should not have been made or of which the system administrator was not notified.
- **Identification of hardware or software failure.** Integrity checkers might also notice a failing disk. File integrity checkers can also be used to determine if an application had changed files because of design faults.
- **Forensic analysis.** If a system were compromised, a "snapshot" of the system could be taken, which would assist forensic activities and in prosecuting offenders.

How the technology works

Integrity checkers identify modifications to critical files by comparing the state of a file system against a trusted state, or a baseline.[94] The baseline is set to reflect the system's state when it has not been modified in any unauthorized way. First, critical files are encrypted through a one-way hash function, making it nearly impossible to derive the original data from the string.[95] The hash function results in a fixed string of digits, which are stored in a database along with other attributes of the files. The database of the original state of critical files is considered the baseline. To be effective, a baseline should be established immediately after the operating system is installed, before an attacker would have the ability to modify the file system.

After a baseline is created, the integrity checker can then compare the current file system against the baseline. Each critical file's hash is compared with the its baseline value. Differences between the hashes indicate that the file has been modified. The user can then determine if the change would have been unauthorized. If so, the user can take action, for example, assessing the damage and restoring the file or system to a good known state.

Effectiveness of the technology

The effectiveness of file integrity checkers depends on the accuracy of the baseline. Comparisons against a corrupted baseline would result in inaccuracy in identifying modified files. The baseline database should be updated

[94] The file system is one of the most important parts of an operating system; and it stores and manages user data on disk drives and ensures that data read from storage are identical to the data that were originally written. In addition to storing user data in files, the file system creates and manages metadata—information about how, when, and by whom a particular set of data was collected and how the data are formatted.

[95] A less secure method uses checksums instead of a hash function.

whenever significant changes are made to the system. Care must be taken to ensure that a baseline is not taken of a compromised system.

Also, although they monitor modifications to files, integrity checkers do not prevent changes from occurring. An administrator will notice that the change has occurred only after the integrity checker has been run. Because of the amount of time it can take to check a file system and the system resources that requires, these tools are typically run at regularly scheduled intervals.

In addition, integrity checkers may generate false alarms when authorized changes are made to monitored files. Not only can investigating false alarms be time-consuming, it could also lead a system administrator to be unwilling to investigate future alarms. As a result, unauthorized changes could go unnoticed.

Cryptography

Cryptography is used to secure transactions by providing ways to assure data confidentiality (assurance that the information will be protected from unauthorized access), data integrity (assurance that data have not been accidentally or deliberately altered), authentication of message originator, electronic certification of data, and nonrepudiation (proof of the integrity and origin of the data that can be verified by a third party). Accordingly, cryptography has had, and will continue to have, an important role in protecting information both within a computer system and when information is sent over the Internet and other unprotected communications channels. Encryption is the process of transforming ordinary data (commonly referred to as plaintext) into code form (ciphertext) using a special value known as a key and a mathematical process called an algorithm. Cryptographic algorithms are designed to produce ciphertext that is unintelligible to unauthorized users. Decryption of ciphertext is possible only with use of the proper key.

A basic premise in cryptography is that good systems depend only on the secrecy of the key used to perform the operations and not on the secrecy of the algorithm. The algorithms used to perform most cryptographic operations over the Internet are well known. However, because the keys used by these algorithms are kept secret, the process is considered secure.

Cryptographic techniques can be divided into two basic types: secret key cryptography and public key cryptography. Each type has its strengths and weaknesses and systems that utilize both forms are used to take advantage of the strengths of a given type.[96]

[96] For additional information on how cryptography works and some of the issues associated with this technology see U.S. General Accounting Office, *Information Security: Advances and Remaining Challenges to Adoption of Public Key Infrastructure Technology*, GAO-01-277 (Washington, D.C.: Feb. 26, 2001), and U.S. General Accounting Office, *Information Security: Status of Federal Public Key Infrastructure Activities at Major Federal Departments and Agencies*, GAO-04-157 (Washington, D.C.: Dec. 15, 2003).

- Secret key or symmetric cryptography employs algorithms in which the key that is used to encrypt the original plaintext message can be calculated from the key that is used to decrypt the ciphertext message, and vice versa. With most symmetric algorithms, the encryption key and the decryption key are the same, and the security of this method rests upon the difficulty of guessing the key. In order to communicate securely, the sender and the receiver must agree on a key and keep the key secret from others. Figure 17 depicts encryption and decryption using a symmetric algorithm. Common symmetric key algorithms include Triple Digital Encryption Standard (3DES) and the Advanced Encryption Standard (AES).

Public key or asymmetric cryptography employs algorithms designed so that the key that is used to encrypt the original plaintext message cannot be calculated from the key that is used to decrypt the ciphertext message. These two keys complement each other in such a way that when one key is used for encryption, only the other key can decrypt the ciphertext. One of these keys is kept private and is known as the *private key*, while the other key is widely publicized and is referred to as the *public key*. Figure 18 depicts one application of encryption and decryption using a public key algorithm. In this process, the public key is used by others to encrypt a plaintext message, but only a specific person with the corresponding private key can decrypt the ciphertext. For example, if fictional character Bob gives his public key to fictional character Alice, only Bob has the private key that can decrypt a message that Alice has encrypted with his public key. Public key algorithms can also be used in an inverse process, whereby the private key is used to encrypt a message and the public key is made freely available. In this process, those who decrypt the message using the corresponding

Figure 17: Encryption and Decryption with a Symmetric Algorithm

Source: GAO analysis and Corel Galley.

Figure 18: Encryption and Decryption with a Key Algorithm

Source: GAO analysis and Corel Galley.

public key can be confident that the message came from a specific person. For example, if Alice decrypts a message that was encrypted with Bob's private key, she has assurance that the message came from Bob. The most popular public key algorithm is RSA, named for its creators—Rivest, Shamir, and Adleman.

Key-based encryption fails if the plaintext or the key are not kept secret from unauthorized users. Such failures often occur not from a weakness in the technology itself, but rather as a result of poor security policies or practices or malicious insiders.

Secret key cryptography has significant limitations that can make it impractical as a stand-alone solution for securing electronic transactions, especially among large communities of users that may have no pre-established relationships. The most significant limitation is that some means must be devised to securely distribute and manage the keys that are at the heart of the system; such a means is commonly referred to as key management. When many transacting parties are involved, key management may create immense logistical problems and delays. Furthermore, in order to minimize the damage that could be caused by a compromised key, the keys may need to be short-lived and therefore frequently changed, adding to the logistical complexity.

Public key cryptography can address many of the limitations of secret key cryptography regarding key management. There is no need to establish a secure channel or physical delivery services to distribute keys. However, public key cryptography has its own challenges, involving the methods of ensuring that the links between the users and their public keys are initially valid and are constantly maintained. For example, it is impractical and unrealistic to expect that each user will have previously established relationships with all of the other potential users in order to obtain their public keys. Digital certificates (discussed further in this appendix) are one solution to this problem. Furthermore, although a sender can provide confidentiality for a message by encrypting it with the recipient's publicly available encryption key using public key algorithms for large messages, this is computationally time-consuming and could make the whole process unreasonably slow.[97]

Instead, it can be better to combine secret and public key cryptography to provide more efficient and effective means by which a sender can encrypt a document so that only the intended recipient can decrypt it. In this case, the sender of a message would generate a onetime secret encryption key (called a session key) and use it to encrypt the body of her message and then encrypt this session key using the recipient's public key. The encrypted message and the encrypted session key necessary to decrypt the message would then be sent to recipient. Because the recipient has the information necessary to decrypt the session key, the sender of a message has reasonable assurance in a properly administered system that only the recipient would be able to successfully decrypt the message.

Cryptographic modules implement algorithms that form the building blocks of cryptographic applications. Using a cryptographic system with cryptographic modules that have been approved by an accredited cryptographic certification laboratory (for example, the NIST Cryptographic Module Validation Program) can help provide assurance that the system will be effective. However, designing, building, and effectively implementing full-featured cryptographic solutions will remain a difficult challenge because it is more than just "installing the technology." Encryption technology is effective only if it is an integral part of an effectively enforced information security policy that includes good key management practices. For example, current public key products and implementations suffer from significant interoperability problems, which make it difficult for officials to make decisions about how to develop a public key infrastructure (PKI) that can be used to perform such functions as encrypting data and providing data integrity.[98]

Cryptographic solutions will continue to be used by systems to help provide the basic data confidentiality, data integrity, authentication of message

[97] Most public key cryptographic methods can be used for both encryption and digital signatures. However, certain public key methods—most notably the Digital Signature Algorithm—cannot be used for encryption, but only for digital signatures.

[98] A PKI is a system of hardware, software, policies, and people that can provide a set of information assurances (identification and authentication, confidentiality, data integrity, and nonrepudiation) that are important in conducting electronic transactions. For more information on PKI, see U.S. General Accounting Office, *Information Security: Advances and Remaining Challenges to Adoption of Public Key Infrastructure Technology*, GAO-01-277 (Washington, D.C.: Feb. 26, 2001).

originator, electronic certification of data, and nonrepudiation. Technologies that use cryptographic algorithms can be used to encrypt message transmissions so that eavesdroppers cannot determine the contents of the message. Hash technologies use cryptography to provide assurance to a message recipient that the contents of the message have not been altered. For example, operating systems use cryptography to protect passwords. Protocols such as IP Security protocol (IPSec) and Secure Sockets Layer (SSL) use cryptographic technologies for confidential communications. SHA and MD5 are examples of hash technology implementations. Digital signature technologies use cryptography to authenticate the sender of a message. Virtual private networks (VPN) use cryptography to establish a secure communications link across unprotected networks.

Digital Signatures and Certificates

What the technology does

Properly implemented digital signatures use public key cryptography to provide authentication, data integrity, and nonrepudiation for a message or transaction. Just as a physical signature provides assurance that a letter has been written by a specific person, a digital signature confirms the identity of a message's sender. Digital signatures are often used in conjunction with a digital certificate. A digital certificate is an electronic credential that guarantees the association between a public key and a specific entity. The most common use of digital certificates is to verify that a user sending a message is who he or she claims to be and to provide the receiver with a means to encode a reply. Certificates can be issued to computer equipment and processes as well as to individuals. For example, companies that do business over the Internet can obtain digital certificates for their computer servers. These certificates are used to authenticate the servers to potential customers, who can then rely on the servers to support the secure exchange of encrypted information, such as passwords and credit card numbers.

How the technology works

The creation of a digital signature can be divided into a two-step process based on public key cryptography, as illustrated in figure 19. As previously noted, for performance reasons, public key cryptography is not used to encrypt large amounts of data. Therefore, the first step involves reducing the amount of data that need to be encrypted. This is typically accomplished by using a cryptographic hash algorithm, which condenses the data into a *message digest*.[99] Then the message digest is encrypted, using the

[99] A hash algorithm compresses the bits of a message to a fixed size. Because any change in the message or the algorithm results in a different value, it is not possible to reverse this process and arrive at the original information.

Figure 19: Creating a Digital Signature

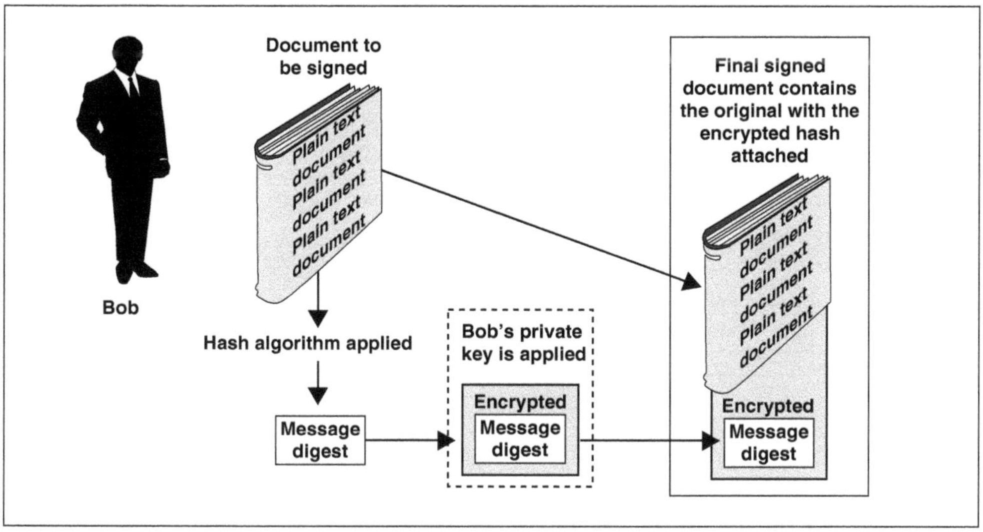

Source: National Institute of Standards Technology and Corel Galley.

sender's private signing key to create a digital signature. Because the message digest will be different for each signature, each signature will also be unique; if a good hash algorithm is used, it is computationally infeasible to find another message that will generate the same message digest.

For example, if Bob wishes to digitally sign an electronic document, he can use his private key to encrypt the message digest of the document. His public key is freely available, so anyone with access to his public key can decrypt the document. Although this seems backward because anyone can read what is encrypted, the fact that Bob's private key is held only by Bob provides the proof that Bob's digital signature is valid.

Alice (or anyone else wishing to verify the document) can compute the message digest of the document and decrypt the signature using Bob's public key (see figure 20). Assuming that the message digests match, Alice then has three kinds of security assurance. First, the digital signature ensures that Bob actually signed the document (authentication). Second, it ensures that Bob in fact sent the message (nonrepudiation). And third, because the message digest would have changed if anything in the message had been modified, Alice knows that no one tampered with the contents of the document after Bob signed it (data integrity). Of course, this assumes that (1) Bob has sole control over his private signing key and (2) Alice is sure that the public key she used to validate Bob's messages really belongs to Bob.

Figure 20: Verifying a Digital Signature

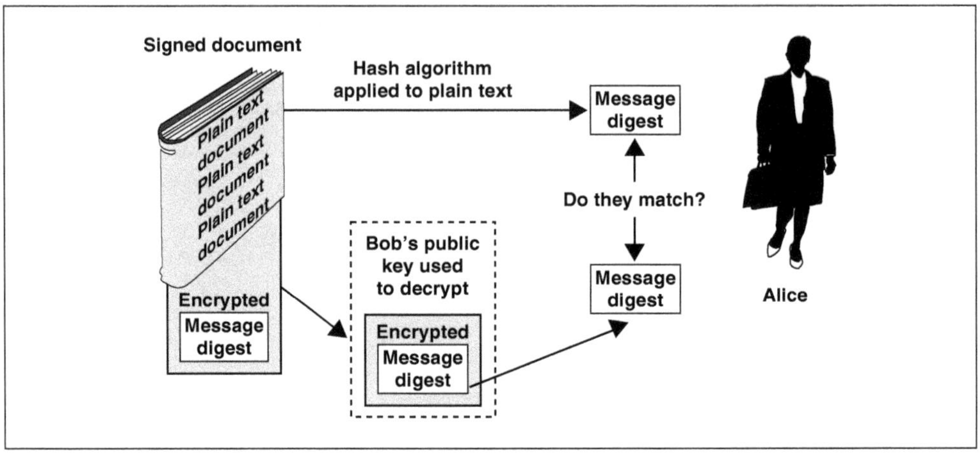

Source: National Institute of Standards Technology and Corel Galley.

Digital certificates address this need to link an individual to his or her public key. A digital certificate is created by placing the individual's name, the individual's public key, and certain other identifying information in a small electronic document that is stored in a directory or other database. Directories may be publicly available repositories kept on servers that act like telephone books in which users can look up others' public keys. The digital certificate itself is created by a trusted third party called a certification authority, which digitally signs the certificate, thus providing assurance that the public key contained in the certificate does indeed belong to the individual named in the certificate. Certification authorities are a main component of a PKI, which uses cryptographic techniques to generate and manage digital certificates.

Effectiveness of the technology

Within an organization, separate key pairs are necessary to support both encryption and digital signatures, and a user's private encryption key should normally be copied to a safe backup location. This provides the organization with the ability to access encrypted data if the user's original private encryption key becomes inaccessible. For example, the organization would have an interest in decrypting data should the private key be destroyed or lost or if the user were fired, incapacitated, or deceased. However, copies of the private keys used for digital signatures should never be made, because they could fall into the wrong hands and be used to forge the owner's signatures.

By linking an individual to his or her public key, digital certificates help to provide assurance that digital signatures are used effectively. However, digital certificates are only as secure as the public key infrastructure that they are based on. For example, if an unauthorized user is able to obtain a private key, the digital certificate could then be compromised. In addition, users of certificates are dependent on certification authorities to verify the digital certificates. If a valid certification authority is not used, or a certification authority makes a mistake or is the victim of a cyber attack, a digital certificate may be ineffective.

Virtual Private Networks

What the technology does

A VPN is a private network that is maintained across a shared or public network, such as the Internet, by means of specialized security procedures. VPNs allow organizations or individuals to connect a network between two or more physical locations (for example, field offices to organization headquarters) without incurring the costs of purchasing or leasing dedicated telephone lines or frame relay circuits[100] (see figure 21). Through measures like authentication and data encryption, cryptographic VPNs can establish a secure virtual connection between physical locations.

VPNs can be implemented through hardware, existing firewalls, and standalone software applications. To a user, VPNs appear no different than traditional networks and can be used normally whether the user is dialing in from home or accessing a field office from headquarters. VPNs are typically used in intranets and extranets and in remote access connections.

Figure 21: Illustration of a Typical VPN

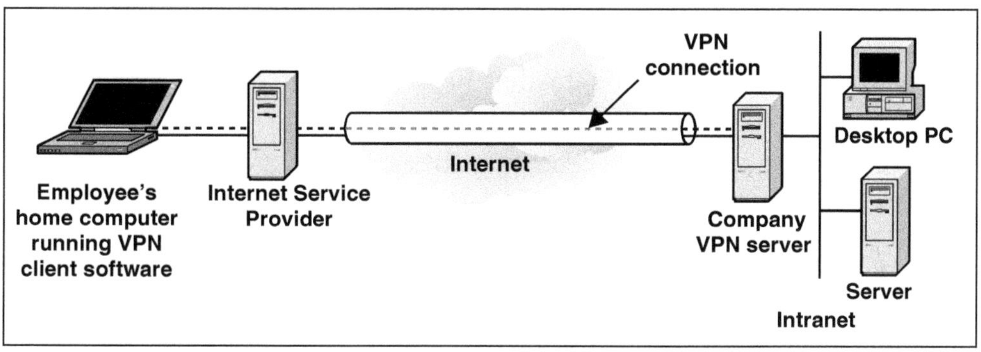

Source: GAO analysis and Microsoft Visio.

[100] Frame relay is a packet-switching protocol for connecting devices on a WAN.

- Intranets are interlinked private networks within an enterprise that allow information and computer resources to be shared throughout an organization. Some organizations have sensitive data on a LAN that is physically disconnected from the rest of the organization's intranet. This lack of connectivity may cause data on the LAN to be inaccessible to users. A VPN can be used to allow the sensitive LAN to be physically connected to the intranet, but separated by a VPN server. Only authorized users would be able to establish a VPN connection with the server to gain access to the sensitive LAN, and all communications across the VPN could be encrypted for data confidentiality.
- Remote access VPNs simplify the process of remote access, allowing off-site users to connect, via the Internet, to a VPN server at the organization's headquarters. Digital subscriber line or cable modem services allow remote VPN users to access the organization's network at speeds comparable to those attained with on-site access.

How the technology works

A VPN works by using shared public networks while maintaining privacy through security procedures and protocols that encrypt communications between two end points. To provide an additional level of security, a VPN can encrypt not only the data, but also the originating and receiving network addresses. There are two main VPN technologies, which differ in their methods of encrypting data for secure transmission over Internet connections. The first method is based on "tunneling" protocols that encrypt packets at the sending end and decrypt them at the receiving end. This process is commonly referred to as *encapsulation*, because the original, unsecured packet is placed within another packet that has been secured by encryption. The encapsulated packets are then sent through a "tunnel" that cannot be traveled by data that have not been properly encrypted. Figure 22 is a depiction of tunneling.

A commonly used tunneling protocol is IPSec.[101] IPSec VPNs connect hosts to entire private networks, encrypt IP packets, and ensure that the packets are not deleted, added to, or tampered with during transmission. Because they are based on the IP protocol, IPSec VPNs can secure any IP traffic and can be configured to support any IP-based application.

In addition to using tunneling protocols, VPNs can also use the SSL protocol, which uses a limited form of public key cryptography. SSL VPNs connect users to services and applications inside private networks, but they secure only the applications' services or data. SSL is a feature of

[101] Other tunneling protocols include Point-to-Point Tunneling Protocol (PPTP) and Layer 2 Tunneling Protocol (L2TP).

Figure 22: Tunneling Establishes a Virtual Connection

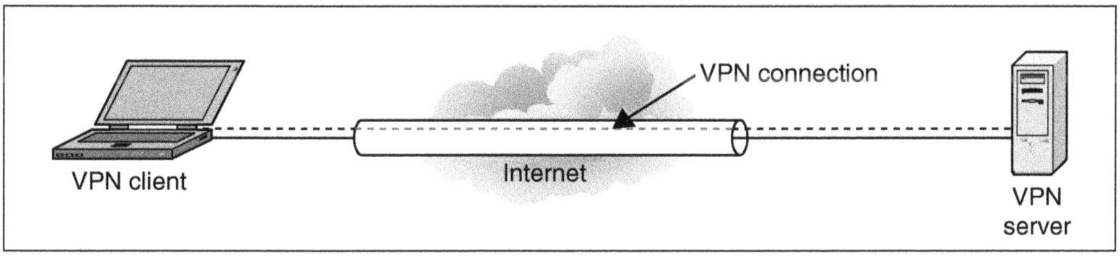

Source: GAO analysis and Microsoft Visio.

commonly available commercial Web browsers (such as Microsoft's Internet Explorer and America Online's Netscape Navigator), and SSL VPNs use standard browsers instead of the specialized client software that is required by IPSec VPNs.

Effectiveness of the technology

VPNs can be a cost-effective way to secure transmitted data across public networks. However, the cost of implementing IPSec VPNs includes the installation and configuration of specialized software that is required on every client computer. SSL VPNs use standard Web browsers, eliminating the need for client administration, but the SSL protocol often requires that applications be customized.

In addition, VPNs are only as secure as the computers that are connected to them. Because of the interconnected environment, any unsecured client computer could be used to launch an attack on the network. In particular, VPNs may be susceptible to man-in-the-middle attacks, message replay attacks, and denial-of-service attacks.[102]

Audit and Monitoring

Audit and monitoring technologies can help security administrators to routinely assess computer security, perform investigations during and after an attack, and even recognize an ongoing attack.

We describe four types of audit and monitoring technologies: intrusion detection systems, intrusion prevention systems, security event correlation tools, and computer forensics. Intrusion detection and intrusion prevention

[102] A *man-in-the-middle attack* is one in which the attacker intercepts messages in a public key exchange and then retransmits them, substituting his or her own public key for the requested one, so that the two original parties still appear to be communicating with each other directly. A *message replay attack* is one in which an attacker eavesdrops, obtains a copy of an encrypted message, and then re-uses the message at a later time in an attempt to trick the cryptographic protocol. A *denial-of-service* attack is one in which an attack from a single source overwhelms a target computer with messages, denying access to legitimate users without actually having to compromise the targeted computer.

systems monitor and analyze events occurring on a system or network and either alert appropriate personnel or prevent an attack from proceeding. Audit logs are produced by many operating systems and software applications. Depending on the configuration of the logging functions, critical activities—such as access to administrator functions—are logged and can be monitored for anomalous activity. Security event correlation tools can help to detect security events and examine logs to determine the method of entry that was used by an attacker and to ascertain the extent of damage that was caused by the attack. Because of the volume of data collected on some systems and networks, these tools can help to consolidate the logs and to identify key information using correlation analysis. Computer forensics involves the identification, preservation, extraction, and documentation of computer-based evidence. Computer forensics tools are used during the investigation of a computer crime to identify the perpetrator and the methods used to conduct the attack.

Intrusion Detection Systems

What the technology does

An intrusion detection system (IDS) detects inappropriate, incorrect, or anomalous activity that is aimed at disrupting the confidentiality, availability, or integrity of a protected network and its computer systems. An IDS collects information on a network, analyzes the information on the basis of a preconfigured rule set, and then responds to the analysis.

A special type of IDS, known as a honeypot, acts as a decoy server or system that gathers information about an attacker or intruder—such as the method of intrusion and the vulnerabilities exploited—in order to improve security methods. To attract attackers, honeypots appear to contain important data, but instead contain false information. A honeypot can be set up to alert a system administrator of an attack via e-mail or pager, allowing the administrator to ensure that the honeypot is not used as a springboard for future attacks.

How the technology works

There are three common types of IDS, classified by the source of information they use to detect intrusion: network-based, host-based, and application-based.

Network-based IDSs detect attacks by capturing and analyzing network packets. When placed in a network segment, one network-based IDS can monitor the network traffic that affects multiple hosts that are connected to that network segment. Network-based IDSs often consist of a set of single-purpose sensors or hosts, placed at various points in a network. These units monitor network traffic, performing local analysis of that traffic and reporting attacks to a central management console. Because these sensors are limited to running the IDS application only, they can more easily be secured against attacks. Many of these sensors are designed to run in "stealth" mode, making it more difficult for an attacker to detect their presence and location.

Host-based IDSs collect information from within an individual computer system and use that information to detect intrusions. Host-based IDSs can determine exactly which processes and user accounts are involved in a particular attack on the system. Furthermore, unlike network-based IDSs, host-based IDSs can more readily "see" the intended outcome of an attempted attack, because they can directly access and monitor the data files and system processes that are usually targeted by attacks. Host-based IDSs normally use two types of information sources: operating system audit trails and system logs. Operating system audit trails are usually generated at the innermost level of the operating system; therefore these trails are more detailed and better protected than system logs. Some host-based IDSs are designed to support a centralized IDS management and reporting infrastructure that can allow a single management console to track many hosts. Others generate messages in formats that are compatible with a network management system.

Application-based IDSs are a special subset of host-based IDSs that analyze the events occurring within a specific software application. The most common information sources used by application-based IDSs are the application's transaction log files. Because they directly interface with the application and use application-specific knowledge, application-based IDSs can detect the actions of authorized users who are attempting to exceed their authorization. This is because such problems are more likely to appear in the interaction among the user, the data, and the application.

These IDSs are characterized by four primary qualities: source of information, method of analysis, timing, and response.

IDSs have two primary methods of performing analysis. Signature-based (sometimes referred to as knowledge-based, or pattern-based) analysis relies on previous known attacks to detect an attack that is occurring. The IDS analyzes system activity, looking for events that match a predefined pattern of events that describes known attacks. If the analysis of data reveals that an attack is ongoing or a vulnerability is being exploited, an alarm is generated. Anomaly-based (also referred to as behavior-based) analysis compares the current operation of a system or network against a valid or accepted system behavior. An anomaly-based IDS creates a baseline of normal (valid or accepted) behavior through various collection methods. If the current behavior of the system is not within the normal boundaries of behavior, then it would be interpreted by the IDS as an attack.

IDSs can use either an interval-based or real-time timing method. The interval-based timing method analyzes the data on a predetermined schedule. This method allows an IDS to collect a large amount of data. The real-time method analyzes and responds to the data as they come in, allowing administrators to respond in real time to attacks.

IDSs can respond to possible attacks using either an active or a passive response strategy. An active response IDS is referred to as an intrusion prevention system (IPS). A passive-response IDS will typically generate an alarm for an administrator. The alarm may appear on the administrator's screen and provide the administrator with information such as the type of attack, the location of the attack, the threat level, how it should be responded to, and possibly whether the attack is successful. A passive response IDS relies on a human to take action in response to the alert.

Effectiveness of the technology

IDSs cannot instantaneously detect, report, or respond to an attack when there is a heavy network or processing load. Therefore, IDSs are vulnerable to denial-of-service attacks; a malicious individual could send large amounts of information through a network to overwhelm the IDS, allowing the individual to launch another attack that would then go unnoticed by the IDS. IDSs rely on available attack information, and they are not as effective when protecting against unknown attacks, newly published attacks, or variants of existing attacks. In addition, IDSs are not always able to automatically investigate attacks without human involvement.

The effectiveness of an IDS can be somewhat determined by the number of false positives and false negatives that it generates. A false positive occurs when the IDS alerts that there is an attack occurring, when in fact there is no attack. A false negative occurs when the IDS fails to alert that an attack is occurring. Overall, with anomaly-based IDSs, false positives are numerous because of the unpredictable behaviors of users and networks. Administrators must devote a fair amount of time to regularly reviewing the IDS logs and to fine-tuning the IDS to limit the number of false alarms. If excessive false alarms occur, future alarms are increasingly likely to be ignored. Sometimes the IDS may be disabled for the sake of convenience. An attacker could exploit this vulnerability by slowly changing the accepted operation of the system or network recognized by the IDS, allowing for a larger attack to occur at a future time. The attacker could accomplish this by affecting the baseline as it is being created or by later slowly attacking the system so that the baseline moves to a new threshold of accepted behavior. Also, if an anomaly-based IDS is used while an attack is occurring, the normal behavior accepted by the IDS will include behaviors that are characteristic of an attack. Anomaly-based IDSs also take a varying amount of time to compute the valid or accepted behavior, so that for a period of time the IDS will not be an effective method of detecting attacks.

Intrusion Prevention Systems

What the technology does

As we have described, intrusion prevention systems (IPSs) are IDSs with an active response strategy. This means that IPSs not only can detect an intrusive activity, they also can attempt to stop the activity—ideally before it reaches its targets. Intrusion prevention is much more valuable than intrusion detection, because intrusion detection simply observes events without making any effort to stop them. IPSs often combine the best of firewall, intrusion detection, antivirus, and vulnerability assessment technologies. Their focus, however, is on the prevention of detected attacks that might exploit an existing vulnerability in the protected network or host system.

How the technology works

Like IDSs, IPSs are either network-based or host-based. They perform IDS functions and when they detect an intrusion, take action such as blocking the network traffic to prevent the attack from progressing. Network-based IPSs may simply monitor the network traffic or they may actually be "in line", which means that activity must pass through them. For example, an IPS that includes a network-based IDS that is integrated with a firewall and a host-based IDS that integrates the detection and prevention functionalities into the kernel of the operating system. Network-based IPSs thoroughly inspect data traffic, typically using specialized hardware to compensate for the processing overhead that inspection consumes.

IPSs actively respond to possible attacks by collecting additional information, changing the current environment, and taking action against the intruder. One of their common responses is to adjust firewall rules to block the offending network traffic. If an IPS responds to an attack by taking action against the intruder (commonly referred to as attack-back or strike-back), it may initiate a launch of attacks against the attacker. In another aggressive response, called "trace back," the IPS attempts to find the source of the attack.

Effectiveness of the technology

Intrusion prevention systems are the logical evolution of intrusion detection systems. Instead of dealing with the constant warning alarms of IDSs, IPSs can prevent attacks by blocking suspicious network traffic. A key value of some IPSs is their ability to "learn" what constitutes acceptable behavior and to halt activity that is not based on rules that were generated during the learning, or profiling, stage.

Network-based IPSs offer in-line monitoring of data streams throughout the network and provide the capability to prevent intrusion attempts. Host-based IPSs allow systems and applications to be configured individually, preventing attacks against the operating system or applications. These IPSs are suitable measures to help guard unpatched and exploitable systems against attacks, but they require substantial user administration.

Unfortunately, IPSs are susceptible to errors in detecting intrusions. If the detection of incidents is not accurate, then an IPS may block legitimate activities that are incorrectly classified as malicious. Any organization that wants to utilize intrusion prevention should pay particular attention to detection accuracy when selecting a product.

Users of IPSs also face the challenge of maintaining a database of recent attack signatures so that systems can be guarded against recent attack strategies. Furthermore, IPSs cause bottlenecks in network traffic, reducing throughput across the network.

Security Event Correlation Tools

What the technology does

Security event correlation tools collect logs, or lists of actions that have occurred, from operating systems, firewalls, applications, IDSs and other network devices. Then the correlation tools analyze the logs in real time, discern whether an attack has occurred, and respond to a security incident.

Review and analysis of logs can provide a dynamic picture of ongoing system activities that can be used to verify that the system is operating according to the organization's policies. Analyzing a single device's logs is insufficient to gain a full understand of all system activity, but the size, number, and difficulty of reading through every tool's log files is a daunting task for an administrator. Security event correlation tools address the need for an administrator to investigate an attack in a real-time setting, through analysis and correlation of all the different IDS, firewall, and server logs. Automated audit tools provide a means to significantly reduce the required review time, and they will print reports (predefined and customized) that summarize the log contents from a set of specific activities (see figure 23).

How the technology works

Security event correlation tools first consolidate the log files from various sources, such as operating systems, firewalls, applications, IDSs, antivirus programs, servers, and virtual private networks. Often, the logs from the various sources come in a variety of proprietary formats that make comparisons difficult. As part of the consolidation process, security event

Figure 23: Typical Operation of Security Event Correlation Tools

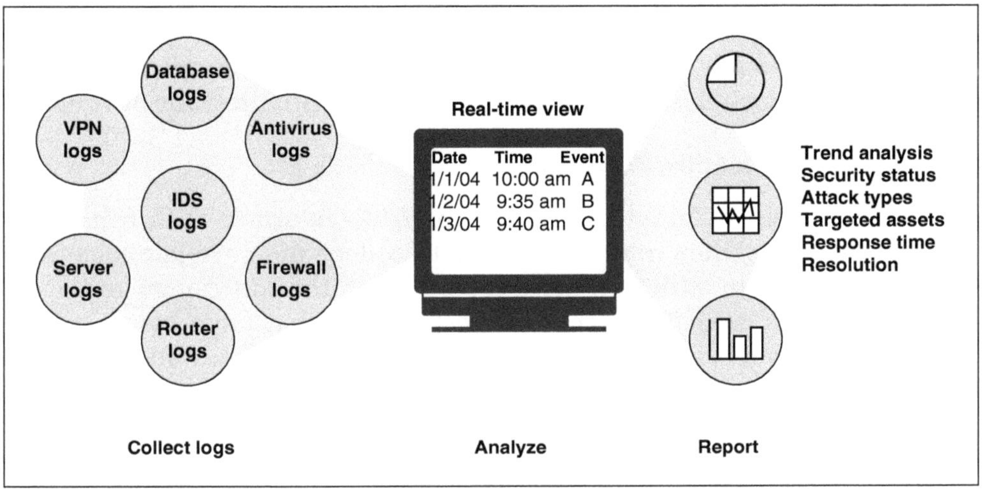

Source: GAO and Corel Draw.

correlation tools normalize the logs into a standard format—for example, Extensible Markup Language (commonly referred to as XML).[103] After the normalization process, unnecessary data can be eliminated in order to decrease the chance of errors.

The normalized logs are then compared (or correlated) to determine whether attacks have occurred. A variety of correlation methods can be used, including sophisticated pattern-based analysis, which can identify similar activity on various logs that have originated from an attack. For example, an IDS might not raise a flag if a single port was being scanned. However, if that port was being scanned on multiple systems, that activity might indicate an attack. By consolidating the logs from the various IDSs, correlation tools may detect this type of attack. A second method of analysis is called anomaly detection. In this method, a baseline of normal user activity is taken, and logged activities are compared against this baseline. Abnormal activity can then be interpreted as potentially indicating an attack. Another correlation method considers the significance of the logged event, which can be calculated as the probability that the attack would have succeeded.

If an attack is detected, the tools can then respond either passively or actively. A passive response means that no action is taken by the tool to

[103] XML is a flexible, nonproprietary set of standards for tagging information so that it can be transmitted over a network such as the Internet and readily interpreted by disparate computer systems.

stop the threat directly. For example, notifications can be sent to system administrators via pagers or e-mail, incidents can be logged, and IP addresses can be added to intruder or asset watch lists. An active response is an automated action taken by the tool to mitigate the risk. For example, one active response is to block the attack through interfaces with firewalls or routers.

Effectiveness of the technology

Correlation tools are limited in their ability to interface with numerous security products; they may not be able to collect and correlate logs from certain products. In addition, these tools rely on the sufficiency and accuracy of the logs, and they cannot detect attacks that have bypassed the various security devices such as the firewall and IDS. If an attacker were able to compromise the logs, then the security event correlation tool could be analyzing false information. Encryption and authentication to ensure the security and integrity of the data may mitigate this risk.

Computer Forensics Tools

What the technology does

Computer forensics tools are used to identify, preserve, extract, and document computer-based evidence. They can identify passwords, logons, and other information in files that have been deleted, encrypted, or damaged. During the investigation of a computer crime, these tools are used to determine the perpetrator and the methods used to conduct the attack.

There are two main categories of computer forensics tools: (1) evidence preservation and collection tools, which prevent the accidental or deliberate modification of computer-related evidence and create a logical or physical copy of the original evidence, and (2) recovery and analysis tools, which provide data recovery and discovery functions. A few commercially available computer forensic products incorporate features of both categories and claim to provide a complete suite of forensic tools.

How the technology works

Evidence Preservation and Collection Tools

Write protection and disk imaging software are used to preserve and copy computer evidence while preserving its integrity.

There are several techniques that are used by write protection software, which prevent or disable a user's attempts to modify data (or perform the "write" operation) on a computer's hard drive or other computer media. In one method, the write protection software attempts to gain exclusive access to the media through mechanisms specific to the operating system. If exclusive access can be gained, all other software applications will be prevented from accessing and modifying the locked media. Another method utilizes a separate software component that is installed as part of the operating system and is loaded when the operating system starts (and before any other application can execute).

Disk imaging is a process that attempts to copy every bit of data from one physical computer medium to another, similar medium. This type of duplication is known as a physical disk copy, and it involves copying all data, including files, file names, and data that are not associated with a file. Disk imaging tools may also perform varying degrees of integrity checking to verify that all data have been copied without error or alteration. The most common technique used to verify data integrity is a digital signature or a checksum algorithm.

Analysis Tools

These tools can recover deleted files by taking advantage of a common technique that is typically employed by commercial operating systems. When a user deletes a file from a computer medium (such as a floppy disk or hard drive), many operating systems do not destroy the data contained in the files. Instead, the space occupied by the deleted file is marked as available, or unallocated, so it can be reused as new files are created. The unallocated data contained in those deleted files may still remain on the medium. Analysis tools that recover unallocated data examine a specific structure and organization of information (called a file system) as it is stored on computer media. Because common operating systems maintain data in unique file systems that vary greatly, these analysis tools are typically designed for a specific file system.

Other analysis tools examine text files to identify the occurrence and frequency of specific words or patterns. They can generate a word index by creating a database of every word or delimited string that is contained within a single file, a collection of files, or an entire medium. They can also search multiple files or entire media for the occurrence of specified strings or words, as well as performing advanced searches using Boolean expressions.[104] Some tools have the capability to perform fuzzy logic searches, which search for derivatives of a word, related words, and misspelled words. For example, when searching for files containing the word "bomb", files that contain "bombed", "explosive", or "bommb" may also be considered as matches.

Other analysis tools identify files by their type or individual identity, a method that can reduce the volume of data that an investigator must analyze.

---

[104] In Boolean searches, an "and" operator between two words or other values (for example, "pear AND apple") means one is searching for documents containing both of the words or values, not just one of them. An "or" operator between two words or other values (for example, "pear OR apple") means one is searching for documents containing either of the words.

File type identification is based on a file signature—a unique sequence of values stored within a file that may be as short as 2 characters or longer than 12 characters. The longer the sequence, the greater the uniqueness of the signature and the less likely it is a file that will be mislabeled. Individual file identification is also signature-based, but the method calculates a signature over an entire file or data unit. One approach utilizes a representation that is both efficient in storage requirements and reliable in terms of its uniqueness, such as hashing algorithms.

Effectiveness of the technology

There are many different automated tools that are routinely used by law enforcement organizations to assist in the investigation of crimes involving computers. These tools are employed to generate critical evidence that is used in criminal cases. However, there are no standards or recognized tests by which to judge the validity of the results produced by these tools. Computer forensic tools must meet the same standards that are applied to all forensic sciences, including formal testable theories, peer-reviewed methodologies and tools, and replicable empirical research. Failing to apply standards may result in contaminating or losing critical evidence. It is important to obtain legal advice and consult with law enforcement officials before undertaking any forensic activities in situations where criminal or civil investigation or litigation is a potential outcome.

Configuration Management and Assurance

Configuration management and assurance technologies help security administrators to view and change the security settings on their hosts and networks, verify the correctness of the security settings, and maintain operations in a secure fashion under duress. Technologies that assist configuration management and assurance include policy enforcement tools, network management, continuity of operations tools, scanners for testing and auditing security, and patch management.

Policy enforcement tools help administrators define and ensure compliance with a set of security rules and configurations, such as a password policy, access to systems and files, and desktop and server configurations. Management and administration tools are used to maintain networks and systems. These tools incorporate functions that facilitate central monitoring of the security posture of networks and systems. Network management tools obtain status data from network components, make configuration changes, and alert network managers of problems.

To provide continuity of operations, there are secure backup tools that can restore system functionality and data in the event of a disruption. These products are used to account for naturally occurring problems, such as power outages, and are now also being applied to help address problems resulting from malicious cyber attacks. Tools are also available to help systems and networks to continue to perform during an ongoing attack.

Scanners are common testing and audit tools that are used to identify vulnerabilities in networks and systems. As part of proactive security testing, scanners are available that can be used to probe modems, Internet ports, databases, wireless access points, and Web pages and applications. These tools often incorporate the capability to monitor the security posture of the networks and systems by testing and auditing their security configurations.

Patch management tools help system administrators with the process of acquiring, testing, and applying fixes to operating systems and applications. Software vendors typically provide these fixes to correct known vulnerabilities in their software.

Policy Enforcement Applications

What the technology does

Policy enforcement technologies allow system administrators to perform centralized monitoring of compliance with an organization's security policies.[105] These tools examine desktop and server configurations that define authorized access to specified devices and compare these settings against a baseline policy. They typically provide multilevel reports on computer configurations, and some products have the capability to fix various identified problems. They also provide a centralized way for administrators to use other security technologies, such as access control and security event and correlation tools.

How the technology works

Policy enforcement tools generally have four main functions:

Policy definition. These tools have the functionality to help establish baseline policy settings. Policies can include features like minimum password requirements and user and group rights to specific applications. Some products include policy templates that can be customized and distributed to users for review and signatures.

Compliance checking. After a security policy has been defined, these tools can compare current system configurations with the baseline settings. Compliance can be monitored across multiple administrative domains and operating systems from a central management console. For example, compliance checking could include testing for a particular setting in multiple

[105] Policy is defined as a set of configurations and access controls that affect the overall security stance of a user, group, device, or application.

systems' configuration files, checking the audit configuration on a subset of computers, or checking that console passwords fit the policies of the organization (for example, using the correct length of characters in a password, using alphanumeric characters, and periodically changing passwords). The tools often allow customized checks to be defined.

Reporting. Basic reporting templates are generally included with these tools, such as templates for configurations, user accounts, access controls, and software patch levels. In addition, users can customize reports and create ad hoc queries for specific information on particular computers.

These reports can consolidate information, such as which users have not recently logged on to a system and which computers are running unpatched applications. The reports can be tailored differently for security personnel and management.

Remediation. Some policy enforcement tools allow problems that have been discovered to be proactively fixed. For example, if the latest security software patch has not been installed for a particular application, some tools automatically download patches from a vendor's Web site and either alert an administrator or install the patches directly onto the system.

Effectiveness of the technology

Policy enforcement software can provide for centralized monitoring, control, and enforcement. However, the software's effectiveness is largely governed by the security policies of the organization. These tools can only assist in monitoring and enforcing those policies that organizations choose to implement. As such, they can be only as good as the policies that the organization defines. In addition, some policy enforcement tools do not work on all operating systems, and installation and configuration can be arduous.

Network Management

What the technology does

Network management is the ability to control and monitor a computer network from a central location. Network management systems consist of software programs and dedicated computer hardware that view the entire network as a unified architecture in order to obtain status data from network components, make configuration changes, and alert network managers to problems. The International Organization for Standardization defines a conceptual model for describing the five key functional areas of network management (and the main functions of network management systems):

- **Fault management** identifies problems in nodes, the network, and the network's operation to determine their causes and to take remedial action.

- **Configuration management** monitors network configuration information so that the effects of specific hardware and software can be managed and tracked.
- **Accounting management** measures network utilization of individual users or groups to provide billing information, regulate users or groups, and help keep network performance at an acceptable level.
- **Performance management** measures various aspects of network performance, including gathering and analyzing statistical system data so that performance may be maintained at an acceptable level.
- **Security management** controls access to network resources by limiting access to network resources and providing notification of security breaches and attempts, so that information cannot be obtained without authorization.

How the technology works

A network management system typically consists of managed devices (the network hosts); software agents, which communicate information about the managed devices; a network management application, which gathers and processes information from agents; and a network management station, which allows an operator to view a graphical representation of the network, control managed devices on the network, and program the network management application. Figure 24 is an example of a typical network management architecture.

The network management station receives and processes events from network elements and acts as the main console for network operations. The network management station displays a graphical network map that highlights the operational states of critical network devices such as routers and switches. Each network device is represented by a graphical element on the management station's console, and different colors are used to represent the current operational status of network devices, based on status notifications sent by the devices. These notifications (usually called events) are placed in a log file.

The functionality of network management software (network management applications and agents) depends on the particular network management protocol that the software is based on. Most systems use open protocols. However, some network management software is based upon vendor-specific proprietary protocols. The two most common network management protocols are the Simple Network Management Protocol (SNMP) and Common Management Information Protocol (CMIP). SNMP is widely used in most LAN environments. CMIP is used in telecommunication environments, where networks tend to be large and complex.

Figure 24: Typical Network Management Architecture

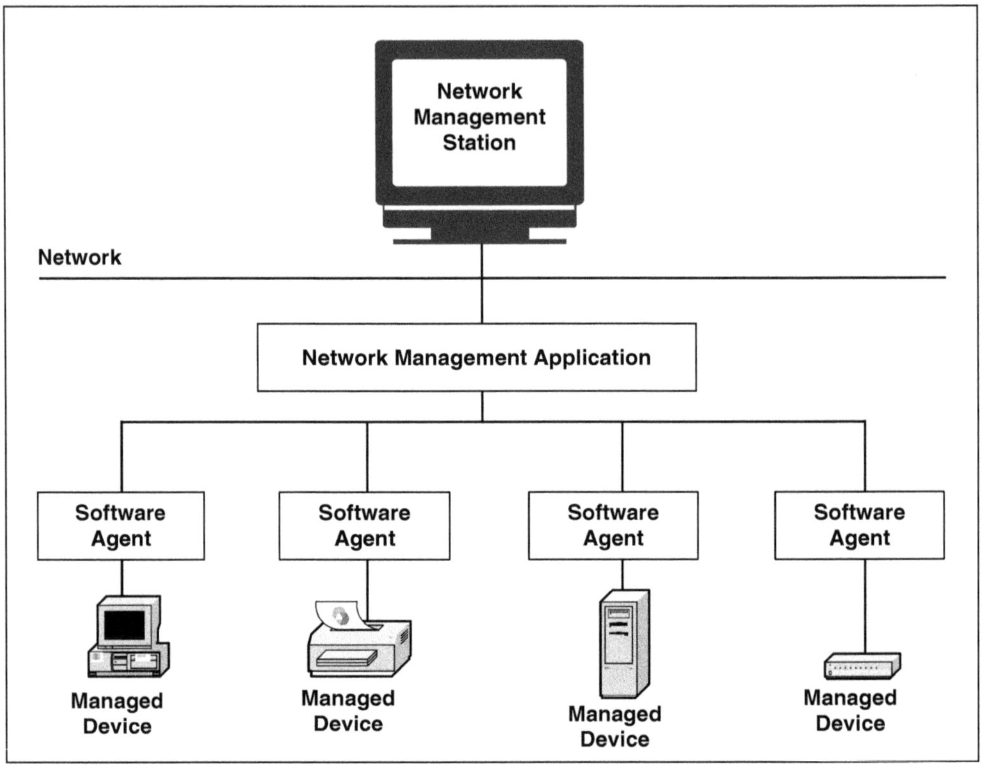

Source: Corel Draw and Microsoft Visio.

Effectiveness of the technology

Network management systems can be quite expensive and they are often complex. The complexity is primarily in the network management protocols and data structures that are associated with the network management information. Also, these systems require personnel with the specialized training to effectively configure, maintain and operate the network management system.

Many network management systems cannot support network devices that use vendor-specific protocols.

Continuity of Operations Tools

What the technology does

Continuity of operations tools provide a complete backup infrastructure to keep the enterprise's data resources online and available at multiple locations in case of an emergency or planned maintenance, such as system or software upgrading. They maintain operational continuity of the storage devices and host and database levels. Continuity-of-operations tools include *high-availability systems,* which link two or more computers together to provide continuous access to data through systems redundancy (known as clustering); *journaling file systems,* which maintain specific information about data to avoid file system errors and corruption; *load-balancing* technology, which distributes traffic efficiently among network servers so that no individual server is overburdened; and *Redundant Array of Independent Disk (RAID)* technology, which allows two or more hard drives to work in concert for increased fault tolerance[106] and performance.

How the technology works

High-availability systems use *clustering,* which refers to two or more servers set up in such a way that if an application running on one server fails then it can be automatically restarted or recovered on another server. This is referred to as fail over from one server or node in the cluster to another. High-availability systems utilize fail over operations to automatically switch to a standby database, server, or network if the primary system fails or is temporarily shut down for servicing. Some high-availability systems can also perform remote backups, remote mutual takeovers, concurrent access operations, and remote system recoveries. These functions are described below:

- In a *remote backup,* a remote geographic site is designated as the hot backup site that is live and ready to take over the current workload. This backup site includes hardware, system and application software, and application data and files. In the event of a failure, the failed site's application workload automatically moves to the remote hot backup site.
- In a *remote mutual takeover,* geographically separated system sites are to be designated as hot backups for each other. Should either site experience a failure, the other acts as a hot backup and automatically takes over the designated application workload of the failed site. Two different workloads running at two different sites are protected.
- In *concurrent access,* systems at both sites are concurrently updating the same database.
- In *remote system recovery,* data can be resynchronized and a failed system that has been restored to operation can be reintegrated with the remote hot backup. In a process known as file mirroring, the failed system is updated with current application data and files that were processed by the backup system after the failed system ceased operations.

[106] Fault tolerance is the ability of a system to respond gracefully to an unexpected hardware or software failure.

Upon completing restoration of an up-to-date data and file mirror, the high-availability system will resume synchronized system operations, including the mirroring of real-time data and files between the system sites. This can occur while the remote backup is in use.

A *journaling file system* ensures that the data on a disk has been restored to its pre-failure configuration. It also recovers unsaved data and stores them in their intended locations (had the computer not failed), making the journaling file system an important feature for mission-critical applications. A journaling file system transaction treats a sequence of changes as a single operation and tracks changes to file system metadata and user data. The transaction guarantees that either all or none of the file system updates are done.

For example, the process of creating a new file modifies several metadata values. Before the file system makes those changes, it creates a transaction to record the intended changes. Once the transaction has been recorded on disk, the file system modifies the metadata and the transaction is stored on the journaling file system. In the event of a system failure, the file system is restored to a consistent state by repeating the transactions listed in the journal. Rather than examining all metadata, the file system inspects only those portions of the metadata that have recently changed.

Load-balancing technology distributes processing and communications activity evenly across a computer network by transferring the tasks from heavily loaded processors to the lightly loaded ones. Load-balancing decisions are based on three policies: an information policy, which specifies the amount of load information made available; a transfer policy, which specifies the current workload of the host and the size of the job; and a placement policy, which specifies proper allocation of processes to the different computer processors.

RAID systems provide large amounts of storage by making the data on many smalls disks readily available to file servers, host computers, or the network as a single unit (known as an *array*). The design of the array of disks is an important determinant of performance and data availability in a RAID system. In addition to the array of multiple disks, RAID systems include a controller—an intelligent electronic device that routes, buffers and manages data flow between the host computer and the network array of disks. RAID controllers can organize data on the disks in several ways in order to optimize the performance and reliability of the system for different types of applications. RAID can also be implemented in software.

Effectiveness of the technology

The continuity-of-operations technologies can help an organization increase the availability of its mission-critical applications. Some of the technologies such as RAID and journaling file system increase the ability of a single server to survive a number of failures. For many businesses, the combination of RAID, journaling file system, and redundant power supply can provide adequate protection against disruptions.

Organizations that cannot tolerate an application outage of more than a few minutes may deploy a high-availability system that uses clustering. Clustering has a proven track record as a good solution for increasing application availability. However, clustering is expensive because it requires additional hardware and clustering software, and is more complex to manage than a single system.

Scanners

What the technology does

Scanners help identify a network's or a system's security vulnerabilities. There are a variety of scanning tools, including port scanners, vulnerability scanners, and modem scanners.[107]

Port scanners are used to map networks and identify the services running on each host by detecting open TCP and UDP ports. Vulnerability scanners are used to identify vulnerabilities on computer hosts and networks and make use of the results generated by a port scanner. The tools have reporting features to list the vulnerabilities they identified and may provide instructions on how to reduce or eliminate the vulnerability. Many scanners are now equipped to automatically fix selected vulnerabilities.

Modem scanners, also known as *war dialers*, are programs that identify phone numbers that can successfully make a connection with a computer modem. Unauthorized modems provide a means to bypass most or all of the security measures in place to stop unauthorized users from accessing a network—such as firewalls and intrusion detection systems.

How the technology works

Port scanners use methods known as *ping sweeps* and *port scans* to map networks and identify services in use. Ping sweeps are considered the most basic technique for scanning a network. A ping sweep determines which range of IP addresses map to computers that are turned on by sending communication requests (known as Internet Control Message Protocol (ICMP) ECHO requests) to multiple IP addresses. If a computer at a target address is turned on, it will return a specific ICMP ECHO reply. In port scanning, the scanner sends a message to a specific port on a target computer and waits for a response. The responses to a scan can allow the scanner to

[107] Other scanning tools include database scanners, Web application scanners, and wireless packet analyzers.

determine (1) which ports are open, and (2) the operating system the computer is running (certain port scans only work on certain operating systems). The type of message sent and the information the scanner receives can distinguish the various types of port scans.

Vulnerability scanners are software applications that can be used to identify vulnerabilities on computer hosts and networks. Host-based scanners must be installed on each host to be tested, and they typically require administrative-level access to operate. Network-based scanners operate on an organization's network and identify vulnerabilities on multiple computers. Whether host-based or network-based, vulnerability scanners automatically identify a host's operating system and active applications; they then compare these with the scanner's database of known vulnerabilities. Vulnerability scanners employ large databases of known vulnerabilities to identify vulnerabilities that are associated with commonly used operating systems and applications. When a match is found, the scanner will alert the operator to a possible vulnerability. Figure 25 shows a sample screen from a vulnerability scanner.

Figure 25: Example of a Vulnerability Scanner Screen

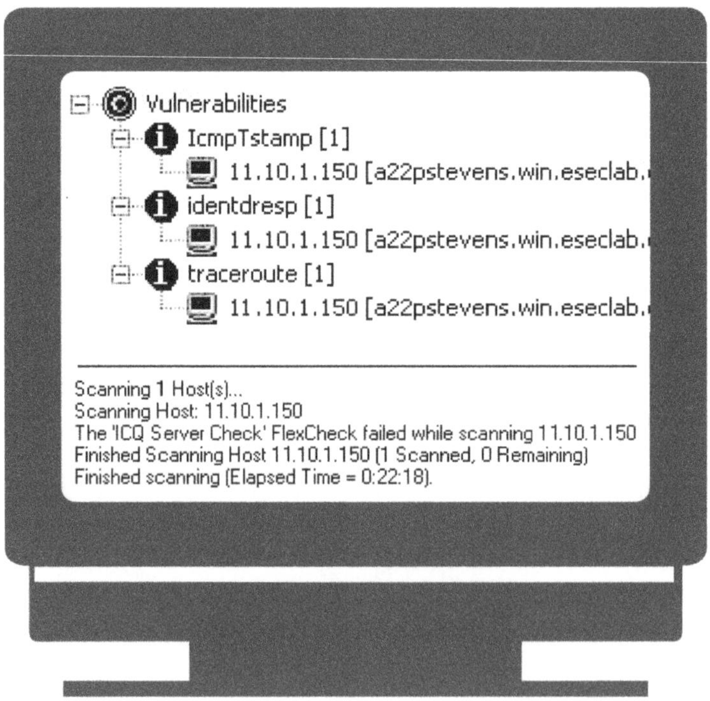

Sources: GAO and Corel Draw.

Modem scanners are software programs that automatically dial a defined range of phone numbers and track successful connections in a database. Some modem scanners can also identify the particular operating system running on the computer, and they may be configured to attempt to gain access to the system by running through a predetermined list of common user names and passwords.

Effectiveness of the technology

Port-scanning applications have the capability to scan a large number of hosts, but they do not directly identify known vulnerabilities. However, some vulnerability scanners can make use of a port scanner's output to target specific network hosts for vulnerability scanning. Vulnerability scanners can identify the vulnerabilities and suggest how to fix them, but they may not themselves have the capability to fix all identified vulnerabilities. They have been known to generate false positives (i.e., detecting a vulnerability that does not exist) and false negatives (i.e., not detecting a vulnerability that exists). While false positives are irrelevant warnings that can be ignored, false negatives can result in overlooking critical security vulnerabilities. Also, their effectiveness is linked to the quality of the database of known vulnerabilities; if the database is not up to date, vulnerability scanners might not identify newly discovered vulnerabilities.

Patch Management

What the technology does

Patch management tools automate the otherwise manual process of acquiring, testing, and applying patches to multiple computer systems.[108] These tools can either be stand-alone patch management products or the patch component of systems management products. Patch management tools are used to identify missing patches on each system, deploy patches to a single or multiple computers, and generate reports to track the status of a patch across a number of computers. Some tools offer customized features, including automated inventorying and immediate notification of new patches. While patch management tools primarily support the Windows operating system, they are expanding to support multiple platforms.

How the technology works

Patch management tools have various system requirements, such as specific applications, servers, and service pack levels, depending on the tool selected. Patch management tools can be either *scanner-based (nonagent)* or

---

[108] A patch is an upgrade designed to fix a serious flaw (that is, a vulnerability) in a piece of software and is typically developed and distributed as a replacement for or an insertion in compiled code.

agent-based. Agent-based tools place small programs, or agents, on each computer. The agents periodically poll a patch database—a server on a network—for new updates and apply the patches pushed out by the administrator. This architecture allows for either the client or the server to initiate communications, which means that individual computers can either query the patch database or allow the server to perform a scan to determine their configuration status. Some patch management vendors have contractual agreements with software vendors to receive pre-notification of vulnerabilities and related patches before they are publicly released. These patch management vendors test the patch before it is made available at a designated location (for example, a server), where they can be automatically downloaded for deployment. The agents will then install the patches for systems meeting the patch requirements.

Scanner-based tools scan the computers on a network according to provided criteria, such as domain or IP range, to determine their configurations. The server initiates communication with the client by logging in and querying each machine as a domain or local administrator. Patches are downloaded from the vendor's Web site and stored at a designated location to be installed to the target machine.

Most tools also have built-in knowledge repositories that compare the systems' established versions against lists that contain the latest vulnerabilities and notifications of fixes. They also have the capability to make recommendations on which patches to deploy on what machines. Additionally, these tools can analyze whether the relevant patch has been deployed to all affected systems. Many tools can also prioritize patch deployment and dependencies on each system. This capability can allow for logical groupings of target machines in order to streamline the patch installation process.

Effectiveness of the technology

While patch management tools can automate patch delivery, it is still necessary to determine if a particular patch is appropriate to apply. In addition, patches may need to be tested against the organization's specific systems configurations. The complexity of the organization's enterprise architecture determines the difficulty of this task. Also, some of these tools are not consistently accurate and will incorrectly report that a patch is missing when it was actually installed (that is, a false negative) or report that patches have been installed on unpatched systems (that is, a false positive). Furthermore, the automated distribution of patches may be a potential security exposure because patches are a potential entry point into an organization's infrastructure.

Agent-based products can reduce network traffic because the processing and analysis are offloaded to the target system and are not done on the network. In this kind of implementation, the work is performed at the client, which offloads the processing and analysis to the individual computers and saves the data until it needs to report to the central server.

Agent-based products, however, require more maintenance, deployment, and labor costs because of their distributed architecture. Additionally, the task of installing agents on each machine requires more work on the front-end. Agent-based tools are better suited for larger networks because they can typically provide a real-time network view.

Scanner-based tools are easier and faster to deploy and do not present distributive management concerns. However, they can significantly increase network traffic because tests and communications travel over the network whenever a scan is requested. Additionally, computers not connected to the network at the time scans are performed are not accounted for. As such, scanner-based tools are recommended for smaller, static networks.

Appendix IV: Comments from the Department of Homeland Security

U.S. Department of Homeland Security
Washington, DC 20528

Homeland Security

April 23, 2004

MEMORANDUM FOR: RICHARD HUNG
ASSISTANT DIRECTOR, CENTER FOR TECHNOLOGY AND ENGINEERING
GENERAL ACCOUNTING OFFICE

FROM: John P. Chase
Chief of Staff
Information Analysis and Infrastructure Protection Directorate
Department of Homeland Security

SUBJECT: Department of Homeland Security Response to the Draft GAO Technology Assessment (GAO-04-321) on Cybersecurity for Critical Infrastructure Protection

Thank you for the opportunity to comment on your draft report, *Technology Assessment: Cybersecurity for Critical Infrastructure Protection (GAO-04-321).* We concur with the purpose of the report and generally concur with its contents. We fully agree that the effective use of cybersecurity technologies is crucial to securing the nation's critical infrastructures. Your report effectively discusses many of the important issues in this area and will be of great value to those entrusted with protecting critical systems and networks.

We would like to offer some recommended changes which we believe will add value to your report. These changes, with supporting explanations, are contained in the attached spreadsheet. We recently developed this spreadsheet to facilitate our responses to GAO reports and recommendations. The empty column to the far right is available for GAO to respond to our comments if and when necessary. We hope you will find the spreadsheet makes it easier for you to process and correlate our responses.

We look forward to receiving your final report. If you or your staff have any questions or need additional information, please contact me or my GAO Liaison, John Daley, at 202-282-8381.

Attachment

www.dhs.gov

Appendix V: Comments from the National Science Foundation

NATIONAL SCIENCE FOUNDATION
4201 WILSON BOULEVARD
ARLINGTON, VIRGINIA 22230

April 12, 2004

OFFICE OF THE DIRECTOR

Mr. Richard Hung
Assistant Director
Center for Technology and Engineering
General Accounting Office
Washington, DC 20548

Dear Mr. Hung:

Thank you very much for providing NSF with the opportunity to comment on the GAO draft report entitled *Technology Assessment: Cybersecurity for Critical Infrastructure Protection* (GAO-04-321). This is an important and timely report that provides broad coverage of current and emerging cybersecurity and infrastructure technologies. As the report documents, NSF has been actively engaged in the intertwined issues of critical infrastructure protection and computing for several years and has stimulated multi-disciplinary research and education in cybersecurity through workshops and programs such as the Information Technology Research (ITR) program, the Scholarships for Service program and the Cyber Trust emphasis area.

The cybersecurity research issues raised in the report are very real. While there is certainly a need to reinforce the technology that is already deployed, simply finding and patching holes in the existing computing fabric may not suffice. NSF advocates research and education that will effectively and efficiently lead to the development and deployment of a secure and trustworthy computing-enabled civil infrastructure. There remain significant challenges in technology deployment and use that lead to security problems. While the report emphasizes mitigating these challenges through after-the-fact application of technology, improvements may also be made through the immediate implementation of relatively simple changes in current infrastructure. This can be accomplished through the widespread deployment of architectures already recognized to be more resistant to attack.

It should also be noted that new technology discoveries are likely to lead to changes in fundamental architectural and implementation strategies for civil infrastructure. These can be expected to present both new security problems and new opportunities for deeper integration of cybersecurity into operational infrastructures. Major information technology shifts, for example, to open systems, decentralization, ad hoc networking, X-by-wire, and dynamically configured infrastructures, are likely to change the nature of cybersecurity problems and will change requirements for future civil infrastructures. For this reason too, NSF emphasizes the critical ongoing role of long range research both for developing newly robust infrastructures and for achieving security as an inherent property of these infrastructures. The preparation of a diverse national workforce equipped to create, develop, configure, operate and evaluate such systems is a similarly critical endeavor.

Finally, NSF notes that an essential component in security is the establishment of credible deterrents. In the realm of cybersecurity, this might be accomplished via strong forensics and effective use in law enforcement. Research in cyberforensics, to provide tools and training to law enforcement professionals, and to adequately fund aggressive investigations and prosecutions of malicious activity, may reduce overall threat and serve as a deterrent to would-be attackers.

Again, NSF very much appreciates the opportunity to comment on the report.

Sincerely,

Arden Bement
Acting Director

Appendix VI: GAO Contacts and Acknowledgments

GAO Contacts

Keith Rhodes (202) 512-6412; rhodesk@gao.gov. Joel Willemssen (202) 512-6408; willemssenj@gao.gov. Robert Dacey (202) 512-3317; daceyr@gao.gov. Naba Barkakati (202) 512-4499; barkakatin@gao.gov.

Acknowledgments

Additional staff who made contributions to this report are Scott Borre, Lon Chin, Joanne Fiorino, Michael Gilmore, Richard Hung, Elizabeth Johnston, Christopher Kovach, Anjalique Lawrence, Stephanie Lee, Laura Nielsen, David Noone, Tracy Pierson, and Harold Podell.

We gratefully acknowledge the time and assistance of the following people who reviewed a draft of this report: Ken Birman, Cornell University; Earl Boebert, Sandia National Laboratories; Stephen Crocker, Shinkuro, Inc.; John Davis, Infosec Research Council; Lars Kjaer, World Shipping Council; Noel Matchett, Information Security Incorporated; and Dan Murray, American Transportation Research Institute. We also gratefully acknowledge the time and assistance provided by officials from the following infrastructure sectors: chemical, defense industrial base, energy, information technology, transportation, and water.

We also appreciate the contributions provided by the following organizations during our meeting on the use of cybersecurity technologies for critical infrastructure protection: American Transportation Research Institute; AT&T Labs Research; Bank of America; Carnegie Mellon University; Cornell University; Dartmouth College; Information Security Incorporated; Ivan Walks and Associates; Johns Hopkins Center for Civilian Biodefense Studies; RAND Corporation; Sandia National Laboratories; Shinkuro, Inc.; University of California at Davis; Washington State University; Wildman Harrold Allen and Dixon; and the World Shipping Council.

Bibliography

Institute for Information Infrastructure Protection. *Cyber Security Research and Development Agenda*. January, 2003.

International Organization for Standardization. *Information Technology—Code of Practice for Information Security Management*, ISO 17799, 2000.

International Organization for Standardization. *Information Technology—Security Techniques—Evaluation Criteria for IT Security—Part 1: Introduction and General Model*, ISO 15408-1, 1999.

International Organization for Standardization. *Information Technology—Security Techniques—Evaluation Criteria for IT Security—Part 2: Security Functional Requirements*, ISO 15408-2, 1999.

International Organization for Standardization. *Information Technology—Security Techniques—Evaluation Criteria for IT Security—Part 3: Security Assurance Requirements*, ISO 15408-3, 1999.

National Institute of Standards and Technology. *Guide to Selecting Information Technology Security Products*, NIST Special Publication 800-36. Gaithersburg, MD: October 2003.

National Institute of Standards and Technology. *Recommended Security Controls for Federal Information Systems*, NIST Special Publication 800-53, Initial Public Draft. Gaithersburg, MD: October 2003.

National Institute of Standards and Technology. *Risk Management Guide for Information Technology Systems*, NIST Special Publication 800-30. Gaithersburg, MD: October 2001.

National Institute of Standards and Technology. *Security Considerations in the Information System Development Life Cycle*, NIST Special Publication 800-64. Gaithersburg, MD: October 2003.

National Institute of Standards and Technology. *Security Metrics Guide for Information Technology Systems*, NIST Special Publication 800-55. Gaithersburg, MD: July 2003.

National Research Council. *Critical Information Infrastructure Protection and the Law: An Overview of Key Issues*. Washington, DC: National Academy Press, 2003.

National Research Council. *Cybersecurity of Freight Information Systems: A Scoping Study*. Washington, DC: National Academy Press, 2003.

National Research Council. *Innovation in Information Technology*. Washington, DC: National Academy Press, 2003.

National Research Council. *Trust in Cyberspace*. Washington, DC: National Academy Press, 1999.

U.S. General Accounting Office. *Combating Terrorism: Selected Challenges and Related Recommendations*. GAO-01-822. Washington, DC: September 20, 2001.

U.S. General Accounting Office. *Critical Infrastructure Protection: Challenges for Selected Agencies and Industry Sectors*. GAO-03-233. Washington, DC: February 28, 2003.

U.S. General Accounting Office. *Critical Infrastructure Protection: Challenges in Securing Control Systems*. GAO-04-140T. Washington, DC: October 1, 2003.

U.S. General Accounting Office. *Critical Infrastructure Protection: Efforts of the Financial Services Sector to Address Cyber Threats*. GAO-03-173. Washington, DC: January 30, 2003.

U.S. General Accounting Office. *Critical Infrastructure Protection: Establishing Effective Information Sharing with Infrastructure Sectors*. GAO-04-699T. Washington, DC: April 21, 2004.

U.S. General Accounting Office. *Critical Infrastructure Protection: Federal Efforts Require a More Coordinated and Comprehensive Approach for Protecting Information Systems.* GAO-02-474. Washington, DC: July 15, 2002.

U.S. General Accounting Office. *High Risk Series: Protecting Information Systems Supporting the Federal Government and the Nation's Critical Infrastructures.* GAO-03-121. Washington, DC: January 2003.

U.S. General Accounting Office. *Information Security: Challenges in Using Biometrics.* GAO-03-1137T. Washington, DC: September 9, 2003.

U.S. General Accounting Office. *Information Security: Code Red, Code Red II, and SirCam Attacks Highlight Need for Proactive Measures.* GAO-01-1073T. Washington, DC: August 29, 2001.

U.S. General Accounting Office. *Information Security: Effective Patch Management is Critical to Mitigating Software Vulnerabilities.* GAO-03-1138T. Washington, DC: September 10, 2003.

U.S. General Accounting Office. *Information Security: Progress Made, But Challenges Remain to Protect Federal Systems and the Nation's Critical Infrastructures.* GAO-03-564T. Washington, DC: April 8, 2003.

U.S. General Accounting Office. *Information Security: Serious Weaknesses Place Critical Federal Operations and Assets at Risk.* GAO/AIMD-98-92. Washington, DC: September 23, 1998.

U.S. General Accounting Office. *Information Security: Technologies to Secure Federal Systems.* GAO-04-467. Washington, DC: March 9, 2004.

U.S. General Accounting Office. *Information Security: Weaknesses Place Commerce Data and Operations at Serious Risk.* GAO-01-751. Washington, DC: August 13, 2001.

U.S. General Accounting Office. *Information Sharing: Practices That Can Benefit Critical Infrastructure Protection.* GAO-02-24. Washington, DC: October 15, 2001.

U.S. General Accounting Office. *National Preparedness: Technologies to Secure Federal Buildings.* GAO-02-687T. Washington, DC: April 25, 2002.

U.S. General Accounting Office. *Technology Assessment: Using Biometrics for Border Security.* GAO-03-174. Washington, DC: November 15, 2002.

The White House. *The National Strategy for the Physical Protection of Critical Infrastructures and Key Assets.* Washington, DC: February 2003.

The White House. *The National Strategy to Secure Cyberspace.* Washington, DC: February 2003.

The White House Office of Homeland Security. *National Strategy for Homeland Security.* Washington, DC: July 2002.

GAO's Mission

The General Accounting Office, the audit, evaluation and investigative arm of Congress, exists to support Congress in meeting its constitutional responsibilities and to help improve the performance and accountability of the federal government for the American people. GAO examines the use of public funds; evaluates federal programs and policies; and provides analyses, recommendations, and other assistance to help Congress make informed oversight, policy, and funding decisions. GAO's commitment to good government is reflected in its core values of accountability, integrity, and reliability.

Obtaining Copies of GAO Reports and Testimony

The fastest and easiest way to obtain copies of GAO documents at no cost is through the Internet. GAO's Web site (www.gao.gov) contains abstracts and full-text files of current reports and testimony and an expanding archive of older products. The Web site features a search engine to help you locate documents using key words and phrases. You can print these documents in their entirety, including charts and other graphics.

Each day, GAO issues a list of newly released reports, testimony, and correspondence. GAO posts this list, known as "Today's Reports," on its Web site daily. The list contains links to the full-text document files. To have GAO e-mail this list to you every afternoon, go to www.gao.gov and select "Subscribe to e-mail alerts" under the "Order GAO Products" heading.

Order by Mail or Phone

The first copy of each printed report is free. Additional copies are $2 each. A check or money order should be made out to the Superintendent of Documents. GAO also accepts VISA and Mastercard. Orders for 100 or more copies mailed to a single address are discounted 25 percent. Orders should be sent to:

U.S. General Accounting Office
441 G Street NW, Room LM
Washington, D.C. 20548

To order by Phone: Voice: (202) 512-6000
TDD: (202) 512-2537
Fax: (202) 512-6061

To Report Fraud, Waste, and Abuse in Federal Programs

Contact:

Web site: www.gao.gov/fraudnet/fraudnet.htm
E-mail: fraudnet@gao.gov
Automated answering system: (800) 424-5454 or (202) 512-7470

Public Affairs

Jeff Nelligan, Managing Director, NelliganJ@gao.gov (202) 512-4800
U.S. General Accounting Office, 441 G Street NW, Room 7149
Washington, D.C. 20548

DOCUMENT NO. 3

DATA SECURITY BREACHES: CONTEXT AND INCIDENT SUMMARIES

CRS Report
RL33199

September 28, 2006

Rita Tehan
Information Research Specialist
Knowledge Services Group

Summary

Personal data security breaches are being reported with increasing regularity. Within the last few years, numerous examples of data such as Social Security numbers, bank account, credit card, driver's license numbers, and medical and student records have been compromised. A major reason for the increased awareness of these security breaches is a California law that requires notice of security breaches to the affected individuals. This law, implemented in July 2003, was the first of its kind in the nation.

State security breach notification laws require companies and other entities that have lost data to notify affected consumers. Over half the states considered security breach notice and security freeze legislation in 2005, and several states passed laws requiring that individuals be notified of security breaches.

Congress is considering legislation to address personal data security breaches, following a series of high-profile data security breaches at major financial services firms, data brokers (including ChoicePoint and LexisNexis), and universities. Multiple measures were introduced in 2005 and 2006, but to date, none have been enacted.

For a discussion of legislative and other issues on this topic, see

- CRS Report RS22374, *Data Security: Federal and State Laws*, by Gina Marie Stevens

- CRS Report RL33273, *Data Security: Federal Legislative Approaches*, by Gina Marie Stevens
- CRS Report RS22484, *Identity Theft Laws: State Penalties and Remedies and Pending Federal Bills*, by Kristin Thornblad
- CRS Report RL31408, *Internet Privacy: Overview and Pending* Legislation in the 109th Congress, 1st Session, by Marcia S. Smith;
- CRS Report RL33005, *Information Brokers: Federal and State Laws*, by Angie A. Welborn;
- and CRS Report RS22082, Identity *Theft: The Internet Connection*, by Marcia S. Smith.

This report will be updated regularly.

Introduction

Personal data security breaches are being reported with increasing regularity. During the past few years, there have been numerous examples of hackers breaking into corporate, government, academic, and personal computers and compromising computer systems or stealing personal data such as Social Security numbers, bank account, credit card, and driver's license numbers, and medical and student records. These breaches occur not only because of illegal or fraudulent attacks by computer hackers, but often because of careless business practices, such as lost or stolen laptops, or the inadvertent posting of personal data on public websites. A recent infamous example occurred in May 2006, when 26.5 million veterans and their spouses were in danger of identity theft because a Veterans Affairs data analyst took home a laptop containing personal data (including names, Social Security numbers, and dates of birth), which was later stolen in a burglary. For additional information on legislative proposals introduced after the VA data theft (and in light of several ongoing information security and information technology management issues at the VA), see CRS Report RL33612, *Department of Veterans Affairs: Information Security and Information Technology Management Reorganization*, by Sidath Viranga Panangala.

A California law that requires notice of security breaches to the affected individuals is the major reason for the increased awareness of these breaches.[1] This law, which was implemented in July 2003, was the first of its kind in the nation.

---

[1] California Department of Consumer Affairs, Office of Privacy Protection, *Notice of Security Breach - Civil Code Sections 1798.29 and 1798.82–1798.84*, updated June 24, 2003, at [http://www.leginfo.ca.gov/cgi-bin/displaycode?section=civ&group=01001-02000&file=1798.25-1798.29], and [http://www.leginfo.ca.gov/cgi-bin/displaycode?section=civ&group=01001-02000&file=1798.80-1798.84] and *Recommended Practices on Notification of Security Breach Involving Personal Information*, Oct. 10, 2003, at [http://www.privacy.ca.gov/recommendations/secbreach.pdf].

State security breach notification laws[2] require companies and other entities that have lost personal data to notify affected consumers. Over half the states considered security breach notice and security freeze[3] legislation in 2005, and several states passed laws requiring that individuals be notified of security breaches.[4]

An estimated 10 million consumers are affected annually by lost or stolen data at a cost to the economy of $53 billion.[5] Moreover, victims spend almost 300 million hours a year trying to clear their names and re-establish good credit ratings.[6] For additional information on this, see CRS Report RL31919, *Remedies Available to Victims of Identity Theft*, by Angie Welborn.

Despite the growing fear of data security breaches, a new study suggests that consumers whose credit cards are lost or stolen or whose personal information is accidentally compromised face little risk of becoming victims of identity theft.[7] After six months of study, an analysis by ID Analytics, a fraud-detection company, found that different breaches pose different degrees of risk. In the research, ID Analytics distinguishes between "identity-level" breaches, where names and Social Security numbers are stolen and "account-level" breaches, where only account numbers—sometimes associated with names—are stolen. The report concludes that even in the most dangerous data breaches, where thieves access Social Security numbers and other sensitive information about consumers they have deliberately targeted, the fraud rate is 0.098%—less than one in 1,000 identities are potentially revealed.[8]

> While initially surprising, the seemingly low misuse rate recognizes a fundamental truth about identity fraud. It is the fraud ring's available resources

---

[2] See also *2005 Breach of Information Legislation*, National Conference of State Legislatures at [http://www.ncsl.org/programs/lis/CIP/priv/breach.htm].

[3] A security freeze law allows a customer to block unauthorized third parties from obtaining his or her credit report or score. A consumer who places a security freeze on his or her credit report or score receives a personal identification number to gain access to credit information or to authorize the dissemination of credit information. Source: CRS Report RS22484, *Identity Theft Laws: State Penalties and Remedies and Pending Federal Bills.*

[4] In 2005, security breach notification legislation was introduced in at least 35 states. At least 22 states have enacted security breach notification laws, and a similar bill awaits gubernatorial action in New Jersey. Security breach notification laws have been enacted in the following states: AK, CA, CT, DE, FL, GA (data brokers only), IL, IN (state agencies only), LA, ME, MN, MT, NV, NJ, NY, NC, ND, OH, RI, TN, TX, WA. *State PIRG Summary of State Security Freeze and Security Breach Notification Laws*, U.S. Public Interest Research Group (USPIRG) at [http://www.pirg.org/consumer/credit/statelaws.htm#breach]. See CRS Report RS22374, *Data Security: Federal and State Laws*, by Gina Marie Stevens.

[5] Federal Trade Commission, *Identity Theft Survey Report*, Sept. 2003, at [http://www.consumer.gov/idtheft/pdf/synovate_report.pdf].

[6] Peter Katel, "Identity Theft: Can Congress Give Americans Better Protection?," *CQ Researcher*, June 10, 2005.

[7] Reuters, "ID Theft Risk Lower in Large-Scale Security Breaches," Computerworld, Dec. 8, 2005, at [http://www.computerworld.com/printthis/2005/0,4814,106854,00.html].

[8] ID Analytics, "ID Analytics' First-Ever National Data Breach Analysis Shows the Rate of Misuse of Breached Identities May be Lower than Anticipated," press release, Dec. 8, 2005, at [http://www.idanalytics.com/news_and_events/20051208.htm].

> that determine how much attempted misuse follows a targeted, identity-level data breach. Fraud rings simply do not have the time or manpower to use hundreds of thousands of identities available to them in their nefarious pursuits. Think about this practically. If a fraudster spent five minutes to fill out a new account application that is likely to be approved, one application per unique identity, worked 6.5 hours per day, it would take that individual over 50 years to utilize a breached file of one million consumer identities. This scenario overlooks other practicalities, such as procuring the applications and the need to launder the proceeds over time. The misuse rate could increase drastically if the current black market for "identities" remains unimpeded and becomes more centralized and efficient.[9]

Crimes involving electronic data can be very labor intensive for the criminal. Account information may be stolen in bulk with a few efficient lines of software code, but it is sold in much smaller numbers to other criminals who withdraw money or buy goods one transaction at a time, and usually only for a short period until the fraudulent activity is detected.[10]

More than three-quarters of companies recently surveyed by Deloitte Touche Tohmatsu said they have suffered a security breach from the outside, up sharply from the 26% that said they have suffered one when polled in 2005. But even for companies, it is difficult to find specific examples where hacking (or other type of breaches, such as lost or stolen laptops or computers, or inadvertent posting of personal data to public websites) resulted in substantial financial losses. Businesses cite high costs associated with replacement of credit/debit cards, remediation outreach programs to notify people of security breaches, and efforts to protect against lawsuits by security breach victims. "Theft of information is out of control, but use of that information to commit fraud is not out of control," says Avivah Litan, senior analyst at Gartner Inc., a technology research firm. The truth is, in the great majority of cases involving consumers, criminals don't have enough data with which to commit a crime."[11]

In addition, an August 2006 study by the Elk Rapids, MI-based privacy management research company Ponemon Institute finds that only 37% of information technology professionals believe their company is effective at preventing data breaches.[12] Citing a lack of resources and high product costs as barriers to preventing data leakages, only 43% believed their

[9] ID Analytics, "National Data Breach Analysis: Frequently Asked Questions," 2006 at [http://www.idanalytics.com/pdf/National_DataBreach_FAQ.pdf]

[10] Henry Fountain, "Worry. But Don't Stress Out," *New York Times*, June 26, 2005, sec. 4, p. 1.

[11] Dean Foust, "ID Theft: More Hype than Harm," *Business Week Online*, July 3, 2006, at [http://www.businessweek.com/magazine/content/06_27/b3991041.htm].

[12] Deborah Rothberg, "IT Pros Say They Can't Stop Data Breaches," eWeek, August 30, 2006 at [http://www.eweek.com/article2/0,1759,2010325,00.asp?kc=EWRSS03129TX1K0000614].

company would detect a large data breach (involving more than 10,000 customer records) more than 80% of the time.[13]

Moreover, according to a June 2005 survey by Gartner, Inc., nearly 60% of consumers say they worry more about thieves getting undetected access to private credit reports and other sensitive financial data than defending against phishing attacks.[14] Nearly one-third are "extremely concerned" that they will suffer some type of identity theft fraud because of unauthorized access to their data.[15]

A fraud specialist with Gartner, Inc., concludes that because the crime is often misclassified, identity thieves have a one out of 700 chance of being caught.[16] In other words, the risk to benefit ratio favors the criminal. "It's a crime in which you can get a lot of money and have a very low probability of ever getting caught," Mari J. Frank, a lawyer and author of several books on identity theft, said in a *New York Times* interview. "Criminals are now saying, Why am I using a gun?"[17]

The Identity Theft and Assumption Deterrence Act of 1998 established the Federal Trade Commission (FTC) as the government entity charged with developing "procedures to . . . log and acknowledge the receipt of complaints by individuals," as well as educate and assist potential victims.[18,19] The FTC compiles annual reports and charts of aggregated statistics on these events, but does not identify which corporations, organizations, or other entities have been victims of security breaches.[20] The FTC is also an enforcement agency and does not release data on companies while an investigation is ongoing. At the completion of the investigation, when there is an enforcement action, the FTC then releases information identifying corporations, organization, or others who have violated data security laws.

---

13 Sponsored by Port Authority Technologies, independently conducted by Ponemon Institute, National Survey on the Detection and Prevention of Data Security Breaches, August 28, 2006, at [http://www.portauthoritytech.com/resources/downloads/wp_Ponemon_Institute_Study.pdf]

14 Phishing is e-mail fraud where the perpetrator sends out legitimate-looking e-mails that appear to come from well-known and trustworthy websites in an attempt to gather personal and financial information from the recipient.

15 "Data Security Lapses, Increased Cyber Attacks Damage Consumer Trust in E-Commerce," *Government Technology*, June 27, 2005, at [http://www.govtech.net/magazine/channel_story.php/94447].

16 Avivah Litan, "Underreporting of Identity Theft Rewards the Thieves," Gartner, Inc., July 7, 2003.

17 Tom Zeller, "For Victims, Repairing ID Theft Can be Grueling," *New York Times*, Oct. 1, 2005.

18 Identity Theft and Assumption Deterrence Act, as amended by P.L. 105-318, 112 Stat. 3007 (Oct. 30, 1998), at [http://www.ftc.gov/os/statutes/itada/itadact.htm].

19 For an overview of the federal laws that could assist victims of identity theft with purging inaccurate information from their credit records and removing unauthorized charges from credit accounts, as well as federal laws that impose criminal penalties on those who assume another person's identity through the use of fraudulent identification documents, see CRS Report RL31919, *Remedies Available to Victims of Identity Theft*, by Angie Welborn. (Relevant state laws are also discussed.)

20 Federal Trade Commission, *ID Theft Data: State Data* website at [http://www.consumer.gov/idtheft/id_state.htm]. *National Data* is available at [http://www.consumer.gov/idtheft/id_federal.htm].

Although a number of federal agencies (e.g., the Federal Trade Commission, Department of Justice, Secret Service, U.S. Postal Service, and Social Security Administration), state attorneys general, and private organizations such as the Electronic Privacy Information Center are involved with data privacy investigations or related consumer assistance, none maintains a comprehensive itemized list of data security breaches.[21] However, the Privacy Rights Clearinghouse maintains a frequently-updated chronology of data breaches from February 2005 to the present.[22]

A number of data security breaches by federal agencies in recent months revealed many agencies do not have security controls in place (see **Table 3**: *Data Security Breaches in State and Federal Government*, below).[23] In the first half of 2006, the list of agencies with incidents of potentially compromised data include the Departments of Agriculture, Defense, Energy, Veterans Affairs, Transportation, the Federal Trade Commission, the Internal Revenue Service, the Government Accountability Office, the National Institutes of Health, and the Department of the Navy. The State Department also suffered a series of hacking attacks. In fiscal 2005, major federal agencies reported about 3,600 incidents that were serious enough to warrant alerting the government's cybersecurity center at the Department of Homeland Security, including 304 instances of unauthorized access and 1,806 cases of malicious computer code, according to a yearly OMB report.[24]

> [E]xperts say the federal government faces special challenges because of the variety of sensitive information it keeps, the increasingly mobile nature of the federal workforce and the pervasive use of contractors, which allow thousands of individuals with varying levels of security clearance to access government databases from remote sites. A 2004 government survey on the work practices of 1.8 million federal workers found that more than 140,000 had clearance to connect with government computer systems from home. The IRS says 50,000 of its employees have laptops allowing them to access personal and business tax information from anywhere. And 133 Education Department personnel can access more than 10,000 records containing student loan recipients' personal information.[25]

---

21 For a brief discussion of federal and state data security laws, see CRS Report RS22374, *Data Security: Federal and State Laws*, by Gina Marie Stevens.

22 Privacy Rights Clearinghouse, *A Chronology of Data Breaches* at [http://www.privacyrights.org/ar/ChronDataBreaches.htm]. The chronology "begins with ChoicePoint's 2/15/05 announcement of its data breaches because it was a watershed event in terms of disclosure to the affected individuals."

23 Rebecca Adams, "Data Drip: How the Feds Handle Personal Data," *CQ Weekly*, July 10, 2006, p. 1846.

24 Office of Management and Budget, *FY 2005 Report to Congress on Implementation of The Federal Information Security Management Act of 2002*, March 1, 2006, at [http://www.whitehouse.gov/omb/inforeg/reports/2005_fisma_report_to_congress.pdf].

25 Zachary Goldfarb, "To Agency Insiders, Cyber Thefts And Slow Response Are No Surprise," *Washington Post*, July 18, 2006, at [http://www.washingtonpost.com/wp-dyn/content/article/2006/07/17/AR2006071701170.html].

The United States Computer Emergency Readiness Team (US-CERT) has recently begun monitoring trends involving the acquisition of personally identifiable information (PII) by unauthorized, malicious users.[26]

On September 19, 2006, the President's Identity Theft Task Force adopted interim recommendations on measures that can be implemented immediately to help address the problem of identity theft. In a September 20, 2006 memo to federal department and agency heads[27], the Office of Management and Budget (OMB) outlined steps agencies should take in responding to an identity theft or ways to prevent one from happening. Clay Johnson, the Office of Management and Budget's deputy director for management, made it clear the administration supports the task force's recommendation that departments establish a "core management group responsible for responding to the loss of personal information . . ."[28]

The Identity Theft Task Force, which was established by Executive Order of the President on May 10, 2006[29], and is now comprised of 17 federal agencies and departments, is scheduled to deliver a final strategic plan to the President in November, 2006. The Identity Theft Task Force's interim recommendations to the Administration include the following:

- Data breach guidance to agencies
- Development of universal police report for identity theft victims
- Extending restitution for victims of identity theft
- Reducing access of identity thieves to Social Security Numbers
- Developing alternative methods of authenticating identities
- Improving data security in the government
- Improving agencies' ability to respond to data breaches in the government.[30]

In June, 2006, the Office of Management and Budget issued new security guidelines requiring federal civilian agencies to implement new measures to protect the security of personal information held by federal agencies.[31]

[26] US-CERT, *Quarterly Trends and Analysis Report*, September 1, 2006, at [http://www.us-cert.gov/press_room/trendsandanalysisQ306.pdf]. This report summarizes and provides analysis of incident reports submitted to US-CERT during the third quarter of FY2006 (April 1, 2006 to June 30th, 2006).

[27] Office of Management and Budget Memorandum for the Heads of Departments and Agencies, *Recommendations for Identity Theft Related Data Breach Notification*, September 20, 2006, at [http://www.whitehouse.gov/omb/memoranda/fy2006/task_force_theft_memo.pdf]

[28] Jason Miller, "OMB Issues Data Breach Guidance," Government Computer News, September 22, 2006, at [http://www.gcn.com/online/vol1_no1/42106-1.html].

[29] Executive Order 13402: *Strengthening Federal Efforts to Protect Against Identity Theft*, May 10, 2006, at [http://www.whitehouse.gov/news/releases/2006/05/20060510-3.html].

[30] U.S. Department of Justice press release, *Identity Theft Task Force Announces Interim Recommendations*, September 19, 2006, at [http://www.usdoj.gov/opa/pr/2006/September/06_ag_635.html].

[31] Office of Management and Budget Memorandum for the Heads of Departments and Agencies, *Protection of Sensitive Agency Information*, June 23, 2006, at [http://www.whitehouse.gov/OMB/memoranda/fy2006/m06-16.pdf].

To comply with the new policy, agencies will have to encrypt all data on laptop or handheld computers unless the data are classified as "non-sensitive" by an agency's deputy director. Agency employees also would need two-factor authentication—a password plus a physical device such as a key card—to reach a work database through a remote connection, which must be automatically severed after 30 minutes of inactivity.[32]

In June 2006, a group of government agencies, corporations, and universities launched a research center dedicated to the study of identity fraud. The Center for Identity Management and Information Protection is dedicated to furthering a national research agenda on identity management, information sharing, and data protection.[33]

Congress is considering legislation to address data security, following a series of high-profile data security breaches at major financial services firms and data brokers, including ChoicePoint and LexisNexis. Multiple measures were introduced in 2005 and 2006, and several have been reported out of committee, but to date, none have been brought to the floor.

For a discussion of legislative and other issues on this topic, see

- CRS Report RS22374, *Data Security: Federal and State Laws*, by Gina Marie Stevens
- CRS Report RL33273, *Data Security: Federal Legislative Approaches*, by Gina Marie Stevens
- CRS Report RS22484, *Identity Theft Laws: State Penalties and Remedies and Pending Federal Bills*, by Kristin Thornblad
- CRS Report RL31408, *Internet Privacy: Overview and Pending Legislation in the 109th Congress, 1st Session*, by Marcia S. Smith;
- CRS Report RL33005, *Information Brokers: Federal and State Laws*, by Angie A. Welborn;
- and CRS Report RS22082, *Identity Theft: The Internet Connection*, by Marcia S. Smith.

Tables 1–5 summarize selected data security or identity theft breaches reported in the press since 2000. A few highlights compiled from the reported incidents:

- Almost half of the security breaches occurred at institutions of higher education. (A *Chronicle of Higher Education* article examines why this is

[32] Brian Krebs, "OMB Sets Guidelines for Federal Employee Laptop Security," *Washington Post*, June 27, 2006, at [http://www.washingtonpost.com/wp-dyn/content/article/2006/06/27/AR2006062700540.html]

[33] Center for Identity Management and Information Protection, at [http://www.utica.edu/academic/institutes/cimip/]

so, noting that while colleges have become better at detecting electronic break-ins, security practices, particularly password protections, are lax.[34] In addition, academic culture embraces the open exchange of information and provides a target-rich environment for data breaches—an abundance of computer equipment filled with sensitive data and a pool of financially naive students.[35]). In September 2006, Louisiana State University (LSU), under a year-long agreement with Equifax Inc., will provide students, faculty and staff members with free daily monitoring of their credit reports and $2,500 in identity-theft insurance. LSU claims this is the first agreement of its kind between a credit agency and a higher-education institution. The university will pay Equifax, Inc. $150,000.[36];

- Other prevalent targets for identity theft are financial institutions (banks, credit card companies, securities companies, etc.), and government agencies (international, federal, state, and local); and
- The AARP analyzed 244 publicly disclosed security breaches from January 1, 2005 through May 26, 2006, identified by the Identity Theft Resource Center (ITRC).[37] An examination of the most frequent cause of reported security breaches reveals that a third (33%) of all breaches were caused by hackers who broke into computer systems to gain access to sensitive personal information. The analysis finds that educational institutions are more likely than any other type of entity to report having had a security breach. In fact, educational institutions were more than twice as likely to report suffering a breach as any other type of entity. Physical theft of computers, computer equipment, or paper files is the next most common cause of security breaches, followed by improper display.

[34] Dan Carnevale, "Why Can't Colleges Hold On to Their Data?," *Chronicle of Higher Education*, May 6, 2005, p. A35.

[35] Reuters, "U.S. Colleges Struggle to Combat Identity Theft," eWeek, Aug. 17, 2005, at [http://www.findarticles.com/p/articles/mi_zdewk/is_200508/ai_n14906864].

[36] Andrea L. Foster, "Louisiana State U. Signs Deal to Protect Students and Employees in Case of Data Breach," *Chronicle of Higher Education*, September 13, 2006, at [http://chronicle.com/daily/2006/09/2006091301t.htm].

[37] AARP, "Into the Breach: Security Breaches and Identity Theft," July 2006, at [http://www.aarp.org/research/frauds-scams/fraud/dd142_security_breach.html].

Table 1. Data Security Breaches in Businesses (2000–2006)

Business Incidents	Date Publicized	Who Was Affected	Number Affected	Type of Data Released/ Compromised	Source(s)
Linden Labs (creator of Second Life virtual community)	September 2006	members of interactive virtual community	650,000	names, addresses, encrypted passwords, payment information	"Second Life' Suffers Real-world Breach," CNET.com, September 10, 2006, at [http://news.com.com/2100 7349_3-6114046.html]
Hospital Corporation of America (HCA)—stolen computers	August 2006	records from 1996 to 2006 for patients who had received treatment at hospitals managed by HCA in eight states (Colorado, Kansas, Louisiana, Mississippi, Oklahoma, Oregon, Texas and Washington)	unknown	billing records (details unknown)	Ferguson, Scott, "FBI Investigating Theft of 10 Hospital Computers," eWeek, August 21, 2006 at [http://www.eweek.com/print_article2/0,1217,a=186560,00.asp]
AT&T—hackers broke into computer system	August 2006	customers who purchased DSL equipment from AT&T online store	19,000	credit card data	*Associated Press*, "Hackers Gain Data on AT&T Shoppers," *New YorkTimes.com*, August 30, 2006.
Automated Data Processing (ADP) (Roseland, NJ)—"an unauthorized party impersonated officers" to obtain information on investors	July 2006	individual investors with 60 companies including Fidelity, UBS, Morgan Stanley, Bear Stearns, Citigroup, Merrill Lynch	hundreds of thousands	names, addresses, number of shares held of investors	Spangler, Todd, "ADP Duped into Disclosing Data,"BaselineMag.com, July 10, 2006, at [http://www.baselinemag.com/article2/0, 1540, 1986655,00.asp].
Kaiser HMO—stolen laptop	July 2006	HMO subscribers to Kaiser health plan	160,000	names, phone numbers, Kaiser numbers	Singel, Ryan, "Kaiser Joins Lost Laptop Crowd," *InfoSecurity*, July 30, 2006, at [http://infosecurity.us/mambo//content/view/90/49/]
C.S. Stars (insurance contractor)—lost computer containing workers' records	July 2006	injured New York state workers (claiming compensation funds)	540,000	SSNs, names, addresses	Hines, Matt, "Insurance Company Loses 540,000 N.Y Employee Records," eWeek, July 26, 2006, at [http://www.eweek.com/article2/0,1895,1994416,00.asp]

Business Incidents	Date Publicized	Who Was Affected	Number Affected	Type of Data Released/ Compromised	Source(s)
National Association of Securities Dealers (NASD)-(Boca Raton, FL)—10 stolen laptops	July 2006	securities dealers who were the subject of investigations involving possible misconduct.	73	SSNs of securities dealers, plus inactive account numbers of about 1,000 consumers	Jamieson, Dan, "Rule Likely on Notification of Data Breaches, Some Say; Theft of NASD Laptops Raises Questions about Regulators' security," *Investment News*, July 10, 2006, p. 2.
American Red Cross, Farmers Branch (Dallas, TX)—3 stolen laptops	July 2006	regional blood donors	8,000	names, SSNs, birth dates, medical information	Schreier, Laura, "Donor Data Stolen at Local Red Cross Exclusive: 3 Laptops from Farmers Branch Office Held Encrypted Records," *Dallas Morning News*, July 1, 2006, p. 1A.
Bisys Group Inc.(Roseland, NJ)—employee's truck carrying backup tapes was stolen	July 2006	hedge fund donors	61,000	SSNs of 35,000 individuals	Clair, Chris, "Bisys Discloses Data Theft," *HedgeWorld Daily News*, July 6, 2006 (no page given).
American International Group (AIG)—burglary of a file server	June 2006	employees of various companies whose insurance information was submitted to AIG	970,000	names, addresses, SSNs, medical information	Smith, Elliot Blair, "AIG: Personal Data on 970,000 Lost in Burglary; Insurer Has Yet to Alert Those Affected by March 31 Break-in," *USA Today*, June 19, 2006, p. 5B.
Ernst & Young— stolen laptop	June 2006	Hotels.com customers	243,000	names, credit card numbers	Reilly, David, "Hotels.com Credit-Card Data Lost in Stolen Laptop Computer," *Wall Street Journal*, June 2, 2006, p. A14.
Union Pacific— stolen laptop	June 2006	employees of the railroad company	30,000	personal data	Vijayan, Jaikumar and Todd Weiss, "Flurry of New Data Breaches Disclosed," Computerworld, June 19, 2006 at [http://www.computerworld.com/action/article.do?command=viewArticleBasic&articleId=9001282].

Business Incidents	Date Publicized	Who Was Affected	Number Affected	Type of Data Released/ Compromised	Source(s)
Ross-Simmons —data breach	April 2006	customers	undisclosed	credit card numbers, financial information, other personal information	"Ross-Simons Says Security Breach Exposes Customers," Computerworld, April 12, 2006, at [http://www.computerworld.com/securitytopics/security/story/0,10801,110425,00.html?source=x3888].
EBay—hackers harvesting and selling user information	March 2006	customers	undisclosed	account information	Niccolai, James, "Russian Web Site Offered eBay Account Info for $5," Computerworld, March 24, 2006, at [http://www.computerworld.com/securitytopics/security/cybercrime/story/0,10801,109881,00.html].
Deloitte & Touche—unencrypted CD left on a plane	February 2006	all U.S. and Canadian employees of McAfee Software hired before April 2005	9,200	names, SSNs, McAfee stock holdings	Kuruvila, Matthai C., "Security Giant's Data Lost," *Silicon Valley*, February 24, 2006.
Atlantis Resort—theft from the hotel's database	January 2006	customers	55,000	names, addresses, credit card details, SSNs, driver's license numbers, bank account data	"IDs of 50,000 Bahamas Resort Guests Stolen," CNet News, January 10, 2006.
Guidance Software—hacker	December 2005	security researchers and law enforcement agencies worldwide	3,800	credit card numbers	Krebs, Brian, "Hackers Break Into Computer-Security Firm's Customer Database," *Washington Post* December 19, 2005, p. D5.
Sam's Club—"card-skimming" devices	December 2005	customers who bought fuel at its gas stations between September 21 and October 2.	600	credit card information	Vijayan, Jaikumar, "Card Skimmers Eyed in Sam's Club Data Theft," Computerworld, December 14, 2005, at [http://www.computerworld.com/databasetopics/data/story/0,10801,107067,00.html].

Business Incidents	Date Publicized	Who Was Affected	Number Affected	Type of Data Released/ Compromised	Source(s)
Marriott Vacation Club International—missing data tapes	December 2005	customers and employees	206,000	addresses and credit card information	"Marriott Vacation Club reports missing data tapes," Computerworld, December 26, 2005, at [http://computerworld.com/securitytopics/security/story/0,10801,107366,00.html?SKC=security-107366].
Ford Motor Company—stolen computer	December 2005	current and former Ford employees	70,000	names and SSNs	"Tech Crime Gets Personal at Ford," CNN Money, December 22, 2005, at [http://money.cnn.com/2005/12/22/news/fortune500/ford_theft/].
Safeway—company laptop stolen from manager's home	November 2005	employees	1,200	names, SSNs, hire dates and work locations	Akkad, Dania, "Safeway Discloses Security Breach," *Monterey County Herald*, November 5, 2005 (no page given).
Boeing—theft of company computer	November 2005	current and former Boeing workers	161,000	names, Social Security numbers (SSNs), some birth dates and banking information for employees who elected to use direct deposit of payroll	Bowermaster, David and Dominic Gates and Melissa Allison, "161,000 Workers' Personal Data on PC Stolen from Boeing," *Seattle Times*, November 19, 2005, p. A1.
Eastman Kodak—laptop stolen from a consultant's locked car trunk.	June 2005	former Eastman Kodak workers	5,800	names, Social Security numbers, birth dates and benefits information	Davia, Joy, "Kodak Warns of Data Theft," *Rochester Democrat and Chronicle (New York)*, June 22, 2005, p. 8D.
Time Warner—loss of 40 computer backup tapes containing sensitive data while being shipped by Iron Mountain to an offsite storage center	May 2005	current and former employees, some of their dependents and beneficiaries, and individuals who provided services for the company	600,000	names, SSNs	Zeller, Tom, "Time Warner Says Data on Employees Is Lost," *New York Times*, May 3, 2005, p. C4.

Business Incidents	Date Publicized	Who Was Affected	Number Affected	Type of Data Released/ Compromised	Source(s)
MCI—laptop stolen from a car that was parked in the garage at the home of a MCI financial analyst	May 2005	current and former employees	16,500	names and SSNs	Young, Shawn, "MCI Reports Loss Of Employee Data On Stolen Laptop," *Wall Street Journal*, May 23, 2005, p. A2.
LEXIS/ NEXIS—intruders used passwords of legitimate customers to get access to a Seisint database called Accurint, which sells reports to law-enforcement agencies and businesses. Later analysis determined that its databases had been fraudulently breached 59 times using stolen passwords.	March 2005	customers	32,000 (subsequent investigation reveals the actual number is 310,000)	names, addresses, passwords, SSNs, drivers license	El-Rashidi, Yasmine, "LexisNexis Reports Data Breach; Personal Records Are Hacked as Concerns About Security and Identity Theft Intensify," *Wall Street Journal*, March 10, 2005, p. A3; and Krim, Jonathan, "LexisNexis Data Breach Bigger Than Estimated: 310,000 Consumers May Be Affected, Firm Says," *Washington Post*, April 13, 2005, p. E1.
DSW Shoe Warehouse store—information stolen from computer database over 3- month period	March 2005	customers of 103 of the chain's 175 stores	initially "hundreds of thousands," then raised to 1.4 million	credit card information	*Associated Press*, "DSW ID Theft May Affect Over 100,000," *Chicago Tribune*, March 11, 2005, p. 4; and "Firm Raises Data Theft Count," *Washington Post*, April 19, 2005, p. E2.
T-Mobile—hacker intrusion into company database	February 2005	T-Mobile customers	400	customer records, passwords, SSNs, private e-mail and candid celebrity photos **note**: data offered for sale via online forum	Poulsen, Kevin, "Known Hole Aided T-Mobile Breach,"Wired News, February 28, 2005, at [http://www.wired.com/news/privacy/0,1 848,66735,00.html].

Business Incidents	Date Publicized	Who Was Affected	Number Affected	Type of Data Released/ Compromised	Source(s)
Motorola—Thieves broke into the offices of Affiliated Computer Services (ACS), a provider of human resources services, and stole two computers	June 2005	Motorola employees	34,000 in U.S.	SSNs and personal information	"Two Computers Stolen with Motorola Staff Data," Reuters, June 10, 2005.
ChoicePoint—criminals used fake documentation to open 50 fraudulent accounts to access consumer data	February 2005	consumers	30,000–35,000 in California; 145,000 nationwide	names, addresses, SSNs, credit reports	Perez, Evan, "ChoicePoint Is Pressed to Explain Database Breach," *Wall Street Journal*, February 5, 2005, p. A6.
Affiliated Computer Services—inmate hacked into county database	October 2004	county employees	900	names, birth dates, SSNs, bank account routing numbers and checking account numbers	Whaley, Monte, "FBI on Weld ID-Theft Case Feds to Analyze Data from Cell of Inmate Who Hacked Computer," *Denver Post*, November 11, 2004, p. B1.
Lowe's (home improvement store)—hacker used vulnerable wireless network to attempt to steal credit card info	June 2004	customers	unknown	skimmed credit account information for every transaction processed at a particular Lowe's store	Roberts, Paul, "Wireless Hacker Pleads Guilty: Man Admits Using Store's Wireless Network to Steal Credit Card Info," PC World, June 7, 2004, at [http: //msn.pcworld. com/news/article/ 0,aid,116411,00.asp].
eBay—hackers tricked online merchants who used the PayPal payment processing system into disclosing their user names and passwords, then logged onto the merchants' accounts	March 2004	several eBay merchants	company did not disclose	customer names, e-mail addresses, home addresses and transactions	Kirby, Carrie, "New Scam Threat at eBay / Hackers Obtained Information on Some Customers," *San Francisco Chronicle*, March 16, 2004, p. C1.

Business Incidents	Date Publicized	Who Was Affected	Number Affected	Type of Data Released/ Compromised	Source(s)
Kinko's—hacker installed a key logger to record every character typed on 13 Kinko's computers	November 2003	Customers at Internet terminals at 13 Kinko's copy shops in Manhattan	450	SSNs, names, passwords, credit cards, bank account data **note:** data was sold	Napoli, Lisa, "A Hacker Masters Keystroke Theft: Personal Data Stolen from 450 Victims," *International Herald Tribune*, August 9, 2003, p. 1.
Acxiom (marketing company)—hacker downloaded data	August 2003	clients include 14 of the top 15 credit card companies, 5 of the top 6 retail banks, IBM, Microsoft, and federal government	10% of clientele (no total number given)	passwords, personal, financial, and company information	Lee, W.A. "Hacker Breaches Acxiom Data," *American Banker*, August 11, 2003, p. 5.
DirecTV—hacker stole trade secrets for access card	April 2003	DirecTV subscribers	50,000 customers used counterfeit access cards to watch programming without paying	details about the design and architecture of DirecTV's "Period 4" cards **note**: data was sold	"U. of C. Student Pleads Guilty to Theft of Direc TV Card Data; Trade Secrets Ended up on Hacker Site, Enabling Free Access," *Chicago Sun-Times*, April 30, 2003, p. 16.
TCI help-desk worker sold client access codes to two others, who then used the codes to obtain more than 15,000 customer credit records	November 2002	credit reporting bureau customers	15,000 (Wired News) 30,000 (*Seattle Times*)	names, addresses, SSNs, credit card **note:** data sold, for $60 per record	Delio, Michelle, "Cops Bust Massive ID Theft Ring," Wired News, November 25, 2002, at [http://www.wired.com/news/privacy/0,1848,56567,00.html]; and Masters, Brooke, "Huge ID-Theft Ring Broken; 30,000 Consumers at Risk; Men Charged with Stealing Personal, Financial Data," *Seattle Times*, November 26, 2002, p. A1.
Midwest Express Airlines and Federal Aviation Administration—hackers posted list of customer names to website and posted a list of airport security screening results taken from the FAA's system	April 2002	Midwest Express Airlines customers; FAA (two separate incidents)	unknown	passenger names and airport security screening results	Larson, Virgil, "Computer Hackers Breach Midwest Express Systems," *Omaha World-Herald*, April 22, 2002, p. 1D.

Business Incidents	Date Publicized	Who Was Affected	Number Affected	Type of Data Released/ Compromised	Source(s)
ChoicePoint—Nigerian-born brother and sister posed as legitimate businesses to set up ChoicePoint accounts	2002	unknown	7,000–10,000 inquiries on names and SSNs, then used identities to commit fraud	names and SSNs **note:** data was sold	*Associated Press*, "ChoicePoint Suffered Previous Breach: Two ID Thieves Arrested in 2002 for Tapping into Data" MSNBC, February 3, 2005, at [http://www.msnbc.msn.com/id/7065902/].
New York City restaurant busboy duped credit reporting companies into providing detailed credit reports	March 2001	chief executives, celebrities and tycoons from Forbes list of richest Americans	200	SSNs, home addresses and birth dates, credit card numbers	Hays, Tom, "Busboy Hacks Only the Richest, Used Forbes' List in Plot to Steal Identity, Credit Info, Big Bucks," *Pittsburgh Post-Gazette*, March 21, 2001, p. A11.
World Economic Forum—hackers broke into computer	February 2001	attendees	3,200	passport numbers, cell phone numbers, credit card numbers, exact arrival and departure times, hotel names, room numbers, number of overnights, sessions attended, plus information on 27,000 people who have attended the global forum in recent years	Higgins, Alexander, "Hackers Steal World Leaders' Personal Data," *Chicago Sun-Times*, February 6, 2001, p. 20.
International credit card ring adds fraudulent charges of 277 Russian rubles ($5-10) to credit cards	January 2001	Internet shopping sites	unknown	credit card numbers **note:** data was sold	James, Michael, "Small-time Thefts Reap Big Net Gain Tens of Thousands of Phony $5-$10 Credit-Card Charges Rake in Millions for Hackers," *Orlando Sentinel*, January 27, 2001, p. E5.
Egghead—hacker attacked computer system	December 2000	customers	3.5 million credit card accounts; 7500 of which showed "suspected fraudulent activity"	credit card info	"Sayer, Peter, "Egghead Says Customer Data Safe After Hack Attack," PC World, January 8, 2001 at [http://msn.pcworld.com/news/article/0,aid,37781,00.asp].

Business Incidents	Date Publicized	Who Was Affected	Number Affected	Type of Data Released/ Compromised	Source(s)
Western Union—hackers made electronic copies of the credit and debit card information	September 2000	customers who transferred money on a company website	15,700	credit and debit card information	Cobb, Alan, "Hackers Steal Credit Card Info from Western Union Site," *Chicago Sun-Times*, September 11, 2000, p. 22.
America Online—AOL customer-service representatives mistakenly downloaded an e-mail attachment sent by hackers	June 2000	customers	500 records were viewed	names, addresses, and credit card numbers	"Hackers Breach Security At America Online Inc," *Wall Street Journal*, June 19, 2000, p. A34.
Two British teens intruded into 9 e-commerce websites in the United States, Canada, Thailand, Japan and Britain	March 2000	customers	26,000 credit card accounts	credit card data **note:** some data was posted on the Web	Sniffen, Michael, "2 Teens Accused of Hacking Charged in $3 Million Credit Card Theft," *Chicago Sun-Times*, March 25, 2000, p. 9.
CD Universe (online music store)—hacker stole credit card numbers and released thousands of them on a website when the company refused to pay a $100,000 ransom	January 2000	customers	300,000	credit card numbers **note**: Maxus Credit Card Pipeline Website posted up to 25,000 stolen numbers	*Associated Press*, "Hacker Said to Steal 300,000 Card Numbers," *Arizona Republic*, January 11, 2000, p. A3.
Pacific Bell—16-year-old teenager hacked into server and stole passwords	January 2000	subscribers	63,000 accounts were decrypted; 330,000 customers told to change passwords	passwords	Gettleman, Jeffrey, "Passwords of PacBell Net Accounts Stolen; Computers: Authorities Say 16-year-old Hacker Took the Data for Fun. Theft Affects 63,000 Customers," *Los Angeles Times*, January 12, 2000, p. 2.

Table 2. Data Security Breaches in Education (2000–2006)

Education Incidents	Date Publicized	Who Was Affected	Number Affected	Type of Data Released/ Compromised	Source(s)
Western Illinois University—hacker accessed several electronic student services systems	July 2006	students, customers of the university's online bookstore, guests of the university hotel	180,000	SSNs, personal data, credit card information	Maguire, John, "Alums Just Told of Computer Breach: Data on 180,000 with Ties to WIU Hacked a Month Ago," *Chicago Sun-Times*, July 5, 2006, p. 8.
University of Tennessee—hacker broke into UT computer	July 2006	past and current employees	36,000	SSNs, names, addresses	Herrington, Angie, "UT Notifies Workers of Computer Hacking,"*Chattanooga Times Free Press*, July 7, 2006, p. O.
Northwestern University (Chicago)—hackers broke into nine desktop computers in the Office of Admissions and Financial Aid	July 2006	students and applicants to the school	17,000	names, addresses, SSNs	"Hackers break into NU Admissions, Financial Aid Computers," *Chicago Sun Times*, July 15, 2006, at [http: //www.suntimes.com/cgi-bin/print.cgi?getReferrer=[http: //www.suntimes.com/output/news/cst-nws-hack15.html].
Moraine Park Technical College (Beaver Dam, Fond du Lac, & West Bend, WI)—missing computer disk	July 2006	apprenticeship students back to 1993	1,500	names, addresses, phone numbers, SSNs	"News Summaries Ozaukee and Washington Counties," *Milwaukee Journal Sentinel*, July 16, 2006, p. Z3
Catawba County Schools (Newton, NC)—website exposed personal data	June 2006	students who had taken keyboarding and computer applications placement test during the 2001–02 school year	619	names, SSNs, test scores	Shain, Andrew, and Hannah Mitchell, "619 Students' Secure Data Revealed Online: Google Page Showed Social Security Numbers, Test Scores, *Charlotte Observer*, June 24, 2006, p. 1B.
San Francisco State University—faculty member's laptop stolen	June 2006	current and former students	3,000	names, SSNs, phone numbers and grade point averages.	Asimov, Nanette, "SFSU students' information stolen; School alerts 3,000 affected by theft of faculty laptop," *San Francisco Chronicle*, June 23, 2006, p. B5.

Education Incidents	Date Publicized	Who Was Affected	Number Affected	Type of Data Released/ Compromised	Source(s)
University of Kentucky—stolen thumb drive	June 2006	current and former students	6,500	SSNs	Kiernan, Vincent, "Incidents at Two Universities Put More Than 200,000 Students at Risk of Data Theft," *The Chronicle of Higher Education*, June 19, 2006, p. A21
Ohio University (Athens, OH)— hackers breach servers in two separate incidents	May 2006	individuals and organizations listed in the alumni database, owners of patents and other intellectual property	300,00	SSNs, personal information, biographical information, patent data, intellectual property files	Vijayan, Jaikumar, "Ohio University Reports Two Separate Security Breaches," Computerworld, May 3, 2006, at [http://www.computerworld.com/action/article.do?command=viewArticleBasic&articleId=111113&intsrc=article_pots_bot].
Sacred Heart University—hackers intrude system	May 2006	students and some individuals not associated with the university	135,000	personal information, SSNs	Sandoval, Greg, "Sacred Heart is Latest University to be Hacked," CNet News, May 26, 2006, at [http://news.com.com/2100-7349_3-6077212.html].
University of Texas, Austin—data breach	April 2006	students, alumni, faculty, and staff of the business school	200,000	SSNs, biographical materials	*Associated Press*, "University of Texas Probes Computer Breach," MSNBC, April 24, 2006, at [http://www.msnbc.msn.com/id/12459840/].
University of Arizona—hackers break into journalism department's computer system	February 2006	journalism students	undisclosed	none so far	Grossman, Djamila, "Romanian Hacker Breaks into UA Journalism Computers," *Arizona Daily Star*, February 14, 2006, p. B2.
Notre Dame—hackers attack server	January 2006	alumni and other donors to the university	undisclosed	SSNs, credit card numbers, check images	Roberts, Paul F., "Hackers Target Notre Dame Donors," eWeek, January 24, 2006, at [http://www.eweek.com/article2/0,1895,1915087,00.asp].
Indiana University—malicious software programs installed on business instructor's computer	November 2005	Kelly School of Business students enrolled in introductory business course between 2001-2005	5,300	personal student information	*Associated Press*,"IU Finds 'Malicious' Software," FortWayne.com, November 18, 2005, at [http://www.fortwayne.com/mld/fortwayne/news/local/13202338.htm].

Education Incidents	Date Publicized	Who Was Affected	Number Affected	Type of Data Released/ Compromised	Source(s)
University of Tennessee Medical Center—laptop computer stolen	November 2005	patients who received treatment in 2003	3,800	names and SSNs	"UT Patients Warned of Stolen Computer," *Chattanooga Times Free-Press*, November 2, 2005, p. B2.
Georgia Institute of Technology Office of Enrollment Services—computer theft	November 2005	past, present, and prospective students	13,000	SSNs, birth dates, names, addresses	Kantor, Arcadiy, "Georgia Tech Computer Theft Compromises Student Data," *The Technique* (via University Wire), November 11, 2005 at [http://www.nique.net/issues/2005-11-11/news/3].
University of Tennessee—inadvertent posting of names and Social Security numbers to Internet lists	October 2005	students and employees	1,900	names and SSNs	"State Briefs: UT Students' Private Data Posted on the 'Net," *The* Tennessean.com, October 29, 2005, at [http://tennessean.com/apps/pbcs.dll/article?AID=/20051029/NEWS01/510290327/1006/NEWS01].
University of Georgia—hacker hits employee records server	September 2005	current and former employees of university's College of Agricultural and Environmental Sciences	1,600	SSNs	Simmons, Kelly, "Hackers Breach Database at UGA," *The Atlanta Journal - Constitution*, September 29, 2005, p. C2.
Miami University (Ohio)—report containing SSNs and grades of more than 20,000 students has been accessible via the Internet since 2002	September 2005	students	21,762	SSNs, grades	Giordano, Joe, "Miami University, Ohio, Finds Huge Online Security Breach," *Journal-News (Hamilton, OH)*, September 16, 2005 (no page given).
Kent State University—five desktop computers stolen from campus	September 2005	students and professors	100,000	names, SSNs, grades	Gonzalez, Jennifer, "Student, Faculty Data on Stolen Computers," *Plain Dealer (Cleveland)*, September 10, 2005, p. B1.
Sonoma State University—hacking	August 2005	people who either attended, applied, graduated or worked at the school from 1995 to 2002	61,709	names, SSNs	Park, Rohnert, "Hackers Hit College Computer System: Identity Theft Fears at Sonoma State," *San Francisco Chronicle*, August 9, 2005, p. B2.

Education Incidents	Date Publicized	Who Was Affected	Number Affected	Type of Data Released/ Compromised	Source(s)
California State University—Office of the Chancellor may have experienced unauthorized access to one of its computers	August 2005	students who receive financial aid and two financial aid administrators	154	names, SSNs	"California State University Chancellor's Office Experiences Potential Computer Security Breach," *U.S. States News*, August 29, 2005 (no page given).
University of Florida Health Sciences Center/ ChartOne—stolen laptop	August 2005	patients and physicians	3,851	names, SSNs, dates of birth, medical records	Chun, Diane, "3,851 Patients at Risk of ID Theft," *Gainesville.com*, August 27, 2005 at [http://www.gainesville.com/apps/pbcs.dll/article?AID=/20050827/LOCAL/208270336/1078/news].
University of Colorado—hacking into campus Card Office (creates IDs for staff and students)	August 2005	students and faculty	36,000	university accounts and personal information	Uhls, Anna, "U. Colorado students getting (re)carded," *University Wire/ Colorado Daily*, August 4, 2005 (no page given).
University of North Texas—hacking	August 2005	current, former and prospective students	38,607	names, addresses, telephone numbers, SSNs, student identification numbers, student ID passwords, student classification information and possibly 524 credit card numbers	Tessyman, Neal, "Hackers Steal Student Info from U. North Texas," *University Wire*, August 11, 2005 (no page given).
University of Colorado—hackers tapped into a database in the registrar's office	August 2005	student records from June 1999 to May 2001 and from fall 2003 to summer 2005.	49,000	names, SSNs, addresses, phone numbers	Mccrimmon, Katie Kerwin, "Hackers Tap CU Registrar's Database; Privacy of 49,000 Students Potentially Invaded in Breach," *Rocky Mountain News* (Denver), August 20, 2005, p. 20A.
California State University, Stanislaus—hacking	August 2005	student workers	900	names, SSNs	Togneri, Chris, "Hacker Breaks into Stan State Computer," *Modesto Bee*, August 16, 2005, p. B1.

Education Incidents	Date Publicized	Who Was Affected	Number Affected	Type of Data Released/ Compromised	Source(s)
University of Southern California—individual hacked into USC's online application system	July 2005	applicants	270,000	name, address, SSNs, e-mail address, phone number, date of birth, login information	Hawkins, Stephanie, "Hacker Hits Application System at USC," *University Wire/ Daily Trojan*, August 18, 2005 (no page given).
California Polytechnic, Pomona—two computers hacked	July 2005	university applicants and current and former faculty, staff and students	31,077	names, SSNs	Ruiz, Kenneth, "Hackers Infiltrate Cal Poly," *Whittier Daily News (CA)*, August 5, 2005 (no page given).
University of Colorado, Boulder—hackers broke into a computer server containing information used to issue identification cards	July 2005	students and professors	29,000 students and 7,000 professors	SSNs, names, photographs	*Associated Press*, "Hackers Break into CU Computers Containing 36k Records," August 1, 2005.
Michigan State University—breach of a server in the College of Education	July 2005	students	27,000	names, addresses, SSNs, course information, personal identification numbers	*Associated Press*, "Students Informed Social Security Numbers Possibly Compromised," July 7, 2005.
University of California, San Diego—hackers broke into university server	July 2005	students, staff, faculty who had attended or worked at UCSD Extension in the past five years	3,300	SSNs, driver license and credit card numbers	"SD UCSD Hackers," *City News Service*, July 1, 2005 (no page given).
California State University Dominguez Hills—hacking	July 2005	students	9613	names, SSNs	*Associated Press*, "Hackers crack computers, access private student information," July 29, 2005.
University of Connecticut—hacking—rootkit (collection of programs that a hacker uses to mask intrusion and obtain computer network) placed on server on October 26, 2003, but not detected until July 20, 2005	June 2005	students, staff, and faculty	72,000	names, SSNs, dates of birth, phone numbers and addresses	Naraine, Ryan, "UConn Finds Rootkit in Hacked Server," eWeek, June 27, 2005, at [http://www.eweek.com/article2/0,1759,1831892,00.asp].

Education Incidents	Date Publicized	Who Was Affected	Number Affected	Type of Data Released/ Compromised	Source(s)
Kent State University—laptop stolen from employee's car	June 2005	full-time faculty members since 2001	1,400	names, SSNs	Hampp, David, "Kent State U. Faculty Affected by Stolen Computer," *Daily Kent Stater* (via University Wire), June 22, 2005 (no page given).
Ohio State University Medical Center—two stolen laptops	June 2005	patients	15,000	patient names, admission and discharge dates, whether the patient had insurance, total charges and adjustments to the account.	Crane, Misti, "Laptop Containing Patients' Billing Information Stolen; Birth Dates, Social Security Numbers Not in Data Taken from Consultant, Osu Says," *Columbus Dispatch (OH)*, June 30, 2005, p. 4C.
University of Hawaii—dishonest library worker indicted on federal charges of bank fraud related to identity theft	June 2005	students, faculty, staff and library patrons at any of the 10 campuses between 1999 and 2003	150,000	SSNs, addresses and phone numbers	*Associated Press*, "UH Warns of Possible Identity Theft," June 19, 2005.
Jackson Community College (MI)—hacker breaks into computer system	May 2005	employees and students of the college	8,000	SSNs	"Computer Crime: Hacker May Have Stolen Social Security Numbers From Jackson Community Collegea," *Computer Crime Research Center*," May 29, 2005 (no page given).
Carnegie Mellon University—security breach of school's computer network	May 2005	graduates of the Tepper School of Business from 1997 to 2004; current graduate students; applicants to the doctoral program from 2003 to 2005; applicants to the MBA program from 2002 to 2004; and administrative employees	5,000	SSNs and personal information	*Associated Press*, "Carnegie Mellon Reports Computer Breach," MSNBC, April 21, 2005, at [http://msnbc.msn.com/id/7590506/]
Stanford University—computer system breach	May 2005	students and recruiters of the university	9,600	SSNs, resumes, financial data, government information	Musil, Steven, "FBI Probes Network Breach at Stanford," CNet News, May 25, 2005.

Education Incidents	Date Publicized	Who Was Affected	Number Affected	Type of Data Released/ Compromised	Source(s)
Florida International University (FIU)—a hacker acquired user names and passwords for 165 computers on campus	May 2005	faculty and students	unknown	SSNs, card numbers	Leyden, John, "Florida Univ on Brown Alert after Hack Attack," *The Register*, April 29, 2005, at [http://www.theregister.com/2005/04/29/fiu_id_fraud_alert/].
Northwestern University (Kellog School of Management)—computer network breach	May 2005	faculty, students, and alumni	17,500	user IDs and passwords	Meglio, Francesca Di, "Hacker Break-In," *Computer Crime Research Center*, May 23, 2005 (no page given).
University of California, San Francisco—hacker gained access to server used by accounting and personnel department	April 2005	students, faculty and staff	7,000	names and SSNs numbers	Lazarus, David, "Another Incident for UC," *San Francisco Chronicle*, April 6, 2005, p. C1.
Tufts University—possible security breach in an alumni and donor database after abnormal activity on the server in October and December, 2004	April 2005	alumni	106,000	SSNs and other unspecified personal information	Roberts, Paul, "Tufts Warns 106,000 Alumni, Donors of Security Breach: Personal Data on a Server Used for Fund Raising May Have Been Exposed," Computerworld, April 13, 2005, at [http://www.computerworld.com/securitytopics/security/privacy/story/0,10801,101043,00.html?source=x10].
University of Nevada, Las Vegas—hackers accessed school's Student and Exchange Visitor Information System (SEVIS) database	March 2005	current and former students and faculty	5,000	personal records, including birth dates, countries of origin, passport numbers, and SSNs	Lipka, Sara, "Hacker Breaks Into Database for Tracking International Students at UNLV," *Chronicle of Higher Education*, March 21, 2005, p. A43.
California State University, Chico—hackers broke into servers	March 2005	students, former students, prospective students, and faculty	59,000	SSNs	*Associated Press*, "Hackers Gain Personal Information of 59,000 People Affiliated with California University," *Grand Rapids Press*, March 22, 2005, p. A2.

Education Incidents	Date Publicized	Who Was Affected	Number Affected	Type of Data Released/ Compromised	Source(s)
University of California, Berkeley laptop stolen from restricted area of campus office	March 2005	alumni, graduate students, and past applicants	100,000	SSNs numbers, names; addresses, and birth dates for 1/3 of affected people	Liedtke, Michael, "Laptop Theft Causes Identity Fraud Worry," *Daily Breeze* (Torrance, CA), March 28, 2005, p. A10.
George Mason University—hackers gained access to information	January 2005	faculty, staff, and students	30,000	names, photos, SSNs, and campus ID numbers	McCullagh, Declan, "Hackers Steal ID Info from Virginia University," Wired News, January 10, 2005, at [http://news.com.com/2100-7349_3-5519592.html].
University of California, San Diego (UCSD)—hacker breached computer system	January 2005	students and alumni of UCSD Extension	3,500	names, SSNs	Yang, Eleanor, "Hacker Breaches Computers That Store UCSD Extension Student, Alumni Data," *San Diego Union Tribune*, January 18, 2005, p. B3.
University of California, Berkeley—hacker compromised the university's computer system	October 2004	Californians participating in California's In-Home Supportive Services program since 2001	1.4 million individuals	SSNs, names, addresses, phone numbers, and dates of birth	Reuters, "Hacker Strikes University Computer System,"CNET News, October 19, 2004, at [http://news.com.com/2100-7349_3-5418388.html].
California State—auditor from chancellor's office lost hard drive containing personal information	August 2004	380,000 current and former students, applicants, staff, faculty and alumni at UC San Diego and 178,000 at San Diego State	23,500	name, address, SSNs	Connell, Sally Ann, "Security Lapses, Lost Equipment Expose Students to Possible ID Theft; in the Latest Incident, a Cal State Hard Drive with Data on 23,500 Individuals Is Missing," *Los Angeles Times*, August 29, 2004, p. B4.
University of California, Los Angeles—stolen laptop w/ blood donor info	June 2004	blood donors	145,000	names, birth dates and SSNs	Becker, David, "UCLA Laptop Theft Exposes ID Info,"CNET News, October 6, 2004, at [http://news.com.com/UCLA+laptop+theft+exposes+ID+info/2100-1029_3-5230662.html?tag=nl].
University of California, San Diego (UCSD)—hackers breacked security at the San Diego Supercomputer Center and the	April 2004	UCSD students, alumni, faculty, employees and applicants	380,000	SSNs, and driver license numbers	Sidener, Jonathan, "SD Supercomputer Center Among Victims of Intrusion," *San Diego Union Tribune*, April 15, 2004, p. B3.

Education Incidents	Date Publicized	Who Was Affected	Number Affected	Type of Data Released/ Compromised	Source(s)
University's Business and Financial Services Department					
Georgia Institute of Technology	March 2003	patrons of art and theatre program	57,000	credit card numbers	Lemos, Robert, "Data Thieves Strike Georgia Tech," Wired News, March 31, 2003, at [http://news.com.com/Data+thieves+strike+Georgia+Tech/2100-1002_3-994821.html?tag=nl].
University of Texas, Austin—computer hackers broke into database on multiple occasions	March 2003	current and former student, faculty and staff members, as well as job applicants	55,200	names, addresses, SSNs, email addresses, office phone numbers **note:** perpetrator claimed he did not distribute the numbers and had not used them "to anyone's detriment"	Read, Brock, "Hackers Steal Data From U. of Texas Database," *Chronicle of Higher Education*, March 21, 2003, p. 35.
University of Kansas—hacker break-in to Student and Exchange Visitor Information System (SEVIS)	January 2003	foreign students	1,400	SSNs, passport numbers, countries of origin, and birth dates.	Arnone, Michael, "Hacker Steals Personal Data on Foreign Students at U. of Kansas,"*Chronicle of Higher Education*, January 24, 2003 (no page given).
College of the Canyons (California)—computer hard drive containing personal student information stolen	October 2001	current and former students	36,000	names, SSNs, and photographs	Mistry, Bhavna, "Identity Theft Alert Issued at College," *Los Angeles Daily News*, October 21, 2001, p. N7.
University of Washington Medical Center—hacker broke into computer system	December 2000	cardiology and rehabilitation patients	5,000	names, addresses, birth dates, heights and weights, SSNs, and the medical procedure undergone	"Hacker Steals Patient Records," *San Diego Union-Tribune*, December 9, 2000, p. A3.

Table 3. Data Security Breaches in Financial Institutions (2001–2006)

Financial Institutions Incidents	Date Publicized	Who Was Affected	Number Affected	Type of Data Released/ Compromised	Source(s)
ING Financial Services—stolen laptop	June 2006	District of Columbia government workers and retirees	13,000	SSNs, personal data	Dwyer, Timothy, "ING Financial to Notify Potential Identity Theft Victims," *Washington Post*, June 19, 2006, p. B4.
Equifax Inc.—stolen laptop	June 2006	nearly all the U.S. employees of the credit reporting bureau	2,500	names, SSNs	Stempel, Jonathan, "Equifax Says Laptop With Employee Data Was Stolen," eWeek, June 20, 2006, at [http://www.eweek.com/article2/0,1759,1979296,00.asp?kc=EWRSS03129TX1K0000614].
Fidelity Investments—stolen laptop	March 2006	Hewlett-Packard employees	196,000	personal data	Hines, Matt, "Stolen Fidelity Laptop Exposes HP Workers," eWeek, March 23, 2006, at [http://www.eweek.com/article2/0,1895,1942049,00.asp].
Bank of America, Washington Mutual—debit cards cancelled	February 2006	customers using debit cards issued by the two banks at Sam's Club gas stations and Office Max	200,000	debit card information which was used to accrue fraudulent charges	Sandoval, Greg "Web of Intrigue Widens in Debit-Card Theft Case," CNet News, February 13, 2006, at [http://news.com.com/Web+of+intrigue+widens+in+debit-card+theft+case/2100-1029_3-6038405.html].
Ameriprise Financial—laptop theft	January 2006	customers and advisers with the financial firm	230,000	names, SSNs, internal account numbers	Dash, Eric, "Ameriprise Loses Data on 230,000 Customers and Advisers," *New York Times*, January 25, 2006.
H&R Block—Social Security numbers printed on unsolicited packages containing free software	January 2006	recipients of the company's tax preparation software	undisclosed	SSNs	Gilbert, Alorie, "H&R Block Blunder Exposes Consumer Data," CNet News, January 3, 2006, at [http://news.com.com/H38R+Block+blunder+exposes+consumer+data/2100-1029_3-6016720.html].

Financial Institutions Incidents	Date Publicized	Who Was Affected	Number Affected	Type of Data Released/ Compromised	Source(s)
Visa USA	December 2005	customers with Visa cards from various financial institutions using a mutual merchant	undisclosed	credit card information	Weinstein, Natalie, "Visa Deals With Possible Data Breach," CNet News, December 24, 2005, at [http://news.com.com/2100-1029_3-6007759.html].
Scottrade Inc.—internet hacker	December 2005	customers of the stock brokerage firm	140,000	names, birth dates, drivers license numbers, phone numbers, bank names, bank routing numbers, bank account numbers, and Scottrade account numbers	"Hackers Reveal 140,000 Customer ID's," *Computer Crime Research Center*, December 2, 2005 (no page given).
TransUnion (credit reporting bureau)—stolen desktop computer	November 2005	customers	3,600	SSNs and personal credit information	Paul, Peralte, "Credit Bureau Burglary Leaves 3,600 Vulnerable," *Atlanta Journal and Constitution*, November 11, 2005, p. 5G.
Choicepoint—Miami-Dade County Police Department may have misused the department's account to illegally access consumer records	September 2005	consumers	5,103	SSNs, driver's license information	Husted, Bill, "Another Breach of Records Feared; Choicepoint Tells 5,103 Customers about Incident," *Atlanta Journal-Constitution*, September 17, 2005, p. 1H.
Bank of America—stolen laptop	September 2005	Visa Buxx card users	undisclosed	names, credit card numbers, bank account numbers, routing transit numbers	McMillan, Robert, "Bank of America Notifying Customers After Laptop Theft," Computerworld, October 7, 2005, at [http://www.computerworld.com/securitytopics/security/story/0,10801,105246,00.html].

Financial Institutions Incidents	Date Publicized	Who Was Affected	Number Affected	Type of Data Released/ Compromised	Source(s)
J.P. Morgan (Dallas)—stolen laptop	August 2005	clients	unknown	personal and financial information	"Security Breach at J.P. Morgan Private Bank," *AFX International Focus*, August 30, 2005 (no page given).
Citigroup—a box of computer tapes with account information for 3.9 million customers was lost in shipment by CitiFinancial, a unit of Citigroup	June 2005	personal and home equity loan customers	3.9 million	names, addresses, SSNs and loan-account data	Krim, Jonathan, "Customer Data Lost, Citigroup Unit Says:3.9 Million Affected As Firms' Security Lapses Add Up, *Washington Post*, June 7, 2005, p. A1.
Japanese credit cardholders—hackers behind U.S. data theft may have compromised the data of Japanese cardholders, according to the government. Fraudulent transactions have now emerged in Japan.	June 2005	customers of 26 domestic Japanese credit card firms	unknown	unknown	"Japan Cardholders 'Hit' by Theft," *BBC News*, June 21, 2005 at [http: //news.bbc. co.uk/2/hi/business/ 4114252.stm].
MasterCard—breach occurred in 2004 at a processing center in Tucson operated by CardSystems Solutions, one of several companies that handle transfers of payment between the bank of a credit card-using consumer and the bank of the merchant where a purchase was made.	June 2005	MasterCard credit card and some debit card customers	40 million	names, account numbers, security codes, expiration dates	Krim, Jonathan and Michael Barbaro, "40 Million Credit Card Numbers Hacked: Data Breached at Processing Center," *Washington Post*, June 18, 2005, p. A1; Zeller, Tom and Eric Dash, "MasterCard Says 40 Million Files Put at Risk," *New York Times*, June 18, 2005, p. A1; and Evers, Joris, "Credit Card Suit Now Seeks Damages," CNET News.com, July 7, 2005, at [http: //news.com. com/Credit+card+suit+ now+seeks+damages/ 2100-7350_3-5777818 .html].

Financial Institutions Incidents	Date Publicized	Who Was Affected	Number Affected	Type of Data Released/ Compromised	Source(s)
CardSystems' computers were breached by malicious code that allowed access to customer data.					
Bank of America—laptop stolen from car in Walnut Creek, CA	June 2005	California customers	18,000	names, addresses, SSNs,	Lazarus, David, "Breaches in Security Require New Laws," *San Francisco Chronicle,* June 29, 2005, p. C1.
New Jersey cybercrime ring stole financial records from bank accounts	May 2005	customers of four banks (Charlotte, North Carolina-based Bank of America and Wachovia, Cherry Hill, New Jersey-based Commerce Bank, and PNC Bank of Pittsburgh)	700,000	names, SSNs, bank account information **note:** bank employees sold financial records to collection agencies and law firms.	Weiss, Todd, "Scope of Bank Data Theft Grows to 676,000 Customers: Bank Employees Used Computer Screen Captures to Snag Customer Data," Computerworld, May 20, 2005, at [http://www.computerworld.com/securitytopics/security/cybercrime/story/0,10801,101903,00.html].
Ameritrade (securities broker)—loses tapes with back-up information on customer accounts	April 2005	Ameritrade current and former customers	200,000	account information	"Ameritrade Loses Customer Account Info," CNN Money, April 19, 2005, at [http://money.cnn.com/2005/04/19/technology/ameritrade/index.htm].
HSBC (global bank) sent out warning letters notifying customers that criminals may have gained access to credit card info	April 2005	holders of General Motors MasterCard who had shopped at Polo Ralph Lauren stores	180,000	credit card information	"Security Scare Hits HSBC's Cards," ***BBC News***, April 14, 2005, at [http://news.bbc.co.uk/2/hi/business/4444477.stm]; and Vijayan, Jaikumar, "Update: Scope of Credit Card Security Breach Expands," Computerworld, April 15, 2005, at [http://www.computerworld.com/securitytopics/security/story/0,10801,101101,00.html].

Financial Institutions Incidents	Date Publicized	Who Was Affected	Number Affected	Type of Data Released/ Compromised	Source(s)
Bank of America—computer data tapes lost during shipment	February 2005	GSA charge card program (Visa cards issued to federal employees)	1.2 million	customer and account information	Carrns, Ann, "Bank of America Is Missing Tapes With Card Data," *Wall Street Journal*, February 28, 2005, p. B2.
Wells Fargo—computers stolen from Wells Fargo vendor	November 2004	mortgage and student-loan customers	company would not disclose	customers' names, addresses, and SSNs, and account numbers	Breyer, R. Michelle, "Wells Fargo Customer Data Stolen in Computer Theft," *Austin-American Statesman*, November 3, 2004, p. D1.
Wells Fargo—hacker arrested with stolen computers and laptop	November 2003	customers with personal lines of credit used for consumer loans and overdraft protection	company would not disclose	names, addresses, account and SSNs	"Suspect Is Arrested in Theft of Bank Data," *Los Angeles Times*, November 27, 2003, p. C2.
Weichert Financial Services—credit profiles were unlawfully accessed from internal computer system	May 2003	clients	3,774	credit reports, driver's license info	*Associated Press*, "Pair Accused of Fraud in Credit Reports' Theft: Allegedly Used Data to Buy Goods over the Internet," *The Record* (Bergen County, NJ), May 2, 2003, p. A10.
Visa, MasterCard, American Express and Discover account numbers—hacker stole 8 million	February 2003	credit card customers	PNC Bank cancelled 16,000 cards; Citizens Bank cancelled 8,000–10,000 cards	ATM/debit/ check cards	Sabatini, Patricia, "PNC Cancels 16,000 Cards After Hacking Theft Incident," *Pittsburgh Post-Gazette*, February 20, 2003, p. C1.
Fullerton, California—bogus credit card ring opened bank accounts, credit lines, auto and home loans	June 2001	impersonated more than 1,500 people nationwide and defrauded 76 financial institutions	1,500	birth dates, SSNs, mothers' maiden names, credit cards, driver's licenses, and receipts for car and home purchases.	Brown, Aldrin and Jeff Collins, "Suspicious Mail Triggered Probe of Identity Theft Crime Losses from the Alleged Ring, Which Used Data Stolen as Far Back as the Early '90s, May Hit $10 Million," *Orange County Register*, June 21, 2001 (no page given).

Table 4. Data Security Breaches in State and Federal Government (2003–2006)

Government (State and Federal) Incidents	Date Publicized	Who Was Affected	Number Affected	Type of Data Released/ Compromised	Source(s)
U.S. Department of Commerce—1,137 stolen, lost, or missing laptops	September 2006	Census Bureau and National Oceanic and Atmospheric Administration	6,200 households (estimated)	unknown	Sipress, Alan, "1,100 Laptops Missing from Commerce Dept.," Washington Post, September 22, 2006, p. A3.
U. S. Department of Veterans Affairs—missing computer from contractor's office	August 2006	patients at VA hospitals in Pennsylvnia	38,000	SSNs, names, addresses, birth dates, insurance carriers, billing information, details of service	Rash, Wayne, "Another VA Computer Goes Missing," eWeek, August 7, 2006, at [http://www.eweek.com/article2/0,1895,2000268,00.asp]
U.S. Department of Transportation—stolen laptop	August 2006	drivers license records of Florida residents	133,000	SSNs, names, addresses	Rash, Wayne, "DOT is the Latest Victim of Computer Theft," eWeek, August 10, 2006, at [http://www.eweek.com/article2/0,1895,2002148,00.asp?kc=EWNAVEMNL081106EOAD]
U.S. Department of Education—exposed loan data	August 2006	students who borrowed money under the Federal Direct Student Loan program	21,000	names, birth dates, SSNs, addresses, phone numbers and in some cases account information for holders of federal direct student loans	Yen, Hope, "Ed. Dept. offers free credit monitoring," *Houston Chronicle*, August 24, 2006 (no page given).
Naval Safety Center—personal data exposed on website and on 1,100 computer discs mailed to naval commands	July 2006	Naval and Marine Corps aviators and air crew, both active and reserve	"more than 100,000"	SSNs, personal information	"Naval Safety Center Finds Personal Data on Website," U.S. Department of Defense press release, July 8, 2006, at [http://www.news.navy.mil/search/display.asp?story_id=24568].
U.S. State Department—hackers	July 2006	Washington headquarters, and the Bureau of East Asian and Pacific Affairs	unknown	access to data and passwords	"State Department Releases Details Of Computer System Attacks," *COMMWEB*, July 13, 2006 (no page given), and Greenemeier, Larry, "State Department Hack Escalates Federal Data Insecurity,"

Government (State and Federal) Incidents	Date Publicized	Who Was Affected	Number Affected	Type of Data Released/ Compromised	Source(s)
					Information Week, July 12, 2006, at [http://www.informationweek.com/news/showArticle.jhtml?articleID=190302905].
Federal Trade Commission	June 2006	subjects of law enforcement investigations	110	names, addresses, SSNs, financial account numbers	*Reuters*, "FTC Laptops Stolen, 110 People at Risk of ID Theft," Baseline.com, June 23, 2006 (no page given).
U.S. Navy—an open website contained five spreadsheet files with personal information	June 2006	Navy members and dependents	30,000	names, birth dates and SSNs	"Navy Personal Data on Web Is Katrina-related," *States News Service*, June 26, 2006 (no page given).
Texas Guaranteed Student Loan—computer equipment lost	June 2006	college students borrowing money from the loan company	1.3 million	names, SSNs	Evers, Joris, "Loan Company Reports Loss of Data on 1.3 Million," CNet News, June 1, 2006, at [http://news.com.com/Loan+company+reports+loss+of+data+on+1.3+million/2100-1029_3-6079261.html].
National Institutes of Health Federal Credit Union (Rockville, MD)	June 2006	credit union members	"small number"	unidentified persμonal information	Trejos, Nancy, "Identity Thieves Hit NIH Credit Union; Scheme Is Latest in Spate of Breaches Affecting Millions," *Washington Post*, June 29, 2006, p. B3.
U.S. Department of Agriculture—external security breach of a workstation and two servers	June 2006	current and retired employees of the department	26,000	names, SSNs, employee photos, internal building locations	Azaroff, Rachel, "Hacker Might Have Breached Personal Data at USDA," *FCW*, June 22, 2006, at [http://www.fcw.com/article94991-06-22-06 Web].
Minnesota Department of Revenue (St. Paul, MN)—missing data tape	June 2006	individuals and businesses (taxpayers)	2,400 individuals and 48,000 businesses	names, addresses, SSNs, employment data	MN Department of Revenue, "Department of Revenue to Assist Taxpayers Whose Private Information Was Included in a Package Lost in the Mail," June 28, 2006, at [http://www.taxes.state.mn.us/taxes/publications/press_releases/content/taxpayer_information.shtml]

Government (State and Federal) Incidents	Date Publicized	Who Was Affected	Number Affected	Type of Data Released/ Compromised	Source(s)
Department of Energy—file stolen by hacker	June 2006	employees of the Energy Department's nuclear weapons agency	1,500	names, SSNs, birth datess, codes showing where the employees worked, codes showing their security clearance	*Associated Press*, "DOE Computers Hacked; Info on 1,500 Taken," June 11, 2006.
Government Accountability Office (GAO)—website exposed data from audit reports on Defense Department travel vouchers from the 1970s	June 2006	DoD employees	"fewer than 1,000"	service members' names, SSNs, addresses	Thormeyer, Rob, "GAO Removes Archived Personal Data from Web Site," Washington Technology.com, June 27, 2006 at [http://www.washingtontechnology.com/news/1_1/daily_news/28845-1.html].
King County Records, Elections, and Licensing Services Division (Seattle, WA)—website exposed personal data	June 2006	current and former county residents	unknown (potentially thousands)	SSNs	*Associated Press*, "Councilman Irked by Data Postings on Web," June 27, 2006.
Internal Revenue Service—lost laptop	June 2006	IRS employees and job applicants	291	names, birth dates, SSNs, fingerprints	Lee, Christopher, "IRS Laptop Lost with Data on 291 People," *Washington Post*, June 8, 2006, p. A4.
Nebraska Treasurer's Office (Lincoln, NE)—hacker broke into a child-support computer system	June 2006	individuals and employers who pay and receive child support payments	300,000 individuals and 9,000 employers	names, SSNs, tax identification numbers for businesses	Nebraska State Treasurer, "Hacker Virus Stopped by Treasurer's Office," June 29, 2006, at [http://www.treasurer.state.ne.us/ie/server.asp]
Pentagon, Tricare Management Activity—hackers break into server	May 2006	Defense Department conference attendees	14,000	names, SSNs, credit card numbers, employer identification, other personal information	Barr, Stephen, "Conference Attendees' Personal Data May Be at Risk," *Washington Post*, May 12, 2006, p. D4.

Government (State and Federal) Incidents	Date Publicized	Who Was Affected	Number Affected	Type of Data Released/ Compromised	Source(s)
Department of Veterans Affairs—laptop and external hard drive stolen	May 2006	military veterans	26.5 million	names, birth dates, SSNs	Lee, Christopher and Steve Vogel, "Personal Data on Veterans is Stolen," *Washington Post*, May 23, 2006, p. A1.
National Institutes of Health (NIH)—posting of confidential grant applications	October 2005	applicants to the NIH	undisclosed	grant proposals and other grant review materials	Pulley, John L., "NIH Accidentally Posts Confidential Grant Applications on the Web," *The Chronicle of Higher Education*, October 31, 2005 (no page given).
U.S. Air Force—records stolen from the Air Force Personnel Center's online Assignment Management System	August 2005	officers and 19 NCOs	33,300	SSNs, birth dates, and other sensitive information	Dorsett, Amy, "Identity theft Threat Hangs over AF Officers," *San Antonio Express-News*, August 24, 2005, p. 1A.
San Diego County Employees Retirement Association—hackers broke into two computers	July 2005	current and retired county government employees	33,000	workers' names, Social Security numbers, addresses and dates of birth	Chacon, Daniel, "Hackers Breach County's Personal Records; 33,000 People at Risk in Retirement Association," *San Diego Union-Tribune*, July 30, 2005, p. B1.
Federal Deposit Insurance Corporation—computer breach in early 2004. The agency wrote to employees that it learned of the breach only "recently", but did not explain how the breach occurred, aside from stating that it was not the result of a computer security failure.	June 2005	FDIC current and former employees or anyone employed at the agency as of July 2002.	6,000	names, birth dates, SSNs, and salary information	Krim, Jonathan, "FDIC Alerts Employees of Data Breach", *Washington Post*, June 16 2005, p. D1.

Government (State and Federal) Incidents	Date Publicized	Who Was Affected	Number Affected	Type of Data Released/ Compromised	Source(s)
Lucas County (OH) Children Services—information from the agency's personnel database was compiled and e-mailed to an outside computer	June 2005	agency's 400 current employees and about 500 others who have worked there since 1991	900	names, telephone numbers, SSNs	Patch, David, "Lucas County Children Services Data Stolen," *Toledo Blade*, June 28, 2005, p. B1.
hackers breached Illinois Employment Development Department server	February 2004	people who work as domestic employees and those who employ them	90,000	SSNs, wages	"Hackers Breach State Files on 90,000," *Chicago Tribune*, February 15, 2004, p. 12.
U.S. Department of Defense—hackers downloaded Navy credit cards	August 2003	Navy's purchase card program, used to order routine office supplies	13,000	credit card numbers	Reddy, Anitha, "Hackers Steal 13,000 Credit Card Numbers; Navy Says No Fraud Has Been Noticed," *Washington Post*, November 23, 2003, p. E1.
Bronx identity theft ring filed thousands of fraudulent income tax returns	February 2003	income tax filers	not specified	SSNs **note:** ID theft ring obtained $7million in tax refunds	Weiser, Benjamin, "19 Charged in Identity Theft That Netted $7 Million in Tax Refunds," *New York Times*, February 5, 2003, p. B3.

Table 5. Data Security Breaches in Health Care (2003–2006)

Healthcare Incidents	Date Publicized	Who Was Affected	Number Affected	Type of Data Released/ Compromised	Source(s)
Medco Health Solutions—stolen laptop	March 2006	Ohio state employees and their dependents	4,600	SSNs, birth dates	Weiss, Todd R., "Vendor Waited Six Weeks to Notify Ohio Officials of Data Breach," Computerworld, March 1, 2006, at [http://www.computerworld.com/printthis/2006/0,4814,109116,00.html].
Children's Health Council, San Jose, California—stolen backup tape	September 2005	patients, employees, and parents of patients	5,000–6,000	psychiatric records, evaluations and SSNs; also payroll data on hundreds of current and former employees and credit card information from parents of patients	Walsh, Diana, "Data Stolen from Children's Psychiatric Center," *San Francisco Chronicle,* September 20, 2005, p. B8.
San Jose Medical Group Management—desktop computers stolen from locked administrative office	April 2005	former patients from last seven years	185,000	names, addresses, SSNs, confidential medical information	Weiss, Todd, "Update: Stolen Computers Contain Data on 185,000 Patients," Computerworld, April 8, 2005, at [http://www.computerworld.com/databasetopics/data/story/0,10801,100961,00.html].
TriWest Healthcare Alliance— theft of a database containing names and SSNs	December 2002	military personnel and their dependents	500,000	names, addresses, SSNs	Gorman, Tom, "Reward Offered in Huge Theft of Identity Data; Stolen Computers Had Names, Social Security Numbers of 500,000 Military Families,"*Los Angeles Times*, January 1, 2003, p. 14.

Source: The tables were prepared by CRS from publicly available and news media sources.The author would like to acknowledge the technical assistance of Carol Glover and Logan Council in preparing these tables.)

Note: URLs are listed for exclusively online sources; other publications are identified by name and date.

CYBERTERRORISM: TERRORIST CAPABILITIES

Commentary

By
Douglas C. Lovelace, Jr.

The next three documents presented in this volume address cyber-terrorist and cyber-criminal capabilities, some of the laws enacted to thwart them, and challenges that remain regarding analysis and warning of cyber-attacks. Together, they provide a relatively up to date assessment of the ability of terrorists to use cyber-space to create terror and of measures taken and needed to deny cyber-terrorists their objectives. The documents suggest, albeit in a fairly general manner, several policy issues for countering cyber-terrorist capabilities. The first document in this section is a Congressional Research Service (CRS) report entitled *Terrorist Capabilities for Cyberattack: Overview and Policy Issues*. It quite accurately reports that terrorists' use of the internet is growing in multiple dimensions. As one could reasonably expect, the cost and risk of attempting to exploit increasingly secure U.S. physical borders have grown considerably. That could have the effect of changing the terrorists' cost/benefit calculus, with respect to cyberterrorism. Additionally, as the internet and world-wide web continue to grow rapidly, cyber-security becomes ever more challenging. Thus the CRS report correctly concludes that internet and computer security vulnerabilities are almost certain to attract more terrorist attention over time.

Another disturbing trend addressed in the report, as well as in the subsequent documents in this section, is the nascent but significant nexus forming between cyber-terrorists and cyber-criminals. While their motivations may differ, their methods are similar in many respects. The report astutely notes that cyber-crime is on the rise and terrorists seem to be turning more to criminal activities to finance their efforts. For example, terrorists are beginning to engage in identity theft, theft of financial information, electronic money laundering, internet facilitated arms and drug trafficking, and counterfeiting of intellectual property. Questioning whether the U.S. government will be able to counter such attacks, the CRS report briefly but effectively addresses selected terrorists' objectives, as well as computer vulnerabilities that could facilitate cyber-terror attacks. The report also correctly notes that countering cyberterrorism is an international vice a domestic challenge, and nations and non-national entities must join together in a common effort, if large scale cyber-terror is to be avoided. Still, the difficulty of establishing sufficient trust between government and business to permit formulation and implementation of an effective strategy to counter cyberterrorism is exacerbated when other nations and global entities are involved.

The report laments that it is difficult to determine whether a cyber-attack is the work of ideologically motivated cyber-terrorists or cyber-criminals motivated by greed and power aspirations. As stated earlier, both employ similar tactics. The report notes that in 2003, the U.S. Drug Enforcement Agency (DEA) reported that almost half of foreign terrorist organizations were involved in criminal activity. That report is consistent with an earlier report by the Library of Congress Federal Research Division. The proportion is almost certainly higher now. The DEA argued for linking the war against terrorists to the war against drug traffickers. Additionally, the CRS report correctly notes that criminal drug traffickers have become quite sophisticated in using computer messaging, encryption, and steganography to conceal their illegal internet communications. One could reasonably conclude that cyber-terrorists have become equally skilled users of the internet, especially considering their constantly improving connections with cyber-criminals.

Given the above discussion of the astute conclusions drawn by the CRS report concerning the intersection of cyberterrorism with cyber-crime, the authors of the report appear overly concerned about the difficulty of distinguishing between cyber-terrorists and cyber-criminals. Both pose threats to U.S. national security. Both conduct illegal activity that subjects them to the police powers of the nation. With the passage and renewal of the USAPATRIOT Act, law enforcement and other agencies of government, to include the Department of Defense, are able to integrate better their respective efforts. Therefore, a comprehensive strategy for countering both cyberterrorism and cyber-crime may be crafted and implemented, even though, during formulation and implementation, one may not know for sure whether the target is a cyber-criminal, cyber-terrorist, or both. By definition, a cyber-terrorist is a cyber-criminal, although a cyber-criminal might not be a terrorist. That distinction need not necessarily be made in advance by the counter terrorist strategist.

This report continues the theme introduced in the preface of this volume and found in previously provided documents; i.e., considerable disagreement exists over the severity of the cyber-terrorist threat. The report's treatment of the differing views is consistent with other documents presented. Concern about cyberterrorism spiked shortly after September 11, 2001, began to wane over a number of years reaching a nadir in 2005, but becoming progressively more pronounced after 2005. The CRS report notes that a "Business Roundtable" report issued in June 2006 concluded that the United States was not prepared to recognize and respond to a cyber-attack for three reasons: it has no established and widely accepted indicators of an attack, it is limited in its ability to determine who is responsible for an attack, and it has not dedicated adequate resources to procedures and capabilities for mitigating the effects of a cyber-attack. While these deficiencies continue to exist, they are not as debilitating as they were two years ago.

The CRS report correctly notes that physical security enhancements for critical infrastructure may be pushing terrorists to exploit the vulnerabilities many analysts claim cyber-space creates. These analysts argue that not enough is being done to reduce the existing and growing vulnerabilities, with the expanding world-wide web creating more every day. Thus, the probability of a significantly damaging cyber-terror attack increases daily and, to some, is virtually assured. Still, others challenge this view, arguing that the owners of critical infrastructure, mostly private commercial entities, have taken steps to recover quickly form a cyber-terrorist attack, in accordance with sound business case analyses. The CRS report introduces these two schools of thought reasonably well, while leaving it to the reader to draw his or her own conclusions.

The next document presented in this section, *Botnets, Cybercrime, and Cyberterrorism: Vulnerabilities and Policy Issues for Congress*, is a very useful updated analysis of cyber-criminals and cyber-terrorists and their use of "botnets." It correctly notes that criminal and terrorist organizations can hire individuals with highly technical internet and computer skills for criminal and terroristic purposes. The report also correctly observes that the sophisticated skills available to criminals and terrorists have largely succeeded in defeating efforts to track and attribute cyber-attacks. This is due, in part, to the innovative use of botnets by cyber-terrorists and cyber-criminals. The report defines a botnet as a network of compromised computers that cyber-terrorists and criminals enslave to do their bidding, inside the government and industry information systems within which the compromised computers reside.

The report provides a useful look at how criminals and terrorists can access internet expertise and to what ends. The report effectively sets the context and provides the basis for the issues it presents by beginning with a background discussion that includes identification of computer system vulnerabilities, definitions of cyber-crime and cyberterrorism, a discussion of botnets, a review of trends in cyber-crime and cyberterrorism, identification of linkages between cyber-crime and cyberterrorism, a description of infrastructure unpredictability, and a discussion of system vulnerabilities, protection problems, measures taken to date, and the need for improved actions. The report's most important contribution should be the extent to which it identifies and develops issues for congressional consideration. In that regard, the report will disappoint many readers.

Clearly the increasing technical skills of cyber-terrorists and the importance of measuring effects, formulating responses, improving software security, educating computer users, coordinating government and private defenses, and better notification to victims are critical considerations. Nonetheless, they are not developed into issues that point toward legislation, and the report's brief treatment of them does little more than increase congressional awareness. One may fairly assume, however, that increased congressional awareness is valuable, in that it enables congress to consider the cyber-terrorist dimension in laws that may be introduced for other purposes, such as protection of personal information legislation.

One observation the report makes is singularly important—that Congress should examine incentives for achieving the goals of the National Strategy for Securing Cyberspace (see Vol. 86, this series). The lack of such incentives has inhibited effective implementation of the strategy. The report offers some specific measure Congress could enact to effectuate the strategy. The limited progress in turning the various strategic concepts that comprise the strategy into action suggest the need for more regulation of cyber-security. That notwithstanding, the report accurately observes that much support remains for the proposition that cyber-security should result from market forces, rather than government action.

The third document presented in this section, *Cybercrime: An Overview of the Federal Computer Fraud and Abuse Statute and Related Federal Criminal Laws*, is a CRS report that outlines and discusses Title 18 of the United States Code, Section 1030, the federal computer fraud and abuse statute. The report conveniently lays-out and discusses the protections the statute provides, within the context of other federal laws enacted, at least in part, to provide for cyber-security. It presents the various violations and discusses them and the respective penalties that may be imposed, which include life imprisonment, in extreme cases. Although the report claims that the statute is not comprehensive and is intended only to fill gaps in cyber-security left by other laws, one is struck by how many cyber-terror and cyber-criminal acts are made explicitly illegal by offenses discussed. Additionally, the gap-filling function of the statute is very significant in that it makes a coherent whole out of what previously were many disparate laws. Although 18 U.S.C. § 1030 is principally a criminal statute, it also creates a civil cause of action for victims.

The coverage of the statute appears somewhat limited since, by its terms, it applies only to the protection of "computers in which there is a federal interest—federal computers, bank computers, and computers used in interstate and foreign commerce." However, the report's authors provide several excellent examples of how the statute is harmonized with other laws to protect against virtually every conceivable act of cyber-crime and cyberterrorism. The reader will find the cross-walks provided in the body and footnotes of the report between the statute and other laws to be very informative and useful. In many respects, the report shows how the statute provides linchpins linking many other cyber-security laws.

The report correctly points out that only two sections of the statute specifically and explicitly address cyberterrorism: 18 U.S.C. 1030(a)(1) and (a)(5). These two explicit categorizations of offenses as cyberterrorism are significant, in that, as the report correctly notes, they trigger several other substantive and procedural criminal statutes, without the need to show any further nexus to terrorism. Therefore, several other deterring considerations come into play. For example, federal crimes of terrorism are subject to an 8-year statute of limitations (vice 5 years), parole or probation may be for life, pre-trial release is normally not permitted, maximum terms of imprisonment may be more than doubled, one who knowingly provides maritime transportation to an individual intending to commit or fleeing from an act of terrorism may be imprisonment for any term of years up to life. Additionally, the report explains that federal crimes of terrorism are considered RICO predicate offenses, conviction of which can result in up to 20 years imprisonment, fines up to $250,000, and civil liability that could include treble damages, costs and attorneys' fees, among other remedies. In sum, this report provides an excellent assessment of how the Federal Computer Fraud and Abuse Statute combine with other federal criminal laws to deter and punish acts of cyberterrorism.

DOCUMENT NO. 4

TERRORIST CAPABILITIES FOR CYBERATTACK: OVERVIEW AND POLICY ISSUES

CRS Report
RL33123

January 22, 2007

John Rollins
Specialist in Terrorism and International Crime
Foreign Affairs, Defense, and Trade Division

Clay Wilson
Specialist in Technology and National Security
Foreign Affairs, Defense, and Trade Division

Summary

Terrorist's use of the internet and other telecommunications devices is growing both in terms of reliance for supporting organizational activities and for gaining expertise to achieve operational goals. Tighter physical and border security may also encourage terrorists and extremists to try to use other types of weapons to attack the United States. Persistent Internet and computer security vulnerabilities, which have been widely publicized, may gradually encourage terrorists to continue to enhance their computer skills, or develop alliances with criminal organizations and consider attempting a cyberattack against the U.S. critical infrastructure.

Cybercrime has increased dramatically in past years, and several recent terrorist events appear to have been funded partially through online credit card fraud. Reports indicate that terrorists and extremists in the Middle East and South Asia may be increasingly collaborating with cybercriminals for the international movement of money, and for the smuggling of arms and illegal drugs. These links with hackers and cybercriminals may be examples of the terrorists' desire to continue to refine their computer skills, and the relationships forged through collaborative drug trafficking efforts may also provide terrorists with access to highly skilled computer programmers. The July 2005 subway and bus bombings in England also indicate that extremists and their sympathizers may already be embedded in societies with a large information technology workforce.

The United States and international community have taken steps to coordinate laws to prevent cybercrime, but if trends continue computer attacks will become more numerous, faster, and more sophisticated. In addition, a recent report by the Government Accountability Office states that, in the future, U.S. government agencies may not be able to respond effectively to such attacks.

This report examines possible terrorists' objectives and computer vulnerabilities that might lead to an attempted cyberattack against the critical infrastructure of the U.S. homeland, and also discusses the emerging computer and other technical skills of terrorists and extremists. Policy issues include exploring ways to improve technology for cybersecurity, or whether U.S. counterterrorism efforts should be linked more closely to international efforts to prevent cybercrime.

This report will be updated as events warrant.

Introduction

Often it is very difficult to determine if a cyber attack or intrusion is the work of a terrorist organization with the objective of doing harm, or a cyber criminal who wishes to steal information for purposes of monetary gain. Just as terrorists and violent extremists often rely on exploiting vulnerabilities of targets seen as soft and easy to access to support possible future cyber attacks, cyber criminals exploit these same vulnerabilities to gain access to information that may lead to monetary gain. Implementation of a stronger policy for domestic physical security has reduced the risk to some targets that may have previously been vulnerable to physical attacks. Also, it is suggested by numerous experts that terrorists may be enhancing their computer skills or forming alliances with cybercriminals that possess a high-level of telecommunications expertise. In addition, continuing publicity about Internet computer security vulnerabilities may encourage terrorists' interest in attempting a possible computer network attack, or cyberattack, against U.S. critical infrastructure.

To date, the Federal Bureau of Investigation (FBI) reports that cyberattacks attributed to terrorists have largely been limited to unsophisticated efforts such as email bombing of ideological foes, or defacing of websites. However, it says their increasing technical competency is resulting in an emerging capability for network-based attacks. The FBI has predicted that terrorists will either develop or hire hackers for the purpose of complimenting large conventional attacks with cyberattacks.[1] Recently, during the Annual Threat Assessment, FBI Director Mueller observed that "terrorists increasingly use the internet to communicate, conduct operational planning, proselytize, recruit, train and to obtain logistical and financial support. That is a growing and increasing concern for us."[2]

IBM has reported that, during the first half of 2005, criminal-driven computer security attacks increased by 50 percent, with government agencies and industries in the United States targeted most frequently.[3] Cybercrime is now a major criminal activity, and it may become increasingly difficult to separate some forms of cybercrime from suspected terrorist activities. For example, in a recent report from the House Homeland Security Committee, FBI officials indicated that extremists have used identity theft and credit card fraud to support recent terrorist activities by Al Qaeda cells.[4] Also, according to press reports Indonesian police officials believe the 2002 terrorist bombings in Bali were partially financed through online credit card fraud.[5]

This report reviews publications and government reports to explore the following: (1) examples of vulnerabilities that may raise the level of interest that terrorists might have in attempting a coordinated cyberattack; (2) effects of the War on Terror that are driving terrorists to use the Internet more; (3) inconsistent reporting about terrorists' cyber activities; and (4) ways that terrorists may be improving their cyber skills.

Background

Distinctions between crime, terrorism, and war tend to blur when attempting to describe a computer network attack (CNA) in ways that parallel the physical world. For example, if a nation state were to secretly sponsor non-state actors who initiate a CNA to support terrorist activities or to create economic disruption, the distinction between cybercrime and cyberwar becomes less clear. Because it is difficult to tell from where a cyberattack

[1] Keith Lourdeau, FBI Deputy Assistant Director, testimony before the U.S. Senate Judiciary Subcommittee on Terrorism, Technology, and Homeland Security, February 24, 2004.

[2] Robert Mueller, FBI Director, testimony before the Senate Select Committee on Intelligence, January 11, 2007.

[3] IBM Press Release, Government, financial services and manufacturing sectors top targets of security attacks in first half of 2005, August 2, 2005, [http://www.ibm.com/news/ie/en/2005/08/ie_en_news_20050804.html].

[4] According to FBI officials, Al Qaeda terrorist cells in Spain used stolen credit card information to make numerous purchases. Also, the FBI has recorded more than 9.3 million Americans as victims of identity theft in a 12-month period; June, 2005. Report by the Democratic Staff of the House Homeland Security Committee, *Identity Theft and Terrorism*, July 1, 2005, p. 10.

[5] Alan Sipress, "An Indonesian's Prison Memoir Takes Holy War Into Cyberspace," *Washington Post*, December 14, 2004, p. A19.

originates, an attacker may direct suspicion toward an innocent third party. Likewise, the interactions between terrorists and criminals who use computer technology may sometimes blur the distinction between cybercrime and cyberterrorism. It also may be the case that individuals providing computer expertise to a criminal or terrorist may not be aware of the intentions of the individual that requested the support. So far, it remains difficult to determine the sources responsible for most of the annoying, yet increasingly sophisticated attacks that plague the Internet. Given the difficulty in determining the originator of the cyber intrusions or attacks, some argue that unlike responding to traditional criminal acts, the focus should be on the act rather than the perpetrator and the threshold for launching defensive and offensive actions should be lowered.

The Internet is now used as a prime recruiting tool for insurgents in Iraq.[6] Insurgents have created many Arabic-language websites that are said to contain coded plans for new attacks. Some reportedly give advice on how to build and operate weapons, and how to pass through border checkpoints.[7] Other news articles report that a younger generation of terrorists and extremists, such as those behind the July 2005 bombings in London, are learning new technical skills to help them avoid detection by law enforcement computer technology.[8]

When is Cyberattack Considered Cyberterrorism?

Some observers feel that the term "Cyberterrorism" is inappropriate, because a widespread cyberattack may simply produce annoyances, not terror, as would a bomb, or other chemical, biological, radiological, or nuclear explosive (CBRN) weapon. However, others believe that the effects of a widespread computer network attack would be unpredictable and might cause enough economic disruption, fear, and civilian deaths, to qualify as terrorism. At least two views exist for defining the term Cyberterrorism:

- **Effects-based**: Cyberterrorism exists when computer attacks result in effects that are disruptive enough to generate fear comparable to a traditional act of terrorism, even if done by criminals.
- **Intent-based**: Cyberterrorism exists when unlawful or politically motivated computer attacks are done to intimidate or coerce a government

[6] Jonathan Curiel, "TERROR.COM: Iraq's tech-savvy insurgents are finding supporters and luring suicide-bomber recruits over the Internet," *San Francisco Chronicle*, July 10, 2005, [http://www.sfgate.com/cgi-bin/article.cgi?f=/c/a/2005/07/10/CURIEL.TMP].

[7] Jonathan Curiel, "Iraq's tech-savvy insurgents are finding supporters and luring suicide-bomber recruits over the Internet," *San Francisco Chronicle*, July 10, 2005, p. A.01.

[8] Michael Evans and Daniel McGrory, "Terrorists Trained in Western Methods Will Leave Few Clues," *London Times*, July 12, 2005.

or people to further a political objective, or to cause grave harm or severe economic damage.[9]

Objectives for a Cyberattack

The Internet, whether accessed by a desktop computer or the many available handheld devices, is the medium through which a cyberattack would be delivered. However, for a targeted attack[10] to be successful, the attackers usually require that the network itself remain more or less intact, unless the attackers assess that the perceived gains from shutting down the network would offset the accompanying loss of communication. A targeted cyberattack could be effective if directed against a portion of the U.S. critical infrastructure, and if timed to amplify the effects of a simultaneous conventional physical or chemical, biological, nuclear, or radiological (CBRN) terrorist attack. The objectives of a cyberattack include the following four areas:[11]

1. Loss of integrity, such that information could be modified improperly;
2. Loss of availability, where mission critical information systems are rendered unavailable to authorized users;
3. Loss of confidentiality, where critical information is disclosed to unauthorized users; and,
4. Physical destruction, where information systems create actual physical harm through commands that cause deliberate malfunctions.

According to Richard Clarke, former Administration Counter Terrorism Advisor and National Security Advisor, if terrorists were to launch a widespread cyberattack against the United States, the economy would be the intended target for disruption, while death and destruction might be considered collateral damage.[12] Many security experts also agree that a cyberattack would be most effective if it were used to amplify a conventional bombing or CBRN attack. Such a scenario might include attempting to disrupt 911 call centers simultaneous with the detonating of an explosives devices. This type of example is usually contrasted to a widespread, coordinated cyberattack, unaccompanied by a physical attack, that would technically be very difficult to orchestrate and unlikely be effective in furthering terrorists' goals. Because such an attack cannot directly cause death and

[9] For a more in-depth discussion of the definition of cyberterrorism, see CRS Report RL32114, *Computer Attack and Cyberterrorism: Vulnerabilities and Policy Issues for Congress*, by Clay Wilson.

[10] A targeted attack is one where the attacker is intentionally attempting to gain access to or disrupt a specific target. This is in contrast to a random attack where the attacker seeks access to or disrupt any target that appears vulnerable.

[11] U.S. Army Training and Doctrine Command, Cyber Operations and Cyber Terrorism, Handbook No. 1.02, August 15, 2005, p.II-1 and II-3

[12] Kevin Rademacher reporting remarks of Richard Clarke at CardTech/SecurTech security conference April 2005, "Clarke: ID Theft Prevention Tied to Anti-terrorism Efforts," *Las Vegas Sun*, April 13, 2005, at [http://www.lasvegassun.com/sumbin/stories/text/2005/apr/13/518595803.html].

destruction, this may explain why there is no evidence that terrorist groups have undertaken a significant cyber attack.[13] However, other observers say that, because of interdependencies among infrastructure sectors, a large-scale cyberattack that affected one sector could also have disruptive, unpredictable, and perhaps devastating effects on other sectors, and possibly long-lasting effects to the economy. These observers assert Al Qaeda and associated terrorist groups are becoming more technically sophisticated, and years of publicity about computer security weaknesses has made them aware that the U.S. economy could be vulnerable to a coordinated cyberattack.[14]

Publicity would be also one of the primary objectives for a terrorist attack. Extensive coverage has been given to the vulnerability of the U.S. information infrastructure and to the potential harm that could be caused by a cyberattack. This might lead terrorists to feel that even a marginally successful cyberattack directed at the United States may garner considerable publicity.[15] Some suggest that were such a cyber attack by a terrorist organization to occur and become known to the general public, regardless of the level of success of the attack, concern by many citizens may lead to widespread withdrawal of funds and selling of equities.

Persistent Computer Security Vulnerabilities

At the July 2005 Black Hat computer security conference (a private sector sponsored annual meeting of organizations focused on cyber-security technology and related issues) Las Vegas, a security expert demonstrated an exploit of what many consider to be a significant Internet security flaw, by showing how the most commonly used Internet routers; the computer's device that forwards data to a desired destination, could quickly be hacked.[16] This router vulnerability could allow an attacker to disrupt

[13] Joris Evers, "Does Cyberterrorism Pose a True Threat?," *PCWorld*, March 14, 2003, at [http://www.peworld.com/news/article/0,aid,109819,00.asp]. Joris Evers, reporting remarks by Bruce Schneier at CeBIT technology trade show in March 2003, "Cyberterror Threat Overblown," *Computerworld*, March 14, 2003, at [http://www.computeworld,com/printthis/2003/0,4814,79368,00.html]. Gabriel Weimann, *Special Report - Cyberterrorism: How Real is the Threat?*, United States Institute of Peace, Washington, D.C., May 2004. Dan Ilett reporting remarks of Richard Clarke at the Oxford University Internet Institute in February 2005, Clarke joins latest cyberterror debate, ZDNet UK, February 11, 2005, at [http://www.zdnet.co.uk/print/?TYPE=story&AT=39187582-39020375t-10000025c].

[14] Dan Verton, *Black Ice: The Invisible Threat of Cyber-Terrorism*, McGraw-Hill, 2003, p. 110. Keith Lourdeau, Deputy Assistant Director of the FBI Cyber Division, testimony before the Senate Judiciary Subcommittee on Terrorism, Technology and Homeland Security, February 24, 2004. Ryan Naraine reporting remarks of Roger Cressey at Infosec World 2005, *Cyber-Terrorism Analyst Warns Against Complacency*, eWEEK.com, April 4, 2005, at [http://www.eweek.com/article2/0,1759,1782288,00.asp].

[15] The Electronic Intrusion Threat to National Security and Emergency Preparedness (NS/EP) Internet Communications, Office of the Manager, National Communications System, December 2000, p.31, at [http://www.ncs.gov/library/reports/electron ic_intrusion_threat2000_final2.pdf].

[16] Amy Storer, Update: *IPv6 risks may outweigh benefits*, SearchSecurity.com, July 29, 2005, at [http://searchsecurity.techtarget.com/originalContent/0,289142,sid14_gci1112459,00.html?track=NL-358&ad=525032USCA].

selected portions of the Internet, or even target specific groups of banks or power stations.[17] Security expert Bruce Schneier, a recent critic of the idea of cyberterrorism, reportedly agreed that the router flaw was a "major" Internet security vulnerability, and could allow criminals to steal identity information, or otherwise attack networks. The company released in April 2005 a software patch to fix the problem, but over the following four months, had apparently not notified its customers and government agencies, including DHS, about the seriousness of the vulnerability.[18]

The United States may provide ample economic targets vulnerable to cyberattack, thus tempting terrorist groups to increase their cyber skills.[19] A February 2005 report by the President's Information Technology Committee (PITAC) stated that the information technology infrastructure of the United States, which is vital for communication, commerce, and control of the physical infrastructure, is highly vulnerable to terrorist and criminal attacks. The report also found that the private sector has an important role in protecting national security by deploying sound security products, and by adopting good security practices.[20] However, a recent survey of 136,000 PCs used in 251 commercial businesses in North America found that a major security software patch, known as SP2, was installed on only nine percent of the systems, despite the fact that Microsoft advertized the importance of installing the security patch one year ago. The remaining 91 percent of commercial businesses surveyed will continue to be exposed to major security threats until they deploy the software patch throughout their organizations.[21] This may bring into question the extent to which the private sector will self-protect without greater incentive.

Several recent studies by global computer security firms found that the highest rates for computer attack activity were directed against critical infrastructures, such as government, financial services, manufacturing, and power. These reports also show that the United States is the most highly targeted nation for computer attacks; during the first half of 2005, United States computer systems were attacked at a rate 10 times higher than the next most highly targeted nation, China (see section titled "Trends

[17] Victor Garza, *Security researcher cause furor by releasing flaw in Cisco Systems IOS*, SearchSecurity.com, July 28, 2005, at [http://searchsecurity.techtarget.com/originalContent/0,289142,sid14_gci1111389,00.html].

[18] Justin Rood, *Cisco Failed to Alert DHS, Other Agencies About Software Security Flaw*, CQ Homeland Security, August 2, 2005, at [http://homeland.cq.com/hs/display.do?docid=1810432&sourcetype=31&binderName=news-all].

[19] Dan Verton, *Black Ice: The Invisible Threat of Cyber-Terrorism*, McGraw-Hill, 2003, p. 110. (Hereafter cited as Verton, *Black Ice*.)

[20] The President's Information Technology Advisory Committee, *Cyber Security: A Crisis of Prioritization*, Report to the President, February 2005, p. 25, [http://www.nitrd.gov/pitac/reports/20050301_cybersecurity/cybersecurity.pdf].

[21] John Foley, "Businesses Slow to Deploy Windows XP SP2," *Information Week*, April 26, 2005, p. 26.

in Cybercrime," below).[22] U.S. federal agencies have come under criticism in past years for the effectiveness of their computer security programs.[23] Further, a May 2005 report by the Government Accountability Office (GAO) stated that because of the growing sophistication of malicious code on the Internet, the federal government may increasingly be limited in its ability to respond to cyber threats.[24]

U.S. Government Cybersecurity Efforts

Many U.S. federal government departments and agencies have responsibilities and have established programs to address various aspects of cybersecurity. Some would argue that this level of federal effort demonstrates the government's view as recognizing cyber-security as a national priority. Others see the many organizations and programs as unnecessarily duplicative with the Nation lacking a coherent strategy for understanding the true cyber security threat or the roles and responsibilities of each federal government organization.

Department of Homeland Security (DHS). Some homeland security experts are concerned that the establishment of DHS has delayed federal government cyber security efforts significantly. It is suggested that during a time when the terrorists appear to be growing more reliant on the internet and gaining valuable expertise and experience, DHS, the lead federal agency responsible for cyber-security, has not progressed to meet the challenges that might lie ahead. Others cite the difficulty of ascertaining the intentions, origination, and groups behind cyber-intrusions and attacks as a reason for DHS and the federal government's lack of progress. In February, 2006, DHS participated in and sponsored exercise Cyber Storm which tested the ability of the U.S. government, international partners, and the private sector to recognize, disrupt, and respond to a large-scale cyber attack. Analysis of the exercise produced eight major findings to better position the United States to "enhance the nation's cyber preparedness and response capabilities."[25] While many were pleased that DHS conducted

---

22 IBM News, *Report Finds Online Attacks Shift Toward Profit*, August 2, 2005, at [http://www.ibm.com/news/us/en/2005/08/2005_08_02.html]. Symantec Press Release, *Symantec Internet Security Threat Report Highlights Rise In Threats To Confidential Information*, March 21, 2005, at [http://www.symantec.com/press/2005/n050321.html].

23 Based on 2002 data submitted by federal agencies to the White House Office of Management and Budget, GAO noted, in testimony before the House Committee on Government Reform (GAO-03-564T, April 8, 2003), that all 24 agencies continue to have "significant information security weaknesses that place a broad array of federal operations and assets at risk of fraud, misuse, and disruption." Christopher Lee, November 20, 2002, *Agencies Fail Cyber Test: Report Notes 'Significant Weaknesses' in Computer Security*, at [http://www.washingtonpost.com/ac2/wp-dyn/A12321-2002Nov19?language=printer.]

24 GAO, *Information Security; Emerging Cybersecurity Issues Threaten Federal Information Systems*, report 05-231, May 2005.

25 DHS, DHS Releases Cyber Storm Public Exercise Report, September 13, 2006 [http://www.dhs.gov/xnews/releases/pr_1158341221370.shtm]. The eight cyber-security enhancement findings

this exercise and recognized areas for improvement, other homeland security observers found the findings to be an acknowledgment of the work that has not been accomplished since the establishment of the Department.

Department of Defense. In August 2005, DOD Directive 3020.40, the "Defense Critical Infrastructure Program," assigned functional responsibility within DOD for coordinating with public and private sector services for protection of defense critical infrastructures from terrorist attacks, including cyberattack.[26] DOD also announced the formation of the Joint Functional Component Command for Network Warfare (JFCCNW) which has responsibility for defending all DOD computer systems. The expertise and tools used in this mission are for both offensive and defensive operations.[27]

FBI. The FBI Computer Intrusion program provides administrative and operational support and guidance to field offices investigating computer intrusions. A Special Technologies and Applications program supports FBI counterterrorism computer intrusion investigations, and the FBI Cyber International Investigative program conducts international investigations through coordination with FBI Headquarters Office of International Operations and foreign law enforcement agencies.[28]

NSA. The National Security Agency (NSA) has created the National Centers of Academic Excellence in Information Assurance Education (CAEIAE) Program, which is intended to reduce vulnerability of national information infrastructure by promoting higher education in information assurance (IA), and by producing more professionals with IA expertise. The NSA and the Department of Homeland Security (DHS) in support of the President's National Strategy to Secure Cyberspace, established in February 2003, now jointly sponsor the program. Under this program, four-year colleges and graduate-level universities are eligible to apply to be designated as a National Center of Academic Excellence in Information Assurance Education (CAEIAE). Students attending CAEIAE schools are eligible to apply for scholarships and grants through the Department of Defense

---

addressed: Interagency Coordination, Contingency Planning, Risk Assessment and Roles and Responsibilities, Correlation of Multiple Incidents between Public and Private Sectors, Exercise Program, Coordination between Entities of Cyber Incidents, Common Framework for Response to Information Access, Strategic Communications and Public Relations, and Improvement of Process, Tools and Technology.

[26] The Defense Critical Infrastructure is defined as those DOD and non-DOD networked assets essential to project, support, and sustain military forces and operations worldwide.

[27] John Lasker, "U.S. Military's Elite Hacker Crew," *Wired News*, April 18, 2005, [http://www.wired.com/news/print/0,1294,67223,00.html].

[28] Keith Lourdeau, testimony before the Senate Judiciary Subcommittee on Terrorism, Technology, and Homeland Security, February 24, 2004, [http://www.fbi.gov/congress/congress04/lourdeau022404.htm].

Information Assurance Scholarship Program and the Federal Cyber Service Scholarship for Service Program (SFS).[29]

CIA. The CIA Information Operations Center, which evaluates threats to U.S. computer systems from foreign governments, criminal organizations and hackers, conducted a cybersecurity exercise in 2005 called "Silent Horizon" to see how government and industry could react to Internet based attacks. One problem the CIA wanted to examine was who would actually deal with a major cyberwar attack. In theory, the government is in charge, but in practice, the defenses are controlled by a number of civilian telecommunications firms. The simulated cyber attacks were set five years into the future. The stated premise of the exercise was that cyberspace would see the same level of devastation as the 9/11 hijackings.[30]

An earlier cyberterrorism exercise called "Livewire" concluded there were serious questions over government's role during a cyberattack depending on who was identified as the culprit—terrorists, a foreign government, or bored teenagers. It also questioned whether the U.S. government would be able to detect the early stages of such an attack without significant help from private technology companies.

Inter-Agency Forums. To improve cybersecurity for federal agencies and the critical infrastructure, the Office of Management and Budget (OMB) has created a task force to investigate how agencies can better coordinate cybersecurity functions such as training, incident response, disaster recovery, and contingency planning. The U.S. Department of Homeland Security has also created a new National Cyber Security Division that will focus on reducing vulnerabilities in the government's computing networks, and in the private sector to help protect the critical infrastructure.[31]

Many security vendors agree that to combat cybercrime more effectively, it must be treated as a global problem. Some of these security vendors have created their own independent advance-warning systems for their customers through linking proprietary security equipment into global networks that share information collected by their distributed customer base. One example is an early-warning cyber-security intrusion program that's composed of a global network of 19,000 firewall and intrusion-detection devices maintained by thousands of volunteer data partners. This early intrusion system correlates global data to detect the start of a possible swarming Internet attack originating simultaneously in different parts of the world,

---

29 National Security Agency, [http://www.nsa.gov/ia/academia/caeiae.cfm].

30 Ted Bridis, "'Silent Horizon' war games wrap up for the CIA," *USA Today*, May 26, 2005, [http://www.usatoday.com/tech/news/techpolicy/2005-05-26-cia-wargames_x.htm].

31 Jason Miller, "New Cybersecurity Team Meets this Week," *Government Computer News*, March 21, 2005. Grant Gross, "Homeland Security to Oversee Cybersecurity," *PC World*, June 9, 2003, at [http://www.pcworld.com/news/article/0,aid,111066,00.asp].

and notifies administrators to help them defend their systems when targeted.[32] A similar public/private partnership security warning program was created through the Cyber Incident Detection Data Analysis Center (CIDDAC).[33] In 2005, CIDDAC will install special sensors on the networks of participating partner companies to automatically detect cyberattacks and notify administrators and law enforcement.

Changing Concerns about Cyberattack, 2001–2006

Following the September 11 attacks, public concerns were high about the threat of a possible follow-on cyberattack from terrorist groups.[34] Subsequently, there has been disagreement among security experts about (1) whether such an attack could possibly be launched by terrorists against U.S. civilian critical infrastructure, or (2) whether such an attack could seriously disrupt the U.S. economy.[35]

Simulated cyberattacks, conducted by the U.S. Naval War College in 2002, indicated that attempts to cripple the U.S. telecommunications infrastructure would be unsuccessful because system redundancy would prevent damage from becoming too widespread. Many observers suggest that evidence from natural disasters shows that many the critical infrastructure systems, including banking, power, water, and air traffic control, would likely recover rapidly from a possible cyberattack.[36]

To date, there has been no published report of a coordinated cyberattack launched against the critical infrastructure by a terrorist or terrorist group. Dennis McGrath of the Institute of Security Technology Studies at Dartmouth College reportedly observed that, "We hear less and less

---

[32] Paul Roberts, "Symantec Offers Early Warning of Net Threats," *PC World*, February 12, 2003, at [http://www.pcworld.com/news/article/0,aid,109322,00.asp].

[33] CIDDAC is a not-for-profit organization that combines private and government perspectives to facilitate automated real-time sharing of cyberattack data. CIDDAC is specifically designed to protect privacy rights while collecting cyber threat information from sensors attached to corporate computer networks.

[34] In July 2002, Gartner Research and the U.S. Naval War College hosted a three-day, seminar-style war game called "Digital Pearl Harbor" (DPH), with the result that 79% of the gamers said that a strategic cyberattack against the United States was likely within the next two years. Gartner Research, 'Digital Pearl Harbor': Defending Your Critical Infrastructure, October 4, 2002, at [http://www.gartner.com/pages/story.php.id.2727.s.8.jsp].

[35] Robert Gates, former CIA director, warned that the threat of cyberterrorism should be taken particularly seriously. Keith Lourdeu, deputy assistant director of the FBI Cyber Division, stated that "our networked systems make inviting targets for terrorists due to the potential for large-scale impact on the nation." Douglas Schweitzer, "Be Prepared for Cyberterrorism," *Computerworld*, April 6, 2005. However, others believe that infrastructure systems are robust and could recover quickly. Richard Forno, "Shredding the Paper Tiger of Cyberterrorism," *Security Focus*, September 25, 2002, at [http://www.securityfocus.com/printable/columnists/111]. See also, CRS Report RL32114, *Computer Attack and Cyberterrorism: Vulnerabilities and Policy Issues for Congress*, by Clay Wilson.

[36] Scott Nance, "Debunking Fears: Exercise Finds 'Digital Pearl Harbour' Risk Small," *Defense Week*, April 7, 2003, at [http://www.kingpublishing.com/publications/dw/]. William Jackson, "War College Calls Digital Pearl Harbor Doable," *Government Computer News*, August 23, 2002, at [http://www.gcn.com/vol1_no1/daily-updates/19792-1.html].

about a digital Pearl Harbor. Cyberterrorism is not at the top of the list of discussions."[37]

In May 2005, the CIA reportedly conducted a classified war game, dubbed "Silent Horizon," to practice defending against a simulated widespread cyberattack directed against the United States. The national security simulation was considered significant because many U.S. counterterrorism experts feel that far-reaching effects from a cyberattack are highly unlikely.[38] However, other observers believe that tests of countermeasures, even for unlikely events, may sometimes be prudent.

Many cyber security observers are concerned that U.S. government efforts to date have not effectively prepared the nation for a catastrophic cyberattack. A Business Roundtable report issued in June 2006 found three "cybergaps" that are keeping the United States from being prepared to recognize and respond to a cyberattack: (1) the lack of established indicators that would indicate an attack is underway; (2) a failure to identify who is responsible for restoring affected infrastructure; and (3) a lack of dedicated resources to assist in returning cyber operations to a pre-attack condition.[39] Due to increased security measures applied to physical facilities and U.S. government efforts to track and engage groups in their home countries, many believe the internet will increasingly play a bigger role in terrorist support and operational efforts. Many observers that monitor the Internet suggest that due to the effects of intensified counterterrorism efforts worldwide, Islamic extremists are gravitating toward the Internet, and are succeeding in organizing online where they have been failing in the physical world. Terrorist groups increasingly use online services for covert messaging, through steganography, anonymous e-mail accounts, and encryption.[40]

Inconsistent Reporting of Terrorists' Cyber Activities

Some security observers argue that a lack of consistent reporting on the true nature of the cyber-security threat is a direct by-product of the federal government's lack of strategy and inability to clarify assignments for the numerous departments and agencies that have some responsibility for the issue. Others note that the numerous recent governmental organizations are the reason for the delay in progress, and also predict that as DHS and

---

[37] "CIA Overseeing 3-Day Wargame on Internet," *Associated Press*, May 25, 2005.

[38] Ted Bridis, "'Silent Horizon' War Games Wrap up for the CIA," *USA Today*, May 26, 2005, at [http://www.usatoday.com/tech/news/techpolicy/2005-05-26-cia-wargames_x.htm].

[39] Business Roundtable, *Essential Steps to Strengthen America's Cyber Terrorism Preparedness*, June 2006, at [http://www.businessroundtable.org/pdf/20060622002CyberReconFinal6106.pdf].

[40] Terrorist suspects are reportedly using encryption techniques to prevent police from accessing vital intelligence on seized computers, according to U.K. police. Stewart Tendler, "Encrypted Files Frustrate Police," *Times Online*, July 20, 2005, at [http://technology.timesonline.co.uk/article/0,,20409-1701405,00.html]. See CryptoHaven, at [http://www.cryptoheaven.com/], and SecretMaker, at [http://www.secretmaker.com/emailsecurer/steganography/default.html].

the Office of the Director of National Intelligence mature, the issue of cybersecurity assessments and reporting may receive a higher priority.

A review of two annual U.S. government reports on terrorism activity shows inconsistent attention to the issue of possible cyberterrorism.[41] Two federal agencies report on terrorism activity annually: (1) the Department of State's (DOS) *Patterns of Global Terrorism*[42] and, (2) the Federal Bureau of Investigation's *Annual Terrorism in the United States.*[43]

In the DOS reports for the years 1996 to 1999, brief mention is made of cyberterrorism issues. In the year 2000, the report acknowledges that "widespread availability of hacking software and its anonymity and increasingly automated design make it likely that terrorists will more frequently incorporate these tools into their online activity." In 2001, however, no mention of cyberterrorism issues appeared in the DOS report, and for the years 2002 to 2004, only mentions of various security forums and international cybersecurity working groups were noted.

The FBI's *Annual Terrorism Report* similarly was inconsistent in mentioning cyberterrorism issues. In the 1996 and 1997 reports, there was no mention of cyberterrorism or related activity. In 1998 the report acknowledged that "cyber tools may find their way in the hands of terrorist" and speculated that "the spread of cyberattack tools, like the proliferation of conventional weapon technology may eventually wind up in the hands of terrorists." The following year, 1999, the Report stated that "the threat of cyberterrorism will grow in the new Millennium, as the leadership positions in extremist organizations are increasingly filled with younger, Internet-savvy individuals." These two reports arguably suggested that the issue of cyberterrorism was being followed closely. The Reports from 2000 to 2003 mentioned cyberterrorism, but only in the programmatic aspect regarding organizational changes the FBI was putting in place to address cybersecurity, with no mention of past or projected cyberterrorism incidents or issues. The FBI did not produce a report in 2004, and one is not yet due for 2005.

Since the attacks of 9/11, many observers are concerned that increased efforts to safeguard facilities, infrastructure, personnel safety, and the decrease in the DOS's and FBI's discussion of cybersecurity issues, together may indicate a lack of appreciation for the threat that may be facing the United States from possible cyberterrorism. Others suggest that although the frequency and severity of cyberattacks are on the rise, the

---

[41] John Rollins, Specialist in Terrorism and International Crime, Congressional Research Service, August 2005.

[42] "Country Reports on Terrorism" is submitted in compliance with Title 22 of the United States Code, Section 2656(f) which requires the Department of State to provide Congress with a full and complete annual report on terrorism for those countries and groups meeting the criteria of Section (a)(1) and (2) of the act, at [http://www.state.gov/s/ct/rls/c14812.htm].

[43] [http://www.fbi.gov/publications.htm].

federal government may not be sufficiently increasing its efforts to improve cybersecurity.[44]

Technical Skills of Terrorists

Through captured literature, it is known that many Al Qaeda members are well educated, and have familiarity with engineering and other technical areas.[45] During a November 2001 attack by U.S. forces, Al Qaeda fighters fled from Kabul, Afghanistan leaving behind many documents and sensitive information that yielded a profile of some Al Qaeda operatives as well-educated and trained in the use of computer systems. "Technical treatises in Arabic, English, German as well a students' notebooks in Arabic, Turkish, Kurdish, and Russian reflected a consistent interest in and widespread familiarity with electrical and chemical engineering, atomic physics, ballistics, computers, and radios," according to researchers and journalists who reportedly examined the documents.[46]

Just as people all over the world now use the Internet, terrorists also use it as a modern tool for communication. Terrorists and extremist groups have reportedly generated thousands of Internet web sites to support psychological operations, fund raising, recruitment, and coordination of activities. Recently, the Department of State's Counterterrorism Director noted "the most worrisome scenario of another attack in the homeland is lone operatives who slip into the country and take directions through cyberspace."[47] A significant concern is that some of these web sites used for the suspected terrorist activity are hosted on Internet Service Providers inside the United States.[48] The level of technical sophistication of the extremist groups that use and operate these web sites has also increased. In 2006 it was reported that an organization linked to al-Qaeda produced a 26-page manual providing instructions on the use of the Google search engine to further the goals of global jihad.[49] Recently British forces in Iraq have found print-outs of Google-Earth pictures that reportedly were to be used for targeting of coalition forces.[50]

---

44 GAO, *Information Security; Emerging Cybersecurity Issues Threaten Federal Information Systems*, report 05-231, May 2005.

45 Tom Spring, "Al Qaeda's Tech Traps," *PC World*, September 1, 2004, [http://www.pcworld.com/news/article/0,aid,117658,00.asp].

46 Anthony Davis, "The Afghan files: Al-Qaeda Documents from Kabul," *Jane's Intelligence Review*, February 1, 2002.

47 Michael Isikoff, Terror: We're Going to Get Hit, *Newsweek*, January 22, 2007.

48 Internet Service Providers (ISPs) are not liable for terrorist propaganda posted on their systems unless they have actual knowledge of it. Once discovered, terrorist web sites can quickly jump to another ISP faster than system administrators, or law enforcement, can track them. Evan Kohlman, Al Qaeda on the Internet, *Washington Post online interview*, August 8, 2005, 3 P.M. E.T.

49 "Terrorists Launch Google Guide," *The Jawa Report*, November 29, 2006, [http://mypetjawa.mu.nu/archives/185504.php].

50 Thomas Harding, "Terrorists use Google Maps to hit UK Troops," *Telegraph*, January 13, 2007, [http://www.telegraph.co.uk/news/main.jhtml?xml=/news/2007/01/13/wgoogle13.xml].

A recent study of more than 200,000 multimedia documents on 86 sample websites concluded that extremists exhibited similar levels of web knowledge as U.S. government agencies, and that the terrorist websites employed significantly more sophisticated multimedia technologies than U.S. government websites. The study concluded that these extremist websites support advanced Internet-based communication tools such as online forums and chat rooms more frequently than U.S. government web sites.[51] Because of perceived anonymity, terrorist likely feel safer when working together on the Internet.

In April 2002, the Central Intelligence Agency (CIA) stated in a letter to the U.S. Senate Select Committee on Intelligence that cyberwarfare attacks against the U.S. critical infrastructure will become a viable option for terrorists as they become more familiar with the technology required for the attacks. Also according to the CIA, various groups, including Al Qaeda and Hizballah, are becoming more adept at using the Internet and computer technologies, and these groups could possibly develop the skills necessary for a cyberattack.[52] In February 2005, FBI director Robert Mueller, testified before the Senate Select Committee on Intelligence that terrorists show a growing understanding of the critical role of information technology in the U.S. economy and have expanded their recruitment to include people studying math, computer science, and engineering.[53]

Senior leadership of al-Qaeda, who reportedly have access to the most modern technology equipment,[54] and other terrorist groups are reportedly building a massive and dynamic online library of training materials, many of which are supported by subject matter experts who answer questions on message boards or in chat rooms. This online library covers such areas as how to mix poisons for chemical attacks, how to ambush U.S. soldiers, how to coordinate a suicide bomb attack, and how to hack computers.[55] One discussion forum popular with supporters of terrorism is called Qalah, or Fortress, where potential al Qaeda recruits can find links to the latest in computer hacking techniques in a discussion area called "electronic jihad."[56]

---

[51] Jialun Qin et al., Analyzing terror campaigns on the internet: Technical sophistication, content richness, and Web interactivity, International Journal of Human-Computer Studies, November 1, 2006, vol. 65, p.71–84.

[52] Verton, *Black Ice*, p. 87.

[53] Testimony before the Senate Select Committee on Intelligence, February 16, 2005.

[54] "Al-Qaida leaders have the best computer technology that money can buy." Evan Kohlmann, terrorism consultant, *Newsday*, Tunnel Plot Talk in Web Chat rooms can net cyber terrorists, July 8, 2006.

[55] Some have described these web training sites as an open university for jihad. Steve Coll and Susan Glasser, "Terrorists Turn to the Web as Base of Operations," *Washington Post*, Aug 7, 2005, A1.

[56] Steve Coll and Susan Glasser, "Terrorists Turn to the Web as Base of Operations," *Washington Post*, Aug 7, 2005, A1.

Some security experts do not think it is worthwhile to hijack or disrupt the web sites created by terrorists. This is because terrorists will usually find a way to quickly put their sites back up under different, multiple names, which may be even more difficult to monitor. Instead, U.S. intelligence sources can gain valuable information by simply monitoring the web sites they already know about. This may also include monitoring the Internet addresses of those who frequent these web sites. However, more skilled analysts are needed to help translate the communications and information that is posted on the many different terrorist web sites.[57]

The *Washington Times* has reported that Islamic extremists are calling for creation of an Islamist hackers' army to plan cyberattacks against the U.S. government and that postings on the extremist bulletin board, al-Farooq, carry detailed cyberattack instructions, and include spyware programs for download that can be used to learn the passwords of targeted users.[58] Other extremist websites reportedly resemble online training camps that may offer instructions for how to create a safe-house, how to clean a rocket-propelled grenade launcher, or what to do if captured.[59]

Iman Samudra, convicted and now awaiting execution for taking part in the 2002 bombings of two Bali nightclubs, has written a book titled "Aku Mekawan Terroris!", which reportedly translates to "Me Against the Terrorist". Samudra advocates that Muslim youth actively develop hacking skills "to attack U.S. computer networks." Samudra names several websites and chat rooms as sources for increasing hacking skills. He urges Muslim youth to obtain credit card numbers and use them to fund the struggle against the United States and its allies.[60] The terrorist attacks in Bali, and recent attacks in several other countries, may have been funded through stolen credit cards.[61]

Cyberterrorism Capability of State Sponsors of Terrorism

Methods for conducting information warfare to advance the goals of a nation state might also involve secretly sponsoring terrorists. In March

[57] Susan Glassar, "The Iraq Insurgency's Online Strategy," *Washington Post online interview*, August 9, 2005, 11 A.M. E.T.

[58] Shaun Waterman, "Islamists Seek To Organize Hackers' Jihad in Cyberspace," *Washington Times*, August 26, 2005, p. 9.

[59] Tom Spring, "Al Qaeda's Tech Traps," *PCWorld*, September 1, 2004, at [http://www.pcworld.com/news/article/0,aid,117658,00.asp].

[60] FBI Report FEA20041222000744, version 17, *Convicted Indonesian Terrorist Calls for Computer Hacking, Jihad Against US*, December 4, 2004, [https://www.fbis.gov/portal/server.pt/gateway/PTARGS_0_22439_246_203_0_43/http%3B/apps.fbis.gov%3B7011/fbis.gov/search/Search?action=viewDocument&holding=5051585].

[61] Richard Clarke, former counterterrorism advisor for Presidents George W. Bush and Bill Clinton, stated that we are vulnerable to people who would use our identities against us. Kevin Rademacher, "Clarke: ID Theft Prevention Tied to Anti-Terrorism Efforts, *Las Vegas Sun*, April 13, 2005, at [http://www.lasvegassun.com/sunbin/stories/text/2005/apr/13/518595803.html].

2005, a Department of Homeland Security (DHS) report indicated that, of the six nations currently listed by the State Department as terrorist sponsors, five of them—North Korea, Sudan, Syria, Libya, and Cuba—are described as a diminishing concern for terrorism. Only Iran remains listed as a nation-state possibly having a future motivation to assist terrorist groups in attacking the United States homeland. However, some experts believe that a decline in state-sponsorship of terrorism may push terrorist organizations to increasingly embrace the drug trade or other forms of cybercrime.[62]

China is often cited as providing government support to computer-hackers. A paper published in 1999 authored by two senior colonels in the Chinese military specifically discusses the need for China to place new emphasis on information warfare methods to attack enemy financial markets, civilian electricity networks, and telecommunications networks by burying ". . . a computer virus and hacker detachment in the opponent's computer systems in advance . . ." of launching the information warfare network attacks.[63]

DOD officials have acknowledged that hackers, apparently based in China, have been successfully penetrating U.S. military networks since 2001, and perhaps earlier. Although some of these successful cyberattacks were directed against unclassified networks, one intrusion reportedly did obtain data about a future Army command and control system.[64] Although the hackers are suspected to be based in China, DOD and security officials remain divided over (1) whether the ongoing cyberattacks are coordinated or sponsored by the Chinese government, (2) whether they are the work of individual and independent hackers, or (3) whether the cyberattacks are being initiated by some third-party organization that is using network servers in China to disguise the true origins of the attacks. It remains very difficult to determine the true identity, purpose, or sponsor (if any) of a cyber attacker.

Trends in Cyberterrorism and Cybercrime

Today, cyberattacks are increasingly designed to silently steal information without leaving behind any damage that would be noticeable to a user. These types of attacks attempt to escape detection in order to remain on host systems for longer periods of time. Research has shown that attackers

[62] Jennifer Hesterman, *Transnational Crime and the Criminal-Terrorist Nexus*, Walker Paper No.1, Air University, Air University Press, May, 2005, p.32.

[63] Qioa Lang and Wang Xiangsui, *Unrestricted Warfare*, Beijing: PLA Literature and Arts Publishing House, February 1999.

[64] Frank Tiboni, "The New Trojan War," *Federal Computer Week*, August 22, 2005, p. 60. Nathan Thornburgh, *Inside the Chinese Hack Attack*, August 25, 2005, at [http://www.time.com/time/nation/printout/0,8816,1098371,00.html].

are now focusing their efforts on infecting home user desktops or taking control of web applications, allowing the attacker to steal confidential information such as passwords or account codes. The attackers are also using new malicious code tools called "bot networks" that attempt to deny Internet service to targeted victims. According to recent studies by the security organization Symantec and the Cyber Security Industry Alliance, in the first six months of 2006 the home user sector accounted for a large percentage of all targeted attacks, and many home users now believe their financial and personal information may be at risk due to cybercrime.[65]

Identity theft involving thousands of victims is enabled by advances in computer technology, and by poor computer security practices.[66] In June 2006, officials from the U.S. Department of Energy acknowledged that names and personal information belonging to more than 1,500 employees of the National Nuclear Security Administration (NNSA) had been stolen in a network intrusion that apparently took place starting in 2004. The NNSA did not discover the security breach until one year after it had occurred.[67]

A series of computer attacks launched in 2003 against DOD systems and computer systems belonging to DOD contractors apparently went undetected for many months. This series of cyberattacks was labeled "Titan Rain," and was suspected by DOD investigators to originate in China. The attacks were directed against the U.S. Defense Information Systems Agency (DISA), the U.S. Redstone Arsenal, the Army Space and Strategic Defense Installation, and several computer systems critical to military logistics. Although no classified systems were breached, many files were copied containing information that is sensitive and subject to export-control laws.

In November 2006, an extended computer attack against the U.S. Naval War College in Newport, Rhode Island, prompted officials to disconnect the entire campus from the Internet.[68] DOD officials acknowledge that the Global Information Grid, which is the main network for the U.S. military,

---

[65] Vincent Weafer, Statement before the House Subcommittee on Telecommunications and the Internet, Committee on Energy and Commerce, September 13, 2006.

[66] On April 12, 2005, personal information, such as Social Security Numbers for 310,000 U.S. citizens, may have been stolen in a data security breach that involved 59 instances of unauthorized access into its corporate databases using stolen passwords. Boston College reported in March 2005 that a hacker had gained unauthorized access to computer database records with personal information for up to 106,000 alumni, and in the same month, Chico State University of California, reported that its databases had been breached containing the names and Social Security numbers for as many as 59,000 current and former students. David Bank and Christopher Conkey, "New Safeguards for Your Privacy," *The Wall Street Journal*, March 24, 2005, p. D1.

[67] Dawn Onley and Patience Wait, DOD's efforts to stave off nation-state cyberattacks begin with China, *Government Computer News*, August 21, 2006.

[68] Chris Johnson, Naval War College Network, Web Site Back Up Following Intrusion, *Inside the Navy*, December 18, 2006.

experiences more than three million daily scans by unknown potential intruders. DOD officials also suspect that most of these scans originated in the United States and in China (although some of the attacks apparently only traversed through networks in China, casting some doubt on the true origin).[69]

Security experts warn that all U.S. federal agencies should now be aware that in cyberspace some countries consider that no boundaries exist between military and civilian targets. According to an August 2005 computer security report by IBM, more than 237 million overall security attacks were reported globally during the first half of the year.[70] Government agencies were targeted the most, reporting more than 54 million attacks, while manufacturing ranked second with 36 million attacks, financial services ranked third with approximately 34 million, and healthcare received more than 17 million attacks. The most frequent targets for these attacks, all occurring in the first half of 2005, were government agencies and industries in the United States (12 million), followed by New Zealand (1.2 million), and China (1 million). These statistics may represent an underestimation, given that most security analysts agree that the number of incidents reported are only a small fraction of the total number of attacks that actually occur.

Usually, a cyberattack is difficult to detect until after it is well underway, and may involve hundreds or thousands of compromised computers from all parts the globe that are directed by a cybercriminal to attack as a swarm. If the attack is directed against a yet-undisclosed, or newly-discovered security vulnerability, the targeted computer systems may be at a significant disadvantage. Most commercial computer security safeguards operate mainly to prevent the types of attacks that are already known to administrators. A new, unique type of attack against computers may encounter inadequate, untested, or non-existent defenses.

A 2004 survey by an internet security company, covering 450 networks in 35 countries, found that hacking had become a profitable criminal pursuit.[71] Hackers sell unknown computer vulnerabilities (commonly called "zero-day exploits") on the black market to criminals who use them for fraud. Hackers with networks of compromised computers (also known as "bot nets") rent them to other criminals who use them to launch

[69] Some estimates say that up to 90% of computer software used in China is pirated, and thus open to hijack through computer viruses. James Lewis, *Computer Espionage, Titan Rain and China*, Center for Strategic and International Studies, December 14, 2005.

[70] The Global Business Security Index reports worldwide trends in computer security from incidents that are collected and analyzed by IBM and other security organizations. IBM press release, *IBM Report: Government, Financial Services and Manufacturing Sectors Top Targets of Security Attacks in First Half of 2005*, IBM, August 2, 2005.

[71] Counterpane Internet Security, *Attack Trends 2005*, June 2005, at [http://www.schneier.com/essay-085.pdf].

coordinated attacks against targeted individuals or businesses, including banks or other institutions that manage financial information.[72]

It has been reported that stolen credit card numbers and bank account information are now traded online in a highly structured arrangement, involving buyers, seller, intermediaries, and service industries. These services include offering to conveniently change the billing address of a theft victim, through manipulation of stolen PINs or passwords. Estimates by some observers are that, in a highly profitable black market, each stolen MasterCard number can be sold for between $42 and $72.[73]

MasterCard International reported that in 2005 more than 40 million credit card numbers belonging to U.S. consumers were accessed by computer hackers and were at risk of being used for fraud.[74] Some of these account numbers were reportedly being sold on a Russian website, and some consumers have reported fraudulent charges on their statements. Officials at the UFJ bank in Japan reportedly stated that some of that bank's customers may also have become victims of fraud related to theft of MasterCard information.[75]

In Autumn 2004, organized cybercriminals appear to have infiltrated the computer systems of the London offices of Sumitomo, the Japanese bank, in an attempt to steal £220 million. The cybercriminals reportedly planned to transfer the money to other bank accounts around the world. Officials at the London police fraud squad reportedly stated that Sumitomo is the only incident so far in which an attack by external cybercriminals has nearly succeeded against a major bank.[76] Figures from the National Hi-Tech Crime Unit in England show that, in 2003, at least 83% of U.K. companies were targeted by hackers in attempts to seize control of their systems.[77]

The Insider Threat

A 2003 study of security incidents, conducted by the U.S. Secret Service and the Carnegie Mellon Software Engineering Institute, found that attacks

[72] Bruce Schneier, *Attack Trends: 2004 and 2005*, June 6, 2005, at [http://www.schneier.com/blog/archives/2005/06/attack_trends_2.html].

[73] CCRC staff, *Russia, Biggest Ever Credit Card Scam*, Computer Crime Research Center, July 8, 2005, at [http://www.crime-research.org/news/08.07.2005/1349/].

[74] Jonathan Krim and Michael Barbaro, "40 Million Credit Card Numbers Hacked," *Washington Post*, June 18, 2005, p. A01. See also the report by the U.S. House of Representative Homeland Security Committee, July 1, 2005, raising concerns about potential ties between identity theft victims and terrorism. Caitlin Harrington, "Terrorists Can Exploit Identity Theft, Report From House Democrats Says," *CQ Homeland Security*, July 1, 2005.

[75] BBC News, "Japan Cardholders 'Hit' by Theft," June 21, 2005, at [http://news.bbc.co.uk/1/hi/business/4114252.stm].

[76] Conal Walsh, "Terrorism on the Cheap—and with No Paper Trail," *The Guardian Observer* (London), July 17, 2005. (Hereafter cited as Walsh, *Terrorism on the Cheap*.)

[77] *Hi-Tech Crime: The Impact on U.K. Business 2005*, 2004 Survey, at [http://www.nhtcu.org/media/documents/publications/8817_Survey.pdf].

on computer systems committed by insiders with authorized access, have reportedly cost industry millions of dollars in fraud and lost data.[78] Insider employees with access to sensitive information systems can initiate threats in the form of malicious code inserted into software that is being developed either locally, or under offshore contracting arrangements. For example, in January 2003, 20 employees of subcontractors working in the United States at the Sikorsky Aircraft Corporation were arrested for possession of false identification used to obtain security access to facilities containing restricted and sensitive military technology. All of the defendants pleaded guilty and have been sentenced, except for one individual who was convicted at trial on April 19, 2004.[79]

Links Between Terrorism and Cybercrime

The proportion of cybercrime that can be directly or indirectly attributed to terrorists is difficult to determine. Linkages between criminal and terror groups may allow terror networks to expand and undertake large attacks internationally by leveraging criminal sources, money, and transit routes. For example, observers speculate that Aftab Ansari, a criminal suspect located in Dubai, used ransom money earned from prior kidnappings to assist with funding for the September 11, 2001 terrorist attacks. Also, London police officials believe that terrorists obtained the high-quality explosives used for the 2005 bombings through involvement with an Eastern European black market.[80] The recent subway and bus bombings in the U.K. also indicate that groups of terrorists may be active within other countries that have large computerized infrastructures, along with a large, highly skilled information technology workforce. A report by the Department of Homeland Security (DHS) predicts that other possible sponsors of terrorist attacks against the United States homeland may include groups such as Jamaat ul-Fuqura, a Pakistani-based organization allegedly linked to Muslims of America; Jamaat al Tabligh, an Islamic missionary organization; and, the American Dar Al Islam Movement.[81]

Officials of the U.S. Drug Enforcement Agency (DEA), reported in 2003 that 14 of the 36 groups found on the U.S. State Department's list of foreign terrorist organizations were involved in drug trafficking. Consequently,

[78] Marisa Randazzo et al., *Insider Threat Study: Illicit Cyber Activity in the Banking and Finance Sector*, Carnegie Mellon Software Engineering Institute, August 2004.

[79] U.S. Attorneys Office District of Connecticut, at [http://www.usdoj.gov/usao/ct/attf.html].

[80] Walsh, *Terrorism on the Cheap*. Rollie Lal, "Terrorists and Organized Crime Join Forces," *International Herald Tribune*, May 25, 2005, at [http://www.iht.com/articles/2005/05/23/opinion/edlal.php]. Barbara Porter, "Forum Links Organized Crime and Terrorism," *By George!*, summer 2004 [http://www2.gwu.edu/~bygeorge/060804/crimeterrorism.html].

[81] The DHS report, dated January 2005, is entitled "Integrated Planning Guidance, Fiscal Years 2005–2011." Justin Rood, "Animal Rights Groups and Ecology Militants Make DHS Terror List, Right-Wing Vigilantes Omitted," *CQ Homeland Security*, March 25, 2005. Eric Lipton, "Homeland Report Says that Threat From Terror-List Nations Is Declining," *The New York Times*, March 31, 2005, p. A9.

DEA officials reportedly argued that the war on drugs and the war on terrorism are and should be linked.[82] A 2002 report by the Library of Congress Federal Research Division, revealed a "growing involvement of Islamic terrorist and extremists groups in drug trafficking", and limited evidence of cooperation between different terrorist groups involving both drug trafficking and trafficking in arms.[83] State Department officials, at a Senate hearing in March 2002, also indicated that some terrorist groups may be using drug trafficking as a way to gain financing while simultaneously weakening their enemies in the West through exploiting their desire for addictive drugs.[84] Western Europe and North America continue to be regions that have major narcotics markets, optimal infrastructure, and open commercial nodes that increasingly serve the transnational trafficking needs of both criminal and terrorist groups.[85]

Drug traffickers are reportedly among the most widespread users of computer messaging and encryption, and often have the financial clout to hire high level computer specialists capable of using steganography (writing hidden messages contained in digital photographs) and other means to make Internet messages hard or impossible to decipher. Access to such high level specialists can allow terrorist organizations to transcend borders and operate internationally without detection. Many highly trained technical specialists available for hire are located in the countries of the former Soviet Union and in the Indian subcontinent. Some specialists will not work for criminal or terrorist organizations willingly, but may be misled or unaware of their employers political objectives. Still, others will agree to provide assistance because well-paid legitimate employment is scarce in their region.[86]

An emerging area of concern is the involvement of terrorist groups in counterfeiting of intellectual property, which can be even more lucrative than

---

[82] Authorization for coordinating the federal war on drugs expired on September 30, 2003. For more information, see CRS Report RL32352, *War on Drugs: Reauthorization of the Office of National Drug Control Policy*, by Mark Eddy. Also, see D.C. Préfontaine, QC and Yvon Dandurand, *Terrorism and Organized Crime Reflections on an Illusive Link and its Implication for Criminal Law Reform*, International Society for Criminal Law Reform Annual Meeting—Montreal, August 8–12, Workshop D-3 Security Measures and Links to Organized Crime, August 11, 2004, at [http://www.icclr.law.ubc.ca/Publications/Reports/International%20Society%20Paper%20of%20Terrorism.pdf].

[83] L. Berry, G.E. Curtis, R.A. Hudson, and N. A. Kollars, *A Global Overview of Narcotics-Funded Terrorist and Other Extremist Groups*, Federal Research Division, Library of Congress, Washington, DC, May 2002.

[84] Rand Beers and Francis X. Taylor, U.S. State Department, *Narco-Terror: The Worldwide Connection Between Drugs and Terror*, testimony before the U.S. Senate Judiciary Committee, Subcommittee on Technology, Terrorism, and Government Information, March 13, 2002.

[85] Glenn Curtis and Tara Karacan, *The Nexus Among Terrorists, Narcotics Traffickers, Weapons Proliferators, and Organized Crime Networks in Western Europe*, A study prepared by the Federal Research Division, Library of Congress, December 2002, p. 22, at [http://www.loc.gov/rr/frd/pdf-files/WestEurope_NEXUS.pdf].

[86] Louise Shelly, *Organized Crime, Cybercrime and Terrorism*, Computer Crime Research Center, September 27, 2004, [http://www.crime-research.org/articles/Terrorism_Cybercrime/].

drug trafficking. In other areas, where criminals and terrorists work together to move money internationally, members of terrorist groups may be given special training in computer software, or in engineering, to facilitate communications through the Internet. In-house financial specialists and experienced advisors may also knowingly, or sometimes unknowingly, help cybercriminals evade the scrutiny of bank regulators and international investigators. These reportedly may include, accountants, bank employees in offshore zones and in major financial centers who may or may not also be terrorists or supportive of the political motives of their clients.[87]

International Efforts to Prevent Cybercrime

Cybercrime is a major international challenge, however attitudes about what composes a criminal act of computer wrongdoing may still vary from country to country. The European Union has set up the Critical Information Infrastructure Research Coordination Office (CI2RCO), which is tasked to examine how its member states are protecting their critical infrastructures from possible cyberattack. The project will identify research groups and programs focused on IT security in critical infrastructures.

The Convention on Cybercrime was adopted in 2001 by the Council of Europe, a consultative assembly of 43 countries, based in Strasbourg. The Convention, effective July 2004, is the first and only international treaty to deal with breaches of law "over the internet or other information networks." The Convention requires participating countries to update and harmonize their criminal laws against hacking, infringements on copyrights, computer facilitated fraud, child pornography, and other illicit cyber activities.[88] To date, eight of the 42 countries that signed the Convention have completed the ratification process.

Although the United States has signed the Convention, it did not sign a complementary protocol that contained provisions to criminalize xenophobia and racism on the Internet, which would likely not be supported by the U.S. Constitution.[89] The complementary protocol could be interpreted as requiring nations to imprison anyone guilty of "insulting publicly, through a computer system" certain groups of people based on characteristics such as race or ethnic origin, a requirement that could make it a crime

[87] Louise I. Shelley and John T. Picarelli, "Methods Not Motives: Implications of the Convergence of International Organized Crime and Terrorism," *Police Practice and Research*, vol. 3, no. 4, 2002 p. 311, at [http://www.american.edu/traccc/Publications/Shelley%20Pubs/To%20Add/MethodsnotMotives.pdf].

[88] Full text for the Convention on Cyber Crime may be found at [http://conventions.coe.int/Treaty/Commun/QueVoulezVous.asp?NT=185&CM=8&DF=18/06/04&CL=ENG].

[89] The U.S. Senate Committee on Foreign Relations held a hearing on the Convention on June 17, 2004. CRS Report RS21208, *Cybercrime: The Council of Europe Convention*, by Kristin Archick. Estelle Durnout, *Council of Europe Ratifies Cybercrime Treaty*, ZDNet, March 22, 2004, at [http://news.zdnet.co.uk/business/legal/0,39020651,39149470,00.htm].

to e-mail jokes about ethnic groups or question whether the Holocaust occurred. The Department of Justice has said that it would be unconstitutional for the United States to sign that additional protocol because of the First Amendment's guarantee of freedom of expression. The Electronic Privacy Information Center, in a June 2004 letter to the Foreign Relations Committee, objected to U.S. ratification of the Convention, because it would "would create invasive investigative techniques while failing to provide meaningful privacy and civil liberties safeguards."[90] However, a coalition of U.S. industry associations, including the Business Software Alliance, the Cyber Security Industry Alliance, the American Bankers Association, the Information Technology Association of America, InfraGard, Verisign, and several others, have urged the U.S. Senate Foreign Relations Committee to recommend ratification of the Convention.[91]

The Bush Administration submitted the Convention on Cybercrime (Treaty Doc. 108-11) to the Senate for hearings and resolution in November 2003. On July 26, 2005, the U.S. Senate Foreign Relations Committee approved the signed Convention. The United States will comply with the Convention based on existing U.S. federal law; and no new implementing legislation will be required. Legal analysts say that U.S. negotiators succeeded in scrapping most objectionable provisions, thereby ensuring that the Convention tracks closely with existing U.S. laws.[92]

Analysis and Policy Issues

Computer security experts disagree about whether a widespread coordinated cyberattack by terrorists is a near-term or long-term possibility. However, terrorists have repeatedly demonstrated a willingness to plan and launch conventional attacks against targets that have easy accessibility and numerous vulnerabilities. Internet and computer system vulnerabilities are persistent and widely publicized. As technology continues to advance, the capability, reliance, and interdependent nature of computer systems likely will be more vulnerable to cyberattack tools that are becoming faster and more sophisticated. Terrorists may also be developing links with cybercriminals that will give them access to high-level computer skills. The time may be approaching when a cyberattack may offer advantages that cause terrorists to act, even if the probability of success, or level of effectiveness, is unknown. Similar to terrorists reconnaissance of physical

---

[90] [http://www.epic.org/privacy/intl/senateletter-061704.pdf].

[91] Patience Wait, "Industry Groups Urge Senate Ratification of Cybercrime Treaty," *Government Computer News*, June 6, 2005, at [http://appserv.gcn.com/vol1_no1/web/362 57-1.html]. Declan McCullagh, *Tech Firms call for approval of cybercrime treaty*, Cnet News.com, June 29, 2005, at [http://news.com.com/2102-7348_3-5768462.html?tag=st.util.print].

[92] For more information about the Convention on Cybercrime, see CRS Report RS21208, *Cybercrime: The Council of Europe Convention*, by Kristin Archick.

targets to assess the level of security prior to an attack, it is suggested that the U.S. may experience a number of small cyber intrusion events prior to an attempt at a larger more devastating attack.

Given the ability of a catastrophic cyber-attack to disrupt a significant portion of the nation's infrastructure, some national security observers suggest that the Director of National Intelligence (DNI) should have the responsibility for monitoring the capabilities and identities of the countries and groups that may wish to cause the Nation harm through cyberattack. The DNI, as the Nation's Chief Intelligence Officer, has the ability to coordinate all known cyber-threat related information and then task the intelligence community to collect information to better understand the groups that may wish to cause the U.S. harm, and to forecast their intentions and capabilities.

One issue is whether DHS has done enough to strengthen computer security for civilian federal agencies and for the private sector. In July 2005, DHS Secretary Michael Chertoff announced creation of the new position of Assistant Secretary for Cyber and Telecommunications Security. In doing so he acknowledged both the efficiencies and vulnerabilities of modern technology upon which so much of society now depends.[93] Many cybersecurity observers hope that by elevating the DHS Cyber Security Officer from a Division Director to an Assistant Secretary level position, the new senior official will become a more effective proponent of federal government efforts to address and manage information technology vulnerabilities, incident response programs, and remediation efforts.

DHS is also supporting efforts to encourage U.S. computer systems to change to the new, reportedly more secure, IPV6 Internet Protocol.[94] Despite these efforts, according to GAO officials, DHS does not have an Internet recovery plan, or a national cybersecurity threat assessment. DHS officials have stated that a draft cybersecurity threat evaluation plan will be available in late 2005, but a finalized cybersecurity plan that pinpoints the nations's weakest security links will likely not be available until 2006.[95] Leaders of the Senate Committee on Homeland Security and Governmental Affairs, Subcommittee on Financial Management, Government Information and International Security, reportedly have stated that DHS does not

---

[93] Secretary Michael Chertoff, U.S. Department of Homeland Security, Second Security Stage Review Remarks, July 13, 2005, at [http://www.dhs.gov/dhspublic/interapp/speech_0255.xml].

[94] IPV6 is the designation for a newer, more secure communications protocol for the Internet. For more information, see CRS Report RL32411, *Network Centric Warfare: Background and Oversight Issues for Congress*, by Clay Wilson.

[95] Wilson Dizard, "Cybersecurity Plans Wait for Dhs to Complete its Evaluation of Threats," *Government Computer News*, July 25, 2005, vol. 24, no. 20.

have a robust way to detect a coordinated attack against the critical infrastructure.[96]

Security vulnerabilities found in the Internet and in critical infrastructure computer systems are widely publicized. Many experts are concerned that private sector cyber security firms do not notify DHS or their customers immediately upon recognition of a potentially serious Internet security vulnerability. If hackers become aware of this vulnerability, observers speculate that these individuals could disable portions of the Internet, or successfully disrupt selected portions of the United States or international critical infrastructure. This raises the following questions:

- Should vendors of computer products be required to quickly report all serious, newly discovered product vulnerabilities to DHS?
- Should computer service providers or businesses be required to report to DHS any major security vulnerabilities that have been newly exploited by cybercriminals?
- Should there be penalties if an organization has a poor security policy that contributes to a major loss of sensitive information?

Some actions are underway that Congress may consider.[97] For example, on September 30, 2005, an interim rule was issued by the Federal Acquisition Regulations Council, outlining several new steps acquisition workers must take to ensure IT security is incorporated into all federal purchases. Under this interim rule, government contracting officers must include additional cybersecurity rules in their acquisition planning, which will require vendors to improve computer security for the IT products and services they supply to the federal government.[98]

Experts now believe that terrorist collaborate with organized crime networks in the Middle East for international smuggling of arms and illegal drugs. Criminal drug traffickers can provide terrorists with access to computer specialists with high-level technical skills. What are the pro's and con's of linking counterterrorism efforts more closely to the efforts of agencies that counter drug trafficking?

Should the counterterrorism efforts be linked more closely with international efforts to prevent cybercrime? What are effective ways to encourage more international cooperation for identifying which activities

[96] Grant Gross, *Senators Call on DHS to Improve Cybersecurity Efforts*, Symantec, at [http://enterprisesecurity.symantec.com/publicsector/article.cfm?articleid=5862&EID=0].

[97] See National Institute of Standards and Technology website for Federal Agency Security Practices, at [http://csrc.nist.gov/fasp/].

[98] Jason Miller, "IT Security Requirements Now Part of the FAR," *Government Computer News*, September 30, 2005, at [http://www.gcn.com/vol1_no1/daily-updates/37162-1.html]. *Federal Register*, September 30, 2005, vol. 70, no. 189, pp. 57449–57452.

should be labeled as cybercrime, and for punishing those who operate as cybercriminals?

Security experts have reportedly stated that, although U.S. military networks are relatively secure, many of those networks remain highly dependent on the civilian communications infrastructure.[99] Should DOD collaborate more closely with DHS for new technologies to strengthen the computer security of civilian agencies and infrastructure?

Trends for cybercrime indicate that computer attacks could increase in number, speed, and sophistication. Will future unknown computer vulnerabilities and sophisticated attacks allow terrorist to launch an effective cyberattack that might overwhelm the ability of civilian agencies to respond effectively? Could a new approach to computer security reduce vulnerabilities? An example of a new approach to improve computer security for computer systems and the Internet might include development and refinement of quantum methods for unbreakable cryptography.[100] However, new approaches to computer security could also lead to the emergence of new threats directed against new vulnerabilities. For example, the proliferation and use of commercial products with unbreakable cryptography could seriously undermine the ability of law enforcement to perform critical missions such as protecting against threats posed by terrorists, organized crime, and foreign intelligence agents.

Related Legislation

The following bills are related to improving national computer security, or the prevention of cybercrime:

H.R. 1. H.R. 1, "Implementing the 9/11 Commission Recommendations Act of 2007," was referred to the Senate Committee on Homeland Security and Governmental Affairs on January 9, 2007. The DHS Secretary shall evaluate and annually prioritize all pending applications for covered grants based upon the degree to which they would lessen the threat to the critical infrastructure, including, but not limited to, cyber threats. Evaluation and prioritization shall be based upon the risk assessment by the Office of Intelligence Analysis and the Office of Infrastructure Protection of the threats of terrorism against the United States.

[99] Barton Reppert, remarks made by Clifford Lau, July 26, 2005, at the Rayburn House Office Building, subsequent to a hearing by the House Science Committee.

[100] Quantum cryptography: In the microscopic world, once a system is observed, it is inevitably affected and changes into another state (Heisenberg's Uncertainty Principle). By incorporating the fact that weak light behaves as "photons" subject to this law, quantum cryptography is an unbreakable cryptography with the photons becoming the information carriers, or information cameras. Press Release, Mitsubishi Electric, 2002, [http://global.mitsubishielectric.com/news/news_releases/2002/mel0560_b.html].

DOCUMENT NO. 5

BOTNETS, CYBERCRIME, AND CYBERTERRORISM: VULNERABILITIES AND POLICY ISSUES FOR CONGRESS

CRS Report
RL32114

January 29, 2008

Clay Wilson
Specialist in Technology and National Security
Foreign Affairs, Defense, and Trade Division

Summary

Cybercrime is becoming more organized and established as a transnational business. High technology online skills are now available for rent to a variety of customers, possibly including nation states, or individuals and groups that could secretly represent terrorist groups. The increased use of automated attack tools by cybercriminals has overwhelmed some current methodologies used for tracking Internet cyberattacks, and vulnerabilities of the U.S. critical infrastructure, which are acknowledged openly in publications, could possibly attract cyberattacks to extort money, or damage the U.S. economy to affect national security.

In April and May 2007, NATO and the United States sent computer security experts to Estonia to help that nation recover from cyberattacks directed against government computer systems, and to analyze the methods used and determine the source of the attacks.[1] Some security experts suspect that political protestors may have rented the services of cybercriminals, possibly a large network of infected PCs, called a "botnet," to help disrupt the computer systems of the Estonian government. DOD officials

---

[1] Larry Greenemeier, "Estonian Attacks Raise Concern Over Cyber 'Nuclear Winter,'" *Information Week*, May 24, 2007, at [http://www.informationweek.com/news/showArticle.jhtml?articleID=199701774].

have also indicated that similar cyberattacks from individuals and countries targeting economic, political, and military organizations may increase in the future.[2]

Cybercriminals have reportedly made alliances with drug traffickers in Afghanistan, the Middle East, and elsewhere where profitable illegal activities are used to support terrorist groups. In addition, designs for cybercrime botnets are becoming more sophisticated, and future botnet architectures may be more resistant to computer security countermeasures.[3]

This report discusses options now open to nation states, extremists, or terrorist groups for obtaining malicious technical services from cybercriminals to meet political or military objectives, and describes the possible effects of a coordinated cyberattack against the U.S. critical infrastructure. This report will be updated as events warrant.

Introduction

The U.S. military is supported partly by civilian high technology services and products, most often in the form of communications systems and computer software.[4] In future conflicts that involve cyberwarfare between nations, the distinction between U.S. military and civilian targets may be blurred and civilian computer systems may increasingly be seen as viable targets vulnerable to attack by adversaries.[5]

Computer networking technology has also blurred the boundaries between cyberwarfare, cybercrime, and cyberterrorism. Officials in government and industry now say that cybercrime and cyberattack services available for hire from criminal organizations are a growing threat to national security as well as to the U.S. economy.[6] New and sophisticated cybercrime tools could operate to allow a nation state or terrorist group to remain unidentified while they direct cyberattacks through the Internet.[7] Many experts

---

[2] Jeanne Meserve, "Official: International Hackers Going After U.S. Networks," CNN.com, October 19, 2007, [http://www.cnn.com/2007/US/10/19/cyber.threats/index.html]. Sebastian Sprenger, "Maj. Gen. Lord Is a Groundbreaker," *Federal Computer Week*, October 15, 2007, vol. 21, no. 34, p. 44.

[3] Tom Espiner, "Security Expert: Storm Botnet 'Services' Could Be Sold," CnetNews.com, October 16, 2007, [http://www.news.com/Security-expert-Storm-botnet-services-could-be-sold/2100-7349_3-6213781.html]. Dan Sullivan, "P2P Botnets Increasingly Sophisticated, Realtime-Websecurity," April 18, 2007, [http://www.realtime-websecurity.com/articles_and_analysis/2007/04/p2p_botnets_increasingly_sophi.html].

[4] Dan Kuehl, professor at the National Defense University School of Information Warfare and Strategy, has pointed out that a high percentage of U.S. military messages flow through commercial communications channels, and this reliance creates a vulnerability during conflict. Eric Naef, "Wanja," *Infocon Magazine*, October 2003, [http://www.iwar.org.uk/infocon/io-kuehl.htm].

[5] Sebastian Sprenger, "Maj. Gen. Lord Is a Groundbreaker," *Federal Computer Week*, October 15, 2007, vol. 21, no. 34, p. 44.

[6] James Lewis, testimony before the House Committee on Homeland Security, Subcommittee on Emerging Threats, Cybersecurity, and Science and Technology, April 15, 2007.

[7] Tim Greene, "Storm Worm Strikes Back at Security Pros," NetworkWorld.com, October 24, 2007, at [http://www.networkworld.com/news/2007/102407-storm-worm-security.html?nlhtsec=1022securityalert4&&nladname=102507securityal].

point out that past incidents of conventional terrorism have already been linked with cybercrime, and that computer vulnerabilities may make government and civilian critical infrastructure systems seem attractive as targets for cyberattack.[8] Some experts argue that the government of Estonia may have already experienced this type of cyberattack directed against their systems and websites in April, 2007.

This report explores the possible connections between cybercriminals and terrorist groups that want to damage the U.S. economy or national security interests. The report also examines the effects of a coordinated cyberattack against the U.S. critical infrastructure, including use of cybercrime tools that could possibly take advantage of openly-publicized cyber vulnerabilities. Trends in cybercrime are described, showing how malicious Internet websites, and other cybercrimes such as identity theft are linked to conventional terrorist activity.

Congress may wish to explore the possible effects on the U.S. economy and on the U.S. military that could result from a coordinated attack against civilian and military computers and communications systems, whether due to cybercrime or cyberterrorism. Congress may also wish to explore the difficulties associated with establishing doctrine for selecting an appropriate military or law enforcement response after such an attack.

Background

It is clear that terrorist groups are using computers and the Internet to further goals associated with spreading terrorism. This can be seen in the way that extremists are creating and using numerous Internet websites for recruitment and fund raising activities, and for Jihad training purposes. Several criminals who have recently been convicted of cybercrimes used their technical skills to acquire stolen credit card information in order to finance other conventional terrorist activities.[9] It is possible that as criminals and terrorist groups explore more ways to work together, a new type of threat may emerge where extremists gain access to the powerful network tools now used by cybercriminals to steal personal information, or to disrupt computer systems that support services through the Internet.

[8] Brian Krebs, "Three Worked the Web to Help Terrorists," *The Washington Post*, July 6, 2007, p. D01. Walsh, *Terrorism on the Cheap*. Rollie Lal, "Terrorists and Organized Crime Join Forces," *International Herald Tribune*, May 25, 2005, at [http://www.iht.com/articles/2005/05/23/opinion/edlal.php]. Barbara Porter, "Forum Links Organized Crime and Terrorism," *By George!*, summer 2004, at [http://www2.gwu.edu/~bygeorge/060804/crimeterrorism.html].

[9] Gregory Crabb, "U.S. Postal Service Global Investigations," and Yuval Ben-Itzhak, "CTO Finjan," Presentation at the Gartner IT Security Summit 2007, Washington, DC, June 4, 2007.

Three Basic Methods for Disrupting Computer Systems

There are several effective methods for disrupting computer systems. This report focuses on the method known as cyberattack, or computer network attack (CNA), which uses malicious computer code to disrupt computer processing, or steal data. A brief description of three different methods are shown here. However, as technology changes, future distinctions between these methods may begin to blur.

An attack against computers may (1) disrupt equipment and hardware reliability, (2) change processing logic, or (3) steal or corrupt data.[10] The methods discussed here are chosen based on the technology asset against which each attack mode is directed, and the effects each method can produce. The assets affected or effects produced can sometimes overlap for different attack methods.

- Conventional kinetic weapons can be directed against computer equipment, a computer facility, or transmission lines to create a physical attack that disrupts the reliability of equipment.
- The power of electromagnetic energy, most commonly in the form of an electromagnetic pulse (EMP), can be used to create an electronic attack (EA) directed against computer equipment or data transmissions. By overheating circuitry or jamming communications, EA disrupts the reliability of equipment and the integrity of data.[11]
- Malicious code can be used to create a cyberattack, or computer network attack (CNA), directed against computer processing code, instruction logic, or data. The code can generate a stream of malicious network packets that can disrupt data or logic through exploiting a vulnerability in computer software, or a weakness in the computer security practices of an organization. This type of cyberattack can disrupt the reliability of equipment, the integrity of data, and the confidentiality of communications.

Cyberattack, Cybercrime, and Cyberterrorism

Labeling a "cyberattack" as "cybercrime" or "cyberterrorism" is problematic because of the difficulty determining with certainty the identity, intent, or the political motivations of an attacker.[12] "Cybercrime" can be very

[10] All methods of computer attack are within the current capabilities of several nations. See CRS Report RL31787, *Information Operations and Cyberwar: Capabilities and Related Policy Issues*, by Clay Wilson.

[11] For more on electromagnetic weapons, see CRS Report RL32544, *High Altitude Electromagnetic Pulse (HEMP) and High Power Microwave (HPM) Devices: Threat Assessments*, by Clay Wilson.

[12] Serge Krasavin, *What is Cyberterrorism?* Computer Crime Research Center, April 23, 2004, [http://www.crime-research.org/analytics/Krasavin/].

broad in scope, and may sometimes involve more factors than just a computer hack. "Cyberterrorism" is often equated with the use of malicious code. However, a "cyberterrorism" event may also sometimes depend on the presence of other factors beyond just a "cyberattack."

Definitions for Cyberterrorism

Various definitions exist for the term "cyberterrorism", just as various definitions exist for the term "terrorism."[13] Security expert Dorothy Denning defines cyberterrorism as ". . . politically motivated hacking operations intended to cause grave harm such as loss of life or severe economic damage."[14] The Federal Emergency Management Agency (FEMA) defines cyberterrorism as "unlawful attacks and threats of attack against computers, networks, and the information stored therein when done to intimidate or coerce a government or its people in furtherance of political or social objectives."[15]

Others indicate that a physical attack that destroys computerized nodes for critical infrastructures, such as the Internet, telecommunications, or the electric power grid, without ever touching a keyboard, can also contribute to, or be labeled as cyberterrorism.[16] Thus, it is possible that if a computer facility were deliberately attacked for political purposes, all three methods described above (physical attack, EA, and cyberattack) might contribute to, or be labeled as "cyberterrorism."

Definitions for Cybercrime

Cybercrime is crime that is enabled by, or that targets computers. Some argue there is no agreed-upon definition for "cybercrime" because "cyberspace" is just a new specific instrument used to help commit crimes that are not new at all. Cybercrime can involve theft of intellectual property, a violation of patent, trade secret, or copyright laws. However, cybercrime also includes attacks against computers to deliberately disrupt processing, or may include espionage to make unauthorized copies of classified data. If a terrorist group were to launch a cyberattack to cause harm, such an

[13] Under 22 USC, Section 2656, "terrorism" is defined as premeditated, politically motivated violence perpetrated against noncombatant targets by sub national groups or clandestine agents, usually intended to influence an audience. The United States has employed this definition of terrorism for statistical and analytical purposes since 1983. U.S. Department of State, 2002, *Patterns of Global Terrorism, 2003*, [http://www.state.gov/s/ct/rls/pgtrpt/2001/html/10220.htm].

[14] Dorothy Denning, "Activism, Hactivism, and Cyberterrorism: The Internet as a tool for Influencing Foreign Policy," in John Arquilla and David Ronfeldt, eds., *Networks and Netwars*, (Rand 2001), p. 241. Dorothy Denning, *Is Cyber War Next?* Social Science Research Council, November 2001, at [http://www.ssrc.org/sept11/essays/denning.htm].

[15] [http://www.fema.gov/pdf/onp/toolkit_app_d.pdf].

[16] Dan Verton, "A Definition of Cyber-terrorism", *Computerworld*, August 11, 2003, [http://www.computerworld.com/securitytopics/security/story/0,10801,83843,00.html].

act also fits within the definition of a cybercrime. The primary difference between a cyberattack to commit a crime or to commit terror is found in the intent of the attacker, and it is possible for actions under both labels to overlap.

Botnets

Botnets are becoming a major tool for cybercrime, partly because they can be designed to very effectively disrupt targeted computer systems in different ways, and because a malicious user, without possessing strong technical skills, can initiate these disruptive effects in cyberspace by simply renting botnet services from a cybercriminal.[17] Botnets, or "Bot Networks," are made up of vast numbers of compromised computers that have been infected with malicious code, and can be remotely-controlled through commands sent via the Internet. Hundreds or thousands of these infected computers can operate in concert to disrupt or block Internet traffic for targeted victims, harvest information, or to distribute spam, viruses, or other malicious code. Botnets have been described as the "Swiss Army knives of the underground economy" because they are so versatile.

Botnet designers, or "botmasters", can reportedly make large sums of money by marketing their technical services. For example, Jeanson Ancheta, a 21-year-old hacker and member of a group called the "Botmaster Underground", reportedly made more than $100,000 from different Internet Advertising companies who paid him to download specially-designed malicious adware code onto more than 400,000 vulnerable PCs he had secretly infected and taken over. He also made tens of thousands more dollars renting his 400,000-unit "botnet herd" to other companies that used them to send out spam, viruses, and other malicious code on the Internet. In 2006, Ancheta was sentenced to five years in prison.[18]

Botnet code was originally distributed as infected email attachments, but as users have grown more cautious, cybercriminals have turned to other methods. When users click to view a spam message, botnet code can be secretly installed on the users' PC. A website may be unknowingly infected with malicious code in the form of an ordinary-looking advertisement banner, or may include a link to an infected website. Clicking on any of these may install botnet code. Or, botnet code can be silently uploaded, even if the user takes no action while viewing the website, merely through some un-patched vulnerability that may exist in the browser. Firewalls and

[17] Jeanne Meserve, "Official: International Hackers Going After U.S. Networks," CNN.com, October 19, 2007, [http://www.cnn.com/2007/US/10/19/cyber.threats/index.html]. Sebastian Sprenger, "Maj. Gen. Lord Is a Groundbreaker," *Federal Computer Week*, October 15, 2007, vol. 21, no. 34, p. 44.

[18] Bob Keefe, "PC Security Still More of a Wish than a Promise," *The Atlanta Journal*, February 3, 2007, p. 1A.

antivirus software do not necessarily inspect all data that is downloaded through browsers. Some bot software can even disable antivirus security before infecting the PC. Once a PC has been infected, the malicious software establishes a secret communications link to a remote "botmaster" in preparation to receive new commands to attack a specific target. Meanwhile, the malicious code may also automatically probe the infected PC for personal data, or may log keystrokes, and transmit the information to the botmaster.

The Shadowserver Foundation is an organization that monitors the number of command and control servers on the Internet, which indicates the number of bot networks that are being controlled online at a given time. From November 2006 through May 2007, approximately 1,400 command and control servers were found to be active on the Internet. The number of individual infected drones that are controlled by these 1,400 servers reportedly grew from half a million to more than 3 million from March to May 2007. Symantec, another security organization, reported that it detected 6 million bot-infected computers in the second half of 2006.[19]

Some botnet owners reportedly rent their huge networks for US$200 to $300 an hour, and botnets are becoming the weapon of choice for fraud and extortion.[20] Newer methods are evolving for distributing "bot" software that may make it even more difficult in the future for law enforcement to identify and locate the originating "botmaster." Some studies show that authors of software for botnets are increasingly using modern, open-source techniques for software development, including the collaboration of multiple authors for the initial design, new releases to fix bugs in the malicious code, and development of software modules that make portions of the code reusable for newer versions of malicious software designed for different purposes. This increase in collaboration among hackers mirrors the professional code development techniques now used to create commercial software products, and is expected to make future botnets even more robust and reliable. This, in turn, is expected to help increase the demand for malware services in future years.[21]

Traditionally, botnets organize themselves in an hierarchical manner, with a central command and control location (sometimes dynamic) for the botmaster. This central command location is useful to security professionals because it offers a possible central point of failure for the botnet. However, in the near future, security experts believe that attackers may use new botnet architectures that are more sophisticated, and more difficult to detect

---

[19] Julie Bort, "Attack of the Killer Bots," *Network World*, Jul 2/9, 2007, p. 29.

[20] Susan MacLean, "Report warns of Organized Cyber Crime," *It World Canada*, August 26, 2005, [http://www.itworldcanada.com/a/IT-Focus/39c78aa4-df47-4231-a083-ddd1ab8985fb.html].

[21] McAfee Virtual Criminology Report: Organized Crime and the Internet, December 2006, [http://www.sigma.com.pl/pliki/albums/userpics/10007/Virtual_Criminology_Report_ 2006.pdf].

and trace. One class of botnet architecture that is beginning to emerge uses peer-to-peer protocol,[22] which, because of its decentralized control design, is expected to be more resistant to strategies for countering its disruptive effects.[23] For example, some experts reportedly argue that a well-designed peer-to-peer botnet may be nearly impossible to shut down as a whole because it may provide anonymity to the controller, who can appear as just another node in the bot network.[24]

Estonia, 2007

In the Spring of 2007, government computer systems in Estonia experienced a sustained cyberattack that has been labeled by various observers as cyberwarfare, or cyberterror, or cybercrime. On April 27, officials in Estonia moved a Soviet-era war memorial commemorating an unknown Russian who died fighting the Nazis. The move stirred emotions, and led to rioting by ethnic Russians, and the blockading of the Estonian Embassy in Moscow. The event also marked the beginning of a series of large and sustained Distributed Denial-Of-Service (DDOS) attacks launched against several Estonian national websites, including government ministries and the prime minister's Reform Party.[25]

In the early days of the cyberattack, government websites that normally receive around 1,000 visits a day reportedly were receiving 2,000 visits every second. This caused the repeated shut down of some websites for several hours at a time or longer, according to Estonian officials.[26] The attacks, which flooded computers and servers and blocked legitimate users, were described as crippling, owing to Estonia's high dependence on information technology, but limited resources for managing their infrastructure. Security experts say that the cyberattacks against Estonia were unusual because the rate of the packet attack was very high, and the series

[22] Gnutella emerged as the first fully decentralized peer-to-peer protocol in 2000, and was used on the Internet to share and swap music files in MP3 compression format. The music industry was often frustrated in their efforts to counter this peer-to-peer technology because it could not identify a main controlling source. Since then, several other peer-to-peer protocols have been developed.

[23] Symantec, *Trojan.Peacomm: Building a Peer-to-Peer Botnet*, 2007, [http://www.symantec.com/enterprise/security_response/weblog/2007/01/trojanpeacomm_building_a_peert.html]. Matthew Broersma, *Peer-to-Peer Botnets a New and Growing Threat*, CSO Online, April 17, 2007, [http://www2.csoonline.com/blog_view.html?CID=32852]. Julian B. Grizzard et. al., *Peer-to-Peer Botnets: Overview and Case Study*, 2007, [http://www.usenix.org/events/hotbots07/tech/full_papers/grizzard/grizzard_html/]. Reinier Schoof and Ralph Koning, *Detecting Peer-to-Peer Botnets*, February 4, 2007,[http://staff.science.uva.nl/~delaat/sne-2006-2007/p17/report.pdf].

[24] Tom Espiner, "Security Expert: Storm Botnet 'services' Could Be Sold," CnetNews.com, October 16, 2007, [http://www.news.com/Security-expert-Storm-botnet-services-could-be-sold/2100-7349_3-6213781.html]. Robert Lemos, *Bot software looks to improve peerage*,The Register, May 4, 2006, [http://www.theregister.co.uk/2006/05/04/nugache_p2p_botnet/].

[25] Robert Vamosi, "Cyberattack in Estonia—What It Really Means," CnetNews.com, May 29, 2007, at [http://news.com.com/Cyberattack+in+Estonia-what+it+really+means/2008–7349_3-6186751.html].

[26] Christopher Rhoads, "Cyber Attack Vexes Estonia, Poses Debate," *The Wall Street Journal*, May 18, 2007, p. A6.

of attacks lasted weeks, rather than hour or days, which is more commonly seen for a denial of service attack.[27] Eventually, NATO and the United States sent computer security experts to Estonia to help recover from the attacks, and to analyze the methods used and attempt to determine the source of the attacks.

This event can serve to illustrate how computer network technology has blurred the boundaries between crime, warfare, and terrorism. A persistent problem during and after any cyberattack is accurate identification of the attacker, by finding out whether it was sponsored by a nation, or was the independent work of a few unconnected individuals, or was initiated by a group to instill frustration and fear by damaging the computerized infrastructure and economy. The uncertainty of not knowing the initiator also affects the decision about whom should ultimately become a target for retaliation, and whether the response should come from law enforcement or the military.

Initially, the Russian government was blamed by Estonian officials for the cyberattacks, and there were charges of cyberwarfare. Other observers argued that the cyberattack involved collusion between the Russian government and transnational cybercriminals who made their large botnets available for short-term rent, either to individuals or to larger groups. They argue that as the rented time expired, the intensity of the persistent cyberattacks against Estonia also began to fall off.[28] However, not all security experts agree, and it remains unclear at this time whether the cyberattacks were sanctioned or initiated by the Russian government, or if a criminal botnet was actually involved.

After some investigation, network analysts later concluded that the cyberattacks targeting Estonia were not a concerted attack, but instead were the product of spontaneous anger from a loose federation of separate attackers. Technical data showed that sources of the attack were worldwide rather than concentrated in a few locations. The computer code that caused the DDOS attack was posted and shared in many Russian language chat rooms, where the moving of the war memorial was a very emotional topic for discussion. These analysts state that although access to various Estonian government agencies was blocked by the malicious code, there was no apparent attempt to target national critical infrastructure other than internet resources, and no extortion demands were made. Their analysis thus far concluded that there was no Russian government connection to the attacks

[27] Carolyn Marsan, "Examining the Reality of Cyberwar in Wake of Estonian Attacks," *Network World*, August 27, 2007, vol. 24, no. 33, p. 24.

[28] Iain Thomson, "Russia 'Hired Botnets' for Estonia Cyber-War," *Computing*, [http://www.computing.co.uk/vnunet/news/2191082/claims-russia-hired-botnets].

against Estonia.[29] However, investigation into the incident continues, and officials from the United States view some aspects of the event as a possible model for future cyberwarfare or cyberterrorism directed against a nation state.

In January 2008, a court in Estonia convicted and fined a local man for bringing down a government website, as part of the extended cyberattack in 2007. The 20-year-old, who is apparently an ethnic Russian Estonian, used his home PC to carry out the attack. The investigation continues, and so far, he is the only person convicted for participating in the cyberattack against Estonia.[30]

Other Trends in Cybercrime Methods

Cybercrime is usually conducted through a connection to the Internet, but can also involve unauthorized removal of data on small, portable flash drive storage devices. Cybercrime, usually in the form of network hacking, has involved persons with strong technical skills, often motivated by the desire to gain popularity among their technology peers. However, the growing trend is now to profit from these network cyberattacks by targeting specific systems, often through collaboration among criminals and technical experts. The motives that drive these cybercriminal groups now may differ from those of their paying customers, who may possess little or no technical skills.

New technologies continue to outpace policy for law enforcement. Problems of coordination among agencies of different countries, along with conflicting national policies about crime in cyberspace, work to the advantage of cybercriminals who can choose to operate from geographic locations where penalties for some forms of cybercrime may not yet exist. Sophisticated tools for cyberattack can now be found for sale or for rent on the Internet, where highly-organized underground cybercrime businesses host websites that advertise a variety of disruptive software products and malicious technical services. High-end cybercrime groups use standard software business development techniques to keep their products updated with the latest anti-security features, and seek to recruit new and talented software engineering students into their organizations.

Where illicit profits are potentially very large, some high-end criminal groups have reportedly adopted standard IT business practices to systematically develop more efficient and effective computer code for cybercrime. Studies also show that organized crime groups now actively recruit college

[29] Heise Security, *Estonian DDoS—a final analysis,* [http://www.heise-security.co.uk/news/print/90461].
[30] Mike Sachoff, *Man Convicted In Estonia Cyber Attack,* WebProNews, January 24, 2008, [http://www.webpronews.com/topnews/2008/01/24/man-convicted-in-estonia-cyber-attack].

engineering graduates and technical expert members of computer societies, and sponsor them to attend more information technology (IT) courses to further their technical expertise. However, in some cases, targeted students maynot realize that a criminal organization is behind the recruitment offer.[31]

Cyberattacks are increasingly designed to silently steal information without leaving behind any damage that would be noticed by a user. These types of attacks attempt to escape detection in order to remain on host systems for longer periods of time. It is also expected that as mobile communication devices are incorporated more into everyday life, they will be increasingly targeted in the future for attack by cybercriminals.[32]

Malicious Code Hosted on Websites. Malicious code, such as viruses or Trojan Horses, are used to infect a computer to make it available for takeover and remote control. Malicious code can infect a computer if the user opens an email attachment, or clicks an innocent-looking link on a website. For example, users who visited the popular MySpace and YouTube websites in 2005, and who lacked important software security patches, reportedly may have had their PCs infected if they clicked on a banner advertisement which silently installed malicious code on their computers to log keystrokes or capture sensitive data. During the first half of 2006, the Microsoft Security Team reported that it had removed 10 million pieces of malicious software from nearly 4 million computers and web servers.[33] Recently, analysts at Google tested several million web pages for the presence of malicious software, and determined that 4.5 million of the web pages examined were suspicious in nature. After further testing of the 4.5 million web pages, over 1 million were found to launch downloads of malicious software, and more than two thirds of those programs were "bot" software that, among other things, collected data on banking transactions and then emailed the information to a temporary email account.[34]

Researchers at the San Jose, Calif.-based security firm, Finjan Inc., after reviewing security data from the first quarter of 2007, found that more malware is hosted on servers in countries such as the U.S. and U.K., than in

[31] McAfee Virtual Criminology Report: Organized Crime and the Internet, December 2006, [http://www.sigma.com.pl/pliki/albums/userpics/10007/Virtual_Criminology_Report_2006.pdf].

[32] A web crawler (also known as a Web spider or Web robot) is a program or automated script that browses the World Wide Web in a methodical, automated manner. Web crawlers are mainly used to create a copy of all the visited pages for later processing by a search engine that will index the downloaded pages to provide fast searches. Wikipedia, [http://en.wikipedia.org/wiki/Web_crawler].

[33] Elise Ackerman, "Hackers' Infections Slither Onto Web Sites," *The Mercury News*, January 3, 2007, p. 1.

[34] Jeff Hecht, "Web Browsers Are New Frontline in Internet War," *NewScientistTech*, May 5, 2007, [http://www.newscientisttech.com/article.ns?id=mg19426026.000&print=true]. Niels Provos et al., *The Ghost in the Browser: Analysis of Web-based Malware*, Google, Inc., [http://www.usenix.org/events/hotbots07/tech/full_papers/provos/provos.pdf].

other countries with less developed e-crime law enforcement policies. Findings from the Finjan 2007 Web Security Trends Report are based on an analysis of more than 10 million unique websites from Internet traffic recorded in the UK, and include the following:

- Attacks that involve the use of code obfuscation through diverse randomization techniques are growing more numerous and complex, making them virtually invisible to pattern-matching/signature-based methods in use by traditional antivirus products.
- Criminals are displaying an increasing level of sophistication when embedding malicious code within legitimate content with less dependence on outlaw servers in unregulated countries.

Finjan found that 90% of the websites examined containing malware resided on servers located in the U.S. or U.K. "The results of this study shatter the myth that malicious code is primarily being hosted in countries where e-crime laws are less developed," Finjan CTO Yuval Ben-Itzhak reportedly stated.[35]

Identity Theft. Botnets and other examples of malicious code can operate to assist cybercriminals with identity theft. Current FBI estimates are that identity theft costs American businesses and consumers $50 billion a year. Individual users are often lured into clicking on tempting links that are found in email or when visiting websites. Clicking on titles such as "Buy Rolex watches cheap," or "Check out my new Photos," can take advantage of web browser vulnerabilities to place malicious software onto a users system which allows a cybercriminal to gather personal information from the user's computer.

Malicious code can scan a victim's computer for sensitive information, such as name, address, place and date of birth, social security number, mother's maiden name, and telephone number. Full identities obtained this way are bought and sold in online markets. False identity documents can then be created from this information using home equipment such as a digital camera, color printer, and laminating device, to make official-looking driver's licences, birth certificates, reference letters, and bank statements.[36]

Identity theft involving thousands of victims is also enabled by inadequate computer security practices within organizations.[37] MasterCard

[35] Finjan, Inc., *Web Security Trends Report, Q2 2007*, [http://www.finjan.com/Content.aspx?id=827].

[36] Lou Bobson, "Identity Theft Ruining Lives," *The Sunday Mail*, May 20, 2007, p. 62.

[37] On April 12, 2005, personal information, such as Social Security Numbers for 310,000 U.S. citizens, may have been stolen in a data security breach that involved 59 instances of unauthorized access into its corporate databases using stolen passwords. Boston College reported in March 2005 that a hacker had gained unauthorized access to computer database records with personal information for up to 106,000 alumni, and in the same month, Chico State University of California, reported that its

International reported that in 2005 more than 40 million credit card numbers belonging to U.S. consumers were accessed by computer hackers.[38] Some of these account numbers were reportedly being sold on a Russian website, and some consumers have reported fraudulent charges on their statements. Officials at the UFJ bank in Japan reportedly stated that some of that bank's customers may also have become victims of fraud related to theft of the MasterCard information.[39] In June 2006, officials from the U.S. Department of Energy acknowledged that names and personal information belonging to more than 1,500 employees of the National Nuclear Security Administration (NNSA) had been stolen in a network intrusion that apparently took place starting in 2004. The NNSA did not discover the security breach until one year after it had occurred.[40]

Some sources report that stolen credit card numbers and bank account information are traded online in a highly structured arrangement, involving buyers, sellers, intermediaries, and service industries. Services include offering to conveniently change the billing address of a theft victim, through manipulation of stolen PINs or passwords. Observers estimated that in 2005 such services for each stolen MasterCard number cost between $42 and $72.[41] Other news articles report that, in 2007, a stolen credit card number sells online for only $1, and a complete identity, including a U.S. bank account number, credit-card number, date of birth, and a government-issued ID number now sells for just $14 to $18.[42]

As of January 2007, 35 states have enacted data security laws requiring businesses that have experienced an intrusion involving possible identity theft to notify persons affected, and to improve security for protection of restricted data. However, existing federal and state laws that impose obligations on information owners, may require harmonization to provide protections that are more uniform.[43]

databases had been breached containing the names and Social Security numbers for as many as 59,000 current and former students. David Bank and Christopher Conkey, "New Safeguards for Your Privacy," *The Wall Street Journal*, March 24, 2005, p. D1.

38 Jonathan Krim and Michael Barbaro, "40 Million Credit Card Numbers Hacked," *Washington Post*, June 18, 2005, p. A01. See also the report by the U.S. House of Representatives Homeland Security Committee, July 1, 2005, raising concerns about potential ties between identity theft victims and terrorism. Caitlin Harrington, "Terrorists Can Exploit Identity Theft, Report From House Democrats Says," *CQ Homeland Security*, July 1, 2005.

39 BBC News, "Japan Cardholders 'Hit' by Theft," June 21, 2005, at [http://news.bbc.co.uk/1/hi/business/4114252.stm].

40 Dawn Onley and Patience Wait, "DOD's Efforts to Stave off Nation-State Cyberattacks Begin with China," *Government Computer News*, August 21, 2006.

41 CCRC staff, *Russia, Biggest Ever Credit Card Scam*, Computer Crime Research Center, July 8, 2005, at [http://www.crime-research.org/news/08.07.2005/1349/].

42 David Hayes, "A Dollar goes a Long Way in Swiping Private Data," *The Kansas City Star*, March 20, 2007, p. 1.

43 For more information about laws related to identity theft, see CRS Report RL34120, *Information Security and Data Breach Notification Safeguards*, by Gina Marie Stevens.

Cyber Espionage. Cyber espionage involves the unauthorized probing to test a target computer's configuration or evaluate its system defenses, or the unauthorized viewing and copying of data files. However, should a terrorist group, nation, or other organization use computer hacking techniques for political or economic motives, their deliberate intrusions may also qualify them, additionally, as cybercriminals. If there is disagreement about this, it is likely because technology has outpaced policy for labeling actions in cyberspace. In fact, industrial cyber espionage may now be considered a necessary part of global economic competition, and secretly monitoring the computerized functions and capabilities of potential adversary countries may also be considered essential for national defense.[44]

U.S. counterintelligence officials reportedly have stated that about 140 different foreign intelligence organizations regularly attempt to hack into the computer systems of U.S. government agencies and U.S. companies. Cyber espionage, which enables the exfiltration of massive amounts of information electronically, has now transformed the nature of counterintelligence, by enabling a reduced reliance on conventional spying operations.[45] The Internet, including satellite links and wireless local networks, now offers new, low cost and low risk opportunities for espionage. In 2001, a Special Committee of Inquiry established by the European parliament accused the United States of using its Echelon electronic spy network to engage in industrial espionage against European businesses. Echelon was reportedly set up in 1971 as an electronic monitoring system during the Cold War. European-Union member Britain helps operate the system, which includes listening posts in Canada, Australia, and New Zealand. Echelon is described as a global spy system reportedly capable of intercepting wireless phone calls, e-mail, and fax messages made from almost any location around the world.[46]

The European parliament Special Committee reported that information gathered on Echelon may have helped the United States beat the European Airbus Consortium in selling aircraft to Saudi Arabia in 1994.[47] In 1995, France expelled five American diplomats and other officials, reportedly

---

[44] U.S. intelligence officials, speaking on background, explained that they have routinely penetrated potential enemies' computer networks. These officials claim that thousands of attacks have taken place and sensitive information was stolen. John Stanton, "Rules of Cyber War Baffle U.S. Government Agencies," *National Defense*, February 2000, [http://www.nationaldefensemagazine.org/issues/2000/Feb/Rules.htm].

[45] Jeanne Meserve, "Official: International Hackers Going after U.S. Netoworks," CNN.com, October 19, 2007, [http://www.cnn.com/2007/US/10/19/cyber.threats/index.html].

[46] Martin Asser, "Echelon: Big brother without a cause?" BBC News, July 6, 2000, [http://news.bbc.co.uk/1/hi/world/europe/820758.stm].

[47] Ron Pemstein, "Europe Spy System," GlobalSecurity.org, March 30, 2000, [http://www.globalsecurity.org/intell/library/news/2000/03/000330-echelon1.htm]. Paul Meller, "European Parliament Adopts 'Echelon' Report," CNN.com, September 7, 2001, [http://archives.cnn.com/2001/TECH/internet/09/07/echelon.report.idg/].

including the Paris station chief for the CIA, because of suspected industrial espionage activities linked to Echelon.[48]

The State Department denied that the U.S. government was engaged in industrial espionage. However, former director of the U.S. Central Intelligence Agency, James Woolsey, has reportedly justified the possibility of industrial espionage by the United States on the basis of the use of bribery by European companies. Officials of the European parliament reportedly expressed outrage about the justification, while not denying that bribery is sometimes used to make sales.[49]

Some government officials warn that criminals now sell or rent malicious code tools for cyber espionage, and the risk for damage to U.S. national security due to cyber espionage conducted by other countries is great. One industry official, arguing for stronger government agency computer security practices, stated that, "If gangs of foreigners broke into the State or Commerce Departments and carried off dozens of file cabinets, there would be a crisis. When the same thing happens in cyberspace, we shrug it off as another of those annoying computer glitches we must live with."[50]

In 2003, a series of cyberattacks designed to copy sensitive data files was launched against DOD systems, and the computers belonging to DOD contractors. The cyber espionage attack apparently wentundetected for many months. This series of cyberattacks was labeled "Titan Rain," and was suspected by DOD investigators to have originated in China. The attacks were directed against the U.S. Defense Information Systems Agency (DISA), the U.S. Redstone Arsenal, the Army Space and Strategic Defense Installation, and several computer systems critical to military logistics. Although no classified systems reportedly were breached, many files were copied containing information that is sensitive and subject to U.S. export-control laws.

In 2006, an extended cyberattack against the U.S. Naval War College in Newport, Rhode Island, prompted officials to disconnect the entire campus from the Internet.[51] A similar attack against the Pentagon in 2007 led

---

[48] Chris Marsden, "European Union to Investigate US-Run Satellite Spy Network," World Socialist Website, July 10, 2000, [http://www.wsws.org/articles/2000/jul2000/eche-j10.shtml].

[49] European Parliament resolution on the existence of a global system for the interception of private and commercial communications (ECHELON interception system) (2001/2098(INI)), European Parliament approved on September 5, 2001, by 367 votes for, 159 against, and 39 abstentions, [http://www.cyber-rights.org/interception/echelon/European_parliament_resolution.htm]. Gerhard SCHMID *Report on the existence of a global system for the interception of private and commercial communications(ECHELON interception system)*, Doc.: A5-0264/2001, May 9, 2001, [http://www.statewatch.org/news/2001/sep/02echelon.htm]. James Woolsey, *Intelligence Gathering and Democracies: The Issue of Economic and Industrial Espionage*, Federation of American Scientists, March 7, 2000, [http://ftp.fas.org/irp/news/2000/03/wool0300.htm].

[50] James Lewis, testimony before the House Committee on Homeland Security, Subcommittee on Emerging Threats, Cybersecurity, and Science and Technology, April 15, 2007.

[51] Chris Johnson, Naval War College Network, "Web Site Back Up Following Intrusion," *Inside the Navy*, December 18, 2006.

officials to temporarily disconnect part of the unclassified network from the Internet. DOD officials acknowledge that the Global Information Grid, which is the main network for the U.S. military, experiences more than three million daily scans by unknown potential intruders.[52]

Accurate attribution is important when considering whether to retaliate using military force or police action. Some DOD officials have indicated that the majority of cyber attacks against DOD and U.S. civilian agency systems are suspected to originate in China, and these attacks are consistently more numerous and sophisticated than cyberattacks from other malicious actors. The motives appear to be primarily cyber espionage against civilian agencies, DOD contractors, and DOD systems. The espionage involves unauthorized access to files containing sensitive industrial technology, and unauthorized research into DOD operations. Some attacks included attempts to implant malicious code into computer systems for future use by intruders.[53]

Security experts warn that all U.S. federal agencies should now be aware that in cyberspace some malicious actors consider that no boundaries exist between military and civilian targets. According to an August 2005 computer security report by IBM, more than 237 million overall security attacks were reported globally during the first half of that year.[54] Government agencies were targeted the most, reporting more than 54 million attacks, while manufacturing ranked second with 36 million attacks, financial services ranked third with approximately 34 million, and healthcare received more than 17 million attacks. The most frequent targets for these attacks, all occurring in the first half of 2005, were government agencies and industries in the United States (12 million), followed by New Zealand (1.2 million), and China (1 million). These figures likely represent an underestimation, given that most security analysts agree that the number of incidents reported are only a small fraction of the total number of attacks that actually occur.

Terrorism Linked to Cybercrime

The proportion of cybercrime that can be directly or indirectly attributed to terrorists is difficult to determine. However, linkages do exist between terrorist groups and criminals that allow terror networks to expand

[52] Some estimates say that up to 90% of computer software used in China is pirated, and thus open to hijack through computer viruses. James Lewis, *Computer Espionage, Titan Rain and China*, Center for Strategic and International Studies, December 14, 2005.

[53] Josh Rogin, "Cyber officials: Chinese hackers attack 'anything and everything,'" FCW.com, Febrary 13, 2007, [http://www.fcw.com/article97658-02-13-07-Web&printLayout].

[54] The Global Business Security Index reports worldwide trends in computer security from incidents that are collected and analyzed by IBM and other security organizations. IBM press release, *IBM Report: Government, Financial Services and Manufacturing Sectors Top Targets of Security Attacks in First Half of 2005*, IBM, August 2, 2005.

internationally through leveraging the computer resources, money laundering activities, or transit routes operated by criminals. For example, the 2005 U.K. subway and bus bombings, and the attempted car bombings in 2007, also in the U.K., provide evidence that groups of terrorists are already secretly active within countries with large communication networks and computerized infrastructures, plus a large, highly skilled IT workforce. London police officials reportedly believe that terrorists obtained high-quality explosives used for the 2005 U.K. bombings through criminal groups based in Eastern Europe.[55]

A recent trial in the U.K. revealed a significant link between Islamic terrorist groups and cybercrime. In June 2007, three British residents, Tariq al-Daour, Waseem Mughal, and Younes Tsouli, pled guilty, and were sentenced for using the Internet to incite murder. The men had used stolen credit card information at online web stores to purchase items to assist fellow jihadists in the field—items such as night vision goggles, tents, global positioning satellite devices, and hundreds of prepaid cell phones, and more than 250 airline tickets, through using 110 different stolen credit cards. Another 72 stolen credit cards were used to register over 180 Internet web domains at 95 different web hosting companies. The group also laundered money charged to more than 130 stolen credit cards through online gambling websites. In all, the trio made fraudulent charges totaling more than $3.5 million from a database containing 37,000 stolen credit card numbers, including account holders' names and addresses, dates of birth, credit balances, and credit limits.[56]

Cybercriminals have made alliances with drug traffickers in Afghanistan, the Middle East, and elsewhere where illegal drug funds or other profitable activities such as credit card theft, are used to support terrorist groups.[57] Drug traffickers are reportedly among the most widespread users of encryption for Internet messaging, and are able to hire high-level computer specialists to help evade law enforcement, coordinate shipments of drugs, and launder money. Regions with major narcotics markets, such as Western Europe and North America, also possess optimal technology infrastructure and open commercial nodes that increasingly serve the transnational trafficking needs of both criminal and terrorist groups.[58] Officials of the U.S.

---

[55] Walsh, *Terrorism on the Cheap*. Rollie Lal, "Terrorists and Organized Crime Join Forces," *International Herald Tribune*, May 25, 2005, at [http://www.iht.com/articles/2005/05/23/opinion/edlal.php]. Barbara Porter, "Forum Links Organized Crime and Terrorism," *By George!* summer 2004 [http://www2.gwu.edu/~bygeorge/060804/crimeterrorism.html].

[56] Brian Krebs, "Three Worked the Web to Help Terrorists," *The Washington Post*, July 6, 2007, p. D01.

[57] Peter Bergen, "The Taliban, Regrouped and Rearmed," *The Washington Post*, September 10, 2006, p. B1. Helen Cooper, "NATO Chief Says More Troops Are Needed in Afghanistan," *The New York Times*, September 22, 2006, p. 10.

[58] Glenn Curtis and Tara Karacan, *The Nexus Among Terrorists, Narcotics Traffickers, Weapons Proliferators, and Organized Crime Networks in Western Europe*, a study prepared by the Federal Research Division,

Drug Enforcement Agency (DEA), reported in 2003 that 14 of the 36 groups found on the U.S. State Department's list of foreign terrorist organizations were also involved in drug trafficking. A 2002 report by the Federal Research Division at the Library of Congress, revealed a "growing involvement of Islamic terrorist and extremists groups in drug trafficking", and limited evidence of cooperation between different terrorist groups involving both drug trafficking and trafficking in arms.[59] Consequently, DEA officials reportedly argued that the war on drugs and the war against terrorism are and should be linked.[60]

State Department officials, at a Senate hearing in March 2002, also indicated that some terrorist groups may be using drug trafficking as a way to gain financing while simultaneously weakening their enemies in the West through exploiting their desire for addictive drugs.[61] The poppy crop in Afghanistan reportedly supplies resin to produce over 90 percent of the world's heroin, supporting a drug trade estimated at $3.1 billion. Reports indicate that money from drug trafficking in Afghanistan is used to help fund terrorist and insurgent groups that operate in that country. Subsequently, U.S. intelligence reports in 2007 have stated that "al Qaeda in Afghanistan" has been revitalized and restored to its pre-September 11, 2001 operation levels, and may now be in a better position to strike Western countries.[62]

Drug traffickers have the financial clout to hire computer specialists with skills for using technologies which make Internet messages hard or impossible to decipher, and which allow terrorist organizations to transcend borders and operate internationally with less chance of detection. Many highly trained technical specialists that make themselves available for hire originally come from the countries of the former Soviet Union and the Indian subcontinent. Some of these technical specialists reportedly will not work

Library of Congress, December 2002, p. 22, at [http://www.loc.gov/rr/frd/pdf-files/WestEurope_NEXUS.pdf].

59 L. Berry, G.E. Curtis, R.A. Hudson, and N. A. Kollars, *A Global Overview of Narcotics-Funded Terrorist and Other Extremist Groups*, Federal Research Division, Library of Congress, Washington, DC, May 2002.

60 Authorization for coordinating the federal war on drugs expired on September 30, 2003. For more information, see CRS Report RL32352, *War on Drugs: Reauthorization of the Office of National Drug Control Policy*, by Mark Eddy. Also, see D.C. Préfontaine, QC and Yvon Dandurand, *Terrorism and Organized Crime Reflections on an Illusive Link and its Implication for Criminal Law Reform*, International Society for Criminal Law Reform Annual Meeting—Montreal, August 8–12, Workshop D-3 Security Measures and Links to Organized Crime, August 11, 2004, at [http://www.icclr.law.ubc.ca/Publications/Reports/International%20Society%20Paper%20of%20Terrorism.pdf].

61 Rand Beers and Francis X. Taylor, U.S. State Department, *Narco-Terror: The Worldwide Connection Between Drugs and Terror*, testimony before the U.S. Senate Judiciary Committee, Subcommittee on Technology, Terrorism, and Government Information, March 13, 2002.

62 Matthew Lee and Katherine Shrader, *Al-Qaida has rebuilt, U.S. intel warns*, Associated Press, July 12, 2007, [http://news.yahoo.com/s/ap/20070712/ap_on_go_pr_wh/us_terror_ threat_32;_ylt=AuURr2eP8AhBrfHyTOdw714Gw_IE]. Associated Press, "Afghanistan's poppy crop could yield more than 2006's record haul, UN says," International Herald Tribune, June 25, 2007, [http://www.iht.com/articles/ap/2007/06/25/asia/AS-GEN-Afghan-Drugs.php].

for criminal or terrorist organizations willingly, but may be misled or unaware of their employers' political objectives. Still, others will agree to provide assistance because other well-paid legitimate employment is scarce in their region.[63]

Terrorist Groups Linked to Hackers. Links between computer hackers and terrorists, or terrorist-sponsoring nations may be difficult to confirm. Membership in the most highly-skilled computer hacker groups is sometimes very exclusive and limited to individuals who develop, demonstrate, and share only with each other, their most closely-guarded set of sophisticated hacker tools. These exclusive hacker groups do not seek attention because maintaining secrecy allows them to operate more effectively. Some hacker groups may also have political interests that are supra-national, or based on religion, or other socio-political ideologies, while other hacker groups may be motivated by profit, or linked to organized crime, and may be willing to sell their computer services, regardless of the political interests involved.

Information about computer vulnerabilities is now for sale online in a hackers' "black market". For example, a list of 5,000 addresses of computers that have already been infected with spyware and which are waiting to be remotely controlled as part of an automated "bot network" reportedly can be obtained for about $150 to $500. Prices for information about computer vulnerabilities for which no software patch yet exists reportedly range from $1,000 to $5,000. Purchasers of this information are often organized crime groups, various foreign governments, and companies that deal in spam.[64]

Terrorist Capabilities for Cyberattack

Some experts estimate that advanced or structured cyberattacks against multiple systems and networks, including target surveillance and testing of sophisticated new hacker tools, might require from two to four years of preparation, while a complex coordinated cyberattack, causing mass disruption against integrated, heterogeneous systems may require 6 to 10 years of preparation.[65] This characteristic, where hackers devote much time to detailed and extensive planning before launching a cyberattack, has also

[63] Louise Shelly, *Organized Crime, Cybercrime and Terrorism*, Computer Crime Research Center, September 27, 2004, [http://www.crime-research.org/articles/Terrorism_Cybercrime/].

[64] Hackers sell their information anonymously through secretive websites. Bob Francis, "Know Thy Hacker," *Infoworld*, January 28, 2005 at [http://www.infoworld.com/article/05/01/28/05OPsecadvise_1.html].

[65] Dorothy Denning, "Levels of Cyberterror Capability: Terrorists and the Internet," [http://www.cs.georgetown.edu/~denning/infosec/Denning-Cyberterror-SRI.ppt], presentation, and Zack Phillips, "Homeland Tech Shop Wants to Jump-Start Cybersecurity Ideas," *CQ Homeland Security*, September 14, 2004 at [http://homeland.cq.com/hs/display.do?docid=1330150&sourcetype=31&binderName=news-all].

been described as a "hallmark" of previous physical terrorist attacks and bombings launched by Al Qaeda.

It is difficult to determine the level of interest, or the capabilities of international terrorist groups to launch an effective cyberattack. A 1999 report by The Center for the Study of Terrorism and Irregular Warfare at the Naval Postgraduate School concluded that it is likely that any severe cyberattacks experienced in the near future by industrialized nations will be used by terrorist groups simply to supplement the more traditional physical terrorist attacks.[66]

Some observers have stated that Al Qaeda does not see cyberattack as important for achieving its goals, preferring attacks which inflict human casualties.[67] Other observers believe that the groups most likely to consider and employ cyberattack and cyberterrorism are the terrorist groups operating in post-industrial societies (such as Europe and the United States), rather than international terrorist groups that operate in developing regions where there is limited access to high technology.

However, other sources report that Al Qaeda has taken steps to improve organizational secrecy through more active and sophisticated use of technology, and evidence suggests that Al Qaeda terrorists used the Internet extensively to plan their operations for September 11, 2001.[68] In past years, Al Qaeda groups reportedly used new Internet-based telephone services to communicate with other terrorist cells overseas. Khalid Shaikh Mohammed, one of the masterminds of the attack against the World Trade Center, reportedly used special Internet chat software to communicate with at least two airline hijackers. Ramzi Yousef, who was sentenced to life imprisonment for the previous bombing of the World Trade Center, had trained as an electrical engineer, and had planned to use sophisticated electronics to detonate bombs on 12 U.S. airliners departing from Asia for the United States. He also used sophisticated encryption to protect his data and to prevent law enforcement from reading his plans should he be captured.[69]

Tighter physical security measures now widely in place throughout the United States may encourage terrorist groups in the future to explore cyberattack as way to lower the risk of detection for their operations.[70] However, other security observers believe that terrorist organizations

---

66 Report was published in 1999, available at [http://www.nps.navy.mil/ctiw/reports/].

67 The Ashland Institute for Strategic Studies has observed that Al Qaeda is more fixated on physical threats than electronic ones. John Swartz, "Cyberterror Impact, Defense Under Scrutiny," *USA Today*, August 3, 2004, p. 2B.

68 David Kaplan, "Playing Offense: The Inside Story of How U.S. Terrorist Hunters Are Going after Al Qaeda," *U.S. News & World Report*, June 2, 2003, pp. 19–29.

69 Robert Windrem, "9/11 Detainee: Attack Scaled Back," September 21, 2003, [http://www.msnbc.com/news/969759.asp].

70 "Terrorism: An Introduction," April 4, 2003 at [http://www.terrorismanswers.com/terrorism].

might be reluctant to launch a cyberattack because it would result in less immediate drama and have a lower psychological impact than a more conventional bombing attack. These observers believe that unless a cyberattack can be made to result in actual physical damage or bloodshed, it will never be considered as serious as a nuclear, biological, or chemical terrorist attack.[71]

Possible Effects of a Coordinated Cyberattack

In March 2007, researchers at Idaho National Laboratories (INL) conducted an experiment labeled the "Aurora Generator Test" to demonstrate the results of a simulated cyberattack on a power network. In a video released by the Department of Homeland Security, a power generator turbine, similar to many now in use throughout the United States, is forced to overheat and shut down dramatically, after receiving malicious commands from a hacker. The researchers at INL were investigating results of a possible cyberattack directed against a vulnerability that, reportedly, has since been fixed.[72] The video, however, implied that other multiple power generators sharing similar cyber vulnerabilities could potentially be disabled the same way.

In July 2002, the U.S. Naval War College hosted a war game called "Digital Pearl Harbor" to develop a scenario for a coordinated cyberterrorism event, where mock attacks by computer security experts against critical infrastructure systems simulated state-sponsored cyberwarfare. The simulated cyberattacks determined that the most vulnerable infrastructure computer systems were the Internet itself, and the computer systems that are part of the financial infrastructure.[73] It was also determined that attempts to cripple the U.S. telecommunications infrastructure would be unsuccessful because built-in system redundancy would prevent damage from becoming too widespread. The conclusion of the exercise was that a "Digital Pearl Harbor" in the United States was only a slight possibility.[74]

---

[71] James Lewis, "Assessing the Risks of Cyber Terrorism, Cyber War and Other Cyber Threats," December 2002 at [http://www.csis.org/tech/0211_lewis.pdf].

[72] Robert Lemos, *DHS Video Shows Potential Impact of Cyberattack*, SecurityFocus.com, September 27, 2007, [http://www.securityfocus.com/brief/597].

[73] At the annual conference of the Center for Conflict Studies, Phil Williams, Director of the Program on Terrorism and Trans-National Crime and the University of Pittsburgh, said an attack on the global financial system would likely focus on key nodes in the U.S. financial infrastructure: Fedwire and Fednet. Fedwire is the financial funds transfer system that exchanges money among U.S. banks, while Fednet is the electronic network that handles the transactions. The system has one primary installation and three backups. "You can find out on the Internet where the backups are. If those could be taken out by a mix of cyber and physical activities, the U.S. economy would basically come to a halt," Williams said. "If the takedown were to include the international funds transfer networks CHIPS and SWIFT then the entire global economy could be thrown into chaos." George Butters, "Expect Terrorist Attacks on Global Financial System," October 10, 2003 at [http://www.theregister.co.uk/content/55/33269.html].

[74] The simulation involved more than 100 participants. Gartner, Inc., "Cyberattacks: The Results of the Gartner/U.S. Naval War College Simulation," July 2002, at [http://www3.gartner.com/2_events/

However, in 2002, a major vulnerability was discovered in switching equipment software that threatened the infrastructure for major portions of the Internet. A flaw in the Simple Network Management Protocol (SNMP) would have enabled attackers to take over Internet routers and cripple network telecommunications equipment globally. Network and equipment vendors worldwide raced quickly to fix their products before the problem could be exploited by hackers, with possible worldwide consequences. U.S. government officials also reportedly made efforts to keep information about this major vulnerability quiet until after the needed repairs were implemented on vulnerable Internet systems.[75] According to an assessment reportedly written by the FBI, the security flaw could have been exploited to cause many serious problems, such as bringing down widespread telephone networks and also halting control information exchanged between ground and aircraft flight control systems.[76]

Security experts agree that a coordinated cyberattack could be used to amplify the effects of a conventional terrorist attack, including a nuclear, biological, or chemical (NBC) attack. However, many of these same experts disagree about the damaging effects that might result from an attack directed against control computers that operate the U.S. critical infrastructure. Some observers have stated that because of U.S. dependency on computer technology, such attacks may have the potential to create economic damage on a large scale, while other observers have stated that U.S. infrastructure systems are resilient and would possibly recover easily, thus avoiding any severe or catastrophic effects.

While describing possible offensive tactics for military cyber operations, DOD officials reportedly stated that the U.S. could confuse enemies by using cyberattack to open floodgates, control traffic lights, or scramble the banking systems in other countries.[77] Likewise, some of China's military journals speculate that cyberattacks could disable American financial markets. China, however, is almost as dependent on these U.S. markets as the United States, and might possibly suffer even more from such a disruption to finances. As to using cyberattack against other U.S. critical infrastructures,

---

audioconferences/dph/dph.html.] War game participants were divided into cells, and devised attacks against the electrical power grid, telecommunications infrastructure, the Internet and the financial services sector. It was determined that "peer-to-peer networking," a special method of communicating where every PC used commonly available software to act as both a server and a client, posed a potentially critical threat to the Internet itself. William Jackson, "War College Calls Digital Pearl Harbor Doable," *Government Computer News*, August 23, 2002, at [http://www.gcn.com/vol1_no1/daily-updates/19792-1.html].

[75] The vulnerability was found in Abstract Syntax Notation One (ASN.1) encoding, and was extremely widespread. Ellen Messmer, "President's Advisor Predicts Cyber-catastrophes Unless Security Improves," *Network World Fusion*, July 9, 2002 at [http://www.nwfusion.com/news/2002/0709schmidt.html].

[76] Barton Gellman, "Cyber-Attacks by Al Qaeda Feared," *Washington Post*, June 27, 2002, p. A01.

[77] Sebastian Sprenger, "Maj.Gen. Lord Is a Groundbreaker," *Federal Computer Week*, October 15, 2007, vol. 21, no. 34, pp. 44–45.

the amount of potential damage that could be inflicted might be relatively trivial compared to the costs of discovery, if engaged in by a nation state. However, this constraint does not apply to non-state actors like Al Qaeda, thus making cyberattack a potentially useful tool for those groups who reject the global market economy.[78]

SCADA Vulnerabilities. Supervisory Control And Data Acquisition (SCADA) systems are the computers that monitor and regulate the operations of most critical infrastructure industries (such as the companies that manage the power grid). These SCADA computers automatically monitor and adjust switching, manufacturing, and other process control activities, based on digitized feedback data gathered by sensors. These control systems are often placed in remote locations, are frequently unmanned, and are accessed only periodically by engineers or technical staff via telecommunications links. However, for more efficiency, these communication links are increasingly connected to corporate administrative local area networks, or directly to the Internet.

Some experts believe that the importance of SCADA systems for controlling the critical infrastructure may make them an attractive target for terrorists.[79] Many SCADA systems also now operate using Commercial-Off-The-Shelf (COTS) software, which some observers believe are inadequately protected against a cyberattack. These SCADA systems are thought to remain persistently vulnerable to cyberattack because many organizations that operate them have not paid proper attention to these systems' unique computer security needs.[80]

The following example may serve to illustrate the possible vulnerability of control systems and highlight cybersecurity issues that could arise for

[78] James Lewis, "Assessing the Risks of Cyber Terrorism, Cyber War and Other Cyber Threats," December 2002, at [http://www.csis.org/tech/0211_lewis.pdf].

[79] Proprietary systems are unique, custom built software products intended for installation on a few (or a single) computers, and their uniqueness makes them a less attractive target for hackers. They are less attractive because finding a security vulnerability takes time, and a hacker may usually not consider it worth their while to invest the pre-operative surveillance and research needed to attack a proprietary system on a single computer. Widely used Commercial-Off-The-Shelf (COTS) software products, on the other hand, are more attractive to hackers because a single security vulnerability, once discovered in a COTS product, may be embedded in numerous computers that have the same COTS software product installed.

[80] Industrial computers sometimes have operating requirements that differ from business or office computers. For example, monitoring a chemical process, or a telephone microwave tower may require 24-hour continuous availability for a critical industrial computer. Even though industrial systems may operate using COTS software (see above), it may be economically difficult to justify suspending the operation of an industrial SCADA computer on a regular basis to take time to install every new security software patch. See interview with Michael Vatis, director of the Institute for Security Technology Studies related to counterterrorism and cybersecurity. Sharon Gaudin, "Security Experts: U.S. Companies Unprepared for Cyber Terror," *Datamation*, July 19, 2002 at [http://itmanagement. earthweb.com/secu/article.php/1429851]. Also, Government Accountability Office, *Information Security: Further Efforts Needed to Fully Implement Statutory Requirements in DOD*, GAO-03-1037 T, July 24, 2003, p. 8.

infrastructure computers when SCADA controls are interconnected with office networks. In August 2003, the "Slammer" Internet computer worm was able to corrupt for five hours the computer control systems at the Davis-Besse nuclear power plant located in Ohio (fortunately, the power plant was closed and off-line when the cyberattack occurred). The computer worm was able to successfully penetrate systems in the Davis-Besse power plant control room largely because the business network for its corporate offices was found to have multiple connections to the Internet that bypassed the control room firewall.[81]

Other observers, however, suggest that SCADA systems and the critical infrastructure are more robust and resilient than early theorists of cyberterror have stated, and that the infrastructure would likely recover rapidly from a cyberterrorism attack. They cite, for example, that water system failures, power outages, air traffic disruptions, and other scenarios resembling possible cyberterrorism often occur as routine events, and rarely affect national security, even marginally. System failures due to storms routinely occur at the regional level, where service may often be denied to customers for hours or days. Technical experts who understand the systems would work to restore functions as quickly as possible. Cyberterrorists would need to attack multiple targets simultaneously for long periods of time to gradually create terror, achieve strategic goals, or to have any noticeable effects on national security.[82]

For more information about SCADA systems, see CRS Report RL31534, *Critical Infrastructure: Control Systems and the Terrorist Threat*, by Dana A. Shea.

Unpredictable Interactions Between Infrastructures. An important area that is not fully understood concerns the unpredictable interactions between computer systems that operate the different U.S. infrastructures. The concern is that numerous interdependencies (where downstream systems may rely on receiving good data through stable links with upstream computers) could possibly build to a cascade of effects that are unpredictable in how they might affect national security.[83] For example, while the "Blaster" worm was disrupting Internet computers over several days in August 2003, some security experts suggest that slowness of communication links, caused by

---

[81] Kevin Poulsen, "Slammer Worm Crashed Ohio Nuke Plant Network," *Security Focus*, August 19, 2003, at [http://www.securityfocus.com/news/6767].

[82] Scott Nance, "Debunking Fears: Exercise Finds 'Digital Pearl Harbor' Risk Small," *Defense Week*, April 7, 2003 at [http://www.kingpublishing.com/publications/dw/].

[83] The most expensive natural disaster in U.S. history, Hurricane Andrew, is reported to have caused $25 billion in damage, while the Love Bug virus is estimated to have cost computer users around the world somewhere between $3 billion and $15 billion. However, the Love Bug virus was created and launched by a single university student in the Philippines, relying on inexpensive computer equipment. Christopher Miller, *GAO Review of Weapon Systems Software*, March 3, 2003, e-mail communication, MillerC@gao.gov.

Blaster worm network congestion, may have contributed to the Eastern United States power blackout that occurred simultaneously on August 14. The computer worm could have degraded the performance of several communications links between data centers normally used to send warnings to other utility managers downstream on the power grid.[84]

Civilian Technology that Supports DOD. DOD uses Commercial-Off-The-Shelf (COTS) hardware and software products in core information technology administrative functions, and also in the combat systems of all services, as for example, in the integrated warfare systems for nuclear aircraft carriers.[85] DOD favors the use of COTS products in order to take advantage of technological innovation, product flexibility and standardization, and resulting contract cost-effectiveness. Nevertheless, DOD officials and others have stated that COTS products are lacking in security, and that strengthening the security of those products to meet military requirements may be too difficult and costly for most COTS vendors. To improve security, DOD Information Assurance practices require deploying several layers of additional protective measures around COTS military systems to make them more difficult for enemy cyberattackers to penetrate.[86]

However, on two separate occasions in 2004, viruses reportedly infiltrated two top-secret computer systems at the Army Space and Missile Defense Command. It is not clear how the viruses penetrated the military systems, or what the effects were. Also, contrary to security policy requirements, the compromised computers reportedly lacked basic anti virus software protection.[87] Security experts have noted that no matter how much protection is given to computers, hackers are always creating new ways to defeat those protective measures.[88]

---

[84] Network congestion caused by the Blaster worm reportedly delayed the exchange of critical power grid control data across the public telecommunications network, which could have hampered the operators' ability to prevent the cascading effect of the blackout. DanVerton, "Blaster Worm Linked to Severity of Blackout," *Computerworld*, August 29, 2003,[http://www.computerworld.com/printthis/2003/0,4814,84510,00.html.].

[85] Some ships of the U.S. Navy use Windows software. Bill Murray, "Navy Carrier to RunWin 2000," *GCN.com*, September 11, 2000, [http://www.gcn.com/vol19_no27/dod/2868–1.html]. Major U.K. naval systems defense contractor, BAE Systems, also tookthe decision to standardize future development on Microsoft Windows. John Lettice, "OSSTorpedoed: Royal Navy Will Run on Windows for Warships," *Register*, September 6, 2004at [http://www.theregister.co.uk/2004/09/06/ams_goes_windows_for_warships/].

[86] Patience Wait, "Defense IT Security Can't Rest on COTS," *GCN.com*, September 27,2004, at [http://www.gcn.com/23_29/news/27422-1.html].

[87] Dawn Onley, "Army Urged to Step Up IT Security Focus," *GCN.com*, September 2, 2004,at [http://www.gcn.com/vol1_no1/daily-updates/27138-1.html].

[88] Patience Wait, "Defense IT Security Can't Rest on COTS," *GCN.com*, September27,2004, at [http://www.gcn.com/23_29/news/27422-1.html].

Why Cyberattacks Are Successful

Networked computers with exposed vulnerabilities may be disrupted or taken over by a hacker, or by automated malicious code. Botnets opportunistically scan the Internet to find and infect computer systems that are poorly configured, or lack current software security patches. Compromised computers are taken over to become slaves in a "botnet", which can include thousands of compromised computers that are remotely controlled to collect sensitive information from each victim's PC, or to collectively attack as a swarm against other targeted computers.

Even computers that have updated software and the newest security patches may still be vulnerable to a type of cyberattack known as a "Zero-Day exploit." This may occur if a computer hacker discovers a new software vulnerability and launches a malicious attack to infect computers before a security patch can be created by the software vendor and distributed to protect users. Zero-day vulnerabilities in increasingly complex software are regularlydiscovered by computer hackers. Recent news articles report that zero-day vulnerabilities are now available at online auctions, where buyers and sellers negotiate with timed bidding periods and minimum starting prices. This allows newly-discovered computer security vulnerabilities to be sold quickly to the highest bidder. Computer security expert Terri Forslof, of Tipping Point, has reportedly said that such practices will ". . . increase the perceived value of vulnerabilities, and the good guys already have trouble competing with the money you can get on the black market."[89]

The Insider Threat. A major threat for organizations is the ease with which data can now be copied and carried outside using a variety of portable storage devices, such as small flash drives. Newer high-density memory stick technology reportedly allows installed computer applications to be run entirely from the flash drive. This means that the entire contents of a PC could possibly be copied to and stored on a small, easily portable, and easily concealed media device.[90]

Employees with access to sensitive information systems can initiate threats in the form of malicious code inserted into software that is being developed either locally, or under offshore contracting arrangements. For example, in January 2003, 20 employees of subcontractors working in the United States at the Sikorsky Aircraft Corporation were arrested for possession of false identification used to obtain security access to facilities containing restricted and sensitive military technology. All of the defendants pleaded

---

[89] Tim Green, *Web Site auctions software vulnerabilities to highest bidder,* Network World, August 8, 2007.

[90] McAfee Virtual Criminology Report: Organized Crime and the Internet, December 2006, [http://www.sigma.com.pl/pliki/albums/userpics/10007/Virtual_Criminology_Report_ 2006.pdf].

guilty and have been sentenced, except for one individual who was convicted at trial on April 19, 2004.[91]

Persistence of Computer System Vulnerabilities. Vulnerabilities in software and computer system configurations provide entry points for a cyberattack. Vulnerabilities persist largely as a result of poor security practices and procedures, inadequate training in computer security, or technical errors in software products.[92] Inadequate resources devoted to staffing the security function may also contribute to poor security practices. Home PC users often have little or no training in best practices for effectively securing home networks and equipment.

Errors in New Software Products. Vendors for Commercial-Off-The-Shelf software (COTS) are often criticized for releasing new products with errors that create the computer system vulnerabilities.[93] Richard Clarke, former White House cyberspace advisor until 2003, has reportedly said that many commercial software products have poorly written, or poorly configured security features.[94] In response to such criticism, the software industry reportedly has made new efforts to design products with architectures that are more secure. For example, Microsoft has created a special Security Response Center and now works with DOD and with industry and government leaders to improve security features in its new products. However, many software industry representatives reportedly agree that no matter what investment is made to improve software security, there will continue to be vulnerabilities in future software because products are becoming increasingly more complex.[95]

---

[91] U.S. Attorneys Office, District of Connecticut, at [http://www.usdoj.gov/usao/ct/attf. html].

[92] The SANS Institute, in cooperation with the National Infrastructure Protection Center (NIPC), publishes an annual list of the 10 most commonly exploited vulnerabilities for Windows systems and for Unix systems. *The SANS/FBI Twenty Most Critical Internet Security Vulnerabilities, 2003*, SANS, April 15, 2003 at [http://www.sans.org/top20/].

[93] In September 2003, Microsoft Corporation announced three new critical flaws in its latest Windows operating systems software. Security experts predicted that computer hackers may possibly exploit these new vulnerabilities by releasing more attack programs, such as the "Blaster worm" that recently targeted other Windows vulnerabilities causing widespread disruption on the Internet. Jaikumar Vijayan, "Attacks on New Windows Flaws Expected Soon," *Computerworld*, September 15, 2003, vol. 37, no. 37, p. 1.

[94] Agencies operating national security systems must purchase software products from a list of lab-tested and evaluated products in a program that requires vendors to submit software for review in an accredited lab, a process (known as certification and accreditation under the Common Criteria, a testing program run by the National Information Assurance Partnership) that often takes a year and costs several thousand dollars. The review requirement previously has been limited to military national security software, however, the administration has stated that the government will undertake a review of the program in 2003 to "possibly extend" it as a new requirement for civilian agencies. Ellen Messmer, White House issue "National Strategy to Secure Cyberspace," *Network World Fusion*, February 14, 2003, [http://www.nwfusion.com/news/2003/0214ntlstrategy.html].

[95] Scott Charney, Chief Security Strategist, Microsoft, Statement before the House Committee on Armed Services, Terrorism, Unconventional Threats and Capabilities Subcommittee, *Information Technology in the 21st Century Battlespace*, hearing, July 24, 2003, p. 9.

Inadequate Resources. Although software vendors periodically release fixes or upgrades to solve newly discovered security problems, an important software security patch might not get scheduled for installation on an organization's computers until several weeks or months after the patch is available.[96] The job may be too time-consuming, too complex, or too low a priority for the system administration staff. With increased software complexity comes the introduction of more vulnerabilities, so system maintenance is never-ending. Sometimes the security patch itself may disrupt the computer when installed, forcing the system administrator to take additional time to adjust the computer to accept the new patch. To avoid such disruption, a security patch may first require testing on a separate isolated network before it is distributed for installation on all other regular networked computers.

Because of such delays, the computer security patches installed in many organizations may lag considerably behind the current cyberthreat situation. Whenever delays are allowed to persist in private organizations, in government agencies, or among PC users at home, computer vulnerabilities that are widely reported may remain unprotected, leaving networks open to possible attack for long periods of time.

Future Attractiveness of Critical Infrastructure Systems

There has yet been no published evidence showing a widespread focus by cybercriminals on attacking the control systems that operate the U.S. civilian critical infrastructure. Disabling infrastructure controls for communications, electrical distribution or other infrastructure systems, is often described as a likely scenario to amplify the effects of a simultaneous conventional terrorist attack involving explosives.

However, in 2006, at a security discussion in Williamsburg, Virginia, a government analyst reportedly stated that criminal extortion schemes may have already occurred, where cyberattackers have exploited control system vulnerabilities for economic gain. And, in December 2006, malicious software that automatically scans for control system vulnerabilities reportedly was made available on the Internet for use by cybercriminals. This scanner software reportedly can enable individuals with little knowledge about infrastructure control systems to locate a SCADA computer connected to the Internet, and quickly identify its security vulnerabilities.

---

[96] A survey of 2000 PC users found that 42% had not downloaded the vendor patch to ward off the recent Blaster worm attack, 23% said they do not regularly download software updates, 21% do not update their anti-virus signatures, and 70% said they were not notified by their companies about the urgent threat due to the Blaster worm. Jaikumar Vijayan, "IT Managers Say They Are Being Worn Down by Wave of Attacks," *Computerworld*, August 25, 2003, vol. 37, no. 34, p. 1.

The Idaho National Laboratory is tasked to study and report on technology risks associated with infrastructure control systems. Past studies have shown that many, if not most, automated control systems are connected to the Internet, or connected to corporate administrative systems that are connected to the Internet, and are currently vulnerable to a cyberattack. And, because many of these infrastructure SCADA systems were not originally designed with security as a priority, in many cases, new security controls cannot now be easily implemented to reduce the known security vulnerabilities.[97] Following past trends, where hackers and cybercriminals have taken advantage of easy vulnerabilities, some analysts now predict that we may gradually see new instances where cybercriminals exploit vulnerabilities in critical infrastructure control systems.[98]

Measuring Cybercrime

New, automated attack methods have outpaced current methods for tracking the number and severity of cyberattacks and cybercrime intrusions. For example, according to a study by the Cooperative Association for Internet Data Analysis (CAIDA), on January 25, 2003, the SQL Slammer worm (also known as "Sapphire") automatically spread to infect more than 90% of vulnerable computers worldwide within 10 minutes of its release on the Internet, making it the fastest-spreading computer worm in history. As the study reports, the Slammer worm doubled in size every 8.5 seconds and achieved its full scanning rate (55 million scans per second) after about 3 minutes. It caused considerable harm through network outages which led to numerous canceled airline flights and automated teller machine (ATM) failures.[99]

The use of automated tools for cybercrime has had a dramatic affect on the Computer Emergency Response Team/ Coordinating Center (CERT/CC). In 2004, CERT/CC announced that it had abandoned its traditional practice of producing an annual report tracking the number of cyber intrusions recorded for each year. For many years prior to 2004, CERT/CC had maintained a database of statistics about security incidents that were reported to it anonymously by businesses and individuals worldwide. The reason given for abandoning its annual tracking report was because the widespread

[97] Testimony of Aaron Turner, House Committee on Homeland Security, Subcommittee on Emerging Threats, Cybersecurity and Science & Technology, Hearing on "Cyber Insecurity: Hackers are Penetrating Federal Systems and Critical Infrastructure," April 19, 2007, [http://homeland.house.gov/SiteDocuments/20070419153130-95132.pdf].

[98] Testimony of Aaron Turner, House Committee on Homeland Security, Subcommittee on Emerging Threats, Cybersecurity and Science & Technology, Hearing on "Cyber Insecurity: Hackers are Penetrating Federal Systems and Critical Infrastructure," April 19, 2007, [http://homeland.house.gov/SiteDocuments/20070419153130-95132.pdf].

[99] "Internet Worm Keeps Striking," January 27, 2003, *CBSNews.com* at [http://www.cbsnews.com/stories/2003/01/28/tech/main538200.shtml].

use of new, automated cyberattack tools had escalated the number of network attacks to such a high level, that the CERT/CC organization determined that traditional methods for counting security incidents had become meaningless as a metric for assessing the scope and effects of attacks against Internet-connected systems.[100] The CERT-CC website currently states, "Given the widespread use of automated attack tools, attacks against Internet-connected systems have become so commonplace that counts of the number of incidents reported provide little information with regard to assessing the scope and impact of attacks. Therefore, beginning in 2004, we stopped publishing the number of incidents reported."[101]

The FBI estimates that all types of computer crime in the U.S. now costs industry about $400 billion, while officials in the Department of Trade and Industry in Britain say computer crime has risen by 50 percent from 2005 to 2006. As one example of costs associated with a recent computer security breach, TJX, the parent company of TJ Maxx, took a $12 million charge in its fiscal first quarter of 2008 due to the theft of more than 45 million credit and debit card numbers, starting in 2006. The money reportedly went to investigating and containing the intrusion, improving computer security, communicating with customers, and other fees. TJX estimates that, adding damages from future lawsuits, the breach may eventually cost $100 per lost record, or a total of $4.5 billion.[102]

It is estimated that only five per cent of cybercriminals are ever arrested or convicted because the anonymity associated with web activity makes them hard to catch, and the trail of evidence needed to link them to a cybercrime is hard to unravel. Studies also show that cybercrime incidents are rarely reported, especially by companies that wish to avoid negative publicity leading to possible loss of confidence by its customers. However, law enforcement officials argue that "maintaining a code of silence" won't benefit a company in the long-run. Steven Martinez, deputy assistant director for the FBI's cyber division, reportedly stated at the 2006 RSI Computer Security Conference that partnerships between law enforcement, the academic community, and the private sector are key to understanding and reducing cybercrime.[103]

Each year, the Computer Security Institute (CSI), with help from the FBI, conducts a survey of thousands of security practitioners from U.S. corporations, government agencies, financial institutions, and universities. The CSI/FBI Computer Crime and Security Survey, published annually, is

---

[100] "CERT/CC Statistics 1988-2004" at [http://www.cert.org/stats/cert_stats.html].

[101] CERT Coordination Center, Carnegie Mellon University, [http://www.cert.org/stats/].

[102] Sharon Gaudin, *Breach Costs Soar at TJX*, Information Week, May 21, 2007, p. 19.

[103] Marcia Savage, "Companies Still Not Reporting Attacks, FBI Director Says," SearchSecurity.com, February 15, 2006, [http://searchsecurity.techtarget.com/originalContent/0,289142,sid14_gci1166845,00.html?bucket=NEWS&topic=299990].

perhaps the most widely-used source of information about how often computer crime occurs and how expensive these crimes can be. The 2006 survey indicated that the average financial loss reported due to security breaches was $167,713, an 18% decrease from the previous year's average loss of $203,606.

However, some observers argue that the analyses reported in the CSI/FBI survey may be questionable, because the survey methodology is not statistically valid.[104] This is because the survey is limited only to CSI members, which reduces the likelihood that respondents are a representative sample of all security practitioners, or that their employers are representative of employers in general. In addition, the 2006 CSI/FBI survey points out that most companies are continuing to sweep security incidents under the rug.

With the apparent absence of statistically valid survey results concerning the financial costs of computer crime, and with an accompanying lack of clear data about the number and types of computer security incidents reported, it appears that there may be no valid way to currently understand the real scope and intensity of cybercrime. The growing use of botnets and sophisticated malicious code also suggests that the percentage of unreported cybercrime, plus the percentage undetected, may both be going up.

Problems Tracing Cybercrime

The challenge of identifying the source of attacks is complicated by the unwillingness of commercial enterprises to report attacks, owing to potential liability concerns. CERT/CC estimates that as much as 80% of all actual computer security incidents still remain unreported.[105] Law enforcement officials concede they are making little progress in tracing the profits and finances of cybercriminals. Online payment services, such as PayPal and E-Gold, enable criminals to launder their profits and exploit the shortcomings of international law enforcement. Recently, Intermix Media was fined $7.5 million in penalties for distribution of spyware which silently captures personal information from user's PCs. However, some adware and spyware purveyors reportedly can still make millions of dollars per year in profits. Many companies who distribute spyware are difficult to pursue legally because they typically also offer some legitimate services. In many cases, the finances that back cybercrimes are so distributed they are hard for law enforcement to figure out.[106]

[104] Bill Brenner, "Security Blog Log: Has CSI/FBI Survey Jumped the Shark?" SearchSecurity.com, July 21, 2006, [http://searchsecurity.techtarget.com /columnItem/0,294698,sid14_gci1202328,00.html].

[105] Many cyberattacks are unreported usually because the organization is unable to recognize that it has been attacked, or because the organization is reluctant to reveal publicly that it has experienced a cyberattack, Government Accountability Office, *Information Security: Further Efforts Needed to Fully Implement Statutory Requirements in DOD*, GAO-031037T, July 24, 2003, p. 6.

[106] Matt Hines, "Malware Money Though to Trace," *Eweek*, September 18, 2006, p. 14.

Organized Cybercrime

Some large cybercriminal groups are transnational, with names like Shadowcrew, Carderplanet, and Darkprofits. Individuals in these groups reportedly operate from locations all over the world, working together to hack into systems, steal credit card information and sell identities, in a very highly structured, organized network.[107] Organized crime is also recruiting teenagers who indicate they feel safer doing illegal activity online than in the street. A recent report from the McAfee security organization, titled the "Virtual Criminology Report", draws on input from Europe's leading high-tech crime units and the FBI, and suggests that criminal outfits are targeting top students from leading academic institutions and helping them acquire more of the skills needed to commit high-tech crime on a massive scale.[108]

In the future, we may see new and different modes of criminal organization evolve in cyberspace. Cyberspace frees individuals from many of the constraints that apply to activities in the physical world, and current forms of criminal organization may not transition well to online crime. Cybercrime requires less personal contact, less need for formal organization, and no need for control over a geographical territory. Therefore, some researchers argue that the classical hierarchical structures of organized crime groups may be unsuitable for organized crime on the Internet. Consequently, online criminal activity may emphasize lateral relationships and networks instead of hierarchies.[109]

Instead of assuming stable personnel configurations that can persist for years, online criminal organization may incorporate the "swarming" model, in which individuals coalesce for a limited period of time in order to conduct a specific task, or set of tasks, and afterwards go their separate ways. The task of law enforcement could therefore become much more difficult. If cybercriminals evolve into the "Mafia of the moment" or the "cartel of the day," police will lose the advantage of identifying a permanent group of participants who engage in a set of routine illicit activities, and this will only contribute to the future success of organized cybercrime.[110]

---

107 Kevin Poulsen, "Feds Square off with Organized Cyber Crime," SecurityFocus, February 17, 2005, [http://www.securityfocus.com/news/10525].

108 Bill Brenner, "Criminals Find Safety in Cyberspace," SearchSecurity.com, December 18, 2006, [http://searchsecurity.techtarget.com/originalContent/0,289142,sid14_gci1235455,00. html?bucket=NEWS &topic=299990].

109 Council of Europe Octopus Programme, *Summary of the Organised Crime Situation Report 2004: Focus on the Threat of Cybercrime*, Strausbourg, September 6, 2004, p. 48.

110 Susan Brenner, "Organized Cybercrime? How Cyberspace May Affect the Structure of Criminal Relationships," *North Carolina Journal of Law and Technology*, 2002, [http://www.jolt.unc.edu/Vol4_I1/Web/Brenner-V4I1.htm].

Federal Efforts to Protect Computers

The federal government has taken steps to improve its own computer security and to encourage the private sector to also adopt stronger computer security policies and practices to reduce infrastructure vulnerabilities. In 2002, the Federal Information Security Management Act (FISMA) was enacted, giving the Office of Management and Budget (OMB) responsibility for coordinating information security standards and guidelines developed by federal agencies.[111] In 2003, the National Strategy to Secure Cyberspace was published by the Administration to encourage the private sector to improve computer security for the U.S. critical infrastructure through having federal agencies set an example for best security practices.[112]

The National Cyber Security Division (NCSD), within the National Protection and Programs Directorate of the Department of Homeland Security (DHS) oversees a Cyber Security Tracking, Analysis and Response Center (CSTARC), tasked with conducting analysis of cyberspace threats and vulnerabilities, issuing alerts and warnings for cyberthreats, improving information sharing, responding to major cybersecurity incidents, and aiding in national-level recovery efforts. In addition, a new Cyber Warning and Information Network (CWIN) has begun operation in 50 locations, and serves as an early warning system for cyberattacks.[113] The CWIN is engineered to be reliable and survivable, has no dependency on the Internet or the public switched network (PSN), and reportedly will not be affected if either the Internet or PSN suffer disruptions.[114]

In January 2004, the NCSD also created the National Cyber Alert System (NCAS), a coordinated national cybersecurity system that distributes information to subscribers to help identify, analyze, and prioritize emerging vulnerabilities and cyberthreats. NCAS is managed by the United States Computer Emergency Readiness Team (US-CERT), a partnership between NCSD and the private sector, and subscribers can sign up to receive notices from this new service by visiting the US-CERT website.[115]

---

[111] GAO has noted that many federal agencies have not implemented security requirements for most of their systems, and must meet new requirements under FISMA. See GAO Report GAO-03-852T, *Information Security: Continued Efforts Needed to Fully Implement Statutory Requirements*, June 24, 2003.

[112] Tinabeth Burton, *ITAA Finds Much to Praise in National Cybersecurity Plan*, May 7, 2003, [http://www.findarticles.com/p/articles/mi_go1965/is_200303/ai_n7418485]

[113] Bara Vaida, "Warning Center for Cyber Attacks is Online, Official Says," *Daily Briefing*, GovExec.com, June 25, 2003.

[114] The Cyber Warning Information Network (CWIN) provides voice and data connectivity to government and industry participants in support of critical infrastructure protection, [http://www.publicsectorinstitute.net/ELetters/HomelandSecurityStrategies/Volume1No1CyberWarningNetLaunch.lsp].

[115] [http://www.us-cert.gov/cas/].

International Convention on Cybercrime

Cybercrime is also a major international challenge, even though attitudes about what comprises a criminal act of computer wrongdoing still vary from country to country. However, the Convention on Cybercrime was adopted in 2001 by the Council of Europe, a consultative assembly of 43 countries, based in Strasbourg. The Convention, effective July 2004, is the first and only international treaty to deal with breaches of law "over the internet or other information networks." The Convention requires participating countries to update and harmonize their criminal laws against hacking, infringements on copyrights, computer facilitated fraud, child pornography, and other illicit cyber activities.[116]

Although the United States has signed and ratified the Convention, it did not sign a separate protocol that contained provisions to criminalize xenophobia and racism on the Internet, which would raise Constitutional issues in the United States.[117] The separate protocol could be interpreted as requiring nations to imprison anyone guilty of "insulting publicly, through a computer system" certain groups of people based on characteristics such as race or ethnic origin, a requirement that could make it a crime to e-mail jokes about ethnic groups or question whether the Holocaust occurred. The Department of Justice has said that it would be unconstitutional for the United States to sign that additional protocol because of the First Amendment's guarantee of freedom of expression. The Electronic Privacy Information Center, in a June 2004 letter to the Foreign Relations Committee, objected to U.S. ratification of the Convention, because it would "create invasive investigative techniques while failing to provide meaningful privacy and civil liberties safeguards."[118]

On August 3, 2006, the U.S. Senate passed a resolution of ratification for the Convention. The United States will comply with the Convention based on existing U.S. federal law; and no new implementing legislation is expected to be required. Legal analysts say that U.S. negotiators succeeded in scrapping most objectionable provisions, thereby ensuring that the Convention tracks closely with existing U.S. laws.[119]

---

116 Full text for the Convention on Cyber Crime may be found at [http://conventions.coe.int/Treaty/Commun/QueVoulezVous.asp?NT=185&CM=8&DF= 18/06/04&CL=ENG].

117 The U.S. Senate Committee on Foreign Relations held a hearing on the Convention on June 17, 2004. CRS Report RS21208, *Cybercrime: The Council of Europe Convention*, by Kristin Archick. Estelle Durnout, *Council of Europe Ratifies Cybercrime Treaty*, ZDNet, March 22, 2004, at [http://news.zdnet.co.uk/business/legal/0,39020651,39149470,00.htm].

118 [http://www.epic.org/privacy/intl/senateletter-061704.pdf].

119 For more information about the Convention on Cybercrime, see CRS Report RS21208, *Cybercrime: The Council of Europe Convention*, by Kristin Archick.

The Need to Improve Cybersecurity

Department of Defense (DOD) officials have stated that, while the threat of cyber attack is "less likely" to appear than conventional physical attack, it could actually prove more damaging because it could involve disruptive technology that might generate unpredictable consequences that give an adversary unexpected advantages.[120] The Homeland Security Presidential Directive 7 required that the Department of Homeland Security (DHS) coordinate efforts to protect the cybersecurity for the nation's critical infrastructure. This resulted in two reports in 2005, titled "Interim National Infrastructure Protection Plan," and "The National Plan for Research and Development in Support of Critical Infrastructure Protection", where DHS provided a framework for identifying and prioritizing, and protecting each infrastructure sector.

However, some observers question why, in light of the many such reports describing an urgent need to reduce cybersecurity vulnerabilities, there is not an apparent perceived sense of national urgency to close the gap between cybersecurity and the threat of cyberattack. For example, despite Federal Information Security Management Act of 2002 (FISMA), some experts argue that security remains a low priority, or is treated almost as an afterthought at some domestic federal agencies.[121] In 2007, the Government Accountability Office issued a report, titled "Critical Infrastructure Protection: Multiple Efforts to Secure Control Systems Are Under Way, but Challenges Remain," which states that cybersecurity risks have actually increased for infrastructure control systems because of the persistence of interconnections with the Internet, and continued open availability of detailed information on the technology and configuration of the control systems. The report states that no overall strategy yet exists to coordinate activities to improve computer security across federal agencies and the private sector, which owns the critical infrastructure.[122] Some observers argue that, as businesses gradually strengthen their security policies for headquarters and administrative systems, the remote systems that control critical infrastructure and manufacturing may soon be seen as easier targets of opportunity for cybercrime.

---

[120] Advantages of EA and CNA might derive from United States reliance on a computer-controlled critical infrastructure, along with unpredictable results depending on severity of the attack. Jason Sherman, "Bracing for Modern Brands of Warfare," *Air Force Times*, September 27, 2004, [http://www.airforcetimes.com/story.php?f=1-AIRPAPER-358727. php].

[121] Statement of James A. Lewis, Senior Fellow and Director, Technology and Public Policy Program, Center for Strategic and International Studies, Committee on House Oversight and Government Reform Subcommittee on Government Management, Organization, and Procurement, Subcommittee on Information Policy, Census, and National Archives, June 7, 2007.

[122] GAO-08-119T, *Critical Infrastructure Protection: Multiple Efforts to Secure Control Systems are Under Way, but Challenges Remain*, October 17, 2007.

Cybercrime is obviously one of the risks of doing business in the age of the internet, but observers argue that many decision-makers may currently view it as a low-probability threat. Some researchers suggest that the numerous past reports describing the need to improve cybersecurity have not been compelling enough to make the case for dramatic and urgent action by decision-makers. Others suggest that even though relevant information is available, future possibilities are still discounted, which reduces the apparent need for present-day action. In addition, the costs of current inaction are not borne by the current decision-makers. These researchers argue that IT vendors must be willing to regard security as a product attribute that is coequal with performance and cost; IT researchers must be willing to value cybersecurity research as much as they value research for high performance or cost-effective computing; and, finally, IT purchasers must be willing to incur present-day costs in order to obtain future benefits.[123]

Issues for Congress

Policy issues for cybercrime and cyberterrorism include a need for the following:

- increase awareness about changing threats due to the growing technical skills of extremists and terrorist groups;
- develop more accurate methods for measuring the effects of cybercrime;
- help to determine appropriate responses by DOD to a cyberattack;
- examine the incentives for achieving the goals of the National Strategy to Secure Cyberspace;
- search for ways to improve the security of commercial software products;
- explore ways to increase security education and awareness for businesses and home PC users; and
- find ways for private industry and government to coordinate to protect against cyberattack.

Congress may also wish to consider ways to harmonize existing federal and state laws that require notice to persons when their personal information

[123] Seymour Goodman and Herber Lin, editors, Toward a Safer and More Secure Cyberspace, *Committee on Improving Cybersecurity Research in the United States, National Research Council*, 2007, pp. 261–267, [http://books.nap.edu/openbook.php?isbn=0309103959].

has been affected by a computer security breach, and that impose obligations on businesses and owners of that restricted information.[124]

Growth in Technical Capabilities of Terrorists

Seized computers belonging to Al Qaeda indicate its members are becoming more familiar with hacker tools and services that are available over the Internet.[125] Could terrorist groups find it advantageous to hire a cybercrime botnet tailored to attack specific targets, possibly including the civilian critical infrastructure of Western nations? Could cybercrime botnets, used strategically, provide a useful way for extremists to amplify the effects of a conventional terrorist attack using bombs?

As computer-literate youth increasingly join the ranks of terrorist groups, will cyberterrorism likely become increasingly more mainstream in the future? Will a computer-literate leader bring increased awareness of the advantages of an attack on information systems, or be more receptive to suggestions from other, newer computer-literate members? Once a new tactic has won widespread media attention, will it likely motivate other rival terrorist groups to follow along the new pathway?[126]

Better Measurement of Cybercrime Trends

Experiences at CERT/CC show that statistical methods for measuring the volume and economic effects of cyberattacks may be questionable. Without sound statistical methods to accurately report the scope and effects of cybercrime, government and legal authorities will continue to have unreliable measures of the effectiveness of their policies and enforcement actions.

Figures from several computer security reports now used for measuring annual financial losses to U.S. industry due to intrusions and cybercrime are believed by some observers to be limited in scope or possibly contain statistical bias.[127] Is there a need for a more statistically reliable analysis of trends

---

[124] For more information about laws related to identity theft, see CRS Report RL34120, *Information Security and Data Breach Notification Safeguards*, by Gina Marie Stevens.

[125] Richard Clarke, "Vulnerability: What Are Al Qaeda's Capabilities?" *PBS Frontline: Cyberwar*, April 2003, at [http://www.pbs.org].

[126] Jerrold M. Post, Kevin G. Ruby, and Eric D. Shaw, "From Car Bombs to Logic Bombs: The Growing Threat From Information Terrorism," *Terrorism and Political Violence*, summer 2000, vol. 12, no. 2, pp. 97–122.

[127] A well known source of information about the costs of cyberattacks is the annual computer security survey published by the Computer Security Institute (CSI), which utilizes data collected by the FBI. However, respondents to the CSI/FBI survey of computer security issues are generally limited only to CSI members, which may create statistical bias that affects the survey findings. Recently, CSI has also conceded weaknesses in its analytical approach and has suggested that its survey of computer security vulnerabilities and incidents may be more illustrative than systematic. However, the CSI/FBI survey remains useful despite its imperfect methodology. Bruce Berkowitz and Robert W. Hahn, "Cybersecurity: Who's Watching the Store?" *Issues in Science and Technology*, spring 2003.

in computer security vulnerabilities and types of cyberattacks to more accurately show the costs and benefits for improving national cybersecurity? Congress may wish to encourage security experts to find more effective ways to collect data that will enable accurate analysis of trends for cyberattacks and cybercrime. Congress may also wish to encourage security researchers to find better ways to identify the initiators of cyberattacks.

DOD and Cyberattack Response

If a terrorist group were to use a cybercrime botnet to subvert computers in a third party country, such as China, to launch a cyberattack against the United States, the U.S. response to the cyberattack must be carefully considered, in order to avoid retaliating against the wrong entity. Would the resulting effects of cyberweapons used by the United States be difficult to limit or control? Would a cyberattack response that could be attributed to the United States possibly encourage other extremists, or rogue nations, to start launching their own cyberattacks against the United States? Would an attempt by the U.S. to increase surveillance of another entity via use of cyberespionage computer code be labeled as an unprovoked attack, even if directed against the computers belonging to a terrorist group? If a terrorist group should subsequently copy, or reverse-engineer a destructive U.S. military cyberattack program, could it be used against other countries that are U.S. allies, or even turned back to attack civilian computer systems in the United States?[128] If the effects become widespread and severe, could the U.S. use of cyberweapons exceed the customary rules of military conflict, or violate international laws.[129]

Commercial electronics and communications equipment are now used extensively to support complex U.S. weapons systems, and are possibly vulnerable to cyberattack. This situation is known to our potential adversaries.[130] To what degree are military forces and national security threatened by computer security vulnerabilities that exist in commercial software systems, and how can the computer industry be encouraged to create new COTS products that are less vulnerable to cyberattack?

---

[128] See CRS Report RL31787, *Information Warfare and Cyberwar: Capabilities and Related Policy Issues*, by Clay Wilson.

[129] The laws of war are international rules that have evolved to resolve practical problems relating to military conflict, such as restraints to prevent misbehavior or atrocities, and have not been legislated by an overarching central authority. The United States is party to various limiting treaties. Sometimes the introduction of new technology tends to force changes in the understanding of the laws of war. Gary Anderson and Adam Gifford, "Order Out of Anarchy: The International Law of War," *The Cato Journal*, August 2004, vol. 15, no. 1, pp. 25–36.

[130] Stanley Jakubiak and Lowell Wood, "DOD Uses Commercial Software and Equipment in Tactical Weapons," Statements before the House Military Research and Development Subcommittee, Hearing on EMP Threats to the U.S. Military and Civilian Infrastructure, October 7, 1999. House Armed Services Committee, *Commission to Assess the Threat to the United States from Electromagnetic Pulse Attack*, hearing, July 22, 2004.

Incentives for the National Strategy to Secure Cyberspace

Does the National Strategy to Secure Cyberspace present clear incentives for achieving security objectives? Suggestions to increase incentives may include requiring that all software procured for federal agencies be certified under the "Common Criteria" testing program, which is now the requirement for the procurement of military software. However, industry observers point out that the software certification process is lengthy and may interfere with innovation and competitiveness in the global software market.[131]

Should the National Strategy to Secure Cyberspace rely on voluntary action on the part of private firms, home users, universities, and government agencies to keep their networks secure, or is there a need for possible regulation to ensure best security practices? Has public response to improve computer security been slow partly because there are no regulations currently imposed?[132] Would regulation to improve computer security interfere with innovation and possibly harm U.S. competitiveness in technology markets? Two of the former cybersecurity advisers to the president have differing views: Howard Schmidt has stated that market forces, rather than the government, should determine how product technology should evolve for better cybersecurity; however, Richard Clarke has stated that the IT industry has done little on its own to improve security of its own systems and products.[133]

---

[131] Agencies operating national security systems are required to purchase software products from a list of lab-tested and evaluated products in a program run by the National Information Assurance Partnership (NIAP), a joint partnership between the National Security Agency and the National Institute of Standards and Technology. The NIAP is the U.S. government program that works with organizations in a dozen other countries around the world which have endorsed the international security-evaluation regimen known as the "Common Criteria." The program requires vendors to submit software for review in an accredited lab, a process that often takes a year and costs several thousand dollars. The review previously was limited to military national security software and equipment, however, the Administration has stated that the government will undertake a review of the program to "possibly extend" this software certification requirement to civilian agencies. Ellen Messmer, White House issue "National Strategy to Secure Cyberspace," *Network World Fusion*, February 14, 2003, at [http://www.nwfusion.com/news/2003/0214ntlstrategy.html].

[132] Business executives may be cautious about spending for large new technology projects, such as placing new emphasis on computer security. Results from a February 2003 survey of business executives indicated that 45% of respondents believed that many large Information Technology (IT) projects are often too expensive to justify. Managers in the survey pointed to the estimated $125.9 billion spent on IT projects between 1977 and 2000 in preparation for the year 2000 (Y2K) changeover, now viewed by some as a non-event. Sources reported that some board-level executives stated that the Y2K problem was overblown and over funded then, and as a result, they are now much more cautious about future spending for any new, massive IT initiatives. Gary H. Anthes and Thomas Hoffman, "Tarnished Image," *Computerworld*, May 12, 2003, vol. 37, no. 19, p. 37.

[133] Howard Schmidt points out that major technology firms now promote anti-virus software and encourage better cybersecurity practices. He stresses that market forces are causing private industry to improve security of products. Martin Kady, "Cybersecurity a Weak Link in Homeland's Armor," *CQ Weekly*, February 14, 2005. Meanwhile, Richard Clarke, who initially opposed regulation during his tenure in the Clinton and Bush administrations, now states that the IT industry only reponds to improve security of its products when regulation is threatened. William Jackson, "To Regulate or Not to Regulate? That Is the Question," *Government Computer News*, February 26, 2005.

Improving Security of Commercial Software

Some security experts emphasize that if systems administrators received the necessary training for keeping their computer configurations secure, then computer security would greatly improve for the U.S. critical infrastructure. However, should software product vendors be required to create higher quality software products that are more secure and that need fewer patches? Could software vendors possibly increase the level of security for their products by rethinking the design, or by adding more test procedures during product development?

Education and Awareness of Cyberthreats

Ultimately, reducing the threat to national security from cybercrime depends on a strong commitment by government and the private sector to follow best management practices that help improve computer security. Numerous government reports already exist that describe the threat of cybercrime and make recommendations for management practices to improve cybersecurity.

A 2004 survey done by the National Cyber Security Alliance and AOL showed that most home PC users do not have adequate protection against hackers, do not have updated antivirus software protection, and are confused about the protections they are supposed to use and how to use them.[134] How can computer security training be made available to all computer users that will keep them aware of constantly changing computer security threats, and that will encourage them to follow proper security procedures?

Coordination Between Private Sector and Government

What can be done to improve sharing of information between federal government, local governments, and the private sector to improve computer security? Effective cybersecurity requires sharing of relevant information about threats, vulnerabilities, and exploits.[135] How can the private sector obtain information from the government on specific threats which the government now considers classified, but which may help the private sector protect against cyberattack? And, how can the government obtain specific information from private industry about the number of successful

[134] A 2004 survey of 329 PC users revealed that most computer users think they are safe but lack basic protections against viruses, spyware, hackers, and other online threats. In addition, large majorities of home computer users have been infected with viruses and spyware and remain highly vulnerable to future infections. AOL and the National Cyber Security Alliance, "Largest In-home Study of Home Computer Users Shows Major Online Threats, Perception Gap," October 2004 at [http://www.staysafeonline.info/news/NCSA-AOLIn-HomeStudyRelease.pdf].

[135] Government Accountability Office, *Homeland Security: Efforts To Improve Information Sharing Need to Be Strengthened*, GAO-03-760, August 2003.

computer intrusions, when companies resist reporting because they want to avoid publicity and guard their trade secrets?[136] Should cybercrime information voluntarily shared with the federal government about successful intrusions be shielded from disclosure through Freedom of Information Act requests?

How can the United States better coordinate security policies and international law to gain the cooperation of other nations to better protect against a cyberattack? Pursuit of hackers may involve a trace back through networks requiring the cooperation of many Internet Service Providers located in several different nations.[137] Pursuit is made increasingly complex if one or more of the nations involved has a legal policy or political ideology that conflicts with that of the United States.[138]

Thirty-eight countries, including the United States, participate in the Council of Europe's Convention on Cybercrime, which seeks to combat cybercrime by harmonizing national laws, improving investigative abilities, and boosting international cooperation. However, how effective will the Convention without participation of other countries where cybercriminals now operate freely? (For more on the Convention, see CRS Report RS21208, *Cybercrime: The Council of Europe Convention*, by Kristin Archick.)

Legislative Activity

H.R. 1525—The Internet Spyware (I-SPY) Prevention Act of 2007, proposes penalties for unauthorized access to computers, or the use of computers to commit crimes. On May 23, 2007, this bill was received in the Senate and referred to the Committee on the Judiciary.

H.R. 1684—The Department of Homeland Security Authorization Act for Fiscal Year 2008 establishes within the Department of Homeland Security an Office of Cybersecurity and Communications, headed by the Assistant Secretary for Cybersecurity and Communications, with responsibility for overseeing preparation, response, and reconstitution for cybersecurity and to protect communications from terrorist attacks, major disasters, and other emergencies, including large-scale disruptions.

---

[136] CRS Report RL30153, *Critical Infrastructures: Background, Policy and Implementation*, by John Moteff.

[137] Trace back to identify a cyberattacker at the granular level remains problematic. Dorothy Denning, *Information Warfare and Security* (Addison-Wesley, 1999), p. 217.

[138] In Argentina, a group calling themselves the X-Team, hacked into the website of that country's Supreme Court in April 2002. The trial judge stated that the law in his country covers crime against people, things, and animals but not websites. The group on trial was declared not guilty of breaking into the website. Paul Hillbeck, "Argentine Judge Rules in Favor of Computer Hackers," February 5, 2002, at [http://www.siliconvalley.com/mld/siliconvalley/news/editorial/3070194.htm].

The bill directs the Assistant Secretary to do the following:

- Establish and maintain a capability within the Department for ongoing activities to identify threats to critical information infrastructure to aid in detection of vulnerabilities and warning of potential acts of terrorism and other attacks.
- Conduct risk assessments on critical information infrastructure with respect to acts of terrorism.
- Develop a plan for the continuation of critical information operations in the event of a cyber attack.
- Define what qualifies as a cyber incident of national significance for purposes of the National Response Plan.
- Develop a national cybersecurity awareness, training, and education program that promotes cybersecurity awareness within the Federal Government and throughout the Nation.
- Consult and coordinate with the Under Secretary for Science and Technology on cybersecurity research and development to strengthen critical information infrastructure against acts of terrorism.

On May 11, 2007, this bill was referred to the Senate Committee on Homeland Security and Governmental Affairs.

H.R. 3221—The New Direction for Energy Independence, National Security, and Consumer Protection Act proposes establishment of the Grid Modernization Commission to facilitate the adoption of Smart Grid standards, technologies, and practices across the Nation's electricity grid. The bill was passed in the House on August 4, 2007. On October 19, 2007, there was a unanimous consent request to consider H.R. 3221 in the Senate, but objection was heard.

H.R. 3237—The Smart Grid Facilitation Act of 2007, proposes to modernize the Nation's electricity transmission and distribution system to incorporate digital information and controls technology. "Smart grid" technology functions will include the ability to detect, prevent, respond to, or recover from cyber-security threats and terrorism. The new Grid Modernization Commission is directed to undertake, and update on a biannual basis, an assessment of the progress toward modernizing the electric system including cybersecurity protection for extended grid systems. On August 24, 2007, the bill was referred to House subcommittee on Energy and Environment.

DOCUMENT NO. 6

CYBERCRIME: AN OVERVIEW OF THE FEDERAL COMPUTER FRAUD AND ABUSE STATUTE AND RELATED FEDERAL CRIMINAL LAWS

CRS Report
97-1025

February 25, 2008

Charles Doyle
Senior Specialist
American Law Division

Summary

The federal computer fraud and abuse statute, 18 U.S.C. 1030, outlaws conduct that victimizes computer systems. It is a computer security law. It protects federal computers, bank computers, and computers connected to the Internet. It shields them from trespassing, threats, damage, espionage, and from being corruptly used as instruments of fraud. It is not a comprehensive provision, but instead it fills crack and gaps in the protection afforded by other federal criminal laws. This is a brief sketch of section 1030 and some of its federal statutory companions.

In their present form, the seven paragraphs of subsection 1030(a) outlaw:

- computer trespassing (e.g., hacking) in a government computer, 18 U.S.C. 1030(a)(3);
- computer trespassing (e.g., hackers) resulting in exposure to certain governmental, credit, financial, or commercial information, 18 U.S.C. 1030(a)(2);
- damaging a government computer, a bank computer, or a computer used in interstate or foreign commerce (e.g., a worm, computer virus, Trojan horse, time bomb, a denial of service attack, and other forms of cyber attack, cyber crime, or cyber terrorism), 18 U.S.C. 1030(a)(5);

- committing fraud an integral part of which involves unauthorized access to a government computer, a bank computer, or a computer used in interstate or foreign commerce, 18 U.S.C. 1030(a)(4);
- threatening to damage a government computer, a bank computer, or a computer used in interstate or foreign commerce, 18 U.S.C. 1030(a)(7);
- trafficking in passwords for a government computer, a bank computer, or a computer used in interstate or foreign commerce, 18 U.S.C. 1030(a)(6); and
- accessing a computer to commit espionage, 18 U.S.C. 1030(a)(1).

Subsection 1030(b) makes it a crime to attempt to commit any of these offenses. Subsection 1030(c) catalogs the penalties for committing them, penalties that range from imprisonment for not more than a year for simple cyberspace trespassing to a maximum of life imprisonment when death results from intentional computer damage. Subsection 1030(d) preserves the investigative authority of the Secret Service. Subsection 1030(e) supplies common definitions. Subsection 1030(f) disclaims any application to otherwise permissible law enforcement activities. Subsection 1030(g) creates a civil cause of action of victims of these crimes.

This report is available in abbreviated form—without the footnotes, citations, quotations, or appendices found in this report—under the title *Cybercrime: A Sketch of 18 U.S.C. 1030 and Related Federal Criminal Laws*, RS20830.

Introduction

The federal computer fraud and abuse statute, 18 U.S.C. 1030,[1] protects computers in which there is a federal interest—federal computers, bank computers, and computers used in interstate and foreign commerce. It shields them from trespassing, threats, damage, espionage, and from being corruptly used as instruments of fraud. It is not a comprehensive provision, instead it fills cracks and gaps in the protection afforded by other state and federal criminal laws. It is a work that over the last three decades, Congress has kneaded, reworked, recast, amended, and supplemented to bolster the uncertain coverage of the more general federal trespassing, threat, malicious mischief, fraud, and espionage statutes.[2] This is a brief

[1] The full text of 18 U.S.C. 1030 is appended. Earlier versions of this report appeared under the title, *Computer Fraud and Abuse: An Overview of 18 U.S.C. 1030 and Related Federal Criminal Laws*.

[2] Congressional inquiry began no later than 1976, S. Comm. on Government Operations, *Problems Associated with Computer Technology in Federal Programs and Private Industry—Computer Abuses*, 94th Cong., 2d Sess. (1976)(Comm.Print). Hearings were held in successive Congresses thereafter until passage of the original version of section 1030 as part of the Comprehensive Crime Control Act of 1984, P.L. 98-473, 98 Stat. 2190; *see e.g., Federal Computer Systems Protection Act: Hearings Before the Subcomm. on Criminal Laws and Procedures of the Senate Comm. on the Judiciary*, 95th Cong., 2d Sess.(1978); *S.240, the Computer Systems Protection Act of 1979: Hearings Before the Subcomm. on Criminal Justice of the Senate Comm. on the Judiciary*, 96th Cong., 2d Sess.(1980); *Federal Computer System Protection Act, H.R. 3970: Hearings Before the House*

description of section 1030 and its federal statutory companions. There are other laws that address the subject of crime and computers. Section 1030 deals with computers as victims; other laws deal with computers as arenas for crime or as repositories of the evidence of crime or from some other perspective. These other laws—laws relating to identity theft, obscenity, pornography, gambling, inter alia—are beyond the scope of this report.[3]

In their present form, the seven paragraphs of subsection 1030(a) outlaw:

- computer trespassing in a government computer, 18 U.S.C. 1030(a)(3);
- computer trespassing resulting in exposure to certain governmental, credit, financial, or commercial information, 18 U.S.C. 1030(a)(2);
- damaging a government computer, a bank computer, or a computer used in interstate or foreign commerce, 18 U.S.C. 1030(a)(5);
- committing fraud an integral part of which involves unauthorized access to a government computer, a bank computer, or a computer used in interstate or foreign commerce, 18 U.S.C. 1030(a)(4);
- threatening to damage a government computer, a bank computer, or a computer used in interstate or foreign commerce, 18 U.S.C. 1030(a)(7);
- trafficking in passwords for a government computer, a bank computer, or a computer used in interstate or foreign commerce, 18 U.S.C. 1030(a)(6); and
- accessing a computer to commit espionage, 18 U.S.C. 1030(a)(1).

Comm. on the Judiciary, 97th Cong., 2d Sess.(1982); *Computer Crime: Hearings Before the House Comm. on the Judiciary*, 98th Cong., 1st Sess. (1983).

Refurbishing of the original 1984 legislation occurred in 1986, 1988, 1989, 1990, 1994, and 1996: P.L. 99-474, 100 Stat. 1213; P.L. 100-690, 102 Stat. 4404; P.L. 101-73, 103 Stat. 502; P.L. 101-647, 104 Stat. 4831; P.L. 103-322, 108 Stat. 2097; P.L. 104-294, 110 Stat. 3491. Most recently, both the USA PATRIOT Act, P.L. 107-56, 115 Stat. 272 (2001) and the Department of Homeland Security Act, P.L. 107-296, 116 Stat. 2135 (2002) amended provisions of section 1030.

For a chronological history of the act up to but not including the 1996 amendments, see Adams, *Controlling Cyberspace: Applying the Computer Fraud and Abuse Act to the Internet*, 12 Santa Clara Computer & High Technology Law Journal 403 (1996). For a general description of the validity and application of this act, see; Buchman, *Validity, Construction, and Application of Computer Fraud and Abuse Act*, 174 ALR Fed. 101 (2004); Berkowitz, *Computer Security and Privacy: The Third Wave of Property Law*, 33 Colorado Lawyer 57 (Feb. 2004); *Prosecuting Intellectual Property Crimes*, Computer Crime and Intellectual Property Section, Criminal Division, United States Department of Justice [(2006)](*DoJ Computer Crime*), available on February 22, 2008 at [http://www.cybercrime.gov/ipmanual/index.html].

[3] For a discussion of these and similar matters see, *Twenty-Second Survey of White Collar Crime: Computer Crimes*, 44 American Criminal Law Review 313 (2007); CRS Report RL31919, *Remedies Available to Victims of Identity Theft*; CRS Report 95-804, *Obscenity and Indecency: Constitutional Principles and Federal Statutes*; CRS Report 95-406, *Child Pornography: Constitutional Principles and Federal*; CRS Report 97-619, *Internet Gambling: Overview of Federal Criminal Law*; Kerr, *The Fourth Amendment and New Technologies: Constitutional Myths and the Case for Caution*, 102 Michigan Law Review 802 (2004); *DoJ Computer Crime.*

Subsection 1030(b) makes it a crime to attempt to commit any of these offenses.[4] Subsection 1030(c) catalogs the penalties for committing them, penalties that range from imprisonment for not more than a year for simple cyberspace trespassing to imprisonment for not more than twenty years for a second espionage-related conviction. Subsection 1030(d) preserves the investigative authority of the Secret Service. Subsection 1030(e) supplies common definitions. Subsection 1030(f) disclaims any application to otherwise permissible law enforcement activities. Subsection 1030(g) creates a civil cause of action for victims of these crimes. And subsection 1030(h) called for annual reports through 1999 from the Attorney General and Secretary of the Treasury on investigations under the damage paragraph (18 U.S.C. 1030(a)(5)).

Trespassing in Government Cyberspace (18 U.S.C. 1030(a)(3))

> *Whoever . . . intentionally, without authorization to access any nonpublic computer[5] of a department or agency of the United States,[6] accesses such a computer of that department or agency that is exclusively for the use of the Government of the United States or, in the case of a computer not exclusively for such use, is used by or for the Government of the United States and such conduct affects that use by or for the Government of the United States . . . shall be punished as provided in subsection (c) of this section.*
>
> *(b) Whoever attempts to commit an offense under subsection (a) of this section shall be punished as provided in subsection (c) of this section.*

Paragraph 1030(a)(3) condemns unauthorized intrusion ("hacking") into federal government computers whether they are used exclusively by the government or the government shares access with others. With the help of subsection 1030(b) it also outlaws attempted intrusions. In the case of shared computers, a crime only occurs if the unauthorized access "affects . . . use by or for" the government or would affect such use if an attempted effort had succeeded.

Broken down into its elements, paragraph (a)(3) makes it unlawful for anyone to:

- without authorization
- intentionally
- either

[4] The Department of Justice maintains a website which provides a list of prosecutions for "computer intrusion", commonly known as "hacking,"as well as cases, statutes and other documentation associated with cybercrime, available on February 22, 2008 at [http://www.cybercrime.gov].

[5] "(e) As used in this section . . . (1) the term 'computer' means an electronic, magnetic, optical, electrochemical, or other high speed data processing device performing logical, arithmetic, or storage functions, and includes any data storage facility or communications facility directly related to or operating in conjunction with such device, but such term does not include an automated typewriter or typesetter, a portable hand held calculator, or other similar device," 18 U.S.C. 1030(e)(1).

[6] "(e) As used in this section . . . (7) the term 'department of the United States' means the legislative or judicial branch of the Government or one of the executive departments enumerated in section 101 of title 5," 18 U.S.C. 1030(e)(7).

> access a government computer maintained exclusively for the use of the federal government, or
>
> access a government computer used, at least in part, by or for the federal government and the access affects use by or for the federal government, or attempt to do so (18 U.S.C. 1030(b)).

This pure trespassing proscription dates from 1986 and its legislative history leaves little doubt that nothing more than unauthorized entry is required:

> "[S]ection 2(b) will clarify the present 18 U.S.C. 1030(a)(3), making clear that it applies to acts of simple trespass against computers belonging to, or being used by or for, the Federal Government. The Department of Justice and others have expressed concerns about whether the present subsection covers acts of mere trespass, i.e., unauthorized access, or whether it requires a further showing that the information perused was 'used, modified, destroyed, or disclosed.' To alleviate those concerns, the Committee wants to make clear that the new subsection will be a simple trespass offense, applicable to persons without authorized access to Federal computers," S.Rept. 99-432 at 7 (1986); see also, H.Rept. 99-612 at 11 (1986).

Intent

The paragraph only bans "intentional" trespassing. The reports are instructive here, for they make it apparent that the element cannot be satisfied by a mere inadvertent trespass and nothing more. It is intended, however, to cover anyone who purposefully accomplishes the proscribed unauthorized entry into a government computer, and, at least in the view of the House report, anyone "whose initial access was inadvertent but who then deliberatively maintains access after a non-intentional initial contact," H.Rept. 99-612 at 9-10 (1986); see also, S.Rept. 99-432 at 5-6 (1986).

Unauthorized Access

While the question of what constitutes "access without authorization" might seem fairly straight forward, Congress was willing to accept a certain degree of trespassing by government employees in order to protect whistleblowers:

> The Committee wishes to be very precise about who may be prosecuted under the new subsection (a)(3). The Committee was concerned that a Federal computer crime statute not be so broad as to create a risk that government employees and others who are authorized to use a Federal Government computer would not face prosecution for acts of computer access and use that, while technically wrong, should not rise to the level of criminal conduct. At the same time, the Committee was required to balance its concern for Federal employees and other authorized users against the legitimate need to protect Government computers against abuse by "outsiders." The Committee struck that balance in the following manner.

In the first place, the Committee has declined to criminalize acts in which the offending employee merely 'exceeds authorized access' to computers in his own department ("department"' is defined in section 2(g) of S.2281 [now 18 U.S.C. 1030(e)(7)]). It is not difficult to envision an employee or other individual who, while authorized to use a particular computer in one department, briefly exceeds his authorized access and peruses data belonging to the department that he is not supposed to look at. This is especially true where the department in question lacks a clear method of delineating which individuals are authorized to access certain of its data. The Committee believes that administrative sanctions are more appropriate than criminal punishment in such a case. The Committee wishes to avoid the danger that every time an employee exceeds his authorized access to his department's computers—no matter how slightly—he could be prosecuted under this subsection. That danger will be prevented by not including "exceeds authorized access" as part of this subsection's offense.

In the second place, the Committee has distinguished between acts of unauthorized access that occur within a department and those that involve trespasses into computers belonging to another department. The former are not covered by subsection (a)(3); the latter are. Again, it is not difficult to envision an individual who, while authorized to use certain computers in one department, is not authorized to use them all. The danger existed that S.2281, as originally introduced, might cover every employee who happens to sit down, within his department, at a computer terminal which he is not officially authorized to use. These acts can also be best handled by administrative sanctions, rather than by criminal punishment. To that end, the Committee has constructed its amended version of (a)(3) to prevent prosecution of those who, while authorized to use some computers in their department, use others for which they lack the proper authorization. By precluding liability in purely 'insider' cases such as these, the Committee also seeks to alleviate concerns by Senators Mathias and Leahy that the existing statute cases a wide net over "whistleblowers". . . .

The Committee has thus limited 18 U.S.C. 1030(a)(3) to cases where the offender is completely outside the Government, and has no authority to access a computer of any agency or department of the United States, or where the offender's act of trespass is interdepartmental in nature. The Committee does not intend to preclude prosecution under this subsection if, for example, a Labor Department employee authorized to use Labor's computers accesses without authorization an FBI computer. An employee who uses his department's computer and, without authorization, forages into data belonging to another department is engaged in conduct directly analogous to an 'outsider' tampering with Government computers. . . .

The Committee acknowledges that in rare circumstances this may leave serious cases of intradepartmental trespass free from criminal prosecution under (a)(3). However, the Committee notes that such serious acts may be subject to other criminal penalties if, for example, they violate trade secrets laws or 18 U.S.C. 1030(a)(1), (a)(4), (a)(5), or (a)(6), as proposed in this legislation. S.Rept. 99-432 at 7-8 (1986); see also, H.Rept. 99-612 at 11 (1986).

Affects the Use

Trespassing upon governmental computer space on computers that are not exclusive for governmental use is prohibited only when it affects use by the government or use for governmental purposes. The committee reports provide a useful explanation of the distinctive, "affects-the-use" element of the trespassing ban:

> [T]respassing in a computer used only part-time by the Federal Government need not be shown to have affected the operation of the government as a whole. The Department of Justice has expressed concerns that the present subsection's language could be construed to require a showing that the offender's conduct would be an exceedingly difficult task for Federal prosecutors. Accordingly, Section 2(b) will make clear that the offender's conduct need only affect the use of the Government''s operation of the computer in question [or the operation of the computer in question on behalf of the Government]. S.Rept. 99-432 at 6-7 (1986); see also, H.Rept. 99-612 at 11 (1986); S.Rept. 104-357 at 9 (1996).

Jurisdiction

The reports offer little insight into the meaning of the third element—what computers are protected from trespassing. There may be two reasons. Paragraph 1030(a)(3) protects only government computers and therefore explanations of the sweep of its coverage in the area of interstate commerce or of financial institutions are unnecessary. Besides, at least for purposes of these trespassing offenses of paragraph 1030(a)(3), the statute itself addresses several of the potentially more nettlesome questions.

First, the construction of the statute itself strongly suggests that it reaches only computers owned or leased by the federal government: "whoever . . . without authorization to access any nonpublic computer *of a department or agency of the United States*, accesses such a computer *of that department or agency. . . .*"

Second, the language of the statute indicates that "nonpublic" computers may nevertheless include government computers that the government allows to be used by nongovernmental purposes: "in the case of *a [government] computer not exclusively for the use of the Government of the United States . . . .*"

Third, the statute covers government computers that are available to non-government users: "accesses such a computer . . . that. . . in the case of a [government] computer not exclusively for the use of the Government of the United States, is used by *or for* the Government of the United States . . . ."

The use of the term "nonpublic," however, makes it clear that this shared access may not be so broad as to include the general public.

Finally, the section supplies a definition of "department of the United States": "[a]s used in this section . . . the term 'department of the United States' means the legislative or judicial branch of the Government or one of the executive departments enumerated in section 101 of title 5," 18 U.S.C. 1030(e) (7);[7] and the title supplies a definition of "agency of the United States": "[a]s used in this title . . . [t]he term 'agency' includes any department, independent establishment, commission, administration, authority, board or bureau of the United States or any corporation in which the United States has a proprietary interest, unless the context shows that such term was intended to be used in a more limited sense," 18 U.S.C. 6.

Extraterritorial Jurisdiction. There is one jurisdictional aspect of paragraph 1030(a)(3) that is unclear. Under what circumstances, if any, does the paragraph reach hacking initiated or occurring overseas? As a general rule, federal criminal laws are presumed to apply within the United States and not overseas. In some instances, Congress explicitly negates the presumption. The treason statute, for example, outlaws the offense whether committed "within the United States or elsewhere," 18 U.S.C. 2381.

In other instances, when the criminal statute is silent, the courts will conclude that Congress must have intended the statute to apply to overseas misconduct because of the nature of the offense and the circumstances under which it was committed. For example, the Supreme Court concluded that Congress must have intended the federal statute that prohibited fraud against the federal government to apply to fraud against the United States committed abroad, particularly when the offenders were Americans.[8] The Court later decided that a federal statute that outlawed conspiracy to violate federal law applied to an overseas conspiracy to smuggle liquor into this country.[9]

---

[7] "The Executive departments are: The Department of State. The Department of the Treasury. The Department of Defense. The Department of Justice. The Department of the Interior. The Department of Agriculture. The Department of Commerce. The Department of Labor. The Department of Health and Human Services. The Department of Housing and Urban Development. The Department of Transportation. The Department of Energy. The Department of Education. The Department of Veterans Affairs. The Department of Homeland Security." 5 U.S.C. 101.

[8] *United States v. Bowman*, 260 U.S. 94, 98 (1922)("But the same rule of [territorial] interpretation should not be applied to criminal statutes which . . . are enacted because of the right of the Government to defend itself against obstruction, or fraud wherever perpetrated, especially if committed by its own citizens, officers or agents. Some such offenses . . . are such that to limit their locus to the strictly territorial jurisdiction would be greatly to curtail the scope and usefulness of the statute and leave open a large immunity for frauds as easily committed by citizens on the high seas and in foreign countries as at home. In such cases, Congress has not thought it necessary to make specific provision in the law that the locus shall include the high seas and foreign countries, but allows it to be inferred from the nature of the offense").

[9] *Ford v. United States*, 273 U.S. 589 (1927)("The principle that a man who outside a country wilfully puts in motion a force to take effect in it is answerable at the place where the evil is done, is recognized in the criminal jurisprudence of all countries").

In the cybercrime context, at least one court determined that paragraph 1030(a)(4), which prohibits unauthorized computer access to defraud, applied to a hacker in Russia who gained unauthorized access to "protected computers" in this country.[10] The court's conclusion was influenced by an amendment in which Congress had added computers used in "foreign commerce or communications" to the definition of "protected computers" and by the legislative history of why it did so.[11] While the case was pending, Congress further amended the definition of "protected computer" to include "a computer located outside the United States that is used in a manner that affects interstate or foreign commerce or communication of the United States," 18 U.S.C. 1030(e)(2)(B).[12]

Paragraph 1030(a)(3) does not cover "protected computers;" it covers non-public, federal government computers. Congress explicitly provided extraterritorial jurisdiction over the computer-related information acquisition, fraud, damage, and extortion offenses by amending the definition of protected computer. It provided no such explicit provision for simple trafficking offense under paragraph 1030(a)(3).

A court might conclude that Congress meant both to grant extraterritorial application in computer-related information acquisition, fraud, damage, and extortion cases under paragraphs 1030(a)(2), (4), (5), and (7) and to foreclose extraterritorial application in simple trespassing cases under paragraph 1030(a)(3)—even under circumstances when the courts would have otherwise found it appropriate in a simple trespassing case.

Penalties

The penalties for violation or attempted violation of paragraph 1030(a)(3) imprisonment for not more than one year and/or a fine of not more than \$100,000 (\$200,000 for organizations) for the first offense and imprisonment for not more than 10 years and/or a fine of not more than \$250,000 (\$500,000 for organizations) for all subsequent convictions, 18 U.S.C. 1030(c), 3571.[13]

---

[10] *United States v. Ivanov*, 175 F.Supp.2d 367, 374-75 (D. Conn. 2001).

[11] *Id.* at 374 ("the Committee specifically noted its concern that the statute as it existed prior to the 1996 amendments did not cover 'computers used in foreign communications or commerce, despite the fact hackers are often foreign-based.' The Committee cited two specific cases in which foreign-based hackers had infiltrated computer systems in the United States, as examples of the kind of situation the amendments were intended to address. . . . Congress has the power to apply its statutes extraterritorially, and in the case of 18 U.S.C. 1030, it has clearly manifested its intention to do so"), quoting and citing, S.Rept. 104-357, at 4-5 (1996).

[12] The amendment appears as paragraph 814(d)(1) of the USA PATRIOT Act, P.L. 107–56, 115 Stat. 384 (2001).

[13] By virtue of 18 U.S.C. 3571, all felonies are subject to fines of not more than the greater of \$250,000 or twice the amount of the pecuniary gain or loss associated with the offense, unless provisions applicable to a specific crime either call for a higher maximum fine or were enacted subsequent to 1984 when the general provisions of section 3571 became effective.

Most federal criminal statutes give the impression that offenders may be sentenced to imprisonment, to a fine or to both imprisonment and a fine. This may be something of an illusion in most serious

Offenses under other paragraphs may trigger forfeiture, restitution, racketeering, money laundering, sentencing guidelines, and civil liability provisions elsewhere in the law. For reasons that will become apparent when they are discussed later in this report, those provisions have little, if any, relevance in case of simple trespassing offenses under paragraph 1030(a)(3).

Juveniles. Historically, federal authorities did not prosecute juvenile offenders. Most federal crimes, including computer hacking, are crimes under the laws of most states. When a juvenile violates a federal law, he must be turned over to state juvenile authorities unless the state is unwilling or unable to proceed against him, or unless the state has inadequate facilities for his treatment, or unless the crime is a violent federal felony or a federal drug or firearms offense, 18 U.S.C. 5032.[14]

Overview. Paragraph 1030(a)(3) has remained essentially unchanged since 1986,[15] and there appear to have been relatively few prosecutions under its provisions.[16] The explanation may be that paragraph 1030(a)(3) tracks paragraph 1030(a)(2) so closely that the prosecution is ordinarily reserved for the more serious cases which warrant the more serious felony sanctions

---

federal cases. Federal sentencing is influenced by sentencing guidelines that calibrate sentencing levels beneath the maximum terms established in the statute for a particular offense, according to the circumstances of the crime and the offender, see generally, CRS Report RL32846, *How the Federal Sentencing Guidelines Work: Two Examples*. While a sentence in compliance with the Guidelines is no longer mandatory, *United States v. Booker*, 543 U.S. 220, 226–27 (2005), federal courts must begin the sentencing process by calculating the applicable sentencing range under the Guidelines and justify any departure from that range, *Gall v. United States*, 128 S.Ct. 586, 596 (2007).

[14] See generally *Juvenile Delinquents and Federal Criminal Law: The Federal Juvenile Delinquency Act and Related Matters*, CRS Rept. RL30822.

[15] In 1994, Congress amended the paragraph to emphasize that trespassing upon computers used part-time for the government required a showing that government use was "adversely" affected rather than merely affected, P.L.103-322, 108 Stat. 2099. Concerned that it might suggest that trespassing could be beneficial, Congress repealed the 1994 amendment in 1996 when it also made changes to make it clear that a person "permitted to access publicly available Government computers. . . may still be convicted under (a)(3) for accessing without authority any nonpublic Federal Government computer" and that a person may be convicted under paragraph (a)(3) for access that affects the use of a computer employed on behalf of the government regardless of whether the computer is actually operated by the government or is merely operated for the government, P.L. 104-294, 110 Stat. 3491; S.Rept. 104-357 at 9 (1996).

[16] Olivenbaum, *<CTRL><ALT><DELETE>: Rethinking Federal Computer Crime Legislation*, 27 Section Hall Law Review 574, 600-1 (1997); *United States v. Rice, aff'g w/o published op.*, 961 F.2d 211 (4th Cir. 1992), subsequent motion for correction of sentence, 815 F.Supp. 158 (W.D.N.C. 1993).

Rice is a curious case. The unpublished opinion indicates that Rice, a long time Internal Revenue Service (IRS) agent, hacked into the IRS computers at the behest of a drug dealer and disclosed to the dealer the status of an IRS investigation of the dealer; the agent also advised the dealer on means of evading forfeiture of his house. For this he was convicted of conspiracy to launder his friend's drug profits (18 U.S.C. 1956(a)(1)(b)(i)), conspiracy to defraud the United States of forfeitable property (26 U.S.C. 7214), computer fraud, i.e., accessing the computer system of a government agency without authority (18 U.S.C. 1030(a)(3)), and unauthorized disclosure of confidential information (18 U.S.C. 1905)(sometimes known as the Trade Secrets Act). The court did not address the apparent conflict between the conviction and the legislative history of paragraph 1030(a)(3) indicating that the paragraph does not govern cases of an employee hacking into the computer systems of his own agency. See also *Brownlee v. Dyncorp*, 349 F.3d 1343, 1346 (Fed Cir. 2003) (noting that the guilty plea to charges under §1030(a)(3) of the employee of a government contractor resulting from the employee's entering false data regarding hours worked into the government computer system).

available under information acquisition offense of paragraph 1030(a)(3), but not the simple trespassing offense of paragraph 1030(a)(2).[17]

Other Crimes[18]

Attempt. An attempt to hack into a federal computer in violation of paragraph 1030(a)(3) is also a federal crime, 18 U.S.C. 1030(b). In fact, subsection 1030(b) makes it a federal crime to attempt to violate any of the paragraphs of subsection 1030(a).[19] The subsection dates from the original enactment and evokes no comment in the legislation history other than the notation of its existence, H.Rept. 98-894 at 22 (1984).

This is not particularly unusual. There is no general federal attempt statute,[20] but Congress has elected to penalize attempts to commit many individual federal crimes.[21] A body of case law has grown up around them that provides a common understanding of their general dimensions. Thus, as a general rule, in order to convict a defendant of attempt, the government must prove beyond a reasonable doubt that, acting with the intent required to commit the underlying offense,[22] the defendant took some substantial step towards the commission of the underlying offense[23] that strongly corroborates his criminal intent.[24] Mere preparation does not constitute a

[17] *DoJ Computer Crime*, at 21 ("Section 11030(a)(3) is not charged often, and few cases interpret it. This lack is probably because section 1030(a)(2) applies in many of the same cases in which section 1030(a)(3) could be charged. In such cases, section 1030(a)(2) may be the preferred charge because statutory sentencing enhancements sometimes allow section 1030(a)(2) to be charged as a felony on the first offense. A violation of section 1030(a)(3), on the other hand, is only a misdemeanor for a first offense").

[18] Throughout this report, "other crimes" refers to closely related crimes. In any given case, a defendant charged under one of the paragraphs of 1030(a) may also be charged under one or more of these other federal companion statutes. As long as there is at least one element required for conviction of one but not the other, a defendant guilty of violating one or more of the various paragraphs of section 1030 may also be held liable for one or more related offenses, see e.g. *United States v. Czubinski*, 106 F.3d 1069 (1st Cir. 1997) (convictions under 18 U.S.C. 1343 (wire fraud) and 18 U.S.C. 1030(a)(4) (computer fraud) overturned for other reasons); *United States v. Petersen*, 98 F.3d 502 (9th Cir. 1996) (upholding a sentence imposed for convictions under 18 U.S.C. 371 (conspiracy), 18 U.S.C. 1343 (wire fraud), and 18 U.S.C. 1030(a)(4) (computer fraud)).

[19] Subsection 1030(b) states in its entirety, "Whoever attempts to commit an offense under subsection (a) of this section shall be punished as provided in subsection (c) of this section."

[20] *United States v. Neal*, 78 F.3d 901, 906 (4th Cir. 1996); *United States v. Adams*, 305 F. 3d 30, 34 (1st Cir. 2002).

[21] See e.g., 18 U.S.C. 1951 (attempt to obstruct interstate commerce by extortion or robbery); 18 U.S.C. 794 (attempt to communicate national defense information to a foreign government). There are separate attempt offenses in over 130 sections of title 18 alone: e.g., 18 U.S.C. 32, 33, 37, 112, 115, 152.

[22] *United States v. Resendiz-Ponce*, 127 S.Ct. 782, 787 (2007); *United States v. Kenyon*, 481 F.3d 1054, 1069 (8th Cir. 2007); *United States v. Coté*, 504 F.3d 682, 687 (7th Cir. 2007); *United States v. Ballinger*, 395 F.3d 1218, 1238 n.8 (11th Cir. 2005).

[23] *United States v. Spurlock*, 495 F.3d 1011, 1014 (8th Cir. 2007); *United States v. Yost*, 479 F.3d 815, 819 (11th Cir. 2007); *United States v. Rankin*, 487 F.3d 229, 231 (5th Cir. 2007); *United States v. Munro*, 394 F.3d 865, 869 (10th Cir. 2005).

[24] *United States v. Lucas*, 499 F.3d 769, 780 (8th Cir. 2007); *United States v. Wesley*, 417 F.3d 612, 618 (6th Cir. 2005); *United States v. Bellew*, 369 F.3d 450, 453 n.2 (5th Cir. 2004).

substantial step.[25] The line between preparation and a substantial step towards final commission depends largely upon the facts of a particular case,[26] and the courts have offered varying descriptions of its location.[27]

Conspiracy. Conspiracy to violate any federal law is a separate federal crime, 18 U.S.C. 371,[28] Thus, if two or more individuals agree to intentionally access a government computer without authorization and one of them takes some affirmative action to effectuate their plan, each of the individuals is guilty of conspiracy under section 371, regardless of whether the scheme is ultimately successful;[29] and if a conspirator manages to "hack" into a government computer, his coconspirators are equally guilty under 18 U.S.C. 1030(a)(3).[30]

Accomplices as Principals. By the same token, one who counsels, commands, aids or abets, or otherwise acts as an accessory before the fact is liable as a principal for the underlying substantive offense to the same extent as the individual who actually commits the offense.[31] More than

[25] *United States v. Turner*, 501 F.3d 59, 68 (1st Cir. 2007); *Doe v. Smith*, 470 F.3d 331, 344 (7th Cir. 2006); *United States v. Murrell*, 368 F.3d 1283, 1286 (11th Cir. 2004).

[26] *United States v. Barnes*, 230 F.3d 311, 315 (7th Cir. 2000); *United States v. Plummer*, 221 F.3d 1298, 1303 (11th Cir. 2000); *United States v. Ramirez*, 348 F.3d. 1175, 1180 (10th Cir. 2003); *United States v. Spenser*, 439 F.3d 905, 915 (8th Cir. 2006).

[27] *United States v. Goetzke*, 494 F.3d 1231, 1237 (9th Cir. 2007)("To constitute a substantial step, a defendant's actions must cross the line between preparation and attempt by unequivocally demonstrating that the crime will take place unless interrupted by independent circumstances"); *United Stats v. Turner*, 501 F.3d 59, 68 (1st Cir. 2007)("While 'mere preparation' does not constitute a substantial step, a defendant does not have to get very far along the line toward ultimate commission of the object crime in order to commit the attempt offense"); *United States v. Ramirez*, 348 F.3d. 1175, 1180 (10th Cir. 2003)(noting that a substantial step "must be an act adapted to, approximating, and which in the ordinary and likely course of things will result in, the commission of the particular crime. A substantial step is an appreciable fragment of a crime and an action of such substantiality that, unless frustrated, the crime would have occurred. The step must be strongly corroborative of the firmness of the defendant's criminal intent and must unequivocally mark the defendant's acts as criminal. It should evidence commitment to the criminal venture")(citing *United States v. Smith*, 264 F.3d 1012, 1016 (10th Cir. 2001)).

[28] "If two or more persons conspire . . . to commit any offense against the United States . . . or any agency thereof in any manner or for any purpose, and one or more of such persons do any act to effect the object of the conspiracy, each shall be fined under this title or imprisoned not more than five years, or both.

"If, however, the offense, the commission of which is the object of the conspiracy, is a misdemeanor only, the punishment for such conspiracy shall not exceed the maximum punishment provided for such misdemeanor," 18 U.S.C. 371; see generally, *Twenty-Second Survey of White Collar Crime: Federal Criminal Conspiracy*, 44 American Criminal Law Review 523 (2007); *Developments in the Law—Criminal Conspiracy*, 72 Harvard Law Review 920 (1959).

[29] *United States v. Shellef*, 507 F.3d 82, 105 (2d Cir. 2007); *United States v. Spano*, 421 F.3d 599, 603 (7th Cir. 2005); *United States v. Tucker*, 376 F.3d 236, 238 (4th Cir. 2004).

[30] *Pinkerton v. United States*, 328 U.S. 640, 645–48 (1946); *United States v. Parkes*, 497 F.3d 220, 232 (2d Cir. 2007)(Under *Pinkerton v. United States*, "a defendant who does not directly commit a substantive offense may nevertheless be liable if the commission of the offense by a co-conspirator in furtherance of the conspiracy was reasonably foreseeable to the defendant as a consequence of their criminal agreement"); *United States v. Moran*, 493 F.3d 1002, 1009–110 (9th Cir. 2007); *United States v. Roberson*, 474 F.3d 432, 433 (7th Cir. 2007).

[31] "(a) Whoever commits an offense against the United States or aids, abets, counsels, commands, induces or procures its commission, is punishable as a principal.

mere inadvertent assistance is required; but an accomplice who embraces the criminal objectives of another and acts to bring about their accomplishment is criminally liable as a principal.[32]

The fact that subsection 1030(b) outlaws attempts to violate any of the prohibitions of subsection 1030(a) raises an interesting question concerning accessories. As a general rule, an accomplice may only be liable as a principal or accessory before the fact, for a completed crime; the aid must be given before the crime is committed, but liability as a principal will not attach until after the crime has been committed.[33] This does not bar conviction of one who aids or abets the commission of a crime that never succeeds beyond the attempt phase, if, as in the case of paragraph 1030(a)(3), attempt to commit the offense has been made a separate crime.[34]

CAN-SPAM & E-mail. Beyond these auxiliary offenses and bases for criminal liability, the simple trespassing crime created in paragraph 1030(a)(3) is the least likely of the seven crimes established in section 1030 to share coverage with other laws outside the section. Simply hacking into government computers—without damage to the system, injury to the government, or gain by the hacker—implicates only a few other laws.

The most likely overlap may be with the CAN-SPAM Act of 2003, 18 U.S.C. 1037. The CAN-SPAM Act offers protection to all "protected computers"[35] and prohibits any unauthorized access of these computers for the purpose of sending commercial electronic messages (paragraph 1037(a)(1)), or the purpose of deceiving or misleading e-mail recipients (paragraph 1037(a)(2)). The penalties involved for a violation of CAN-SPAM can be as high as five

"(b) Whoever willfully causes an act to be done which if directly performed by him or another would be an offense against the United States, is punishable as a principal," 18 U.S.C. 2; see generally, Blakey & Roddy, *Reflections on* Reves v. Ernst & Young: *Meaning and Impact on Substantive, Accessory, Aiding Abetting and Conspiracy Liability Under RICO*, 33 American Criminal Law Review 1345, 1385-418 (1996); see also, *United States v. Yakou*, 393 F.3d 231, 242 (D.C. Cir. 2005)("The statute typically applies to any criminal statute unless Congress specifically carves out an exception that precludes aiding and abetting liability, and it long has been established that a person can be convicted of aiding and abetting another person's violation of a statute even if it would be impossible to convict the aider and abettor as a principal")(citations omitted).

32 *United States v. Pando Franco*, 503 F.3d 389, 394 (5th Cir. 2007)("to prove the crime of aiding and abetting, the government must establish that the substantive offense occurred and that the defendant (1) associated with a criminal venture, (2) purposefully participated in the crime, and (3) sought by action for it to succeed"); *United States v. Lopez*, 484 F.3d 1186, 1199 (9th Cir. 2007); *United States v. Garcia-Carrasquillo*, 483 F.3d 124, 130 (1st Cir. 2007).

33 *Id.* at 130; *United States v. Sutcliffe*, 505 F.3d 944, 959 (9th Cir. 2007); *United States v. Gardner*, 488 F.3d 700, 713 (6th Cir. 2007).

34 *United States v. Washington*, 106 F.3d 983, 1004-5 (D.C.Cir. 1997)("if the principal had actually attempted to commit a crime but had failed, the aider and abettor would be charged with the same offense as the principal (attempt to commit the crime)"). See also *United States v. Villanueva*, 408 F.3d 193, 202 (5th Cir. 2005) (finding defendant guilty of aiding and abetting an attempted crime); *United States v. Gardner*, 488 F.3d 700, 711 (6th Cir. 2007)(aiding and abetting attempted possession of cocaine).

35 The definition of "protected computer" in section 1037 defers to the definition in 1030(e)(2(B), which covers any computer "used in interstate or foreign commerce or communication" and implicates any computer connected to the Internet.

years imprisonment, if done in furtherance of a felony, or three years for a violation of paragraph 1037(a)(1) or if there is any financial loss by the victim or gain by the hacker, or one year "in any other case," 18 U.S.C. 1037(b).[36]

Of course computer trespassing in one form or another is an element of most of the offenses proscribed in 18 U.S.C. 1030. In addition, each of the states has an anti-hacking statute.[37] Moreover, hacking into someone else's e-mail stored in a government computer system is likely to offend the federal statute that protects e-mail and stored telephone company records, 18 U.S.C. 2701.[38] Hackers who misidentify themselves in order to gain

[36] CAN-SPAM is discussed more in depth *infra* in relation to section 1030(a)(4) on Computer Fraud.

[37] Most states have statutes that outlaw simple computer trespassing: ALA.CODE §13A-8102; ALASKA STAT. §11.46.484; ARIZ.REV.STAT.ANN. §13-2316; ARK.CODE ANN. §5-41104; CAL. PENAL CODE §502; COLO.REV.STAT.ANN. §18-5.5-102; CONN.GEN.STAT.ANN. §53a-251; DEL.CODE ANN. tit.11 §932; FLA. STAT.ANN. §815.06; HAWAII REV.STAT. §708895.5 to 708-895.7; IDAHO CODE §18-2202; ILL.COMP. STAT. ANN. ch.720 §5/16D-3; IND.CODE ANN. §35-43-2-3; IOWA CODE ANN. §716.6B, 702.1A; KAN. STAT. ANN. §213755(d); KY.REV.STAT.ANN. §434.853; LA.REV.STAT.ANN. §14:73.7; ME.REV.STAT.ANN. tit.17-A §432; MD.CRIM.CODE ANN. §7-302; MASS.GEN. LAWS ANN. ch.266 §120F; MINN.STAT.ANN. §609.891; MISS.CODE Ann. §97-45-9; MO.ANN.STAT. §569.099; MONT.CODE ANN. §45-6-311; NEB.REV.STAT. §28-1347; NEV.REV.STAT. §205.4765; N.H. REV.STAT.ANN. §638:17; N.J.STAT.ANN. §2C:20-25; N.Y.PENAL LAW §156.10; N.C.GEN. STAT. §14-454; N.D.CENT. CODE §12.1-06.1-08; OHIO REV. CODE ANN. §2913.04(B); OKLA.STAT.ANN. tit.21 §1953; ORE.REV.STAT. §164.377; PA. STAT.TAT.ANN. tit.18 §§7611, 7615; R.I.GEN. LAWS §11-52-3; S.C.CODE ANN. §16-16-20(4); S.D.COD.LAWS §43-43B-1; TENN.CODE ANN. §39-14-602; TEX.PENAL CODE ANN. §33.02; UTAH CODE ANN. §76-6703; VT.STAT. ANN. tit.13 §4102; WASH. REV.CODE ANN. §9A.52.110; W.VA.CODE ANN. §61-3C-5; WIS. STAT.ANN. §943.70; WYO. STAT. §6-3-504. Analysis of state law is generally beyond the scope of this report.

Members of the military may also incur liability under the Uniform Code of Military Justice for various forms of computer abuse. See *United States v. Wiest*, 59 M.J. 276 (Ct. App. Armed Forces 2004) (reversing lower court on other grounds) in which an Air Force Academy cadet was convicted of a violation of Article 134 of the Uniform Code of Military Justice, for accessing a protected computer without authorization and recklessly damaging a computer in violation of 18 U.S.C. § 1030(a)(5)(B)). See also, *United States v. Mervine*, 26 M.J. 482 (1988)(suggesting that various computer crimes might be charged under Article 134, the general article: "Though not specifically mentioned in this chapter, all disorders and neglects to the prejudice of good order and discipline in the armed forces, all conduct of a nature to bring discredit upon the armed forces, and crimes and offenses not capital, of which persons subject to this chapter may be guilty, shall be taken cognizance of by a general, special, or summary court-martial, according to the nature and degree of the offense, and shall be punished at the discretion of that court").

[38] "(a) Offense.—Except as provided in subsection (c) of this section whoever—(1) intentionally accesses without authorization a facility through which an electronic communication service is provided; or (2) intentionally exceeds an authorization to access that facility; and thereby obtains, alters, or prevents authorized access to a wire or electronic communication while it is in electronic storage in such system shall be punished as provided in subsection (b) of this section.

"(b) Punishment.—The punishment for an offense under subsection (a) of this section is—(1) if the offense is committed for purposes of commercial advantage, malicious destruction or damage, or private commercial gain or in furtherance of any criminal or tortious act in violation of the Constitution or laws of the United States or any State—(A) a fine under this title or imprisonment for not more than 5 years, or both, in the case of a first offense under this subparagraph; and (B) a fine under this title or imprisonment for not more than 10 years, or both, for any subsequent offense under this subparagraph; and (2) in any other case—(A) a fine under this title or imprisonment for not more than 1 year or both, in the case of a first offense under this paragraph; and (B) a fine under this title or imprisonment for not more than 5 years, or both, in the case of an offense under this subparagraph that occurs after a conviction of another offense under this section.

"(c) Exceptions.—Subsection (a) of this section does not apply with respect to conduct authorized—(1) by the person or entity providing a wire or electronic communications service; (2) by a user of that

access to a federal computer may be guilty of violating 18 U.S.C. 1001[39] and 18 U.S.C. 912[40] in the view of at least one commentator.[41] The case law may make the claim difficult to defend. The Supreme Court has suggested that section 1001 should be constructed narrowly,[42] and the courts have consistently held that the false statement must somehow tend to adversely impact the functioning of a governmental agency or department to trigger coverage under section 1001.[43] Cases in other contexts demonstrate the difficulty

---

service with respect to a communication of or intended for that user; or (3) in section 2703, 2704 or 2518 of this title," 18 U.S.C. 2701.

The provisions of 18 U.S.C. 2511 (wiretapping) may apply to the unlawful interception of e-mail transmissions while in transit and 18 U.S.C. 2701 may apply to the unlawful seizure of stored e-mail. Offenses under §2511 are punishable by imprisonment for not more than 5 years as well, 18 U.S.C. 2511(4).

[39] "(a) Except as otherwise provided in this section, whoever, in any matter within the jurisdiction of the executive, legislative, or judicial branch of the Government of the United States, knowingly and willfully—(1) falsifies, conceals, or covers up by any trick, scheme, or device a material fact; (2) makes any materially false, fictitious, or fraudulent statement or representation; or (3) makes or uses any false writing or document knowing the same to contain any materially false, fictitious, or fraudulent statement or entry; shall be fined under this title or imprisoned not more than 5 years or, if the offense involves international or domestic terrorism (as defined in section 2331), imprisoned not more than 8 years, or both.

"(b) Subsection (a) does not apply to a party to a judicial proceeding, or that party's counsel, for statements, representations, writings or documents submitted by such party or counsel to a judge or magistrate in that proceeding.

"(c) With respect to any matter within the jurisdiction of the legislative branch, subsection (a) shall apply only to—(1) administrative matters, including a claim for payment, a matter related to the procurement of property or services, personnel or employment practices, or support services, or a document required by law, rule, or regulation to be submitted to the Congress or any office or officer within the legislative branch; or (2) any investigation or review, conducted pursuant to the authority of any committee, subcommittee, commission or office of the Congress, consistent with applicable rules of the House or Senate," 18 U.S.C. 1001; see generally, *Twenty-Second Survey of White Collar Crime: False Statements and False Claims*, 44 AMERICAN CRIMINAL LAW REVIEW 491 (2007).

[40] "Whoever falsely assumes or pretends to be an officer or employee acting under the authority of the United States or any department, agency or officer thereof, and acts as such, or in such pretended character demands or obtains any money, paper, document, or thing of value, shall be fined under this title or imprisoned not more than three years, or both," 18 U.S.C. 912.

[41] Olivenbaum, *<CTRL><ALT><DELETE>: Rethinking Federal Computer Legislation*, 27 SETON HALL LAW REVIEW 574, 600 (1997)(citing an instance from the infancy of section 1030 where a hacker was indicted under the false statement, 18 U.S.C. 1001, and wire fraud, 18 U.S.C. 1343, statute. The case ended when the defendant pled to a misdemeanor fraud charge). No comparable prosecutions followed and so the author's thesis remains unproven.

[42] *Hubbard v. United States*, 514 U.S. 695 (1995)(overturning an earlier holding that section 1001 applied to false statements made to federal courts and to Congress as well as those made to the executive branch)(superceded by statute, P.L. 104-292, 110 Stat. 3459 (1996)(the modification preserved the exception that it did not apply "to a party to a judicial proceeding, or that party's counsel, for statements, representations, writings or documents submitted by such party or counsel to a judge or magistrate in that proceeding.")(section 1001(b)); *United States v. Gaudin*, 515 U.S. 509 (1995)(holding that materiality of the false statement, as an element of section 1001, is a question for the jury to decide).

[43] *United States v. Gaudin*, 515 U.S. 506, 509 (1995)("the statement must have a natural tendency to influence, or be capable of influencing the decision of the decisonmaking body to which it was addressed"); *United States v. Baker*, 200 F.3d 558, 561 (8th Cir. 2000) ("The materiality inquiry focuses on whether the false statement had a natural tendency to influence or was capable of influencing the government agency or official"). *United States v. Mitchell*, 388 F.3d 1139, 1143 (8th Cir. 2004) (noting that a false statement must have "a natural tendency to influence or is capable of influencing the government agency or official" and that "[m]ateriality does not require proof that the government actually relied on the statement.").

of convincing the courts that simple trespassing in government cyberspace has an adverse impact upon the government.[44]

The difficulty with using the impersonation statute, 18 U.S.C. 912, is that it requires a showing of an official act or of a fraud; something that need not be proven for conviction under paragraph 1030(a)(3).[45] Like 18 U.S.C. 1001, section 912 may be more appropriately employed in cases falling under the ambit of paragraph 1030(a)(4) (unauthorized access of a government computer, bank computer or computer in interstate or foreign commerce as integral part of a scheme to fraud).

Obtaining Information by Unauthorized Computer Access (18 U.S.C. 1030(a)(2))

> (a) Whoever. . . (2) intentionally accesses a computer without authorization or exceeds authorized access, and thereby obtains—
> (A) information contained in a financial record of a financial institution, or of a card issuer as defined in section 1602(n) of title 15,[46] or contained in a file of a consumer reporting agency on a consumer, as such terms are defined in the Fair Credit Reporting Act (15 U.S.C. 1681 et seq.);[47]

---

[44] *United States v. Collins*, 56 F.3d 1416 (D.C.Cir. 1995) and *United States v. Czubinski*, 106 F.3d 1069 (1st Cir. 1997), overturned convictions under 18 U.S.C. 641 (theft of government property), and 18 U.S.C. 1343 (wire fraud) and 1030(a)(4)(computer fraud) respectively, on the ground that the prosecution had failed to show any adverse impact upon the government caused by the defendant's unauthorized access of government computer files.

[45] "Whoever . . . pretends to be an officer. . . acting under the authority of the United States . . . *and acts as such, or in such pretended character demands or obtains any. . . thing of value*," 18 U.S.C. 912 (emphasis added).

[46] "The term 'card issuer' means any person who issues a credit card, or the agent of such person with respect to such card," 15 U.S.C. 1602(n).

"The term 'person' means a natural person or an organization. The term 'organization' means a corporation, government or governmental subdivision or agency, trust, estate, partnership, cooperative, or association. The term 'credit card' means any card, plate, coupon book or other credit device existing for the purpose of obtaining money, property, labor, or services on credit. The term 'credit' means the right granted by a creditor to a debtor to defer payment of debt or to incur debt and defer its payment.

"The term 'creditor' refers only to a person who both (1) regularly extends, whether in connection with loans, sales of property or services, or otherwise, consumer credit which is payable by agreement in more than four installments or for which the payment of a finance charge is or may be required, and (2) is the person to whom the debt arising from the consumer credit transaction is initially payable on the face of the evidence of indebtedness or, if there is no such evidence of indebtedness, by agreement. Notwithstanding the preceding sentence, in the case of an open-end credit plan involving a credit card, the card issuer and any person who honors the credit card and offers a discount which is a finance charge are creditors . . ." 15 U.S.C. 1602(d), (c),(k), (e), and (f), respectively.

[47] "The term 'file', when used in connection with information on any consumer, means all of the information on that consumer recorded and retained by a consumer reporting agency regardless of how the information is stored.

"The term 'consumer reporting agency' means any person which, for monetary fees, dues, or on a cooperative nonprofit basis, regularly engages in whole or in part in the practice of assembling or evaluating consumer credit information or other information on consumers for the purpose of furnishing consumer reports to third parties, and which uses any means or facility of interstate commerce for the purpose of preparing or furnishing consumer reports.

"The term 'consumer' means an individual," 15 U.S.C. 1681a(g), (f) and (c), respectively.

(B) information from any department or agency of the United States; or
(C) information from any protected computer if the conduct involved an interstate or foreign communication . . .
shall be punished as provided in subsection (c) of this section.

One step beyond simple hacking is the prohibition against acquiring certain protected information by intentional unauthorized access.[48] As a practical matter, in any instance involving a government computer it may be very difficult to distinguish between cases evidencing a violation of the simple trespass proscriptions of paragraph 1030(a)(3) and the trespassing-with-information-acquisition prohibitions of paragraph 1030(a)(2). The history of the trespass provisions speaks clearly of an intent to place beyond their reach whistleblowers and other federal employees for simple trespassing with respect to computers within their own an agency. This explains the absence of an "exceeds-authorized-access" provision in the trespassing provisions of paragraph 1030(a)(3). But the trespass-and-be-exposed-to-information provisions of paragraph 1030(a)(2) *do* feature a "exceeds-authorized-access" clause and seem facially applicable to whistleblowers. It remains to be seen whether the courts will read paragraph 1030(a)(2) as effectively amending the simple trespassing provisions of paragraph 1030(a)(3) or will attempt to reconcile the two.

Intent

The intent requirement is the same as that required in the case of simple trespassing. The offender must have "intentionally" gained access. The paragraph only bans "intentional" trespassing. As in the case of the simple trespassing the intent element can be satisfied by anyone who purposefully gains access to a computer covered by the paragraph or by anyone "whose initial access was inadvertent but who then deliberatively maintain access after a non-intentional initial contact."[49] The government, however, need not show that the trespass was committed to defraud or for any other purpose for that matter.[50]

---

[48] "To prove a violation of [subparagraph 1030](a)(2)(C), the Government must show that the defendant (1) intentionally accessed a computer, (2) without authorization (or exceeding authorized access), (3) and thereby obtained information from any protected computer if the conduct involved interstate or foreign communication," *United States v. Willis*, 476 F.3d 1121, 1125 (10th Cir. 2007); *Ticketmaster L.L.C. v. RMG Technologies, Inc.*, 507 F.Supp.2d. 1096, 1113 (C.D. Cal. 2007). The third element of the offense becomes—"thereby obtained information from a financial institution" or "thereby obtained information from a federal agency"—when the violation involves subparagraphs 1030(a)(2)(A)(relating to obtaining financial institution information) or 1030(a)(2)(B)(relating to obtaining federal agency information).

[49] H.Rept. 99-612 at 9-10 (1986); see also, S.Rept. 99-432 at 5-6 (1986)("such conduct . . . must have been the person's conscious objective"); *Butera & Andrews v. IBM, Inc.*, 456 F.Supp. 104, 110 (D.D.C. 2006).

[50] *United States v. Willis*, 476 F.3d 1121, 1125 (10th Cir. 2007).

Unauthorized Access

"Without authorization" or "exceeds authorized access" under 1030(a)(2) has been construed to apply to access by authorized current employees who use their access in any unauthorized manner or for unauthorized purposes, to former employees, and to outsiders who have been granted access subject to explicit reservations.[51] Access within the statute, however, does not mean simply passively receiving information from a computer.[52]

Obtaining Information & Jurisdiction

Paragraph 1030(a)(2) is at once more and less restricted than the simple trespassing proscription of paragraph 1030(a)(3). On one hand, its prosecution requires more than simple trespass.[53] On the other hand, it covers a wider range of computers. Paragraph 1030(a)(2), unlike 1030(a)(3), covers more than government computers. It covers computers from which three types of information may be obtained—information of the federal government, consumer credit or other kinds of financial information, and information acquired from a protected computer through interstate or foreign access.

The protection for financial information has its origins in the initial legislation and was among the first adjusted. Comments from the Senate report accompanying the 1986 amendments illustrate the intended scope of the protection for financial information:

> "The premise of 18 U.S.C. 1030(a)(2) will remain the protection, for privacy reasons, of computerized credit records and computerized information relating to customers' relationships with financial institutions. This protection is imperative in light of the sensitive and personal financial information contained in such computer files. However, by referring to the Right to Financial Privacy Act, the current statute limits its coverage to financial institution customers who are individuals, or are partnerships with five or fewer partners. The Committee intends . . . to extend the same privacy

---

[51] *Shurgard Storage Centers v. Safeguard Self Storage*, 119 F. Supp. 2d 1121 (W.D. Wash. 2000) (unauthorized access found when employees used their access to benefit a competitor); *YourNetDating v. Mitchell*, 88 F. Supp. 2d 870 (N.D. Ill. 2000) (former employee found to be exceeding authorized access because he used his access codes to divert users from his ex-employers website). *Southwest Airlines Co. v. Farecase, Inc.*, 318 F.Supp.2d 435, 439–40 (N.D. Tex. 2004)(use of software to gather fare information from airline's website in spite of "no scrapping" warnings constitutes a violation of paragraph 1030(a)(2)).

[52] *Role Models America v. Jones*, 305 F. Supp. 2d 564, 566–7 (D.Md.2004) (the court rejected the claim that a university "accessed" a computer when a high school employee sent them information from the high school computer). For additional analysis on the meanings of these terms, see generally, Orin S. Kerr, *Cybercrime's Scope: Interpreting "Access" & "Authorization" in Computer Misuse Statutes*, 78 N.Y.U.L.R. 1596 (2003).

[53] Yet it may not require a great deal more than a paragraph 1030(a)(3) prosecution, since merely viewing material on a computer screen has been found to constitute obtaining information for purposes of paragraph 1030(a)(2), *Healthcare Advocates, Inc. v. Harding, Early, Follmer & Frailey*, 497 F.Supp.2d 927, 648 (E.D. Pa. 2007), citing S.Rept. 99-432 at 6-7 (1986).

protections to the financial records of all customers—individual, partnership, or corporate—of financial institutions.

"The Department of Justice has expressed concerns that the term 'obtains information' in 18 U.S.C. 1030(a)(2) makes that subsection more than an unauthorized access offense, i.e., that it might require the prosecution to prove asportation of the data in question. Because the premise of this subsection is privacy protection, the Committee wishes to make clear that 'obtaining information' in this context includes mere observation of the data. Actual asportation, in the sense of physically removing the data from its original location or transcribing the data, need not be proved in order to establish a violation of this subsection," S.Rept. 99-432 at 6-7 (1986).

The committee explanation of the language amending paragraph 1030(a)(2), ultimately enacted as part of the Economic Espionage Act of 1996, endorsed this reading and extended it to cover information obtained from federal computers and information secured by interstate or overseas cyberspace trespassing:

"'Information' as used in this subsection [1030(a)(2)] includes information stored in intangible form. Moreover, the term 'obtaining information' includes merely reading it. There is no requirement that the information be copied or transported. This is critically important because, in an electronic environment, information can be 'stolen' without asportation, and the original usually remains intact. This interpretation of 'obtaining information' is consistent with congressional intent expressed . . . in connection with 1986 amendments to the Computer Fraud and Abuse statute . . . .

"The proposed subsection 1030(a)(2)(C) is intended to protect against the interstate or foreign theft of information by computer. This information, stored electronically, is intangible, and it has been held that the theft of such information cannot be charged under more traditional criminal statutes such as Interstate Transportation of Stolen Property Act, 18 U.S.C. 2314. See *United States v. Brown*, 925 F.2d 1301, 1308 (10th Cir. 1991). This subsection would ensure that the theft of intangible information by the unauthorized use of a computer is prohibited in the same way theft of physical items are protected. In instances where the information stolen is also copyrighted, the theft may implicate certain rights under the copyright laws. The crux of the offense under subsection 1030(a)(2)(C), however, is the abuse of a computer to obtain the information," S.Rept. 104-357 at 6-7 (1996).

The Patriot Act amendment of the definition of "protected computer" confirmed Congress' intent to proscribe unauthorized access and information acquisition from abroad with respect to protected computers.[54] A closer question may be whether in doing so it forecloses extraterritorial application

[54] "As used in this section . . . (2) the term 'protected computer' means a computer . . . (B) which is used in interstate or foreign commerce or communication, *including a computer located outside the Untied States that is used in a manner that affects interstate or foreign commerce or communication of the United States*," 18 U.S.C. 1030(e)(2)(B)(language of the amendment in italics)

of paragraph 1030(a)(2) in other situations, *e.g.*, unauthorized access to federal computer or computer networks located overseas.

Consequences

The simple trespass offenses condemned in paragraph 1030(a)(3) are unlikely to significantly implicate the Sentencing Guidelines, restitution, forfeiture, or civil liability provisions elsewhere in the law. Not so paragraph 1030(a)(2) offenses. Criminal penalties attend it, but so do other consequences.

Penalties. Paragraph 1030(a)(2) has a three tier sentencing structure. Simple violations are punished as misdemeanors, imprisonment for not more than one year and/or a fine of not more than $100,000 ($200,000 for organizations), 18 U.S.C. 1030(c)(2)(A).

The second tier carries penalties of imprisonment for not more than five years and/or a fine of not more $250,000 ($500,000 for organizations) and is reserved for cases in which: "(i) the offense was committed for purposes of commercial advantage or private financial gain; (ii) the offense was committed in furtherance of any criminal or tortious act in violation of the Constitution or laws of the United States or of any State; or (iii) the value of the information obtained exceeds $5,000," 18 U.S.C. 1030(c)(2) (B).

This second level was added in 1996. The $5,000 threshold is the same one the section uses to separate serious from less serious fraud and destruction cases in paragraphs 1030(a)(4) and 1030(a)(5). With respect to the alternative thresholds, (i) and (ii), "[t]he terms 'for purposes of commercial advantage or private financial gain' and 'for the purpose of committing any criminal or tortious act' are taken from the copyright statute (17 U.S.C. 506(a)) and the wiretap statute (18 U.S.C. 2511[(2)] (d)), respectively, and are intended to have the same meaning as in those statutes," S.Rept. 104-357 at 8 (1996). The references to copyright and wiretap law may be less instructive than Congress anticipated for the phrases in question are of uncertain meaning in their original settings.[55] Nevertheless, they clearly contemplate some criminal, tortious, or financially advantageous purpose beyond the computer-trespassing-and-obtaining-information misconduct outlawed in the paragraph generally. Otherwise nothing would be left to be punished as a misdemeanor and the $5,000 distinction of exception (iii) would be swallowed up as well.

[55] 4 Nimmer & Nimmer, Nimmer on Copyright §15.01 n.1.2 (1997) (emphasis added)("*Apparently*, the phrase 'commercial advantage or private financial gain' is intended as the equivalent of 'for profit'"); 1 Fishman & Mckenna, Wiretapping and Eavesdropping,Second Edition §4:29 *b*. (1995) comparing, *Stockler v. Garratt*, 893 F.2d 856 (6th Cir. 1990), with, *By-Product Corp. v. Armen-Berry Co.*, 668 F.2d 956 (7th Cir. 1982)(in disagreement over whether an offender must act upon his or her criminal or tortious purpose after recording a conversation to which they are a party or where one party to the conversation has consented to the recording).

The third tier is for repeat offenders whose punishment is increased to imprisonment of not than 10 years and/or a fine of not more than $250,000 ($500,000 or organizations) for a second or subsequent conviction, 18 U.S.C. 1030(c).

Federal law is no more hospitable to the prosecution of juveniles for the intrusion plus information acquisition offenses under paragraph 1030(a)(2) than it is for the simple trespass offenses under paragraph 1030(a)(3). Essentially, federal proceedings are only possible if the state in which the offense occurs is unwilling or unable to proceed, 18 U.S.C. 5032.

Sentencing Guidelines. The Sentencing Guidelines color the procedure under which the penalties for serious federal crimes are imposed.[56] They were established to eliminate sentencing disparity among cases involving the same offense and to ensure that the sentences imposed reflect the relative seriousness of the circumstances under which the offense was committed in a given case.[57] As a general rule, the Guidelines assign each federal crime to a particular guideline.[58] The individual guideline in turn assigns a beginning number (base offense level) and then adds and subtracts from that number based on the presence of designated aggravating or mitigating circumstances.[59] The final total translates to an authorized sentencing range in months of imprisonment and dollars of fines.[60]

Violations of paragraph 1030(a)(2) are governed by U.S.S.G. §2B1.1 which sets the base offense level at 6. The Tenth Circuit's opinion in *Willis* provides an example of the process from that point:

> The District Court agreed with the Government and found Ms. Fischer's conduct [which resulted in losses of more than $10,000] foreseeable to [her accomplice] Mr. Willis. It therefore imposed a 4-level enhancement on Mr. Willis's base offense level.[61]
>
> It also applied the §2B1.1(b)(10)(C)(i) enhancement because the offense involved using a means of identification to produce another means of

---

[56] At one time, federal sentencing courts were essentially bound by the Guidelines, 18 U.S.C. 3553(b)(1). *Booker* changed that, see *United States v. Booker*, 543 U.S. 220, 245 (2005)("We answer the question of remedy by finding the provision of the federal sentencing statute that makes the Guidelines mandatory, 18 U.S.C.A. 3553(b)(1)(Supp. 2004), incompatible with today's constitutional holding. We conclude that this provision must be severed and excised. . . ."). Now, federal sentencing courts must begin by identifying the appropriate sentencing range under the Guidelines, but enjoy discretion to make justifiable reasonable departures, *Gall v. United States*, 128 S.Ct. 586, 596–97 (2007).

[57] S.Rept. 98-225, at 50-2 (1983).

[58] U.S.S.G. §§1B1.1, 8A1.2.

[59] *Id.*

[60] U.S.S.G. ch.5, pt.A, §5E1.2, ch.8 pt.C.

[61] *United States v. Willis*, 476 F.3d 1121, 1127–128 (10th Cir. 2007), citing U.S.S.G. §2B1.1(b)(1)(C). Paragraph 2B1.1(b)(1) instructs a sentencing court to increase to an offender's offense level under section 2B1.1 according to the amount of the loss associated with the offense. In Mr. Willis's case, the loss was more than $10,000 but less than $30,000. Had it been more than $30,000 but less than $70,000 an increase of 6 would have been appropriate. The enhancements are calibrated to account for losses from $5,000 (add 2) to more than $4 million (add 30).

identification,[62] as well as the §3B1.3 enhancement because Mr. Willis abused a position of trust.[63] This produced an adjusted offense level of 14, which when coupled with his criminal history category of V, resulted in an advisory Guideline range of 33 to 41 months. The District Court sentenced Mr. Willis to 41 months' imprisonment.[64]

Forfeiture. "Any property, real or personal, which constitutes or is derived from proceeds traceable, to a violation of section. . . 1030" is subject to confiscation by the United States under either civil or criminal forfeiture procedures.[65]

Restitution. Restitution is an offender's compensation of the victim for loss or damage associated with the offense.[66] It is mandatory in the case of federal crimes of violence or federal crimes involving fraud or property damage, 18 U.S.C. 3663A.[67] It is within the discretion of the court in the case of all other federal crimes proscribed in title 18 of the United States Code, 18 U.S.C. 3663.

Paragraph 1030(a)(2) acquisition offenses are not crimes of violence and restitution is therefore not mandatory. They come within the discretionary restitution provisions of section 3663, but those provisions have a limitation on the type of losses for which restitution may be ordered.[68] The limitation,

---

[62] *Id.* at 1128. U.S.S.G. §2B1.1(b)(10)(C)(i) states, "If the offense involved . . . (C)(i) the unauthorized transfer or use of any means of identification unlawfully to produce or obtain any other means of identification . . . increase by 2 levels." Mr. Willis had given Ms. Fischer a username and password that gave her unauthorized access to a financial information database, which she used in an identity theft scheme.

[63] *Id.* U.S.S.G. §3b1.3 states, "If the defendant abused a position of public or private trust, or used a special skill, in a manner that significantly facilitated the commission or concealment of the offense, increase by 2 levels." Mr. Willis acquired in his position as supervisor in a debt collection agency the username and password which he had then passed on to his accomplice. Although not implicated here, the special skill enhancement often implicated in the offenses outlawed in the various paragraphs of 18 U.S.C. 1030.

[64] *Id.* Mr. Willis had a fairly extensive record of previous convictions. Had he been a first time offender, his criminal history category would have been I and his sentencing range at an offense level of 14 would have been 15 to 21 months, U.S.S.G. Ch.5, Pt. A (Sentencing Table).

[65] 18 U.S.C. 981(a)(1)(C), 982(a)(2)(B). Criminal forfeiture is accomplished following the criminal prosecution of the property owner, 18 U.S.C. 982. Civil forfeiture is accomplished through an in rem proceeding directed against the property itself, 18 U.S.C. 983. See generally, *Crime and Forfeiture*, CRS Rept. 97-139.

[66] See generally, *Restitution in Federal Criminal Cases*, CRS Rept. RL34138.

[67] E.g., *United States v. Phillips*, 477 F.3d 215, 224–25 (5th Cir. 2007)(restitution ordered for violations of paragraph 1030(a)(5)(damage of a protected computer)).

[68] "(b) The [restitution] order may require that such defendant—(1) in the case of an offense resulting in damage to or loss or destruction of property of a victim of the offense—(A) return the property to the owner of the property or someone designated by the owner; or (B) if return of the property under subparagraph (A) is impossible, impractical, or inadequate, pay an amount equal to the greater of—(i) the value of the property on the date of the damage, loss, or destruction, or (ii) the value of the property on the date of sentencing, less the value (as of the date the property is returned) of any part of the property that is returned," 18 U.S.C. 3663(b)(1).

however, does not apply in the case of a plea bargain[69] or when restitution is orders as a condition of probation or supervised release.[70]

Civil Cause of Action. Subsection 1030(g) creates a cause of action for compensatory damages and injunctive relief for the benefit of victims of a violation of any the paragraphs of 18 U.S.C. 1030, but only if violation results in the kind of loss or damage described in clauses 1030(a)(5)(B)(i) through (v),[71] that is:

> (i) loss to 1 or more persons during any 1-year period (and, for purposes of an investigation, prosecution, or other proceeding brought by the United States only, loss resulting from a related course of conduct affecting 1 or more other protected computers) aggregating at least $5,000 in value;
>
> (ii) the modification or impairment, or potential modification or impairment, of the medical examination, diagnosis, treatment, or care of 1 or more individuals;
>
> (iii) physical injury to any person;
>
> (iv) a threat to public health or safety; or
>
> (v) damage affecting a computer system used by or for a government entity in furtherance of the administration of justice, national defense, or national security.[72]

There is no need to prove that a violation of paragraph 1030(a)(5) has occurred. As long as this type of loss or damage has been suffered, a violation of any of the paragraphs will suffice, including a violation of paragraph 1030(a)(2).[73]

At one time there may have been some uncertainty over the range of victims and losses envisioned in subsection 1030(g). Victims entitled to relief are described as "any person who suffers loss or damage by reason of a violation of this section," but until recently there was no specific definition of

---

[69] 18 U.S.C. 3663(a)(3).

[70] 18 U.S.C. 3563(b)(2), 3583(d)(3). Supervised release is a period of supervision to be served after an individual is released from prison, 18 U.S.C. 3583(a).

[71] "Any person who suffers damage or loss by reason of a violation of this section may maintain a civil action against the violator to obtain compensatory damages and injunctive relief or other equitable relief. A civil action for a violation of this section may be brought only if the conduct involves 1 of the factors set forth in clause (i), (ii), (iii), (iv), or (v) of subsection (a)(5)(B). . . ." 18 U.S.C. 1030(g).

[72] 18 U.S.C. 1030(a)(5)(B).

[73] *Theofel v. Farey-Jones*, 359 F.3d 1066, 1078 n.5 (9th Cir. 2004)("Defendants argue that subsection (a)(5)(A) prescribes the act's only civil offenses. But subsection (g) applies to any violation of 'this section' and, while the offenses must involve one of the five factors in (a)(5)(B), it need not be one of three offenses in (a)(5)(A)"); *Bansal v. Russ*, 513 F.Supp.2d 264, 278 n. 11 (E.D. Pa. 2007); *America Online, Inc. v. National Health Care Discount, Inc.*, 174 F.Supp.2d 890, 899 (N.D. Iowa 2001); cf., *P.C. Yonkers, Inc. v. Celebrations, the Party, and Seasonal Superstore, LLC*, 428 F.3d 504, 512 (3d Cir. 2005) (reaching the same conclusion in the context of a suit under paragraph (a)(4)); *Nexans Wires S.A. v. Sark-USA, Inc.*, 319 F.Supp.2d 468, 472 (S.D.N.Y. 2004)(holding that plaintiffs must satisfy the 1030(a)(5)(B) threshold for each of several claims under 1030(a)(2), (a)(4), and (a)(5)).

the term "person" in either section 1030 or in the definitions applicable to Title 18 generally.[74] The legislative history offered no further edification and the courts had not addressed the issue. "Person" can mean individuals, or individuals and other legal entities including governmental entities, or individuals and other legal entities but not including governmental entities.[75] Credible arguments might have been made for each of the possible definitions, but the fact that Congress elected to use the term "person" to mean only individuals in paragraph 1030(a)(7)(extortionate threats)[76] might seem to favor those who call for a similar interpretation of subsection 1030(g). The USA PATRIOT Act resolved the issue by supplying a definition: "the term 'person' means any individual, firm, corporation, educational institution, governmental entity, or legal or other entity," 18 U.S.C. 1030(e)(12).

It also added a generous definition of the kinds of losses that might give rise to civil liability—"the term 'loss' means any reasonable cost to any victim, including the cost of responding to an offense, conducting a damage assessment, and restoring the data, program, system, or information to its condition prior to the offense, and any revenue lost, cost incurred, or other consequential damages incurred because of interruption of service," 18 U.S.C. 1030(e)(11). The amendment has obvious benefits for the victims of a paragraph (a)(2) intrusion and information acquisition offense with post-intrusion investigation and system evaluation costs but who otherwise would be unable to meet the $5,000 loss requirement of clause 1030 (a)(5)(B)(i).

Subsection 1030(g) suits must be brought within two years of the offense, and compensatory damages are limited to economic damages, 18 U.S.C. 1030(g).

Other Crimes

Attempt, Conspiracy, and Complicity. The same general observations concerning attempt, conspiracy and aiding and abetting noted for the simple trespass offense apply here. It is a separate crime to attempt to violate paragraph 1030(a)(2) under 18 U.S.C. 1030(b). Those who attempt to violate its provisions or aid and abet the violation of another are subject to the same penalties as those who commit the substantive offense, 18 U.S.C. 1030(c)(2).

---

[74] The courts have concluded that the civil remedies under the statute are available to third parties. The court in *Theofel v. Farey-Jones*, 359 F.3d 1066, 1078 (9th Cir. 2004), emphasized that the statute extends a civil remedy to *any* individual who suffers loss or damage, thus "[i]ndividuals other than the computer's owner may be proximately harmed by unauthorized access, particularly if they have rights to data stored on it."

[75] The Dictionary Act, for example, defines the term to include "corporations, associations, firms, partnerships, societies, and joint stock companies, as well as individuals," unless the context suggests otherwise, 1 U.S.C. 1.

[76] "Whoever . . . (7) with intent to extort from any *person, firm, association, educational institution, financial institution, government entity, or other legal entity*, any money or other thing of value . . ." 18 U.S.C. 1030(a)(7)(emphasis added)(the 2002 amendments struck out "firm, association, educational institution, financial institution, government entity, or other legal entity").

Conspirators to violate paragraph 1030(a)(2) are subject to the same penalties as the underlying offense, and to liability for any foreseeable crime committed in furtherance of the scheme.[77]

Paragraph 1030(a)(2) is somewhat unique. There are a host of other federal conversion statutes, but all of the others appear to require that the offender either commit embezzlement by failing to comply with some fiduciary obligation or commit larceny by intending to acquire the property or to deprive another of it. Paragraph 1030(a)(2) in contrast to the conversion statutes and to the computer fraud provisions of paragraph 1030(a)(4) requires no larcenous intent.[78] As a practical matter, it essentially gives prosecutors a more serious charge against hackers, who do more than simply breach the outskirts of a governmental system, than would be available under the pure trespassing provisions of paragraph 1030(a)(3). And it gives them an alternative or additional charge, along with conversion and fraud statutes, against hackers who "steal" information from a protected computer.[79] It affords victims similar latitude in civil litigation under subsection 1030(g).

Paragraph 1030(a)(2) is essentially paragraph 1030(a)(3) plus an information acquisition element and with a broader jurisdictional base. Criminal prohibitions like those of 18 U.S.C. 1001 (false statements on a matter with the jurisdiction of a federal agency) or 912 (impersonating a federal official) which overlap with paragraph 1030(a)(3) at the point of unauthorized entry will overlap with paragraph 1030(a)(2) at the same point. If unauthorized access in violation of paragraph 1030(a)(3) is acquired by false statement under facts sufficient supporting a prosecution under 18 U.S.C. 1001 (false statements) or 18 U.S.C. 912 (false impersonation), unauthorized access and the acquisition of information in violation of paragraph 1030(a)(2) acquired by false statement or impersonation is likely to subject offender to prosecution under sections 1001 or 912 as well. By the same token, if unauthorized computer access to a voice mail or e-mail communication that violates paragraph 1030(a)(3) offends 18 U.S.C. 2511 (interception of wire or electronic communications) and 2701 (unauthorized acquisition of communications in electronic storage), unauthorized computer access and

[77] *Pinkerton v. United States*, 328 U.S. 640, 645–48 (1946); *United States v. Parkes*, 497 F.3d 220, 232 (2d Cir. 2007)(Under *Pinkerton v. United States*, "a defendant who does not directly commit a substantive offense may nevertheless be liable if the commission of the offense by a co-conspirator in furtherance of the conspiracy was reasonably foreseeable to the defendant as a consequence of their criminal agreement"); *United States v. Moran*, 493 F.3d 1002, 1009–110 (9th Cir. 2007); *United States v. Roberson*, 474 F.3d 432, 433 (7th Cir. 2007).

[78] *United States v. Willis*, 476 F.3d 1121, 1125 (10th Cir. 2007).

[79] See, *United States v. Jordan*, 316 F.3d 1215, 1223–224 (11th Cir. 2003)(noting the indictment of a sheriff, for improper use of access to the FBI's NCIC database, under paragraph 1030(a)(2), 18 U.S.C. 2 (aiding and abetting), 371 (conspiracy), and 641 (theft of federal property); the overlap between section 1030 and federal laws that prohibit the theft of intangible property under various circumstances is discussed at greater length in the examination of paragraph 1030(a)(4)(fraud), *infra*.

acquisition of information in violation of paragraph 1030(a)(2) is likely to violate sections 2511 and 2701.[80]

In fact, overlap is even more likely. Paragraph 1030(a)(3) protects only federal computers. Paragraph 1030(a)(2) protectsnot only federal computer information, but information from "protected computers" (computers used in interstate and foreign commerce) when the unauthorized access involves an interstate or foreign communication. Due to the nature of Internet communications, a communication may involve interstate communications even if the both the parties are located within the same state;[81] and, by virtue of an amendment in the USA PATRIOT Act, protected computer information may include information on computers located overseas as long as they involve or affect the foreign commerce or communications of the United States.[82]

Interstate or Foreign Transportation of Stolen Property. Whether a hacker, who steals information stored in a computer, violates any of the general federal theft statutes depends upon whether the particular statute covers intangible property, and if not, whether the victim has been defrauded of tangible in addition to intangible property. For instance, the Supreme Court has noted that 18 U.S.C. 2314, that outlaws the interstate transportation of stolen goods, wares, or merchandise,[83] "contemplate[s] a physical identity

[80] See, *Konop v. Hawaiian Airlines, Inc.*, 302 F.3d 868, 875–80 (9th Cir. 2002)(discussing the application of 18 U.S.C. 2511 and 2701 to a case of unauthorized access to a secure website). See also *Motorola Credit Corp. v. Uzan*, 388 F.3d 39, 44 (2d Cir. 2004) (discussing civil suit claiming violations of sections 1030, 2511, and 2701).

[81] *United States v. Kammersell*, 196 F.3d 1137, 1138–140 (10th Cir. 1999)(a threat communicated between two computers in Utah involved interstate communications because the communication was forwarded by way of AOL's server in Virginia); *United States v. Trotter*, 478 F.3d 918, 921, 922 (8th Cir. 2007)("As both the means to engage in commerce and the method by which transactions occur, the Internet is an instrumentality and channel of interstate commerce. . . [O]nce the computer is used in interstate commerce, Congress has the power to protect it"); *United States v. Sutcliffe*, 505 F.3d 944, 953 (9th Cir. 2007); *United States v. Mitra*, 405 F.3d 492, 496 (7th Cir. 2005).

[82] "[T]he term 'protected computer' means a computer—(A) exclusively for the use of a financial institution or the United States Government, or, in the case of a computer not exclusively for such use, used by or for a financial institution or the United States Government and the conduct constituting the offense affects that use by or for the financial institution or the Government; or (B) which is used in interstate or foreign commerce or communication, *including a computer located outside the United States that is used in a manner that affects interstate or foreign commerce or communication of the United States*," 18 U.S.C. 1030(e)(2)(language added in the USA PATRIOT Act in italics).

[83] "Whoever transports, transmits, or transfers in interstate or foreign commerce any goods, wares, merchandise, securities or money, of the value of $5,000 or more, knowing the same to have been stolen, converted or taken by fraud; or

"Whoever, having devised or intending to devise any scheme or artifice to defraud, or for obtaining money or property by means of false or fraudulent pretenses, representations, or promises, transports or causes to be transported, or induces any person or persons to travel in, or to be transported in interstate or foreign commerce in the execution or concealment of a scheme or artifice to defraud that person or those persons of money or property having a value of $5,000 or more; or

"Whoever, with unlawful or fraudulent intent, transports in interstate or foreign commerce any falsely made, forged, altered, or counterfeited securities or tax stamps, knowing the same to have been falsely made, forged, altered, or counterfeited; or

between the items unlawfully obtained and those eventually transported."[84] Thus, the theft of information stored in a computer may be prosecuted under section 2314 only if the government can establish that it was accomplished in conjunction with the theft and transportation of a physical item. Downloading information onto a stolen computer disk and then transporting the disk across a state line is covered, yet downloading information onto a computer disk that is transported but not stolen is not covered; however, courts have begun to differ in this interpretation and some have found an electronic file to be a tangible good within the meaning of section 2314.[85]

The federal statute proscribing theft from interstate carriers, 18 U.S.C. 659, speaks in terms of stealing "goods and chattels" under a variety of circumstances.[86] And it is presumably subject to the same analysis: section 659

"Whoever, with unlawful or fraudulent intent, transports in interstate or foreign commerce any traveler's check bearing a forged countersignature; or

"Whoever, with unlawful or fraudulent intent, transports in interstate or foreign commerce, any tool, implement, or thing used or fitted to be used in falsely making, forging, altering, or counterfeiting any security or tax stamps, or any part thereof—

"Shall be fined under this title or imprisoned not more than ten years, or both. . . ." 18 U.S.C. 2314.

84 *Dowling v. United States*, 473 U.S. 207, 216 (1985). *Dowling* involved the transportation of bootleg phonograph records which were not themselves stolen.

85 *United States v. Brown*, 925 F.2d 1301, 1305–309 (10th Cir. 1991); *United States v. Lyons*, 992 F.2d 1029, 1033 (10th Cir. 1993)("In *Brown*, we applied the Supreme Court's decision in *Dowling v. United States*, 474 U.S. 207 (1985) to computer software, and held that the intangible intellectual property of a computer program standing alone cannot constitute goods, wares or merchandise within the meaning of 18 U.S.C. 2314. The fact that Mr. Lyons stole the software in conjunction with the theft of tangible hardware distinguishes this case from *Brown*. *Brown* recognizes that the theft of intangible intellectual property in conjunction with the theft of tangible property falls within the ambit of §2314. Unlike the present case, there was no evidence in *Brown* that [the] defendant was involved in the physical theft or transportation of stolen tangible property"); *United States v. Martin*, 228 F.3d 1, 14 (1st Cir. 2000)(section 2314 applies "when there has been some tangible item taken, however insignificant or valueless it may be, absent the intangible component"). But see *United States v. Riggs*, 739 F. Supp 414, 420 (N.D. Ill. 1990) which found the electronic transfer of proprietary information to be covered by this statute ("if the information in [the plaintiff's] text file had been affixed to a floppy disk, or printed out on a computer printer, then [defendant's] transfer of that information across state lines would clearly constitute the transfer of goods, wares, or merchandise within the meaning of § 2314. This court sees no reason to hold differently simply because [defendant] stored the information inside computers instead of printing it out on paper. In either case, the information is in a transferrable, accessible, even salable form."). See also *United States v. Farraj*, 142 F. Supp. 2d 484 (S.D.N.Y. 2001)(the court disagreed with *Brown* and the 10th Circuit line of cases, and instead determined "the view most closely analogous to Second Circuit doctrine is that which holds that the transfer of electronic documents via the internet across state lines does fall within the purview of § 2314").

If section 2314 does apply to a given case, then section 2315 that prohibits receipt of stolen property may also be implicated.

86 "Whoever embezzles, steals, or unlawfully takes, carries away, or conceals, or by fraud or deception obtains from any pipeline system, railroad car . . . with intent to convert to his own use any goods or chattels moving as or which are a part of or which constitute an interstate or foreign shipment of freight, express, or other property; or

"Whoever buys or receives or has in his possession any such goods or chattels, knowing the same to have been embezzled or stolen; or

"Whoever embezzles, steals, or unlawfully takes, carries away, or by fraud or deception obtains with intent to convert to his own use any baggage which shall have come into the possession of any common carrier for transportation in interstate or foreign commerce . . .

or

applies only to the theft of physical items; even if all of the other elements are satisfied, computer fraud is proscribed by section 659 only where in involves the theft of physical item.

Theft of Federal Government Information. Prosecuting computer fraud under a statute that outlaws the interstate transportation of stolen "goods, wares, merchandise, securities or money" may be an awkward fit. The general theft of government property statute, 18 U.S.C. 641, seems a better match, however, for that provision outlaws the misappropriation of any "thing of value" belonging to or in the possession of the federal government.[87] The courts have applied section 641 to the misappropriation of property that lacks any necessary corporal features.[88]

Economic Espionage. Paragraph 1030(a)(2) overlaps with the Economic Espionage Act when the information acquired through unauthorized access is a trade secret.[89] The Economic Espionage Act, among other things, outlaws computerized burglary committed in a commercial setting, 18 U.S.C. 1832.[90] It makes it a federal crime to steal certain trade secrets, or to receive

---

"Whoever embezzles, steals, or unlawfully takes by any fraudulent device, scheme, or game, from any railroad car, bus, vehicle, steamboat, vessel, or aircraft operated by any common carrier moving in interstate or foreign commerce or from any passenger thereon any money, baggage, goods, or chattels . . . .

"Shall in each case be fined under this title or imprisoned not more than ten years, or both; but if the amount or value of such money, baggage, goods or chattels does not exceed $1,000, he shall be fined under this title or imprisoned not more than one year, or both . . . ." 18 U.S.C. 659.

87 "Whoever embezzles, steals, purloins, or knowingly converts to his use or the use of another, or without authority, sells, conveys or disposes of any record, voucher, money, or thing of value of the United States or of any department or agency thereof, or any property made or being made under contract for the United States or any department or agency thereof; or

"Whoever receives, conceals, or retains the same with intent to convert it to his use or gain, knowing it to have been embezzled, stolen, purloined or converted—

"Shall be fined under this title or imprisoned not more than ten years, or both; but if the value of such property in the aggregate, combining amounts from all the counts for which the defendant is convicted in a single case, does not exceed the sum of $1,000, he shall be fined under this title or imprisoned not more than one year, or both."

"The word 'value' means face, par, or market value, or cost price, either wholesale or retail, whichever is greater," 18 U.S.C. 641.

88 See e.g., *United States v. Forman*, 180 F.3d 766, 767–68 (6th Cir. 1999)(information from a confidential government report concerning a criminal investigation); *United States v. Collins*, 56 F.3d 1416, 1419–420 (D.C.Cir. 1995)(computer time and storage); *United States v. Martzkin*, 14 F.3d 1014, 1018–21 (4th Cir. 1994)(bids on government contracts); *United States v. Jeter*, 775 F.2d 670, 680 (6th Cir. 1985)(information as to matters occurring before a federal grand jury); *United States v. Girard*, 601 F.2d 69, 70–1 (2d Cir. 1979) (identity of government undercover agents); *United States v. Lambert*, 446 F.Supp. 890, 892–95 (D.Conn. 1978)(information stolen from a DEA computer data base).

89 *E.g., United States v. Genovese*, 409 F.Supp.2d 253 (S.D.N.Y. 2005)(refusing to dismiss on the bases of overbreadth and vagueness grounds an indictment under section 1832 for downloading Miscrosoft source code without authorization).

90 "(a) Whoever, with intent to convert a trade secret,*, that is related to or included in a product that is produced for or placed in interstate or foreign commerce, to the economic benefit of anyone other than the owner thereof, and intending or knowing that the offense will, injure any owner of that trade secret, knowingly—(1) steals, or without authorization appropriates, takes, carries away, or conceals, or by fraud, artifice, or deception obtains such information; (2) without authorization copies, duplicates, sketches, draws photographs, downloads, uploads, alters, destroys, photocopies,

such trade secrets with the knowledge they have been stolen, or to conspire or attempt to steal them, or to conspire or attempt to receive them knowing they have been stolen. To be covered by the protective umbrella of section 1832, information must (1) have a nexus interstate or foreign commerce; (2) be a secret; and (3) have some trade value.

Information meets the commerce nexus when it is associated with a product that is marketed across state lines, i.e., if it is "related to or included in a product that is produced for or placed in interstate or foreign commerce," 18 U.S.C. 1832(a). Information is considered "secret" if it is "not generally known to the public or to the business, scientific, or education community in which [its] owner might seek to use the information" and its owner takes reasonable steps to maintain its confidentiality, H.Rept. 788 at 12; 18 U.S.C. 1839(3).

But what makes section 1832 a particularly effective shield against computerized burglary in a commercial setting is that the trade secret information it protects includes "all forms and types of financial, business, scientific, technical, economic, or engineering information, including patterns, plans, compilations, program devices, formulas, designs, prototypes, methods, techniques, processes, procedures, programs, or codes, whether tangible or intangible, and whether or how stored, compiled, or memorialized physically, electronically, graphically, photographically, or in writing," 18 U.S.C. 1839(3).

Violations of section 1832 are punishable by imprisonment for not more than 10 years and/or a fine of not more than the greater of twice the amount of pecuniary gain or loss resulting from the offense or $250,000 (not more than $5 million if the offender is an organization).

---

replicates, transmits, delivers, sends, mails, communicates, or conveys such information; (3) receives, buys, or possesses such information, knowing the same to have been stolen or appropriated, obtained, or converted without authorization; (4) attempts to commit any offense described in paragraphs (1) through (3); or (5) conspires with one or more other persons to commit any offense described in paragraphs (1) through (3), and one or more of such persons do any act to effect the object of the conspiracy,—shall, except as provided in subsection (b), be fined under this title or imprisoned not more than 10 years, or both.

"(b) Any organization that commits any offense described in subsection (a) shall be fined not more than $5,000,000," 18 U.S.C. 1832.

* "'[T]rade secret' means all forms and types of financial, business, scientific, technical, economic, or engineering information, including patterns, plans, compilations, program devices, formulas, designs, prototypes, methods, techniques, processes, procedures, programs, or codes, whether tangible or intangible, and whether or how stored, compiled, or memorialized physically, electronically, graphically, photographically, or in writing if—(A) the owner thereof has taken reasonable measures to keep such information secret; and (B) the information derives independent economic value, actual or potential, from not being generally known to, and not being readily ascertainable through proper means by, the public," 18 U.S.C. 1839(3); see generally, *Twenty-Second Survey of White Collar Crime, Intellectual Property Crimes*, 44 AMERICAN CRIMINAL LAW REVIEW 693 (2007); Pooley, Lemley & Toren, *Understanding the Economic Espionage Act of 1996*, 5 TEXAS INTELLECTUAL PROPERTY LAW JOURNAL 177 (1997).

Copyright infringement. Downloading information after unauthorized access to a protected computer may violate not only paragraph 1030(a)(2) but may constitute copyright infringement as well. Computer software programs are ordinarily protected by copyright which generally precludes copying of protected material without the consent of the holder of the copyright. Copyright law outlaws three forms of willful copyright infringement: (A) infringement for "commercial advantage or private financial gain," 17 U.S.C. 506(a)(1)(A); (B) infringement by reproduction of distribution of protected works worth more than $1,000, 17 U.S.C. 506(a)(1)(B); and (C) infringement by "distribution of a work being prepared for commercial distribution, by making it available on a computer network accessible to members of the public, if such person knew or should have known that the work was intended for commercial distribution," 17 U.S.C. 506(a)(1)(C).

Each of the three forms of infringement has its own penalty structure under 18 U.S.C. 2319. Infringement for profit or commercial advantage is punishable by imprison terms with maximum limits of 1 to 10 years depending on the extent of the violation.[91] The maximum term of imprisonment for infringement on works worth more than $1,000 ranges from 1 to 6 years.[92] Finally, the infringement involving works in preparation for distribution carries maximum penalties ranging from 3 to 10 years.[93] The offenses are also subject to fines of not more than $250,000 (not more than $500,000 for organizations) if the maximum term of imprisonment is more than 1 year, and otherwise of not more than $100,000 (not more than $200,000 for organizations).[94]

---

[91] 18 U.S.C. 2319(b)("(b) Any person who commits an offense under section 506(a)(1)(A) of title 17—(1) shall be imprisoned not more than 5 years, or fined in the amount set forth in this title, or both, if the offense consists of the reproduction or distribution, including by electronic means, during any 180-day period, of at least 10 copies or phonorecords, of 1 or more copyrighted works, which have a total retail value of more than $2,500; (2) shall be imprisoned not more than 10 years, or fined in the amount set forth in this title, or both, if the offense is a second or subsequent offense under paragraph (1); and (3) shall be imprisoned not more than 1 year, or fined in the amount set forth in this title, or both, in any other case").

[92] 18 U.S.C. 2319(c)("Any person who commits an offense under section 506(a)(1)(B) of title 17—(1) shall be imprisoned not more than 3 years, or fined in the amount set forth in this title, or both, if the offense consists of the reproduction or distribution of 10 or more copies or phonorecords of 1 or more copyrighted works, which have a total retail value of $2,500 or more; (2) shall be imprisoned not more than 6 years, or fined in the amount set forth in this title, or both, if the offense is a second or subsequent offense under paragraph (1); and (3) shall be imprisoned not more than 1 year, or fined in the amount set forth in this title, or both, if the offense consists of the reproduction or distribution of 1 or more copies or phonorecords of 1 or more copyrighted works, which have a total retail value of more than $1,000").

[93] 18 U.S.C. 2319(d)("(d) Any person who commits an offense under section 506(a)(1)(C) of title 17—(1) shall be imprisoned not more than 3 years, fined under this title, or both; (2) shall be imprisoned not more than 5 years, fined under this title, or both, if the offense was committed for purposes of commercial advantage or private financial gain; (3) shall be imprisoned not more than 6 years, fined under this title, or both, if the offense is a second or subsequent offense; and (4) shall be imprisoned not more than 10 years, fined under this title, or both, if the offense is a second or subsequent offense under paragraph (2)").

[94] 18 U.S.C. 3571.

Money Laundering. The principal federal money laundering statutes, 18 U.S.C. 1956 and 1957, outlaw various financial activities that involve the proceeds from other federal crimes.[95] They prohibit:

- domestic laundering of the proceeds of these predicate offenses, referred to as "specified unlawful activities;"
- international laundering of the proceeds of predicate offenses;
- using the proceeds of predicate offenses to promote further predicate offenses;[96] or
- spending or depositing more than $10,000 of the proceeds of predicate offenses.[97]

Offenses under the various paragraphs of 18 U.S.C. 1030 are all money laundering predicate offenses,[98] although paragraph 1030(a)(2) information acquisition offenses are less likely to generate proceeds than are the fraud and espionage offenses of paragraphs 1030(a)(4) and 1030(a)(1).

Causing Computer Damage (18 U.S.C. 1030(a)(5))

> *Whoever . . . (5)(A)(i) knowingly causes the transmission of a program, information, code, or command, and as a result of such conduct, intentionally causes damage*[99] *without authorization, to a protected computer;*[100]
>
> > *(ii) intentionally accesses a protected computer without authorization, and as a result of such conduct, recklessly causes damage; or*
> >
> > *(iii) intentionally accesses a protected computer without authorization, and as a result of such conduct, causes damage; and*
>
> *(B) by conduct described in clause (i), (ii), or (iii) of subparagraph (A), caused (or, in the case of an attempted offense, would, if completed, have caused)—(i) loss to 1 or more persons during any 1-year period (and, for purposes of an investigation, prosecution, or other proceeding brought by the United States only, loss resulting*

---

[95] See generally, *Twenty-Second Survey of White Collar Crime: Money Laundering*, 44 AMERICAN CRIMINAL LAW REVIEW 769 (2007); *Money Laundering: an Overview of 18 U.S.C. 1956 and Related Federal Criminal Law*, RL33315.

[96] 18 U.S.C. 1956 (text appended).

[97] 18 U.S.C. 1957.

[98] 18 U.S.C. 1956(c)(7)(D), 1957(f)(3).

[99] "The term 'damage' means any impairment to the integrity or availability of data, a program, a system, or information . . . the term 'loss' means an reasonable cost to any victim, including the cost of responding to an offense, conducting a damage assessment, and restoring the data, program, system, or information to its condition prior to the offense, and any revenue lost, cost incurred, or other consequential damages incurred because of interruption of service," 18 U.S.C. 1030(e)(8), (11).

[100] "As used in this section . . . (2) the term 'protected computer' means a computer - (A) exclusively for the use of a financial institution or the United States Government, or, in the case of a computer not exclusively for such use, used by or for a financial institution or the United States Government and the conduct constituting the offense affects that use by or for the financial institution or the Government; or (B) which is used in interstate or foreign commerce or communication including a computer located outside the United States that is used in a manner that affects interstate or foreign commerce or communication of the United States," 18 U.S.C. 1030(e)(2).

from a related course of conduct affecting 1 or more other protected computers) aggregating at least $5,000 in value;

(ii) the modification or impairment, or potential modification or impairment of medical examination, diagnosis, treatment, or care of 1 or more individuals;

(iii) physical injury to any person;

(iv) a threat to public health or safety; or

(v) damage affecting a computer system used by or for a government entity in furtherance of the administration of justice, national defense, or national security . . . shall be punished as provided in subsection (c) of this section.

Intent

Paragraph 1030(a)(5) establishes crimes of dual intent—the intent to knowingly intrude and the intent to damage. Hackers or the creators of viruses, worms and the like may trigger paragraph 1030(a)(5), when they damage, even unintentionally, the systems they have knowingly invaded.[101] Paragraph 1030(a)(5) establishes three computer damage offenses, distinguishable on the basis of the offender's intent to cause damage: (1) *causing damage* to a protected computer by intentional unauthorized access; (2) *recklessly causing damage* to a protected computer by intentional unauthorized access; and (3) *intentionally causing damage* to a protected computer through a knowing transmission. This feature, added in 1996 and amended in the USA PATRIOT and Homeland Security Acts, punishes recklessly and intentionally caused damage more seriously but preserves the earlier understanding that anyone who intentionally secures unauthorized access is punishable for any resulting damage regardless of whether they intended to cause it, or were recklessly indifferent as to whether they did so.[102] In simple terms, to establish a violation a defendant must shown to have " (1) intentionally accessed (2) a protected computer (3) without authorization,

---

[101] *United States v. Lloyd*, 269 F.3d 228, 231 (3d Cir. 2001) involved a former employee charged with triggering a "time bomb" which purged the design and production computer files of the company that fired him. See also, *United States v. Mitra*, 405 F.3d 492 (7th Cir. 2005)(where defendant was found guilty of violating 1030(a)(5) after he disrupted police department's computer-based radio systemand thus created public safety problems because the officers could no longer communicate with each other).

[102] Even under an earlier version of the paragraph 1030(a)(5) that outlawed "intentional access. . . without authorization, and by means of. . . such conduct. . . prevent[ing] authorized use of any such computer. . . and thereby causes loss to one or more others of a value aggregating $1,000 or more . . .," the government was not required to show that the defendant intentionally prevented use nor that he intentionally caused damage "aggregating $1,000 or more"; a demonstration that he intentionally accessed a protected computer without authorization was sufficient, *United States v. Morris*, 928 F.2d 504 (2d Cir. 1991)(Morris, a computer graduate student, was convicted under 18 U.S.C. 1030(a)(5) for releasing a "worm" on the Internet that "spread and multiplied, eventually causing computers at various educational institution and military sites to crash or cease functioning," 928 F.2d at 505); *United States v. Sablan*, 92 F.3d 865, 868 (9th Cir. 1996). Sablan, a disgruntled former bank employee, surreptitiously entered the bank after hours and "called up" and damaged several files from the bank's mainframe on the computer to which she had been assigned prior to her discharge.

and (4) as a result of such conduct, has (5) intentionally, recklessly, or otherwise caused (6) damage."[103]

Unauthorized Activity

Unauthorized activity under paragraph 1030(a)(5) takes two forms. For the intentional damage offense of clause 1030(a)(5)(A)(i), the offender must knowingly transmit a command, program, information or code thereby intentionally causing unauthorized damage. For the reckless or simple damage offenses of clauses 1030(a)(5)(A)(ii) and (iii), the offender must intentionally access a computer without authorization and thereby cause damage either recklessly or unintentionally. In the first instance, it is the damage that is unauthorized; in the second and third it is the access to the computer. The Justice Department suggests that one reason for the distinction is that damage can be intentionally caused without having to access the victimized computer directly,[104] so that the clause reaches intentional damage whether through direct access or not.[105] The legislative history seems to confirm this view.[106] Of course, the clause applies to direct access as well. It reach any individual who intentionally causes damage by issuing a destructive command or downloading a destructive program, after having accessed the victimized computer whether with authorization, without authorization, or in excess of authorization. While the other clauses refer to unauthorized access and exceeding authorized access, clause (a)(5)(a)(i) speaks of unauthorized damage. There is some precedent for the view that "unauthorized damage" includes by implication damage in excess of authorization.[107]

To establish the transmission element of the intentional damage offense, "the government must offer sufficient proof that the person charged is the same person who sent the transmission. Circumstantial evidence is sufficient to prove that the transmission occurred."[108]

---

[103] *ViChip v. Lee*, 438 F.Supp.2d 1087, 1100 (N.D. Cal. 2006).

[104] *DoJ Computer Crimes*, at 32 ("section 1030(a)(5)(A)(i) requires proof only of the knowing transmission of something to damage a computer without authorization. The government does not need to prove 'access.' Because it is possible to damage a computer without 'accessing' it, this element is easier to prove (except for the mental state requirement). For example, most worms and trojans spread through self-replication, without personally accessing the affected systems").

[105] *See e.g., United States v. Mitra*, 405 F.3d 492, 494–95 (7th Cir. 2005)(paragraph 1030(a) (5) covers jamming a city's computer-operated radio traffic communications system).

[106] S.Rept. 104-357 at 10 (1996)(This would penalize "anyone who knowingly causes the transmission of a program, information, code, or command and intentionally causes damage to a protected computer. This would cover anyone who intentionally damages a computer, regardless of whether they were an outsider or an insider otherwise authorized to access the computer").

[107] *International Airport Centers, L.L.C. v. Citrin*, 440 F.3d 418, 421 (7th Cir. 2006)("Citrin points out that his employment contract authorized him to 'return or *destroy*' data in the laptop when he ceased being employed. But it is unlikely to say the least, that the provision was intended to authorize him to destroy data that he knew the company had no duplicates of and would have wanted to have. . .").

[108] *United States v. Shea*, 493 F.3d 1110, 1115 (9th Cir. 2007).

As for unauthorized access element of clauses (a)(5)(A)(ii) and (iii), when the other paragraphs of 18 U.S.C. 1030 speak of unauthorized access, they mention "exceeding authorized access" as an alternative.[109] Clauses (a)(5)(A)(ii) and (iii) do not; they speak only of unauthorized access. The difference has been construed to mean that only outsiders may violation the reckless and simple damage clauses.[110]

Damage

Not all computer damage qualifies as the damage element of a paragraph 1030(a)(5) offense. The paragraph extends to only five specific kinds of damage inflicted upon a specific class of computers. The damage must be an "impairment to the integrity or availability of data, a program, a system, or information,"[111] that:

- causes a loss over the course a year exceeds $5,000;[112]
- modifies, impairs, or could modify or impair medical services;
- causes physical injury;
- threatens public health or safety; or
- affects a justice, national defense, or national security entity computer, 18 U.S.C. 1030(a)(5)(B).

The elements were added in 1996 without a great deal of individual commentary,[113] but the 1996 legislative history of related segments of the statute is informative. An earlier prohibition spoke of intrusions that "cause[d] *loss or damage* to one or more other persons of value aggregating $1,000 or more during any 1-year period," 18 U.S.C. 1030(a)(5)(A)(ii)(II)(1994 ed.) (emphasis added). The Senate Committee report observes that use of the

---

[109] E.g., 18 U.S.C. 1030(a)(4)(emphasis added)("Whoever. . .(4) knowingly and with intent to defraud, accesses a protected computer *without authorization, or exceeds authorized access. . .*")

[110] S.Rept. 104-357, at 11 (1996)("In sum, under the bill insiders, who are authorized to access a computer, face criminal liability only if they intend to cause damage to a computer, not for recklessly or negligently causing damage. By contrast, outside hackers who break into a computer could be punished for any intentional, reckless, or other damage they cause by their trespass"), quoted in, *United States v. Phillips*, 477 F.3d 215, 219 (5th Cir. 2007); *DoJ Computer Crimes*, at 33 ("Subsections 1030(a)(5)(A)(ii) and (iii) require proof that the defendant intentionally accessed a protected computer without authorization. These subsections do not include the phrase 'exceeds authorized access.' Thus, these subsections do not apply to authorized users of a computer who exceed their authorization (insiders)").

[111] 18 U.S.C. 1030(e)(8). Impairment of the integrity of data or information includes disclosure of confidential information secured through unauthorized access, *Therapeutic Research Facilty v. NBTY, Inc.*, 488 F.Supp.2d 991, 996 (E.D. Cal. 2007); *Shurgard Storage Centers, Inc. v. Safeguard Self Storage, Inc.*, 119 F.Supp.2d 1121, 1126 (W.D. Wash. 2000).

[112] More precisely, "(B) by conduct described in clause (i), (ii), or (iii) of subparagraph (A), caused (or, in the case of an attempted offense, would, if completed, have caused)—(i) loss to 1 or more persons during any 1-year period (and, for purposes of an investigation, prosecution, or other proceeding brought by the United States only, loss resulting from a related course of conduct affecting 1 or more other protected computers) aggregating at least $5,000 in value," 18 U.S.C. 1030(a)(5)(B)(i).

[113] See S.Rept. 104-357 at 13-4 (1996) (simply paraphrasing the language of the definition).

term "damage" contemplates the inclusion of all economic harm attributable to the intrusion and that the increased dollar limitation is expected to restrict federal felony prosecutions to the more serious cases:

> "The 1994 amendment required both 'damage' and 'loss,' but it is not always clear what constitutes 'damage.' For example, intruders often alter existing log-on programs so that user passwords are copied to a file which the hackers can retrieve later. After retrieving the newly created password file, the intruder restores the altered log-on file to its original condition. Arguably, in such a situation, neither the computer nor its information is damaged. Nonetheless, this conduct allows the intruder to accumulate valid user passwords to the system, requires all system users to change their passwords, and requires the system administrator to devote resources to resecuring the system. Thus, although there is arguably no 'damage,' the victim does suffer 'loss.' If the loss to the victim meets the required monetary threshold, the conduct should be criminal, and the victim should be entitled to relief. The bill therefore defines 'damage' in new subsection 1030(e)(8), with a focus on the harm that the law seeks to prevent. As in the past, the term 'damage' will require . . . significant financial losses," S.Rept. 104-357 at 11 (1996).

Ordinarily, the presence of a separate hacker prohibition with less severe penalties would argue against allowing "damage assessment" and "security enhancement" costs to be used to reach the $5,000 threshold for the more severe penalty. The report language might be read to rebut such a presumption, but it might also be characterized as asserting no more than that the cost of new locks ("resecuring the system") can be considered damage when the keys ("passwords") are stolen.

The USA PATRIOT Act reduced the prospect of misconception by supplying an explicit definition of "loss" as used here; "the term 'loss' means any reasonable cost to any victim, including the cost of responding to an offense, conducting a damage assessment, and restoring the data, program, system, or information to its condition prior to the offense, and any revenue lost, cost incurred, or other consequential damages incurred because of interruption of service," 18 U.S.C. 1030(e)(11). Thus, the losses incurred by a contractor employed to manage the damaged computer system may properly be included to reach the $5,000 threshold.[114]

It also eliminated a second potential problem. The 1996 amendments, perhaps inadvertently, rephrased the aggregate $5,000 damage-loss threshold describing the victims as "individuals" rather than the term previously employed, "persons."[115] The change stimulated contentions that Congress

[114] *United States v. Millot*, 433 F.3d 1057, 1060–61 (8th Cir. 2006).

[115] Compare "causes loss or damage to one or more other *persons* of value aggregating $1,000 or more during any 1-year period," 18 U.S.C. 1030(a)(5)(A)(ii)(II)(aa)(1994 ed.) (emphasis added), with "causes loss aggregating at least $5,000 in value during any 1-year period to one of more *individuals*," 18 U.S.C. 1030(e)(8)(A)(2000 ed.)(emphasis added).

intended to limit the cases where the threshold could be reached entirely to the damages and losses suffered by human beings without any reference to the damages and losses suffered by corporate or other legal entities.[116] The USA PATRIOT Act negated the problem by describing the damage-loss victims as "persons" and by defining persons to include individuals and any "legal or other entity," 18 U.S.C. 1030(a)(5)(B)(i), (e)(12).

The long standing medical tampering element has no monetary threshold and has remained essentially unchanged since it was added in response to an incident in which juvenile hackers broke into the computer system of the Sloan-Kettering Cancer Center.[117]

The inclusion of computer tampering that causes physical injuries or threatens public health or safety, on the other hand, is new with the 1996 amendments and is designed to reach more general threats:

> As the NII [National Information Infrastructure] and other network infrastructures continue to grown, computers will increasingly be used for access to critical services such a emergency response systems and air traffic control, and will be critical to other systems which we cannot yet anticipate. S.Rept. 104-357 at 11 (1996).

Jurisdiction

These kinds of damage are only federal crimes under paragraph 1030(a)(5) if they involve a *protected computer*. There are five types of protected computers or computer systems. The five include computers:

- used exclusively for or by the United States government;
- used exclusively for or by a bank or other financial institution;
- used in part for or by the United States government where the damage "affects" the government use or use of the government's behalf;
- used in part for or by a bank or other financial institution where the damage "affects" use by or on behalf of the institution; and
- used in interstate or foreign commerce or communications including a computer outside the country whose use affects U.S. commerce, 18 U.S.C. 1030(e)(2).

What is a "computer . . . used in interstate or foreign commerce or communications"? The legislative history shows that the phrase means computer damage which might affect interstate or foreign commerce or interstate or

[116] The argument was made but rejected in *United States v. Middleton*, 231 F.3d 1207, 1210 (9th Cir. 2000).

[117] S.Rept. 99-432 at 2-3 (1986). The medical records offense had always been tied to the use of interstate computers; 1996 amendments also permit prosecution when the medical records tampering involves one of the other four jurisdictional moorings (i.e., the involvement of federal computers or the computers of financial institutes, or adversely affecting the use of computers by the government or financial institutions).

foreign communications. The phrase appears in section 1030 after the 1994 amendments when it was first used to supplement (and in the 1996 amendments to replace) the phrase "computer . . . which is one of two or more computers used in committing the offense, not all of which are located in the same State," compare 18 U.S.C. 1030(a)(5), (e)(2)(1986 Supp.), with 18 U.S.C. 1030(a)(5), (e)(2)(1994 ed.). The change was made because under the earlier language "hackers who attacked other computers in their own State were not subject to Federal jurisdiction, notwithstanding the fact that their actions may have severely affected interstate or foreign commerce. For example, individuals who attack[ed] telephone switches m[ight] disrupt interstate and foreign calls. The 1994 change remedied that defect," S.Rept. 104-357 at 10 (1996). The inherently interstate nature of the Internet is such that a computer used to access the Internet is a computer used in interstate or foreign commerce, and consequently a computer whose protection is within Congress' power to regulate.[118]

Precisely which government computers are protected is a bit more uncertain. Although terms used elsewhere in section 1030 such as "governmental entity"[119] and "department of the United States," are expressly defined, there is no definition of either the phrase "United States Government" or the phrase "Government of the United States" used from the beginning to described the scope of protection provided federal computers. The reports do not explain its meaning. In the trespassing provisions of paragraph 1030(a)(3), however, the phrase is used in juxtaposition with the phrase "department or agency of the United States"[120] suggesting that the term embodies the meaning assigned to that phrase by the definitions subsection of section 1030[121] and by the definition section generally applicable to title 18 of the United States Code.[122] On the other hand, it would not be unreasonable for a court to conclude that the phases "United States

[118] *United States v. Trotter*, 478 F.3d 918, 921, 922 (8th Cir. 2007); *United States v. Sutcliffe*, 505 F.3d 944, 953 (9th Cir. 2007); *United States v. Mitra*, 405 F.3d 492, 496 (7th Cir. 2005).

[119] "As used in this section. . . (9) the term 'government entity' includes the Government of the United States, any State or political subdivision of the United States, any foreign country, and any state, province, municipality, or other political subdivision of a foreign country," 18 U.S.C. 1030(e)(9).

[120] "Whoever. . . intentionally, without authorization to access any nonpublic computer of a *department or agency of the United States*, accesses such a computer of *that department or agency that is exclusively for the use of the Government of the United States* or, in the case of a computer not exclusively for such use, is used by or for the Government of the United States and such conduct affects that use by or for the Government of the United States. . . ." 18 U.S.C. 1030(a)(3)(emphasis added).

[121] "(e) As used in this section. . . (7) the term 'department of the United States' means the legislative or judicial branch of the Government or one of the executive departments enumerated in section 101 of title 5," 18 U.S.C. 1030(e)(7).

[122] "As used in this title: The term 'department' means one of the executive departments enumerated in section 1 [now section 1010] of Title 5, unless the context shows that such term was intended to describe the executive, legislative, or judicial branches of the government. The term 'agency' includes any department, independent establishment, commission, administration, authority, board or bureau of the United States or any corporation in which the United States has a proprietary interest, unless the context shows that such term was intended to be used in a more limited sense," 18 U.S.C. 6.

Government" and "Government of the United States" should be construed narrowly since when Congress intended an expansive definition it provided one. The definition of financial institutions whose computers are protected[123] differs only slightly from the definition generally applicable in title 18.[124]

The question persists as to whether by specifically mentioning overseas computers in the interstate and foreign commerce basis for jurisdiction ("including a computer outside the country whose use affects U.S. commerce"), Congress intended to preclude overseas application of the other bases for jurisdiction (e.g., damage to government computers).

Consequences

Penalties. The paragraph punishes causing damage recklessly or intentionally more severely than causing damage without necessarily intending to do. Causing damage, without necessarily intending to do so, by intentionally gaining access, or attempting to gain access, to a protected computer is punishable by imprisonment of not more than one year (not more than 10 years for a second or subsequent offense) and/or a fine of not more than $100,000 ($200,000 for organizations)(not more than $250,000/$500,0,00 for a second or subsequent offense) 18 U.S.C. 1030(c)(2)(A), (c)(3)(B); 18 U.S.C. 3571.[125]

---

[123] "(e) As used in this section . . . (4) the term financial institution' means—(A) an institution with deposits insured by the Federal Deposit Insurance Corporation; (B) the Federal Reserve or a member of the Federal Reserve including any Federal Reserve Bank; (C) a credit union with accounts insured by the National Credit Union Administration; (D) a member of the Federal home loan bank system and any home loan bank; (E) any institution of the Farm Credit System under the Farm Credit Act of 1971; (F) a broker-dealer registered with the Securities and Exchange Commission pursuant to section 15 of the Securities Exchange Act of 1934; (G) the Securities Investor Protection Corporation; (H) a branch or agency of a foreign bank (as such terms are defined in paragraphs (1) and (3) of section 1(b) of the International Banking Act of 1978); (I) an organization operating under section 25 or section 25(a) of the Federal Reserve Act," 18 U.S.C. 1030(e)(4).

[124] "As used in this title, the term 'financial institution' means—(1) an insured depository institution (as defined in section 3(c)(2) of the Federal Deposit Insurance Act); (2) a credit union with accounts insured by the National Credit Union Share Insurance Fund; (3) a Federal home loan bank or a member, as defined in section 2 of the Federal Home Loan Bank Act (12 U.S.C. 1422), of the Federal home loan bank system; (4) a System institution of the Farm Credit System, as defined in section 5.35(3) of the Farm Credit Act of 1971; (5) a small business investment company, as defined in section 103 of the Small Business Investment Act of 1958 (15 U.S.C. 662); (6) a depository institution holding company (as defined in section 3(w)(1) of the Federal Deposit Insurance Act; (7) a Federal Reserve bank or a member bank of the Federal Reserve System; (8) an organization operating under section 25 or section 25(a) of the Federal Reserve Act; or (9) a branch or agency of a foreign bank (as such terms are defined in paragraphs (1) and (3) of section 1(b) of the International Banking Act of 1978)," 18 U.S.C. 20.

[125] Section 805(c) of the Antiterrorism and Effective Death Penalty Act of 1996, 110 Stat. 1305, instructed the United States Sentencing Commission to adjust the applicable sentencing guidelines so that any violation of paragraph 1030(a)(5) would be punishable by imprisonment for not less than six months. The Commission did so with respect to any violations occurring on or after November 1, 1997, U.S.S.G. §2b1.3(d), 62 *Fed.Reg*. 26620621 (May 14, 1997). Section 814(f) of the USA PATRIOT Act, 28 U.S.C. 994 note, instructed the Commission to amend the Guidelines to ensure the imposition of appropriate penalties "without regard to any mandatory minimum term of imprisonment." For a

Recklessly causing damage by intentionally gaining access, or attempting to gain access, to a protected computer is punishable by imprisonment for not more than five years (not more than 20 years for a second or subsequent offense) and/or a fine of not more than $250,000 (not more than $500,000 for an organization), 18 U.S.C. 1030(c)(4)(B); 18 U.S.C. 3571.

Intentionally causing damage through a knowing transmission to a protected computer is punishable by imprisonment for not more than *10* years (not more than 20 years for a second or subsequent offense) and/or a fine of not more than $250,000 (not more than $500,000 for an organization), 18 U.S.C. 1030(c)(4)(A); 18 U.S.C. 3571. An offender who knowingly or recklessly causes or attempts to cause serious bodily injury or death by knowingly causing an intentionally damaging transmission to a protected computer is punishable by imprisonment for not more than of 20 years (any term of years or life if death results) and/or fine of $250,000 ($500,000 for an organization), 18 U.S.C. 1030(c)(5), 18 U.S.C. 3571.[126]

Here as elsewhere, offenses committed by juveniles are more likely to result in state rather than federal proceedings.[127] Many of the other auxiliary provisions of law such as those relating to the Sentencing Guidelines, forfeiture, and the like, which have little relevance in the case of simple trespassing, may have real consequences in the case of the damage offenses proscribed in paragraph 18 U.S.C. 1030(a)(5).

Sentencing Guidelines. The Sentencing Guidelines operate in paragraph 1030(a)(5) damage cases much as they do in paragraph 1030(a)(2) information acquisition cases.[128] The offenses are assigned to the same guideline, U.S.S.G. §2B1.1. Some of that guideline's escalators, however, are more obviously relevant in damage cases. For example, there is a minimum enhancement of 4 levels when a paragraph 1030(a)(5) offense involves the intentional infliction of damage,[129] and another range of enhancements

criticism of these increased penalties, see Skibell, *Cybercrimes & Misdemeanors: A Reevaluation of the Computer Fraud and Abuse Act*, 18 Berkeley Technology Law Journal 909, 934 (2003).

126 The Homeland Security Act added this provision; the USA PATRIOT Act increased the penalty for second or subsequent offenses from imprisonment for not more than 10 to imprisonment for not more than 20 years, and the penalty for intentionally causing damage to a protected computer through a knowing transmission from imprisonment for not more than five years to imprisonment for not more than 10 years. The applicable Sentencing Guideline sets the sentencing ranges for paragraph 1030(a)(5) violations according to the amount of damage done, the number of victims, and any risk of death or serious injury, U.S.S.G. §2B1.1.

127 18 U.S.C. 5032.

128 See e.g., *United States v. O'Brien*, 435 F.3d 36, 41 (1st Cir. 2006)("The district judge calculated the guideline range. . . adding 6 levels for a loss of $25,000–$40,000, U.S.S.G. §2B1.1, and then adding 2 levels for obstruction of justice, U.S.S.G. §3C1.1, and 2 levels for use of a special skill, U.S.S.G. §3B1.3"). The court noted that the special skill finding was warranted given the defendant's proficiency in the victimized software which permitted him to instruct others on its use, *id*.

129 "(Apply the greatest) If the defendant was convicted of an offense under. . . (ii) 18 U.S.C. 1030(a)(5)(A)(i)[intentionally damaging a protected computer], increase by 4 levels. (iii) 18 U.S.C. 1030, and the offense caused a substantial disruption of a critical infrastructure, increase by 6 levels," U.S.S.G. §2B1.1(b)(14)(A)(ii), (iii).

when an offense has multiple victims.[130] In addition, although the two offenses trigger the same range of enhancements based on the extent of loss or damage caused by the offense, the amount of damage or loss is often greater in a damage case.[131]

Forfeiture & Restitution. Property derived from a violation of any paragraph of 18 U.S.C. 1030 is subject to confiscation.[132] Restitution is mandatory when related to a violation of a paragraph which proscribes fraud or property damage.[133] Forfeiture is judged largely by the extent of the offender's ill-gotten gains; restitution by the extent of the injuries caused by his offense. Thus, restitution is more commonly found in paragraph 1030(a)(5) damages cases than is forfeiture.[134]

Cause of Action. Regardless of the criminal sanctions imposed, offenders of paragraph 1030(a)(2) may also incur civil liability for damage caused, 18 U.S.C. 1030(g).[135]

---

[130] "(Apply the greatest) If the offense—(A) (i) involved 10 or more victims. . . increase by 2 levels; (B) involved 50 or more victims, increase by 4 levels; or (C) involved 250 or more victims, increase by 6 levels," U.S.S.G. §2B1.1(b)(2).

[131] U.S.S.G. §2B1.1(b)(1). Accompanying Application Note (3)(A)(iii) provides, "*Offenses Under 18 U.S.C. §1030.*—In the case of an offense under 18 U.S.C. §1030, actual loss includes the following pecuniary harm, regardless of whether such pecuniary harm was reasonably foreseeable: any reasonable cost to any victim, including the cost of responding to an offense, conducting a damage assessment, and restoring the data, program, system, or information to its condition prior to the offense, and any revenue lost, cost incurred, or other damages incurred because of interruption of service."

[132] 18 U.S.C. 981(a)(1)(C), 982(a)(2)(B).

[133] 18 U.S.C. 3663A(c)(1)(A)(ii).

[134] E.g., *United States v. Shea*, 493 F.3d 1110, 1114 (9th Cir. 2007); *United States v. Perry*, 479 F.3d 885, 888 (D.C. Cir. 2007); *United States v. Phillips*, 477 F.3d 215, 217 (5th Cir. 2007); *United States v. Schuster*, 467 F.3d 614, 616 (7th Cir. 2006); *United States v. Millot*, 433 F.3d 1057, 1060 (8th Cir. 2006).

[135] "(g) Any person who suffers damage or loss by reason of a violation of this section may maintain a civil action against the violator to obtain compensatory damages and injunctive relief or other equitable relief. A civil action for a violation of this section may be brought only if the conduct involves 1 of the factors set forth in clause (i), (ii), (iii), (iv), or (v) of subsection (a)(5)(B). Damages for a violation involving only conduct described in subsection (a)(5)(B)(i) are limited to economic damages. No action may be brought under this subsection unless such action is begun within 2 years of the date of the act complained of or the date of the discovery of the damage. No action may be brought under this subsection for the negligent design or manufacture of computer hardware, computer software, or firmware," 18 U.S.C. 1030(g).

The damages described in clauses (a)(5)(B)(i) through (v) are: "(i) loss to 1 or more persons during any 1-year period (and, for purposes of an investigation, prosecution, or other proceeding brought by the United States only, loss resulting from a related course of conduct affecting 1 or more other protected computers) aggregating at least $5,000 in value; (ii) the modification or impairment, or potential modification or impairment, of the medical examination, diagnosis, treatment, or care of 1 or more individuals; (iii) physical injury to any person; (iv) a threat to public health or safety; or (v) damage affecting a computer system used by or for a government entity in furtherance of the administration of justice, national defense, or national security." See, *America Online, Inc. v. National Health Care Discount, Inc.*, 174 F.Supp.2d 890, 899 (N.D. Iowa 2001)(sending bulk unauthorized and unsolicited e-mail to the Internet service provider's customers violated paragraph 1030(a)(2)).

Although subsection 1030(g) applies to any violation under any of the paragraphs of section 1030, it is discussed at greater length below in connection with paragraph 1030(a)(5)(relating to inflicting damage upon a computer).

Victims of a violation of paragraph 1030(a)(5) or any violation of subsection 1030(a) resulting in the requisite harm have a cause of action for compensatory damages and equitable relief if suit is brought within two years.[136] Damages to medical records, or damage causing physical injury or endangering public safety may also subject the offender to "compensatory" damages beyond "economic" damages—a difference that may entitle a victim to pecuniary damages as well as damages for pain and suffering but probably not exemplary damages.[137] Damages caused by a simply knowing violation of paragraph 1030(a)(5) (as opposed to reckless and intentional violations) are limited to economic damages.

Victims are described as "any person who suffers loss or damage by reason of a violation of this section," but until recently there was no specific definition of the term "person" in either section 1030 or in the definitions applicable to Title 18 generally.[138] The legislative history offered no further edification and the provision has yet to be construed by the courts. "Person" could mean individuals, or individuals and other legal entities including governmental entities, or individuals and other legal entities but not including governmental entities. Creditable arguments can be made for each of the possible definitions, but the fact that Congress elected to use the term "person" to mean only individuals in paragraph 1030(a)(7)(extortionate

[136] "Any person who suffers damage or loss by reason of a violation of this section may maintain a civil action against the violator to obtain compensatory damages and injunctive relief or other equitable relief. A civil action for a violation of this section may be brought only if the conduct involves 1 of the factors set forth in clause (i), (ii), (iii), (iv), or (v) of subsection (a)(5)(B). Damages for a violation involving only conduct described in subsection (a)(5)(B)(i) are limited to economic damages. No action may be brought under this subsection unless such action is begun within two years of the date of the act complained of or the date of the discovery of the damage. No action may be brought under this subsection for the negligent design or manufacture of computer hardware, computer software, or firmware,"18 U.S.C. 1030(g).

The damages described in clauses 1030(a)(5)(B)(i) through (v) are: "(i) loss to 1 or more persons during any 1-year period (and, for purposes of an investigation, prosecution, or other proceeding brought by the United States only, loss resulting from a related course of conduct affecting 1 or more other protected computers) aggregating at least $5,000 in value; (ii) the modification or impairment, or potential modification or impairment, of the medical examination, diagnosis, treatment, or care of 1 or more individuals; (iii) physical injury to any person; (iv) a threat to public health or safety; or (v) damage affecting a computer system used by or for a government entity in furtherance of the administration of justice, national defense, or national security." Under section 1030(g) the plaintiffs must show actual "quantifiable" damage. See e.g., *Pearl Investments v. Standard I/O*, 257 F.Supp.2d 326, 349 (D.Me. 2003) (slowing of system's speed and operation did not meet monetary threshold for civil action under 1030(g)).

[137] Black's defines compensatory damages as those damages "sufficient in amount to indemnify the injured person for the loss suffered," BLACK'S LAW DICTINARY, *Damages* (8th ed. 2004). It recognizes no separate definition for "economic damages," but the term is defined elsewhere in Title 18 of the United States Code as "the replacement costs of lost or damaged property or records, the cost of repeating an interrupted or invalidated experiment, or the loss of profits," 18 U.S.C. 43(d)(3).

[138] Who can be a victim has also been broadly defined by the courts, and rights to civil remedies under the statute have been extended to third parties. The court in *Theofel v. Farey-Jones*, 359 F.3d 1066, 1078 (9th Cir. 2004), emphasized that the statute extends a civil remedy to *any* person who suffers loss or damage, thus "[i]ndividuals other than the computer's owner may be proximately harmed by unauthorized access, particularly if they have rights to data stored on it."

threats)[139] might seem to favor a similar interpretation in subsection 1030(g). The USA PATRIOT Act resolved the question and answered several others.

First, it supplied a definition of person—"the term 'person' means any individual, firm, corporation, educational institution, governmental entity, or legal or other entity," 18 U.S.C. 1030(e)(12). Then, it added an equally generous definition of the kinds of losses that might give raise to civil liability—"the term 'loss' means any reasonable cost to any victim, including the cost of responding to an offense, conducting a damage assessment, and restoring the data, program, system, or information to its condition prior to the offense, and any revenue lost, cost incurred, or other consequential damages incurred because of interruption of service," 18 U.S.C. 1030(e)(11). Finally, it made clear that subsection 1030(g) does not create a cause of action for loss or damage attributable to "the negligent design or manufacture of computer hardware, computer software, or firmware," 18 U.S.C. 1030(g).[140]

Crimes of Terrorism. Paragraph (1) espionage offenses and paragraph (5) intentional damage offenses (other than those based on cause $5,000 in damage) are the only crimes under 18 U.S.C. 1030 classified as federal crimes of terrorism.[141] Designation as a federal crime of terrorism triggers the application of several other substantive and procedural criminal statutes, without any further nexus to terrorism. Federal crimes of terrorism are subject to an 8-year statute of limitations rather than the 5-year period that governs most federal crimes.[142] The maximum term of supervised release for a federal crime of terrorism is life, rather than the 5-year maximum that applies in most other instances.[143] An individual charged with a federal crime of terrorism is presumed to be an inappropriate subject for

---

[139] "Whoever. . . (7) with intent to extort from any *person, firm, association, educational institution, financial institution, government entity, or other legal entity,* any money or other thing of value. . ." 18 U.S.C. 1030(a)(7)(emphasis added)(the 2002 amendments struck out "firm, association, educational institution, financial institution, government entity, or other legal entity").

[140] For some of the difficulties associated with possible manufacturer liability under subsection 1030(g) prior to amendment see, *In re America Online, Inc.*, 168 F.Supp.2d 1359 (S.D.Fla. 2001)(allegations that provider's software damaged customers' computers); *Thurmond v. Compaq Computer Corp.*, 171 F. Supp.2d 667 (E.D. Tex. 2001)(floppy disk controllers that allegedly corrupted or destroyed data); *Hayes v. Packard Bell NEC, Inc.*, 193 F.Supp.2d 910 (E.D.Tex. 2001)(same); *Christian v. Sony Corp. of America*, 152 F.Supp.2d 1184 (D.Minn. 2001)(same).

[141] The USA PATRIOT Act enlarged the definition of federal crimes of terrorism, 18 U.S.C. 2332b(g)(5)(B), to include intentionally damaging a protected computer if the offense involves either impairing medical care, causing physical injury, threatening public health or safety, or damaging a governmental justice, national defense, or national security computer system, 18 U.S.C. 2332b(g)(5)(B)(i)("the term 'federal crime of terrorism means' means an offense that. . . (B) is a violation of—(i) section. . . 1030(a)(5)(A)(i) resulting in damage as defined in 1030(a)(5)(B)(ii) through (v). . . of this title").

[142] 18 U.S.C. 3286(a). A federal crime of terrorism that results in or involves the risk of serious injury can be prosecuted at any time, 18 U.S.C. 3286(b).

[143] 18 U.S.C. 3583. Federal courts generally impose a term of supervised release whenever they sentence an offender to prison for more than one year, *id.*, U.S.S.G. §5D1.1. Other than for certain drug offenses and sex crimes, the maximum length of a term of supervised release is 5 years, 18 U.S.C. 3583(b). Conditions of supervised release are not unlike those for probation or parole; the offender comes under the supervision of the Probation Service subject court designated restrictions and obligations, 18 U.S.C. 3583(d).

release on bail prior to his criminal trial, 18 U.S.C. 3143(e). The maximum term of imprisonment for aggravated identity theft is 5 years when the offense is committed in relation to a federal crime of terrorism rather than the 2-year maximum that would otherwise apply, 18 U.S.C. 1028A. It is a separate federal crime punishable by imprisonment for any term of years or for life to knowingly provide maritime transportation to an individual intending to commit, or in flight from the commission of, a federal crime of terrorism, 18 U.S.C. 2284.

Federal crimes of terrorism are also by definition RICO predicate offenses, 18 U.S.C. 1961(1). Among other things, RICO outlaws the patterned commission of predicate offenses ("racketeering activities") in order to acquire or conduct the affairs of an enterprise whose activities affect interstate or foreign commerce.[144] Offenders face imprisonment for up to 20 years, 18 U.S.C. 1963, as well as civil liability.

Other Crimes

Attempt, Conspiracy, and Complicity

The same general observations concerning attempt, conspiracy and aiding and abetting noted for the simple trespass paragraph apply here. It is a separate crime to attempt to violate paragraph 1030(a)(5) or any of the other paragraphs of subsection 1030(a), 18 U.S.C. 1030(b). Those who attempt to violate or who aid and abet the violation of another are subject to the same penalties as those commit the substantive offense, 18 U.S.C. 1030(c), 2. The same is true of conspiracies except that conspiracy to commit a felony carries a five year maximum of imprisonment, 18 U.S.C. 371.

Damage or Destruction of Federal Property

There are more than a few other federal statutes that might be implicated by damage or destruction of federal property, of the property of financial institutions, or of property used in interstate or foreign commerce. The principal uncertainty is whether these general statutes can be applied to protect intangible property, like information in computer storage. Even if computer-stored data is considered tangible property (electronic files rather than paper files), several statutes that outlaw damage or destruction may be unavailable because they either call for a specific means of destruction—

[144] "(b) It shall be unlawful for any person through a pattern of racketeering activity or through collection of an unlawful debt to acquire or maintain, directly or indirectly, any interest in or control of any enterprise which is engaged in, or the activities of which affect, interstate or foreign commerce.

"(c) It shall be unlawful for any person employed by or associated with any enterprise engaged in, or the activities of which affect, interstate or foreign commerce, to conduct or participate, directly or indirectly, in the conduct of such enterprise's affairs through a pattern of racketeering activity or collection of unlawful debt," 18 U.S.C. 1962(b), (c).

destruction by fire or explosives—or because they protect a particular kind of property—timber or buildings.[145]

Destruction of Government Records. It is a federal crime for anyone to unlawfully "conceal, remove, mutilate, obliterate, or destroy . . . any record, proceeding, map, book, paper, document, or other thing, filed or deposited with . . . any judicial or public officer of the United States."[146] The damage or destruction of government, computer-stored records will fall within the coverage of Section 2071 only if it can meet each of the action (obliterate or destroy), object (any record or other thing) and place (filled with a federal judicial or public officer) tests.

The phrase "conceal, remove, mutilate, obliterate, or destroy" may lend itself to the argument that it extends to destruction or complete inaccessibility, but perhaps not to less than totally destructive damage, of computerized records. Electronic destruction seems to fit under either "obliterate" ("to make undecipherable by obscuring")[147] or "destroy." Absent obliteration or destruction, the section may be thought to protect only tangibles, since the word "mutilate" has obvious physical connotations. Yet one court among the few to construe section 2071 held that it did not prohibit photocopying of government records—not because that would constitute the removal of an intangible (information), but because the statute was designed to prevent "any conduct which deprives the Government of the use of its documents."[148]

The phrase "any record, proceeding, map, book, paper, document, or other thing, filed or deposited with" would seem to cover any "thing" capable of

---

145 "(f)(1) Whoever maliciously damages or destroys, or attempts to damage or destroy, *by means of fire or an explosive*, any building, vehicle, or other personal or real property in whole or in part owned or possessed by, or leased to, the United States, or any department or agency thereof, shall be imprisoned for not less than 5 years and not more than 20 years, fined under this title, or both. . . . 18 U.S.C. 844(f)(emphasis added).

"Whoever unlawfully cuts, or wantonly injures or destroys any tree growing, standing, or being upon any land of the United States. . . shall be fined under this title or imprisoned not more than one year, or both," 18 U.S.C. 1853.

146 "(a) Whoever willfully and unlawfully conceals, removes, mutilates, obliterates, or destroys, or attempts to do so, or, with intent to do so takes and carries away any record, proceeding, map, book, paper, document, or other thing, filed or deposited with any clerk or officer of any court of the United States, or in any public office, or with any judicial or public officer of the United States, shall be fined under this title or imprisoned not more than three years, or both.

"(b) Whoever, having the custody of any such record, proceeding, map, book, document, paper, or other thing, willfully and unlawfully conceals, removes, mutilates, obliterates, falsifies, or destroys the same, shall be fined under this title or imprisoned not more than three years, or both; and shall forfeit his office and be disqualified from holding any office under the United States. As used in this subsection, the term "office" does not include the office held by any person as a retired officer of the Armed Forces of the United States," 18 U.S.C. 2071.

147 MERRIAM WEBSTER'S COLLEGIATE DICTIONARY, 802 (10th ed. 1996).

148 *United States v. Rosner*, 352 F.Supp. 915, 919 (S.D.N.Y. 1972).

being "filed or deposited". In these days of "electronic filing"[149] any contention that federal computer records do not fit the phrase seems untenable.

The final requirement might appear to protect only those records based on deposits with federal court or administrative officials, but the scant case law available suggests coverage extends to any record maintained by the government.[150]

Violations of section 2071 are punishable by imprisonment for not more than three years and/or a fine of not more than $250,000, or both fine and imprisonment, 18 U.S.C. 2071, 3571.

Destruction of Federal Property. It is a federal crime to "willfully injure or commit any depredation against any property of the United States. . . ."[151] Although an offender must be shown to have to injure or depredate property, the government need not show that the defendant knew the property belonged to the government.[152] The federal courts have permitted prosecution under section 1361 of a defendant who used a hammer and drill to destroy a federal computer.[153] There are no reported cases in which section 1361 was used to prosecute electronic computer abuse for damaging federal property, and federal authorities used an earlier version of the computer abuse statute, section 1030, to prosecute one of the first cases of electronic computer abuse resulting in damage.[154]

Damage or destruction of federal property is punishable by imprisonment for not more than 10 years and/or a fine of not more than $250,000 (or not more than one year and/or a fine of not more than $100,000 if the damage

---

149 See, e.g., 26 U.S.C. 6011(e)(1)("The Secretary shall prescribe regulations providing standards for determining which returns must be filed on magnetic media or in other machine-readable form."); IRS Pub. 3112 (2007); 26 C.F.R. §301.7502—1(d) ("Electronically filed documents—(1) In general. A document filed electronically with an electronic return transmitter. . . in the manner and time prescribed by the Commissioner is deemed to be filed on the date of the electronic postmark. . .given by the authorized electronic return transmitter. Thus, if the electronic postmark is timely, the document is considered filed timely although it is received by the agency, officer, or office after the last date, or the last day of the period, prescribed for filing such document.")

150 *United States v. Lang*, 364 F.3d 1210 (10th Cir. 2004)(copy of officially filed court document), rem'd for reconsideration in light of *United States v. Booker*, 543 U.S. 220 (2005), reinstated in part, 405 F.3d 1060 (10th Cir. 2005);*United States v. Poindexter*, 725 F.Supp. 13, 19 (D.D.C. 1989)(National Security Council records); *Coplon v. United States*, 191 F.2d 749 (D.C.Cir. 1951)(FBI counter-intelligence reports).

151 "Whoever willfully injures or commits any depredation against any property of the United States, or of any department or agency thereof, or any property which has been or is being manufactured or constructed for the United States, or any department or agency thereof, or attempts to commit any of the foregoing offenses, shall be punished as follows:

"If the damage or attempted damage to such property exceeds the sum of $1,000, by a fine under this title or imprisonment for not more than ten years, or both; if the damage or attempted damage to such property does not exceed the sum of $1,000, by a fine under this title or by imprisonment for not more than one year, or both." 18 U.S.C. 1361.

152 *United States v. Urfer* 287 F.3d 663, 666 (7th Cir. 2002); but see, *United States v. Bangert*, 645 F.2d 1297, 1305 (8th Cir. 1981).

153 *United States v. Komisaruk*, 885 F.2d 490 (9th Cir. 1989).

154 *United States v. Morris*, 928 F.2d 504 (2d Cir. 1991).

causes amounts to $1,000 or less and no one dies as a result of the offense), 18 U.S.C. 1361; 18 U.S.C. 3571.

Destruction of Federal Communications Systems. Willful or malicious interference or disruption "in any way" with any communications system owned by the United States or used by the United States for military or civil defense purposes is punishable by imprisonment for not more than 10 years and/or a fine of not more than $250,000.[155] The language of section 1362 leaves little room for any contention that it does not apply to computer abuse aimed at federal communications facilities.

Damage or Destruction of Financial Institution Property

A handful of federal statutes protect financial institutions from theft in one form or another, but not property damage or destruction. Section 1030 appears to be the only statute that includes a specific provision designed to protect the property of financial institutions from damage or destruction. As with *Morris*, a defendant prosecuted under an earlier version of paragraph 1030(a)(5) questioned what level of intent was required with respect to the damage caused.[156]

Damage or Destruction to Property in Interstate Commerce

Transportation. The federal statutes, other than paragraph 1030(a)(5), most likely to cover the computerized damage or destruction to property in interstate commerce involve transportation. Each of the provisions that proscribe interference with air, motor, rail and sea transportation appear to have been drafted with sufficient breadth to reach damage or destruction of at least some of the computer systems incidental to those transportation facilities.

---

[155] 18 U.S.C. 1362; 18 U.S.C. 3571. Section 1362 provides in full that: "Whoever willfully or maliciously injures or destroys any of the works, property, or material of any radio, telegraph, telephone or cable, line, station, or system, or other means of communication, operated or controlled by the United States, or used or intended to be used for military or civil defense functions of the United States, whether constructed or in process of construction, or willfully or maliciously interferes in any way with the working or use of any such line, or system, or willfully or maliciously obstructs, hinders, or delays the transmission of any communication over any such line, or system, or attempts or conspires to do such an act, shall be fined under this title or imprisoned not more than ten years, or both

"In the case of any works, property, or material, not operated or controlled by the United States, this section shall not apply to any lawful strike activity, or other lawful concerted activities for the purposes of collective bargaining or other mutual aid and protection which do not injure or destroy any line or system used or intended to be used for the military or civil defense functions of the United States."

[156] *United States v. Sablan*, 92 F.3d 865, 867–69 (9th Cir. 1996). As originally worded, the paragraph penalized anyone who "intentionally accesse[d] a Federal interstate computer. . . and by means of. . . such conduct. . . damage[d]. . . information in such. . . computer," 18 U.S.C. 1030(a)(5)(1988 ed.). Defendants in *Morris* and *Sablan* argued unsuccessfully that the government was required to show that offender had both intentionally accessed a federal computer *and* had intentionally damaged information in the computer. The current wording eliminates the grounds for such contentions.

For example, the provisions applicable to the destruction of aircraft and aircraft facilities penalize anyone who "damages, destroys, or disables any air navigation facility. . . if such. . . damaging, destroying, [or] disabling. . . is likely to endanger the safety of any such aircraft," 18 U.S.C.32(a)(3).[157] This would presumablyprotect air traffic control systems, but not computerized passenger information, i.e., gridlock is not proscribed unless it "endanger[s] the safety" of air travel.

The language of the provisions outlawing interference with maritime navigation are strikingly comparable: "a person who unlawfully and intentionally. . . destroys or seriously damages maritime navigational facilities or serious interferes with their operation, is such act is like to endanger the safe navigation of a ship" or attempts or conspires to do so is punishable by imprisonment for not more than 20 years and/or a fine of not more than $250,000, or if death results form commission of the offense, by imprisonment

[157] Violations, attempted violations, and conspiracies to violate the provisions of section 32 are all punishable by imprisonment for not more than 20 years and/or a fine of not more than $250,000, 18 U.S.C. 32(a); 18 U.S.C. 3571; violations that result in death are punishable by life imprisonment or death, 18 U.S.C. 34. Section 32 reads in pertinent part: "(a) Whoever willfully—(1) sets fire to, damages, destroys, disables, or wrecks any aircraft in the special aircraft jurisdiction of the United States or any civil aircraft used, operated, or employed in interstate, overseas, or foreign air commerce; (2) places or causes to be placed a destructive device or substance in, upon, or in proximity to, or otherwise makes or causes to be made unworkable or unusable or hazardous to work or use, any such aircraft, or any part or other materials used or intended to be used in connection with the operation of such aircraft, if such placing or causing to be placed or such making or causing to be made is likely to endanger the safety of any such aircraft; (3) sets fire to, damages, destroys, or disables any air navigation facility, or interferes by force or violence with the operation of such facility, if such fire, damaging, destroying, disabling, or interfering is likely to endanger the safety of any such aircraft in flight; (4) with the intent to damage, destroy, or disable any such aircraft, sets fire to, damages, destroys, or disables or places a destructive device or substance in, upon, or in proximity to, any appliance or structure, ramp, landing area, property, machine, or apparatus, or any facility or other material used, or intended to be used, in connection with the operation, maintenance, loading, unloading or storage of any such aircraft or any cargo carried or intended to be carried on any such aircraft; (5) interferes or disables, with intent to endanger the safety of any person or with a reckless disregard for the safety of human life, anyone engaged in the authorized operation of such aircraft or any air navigation facility aiding in the navigation of any such aircraft; (6)performs an act of violence against or incapacitates any individual on any such aircraft, if such act of violence or incapacitation is likely to endanger the safety of such aircraft; (7) communicates information, knowing the information to be false and under circumstances in which such information may reasonably be believed, thereby endangering the safety of any such aircraft in flight; or (8) attempts or conspires to do anything prohibited under paragraphs (1) through (7) of this subsection;

shall be fined under this title or imprisoned not more than twenty years or both.

"(b) Whoever willfully—. . . (2) destroys a civil aircraft registered in a country other than the United States while such aircraft is in service or causes damage to such an aircraft which renders that aircraft incapable of flight or which is likely to endanger that aircraft's safety in flight;. . . or (4) attempts or conspires to commit an offense described in paragraphs (1) through (3) of this subsection;

shall be fined under this title or imprisoned not more than twenty years, or both. There is jurisdiction over an offense under this subsection if a national of the United States was on board, or would have been on board, the aircraft; an offender is a national of the United States; or an offender is afterwards found in the United States. . . .

"(c) Whoever willfully imparts or conveys any threat to do an act which would violate any of paragraphs (1) through (5) of subsection (a) or any of paragraphs (1) through (3) of subsection (b) of this section, with an apparent determination and will to carry the threat into execution shall be fined under this title or imprisoned not more than five years, or both."

for life or death.[158] Federal jurisdiction for prosecution exists if the offense occurs within American territorial waters, if the vessel or vessels engaged are of American registry, or if committed by American or by someone later found in this country, 18 U.S.C. 2280(b).

Similarly, attacks on mass transit are punishable by imprisonment for not more than 20 years and/or a fine of not more than $250,000, if death results from commission of the offense, by imprisonment for life or death.[159] Once again, computer abuse that targets rail traffic control is almost certainly covered; computer abuse that targets ticket control is almost certainly not.

---

[158] 18 U.S.C. 2280; 18 U.S.C. 3571. Section 2280 provides in pertinent part: "(a)(1) In general.— A person who unlawfully and intentionally. . . (C) destroys a ship or causes damage to a ship or to its cargo which is likely to endanger the safe navigation of that ship; (D) places or causes to be placed on a ship, by any means whatsoever, a device or substance which is likely to destroy that ship, or cause damage to that ship or its cargo which endangers or is likely to endanger the safe navigation of that ship; (E) destroys or seriously damages maritime navigational facilities or seriously interferes with their operation, if such act is likely to endanger the safe navigation of a ship; (F) communicates information, knowing the information to be false and under circumstances in which such information may reasonably be believed, thereby endangering the safe navigation of a ship; (G) injures or kills any person in connection with the commission or the attempted commission of any of the offenses set forth in subparagraphs (A) through (F); or (H) attempts or conspires to do any act prohibited under subparagraphs (A) through (G),

shall be fined under this title, imprisoned not more than 20 years, or both; and if the death of any person results from conduct prohibited by this paragraph, shall be punished by death or imprisoned for any term of years or for life.

"(2) Threat to navigation.—A person who threatens to do any act prohibited under paragraph (1) (B), (C) or (E), with apparent determination and will to carry the threat into execution, if the threatened act is likely to endanger the safe navigation of the ship in question, shall be fined under this title, imprisoned not more than 5 years, or both.

"(b) Jurisdiction.—There is jurisdiction over the activity prohibited in subsection (a)—(1) in the case of a covered ship, if—(A) such activity is committed—(i) against or on board a ship flying the flag of the United States at the time the prohibited activity is committed; (ii) in the United States; or (iii) by a national of the United States or by a stateless person whose habitual residence is in the United States; (B) during the commission of such activity, a national of the United States is seized, threatened, injured or killed; or (C) the offender is later found in the United States after such activity is committed;

"(2) in the case of a ship navigating or scheduled to navigate solely within the territorial sea or internal waters of a country other than the United States, if the offender is later found in the United States after such activity is committed; and

"(3) in the case of any vessel, if such activity is committed in an attempt to compel the United States to do or abstain from doing any act. . . .

"(e) Definitions.— In this section—'covered ship' means a ship that is navigating or is scheduled to navigate into, through or from waters beyond the outer limit of the territorial sea of a single country or a lateral limit of that country's territorial sea with an adjacent country; 'national of the United States' has the meaning stated in section 101(a)(22) of the Immigration and Nationality Act (8 U.S.C. 1101(a)(22)); 'territorial sea of the United States' means all waters extending seaward to 12 nautical miles from the baselines of the United States determined in accordance with international law; 'ship' means a vessel of any type whatsoever not permanently attached to the sea-bed, including dynamically supported craft, submersibles or any other floating craft, but does not include a warship, a ship owned or operated by a government when being used as a naval auxiliary or for customs or police purposes, or a ship which has been withdrawn from navigation or laid up; 'United States,' when used in a geographical sense, includes the Commonwealth of Puerto Rico, the Commonwealth of the Northern Mariana Islands and all territories and possessions of the United States."

[159] 18 U.S.C. 1992; 18 U.S.C. 3571.

The language of the federal law outlawing the destruction of motor vehicle facilities seems only slightly more modest, for it extends to anyone who "with a reckless disregard for the safety of human life," willfully "damages, destroys . . . tampers with," or otherwise makes "unworkable, unusable, or hazardous to work or use" any "facility used in the operation of, or in support of the operation of, motor vehicles engaged in interstate or foreign commerce," 18 U.S.C. 33(a).[160] Computer abuse that damages or destroys motor traffic control systems in a manner threatening to human safety would seem to fall within the reach of section 33.

Other Damage Crimes. Other federal crimes that might be implicated by damaging computer systems used in interstate or foreign commerce include those that cover damage to an energy facility[161] or proscribe interference

[160] Violations are punishable by imprisonment for not more than 20 years and/or a fine of not more than $250,000 or, if death results from commission of the offense, by imprisonment for life or death, 18 U.S.C. 33(a); 18 U.S.C. 34; 18 U.S.C. 3571.

Section 18 U.S.C. 33 states in full: "(a) Whoever willfully, with intent to endanger the safety of any person on board or anyone who he believes will board the same, or with a reckless disregard for the safety of human life, damages, disables, destroys, tampers with, or places or causes to be placed any explosive or other destructive substance in, upon, or in proximity to, any motor vehicle which is used, operated, or employed in interstate or foreign commerce, or its cargo or material used or intended to be used in connection with its operation; or

"Whoever willfully, with like intent, damages, disables, destroys, sets fire to, tampers with, or places or causes to be placed any explosive or other destructive substance in, upon, or in proximity to any garage, terminal, structure, supply, or facility used in the operation of, or in support of the operation of, motor vehicles engaged in interstate or foreign commerce or otherwise makes or causes such property to be made unworkable, unusable, or hazardous to work or use; or

"Whoever, with like intent, willfully disables or incapacitates any driver or person employed in connection with the operation or maintenance of the motor vehicle, or in any way lessens the ability of such person to perform his duties as such; or

"Whoever willfully attempts to do any of the aforesaid acts—

shall be fined under this title or imprisoned not more than twenty years, or both.

"(b) Whoever is convicted of a violation of subsection (a) involving a motor vehicle that, at the time the violation occurred, carried high-level radioactive waste (as that term is defined in section 2(12) of the Nuclear Waste Policy Act of 1982 (42 U.S.C. 10101(12))) or spent nuclear fuel (as that term is defined in section 2(23) of the Nuclear Waste Policy Act of 1982 (42 U.S.C. 10101(23))), shall be fined under this title and imprisoned for any term of years not less than 30, or for life.

[161] "(a) Whoever knowingly and willfully damages or attempts to damage the property of an energy facility in an amount that in fact exceeds or would if the attempted offense had been completed have exceeded $100,000, or damages or attempts to damage the property of an energy facility in any amount and causes or attempts to cause a significant interruption or impairment of a function of an energy facility, shall be punishable by a fine under this title or imprisonment for not more than 20 years, or both.

"(b) Whoever knowingly and willfully damages or attempts to damage the property of an energy facility in an amount that in fact exceeds or would if the attempted offense had been completed have exceeded $5,000 shall be punishable by a fine under this title, or imprisonment for not more than five years, or both.

"(c) For purposes of this section, the term 'energy facility' means a facility that is involved in the production, storage, transmission, or distribution of electricity, fuel, or another form or source of energy, or research, development, or demonstration facilities relating thereto, regardless of whether such facility is still under construction or is otherwise not functioning, except a facility subject to the jurisdiction, administration, or in the custody of the Nuclear Regulatory Commission or an interstate gas pipeline facility as defined in section 60101 of title 49.

with the operation of a communications or weather satellite.[162] Most of the states also outlaw damaging computer equipment, software, or systems.[163]

RICO. Those paragraph 1030(a)(5) damage offenses that qualify as federal crimes of terrorism—damaging a protected computer and thereby impairing medical care, causing physical injury, or threatening public health or safety; or damaging a governmental justice, national defense, or national security computer system—are by virtue of that fact RICO predicate offenses.[164] Among other things, RICO outlaws conducting the business of a commercial enterprise through the patterned commission of predicate offenses.[165]

Violations are punishable by (a) forfeiture of any property acquired through a RICO violation and of any property interest in the enterprise involved in the violation, and (b) imprisonment for not more than 20 years, or life if one of the predicate offenses carries such a penalty, and/or a fine of not more than $250,000, 18 U.S.C. 1963.

RICO violations also subject the offender to civil liability. The courts may award anyone injured by a RICO violation treble damages, costs and attorneys' fees, and may enjoin RICO violations, order divestiture, dissolution or reorganization, or restrict an offender's future professional or investment activities, 18 U.S.C. 1964.

"(d) Whoever is convicted of a violation of subsection (a) or (b) that has resulted in the death of any person shall be subject to imprisonment for any term of years or life," 18 U.S.C. 1366.

162 (a) Whoever, without the authority of the satellite operator, intentionally or maliciously interferes with the authorized operation of a communications or weather satellite or obstructs or hinders any satellite transmission shall be fined in accordance with this title or imprisoned not more than ten years or both," 18 U.S.C. 1367.

163 See, e.g., ALA.CODE 1975 §§13A-8-102, 13A-8-103; ALASKA STAT. §11.46.740; ARIZ. REV.STAT.ANN. §13-2316; ARK.CODEANN. §5-41-202; CAL.PENAL CODE §502; COLO.REV. STAT.ANN. §18-5.5-102; CONN. GEN.STAT.ANN. §53a-251; DEL.CODEANN. tit.11 §§934, 936; FLA. STAT.ANN. §§815.04, 815.06; GA. CODEANN. §16-9-93; HAWAII REV.STAT. §§708-892, 708-892.5; IDAHO CODE §18-2202; ILL.COMP.LAWS ANN. ch.720 ¶5, §§16D-3, 16D-4; IND.CODE ANN. §35-43-1-4; IOWA CODE ANN. §716.6B; KAN.STAT. ANN. §21-3755; KY. REV.STAT.ANN. §§434.845, 434.851; LA.REV.STAT.ANN. §§14:73.2 to 14:73.4, 14:73.7; ME. REV.STAT.ANN. tit.17-A §433; MD.CRIM.CODE ANN. §7-302; MICH.COMP.LAWS ANN. §752.795; MINN. STAT.ANN. §609.88; MISS.CODEANN. §§97-457, 97-45-9; MO.ANN.STAT. §§569.095 to 569.099; MONT.CODE ANN. §45-6-311; NEB.REV.STAT. §28-1345; NEV.REV. STAT. 205.4765; N.H. REV.STAT.ANN. §638:17;N.J.STAT.ANN. §2C:20-25; N.MEX.STAT. ANN. §30-45-4; N.Y.PENAL LAW §§156.10 to 156.27; N.C.GEN.STAT. §§14-455 to 14-458; N.D. CENT. CODE §12.1-06.1-08; OKLA.STAT.ANN. tit.21 §1953; ORE.REV.STAT. §164.377; PA. STAT. ANN. tit.18 §§ 7612, 7615, 7616; R.I.GEN.LAWS §11-52-4.1; S.C.CODE ANN. §16-16-20; S.D.COD. LAWS §4343B-1; TENN.CODE ANN. §39-14-602; TEX.PENAL CODE ANN. §33.02; UTAH CODE ANN. §76-6-703; VT.STAT.ANN. tit.13 §§4105-4105; VA.CODE. §18.2-152.4; WASH. REV.CODE ANN. §§9A.48.070 to 9A.48.100; W.VA.CODE ANN. §61-3C-7; WIS.STAT.ANN. §943.70; WYO. STAT. §§6-3-501 to 6-3-504.

164 18 U.S.C. 1961(1), 2332b(g)(5)(B).

165 "It shall be unlawful for any person employed by or associated with any enterprise engaged in, or the activities of which affect, interstate or foreign commerce, to conduct or participate, directly or indirectly, in the conduct of such enterprise's affairs through a pattern of racketeering activity or collection of unlawful debt.

"(d) It shall be unlawful for any person to conspire to violate any of the provisions of subsection. . . (c) of this section," 18 U.S.C. 1962(c)(d). See generally, *RICO: A Brief Sketch*, CRS Rept. 96-950.

Computer Fraud (18 U.S.C. 1030(a)(4))

(a) Whoever. . . (4) knowingly and with intent to defraud, accesses a protected computer without authorization, or exceeds authorized access, and by means of such conduct furthers the intended fraud and obtains anything of value, unless the object of the fraud and the thing obtained consists only of the use of the computer and the value of such use is not more than $5,000 in any 1-year period. . . shall be punished as provided in subsection (c) of this section.

Paragraph 1030(a)(4) outlaws fraud by computer intrusion. Its elements consist of:

- knowingly and with intent to defraud;
- accessing a protected computer without authorization, or exceeding authorization;
- thereby furthering a fraud and obtaining anything of value (other than a minimal amount of computer time, i.e., more than $5,000 over the course of a year).[166]

Jurisdiction

Paragraph 1030(a)(4) outlaws fraud against "protected computers," i.e., computers used in interstate or foreign commerce, 18 U.S.C. 1030(e)(2)(B), those used by or for "the United States Government," or those used by or for a financial institution, 18 U.S.C. 1030(e)(2)(A). As noted earlier, there may be some real doubt whether in doing so it reaches computers of the legislative and judicial branches or of the independent federal agencies, or whether it shields only those within the executive branch. The wording of some of the paragraphs of section 1030 clearly anticipates expansive coverage. Having declined to take advantage of those terms of art with respect to paragraph 1030(a)(4), should Congress be presumed to have intended a more limited reach? As noted earlier, the counterpoint is that in one paragraph of section 1030, Congress uses the phrase "Government of the United States" interchangeably with the more expansive phrase "department or agency of the United States," 18 U.S.C. 1030(a)(3). If the terms are interchangeable at one point within the section should they not be construed as interchangeable through out?

The Committee reports indicate that Congress understood the phrase "used in interstate or foreign commerce" to be the equivalent of "affecting interstate or foreign commerce," S.Rept. 104-357 at 10 (1996).

---

[166] *P.C. Yonkers, Inc. v. Celebrations the Party and Seasonal Superstore, LLC*, 428 F.3d 504, 508 (3d Cir. 2005) (A claim under CFAA §1030(a)(4) has four elements: (1) defendant has accessed a 'protected computer;' (2) has done so without authorization or by exceeding such authorization as was granted; (3) has done so 'knowingly' and with 'intent to defraud;' and (4) as a result has 'furthered the intended fraud and obtained anything of value").

Congress amended the definition of protected computer used in interstate or foreign commerce by adding the phrase "including a computer located outside the United State that is used in a manner that affects interstate or foreign commerce," 18 U.S.C. 1030(e)(2). In doing so, it might be thought to have intended to preclude overseas application of the paragraphs of 18 U.S.C. 1030 under any other circumstances, e.g., a federal computer located outside the United States that is not used in a manner that affects commerce.

Intent

Paragraph 1030(a)(4) was proposed as part of the original statute in 1984, H.Rept. 98-894 at 27 (1984), but only enacted with the 1986 amendments, P.L. 99474, 100 Stat. 1213 (1986), 18 U.S.C. 1030 (1986 Supp.). The reports accompanying the 1986 amendments note that the intent element—"knowingly and with intent to defraud"—"is the same standard used for 18 U.S.C. 1029 relating to credit card fraud," S.Rept. 99-432 at 10 (1986); H.Rept. 99-612 at 12 (1986). The phrase as used in the credit card fraud statute means that the offender is conscious of the natural consequences of his action (i.e. that it is likely that someone will be defrauded) and intends that those consequences should occur (i.e., he intends that someone should be defrauded).[167]

The phrase "thereby furthers a fraud" insures that prosecutions are limited to cases where use of a computer is central to a criminal scheme rather those where a computer is used simply as a record-keeping convenience.[168]

[167] H.Rept. 98-894 at 16-7 (1984)("A knowing state of mind with respect to an element of the offense is (1) an awareness of the nature of one' conduct, and (2) an awareness of or a firm belief in the existence of a relevant circumstance such as whether an access device was counterfeit before it was used or trafficked in. The Committee intends that the knowing state of mind requirement may be satisfied by proof that the actor was aware of a high probability of the existence of the circumstances, although a defense should succeed if it is proven that the actor actually believed that the circumstance did not exist after taking reasonable steps to warrant such belief. . . . The Committee intends that the term 'with the intent' have the same culpable state of mind as the term 'purpose' as used in the proposed Model Penal Code (§2.02). The distinction from a knowing state of mind was recently restated by Justice Rehnquist, '. . . a person who causes a particular result is said to act purposefully if he consciously desires that result, whatever the likelihood of that result happening from his conduct, while he is aid to act knowingly if he is aware that result is practically certain to follow from his conduct, whatever his desire may be as to that result.' *United States v. Bailey*, 444 U.S. 394, 404 (1980)").

[168] S.Rept. 99-432 at 9 (1986)("The Committee was concerned that computer usage that is wholly extraneous to an intended fraud might nevertheless be covered by this subsection if the subsection were patterned directly after the current mail fraud and wire fraud laws. If it were so patterned, the subsection might be construed as covering an individual who had devised a scheme or artifice to defraud solely because used a computer to keep records or to add up his potential 'take' from the crime. The Committee does not believe that a scheme or artifice to defraud should fall under the ambit of subsection (a)(4) merely because the offender signed onto a computer at some point near to the commission or execution of the fraud. While such a tenuous link might be covered under current law where the instrumentality used is the mails or the wires, the Committee does not consider that link sufficient with respect to computers. To be prosecuted under this subsection, the use of the computer must be more directly linked to the intended fraud. That is, it must be used by the offender without authorization or in excess of his authorization to obtain property of another, which property furthers in the intended fraud").

Similarly, the demand that the value of converted property exceed $5,000 avoids the possibility that mere computer trespassing would be prosecuted as fraud under the theory that lost computer time could satisfy the "thing of value" element that separates the two offenses. The $5,000 threshold overcomes this problem while permitting prosecution for repeated intrusions, S.Rept. 104-357 at 9 (1996).

The case law available thus far confirms that the difficulty of maintaining a prosecution against even a repeated trespasser under paragraph 1030(a)(4). As *United States v. Czubinski*, 106 F.3d 1069 (1st Cir. 1997), demonstrates. *Czubinski* involved an Internal Revenue Service employee who conducted a number of unauthorized searches of taxpayer files in an IRS computer system. The Court of Appeals overturned his conviction on four counts of violating paragraph 1030(a)(4) because it felt the government had failed to prove that the government had been defrauded, i.e, deprived of anything of value.[169]

Consequences

Violations are punishable by imprisonment for not more than five years (not more than 10 years for subsequent offenses) and/or a fine of not more than $250,000 (not more than $500,000 for organizations), 18 U.S.C. 1030(c)(4); 18 U.S.C. 3571.[170] The same sentencing guideline, U.S.S.G. §2B1.1, covers both fraud under paragraph 1030(a)(4), and damage under paragraph 1030(a)(5), although the escalators based on the amount of loss inflicted are likely to be more telling in the case of wide-spread damage caused by the release of a worm or virus. As discussed earlier, conviction of a paragraph 1030(a)(4) offense requires an order to make restitution and may lead to the confiscation of the fruits of the offense, 18 U.S.C. 981(a)(1)(C),

[169] "The plain language of section 1030(a)(4) emphasizes that more than mere unauthorized use is required: the 'thing obtained' may not merely be the unauthorized use. It is the showing of some additional end—to which the unauthorized access is a means—that is lacking here. The evidence did not show that Czubinski's end was anything more than to satisfy his curiosity by viewing information about friends, acquaintances, and political rivals. No evidence suggests that he printed out, recorded, or sued the information he browsed. No rational jury could conclude beyond a reasonable doubt that Czubinski intended to use or disclose that information, and merely viewing information cannot be deemed the same as obtaining something of value for the purposes of this statute. [The district court, in denying a motion to dismiss the computer fraud counts in the indictment, found that the indictment sufficiently alleged that the confidential taxpayer information was itself a thing of value to Czubinski, given his ends. The indictment, or course, alleged specific uses for the information, such as creating dossiers on KKK members, that were not proven at trial]," *United States v. Czubinski*, 106 F.3d at 1078 (portions of footnote 15 of the Court's opinion in brackets). See also, *United States v. DeMonte*, 25 F.3d 343 (6th Cir. 1994)(authority of sentencing court to order probation instead of imprisonment pursuant to a downward departure, on the basis of extraordinary circumstances, from the applicable sentencing guidelines for a violation of 18 U.S.C. 1030(4) that occurred when the defendant, a Veterans' Administration supervisory accountant made fraudulent entries in a VA computer system that result in payments to a fictitious company).

[170] The governing Sentencing Guideline calculates the applicable sentencing ranges below the statutory 5 and 10 year maximum penalties based on the amount of loss and the number of victims related to the offense, U.S.S.G. §2B1.1.

982(a)(2)(B), 3663A. Victims may sue for compensatory damages and/or injunctive relief under subsection 1030(g).[171]

Other Crimes

Paragraph 1030(a)(4) prohibits unauthorized use of a government computer, a bank computer or a computer used in interstate or foreign commerce as an integral part of a fraud. Its companions at federal criminal law include general criminal statutes, statutes proscribing theft or fraud of federal property, those that outlaw the theft or fraud of the property of financial institutions, and those that prohibit theft or fraud involving property with an interstate or foreign commerce nexus.

Interstate & Foreign Commerce

Wire Fraud. Although the wire fraud statute, 18 U.S.C. 1343, does not refer to "things of value," a phrase that encompass both the tangible and the intangible, neither does it refer exclusively to physical items such as "goods, wares, merchandises, securities or money." Rather it condemns the use of interstate or foreign wire communications pursuant to a scheme to defraud another of "money or property."[172] The Supreme Court has made it clear that "property" within its purview may include confidential information,[173] and various federal courts have made it clear that confidential information in computer storage is no less favored.[174] In fact, one commentator claims that "[t]he wire fraud statute, 18 U.S.C. 1343, has produced more convictions for computer-related crimes than §1030 or any other computer-specific statute."[175]

---

[171] Civil plaintiffs utilizing 1030(g) tend to have been more likely to successfully litigate under a violation of 1030(a)(4) than in the criminal context. See, e.g., *Creative Computing v. Getloaded.com*, 386 F.3d 930 (9th Cir. 2004)(court found that plaintiff successfully demonstrated loss of business as economic damages, and that the evidence supported a damage award and injunctive relief).

[172] "Whoever, having devised or intending to devise any scheme or artifice to defraud, or for obtaining money or property by means of false or fraudulent pretenses, representations, or promises, transmits or causes to be transmitted by means of wire, radio, or television communication in interstate or foreign commerce, any writings, signs, signals, pictures, or sounds for the purpose of executing such scheme or artifice, shall be fined under this title or imprisoned not more than five years, or both. If the violation affects a financial institution, such person shall be fined not more than $1,000,000 or imprisoned not more than 30 years, or both," 18 U.S.C. 1343; see generally, *Twenty-Second Survey of White Collar Crime: Mail and Wire Fraud*, 44 American Criminal Law Review 745 (2007); *Criminal and Civil RICO: Traditional Canons of Statutory Interpretation and the Liberal Construction Clause*, 30 Columbia Journal of Law & Social Problems 41 (1996); Lynch, *RICO: The Crime of Being a Criminal*, 87 Columbia Law Review 661 (Pts. I & II), 920 (Pts. III & IV) (1987).

[173] *Carpenter v. United States*, 484 U.S. 19, 26 (1987).

[174] *United States v. Martin*, 228 F.3d 1, 16 (1st Cir. 2000); *United States v. Czubinski*, 106 F.3d 1069, 1073–76 (1st Cir. 1997); *United States v. Wang*, 898 F.Supp. 758, 760 (D.Colo. 1995); *United States v. Seidlitz*, 589 F.2d 152, 160 (4th Cir. 1978).

[175] Olivenbaum, *<CTRL><ALT><DELETE>: Rethinking Federal Computer Crime Legislation*, Seton Hall Law Review 574, 625 (1997).

Credit Card Fraud. Section 1029 of title 18 (credit card fraud) and section 1030 (computer fraud) share a common recent history.[176] Like section 1030, section 1029 has undergone rather regular fine-tuning since its initial passage in 1984 as part of the Comprehensive Crime Control Act of that year.[177] Unlike section 1030, it has a single, uniformly applicable jurisdictional base: it applies to offenses that "affect interstate or foreign commerce."[178]

The two overlap where Section 1029 outlaws the deception of commercial computer systems through the improper use of an "access device" to acquire cash, credit, merchandise, or services.[179]

An access device is (1) any—

- card,
- personal identification number,
- plate,
- electronic serial number,
- code,
- mobile identification number, or
- any account number or other telecommunications service, equipment, or instrument identifier, or other means of account access;

[176] Each was enacted in part due to concerns about the breadth of a more narrowly crafted ancestor whose prohibitions continue in effect. In the case of section 1029, there were questions whether 15 U.S.C. 1644 (Truth in Lending Act) that outlaws the fraudulent use of credit cards could reach counterfeiting or the use of stolen credit card account numbers, H.Rept. 894, 98th Cong., 2d Sess. 5 (1984). In the case of section 1030, similar questions were raised about sweep of 15 U.S.C. 1693n (Electronic Funds Transfer Act) that outlaws the fraudulent use of bank debit cards), Id. See generally, *What Constitutes Violation of 18 USCS §1029, Prohibiting Fraud or Related Activity in Connection with Credit Card or Other Credit Access Device*, 115 ALR FED 213 (2005).

[177] P.L. 98-473, 98 Stat. 2183, 2190 (1984). Section 1029 was amended by P.L. 99-646, 100 Stat. 3601 (1986); P.L. 101-647, 104 Stat. 4831 (1990); P.L. 103-322, 108 Stat. 2087, 2148 (1994); P.L. 103-414, 108 Stat. 4291 (1994); P.L. 104-294, 110 Stat. 3501 (1996); P.L. 105172, 112 Stat. 53 (1998); P.L. 107-25,115 Stat. 342 (2001); P.L. 107-273, 116 Stat. 1808 (2002).

[178] The cases suggest that the interstate nexus must be clearly identifiable but have yet to identify the point, if any, at which the connection becomes too tenuous to support a claim of an affect on interstate commerce, see e.g., *United States v. Bolton*, 68 F.3d 396, 400 n.3 (10th Cir. 1995)(large majority of stolen credit cards in the defendant's possession had out of state addresses printed on them); *United States v. Clayton*, 108 F.3d 1114, 1118 (9th Cir. 1997). Since the misconduct proscribed is commercial in nature the question is not one of Congressional power but whether in a given case the government can and has proven that the particular misconduct "affects interstate or foreign commerce," compare *United States v. Morrison*, 529 U.S. 598, 608–9 (2000) and *United States v. Lopez*, 514 U.S. 549, 558–59 (1995)(Congress may regulate the instrumentalities and use of the channels of interstate commerce and activities that have a substantial relation to interstate commerce), with, *Jones v. United States*, 529 U.S. 848, 852 (2000) (a statute that outlaws the destruction of property "used" in commerce does not protect residential property not shown to have been used for any commercial purpose) and *Gonzales v. Raich*, 545 U.S. 1, 17 (2005) (federal government may regulate "an economic class" of intrastate activities—even if the activity itself, is noncommercial—if they are rationally related to or substantially effecting interstate commerce).

[179] As discussed below section 1029 also overlaps paragraph 1030(a)(6) that relates to trafficking in a particular access device, computer passwords.

(2) that either

(a) can be used, alone or in conjunction with another access device, to obtain money, goods, services, or any other thing of value, or

(b) can be used to initiate a transfer of funds (other than a transfer originated solely by paper instrument), 18 U.S.C. 1029(e)(1).

The level of intent for each of the several crimes established in section 1029 is the same as that often used for section 1030—"knowing and with the intent to defraud." Thus, criminal liability under section 1029 requires that the offender know that his or her actions are likely to deprive another of something of value and demands that the offender means for that deprivation to occur.[180]

Section 1029 establishes three types of crimes: misuse of access devices, conduct in anticipation of misuse of access devices, and attempts or conspiracies to commit one of these substantive violations. The misuse crimes include:

- use of a *counterfeit* access device;[181] a counterfeit access device is one that is "counterfeit, fictitious, altered, or forged, or an identifiable component of an access device or a counterfeit access device" (§1029(e)(2)(emphasis added));[182]
- use of a *unauthorized* access device resulting in a loss or gain over the course of one year worth than $1,000;[183] an unauthorized access device is one that has been "lost, stolen, expired, revoked, canceled, or obtained with intent to defraud" (§1029(e)(3)(emphasis added)); and

[180] "'With intent to defraud' means that the offender has a conscious objective, desire or purpose to deceive another person, and to induce such other person, in reliance upon such deception, to assume, create, transfer, alter or terminate a right, obligation, or power with reference to property," S.Rept. 368 at 7.

[181] "Whoever—(1) knowingly and with intent to defraud produces, uses, or traffics in one or more counterfeit access devices. . . shall, if the offense affects interstate or foreign commerce, be punished as provided in subsection (c) of this section," 18 U.S.C. 1029(a)(1).

[182] "The term 'fictitious' is intended to cover a number of different types of counterfeit devices, including representations, depictions or facsimiles of an access device. The definition is intended to be sufficiently broad to cover components of an access device or a counterfeit access device, but would exclude indistinguishable raw materials. The components would include elements of devices that are legitimate but obtained or used with an intent to defraud. Thus, any identifiable component, whether it is in fact an actual component that has been obtained in some fashion by a perpetrator with an intent to defraud or a false or counterfeit substitute for a legitimate component, would fall within the definition of counterfeit access device. The committee intends the term 'component' to include incomplete access devices or counterfeit access devices, such as any mag strips, holograms, signature panels, microchips, and blank cards of so-called 'white plastic.'" H.Rept. 98-894 at 19 (1984).

[183] "Whoever. . . knowingly and with intent to defraud traffics in or uses one or more unauthorized access devices during any one-year period, and by such conduct obtains anything of value aggregating $1,000 or more during that period. . . shall, if the offense affects interstate or foreign commerce, be punished as provided in subsection (c) of this section," 18 U.S.C. 1029(a)(2).

- use of an access device "issued to another person" resulting in a loss or gain over the course of one year worth than $1,000; again each of the uses is only criminal if done knowingly and with an intent to defraud;[184]

The "preparation" offenses of section 1029 each extend only to misconduct that affects interstate or foreign commerce and only to misconduct committed knowingly and with an intent to defraud, 18 U.S.C. 1029(a). They include:

- possession of 15 or more counterfeit or unauthorized access devices;[185]
- possession of "device-making" equipment (§1029(a)(4);[186] essentially counterfeiting paraphernalia;[187]
- offering another an access device or offering to sell information concerning an access device, without the authorization of the issue of the device;[188]
- use of a telecommunications device modified or altered to permit the unauthorized receipt of telecommunications services;[189]
- use of a scanner;[190] i.e., illegal wiretapping or electronic eavesdropping equipment;[191]

---

184 "Whoever. . . knowingly and with intent to defraud effects transactions, with 1 or more access devices issued to another person or persons, to receive payment or any other thing of value during any 1-year period the aggregate value of which is equal to or greater than $1,000. . . shall, if the offense affects interstate or foreign commerce, be punished as provided in subsection (c) of this section," 18 U.S.C. 1029(a)(5).

185 "Whoever. . . knowingly and with intent to defraud possesses fifteen or more devices which are counterfeit or unauthorized access devices. . . shall, if the offense affects interstate or foreign commerce, be punished as provided in subsection (c) of this section," 18 U.S.C. 1029(a)(3).

186 "Whoever. . . knowingly, and with intent to defraud, produces, traffics in, has control or custody of, or possesses device-making equipment. . . shall, if the offense affects interstate or foreign commerce, be punished as provided in subsection (c) of this section," 18 U.S.C. 1029(a)(4).

187 "As used in this section. . . the term 'device-making equipment' means any equipment, mechanism, or impression designed or primarily used for making an access device or a counterfeit access device," 18 U.S.C. 1029(e)(6).

188 "Whoever. . . without the authorization of the issuer of the access device, knowingly and with intent to defraud solicits a person for the purpose of -- (A) offering an access device; or (B) selling information regarding or an application to obtain an access device. . . shall, if the offense affects interstate or foreign commerce, be punished as provided in subsection (c) of this section," 18 U.S.C. 1029(a)(6).

189 "Whoever. . . knowingly and with intent to defraud uses, produces, traffics in, has control or custody of, or possesses a telecommunications instrument that has been modified or altered to obtain unauthorized use of telecommunications services. . . shall, if the offense affects interstate or foreign commerce, be punished as provided in subsection (c) of this section," 18 U.S.C. 1029(a)(7).

190 "Whoever. . . knowingly and with intent to defraud uses, produces, traffics in, has control or custody of, or possesses a scanning receiver. . . shall, if the offense affects interstate or foreign commerce, be punished as provided in subsection (c) of this section," 18 U.S.C. 1029(a)(8).

191 "The term 'scanning receiver' means a device or apparatus that can be used to intercept a wire or electronic communication in violation of chapter 119 or to intercept an electronic serial number, mobile identification number, or other identifier of any telecommunications service, equipment, or instrument," 18 U.S.C. 1029(e)(8).

- possession of computer equipment used to avoid telecommunications charges, i.e., possession of "hardware or software used for altering or modifying telecommunications instruments to obtain unauthorized access to telecommunications services";[192] and
- causing another to present credit card slips for payment with the intent to defraud.[193]

Paragraph 1029(b)(1) makes it a separate offense to attempt to commit any of the substantive crimes in subsection 1029(a) just described.[194] Paragraph 1029(b)(2) makes it a separate offense to conspire to commit any of them.[195] Attempt to carries the same penalties as the completed offense (imprisonment either for not more than 10 or not more than 15 years), but conspiracy is punishable by imprisonment for not more than half the maximum terms applicable to the underlying offense (imprisonment for not more than 5 or not more than 7.5 years), 18 U.S.C. 1029(b). One reason for the distinction may be that while attempt is merged in the completed offense so that an offender may be punished for either but not both, the crime of conspiracy is ordinarily not merged in the substantive offense so that punishment for either or both is permitted.

In any event, the maximum penalties are determined by those set for the underlying violations of subsection 1029: (1) imprisonment for not more than 10 years for first time offenses involving:

- use of counterfeit access devices, 18 U.S.C. 1029(a)(1);
- use of unauthorized access devices, 18 U.S.C. 1029(a)(2);

---

[192] "Whoever. . . knowingly and with intent to defraud uses, produces, traffics in, has control or custody of, or possesses hardware or software, knowing it has been configured to insert or modify telecommunication identifying information associated with or contained in a telecommunications instrument so that the instrument may be used to obtain telecommunications service without authorization . . . shall, if the offense affects interstate or foreign commerce, be punished as provided in subsection (c) of this section," 18 U.S.C. 1029(a)(9).

[193] "Whoever. . . without the authorization of the credit card system member* or its agent, knowingly and with intent to defraud causes or arranges for another person to present to the member or its agent, for payment, 1 or more evidences or records of transactions made by an access device; shall, if the offense affects interstate or foreign commerce, be punished as provided in subsection (c) of this section," 18 U.S.C. 1029(a)(10).

* "As used in this section. . . [t]he term 'credit card system member' means a financial institution or other entity that is a member of a credit card system, including an entity, whether affiliated with or identical to the credit card issuer, that is the sole member of a credit card system," 18 U.S.C. 1029(e)(7).

[194] "Whoever attempts to commit an offense under subsection (a) of this section shall be punished as provided in subsection (c) of this section," 18 U.S.C. 1029(b)(1).

[195] "Whoever is a party to a conspiracy of two or more persons to commit an offense under subsection (a) of this section, if any of the parties engages in any conduct in furtherance of such offense, shall be fined an amount not greater than the amount provided as the maximum fine for such offense under subsection (c) of this section or imprisoned not longer than one-half the period provided as the maximum imprisonment for such offense under subsection (c) of this section, or both," 18 U.S.C. 1029(b)(2).

- possession of 15 or more counterfeit or unauthorized access devices, 18 U.S.C. 1029(a)(3);
- unauthorized sale of an access device, 18 U.S.C. 1029(a)(6);
- possession of a device designed to avoid telephone charges, 18 U.S.C. 1029(a)(7); or
- fraudulently causing another to present credit car slips for payment, 18 U.S.C. 1029(a)(10);
- and imprisonment for not more than 15 years for first time offenses involving:
- possession of counterfeiting equipment, 18 U.S.C. 1029(a)(4);
- use of another's access device to defraud, 18 U.S.C. 1029(a)(5);
- possession of a scanner, 18 U.S.C. 1029(a)(8); or
- possession of equipment designed to avoid communications service charges, 18 U.S.C. 1029(a)(9).[196]

Defrauding the Federal Government

Conspiracy. The same statute that makes it a crime to conspire to violate federal law also makes it a federal crime to conspire to defraud the United States, 18 U.S.C. 371.[197] Unlike the mail and wire fraud statutes, a successful prosecution for conspiracy to defraud the United States does not require a showing that the defendant sought to deprive the United States or anyone else of money or property.[198] This lesser known branch of the statute has extraordinary range and "reaches any conspiracy for the purpose of

[196] Offenders are subject to fines and forfeiture as well, "(1). . . The punishment for an offense under subsection (a) of this section is—(A) in the case of an offense that does not occur after a conviction for another offense under this section—"(i) if the offense is under paragraph (1), (2), (3), (6), (7), or (10) of subsection (a), a fine under this title or imprisonment for not more than 10 years, or both; and (ii) if the offense is under paragraph (4), (5), (8), or (9), of subsection (a), a fine under this title or imprisonment for not more than 15 years, or both;

"(B) in the case of an offense that occurs after a conviction for another offense under this section, a fine under this title or imprisonment for not more than 20 years, or both; and

"(C) in either case, forfeiture to the United States of any personal property used or intended to be used to commit the offense.

"(2) Forfeiture procedure.—The forfeiture of property under this section, including any seizure and disposition of the property and any related administrative and judicial proceeding, shall be governed by section 413 of the Controlled Substances Act, except for subsection (d) of that section," 18 U.S.C. 1029(c).

[197] "If two or more persons conspire. . . to defraud the United States, or any agency thereof in any manner or for any purpose, and one or more of such persons do any act to effect the object of the conspiracy, each shall be fined under this title or imprisoned not more than five years, or both," 18 U.S.C. 371.

[198] *United States v. Goldberg*, 105 F.3d 770, 773 (1st Cir. 1997); *United States v. Clark*, 139 F.3d 485, 488–89 (5th Cir. 1998); *United States v. Gosselin World Wide Moving*, 411F.3d 502, 516 (4th Cir. 2005); *United States v. Shellef*, 507 F.3d 82, 104 (2d Cir. 2007).

impairing, obstructing or defeating the lawful function of any department of the Government."[199] There need be no evidence of any other underlying substantive offense or purpose.[200] "The government need only show (1) that the defendant entered into an agreement (2) to obstruct a lawful function of the government (3) by deceitful or dishonest means and (4) at least one overt act in furtherance of the conspiracy."[201]

Fraud Involving Government Computers. There are also a host of federal criminal statutes that proscribe fraud in one form or other, more than a few of which would cover the unauthorized manipulation of federal computers as an integral part of a scheme to defraud. Two of the more prominent, the false statement statute, 18 U.S.C. 1001 (false statements on a matter within the jurisdiction of a federal agency or department) and conspiracy to defraud the United States, 18 U.S.C. 371, have already been mentioned. Others include 18 U.S.C. 1031 (major procurement fraud against the United States);[202] 18 U.S.C. 1035 (false statements relating to health care);[203] 18 U.S.C. 1014 (false statements on federally insured loan and credit applications);[204]

---

[199] *Tanner v. United States*, 483 U.S. 107, 128 (1987), citing, *Dennis v. United States*, 384 U.S. 855, 861 (1966); *Hass v. Henkel*, 216 U.S. 462, 479 (1910); *Glasser v. United States*, 315 U.S. 60, 66 (1942); *Hammerschmidt v. United States*, 265 U.S. 182, 188 (1924); *Gosselin World Wide Moving*, 411 F.3 502, 516 (4th Cir.2005); *United States v. McKee*, 506 F.3d 225, 238 (3d Cir. 2007).

[200] *United States v. Ballistrea*, 101 F.3d 827, 832 (2d Cir. 1996)("so long as deceitful or dishonest means are employed to obstruct governmental functions, the impairment need not involve the violation of a separate statute"); *United States v. Khalife*, 106 F.3d 1300, 1303 (6th Cir. 1997); *United States v. Douglas*, 398 F.3d 407, 412 (6th Cir. 2005)("a conviction under section 371 does not require the government to prove a violation of a separate substantive statute").

[201] *United States v. Shellef*, 507 F.3d 82, 107 (2d Cir. 2007); *United States v. Dean*, 55 F.3d 640, 647 (D.C.Cir. 1994); *United States v. Hansen*, 262 F.3d 1217, 1246 (11th Cir. 2001)("To obtain a conviction under 18 U.S.C. § 371, the government must show: (1) the existence of an agreement to achieve an unlawful objective; (2) the defendant's knowing and voluntary participation in the conspiracy; and (3) the commission of an overt act in furtherance of the conspiracy").

[202] "(a) Whoever knowingly executes, or attempts to execute, any scheme or artifice with the intent—(1) to defraud the United States; or (2) to obtain money or property by means of false or fraudulent pretenses, representations, or promises—in any procurement of property or services as a prime contractor with the United States or as a subcontractor or supplier on a contract in which there is a prime contract with the United States, if the value of the contract, subcontract, or any constituent part thereof, for such property or services is $1,000,000 or more shall, subject to the applicability of subsection (c) of this section, be fined not more than $1,000,000, or imprisoned not more than 10 years, or both.

"(b) The fine imposed for an offense under this section may exceed the maximum otherwise provided by law, if such fine does not exceed $5,000,000 and—(1) the gross loss to the Government or the gross gain to a defendant is $500,000 or greater; or (2) the offense involves a conscious or reckless risk of serious personal injury.

"(c) The maximum fine imposed upon a defendant for a prosecution including a prosecution with multiple counts under this section shall not exceed $10,000,000. . . ." 18 U.S.C. 1031.

[203] "Whoever, in any matter involving a health care benefit program, knowingly and willfully— (1) falsifies, conceals, or covers up by any trick, scheme, or device a material fact; or (2) makes any materially false, fictitious, or fraudulent statements or representations, or makes or uses any materially false writing or document knowing the same to contain any materially false, fictitious, or fraudulent statement or entry, in connection with the delivery of or payment for health care benefits, items, or services, shall be fined under this title or imprisoned not more than five years, or both," 18 U.S.C. 1035(a).

[204] "Whoever knowingly makes any false statement or report, or willfully overvalues any land, property or security, for the purpose of influencing in any way the action of the Farm Credit Administration, Federal Crop Insurance Corporation or a company the Corporation reinsures, the Secretary of

18 U.S.C. 1010, 1012 (false statements concerning various HUD transactions);[205] and 18 U.S.C. 287 (false claims against the United States).[206]

Bank Fraud. Although less numerous, several federal criminal statutes outlaw defrauding financial institutions in language similar to the prohibitions against defrauding the United States, most notably the general bank

Agriculture acting through the Farmers Home Administration or successor agency, the Rural Development Administration or successor agency, any Farm Credit Bank, production credit association, agricultural credit association, bank for cooperatives, or any division, officer, or employee thereof, or of any regional agricultural credit corporation established pursuant to law, or a Federal land bank, a Federal land bank association, a Federal Reserve bank, a small business investment company, as defined in section 103 of the Small Business Investment Act of 1958 (15 U.S.C. 662), or the Small Business Administration in connection with any provisions of that act, a Federal credit union, an insured State-chartered credit union, any institution the accounts of which are insured by the Federal Deposit Insurance Corporation, the Office of Thrift Supervision, any Federal home loan bank, the Federal Housing Finance Board, the Federal Deposit Insurance Corporation, the Resolution Trust Corporation, the Farm Credit System Insurance Corporation, or the National Credit Union Administration Board, a branch or agency of a foreign bank (as such terms are defined in paragraphs (1) and (3) of section 1(b) of the International Banking Act of 1978), or an organization operating under section 25 or section 25(a) of the Federal Reserve Act, upon any application, advance, discount, purchase, purchase agreement, repurchase agreement, commitment, or loan, or any change or extension of any of the same, by renewal, deferment of action or otherwise, or the acceptance, release, or substitution of security therefor, shall be fined not more than $1,000,000 or imprisoned not more than 30 years, or both. . . ." 18 U.S.C. 1014.

205 "Whoever, for the purpose of obtaining any loan or advance of credit from any person, partnership, association, or corporation with the intent that such loan or advance of credit shall be offered to or accepted by the Department of Housing and Urban Development for insurance, or for the purpose of obtaining any extension or renewal of any loan, advance of credit, or mortgage insured by such Department, or the acceptance, release, or substitution of any security on such a loan, advance of credit, or for the purpose of influencing in any way the action of such Department, makes, passes, utters, or publishes any statement, knowing the same to be false, or alters, forges, or counterfeits any instrument, paper, or document, or utters, publishes, or passes as true any instrument, paper, or document, knowing it to have been altered, forged, or counterfeited, or willfully overvalues any security, asset, or income, shall be fined under this title or imprisoned not more than two years, or both," 18 U.S.C. 1010.

"Whoever, with intent to defraud, makes any false entry in any book of the Department of Housing and Urban Development or makes any false report or statement to or for such Department; or whoever receives any compensation, rebate, or reward, with intent to defraud such Department or with intent unlawfully to defeat its purposes; or whoever induces or influences such Department to purchase or acquire any property or to enter into any contract and willfully fails to disclose any interest which he has in such property or in the property to which such contract relates, or any special benefit which he expects to receive as a result of such contract—shall be fined under this title or imprisoned not more than one year, or both," 18 U.S.C. 1012.

206 "Whoever makes or presents to any person or officer in the civil, military, or naval service of the United States, or to any department or agency thereof, any claim upon or against the United States, or any department or agency thereof, knowing such claim to be false, fictitious, or fraudulent, shall be imprisoned not more than five years and shall be subject to a fine in the amount provided in this title," 18 U.S.C. 287; see generally, *Twenty-Second Survey of White Collar Crime: False Statements and False Claims*, 44 American Criminal Law Review 491 (2007).

fraud provision, 18 U.S.C. 1344[207] and the laws that proscribe embezzlement and similar misconduct by bank officers and employees.[208]

General crimes

CAN-SPAM Act. The criminal provisions of the Controlling the Assault of Non-Solicited Pornography and Marketing Act of 2003 (CAN-SPAM), 18 U.S.C. 1037, generally broadens the type of coverage given by section 1030 and adds to the federal government's ability to prosecute hackers who use e-mail for fraudulent purposes. More precisely, it proscribes, when done knowingly and in a manner in or affecting interstate or foreign commerce:

- accessing a protected computer and intentionally sending multiple e-mails (100 a day month, 1,000 a month, or 10,000 a year), 18 U.S.C. 1037(a)(1), (d)(3);
- using a protected computer to send commercial e-mails with the intent to deceive or mislead as to their source, 18 U.S.C. 1037(a)(2);
- materially altering an e-mail header and sending out multiple e-mails under the falsified header, 18 U.S.C. 1037(a)(3), (d)(3);
- registering for 5 or more e-mail accounts or 2 or domain names providing false identification and using them to send out multiple commercial e-mails, 18 U.S.C. 1037(a)(4), (d)(3); or
- providing false identification to registrant of 5 or more IP addresses and using the addresses to send out multiple commercial e-mails, or conspires to do so, 18 U.S.C. 1037(a)(5), (d)(3).

---

[207] "Whoever knowingly executes, or attempts to execute, a scheme or artifice—(1) to defraud a financial institution; or (2) to obtain any of the moneys, funds, credits, assets, securities, or other property owned by, or under the custody or control of, a financial institution, by means of false or fraudulent pretenses, representations, or promises—shall be fined not more than $1,000,000 or imprisoned not more than 30 years, or both," 18 U.S.C. 1344; see generally, *Twenty-Second Survey of White Collar Crime: Financial Institution Fraud*, 44 American Criminal Law Review 555 (2007).

[208] Whoever, being an officer, director, agent or employee of, or connected in any capacity with any Federal Reserve bank, member bank, depository institution holding company, national bank, insured bank, branch or agency of a foreign bank, or organization operating under section 25 or section 25(a) of the Federal Reserve Act [12 U.S.C.A. ss 601 et seq., 611 et seq.], or a receiver of a national bank, insured bank, branch, agency, or organization or any agent or employee of the receiver, or a Federal Reserve Agent, or an agent or employee of a Federal Reserve Agent or of the Board of Governors of the Federal Reserve System, embezzles, abstracts, purloins or willfully misapplies any of the moneys, funds or credits of such bank, branch, agency, or organization or holding company or any moneys, funds, assets or securities intrusted to the custody or care of such bank, branch, agency, or organization, or holding company or to the custody or care of any such agent, officer, director, employee or receiver, shall be fined not more than $1,000,000 or imprisoned not more than 30 years, or both; but if the amount embezzled, abstracted, purloined or misapplied does not exceed $1,000, he shall be fined under this title or imprisoned not more than one year, or both," 18 U.S.C. 656; see also, 18 U.S.C. 657 (theft or embezzlement by officer or employee of lending, credit or insurance institution); 1005 (false entries by bank officers or employees); 1006 (false entries by officers or employees of federal credit institutions); 1007 (false statemetns to influence the Federal Deposit Insurance Corporation).

Offenders face one of a number of sentences ranging from imprisonment for not more than a year to imprisonment for not more than 5 years depending on the extent and regularity of the offense, among other factors.[209] When the offense is punishable by imprisonment for not more than a year, offenders also face to a fine of not more than $100,000 (not more than $200,000 for organizations); those guilty of other violations of section 1037 face fines of not more than $250,000 (not more than $500,000 for organizations), 18 U.S.C. 3571. Any property used in, or realized through, the commission of the offense is subject to confiscation, 18 U.S.C. 1037(c).

Attempt, Conspiracy, and Complicity. The same general observations concerning attempt, conspiracy and aiding and abetting noted for the simple trespass paragraph apply here. It is a separate crime to attempt to violate paragraph 1030(a)(4), 18 U.S.C. 1030(b). Those who attempt to do so or who aid and abet the violation of another are subject to the same penalties as those commit the substantive offense, 18 U.S.C. 1030(c), 2. The same is true of conspiracies except that conspiracy to commit a felony carries a five year maximum of imprisonment, 18 U.S.C. 371.

Money Laundering. The principal federal money laundering statutes, 18 U.S.C. 1956 and 1957, outlaw various financial activities that involve the proceeds from other federal crimes. They prohibit:

- domestic laundering the proceeds of these predicate offenses, referred to as "specified unlawful activities;"
- international laundering the proceeds of predicate offenses;
- using the proceeds of predicate offenses to promote further predicate offenses;[210] or

[209] "The punishment for an offense under subsection (a) is—(1) a fine under this title, imprisonment for not more than 5 years, or both, if—(A) the offense is committed in furtherance of any felony under the laws of the United States or of any State; or (B) the defendant has previously been convicted under this section or section 1030, or under the law of any State for conduct involving the transmission of multiple commercial electronic mail messages or unauthorized access to a computer system;

"(2) a fine under this title, imprisonment for not more than 3 years, or both, if—(A) the offense is an offense under subsection (a)(1); (B) the offense is an offense under subsection (a)(4) and involved 20 or more falsified electronic mail or online user account registrations, or 10 or more falsified domain name registrations; (C) the volume of electronic mail messages transmitted in furtherance of the offense exceeded 2,500 during any 24-hour period, 25,000 during any 30-day period, or 250,000 during any 1-year period; (D) the offense caused loss to one or more persons aggregating $5,000 or more in value during any 1-year period; (E) as a result of the offense any individual committing the offense obtained anything of value aggregating $5,000 or more during any 1-year period; or (F) the offense was undertaken by the defendant in concert with three or more other persons with respect to whom the defendant occupied a position of organizer or leader; and

"(3) a fine under this title or imprisonment for not more than 1 year, or both, in any other case, " 18 U.S.C. 1037(b).

[210] 18 U.S.C. 1956 (text appended).

- spending or depositing more than $10,000 of the proceeds of predicate offenses.[211]

Offenses under the various paragraphs of 18 U.S.C. 1030 are all money laundering predicate offenses, 18 U.S.C. 1956(c)(7)(D), 1957(f)(3). Directly or indirectly they will support a money laundering prosecution as will several of the crimes that may be implicated whenever a paragraph 1030(a)(4) fraud offense is involved: i.e., credit card fraud (18 U.S.C. 1029), and wire fraud (18 U.S.C. 1343).

Financial transactions are defined broadly for money laundering purposes to encompass virtually every possible transfer of wealth,[212] as long as they "in any way or degree affect[] interstate or foreign commerce . . . or . . . involving the use of a financial institution which is engaged in, or the activities of which affect, interstate or foreign commerce in any way or degree," 18 U.S.C. 1956(c)(4). The proof required to satisfy this "any way or degree" jurisdictional element, even after *Lopez*, has been characterized as "de minimis," "minimal," "slight," or "incidental."[213]

To establish "promotion" the government need show little more than that the transaction is intended to further the illicit scheme, activity or business.[214]

---

[211] 18 U.S.C. 1957.

[212] "(4) the term 'financial transaction' means (A) a transaction* which in any way or degree affects interstate or foreign commerce (i) involving the movement of funds by wire or other means or (ii) involving one or more monetary instruments,** or (iii) involving the transfer of title to any real property, vehicle, vessel, or aircraft, or (B) a transaction involving the use of a financial institution which is engaged in, or the activities of which affect, interstate or foreign commerce in any way or degree," 18 U.S.C. 1956(c)(4).

* "The term 'transaction' includes a purchase, sale, loan, pledge, gift, transfer, delivery, or other disposition, and with respect to a financial institution includes a deposit, withdrawal, transfer between accounts, exchange of currency, loan, extension of credit, purchase or sale of any stock, bond, certificate of deposit, or other monetary instrument, use of a safe deposit box, or any other payment, transfer, or delivery by, through, or to a financial institution, by whatever means effected," 18 U.S.C. 1956(c)(3).

** "The term 'monetary instruments' means (i) coin or currency of the United States or of any other country, travelers' checks, personal checks, bank checks, and money orders, or (ii) investment securities or negotiable instruments, in bearer form or otherwise in such form that title thereto passes upon delivery," 18 U.S.C. 1956(c)(5).

[213] *United States v. Ables*, 167 F.3d 1021, 1029 (6th Cir. 1999); *United States v. Owens*, 167 F.3d 739, 755 (1st Cir. 1999); *United States v. Meshack*, 225 F.3d 556, 572 (5th Cir. 2000); *United States v. Oliveros*, 275 F.3d 1299, 1303 (11th Cir. 2001); *United States v. Ramerez*, 313 F. Supp. 2d 276, 279 (S.D.N.Y. 2004) In *United States v. Lopez*, 514 U.S. 549 (1995), the United States Supreme Court held that Gun Free School Zone Act, which purported to make it a federal crime to possess a gun in or near a school, failed to claim or exhibit the nexus to interstate or foreign commerce necessary to constitute the valid exercise of Congress' legislative authority under the Constitution's commerce clause.

[214] *United States v. Williamson*, 339 F.3d 1295, 1302 (11th Cir. 2003) (depositing and cashing checks of proceeds of fraud promoted present and future unlawful activities); *United States v. Rivera*, 295 F.3d 461, 469 (5th Cir. 2002)(bank withdrawal of a portion of the proceeds of a fraudulent scheme to pay a co-conspirator his share constituted "promotion"); see also, *United States v. Febus*, 218 F.3d 784, 790 (7th Cir. 1999) (operator of illegal gambling enterprise "promoted" the venture for money laundering purposes by paying off winning customers and thereby ensuring their continued patronage); *United States v. Meshack*, 225 F.3d 556, 573 (5th Cir. 2000)(defendant's use of drug money to pay the rent on his girlfriend's apartment where drugs were stored and which was used "in an attempt to conceal the conspiracy" was sufficient to establish promotion of the drug trafficking conspiracy);

"The elements necessary to prove a violation of §1957 are that:

(1) the defendant engage or attempt to engage

(2) in a monetary transaction

(3) in criminally derived property that is of a value greater than $10,000

(4) knowing that the property is derived from unlawful activity, and

(5) the property is, in fact, derived from 'specified unlawful activity.'"[215]

The predicate offenses are the same as those for section 1956, 18 U.S.C. 1957(f)(3), the meaning of "monetary transaction" closely tracks that of a "financial transaction" in section 1956,[216] and the definition of monetary transaction includes the jurisdiction component of the offense, that is, that the transaction occurs "in or affecting interstate or foreign commerce," 18 U.S.C. 1957(f)(1), which requires no more than the de minimis nexus demanded of section 1956.[217]

State Computer Fraud Law. Although the elements vary considerably, most states have explicit statutory prohibitions against computer fraud.[218]

United States v. Bockius, 228 F.3d 305, 310 n.8 (3d Cir. 2000)(noting its holding in *United States v. Paramo*, 998 F.2d 1212, 1218 (3d Cir. 1993) (that a rationale jury could have concluded that cashing embezzled IRS checks was intended to promote the antecedent frauds).

[215] *United States v. Sokolow*, 91 F.3d 396, 408 (3d Cir. 1996); *United States v. Rivera-Hernandez*, 497 F3d 71,76 (1st Cir. 2007); *United States v. Rayborn*, 491 F.3d 513, 517 (6th Cir. 2007). Or more precisely, " (a) Whoever, in any of the circumstances set forth in subsection (d), knowingly engages or attempts to engage in a monetary transaction in criminally derived property that is of a value greater than $10,000 and is derived from specified unlawful activity, shall be punished as provided in subsection (b). "(b)(1) Except as provided in paragraph (2), the punishment for an offense under this section is a fine under title 18, United States Code, or imprisonment for not more than ten years or both. (2) The court may impose an alternate fine to that imposable under paragraph (1) of not more than twice the amount of the criminally derived property involved in the transaction.

"(c) In a prosecution for an offense under this section, the Government is not required to prove the defendant knew that the offense from which the criminally derived property was derived was specified unlawful activity.

"(d) The circumstances referred to in subsection (a) are—(1) that the offense under this section takes place in the United States or in the special maritime and territorial jurisdiction of the United States; or (2) that the offense under this section takes place outside the United States and such special jurisdiction, but the defendant is a United States person (as defined in section 3077 of this title, but excluding the class described in paragraph (2)(D) of such section). . ." 18 U.S.C. 1957(a)-(d).

[216] "As used in this section—(1) the term 'monetary transaction' means the deposit, withdrawal, transfer, or exchange, in or affecting interstate or foreign commerce, of funds or a monetary instrument (as defined in section 1956(c)(5) of this title) by, through, or to a financial institution (as defined in section 1956 of this title), including any transaction that would be a financial transaction under section 1956(c)(4)(B) of this title, but such term does not include any transaction necessary to preserve a person's right to representation as guaranteed by the sixth amendment to the Constitution," 18 U.S.C. 1957(f)(1).

[217] *United States v. Aramony*, 88 F.3d 1369, 1386 (4th Cir. 1996); *United States v. Kunzman*, 54 F.3d 1522, 1527 (10th Cir. 1995); it is enough, for example, for the government to show that the transaction involved a federally insured bank, *United States v. Benjamin*, 252 F.3d 1, 8 (1st Cir. 2001); *United States v. Ford*, 184 F.3d 566, 583–84 (6th Cir. 1999); *United States v. Wadena*, 152 F.3d 831, 853 (8th Cir. 1998).

[218] Ala.Code §§13A-8-102, 13A-8-103; Alaska Stat. §11.46.740; Ariz.Rev. Stat.Ann. §13-2316, 2316.02; Ark.Code Ann. §5-41-103; Cal.Penal Code §502; Colo.Rev. Stat.Ann. §18-5.5-102; Conn.Gen. Stat.Ann. §53a-251; Del.CodeAnn. tit.11 §§933; Fla.Stat. Ann. §815.04; Ga.Code Ann. §16-9-93, 93.1; Hawaii Rev.Stat. §708-891, 891.5; Idaho Code §18-2202; Ill. Comp.Stat.Ann. 720 5/16D-5;

Extortionate Threats (18 U.S.C. 1030(a)(7))

Whoever. . . (7) with intent to extort from any person any money or other thing of value, transmits in interstate or foreign commerce any communication containing any threat to cause damage to a protected computer. . . shall be punished as provided in subsection (c) of this section.

Congress added paragraph 1030(a)(7) in 1996 out of concern that "the 'property' protected under existing laws, such as the Hobbs Act, 18 U.S.C. 1951 (interference with commerce by extortion), or 18 U.S.C. 875(d)(interstate communication of threat to injury property of another), does not clearly include the operation of a computer, the data or programs stored in a computer or its peripheral equipment, or the decoding keys to encrypted data," S.Rept. 357 at 12. The paragraph provides that no one shall

- transmit in interstate or foreign commerce
- any communication containing any threat
- to cause damage, (i.e., "any impairment to the integrity or availability of data, a program, a system, or information," (1030(e)(8)))
- to a protected computer, [i.e. one
  - — used exclusively for or by the federal government;
  - — used exclusively for or by a bank or other financial institution;
  - — used in part for or by the federal government where the damage would "affect" government use or use of the government's behalf;
  - — used in part for or by a bank or other financial institution where the damage would "affect" use by or on behalf of the institution; or
  - — used in interstate or foreign commerce or communications (1030(e)(2))]
- with the intent to extort money or a thing of value
- from any person [i.e. any individual, firm, association, educational institution, financial institution, government entity, legal or other entity (1030(3)(12))].

KAN.STAT.ANN. §213755; KY.REV.STAT.ANN. §434.845; LA. REV.STAT.ANN. §14:73.5; ME. REV.STAT. ANN. tit.17-A §433; MICH.COMP.LAWS ANN. §752.794; MINN.STAT.ANN. §609.89; MISS. CODE ANN. §97-45-3; MONT.CODE ANN. §45-6-311; NEB.REVSTAT. §28-1344; NEV.REV. STAT. 205.4765, 481; N. H.REV.STAT.ANN. §638:17; N.J.STAT.ANN. §2C:20–25; N.MEX.STAT. ANN.§30-45-3; N.Y. PENAL LAW §§156.10 to 156.30; N.C.GEN.STAT. §§14-454, 14-454.1, 14-458; N.D. CENT.CODE §12.1-06.1-08; OKLA. STAT.ANN. tit.21 § 1953; ORE.REV.STAT. §164.377; PA.STAT.ANN. tit.18 §§7611, 7613; R.I.GEN.LAWS §11-52-2; S.C. CODE ANN. §16-16-20; S.D.COD.LAWS §43-43B-1; TENN.CODE ANN. §39-14-602; TEX.PENAL CODE ANN. §33.02; UTAH CODE ANN. §76-10-1801; VT.STAT.ANN. tit.13 §4103; VA.CODE §18.2152.3; WASH. REV.CODE ANN. §9A.52.110; W.VA.CODE ANN. §61-3C-4; WIS.STAT.ANN. §943.70; WYO.STAT. §6-3-502.

Jurisdiction

Paragraph 1030(a)(7) stands on dual jurisdictional footings. First, a successful prosecution is only possible if a threat with intent to extort has been transmitted in interstate or foreign commerce, an element that may be satisfied even in the case of intrastate communications under some circumstances.[219] Second, conviction can only be had if the transmitted threat is directed against a protected computer, i.e., one used in or for interstate or foreign commerce, one used by or for the federal government, or one used by or for a financial institution, 18 U.S.C. 1030(e)(2).

Prior to the 2001 amendment to the definition of "protected computer," a paragraph 1030(a)(7) extortion proscription was said to apply to an extortionate threat initiated overseas but directed at a computer within this country.[220] Then in 2001, Congress noted that the class of computers protected because of their use in interstate or foreign commerce, 18 U.S.C. 1030(e)(2)(B)(2000 ed.), should be understood to "include a computer located outside the United States that is used in a manner than affects interstate or foreign commerce or communication of the United States."[221] The question arises whether by specifying this particular form of overseas application Congress intended to exclude all others left unmentioned.

Threat of "Damage"

Paragraph 1030(a)(7) proscribes threats to cause computer "damage" and the legislative history describes its reach in terms consistent with the common understanding of the word "damage":

> "New section 1030(a)(7) would close [the] gap in the law and provide penalties for the interstate or international transmission of threats directed against computers and computer systems. This covers any interstate or international transmission of threats against computers, computer networks, and their data and programs whether the threat is received by mail, a telephone call, electronic mail, or through a computerized massaging service. *Unlawful threats could include interference in any way with the normal operation of the computer or system in question*, such as denying access to authorized users, erasing or corrupting data or programs, slowing down the operation of the computer or system, or encrypting data and then demanding money for the key," S.Rept. 357 at 12 (emphasis added).

Prior to the USA PATRIOT Act amendments, the paragraph did not cover all threats to interfere with the normal operation of protected computers, but only threats to "damage" protected computers and only "damage" as

[219] See e.g., *United States v. Kammersell*, 196 F.3d 1137, 1138-140 (10th Cir. 1999)(a threat communicated between two computers in Utah involved interstate communications because the communications was forwarded by way of AOL's server in Virginia).

[220] *United States v. Ivanov*, 175 F.Supp.2d 367, 374 (D.Conn. 2001).

[221] Section 814(d)(1), P.L. 107-56, 115 Stat. 384 (2001), amending 18 U.S.C. 1030j(e)(2)(B).

then defined in section 1030, i.e., "any impairment to the integrity or availability of data, a program, a system, or information, that—(A) causes loss aggregating at least $5,000 in value during any 1-year period to one or more individuals; (B) modifies or impairs, or potentially modifies or impairs, the medical examination, diagnosis, treatment, or care of one or more individuals; (C) causes physical injury to any person; or (D) threatens public health or safety," 18 U.S.C. 1030(e)(8)(2000 ed.). The act expanded the damage definition and thus the coverage of the paragraph by reducing the definition to "any impairment to the integrity or availability of data, a program, a system, or information," 18 U.S.C. 1030(e)(8).

Intent

The level of intent required for a violation of paragraph 1030(a)(7) differs from the level used for the fraud provisions of section 1030. Rather than the demand that the offense be committed "knowingly and with an intent to defraud;" offenses under paragraph 1030(a)(7) must be committed "with the intent to extort." Because the crime is only complete if committed with this intent to extort, it anticipates that the offender will have intended his victim to feel threatened. The paragraph thereby avoids some of the uncertainty that has plagued the threat statutes.[222]

Threats

Construction of the threat statutes may provide useful insight, however, into what constitutes a "threat" for purposes of paragraph 1030(a)(7). Although statements of political hyperbole may not always constitute true threats,[223] a threat is no less a threat because it is contingent,[224] because the

[222] The circuits are divided over the question of whether in order to convict under some of the threat statutes, the government must show that the defendant intended the victim to feel threatened or merely intended the conduct that a reasonable person would consider threatening. *United States v. Darby*, 37 F.3d 1059, 1963–66 (4th Cir. 1994)(and the conflicting cases cited there)("to establish a violation of section 875(c) the government must establish that the defendant intended to transmit the interstate communication and that the communication contained a true threat. . . . The government does not have to prove that the defendant subjectively intended for the recipient to understand the communication as a threat"); *United States v. Alkhabaz (Baker)*, 104 F.3d 1492, 1495 (6th Cir. 1997)("to constitute a communication containing a threat under Section 875(c), a communication must be such that a reasonable person (1) would take the statement as a serious express of an intention to inflict bodily harm (the mens rea), and (2) would perceive such expression as being communicated to effect some change or achieve some goal through intimidation (the actus reus)"); *United States v. Stewart*, 411 F.3d 825, 828 (7th Cir. 2005)("guilt is not dependent upon what the defendant intended, but whether the recipient could reasonably have regarded the defendant's statement as a threat")(court declines to follow contradictory Ninth Circuit precedent, *id*. at 828 n4).

[223] *United States v. Hinkson*, 349 F.Supp.2d 1350, 1355 (D. Idaho 2004) ("Certain expressions, including 'vehement, caustic, and sometimes unpleasantly sharp attacks on Government and public officials[,]' may be protected free speech")(citing *Watts v. United States*, 394 U.S. 705, 708 (1969)); *United States v. Bly*, 510 F.3d 453, 458 (4th Cir. 2007). Moreover, "generally, a person who informs someone that he or she is in danger from a third party has not made a threat," *New York ex rel. Spitzer v. Operation Rescue National*, 273 F.3d 184, 196 (2d Cir. 2001).

[224] *United States v. Patrick*, 117 F.3d 375, 377 (8th Cir. 1997)("that Patrick's threat was contingent upon his release from prison does not save him from violating section 876"); *United States v. Viefhaus*,

speaker does not intend or is unable to carry it out,[225] because the threat was not directly communicated to the target,[226] or because the language used might be considered cryptic or ambiguous.[227] Whether a particular communication constitutes a threat is a question determined by whether a reasonable person, considering all the circumstances, would regard the communication as a threat.[228] While the jurisdictional element, such as transmission in interstate commerce, must be established,[229] the government need not show the defendant knew that the threat had been transported interstate commerce.[230]

Consequences

Penalties & Civil Liability. Violations are punishable by imprisonment for not more than five years (not more than 10 years for second and subsequent offenses) and/or a fine of not more than $250,000, and in cases involving more than $5000 damage or some other qualifying circumstance, victims may claim the advantages of the civil cause of action for damages available under 18 U.S.C. 1030(g).[231] The general fraud/damage sentencing guideline, U.S.S.G. §2B1.1, applies to violations of paragraph (a)(7).

168 F.3d 392, 396 (10th Cir. 1999); *United States v. Bly*, 510 F.3d 453, 459 (4th Cir. 2007); as the phrase "your money or your life" demonstrates, contingent threats are an essential component of robbery and extortion.

225 *United States v. Cassel*, 408 F.3d 622, 627–28 (9th Cir. 2005);*United States v. Saunders*, 166 F.3d 907, 914 (7th Cir. 1999); *United States v. Martin*, 163 F.3d 1212, 1216 (10th Cir. 1998).

226 *United States v. Floyd*, 458 F.3d 844, 849 (8th Cir. 2006); *United States v. Hinkson*, 349 F. Supp. 2d 1350, 1355 (D. Idaho 2004).

227 *United States v. Fulmer*, 108 F.3d 1486, 1492 (1st Cir. 1997); *United States v. Malik*, 16 F.3d 45, 49 (2nd Cir. 1994).

228 *United States v. England*, 507 F.3d 581, 589 (7th Cir. 2007); *United States v. Francis*, 164 F.3d 120, 123 (2d Cir. 1999); *United States v. Morales*, 272 F.3d 284, 287 (5th Cir. 2001). *United States v. Stewart*, 411 F.3d 825, 828 (7th Cir. 2005) ("the government must prove that the statement came in a context or under such circumstances wherein a reasonable person would foresee that the statement would be interpreted by those to whom the maker communicates a statement as a serious expression of an intention to inflict bodily harm upon or to take the life of [another individual].")

229 *United States v. Korab*, 893 F.2d 212, 214–15 (9th Cir. 1989).

230 *United States v. Darby*, 37 F.3d at 1063–64; see also, *United States v. Kammersell*, 196 F.3d 1137, 1139–140 (10th Cir. 1999)(a threatening computer message from defendant in Utah to his girlfriend's place of employment within the same state constituted transmission of a threatening communication in interstate commerce because the message was transmitted by way of the defendant's service provider's main server in Virginia; see also *United States v. Guerva*, 408 F.3d 252, 259 (5th Cir. 2005)(court finding that threat that led to the temporary closing of a federal building and the shutting down of various federal agencies resulted in threat affecting interstate commerce).

231 ". . . A civil action for a violation of this section may be brought only if the conduct involves 1 of the factors set forth in clause (i), (ii), (iii), (iv), or (v) of subsection (a)(5)(B). . ." 18 U.S.C. 1030(g). The qualifying circumstances described in clauses (a)(5)(B)(i) through (v) are: "(i) loss to 1 or more persons during any 1-year period (and, for purposes of an investigation, prosecution, or other proceeding brought by the United States only, loss resulting from a related course of conduct affecting 1 or more other protected computers) aggregating at least $5,000 in value; (ii) the modification or impairment, or potential modification or impairment, of the medical examination, diagnosis, treatment, or care of 1 or more individuals; (iii) physical injury to any person; (iv) a threat to public health or safety; or (v) damage affecting a computer system used by or for a government entity in furtherance of the administration of justice, national defense, or national security."

Other Consequences. Property derived from an extortion offense under paragraph 1030(a)(7) is subject to confiscation, 18 U.S.C. 981(a)(1)(C), 982(a)(2)(B). Offenders may also be ordered to pay restitution, 18 U.S.C. 3663. Offenses under the paragraph are not considered federal crimes of terrorism, however, 18 U.S.C. 2332b(g)(5).

Other Crimes

Attempt, Conspiracy and Complicity. The same general observations concerning attempt, conspiracy and aiding and abetting noted with respect to the other paragraphs of 1030(a) apply here. It is a separate crime to attempt to violate paragraph 1030(a)(7), 18 U.S.C. 1030(b). Those who attempt or aid and abet the violation of another are subject to the same penalties as those commit the substantive offense, 18 U.S.C. 1030(c), 2. The same is true of conspiracies except that conspiracy to commit a felony carries a five year maximum of imprisonment, 18 U.S.C. 371.

Hobbs Act. The Hobbs Act, 18 U.S.C. 1951, prohibits extortion that affects commerce. More precisely, among other things, it declares that "Whoever in any way or degree obstructs, delays, or affects commerce or the movement of any article or commodity in commerce, by... extortion or attempts or conspires so to do. . . shall be fined under this title or imprisoned not more than twenty years, or both," 18 U.S.C. 1951(a).[232] For purpose of section 1951, "'extortion' means the obtaining of property from another, with his consent, induced by wrongful use of... fear," 18 U.S.C. 1951(b)(2). The government need show only a minimal impact on interstate or foreign commerce to satisfy the jurisdictional element of the Hobbs Act.[233]

Facially, paragraph 1030(a)(7) might seem little more than a more specific version of the Hobbs Act: the Hobbs Act prohibits extortionate acquisition of property, generally, in a manner that affects interstate or foreign commerce; while paragraph 1030(a)(7) prohibits extortionate acquisition of property, specifically acquired by a threat to damage computers, in a manner that affects interstate or foreign commerce. But much of section 1030 can be explained by Congress' concern that its purposes could be frustrated by too narrow a definition of "property." In most instances, the fear has been that computer systems or information in computer storage or on computer disks will be considered too intangible to claim the legal protection

---

[232] For a general discussion see *Elements of Offense Proscribed by the Hobbs Act (18 USCS §1951) Against Racketeering in Interstate or Foreign Commerce*, 4 ALR FED. 881.

[233] *United States v. Davis*, 473 F.3d 680, 681–83 (6th Cir. 2007); *United States v. Mitov*, 460 F.3d 901, 908 (7th Cir. 2006); *United States v. Vega Molina*, 407 F.3d 511, 526 (1st Cir 2005); *United States v. Vallejo*, 297 F.3d 1154, 1166 (11th Cir. 2002); *United States v. Malone*, 222 F.3d 1286, 1294–295 (10th Cir. 2000). Some circuits may be more demanding where the victim is an individual rather than a business, *United States v. Lynch*, 282 F.3d 1049, 1052–55 (9th Cir. 2002) (requiring greater commerce showing the case of individual victims and describing views of other circuits); *United States v. Mann*, 493 F.3d 484, 494–95 (5th Cir. 2007).

available to more tangible property. The applicability of the Hobbs Act and of the various "threats with intent to extort" statutes present an additional "property" complication, for they may involve both property under threat and property sought by the extortionist.

There is little question that the act guards against threats to both tangible and intangible property. The cases are replete with the observation that wrongful exploitation of a reasonable fear of economic loss in order to obtain property constitutes extortion for purposes of section 1951.[234] The case law gives credence to Congress' concern that some may conclude that the Hobbs Act does not always reach cases where the "property" obtained by the extortionist is an intangible benefit rather than tangible property like money.[235]

Threat Statutes. Several federal statutes prohibit threats against "property" made with extortionate intent. Here the Hobbs Act puzzle is reversed. Here it is the meaning of the "property" protected from threat that is uncertain; while the meaning of "property" sought by the extortionist is conceded and spacious.

The statutes in question include at a minimum 18 U.S.C. 875 (threats transmitted in interstate commerce),[236] 18 U.S.C. 876 (mailing threatening

[234] *Sanchez v. Triple-S Management, Corp.*, 492 F.3d 1, 12 (1st Cir. 2007); *United States v. Mitov*, 460 F.3d 901, 907 (7th Cir. 2006); *United States v. Cruzado-Laureano*, 404 F.3d 470, 481 (1st Cir. 2005); *United States v. Edwards*, 303 F.3d 606, 635 (5th Cir. 2002); *United States v. Collins*, 78 F.3d 1021, 1029–30 (6th Cir. 1996); *United States v. Middlemiss*, 217 F.3d 112, 118 (2nd Cir. 2000).

[235] Compare *National Organization for Women, Inc. v. Scheidler*, 267 F.3d 687, 709 (7th Cir. 2001), rev'd, 537 U.S. 393 (2003)(rejecting a contention that neither women's right to receive medical services from abortion clinics nor the clinics' right to provide such services constituted "property" received under threat for Hobbs Act purposes), and *United States v. Gigante*, 39 F.3d 42, 49–51 (2d Cir. 1994)(holding that the act extended to a benefit realized when the victim of the threat agreed not to engage in competition bidding on a public contract against with firms paying kickbacks to the extortionists); with *Town of West Hartford v. Operation Rescue*, 915 F.2d 92, 101–2 (2nd Cir. 1990)(despite recognition that "'property' under the [Hobbs] Act 'includes in a broad sense, any valuable right considered as a source or element of wealth' including a right to solicit business. . . the term 'property' cannot plausible be construed to encompass altered official conduct," i.e., increased police and other emergency services), and *United States v. Edwards*, 303 F.3d 606, 635 (5th Cir. 2002)(noting that the "property" threatened for Hobbs Act purposes does not include potential benefits or opportunities). The Supreme Court subsequently resolved the Hobbs Act issue—not by determining whether the extraction of intangible property is sufficient to constitute extortion under the act—but by concluding that the Hobbs extortion requires that the offender "obtain" something, merely compelling the victim to forego the exercise of a prerogative is insufficient, *Scheidler v. National Organization for Women, Inc.*, 537 U.S. 393, 402–10 (2003). For a discussion on the Hobbs Act in relation to social protest activity and the meaning of property in that context, see Kristal S. Stippich, *Behind the Words: Interpreting the Hobbs Act Requirement of "Obtaining of Property From Another,"* 36 JOHN MARSHALL LAW REVIEW 295 (2003).

Congress' uncertainty notwithstanding, at least one district court has confirmed the extraterritorial application of the Hobbs Act, 18 U.S.C. 371 (conspiracy), 18 U.S.C. 1029 (access device offenses), as well as paragraphs 1030(a)(7)(extortion) and 1030(a)(4)(fraud) to misconduct arising out of an overseas extortionate threat against a commercial computer system in this country, *United States v. Ivanov*, 175 F.Supp.2d 367 (D.Conn. 2001).

[236] "Whoever, with intent to extort from any person, firm, association, or corporation, any money or other thing of value, transmits in interstate or foreign commerce any communication containing any

communications),[237] 18 U.S.C. 877 (mailing threatening communications from a foreign country),[238] and 18 U.S.C. 880 (receipt of the proceeds of extortion).[239] Other than the receipt statute, they are all essentially alike except for their jurisdictional elements. Each prohibits the communication of a threat to injure the property of the addressee or of another conveyed with extortionate intent. Each identifies "money or other thing of value" as the extortionist's objective, and each punishes offenders by imprisonment for not more than two years and/or a fine of not more than $250,000.

As noted earlier, the courts see extraordinary elasticity in the term "thing of value" as used in federal criminal law,[240] but not infrequently are divided over which intangibles may legitimately be considered "property" for purposes of federal criminal statutes.[241] Again even in the case of the "property"

---

threat to injure the property. . . of the addressee or of another. . . shall be fined under this title or imprisoned not more than two years, or both," 18 U.S.C. 875(d).

[237] "Whoever, with intent to extort from any person any money or other thing of value, knowingly so deposits or causes to be delivered, as aforesaid, any communication, with or without a name or designating mark subscribed thereto, addressed to any other person and containing any threat to injure the property. . . of the addressee or of another. . . . shall be fined under this title or imprisoned not more than two years, or both. If such a communication is addressed to a United Stats judge, a federal law enforcement officer, or an official who is covered by section 1114 [any federal employee], the individual shall be fined under this title, imprisoned not more than 10 years, or both," 18 U.S.C. 876(d).

[238] ". . . Whoever, with intent to extort from any person any money or other thing of value, knowingly so deposits as aforesaid, any communication, for the purpose aforesaid, containing any threat to injure the property. . . of the addressee or of another. . . shall be fined under this title or imprisoned not more than two years, or both," 18 U.S.C. 877.

[239] "A person who receives, possesses, conceals, or disposes of any money or other property which was obtained from the commission of any offense under this chapter that is punishable by imprisonment for more than 1 year, knowing the same to have been unlawfully obtained, shall be imprisoned not more than 3 years, fined under this title, or both," 18 U.S.C. 880.

[240] See *United States v. Maneri*, 353 F.3d 165, 168 (2d Cir. 2003)(thing of value included opportunity for sexual encounter);*United States v. Freeman*, 208 F.3d 332, 341 (1st Cir. 2000)(night club owner's special treatment of police officer including access to dancers' dressing room constituted a thing of value); *United States v. Marmolejo*, 89 F.3d 1185, 1192–193 (5th Cir. 1996)(citing a wide range of intangible property benefits found to constitute "things of value" under various federal criminal statutes); *United States v. Bryant*, 117 F.3d 1464, 1468 n.7 (D.C.Cir. 1997)(noting that a forbearance from arrest constitutes a "thing of value" for purposes of 18 U.S.C. 912 even in a case where two members of the three judge panel expressed the view that the defendant should never have been charged, prosecuted or convicted); *United States v. Collins*, 56 F.3d 1416, 1420 (D.C.Cir. 1995)(noting the widespread acceptance of an expansive reading of the term "thing of value" the purposes of the theft of federal property statute, 18 U.S.C. 641). The things of value are not limited to those things that can be lawfully possessed, see e.g., *United States v. Sargent*, 504 F.3d 767, 770–71 (9th Cir. 2007)(marijuana); *United States v. Fink*, 502 F.3d 585, 586 (6th Cir. 2007)(child pornography).

[241] *United States v. Salvatore*, 110 F.3d 1131, 1139–141 (5th Cir. 1997)(noting the *McNally-Carpenter* distinction and the split of appellate courts on the question of whether unissued licenses may constitute "property" interests for purposes of the mail fraud statute, 18 U.S.C. 1341, a conflict which the Supreme Court subsequently resolved in *Cleveland v. United States*, 531 U.S. 12, 26–7 (2000) when it concluded that a state had not been defrauded of "property" for the purposes of section 1341 when it was fraudulently induced by issue a license); *United States v. Delano*, 55 F.3d 720, 726–27 (2d Cir. 1995)(holding that labor or services cannot be considered "property" for purposes of a RICO charged based on an extortionate predicate offense). *United States v. Hedaithy*, 392 F.3d 580, 584 (3d Cir. 2004) (court found that mail fraud violation occurred when would-be test takers had others take a standardized test in their place; the court found that the testing service's property interests were violated because of the unauthorized use of its copyrighted and confidential materials and because, in obtaining a score report, the defendants possessed the "embodiment of the services that ETS provides").

statutes, however, the intangibles at issue in computer cases would seem to fall more clearly on the *Carpenter* "confidential information" side of the line than on the *McNally* "honest public services" or the *Cleveland* "unissued license" side.

RICO, Money Laundering, and the Travel Act. Section 1030 is a money laundering predicate offense, 18 U.S.C. 1956(c)(7)(D), 1957(f)(3). Thus, financial transactions involving the proceeds from computer-related extortion that violates paragraph 1030(a)(7) may support a prosecution under 18 U.S.C. 1956 or 1957. Moreover, a violation of paragraph 1030(a)(7) may at the same time offend one of its companions that is a RICO predicate, e.g., the Hobbs Act, 18 U.S.C. 875 (extortion affecting in interstate or foreign commerce), or the Travel Act (extortion is a Travel Act predicate), thereby rising the prospect of a RICO prosecution.

Trafficking in Computer Access (18 U.S.C. 1030(a)(6))

> *Whoever . . . (6) knowingly and with intent to defraud traffics (as defined in section 1029) in any password or similar information through which a computer may be accessed without authorization, if—(A) such trafficking affects interstate or foreign commerce; or (B) such computer is used by or for the Government of the United States . . . shall be punished as provided in subsection (c) of this section.*

Paragraph 1030(a)(6) outlaws misconduct similar to the access device proscriptions of section 1029.[242] It was enacted to deal with the practice of hackers of posting the passwords of various computer systems on electronic bulletin boards, S.Rept. 99-432 at 13 (1986); H.Rept. 99-612 at 12-3 (1986). Although limited, it provides several distinct advantages. First, it covers passwords to government computers more clearly than does section 1029. Second, as something of a lesser included offense to section 1029, it affords the government plea bargain room in a case that it might otherwise be forced to bring under section 1029 or abandon. Third, it contributes a means of cutting off the practice of publicly posting access to confidential computer systems without imposing severe penalties unless the misconduct persists. Fourth, it supplies a basis for private enforcement through the civil liability provisions of subsection 1030(g) for misconduct that may be more appropriately addressed by the courts as a private wrong. The elements of the crime are:

- knowingly and with an intent to defraud;

[242] "Whoever. . . knowingly and with intent to defraud traffics in or uses one or more unauthorized access devices during any one-year period, and by such conduct obtains anything of value aggregating $1,000 or more during that period. . . shall, if the offense affects interstate or foreign commerce, be punished as provided in subsection (c) of this section," 18 U.S.C. 1029(a)(2). Violations are punishable by imprisonment for not more than 10 years and/or a fine of not more than $250,000, 18 U.S.C. 1029(c)(1).

- trafficking in (i.e. "to transfer, or otherwise dispose of, to another, or obtain control of with intent to transfer or dispose of" (18 U.S.C. 1029(e)(5));
- a computer password or similar computer key; and
- either
  - of a federal computer or
  - in a manner that affects interstate or foreign commerce.

Jurisdiction

Federal jurisdiction exists where the traffic affects interstate or foreign commerce, 18 U.S.C. 1030(a)(6)(A) or where the password or key is to a computer used by or for the Government of the United States, 18 U.S.C. 1030(a) (6)(B). As has been said of other paragraphs and government computers, it is unclear whether the protection of paragraph 1030(a)(6) cloaks legislative and judicial branch computers or is limited to those of the executive branch. The uncertainty is born of the section's care to define the phrase "department or agency of the United States" to include all three branches and its use of that phrase in establishing some crimes, contrasted with its failure to use that phrase in paragraph 1030(a)(6), discussed *supra*. The explicit reference to overseas application of offenses affecting commerce, 18 U.S.C. 1030(e)(2), without a similar statement concerning government computers may raise further uncertainty. Was the omission an oversight or intended to signal a limitation?

Intent

The intent element is the same as that used in paragraph 1030(a)(4)(fraud), and in the credit card fraud proscriptions of 18 U.S.C. 1029: knowingly and with the intent to defraud, S.Rept. 99-432 at 10 (1986); H.Rept. 99-612 at 12 (1986). The phrase as used in the credit card fraud statute means that the offender is conscious of the natural consequences of his action (i.e., that it likely that someone will be defrauded) and intends that those consequences should occur (i.e., he intends that someone should be defrauded), H.Rept. 98-894 at 16-7 (1984).

Consequences

Penalties. The first offense is punishable by imprisonment for not more than one year and/or a fine of not more than $100,000; subsequent offenses are punishable by imprisonment for not more than 10 years and/or a fine of not more than $250,000, 18 U.S.C. 1030(c)(2); 18 U.S.C. 3571. The general theft/damage sentencing guideline, U.S.S.G. §2B1.1, covers violations of paragraph 1030(a)(6)(traffic in passwords) as it does fraud and damage under paragraphs 1030(a)(4) and 1030(a)(5).

Other Consequences. Proceeds and property traceable to the proceeds of a violation of paragraph 1030(a)(6) trafficking offenses are subject to confiscation, 18 U.S.C. 981(a)(1)(C), 982(a)(2)(B). Upon conviction, defendants are ordered to pay restitution, 18 U.S.C. 3663A(c)(1)(A)(ii). And offenders may also be subject to a cause of action for damages or injunctive relief, 18 U.S.C. 1030(g).

Other Crimes

The generally applicable provisions dealing with attempt, conspiracy and complicity will apply with equal force in cases involving paragraph 1030(a)(6). Paragraph 1030(a)(6) appears to have few counterparts in federal law, other than the prohibition against trafficking in access devices (credit card fraud) under 18 U.S.C. 1029(a)(2)[243] and the wire fraud provisions of 18 U.S.C. 1343.[244] Nevertheless, violations of either of these—or of the money laundering proscriptions (18 U.S.C. 1956, 1957) for which section 1030 is a predicate—may provide the foundation for a RICO (18 U.S.C. 1962) prosecution, so that should conduct in violation of paragraph 1030(a)(6) also offend either the mail fraud, credit card fraud or money laundering prohibitions, a criminal breach of RICO may also have occurred. Brokering computer passwords without more may not be the ground upon which a sprawling criminal enterprise might be built, but violations of paragraph 1030(a)(6), with other crimes, might be part of a pattern of criminal activity used to operate such an enterprise.

Computer Espionage (18 U.S.C. 1030(a)(1))

Whoever . . . (1) having knowingly accessed a computer without authorization or exceeding authorized access, and by means of such conduct having obtained information that has been determined by the United States Government pursuant to an Executive order or statute to require protection against unauthorized disclosure for reasons of national defense or foreign relations, or any restricted data, as defined in paragraph y of section 11 of the Atomic Energy Act of 1954, with reason to believe that such information so obtained could be used to the injury of the United States, or to the advantage of any foreign nation willfully communicates, delivers, transmits, or causes to be communicated, delivered, or transmitted, or attempts to communicate, deliver, transmit or cause to be communicated, delivered, or transmitted the same to any person not entitled to receive it, or willfully retains the same and

---

[243] Prosecution under paragraph 1029(a)(2) requires a loss of at least $1,000 over the course of a year and that the device permit access to an "account," 18 U.S.C. 1029(e)(1)(defining "access device"); paragraph 1030(a)(6) imposes neither burden upon a prosecution. This is probably why paragraph 1030(a)(6) is punishable as a misdemeanor while paragraph 1029(a)(2) is a 10 year felony.

[244] To establish wire fraud, the government must show an interstate wire transmission in furtherance of a scheme to defraud another of money or property, *United States v. Mann*, 493 U.S. 484, 493 (5th Cir. 2007); *United States v. Allen*, 491 F.3d 178, 185 (4th Cir. 2007); *United States v. Dowlin*, 408 F.3d 647, 658 n.5 (10th Cir. 2005); *United States v. Owens*, 301 F.3d 521, 528 (7th Cir. 2002).

fails to deliver it to the officer or employee of the United States entitled to receive it . . . shall be punished as provided in subsection (c) of this section.

Paragraph 1030(a)(1) essentially tracks existing federal espionage laws, 18 U.S.C. 793, 794 and 798, that ban disclosure of information potentially detrimental to our national defense and well being, or more simply laws that outlaw spying.[245] The paragraph was enacted as part of the original act and has been amended primarily to more closely track other espionage laws.[246] The distinctive feature of paragraph 1030(a)(1) is its merger of elements of espionage and computer abuse.[247] Broken down into a simplified version of its constituent elements it bars anyone from:

- either
  - willfully disclosing,
  - willfully attempting to disclose, or
  - willfully failing to return
- classified information concerning national defense, foreign relations or atomic energy
- with reason to believe that the information either
  - could to used to injure the United States, or
  - could be used to the advantage of the a foreign nation
- when the information was acquired by unauthorized computer access.

[245] For a discussion of federal espionage laws generally see, 70 AMERICAN JURISPRUDENCE, 2D EDITION, *Sedition, Subversive Activities, and Treason* §§17–44; see also, Bazan, *Espionage and the Death Penalty*, 41 FEDERAL BAR NEWS &JOURNAL 615 (1994); Vladeck, *Inchoate Liability and the Espionage Act: The Statutory Framework and the Freedom of the Press*, 1 HARVARD LAW &J POLICY REVIEW 219 (2007).

[246] 18 U.S.C. 1030 (1982 ed. & 1984 Supp.); H.Rept. 98-894 at 21 (1984). Compare the language of 1030(a)(1) with that of 18 U.S.C. 793(e)("Whoever having unauthorized possession of, access to, or control over any document, writing, code book, signal book, sketch, photograph, photographic negative, blueprint, plan, map, model, instrument, appliance, or note relating to the national defense, or information relating to the national defense which information the possessor has reason to believe could be used to the injury of the United States or to the advantage of any foreign nation, willfully communicates, delivers, transmits or causes to be communicated, delivered, or transmitted, or attempts to communicate, deliver, transmit or cause to be communicated, delivered, or transmitted the same to any person not entitled to receive it, or willfully retains the same and fails to deliver it to the officer or employee of the United States entitled to receive it").

[247] "Although there is considerable overlap between 18 U.S.C. 793(3) and section 1030(a)(1), as amended by the NII Protection Act, the two statutes would not reach exactly the same conduct. Section 1030(a)(1) wold target those persons who deliberately break into a computer to obtain properly classified Government secrets then try to peddle those secrets to others, including foreign governments. In other words, unlike existing espionage laws prohibiting the theft and peddling of Government secrets to foreign agents, section 1030(a)(1) would require proof that the individual knowingly used a computer without authority, or in excess of authority, for the purpose of obtaining classified information. In this sense then, it is the use of the computer which is being proscribed, not the unauthorized possession of, access to, or control over the classified information itself," S.Rept. 104-357 at 6-7.

Jurisdiction

The federal government is a creature of the Constitution. It enjoys only those powers that the Constitution grants it, U.S.Const. Amend. IX, X. Since states are primarily responsible for the enactment and enforcement of criminal law, the validity of any federal criminal law depends upon a clear nexus some power that the Constitution vests in the national government. Most of section 1030 represents the execution of Congress' authority to enact laws for the regulation interstate and foreign commerce, for example, U.S.Const. Art.I, §8, cl.3. Paragraph 1030(a)(1), on the other hand, is anchored in the protection of defense and foreign relations of the nation and so jurisdictional ties to interstate or foreign commerce are unnecessary.

Intent

The state of mind element for a breach of paragraph 1030(a)(1) is pegged high. The offender must (1) purposefully transmit or retain information that (2) he has reason to believe could be used to the injure the United States or benefit another country, and (3) that he has obtained through access to a computer that he knows he had no authority to access.[248]

Consequences

Penalties & Sentencing Guidelines. Violations are punishable by imprisonment for not more than 10 years (not more than 20 years for second and subsequent offenses) and/or a fine of not more than $250,000, 18 U.S.C. 1030(c)(1), 3571. The general espionage sentencing guideline, U.S.S.G. §2M3.2, applies to violations of paragraph (a)(1) which calls for a base sentencing level of 30 (carrying an initial sentencing range beginning at 8 years imprisonment) and of 35 (an initial sentencing range beginning at 14 years) if top secret information is involved. Since paragraph 1030(a)(1) offenses are federal crimes of terrorism, the minimum sentencing level is 32 and the criminal history category is VI which means the sentencing range begins at 17.5 years imprisonment (and begins at 24.33 years imprisonment if top secret information is involved), U.S.S.G. §3A1.4.

Federal crime of terrorism. Paragraph 1030(a)(1) is a federal crime of terrorism, 18 U.S.C. 2332b(g)(5)(B). Therefore:

- the applicable statute of limitations is 8 years rather than 5 years, 18 U.S.C. 3286;
- pretrial detention of defendants charged with a violation of paragraph 1030(a)(1) is presumed, 18 U.S.C. 3142;

[248] H.Rept. 98-894 at 21 (1984)("As the Supreme Court stated in *Gorin v. U.S.*, (312 U.S. 19, 28), 'This requires those prosecuted to have acted in bad faith. The sanctions apply only when scienter is established'").

- conviction carries the prospect of life-time supervision by probation authorities, 18 U.S.C. 3583;
- a paragraph 1030(a)(1) offense is a ground for sentencing enhancement in the case of, or is a predicate offense for:
  - aggravated identity theft, 18 U.S.C. 1028;
  - RICO, 18 U.S.C. 1961;
  - maritime transportation of terrorists, 18 U.S.C. 2284; and
  - providing material support for terrorist organizations, 18 U.S.C. 2339A.

Other Consequences. Proceeds from a paragraph 1030(a)(1) espionage offense are subject to confiscation, 18 U.S.C. 981(a)(1)(C), 982(a)(2)(B). Upon conviction, defendants are ordered to pay restitution, 18 U.S.C. 3663A(c)(1)(A)(ii). And offenders may also be subject to a cause of action for damages or injunctive relief, 18 U.S.C. 1030(g).

Other Crimes

Espionage prosecutions are not common.[249] And there do not appear to have been any reported cases brought under paragraph 1030(a)(1). The overlap between paragraph 1030(a)(1) and the espionage laws is such, however, that any case prosecutable under paragraph 1030(a)(1) would like also be prosecutable under one or more of the espionage statutes; in fact "the only reported 'espionage' case involving the unauthorized use of computers was prosecuted under §793, the much older, pre-electronic espionage statute and not under §1030(a)(1)."[250]

Attempt, Conspiracy, and Complicity. Subsection 1030(b) makes it a separate crime to attempt to commit a violation of paragraph 1030(a)(1) punishable to the same extent as the underlying offense, 18 U.S.C. 1030(c). Anyone who commands, counsels, aids or abets a violation of the paragraph assumes is as a principal and is therefore likewise subject to the same penalties, 18 U.S.C. 2. Conspirators to violate paragraph 1030(a)(1) are subject to imprisonment for not more than five years and/or a fine of not more than $250,000, 18 U.S.C. 371, and are each liable for the underlying offense and any other foreseeable crimes committed in furtherance of the conspiracy.

Espionage Offenses. The three espionage statutes themselves share common ground under some circumstances. In general terms, they outlaw gathering

[249] See generally, CRS Report 97-805, *Espionage in the United States: Individuals Arrested 1993–1998*, by Suzanne Cavanagh and Stephanie Flagg; and CRS Report 93-531, *Individuals Arrested on Charges of Espionage Against the United States Government*, by Suzanne Cavanagh.

[250] Olivenbaum, *<CTRL><ALT><DELETE>: Rethinking Federal Computer Crime Legislation*, 27 Setion Hall Law Review 574, 594-95 (1997), citing *United States v. Poulsen*, 41 F.3d 1330 (9th Cir. 1994).

and disseminating defense information (18 U.S.C. 793), gathering and disseminating defense information for a foreign country (18 U.S.C. 794), and disclosing classified information concerning government cryptography or communications intelligence (18 U.S.C. 798).

As already noted 18 U.S.C. 793(e) is the generic twin of 1030(a)(1), but section 793 has several other provisions that might also be implicated by a fact pattern sufficient to establish criminal liability under paragraph 1030(a)(1). Section 793 establishes six distinct offenses:

- intruding upon military facilities to gather national defense information (18 U.S.C. 793(a));[251]
- copying documents containing national defense information (18 U.S.C. 793(b));[252]
- unlawful receipt of national defense information (18 U.S.C. 793(c));[253]
- unlawful dissemination of national defense information by a lawful custodian (18 U.S.C. 793(d));[254]

251 "Whoever, for the purpose of obtaining information respecting the national defense with intent or reason to believe that the information is to be used to the injury of the United States, or to the advantage of any foreign nation, goes upon, enters, flies over, or otherwise obtains information concerning any vessel, aircraft, work of defense, navy yard, naval station, submarine base, fueling station, fort, battery, torpedo station, dockyard, canal, railroad, arsenal, camp, factory, mine, telegraph, telephone, wireless, or signal station, building, office, research laboratory or station or other place connected with the national defense owned or constructed, or in progress of construction by the United States or under the control of the United States, or of any of its officers, departments, or agencies, or within the exclusive jurisdiction of the United States, or any place in which any vessel, aircraft, arms, munitions, or other materials or instruments for use in time of war are being made, prepared, repaired, stored, or are the subject of research or development, under any contract or agreement with the United States, or any department or agency thereof, or with any person on behalf of the United States, or otherwise on behalf of the United States, or any prohibited place so designated by the President by proclamation in time of war or in case of national emergency in which anything for the use of the Army, Navy, or Air Force is being prepared or constructed or stored, information as to which prohibited place the President has determined would be prejudicial to the national defense. . . Shall be fined under this title or imprisoned not more than ten years, or both," 18 U.S.C. 793(a).

252 "Whoever, for the purpose aforesaid, and with like intent or reason to believe, copies, takes, makes, or obtains, or attempts to copy, take, make, or obtain, any sketch, photograph, photographic negative, blueprint, plan, map, model, instrument, appliance, document, writing, or note of anything connected with the national defense. . . Shall be fined under this title or imprisoned not more than ten years, or both,"18 U.S.C. 793(b).

253 "Whoever, for the purpose aforesaid, receives or obtains or agrees or attempts to receive or obtain from any person, or from any source whatever, any document, writing, code book, signal book, sketch, photograph, photographic negative, blueprint, plan, map, model, instrument, appliance, or note, of anything connected with the national defense, knowing or having reason to believe, at the time he receives or obtains, or agrees or attempts to receive or obtain it, that it has been or will be obtained, taken, made, or disposed of by any person contrary to the provisions of this chapter. . . Shall be fined under this title or imprisoned not more than ten years, or both,"18 U.S.C. 793(c).

254 "Whoever, lawfully having possession of, access to, control over, or being entrusted with any document, writing, code book, signal book, sketch, photograph, photographic negative, blueprint, plan, map, model, instrument, appliance, or note relating to the national defense, or information relating to the national defense which information the possessor has reason to believe could be used to the injury of the United States or to the advantage of any foreign nation, willfully communicates, delivers, transmits or causes to be communicated, delivered, or transmitted or attempts to communicate, deliver, transmit or cause to be communicated, delivered or transmitted the same to any person not entitled to receive it, or willfully retains the same and fails to deliver it on demand to the officer or

- unauthorized possession of national defense information (18 U.S.C. 793(e));[255] and
- negligently losing national defense information (18 U.S.C. 793(f)).[256]

Conspiracy to violate section 793 is likewise punishable by imprisonment for not more than 10 years (not more than 20 years for a subsequent offense) and/or a fine of not more than $250,000, 18 U.S.C. 793(g), and criminal forfeiture of any proceeds derived from the offense, 18 U.S.C. 793(h).

Section 794 essentially subjects transgressions similar to those banned in section 793 to more severe penalties if they involve gathering national defense information for a foreign nation or to injure the United States,[257] particularly if the offense is committed in war time.[258] Conspirators are subject to

---

employee of the United States entitled to receive it. . . Shall be fined under this title or imprisoned not more than ten years, or both,"18 U.S.C. 793(d).

[255] Whoever having unauthorized possession of, access to, or control over any document, writing, code book, signal book, sketch, photograph, photographic negative, blueprint, plan, map, model, instrument, appliance, or note relating to the national defense, or information relating to the national defense which information the possessor has reason to believe could be used to the injury of the United States or to the advantage of any foreign nation, willfully communicates, delivers, transmits or causes to be communicated, delivered, or transmitted, or attempts to communicate, deliver, transmit or cause to be communicated, delivered, or transmitted the same to any person not entitled to receive it, or willfully retains the same and fails to deliver it to the officer or employee of the United States entitled to receive it. . . Shall be fined under this title or imprisoned not more than ten years, or both," 18 U.S.C. 793(e)

[256] "Whoever, being entrusted with or having lawful possession or control of any document, writing, code book, signal book, sketch, photograph, photographic negative, blueprint, plan, map, model, instrument, appliance, note, or information, relating to the national defense, (1) through gross negligence permits the same to be removed from its proper place of custody or delivered to anyone in violation of his trust, or to be lost, stolen, abstracted, or destroyed, or (2) having knowledge that the same has been illegally removed from its proper place of custody or delivered to anyone in violation of his trust, or lost, or stolen, abstracted, or destroyed, and fails to make prompt report of such loss, theft, abstraction, or destruction to his superior officer. . . Shall be fined under this title or imprisoned not more than ten years, or both," 18 U.S.C. 793(f).

[257] "Whoever, with intent or reason to believe that it is to be used to the injury of the United States or to the advantage of a foreign nation, communicates, delivers, or transmits, or attempts to communicate, deliver, or transmit, to any foreign government, or to any faction or party or military or naval force within a foreign country, whether recognized or unrecognized by the United States, or to any representative, officer, agent, employee, subject, or citizen thereof, either directly or indirectly, any document, writing, code book, signal book, sketch, photograph, photographic negative, blueprint, plan, map, model, note, instrument, appliance, or information relating to the national defense, shall be punished by death or by imprisonment for any term of years or for life, except that the sentence of death shall not be imposed unless the jury or, if there is no jury, the court, further finds that the offense resulted in the identification by a foreign power (as defined in section 101(a) of the Foreign Intelligence Surveillance Act of 1978) of an individual acting as an agent of the United States and consequently in the death of that individual, or directly concerned nuclear weaponry, military spacecraft or satellites, early warning systems, or other means of defense or retaliation against large-scale attack; war plans; communications intelligence or cryptographic information; or any other major weapons system or major element of defense strategy," 18 U.S.C. 794(a).

[258] "Whoever, in time of war, with intent that the same shall be communicated to the enemy, collects, records, publishes, or communicates, or attempts to elicit any information with respect to the movement, numbers, description, condition, or disposition of any of the Armed Forces, ships, aircraft, or war materials of the United States, or with respect to the plans or conduct, or supposed plans or conduct of any naval or military operations, or with respect to any works or measures undertaken for or connected with, or intended for the fortification or defense of any place, or any other information relating to the public defense, which might be useful to the enemy, shall be punished by death or by imprisonment for any term of years or for life," 18 U.S.C. 794(b).

the same penalties, 18 U.S.C. 794(c), and property derived from a violation or used to facilitate a violation is subject to forfeiture, 18 U.S.C. 794(d).

Section 798 protects military and diplomatic codes and government code-breaking. It proscribes unlawful dissemination of classified information concerning communications intelligence and government cryptography.[259] Violations are punishable by imprisonment for not more than 10 years and/or a fine of not more than $250,000, 18 U.S.C. 798(a), 3571, and the confiscation of any property derived from the offense or used to facilitate its commission, 18 U.S.C. 798(d).

Economic Espionage. The economic espionage prohibition, 18 U.S.C. 1831, outlaws stealing, copying, or unlawfully possessing a trade secret for the benefit of a foreign entity or attempting or conspiring to do so.[260] Offenders face

[259] "(a) Whoever knowingly and willfully communicates, furnishes, transmits, or otherwise makes available to an unauthorized person, or publishes, or uses in any manner prejudicial to the safety or interest of the United States or for the benefit of any foreign government to the detriment of the United States any classified information—(1) concerning the nature, preparation, or use of any code, cipher, or cryptographic system of the United States or any foreign government; or (2) concerning the design, construction, use, maintenance, or repair of any device, apparatus, or appliance used or prepared or planned for use by the United States or any foreign government for cryptographic or communication intelligence purposes; or (3) concerning the communication intelligence activities of the United States or any foreign government; or (4) obtained by the processes of communication intelligence from the communications of any foreign government, knowing the same to have been obtained by such processes—Shall be fined under this title or imprisoned not more than ten years, or both.

"(b) As used in subsection (a) of this section—The term 'classified information' means information which, at the time of a violation of this section, is, for reasons of national security, specifically designated by a United States Government Agency for limited or restricted dissemination or distribution; The terms 'code,' 'cipher,' and 'cryptographic system' include in their meanings, in addition to their usual meanings, any method of secret writing and any mechanical or electrical device or method used for the purpose of disguising or concealing the contents, significance, or meanings of communications; The term `foreign government' includes in its meaning any person or persons acting or purporting to act for or on behalf of any faction, party, department, agency, bureau, or military force of or within a foreign country, or for or on behalf of any government or any person or persons purporting to act as a government within a foreign country, whether or not such government is recognized by the United States; The term 'communication intelligence' means all procedures and methods used in the interception of communications and the obtaining of information from such communications by other than the intended recipients; The term 'unauthorized person' means any person who, or agency which, is not authorized to receive information of the categories set forth in subsection (a) of this section, by the President, or by the head of a department or agency of the United States Government which is expressly designated by the President to engage in communication intelligence activities for the United States.

"(c) Nothing in this section shall prohibit the furnishing, upon lawful demand, of information to any regularly constituted committee of the Senate or House of Representatives of the United States of America, or joint committee thereof."

[260] "Whoever, intending or knowing that the offense will benefit any foreign government, foreign instrumentality, or foreign agent, knowingly—(1) steals, or without authorization appropriates, takes, carries away, or conceals, or by fraud, artifice, or deception obtains a trade secret; (2) without authorization copies, duplicates, sketches, draws, photographs, downloads, uploads, alters, destroys, photocopies, replicates, transmits, delivers, sends, mails, communicates, or conveys a trade secret; (3) receives, buys, or possesses a trade secret, knowing the same to have been stolen or appropriated, obtained, or converted without authorization; (4) attempts to commit any offense described in any of paragraphs (1) through (3); or (5) conspires with one or more other persons to commit any offense described in any of paragraphs (1) through (3), and one or more of such persons do any act to effect the object of the conspiracy,—shall, except as provided in subsection (b), be fined not more than $500,000 or imprisoned not more than 15 years, or both," 18 U.S.C. 1831(a).

imprisonment for not more than 15 years and a higher fine that permitted for most felonies—not more than $500,000 (not more than $10 million for organizations), *id.*

RICO and Money Laundering. Violations of Section 793, 794, 798 or 1030 are money laundering predicate offenses, 18 U.S.C. 1956(c)(7)(D). Moreover, violations of paragraph 1030(a)(1) are among the offenses listed in 18 U.S.C. 2332b(g)(5)(B) (federal crimes of terrorism) and are consequently RICO predicate offenses, 18 U.S.C. 1961(1)(G).

Appendices

Selected Bibliography

Articles

Friendman & Bissinger, *"Infojacking": Crimes on the Information Super Highway*, 9 Journal of Property Rights 2 (1997)

Heymann, *Legislating Computer Crime*, 34 Haravard Journal on Legislation 373 (1997)

Kerr, *Search and Seizing Computers and Obtaining Electronic Evidence in Criminal Investigations*, Computer Crime and Intellectual Property Section, Criminal Division, United States Department of Justice (July, 2002), on [http://www.cybercrime.gov] (Nov.21, 2003)

Levinson & Paetsch, *The Computer Fraud and Abuse Act: A Powerful New Way to Protect Information*, 19 Computer & Internet Lawyers 11 (Sept. 2002)

Olivenbaum, *<CTRL><ALT><DELETE>: Rethinking Federal Computer Crime Legislation*, 27 Seton Hall Law Review 574 (1997)

Sinrod & Reilly, *Cyber-Crime: A Practical Approach to the Application of Federal Computer Crime Laws*, 16 Santa Clara Computer & High Technology Law Journal 177 (2000)

Soma, Banker & Smith, *Computer Crime: Substantive Statutes and Technical and Legal Search Considerations*, 39 Air Force Law Review 225 (1996)

United States Department of Justice, *Prosecuting Computer Crimes* (2006)

Notes

Controlling Cyberspace: Applying the Computer Fraud and Abuse Act to the Internet, 12 Santa Clara Computer & High Technology Law Journal 403 (1996)

The Limits of Computer Conversion: United States v. Collins, 9 Harvard Journal of Law & Technology 205 (1996)

Twenty-Second Survey of White Collar Crime, 44 American Criminal Law Review 241 (2007)

18 U.S.C. 1030

(a) Whoever—

(1) having knowingly accessed a computer without authorization or exceeding authorized access, and by means of such conduct having obtained information that has been determined by the United States Government pursuant to an Executive order or statute to require protection against unauthorized disclosure for reasons of national defense or foreign relations, or any restricted data, as defined in paragraph y. of

section 11 of the Atomic Energy Act of 1954, with reason to believe that such information so obtained could be used to the injury of the United States, or to the advantage of any foreign nation willfully communicates, delivers, transmits, or causes to be communicated, delivered, or transmitted, or attempts to communicate, deliver, transmit or cause to be communicated, delivered, or transmitted the same to any person not entitled to receive it, or willfully retains the same and fails to deliver it to the officer or employee of the United States entitled to receive it;

(2) intentionally accesses a computer without authorization or exceeds authorized access, and thereby obtains—

(A) information contained in a financial record of a financial institution, or of a card issuer as defined in section 1602(n) of title 15, or contained in a file of a consumer reporting agency on a consumer, as such terms are defined in the Fair Credit Reporting Act (15 U.S.C. 1681 et seq.);

(B) information from any department or agency of the United States; or

(C) information from any protected computer if the conduct involved an interstate or foreign communication;

(3) intentionally, without authorization to access any nonpublic computer of a department or agency of the United States, accesses such a computer of that department or agency that is exclusively for the use of the Government of the United States or, in the case of a computer not exclusively for such use, is used by or for the Government of the United States and such conduct affects that use by or for the Government of the United States;

(4) knowingly and with intent to defraud, accesses a protected computer without authorization, or exceeds authorized access, and by means of such conduct furthers the intended fraud and obtains anything of value, unless the object of the fraud and the thing obtained consists only of the use of the computer and the value of such use is not more than $5,000 in any 1-year period;

(5)(A)(i) knowingly causes the transmission of a program, information, code, or command, and as a result of such conduct, intentionally causes damage without authorization, to a protected computer;

(ii) intentionally accesses a protected computer without authorization, and as a result of such conduct, recklessly causes damage; or

(iii) intentionally accesses a protected computer without authorization, and as a result of such conduct, causes damage; and

(B) by conduct described in clause (i), (ii), or (iii) of subparagraph (A), caused (or, in the case of an attempted offense, would, if completed, have caused)—

(i) loss to 1 or more persons during any 1-year period (and, for purposes of an investigation, prosecution, or other proceeding brought by the United States only, loss resulting from a related course of conduct affecting 1 or more other protected computers) aggregating at least $5,000 in value;

(ii) the modification or impairment, or potential modification or impairment, of the medical examination, diagnosis, treatment, or care of 1 or more individuals;

(iii) physical injury to any person;

(iv) a threat to public health or safety; or

(v) damage affecting a computer system used by or for a government entity in furtherance of the administration of justice, national defense, or national security;

(6) knowingly and with intent to defraud traffics (as defined in section 1029) in any password or similar information through which a computer may be accessed without authorization, if—

(A) such trafficking affects interstate or foreign commerce; or

(B) such computer is used by or for the Government of the United States;

(7) with intent to extort from any person any money or other thing of value, transmits in interstate or foreign commerce any communication containing any threat to cause damage to a protected computer;

shall be punished as provided in subsection (c) of this section.

(b) Whoever attempts to commit an offense under subsection (a) of this section shall be punished as provided in subsection (c) of this section.

(c) The punishment for an offense under subsection (a) or (b) of this section is—

(1)(A) a fine under this title or imprisonment for not more than ten years, or both, in the case of an offense under subsection (a)(1) of this section which does not occur after a conviction for another offense under this section, or an attempt to commit an offense punishable under this subparagraph; and

(B) a fine under this title or imprisonment for not more than twenty years, or both, in the case of an offense under subsection (a)(1) of this section which occurs after a conviction for another offense under this section, or an attempt to commit an offense punishable under this subparagraph;

(2)(A) except as provided in subparagraph (B), a fine under this title or imprisonment for not more than one year, or both, in the case of an offense under subsection (a)(2), (a)(3), (a)(5)(A)(iii), or (a)(6) of this section which does not occur after a conviction for another offense under this section, or an attempt to commit an offense punishable under this subparagraph;

(B) a fine under this title or imprisonment for not more than 5 years, or both, in the case of an offense under subsection (a)(2), or an attempt to commit an offense punishable under this subparagraph, if—

(i) the offense was committed for purposes of commercial advantage or private financial gain;

(ii) the offense was committed in furtherance of any criminal or tortious act in violation of the Constitution or laws of the United States or of any State; or

(iii) the value of the information obtained exceeds $5,000; and

(C) a fine under this title or imprisonment for not more than ten years, or both, in the case of an offense under subsection (a)(2), (a)(3) or (a)(6) of this section which occurs after a conviction for another offense under this section, or an attempt to commit an offense punishable under this subparagraph;

(3)(A) a fine under this title or imprisonment for not more than five years, or both, in the case of an offense under subsection (a)(4) or (a)(7) of this section which does not occur after a conviction for another offense under this section, or an attempt to commit an offense punishable under this subparagraph; and

(B) a fine under this title or imprisonment for not more than ten years, or both, in the case of an offense under subsection (a)(4) [FN2] (a)(5)(A)(iii), or (a)(7) of this section which occurs after a conviction for another offense under this section, or an attempt to commit an offense punishable under this subparagraph;

(4)(A) except as provided in paragraph (5), a fine under this title, imprisonment for not more than 10 years, or both, in the case of an offense under subsection (a)(5)(A)(i), or an attempt to commit an offense punishable under that subsection;

(B) a fine under this title, imprisonment for not more than 5 years, or both, in the case of an offense under subsection (a)(5)(A)(ii), or an attempt to commit an offense punishable under that subsection;

(C) except as provided in paragraph (5), a fine under this title, imprisonment for not more than 20 years, or both, in the case of an offense under subsection (a)(5)(A)(i) or (a)(5)(A)(ii), or an attempt to commit an offense punishable under either subsection, that occurs after a conviction for another offense under this section; and

(5)(A) if the offender knowingly or recklessly causes or attempts to cause serious bodily injury from conduct in violation of subsection (a)(5)(A)(i), a fine under this title or imprisonment for not more than 20 years, or both; and

(B) if the offender knowingly or recklessly causes or attempts to cause death from conduct in violation of subsection (a)(5)(A)(i), a fine under this title or imprisonment for any term of years or for life, or both.

(d)(1) The United States Secret Service shall, in addition to any other agency having such authority, have the authority to investigate offenses under this section.

(2) The Federal Bureau of Investigation shall have primary authority to investigate offenses under subsection (a)(1) for any cases involving espionage, foreign counterintelligence, information protected against unauthorized disclosure for reasons of national defense or foreign relations, or Restricted Data (as that term is defined in section 11y of the Atomic Energy Act of 1954 (42 U.S.C. 2014(y)), except for offenses affecting the duties of the United States Secret Service pursuant to section 3056(a) of this title.

(3) Such authority shall be exercised in accordance with an agreement which shall be entered into by the Secretary of the Treasury and the Attorney General.

(e) As used in this section—

(1) the term "computer" means an electronic, magnetic, optical, electrochemical, or other high speed data processing device performing logical, arithmetic, or storage functions, and includes any data storage facility or communications facility directly related to or operating in conjunction with such device, but such term does not include an automated typewriter or typesetter, a portable hand held calculator, or other similar device;

(2) the term "protected computer" means a computer—

(A) exclusively for the use of a financial institution or the United States Government, or, in the case of a computer not exclusively for such use, used by or for a financial institution or the United States Government and the conduct constituting the offense affects that use by or for the financial institution or the Government; or

(B) which is used in interstate or foreign commerce or communication, including a computer located outside the United States that is used in a manner that affects interstate or foreign commerce or communication of the United States;

(3) the term "State" includes the District of Columbia, the Commonwealth of Puerto Rico, and any other commonwealth, possession or territory of the United States;

(4) the term "financial institution" means—

(A) an institution, with deposits insured by the Federal Deposit Insurance Corporation;

(B) the Federal Reserve or a member of the Federal Reserve including any Federal Reserve Bank;

(C) a credit union with accounts insured by the National Credit Union Administration;

(D) a member of the Federal home loan bank system and any home loan bank;

(E) any institution of the Farm Credit System under the Farm Credit Act of 1971;

(F) a broker-dealer registered with the Securities and Exchange Commission pursuant to section 15 of the Securities Exchange Act of 1934;

(G) the Securities Investor Protection Corporation;

(H) a branch or agency of a foreign bank (as such terms are defined in paragraphs (1) and (3) of section 1(b) of the International Banking Act of 1978); and

(I) an organization operating under section 25 or section 25(a) of the Federal Reserve Act;

(5) the term "financial record" means information derived from any record held by a financial institution pertaining to a customer's relationship with the financial institution;

(6) the term "exceeds authorized access" means to access a computer with authorization and to use such access to obtain or alter information in the computer that the accesser is not entitled so to obtain or alter;

(7) the term "department of the United States" means the legislative or judicial branch of the Government or one of the executive departments enumerated in section 101 of title 5;

(8) the term "damage" means any impairment to the integrity or availability of data, a program, a system, or information;

(9) the term "government entity" includes the Government of the United States, any State or political subdivision of the United States, any foreign country, and any state, province, municipality, or other political subdivision of a foreign country;

(10) the term "conviction" shall include a conviction under the law of any State for a crime punishable by imprisonment for more than 1 year, an element of which is unauthorized access, or exceeding authorized access, to a computer;

(11) the term "loss" means any reasonable cost to any victim, including the cost of responding to an offense, conducting a damage assessment, and restoring the data, program, system, or information to its condition prior to the offense, and any revenue lost, cost incurred, or other consequential damages incurred because of interruption of service; and

(12) the term "person" means any individual, firm, corporation, educational institution, financial institution, governmental entity, or legal or other entity.

(f) This section does not prohibit any lawfully authorized investigative, protective, or intelligence activity of a law enforcement agency of the United States, a State, or a political subdivision of a State, or of an intelligence agency of the United States.

(g) Any person who suffers damage or loss by reason of a violation of this section may maintain a civil action against the violator to obtain compensatory damages and injunctive relief or other equitable relief. A civil action for a violation of this section may be brought only if the conduct involves 1 of the factors set forth in clause (i), (ii), (iii), (iv), or (v) of subsection (a)(5)(B). Damages for a violation involving only conduct described in subsection (a)(5)(B)(i) are limited to economic damages. No action may be brought under this subsection unless such action is begun within 2 years of the date of the act complained of or the date of the discovery of the damage. No action may be brought under this subsection for the negligent design or manufacture of computer hardware, computer software, or firmware.

(h) The Attorney General and the Secretary of the Treasury shall report to the Congress annually, during the first 3 years following the date of the enactment of this subsection, concerning investigations and prosecutions under subsection (a)(5).

18 U.S.C.1956. Laundering of monetary instruments

(a)(1) Whoever, knowing that the property involved in a financial transaction represents the proceeds of some form of unlawful activity, conducts or attempts to conduct such a financial transaction which in fact involves the proceeds of specified unlawful activity—

(A)(i) with the intent to promote the carrying on of specified unlawful activity; or

(ii) with intent to engage in conduct constituting a violation of section 7201 or 7206 of the Internal Revenue Code of 1986; or

(B) knowing that the transaction is designed in whole or in part—

(i) to conceal or disguise the nature, the location, the source, the ownership, or the control of the proceeds of specified unlawful activity; or

(ii) to avoid a transaction reporting requirement under State or Federal law, shall be sentenced to a fine of not more than $500,000 or twice the value of the property involved in the transaction, whichever is greater, or imprisonment for not more than twenty years, or both. For purposes of this paragraph, a financial transaction shall be considered to be one involving the proceeds of specified unlawful activity if it is part of a set of parallel or dependent transactions, any one of which involves the proceeds of specified unlawful activity, and all of which are part of a single plan or arrangement.

(2) Whoever transports, transmits, or transfers, or attempts to transport, transmit, or transfer a monetary instrument or funds from a place in the United States to or through a place outside the United States or to a place in the United States from or through a place outside the United States—

(A) with the intent to promote the carrying on of specified unlawful activity; or

(B) knowing that the monetary instrument or funds involved in the transportation, transmission, or transfer represent the proceeds of some form of unlawful activity and knowing that such transportation, transmission, or transfer is designed in whole or in part—

(i) to conceal or disguise the nature, the location, the source, the ownership, or the control of the proceeds of specified unlawful activity; or

(ii) to avoid a transaction reporting requirement under State or Federal law, shall be sentenced to a fine of not more than $500,000 or twice the value of the monetary instrument or funds involved in the transportation, transmission, or transfer whichever is greater, or imprisonment for not more than twenty years, or both. For the purpose of the offense described in subparagraph (B), the defendant's knowledge may be established by proof that a law enforcement officer represented the matter specified in subparagraph (B) as true, and the defendant's subsequent statements or actions indicate that the defendant believed such representations to be true.

(3) Whoever, with the intent—

(A) to promote the carrying on of specified unlawful activity;

(B) to conceal or disguise the nature, location, source, ownership, or control of property believed to be the proceeds of specified unlawful activity; or

(C) to avoid a transaction reporting requirement under State or Federal law, conducts or attempts to conduct a financial transaction involving property represented to be the proceeds of specified unlawful activity, or property used to conduct or facilitate specified unlawful activity, shall be fined under this title or imprisoned for not more than 20 years, or both. For purposes of this paragraph and paragraph (2), the term "represented" means any representation made by a law enforcement officer or by another person at the direction of, or with the approval of, a Federal official authorized to investigate or prosecute violations of this section.

(b) Penalties.—

(1) In general.—Whoever conducts or attempts to conduct a transaction described in subsection (a)(1) or (a)(3), or section 1957, or a transportation, transmission, or transfer described in subsection (a)(2), is liable to the United States for a civil penalty of not more than the greater of—

(A) the value of the property, funds, or monetary instruments involved in the transaction; or

(B) $10,000.

(2) Jurisdiction over foreign persons.—For purposes of adjudicating an action filed or enforcing a penalty ordered under this section, the district courts shall have jurisdiction over any foreign person, including any financial institution authorized under the laws of a foreign country, against whom the action is brought, if service of process upon the foreign person is made under the Federal Rules of Civil Procedure or the laws of the country in which the foreign person is found, and—

(A) the foreign person commits an offense under subsection (a) involving a financial transaction that occurs in whole or in part in the United States;

(B) the foreign person converts, to his or her own use, property in which the United States has an ownership interest by virtue of the entry of an order of forfeiture by a court of the United States; or

(C) the foreign person is a financial institution that maintains a bank account at a financial institution in the United States.

(3) Court authority over assets.—A court may issue a pretrial restraining order or take any other action necessary to ensure that any bank account or other property held by the defendant in the United States is available to satisfy a judgment under this section.

(4) Federal receiver.—

(A) In general.—A court may appoint a Federal Receiver, in accordance with subparagraph (B) of this paragraph, to collect, marshal, and take custody, control, and possession of all assets of the defendant, wherever located, to satisfy a civil judgment under this subsection, a forfeiture judgment under section 981 or 982, or a criminal sentence under section 1957 or subsection (a) of this section, including an order of restitution to any victim of a specified unlawful activity.

(B) Appointment and authority.—A Federal Receiver described in subparagraph (A)—

(i) may be appointed upon application of a Federal prosecutor or a Federal or State regulator, by the court having jurisdiction over the defendant in the case;

(ii) shall be an officer of the court, and the powers of the Federal Receiver shall include the powers set out in section 754 of title 28, United States Code; and

(iii) shall have standing equivalent to that of a Federal prosecutor for the purpose of submitting requests to obtain information regarding the assets of the defendant—

(I) from the Financial Crimes Enforcement Network of the Department of the Treasury; or

(II) from a foreign country pursuant to a mutual legal assistance treaty, multilateral agreement, or other arrangement for international law enforcement assistance, provided that such requests are in accordance with the policies and procedures of the Attorney General.

(c) As used in this section—

(1) the term "knowing that the property involved in a financial transaction represents the proceeds of some form of unlawful activity" means that the person knew the property involved in the transaction represented proceeds from some form, though not necessarily which form, of activity that constitutes a felony under State, Federal, or foreign law, regardless of whether or not such activity is specified in paragraph (7);

(2) the term "conducts" includes initiating, concluding, or participating in initiating, or concluding a transaction;

(3) the term "transaction" includes a purchase, sale, loan, pledge, gift, transfer, delivery, or other disposition, and with respect to a financial institution includes a deposit, withdrawal, transfer between accounts, exchange of currency, loan, extension of credit, purchase or sale of any stock, bond, certificate of deposit, or other monetary instrument, use of a safe deposit box, or any other payment, transfer, or delivery by, through, or to a financial institution, by whatever means effected;

(4) the term "financial transaction" means (A) a transaction which in any way or degree affects interstate or foreign commerce (i) involving

the movement of funds by wire or other means or (ii) involving one or more monetary instruments, or (iii) involving the transfer of title to any real property, vehicle, vessel, or aircraft, or (B) a transaction involving the use of a financial institution which is engaged in, or the activities of which affect, interstate or foreign commerce in any way or degree;

(5) the term "monetary instruments" means (i) coin or currency of the United States or of any other country, travelers' checks, personal checks, bank checks, and money orders, or (ii) investment securities or negotiable instruments, in bearer form or otherwise in such form that title thereto passes upon delivery;

(6) the term "financial institution" includes—

(A) any financial institution, as defined in section 5312(a)(2) of title 31,United States Code, or the regulations promulgated thereunder; and

(B) any foreign bank, as defined in section 1 of the International Banking Act of 1978 (12 U.S.C. 3101);

(7) the term "specified unlawful activity" means—

(A) any act or activity constituting an offense listed in section 1961(1) of this title except an act which is indictable under subchapter II of chapter 53 of title 31;

(B) with respect to a financial transaction occurring in whole or in part in the United States, an offense against a foreign nation involving—

(i) the manufacture, importation, sale, or distribution of a controlled substance (as such term is defined for the purposes of the Controlled Substances Act);

(ii) murder, kidnapping, robbery, extortion, destruction of property by means of explosive or fire, or a crime of violence (as defined in section 16);

(iii) fraud, or any scheme or attempt to defraud, by or against a foreign bank (as defined in paragraph 7 of section 1(b) of the International Banking Act of 1978));

(iv) bribery of a public official, or the misappropriation, theft, or embezzlement of public funds by or for the benefit of a public official;

(v) smuggling or export control violations involving—

(I) an item controlled on the United States Munitions List established under section 38 of the Arms Export Control Act (22 U.S.C. 2778); or

(II) an item controlled under regulations under the Export Administration Regulations (15 C.F.R. Parts 730–774);

(vi) an offense with respect to which the United States would be obligated by a multilateral treaty, either to extradite the alleged offender or to submit the case for prosecution, if the offender were found within the territory of the United States; or

(vii) trafficking in persons, selling or buying of children, sexual exploitation of children, or transporting, recruiting or harboring a person, including a child, for commercial sex acts;

(C) any act or acts constituting a continuing criminal enterprise, as that term is defined in section 408 of the Controlled Substances Act (21 U.S.C. 848);

(D) an offense under section 32 (relating to the destruction of aircraft), section 37 (relating to violence at international airports), section 115 (relating to influencing, impeding, or retaliating against a Federal official by threatening or injuring a family member), section 152 (relating to concealment of assets; false oaths and claims; bribery), section 175c (relating to the variola virus), section 215 (relating to commissions or gifts for procuring loans), section 351 (relating to congressional or Cabinet officer assassination), any of sections 500 through 503 (relating to certain counterfeiting offenses), section 513 (relating to securities of States and private entities), section 541 (relating to goods falsely classified), section 542 (relating to entry of goods by means of false statements), section 545 (relating to smuggling goods into the United States), section 549 (relating to removing goods from Customs custody), section 554 (relating to smuggling goods from the United States), section 641 (relating to public money, property, or records), section 656 (relating to theft, embezzlement, or misapplication by bank officer or employee), section 657 (relating to lending, credit, and insurance institutions), section 658 (relating to property mortgaged or pledged to farm credit agencies), section 666 (relating to theft or bribery concerning programs receiving Federal funds), section 793, 794, or 798 (relating to espionage), section 831 (relating to prohibited transactions involving nuclear materials), section 844(f) or (i) (relating to destruction by explosives or fire of Government property or property affecting interstate or foreign commerce), section 875 (relating to interstate communications), section 922(1) (relating to the unlawful importation of firearms), section 924(n) (relating to firearms trafficking), section 956 (relating to conspiracy to kill, kidnap, maim, or injure certain property in a foreign country), section 1005 (relating to fraudulent bank entries), 1006 [FN3] (relating to fraudulent Federal credit institution entries), 1007 (relating to fraudulent Federal Deposit Insurance transactions), 1014 (relating to fraudulent loan or credit applications), section 1030 (relating to computer fraud and abuse), 1032 (relating to concealment of assets from conservator, receiver, or liquidating agent of financial institution), section 1111 (relating to murder), section 1114 (relating to murder of United States law enforcement officials), section 1116 (relating to murder of foreign officials, official guests, or internationally protected persons), section 1201 (relating to kidnaping), section 1203 (relating to hostage taking), section 1361 (relating to willful injury of Government property), section 1363 (relating to destruction of property within the special maritime and territorial jurisdiction), section 1708 (theft from the mail), section 1751 (relating to Presidential assassination), section 2113 or 2114 (relating to bank and postal robbery and theft), section 2280 (relating to violence against maritime navigation), section 2281 (relating to violence against maritime fixed platforms), section 2319 (relating to copyright infringement), section 2320 (relating to trafficking in counterfeit goods and services), section 2332 (relating to terrorist acts abroad against United States nationals), section 2332a (relating to use of weapons of mass destruction), section 2332b (relating to international terrorist acts transcending national boundaries), section 2332g (relating to missile systems designed to destroy aircraft), section 2332h (relating to radiological dispersal devices), section 2339A or 2339B (relating to providing material support to terrorists), section 2339C (relating to financing of terrorism), or section 2339D (relating to receiving military-type training from a foreign terrorist organization) of this title, section 46502 of title 49, United States Code, a felony violation of the Chemical Diversion and Trafficking Act of 1988 (relating to precursor and essential chemicals), section 590 of the Tariff Act of 1930 (19 U.S.C. 1590) (relating to aviation smuggling), section 422 of the Controlled Substances Act (relating to transportation of drug paraphernalia), section 38(c) (relating to criminal violations) of the Arms Export Control Act, section 11 (relating to violations) of the Export Administration Act of 1979, section 206 (relating to penalties) of the International Emergency Economic Powers Act, section 16 (relating to offenses and punishment) of the Trading with the Enemy Act, any felony violation of section 15 of the Food Stamp Act of 1977 [7 U.S.C.A. § 2024] (relating to food stamp fraud) involving a quantity of coupons having a value of not less than $5,000, any violation of section 543(a)(1) of the Housing Act of 1949 42 U.S.C.A. § 1490s(a)(1)] (relating to equity skimming), any felony violation of the Foreign Agents Registration Act of 1938, any felony violation of the Foreign Corrupt Practices Act, or section 92 of the Atomic Energy Act of 1954 (42 U.S.C. 2122) (relating to prohibitions governing atomic weapons)

ENVIRONMENTAL CRIMES

(E) a felony violation of the Federal Water Pollution Control Act (33 U.S.C. 1251 et seq.), the Ocean Dumping Act (33 U.S.C. 1401 et seq.), the Act to Prevent Pollution from Ships (33 U.S.C. 1901 et seq.), the Safe Drinking Water Act (42 U.S.C. 300f et seq.), or the Resources Conservation and Recovery Act (42 U.S.C. 6901 et seq.); or

(F) any act or activity constituting an offense involving a Federal health care offense;

(8) the term "State" includes a State of the United States, the District of Columbia, and any commonwealth, territory, or possession of the United States.

(d) Nothing in this section shall supersede any provision of Federal, State, or other law imposing criminal penalties or affording civil remedies in addition to those provided for in this section.

(e) Violations of this section may be investigated by such components of the Department of Justice as the Attorney General may direct, and by such components of the Department of the Treasury as the Secretary of the Treasury may direct, as appropriate, and, with respect to offenses over which the Department of Homeland Security has jurisdiction, by such components of the Department of Homeland Security as the Secretary of Homeland Security may direct, and, with respect to offenses over which the United States Postal Service has jurisdiction, by the Postal Service. Such authority of the Secretary of the Treasury, the Secretary of Homeland Security, and the Postal Service shall be exercised in accordance with an agreement which shall be entered into by the Secretary of the Treasury, the Secretary of Homeland Security, the Postal Service, and the Attorney General. Violations of this section involving offenses described in paragraph (c)(7)(E) may be investigated by such components of the Department of Justice as the Attorney General may direct, and the National Enforcement Investigations Center of the Environmental Protection Agency.

(f) There is extraterritorial jurisdiction over the conduct prohibited by this section if—

(1) the conduct is by a United States citizen or, in the case of a non-United States citizen, the conduct occurs in part in the United States; and

(2) the transaction or series of related transactions involves funds or monetary instruments of a value exceeding $10,000.

(g) Notice of conviction of financial institutions.—If any financial institution or any officer, director, or employee of any financial institution has been found guilty of an offense under this section, section 1957 or 1960 of this title, or section 5322 or 5324 of title 31, the Attorney General shall provide written notice of such fact to the appropriate regulatory agency for the financial institution.

(h) Any person who conspires to commit any offense defined in this section or section 1957 shall be subject to the same penalties as those prescribed for the offense the commission of which was the object of the conspiracy.

(i) Venue.—(1) Except as provided in paragraph (2), a prosecution for an offense under this section or section 1957 may be brought in—

(A) any district in which the financial or monetary transaction is conducted; or

(B) any district where a prosecution for the underlying specified unlawful activity could be brought, if the defendant participated in the transfer of the proceeds of the specified unlawful activity from that district to the district where the financial or monetary transaction is conducted.

(2) A prosecution for an attempt or conspiracy offense under this section or section 1957 may be brought in the district where venue would lie for the completed offense under paragraph (1), or in any other district where an act in furtherance of the attempt or conspiracy took place.

(3) For purposes of this section, a transfer of funds from 1 place to another, by wire or any other means, shall constitute a single, continuing transaction. Any person who conducts (as that term is defined in subsection (c)(2)) any portion of the transaction may be charged in any district in which the transaction takes place.

RICO Predicate Offenses ("Racketeering Activities")

8 U.S.C. 1961(1)

(A) any act or threat involving murder, kidnapping, gambling, arson, robbery, bribery, extortion, dealing in obscene matter, or dealing in a controlled substance or listed chemical (as defined in section 102 of the Controlled Substances Act), which is chargeable under State law and punishable by imprisonment for more than one year;

(B) any act which is indictable under any of the following provisions of title 18, United States Code: Section 201 (bribery), section 224 (sports bribery), sections 471, 472, and 473 (counterfeiting), section 659 (theft from interstate shipment) if the act indictable under section 659 is felonious, section 664 (embezzlement from pension and welfare funds), sections 891–894 (extortionate credit transactions), section 1028 (fraud and related activity in connection with identification documents), section 1029 (fraud and related activity in connection with access devices), section 1084 (the transmission of gambling information), section 1341 (mail fraud), section 1343 (wire fraud), section 1344 (financial institution fraud), section 1425 (the procurement of citizenship or nationalization unlawfully), section 1426 (the reproduction of naturalization or citizenship papers), section 1427 (the sale of naturalization or citizenship papers), sections 1461–1465 (obscene matter), section 1503 (obstruction of justice), section 1510 (obstruction of criminal investigations), section 1511 (the obstruction of State or local law enforcement), section 1512 (tampering with a witness, victim, or an informant), section 1513 (retaliating against a witness, victim, or an informant), section 1542 (false statement in application and use of passport), section 1543 (forgery or false use of passport), section 1544 (misuse of passport), section 1546 (fraud and misuse of visas, permits, and other documents), sections 1581-1592 (peonage, slavery, and trafficking in persons), section 1951 (interference with commerce, robbery, or extortion), section 1952 (racketeering), section 1953 (interstate transportation of wagering paraphernalia), section 1954 (unlawful welfare fund payments), section 1955 (the prohibition of illegal gambling businesses), section 1956 (the laundering of monetary instruments), section 1957 (engaging in monetarytransactions in property derived from specified unlawful activity), section 1958 (use of interstate commerce facilities in the commission of murder-for-hire), section 1960 (illegal money transmitters), sections 2251, 2251A, 2252, and 2260 (sexual exploitation of children), sections 2312 and 2313 (interstate transportation of stolen motor vehicles), sections 2314 and 2315 (interstate transportation of stolen property), section 2318 (trafficking in counterfeit labels for phonorecords, computer programs or computer program documentation or packaging and copies of motion pictures or other audiovisual works), section 2319 (criminal infringement of a copyright), section 2319A (unauthorized fixation of and trafficking in sound recordings and music videos of live musical performances), section 2320 (trafficking in goods or services bearing counterfeit marks), section 2321 (trafficking in certain motor vehicles or motor vehicle parts), sections 2341–2346 (trafficking in contraband cigarettes), sections 2421-24 (white slave traffic), sections 175–178 (biological weapons), sections 229–229F (chemical weapons), section 831 (nuclear materials),

(C) any act which is indictable under title 29, United States Code, section 186 (dealing with restrictions on payments and loans to labor organizations) or section 501(c) (embezzlement from union funds),

(D) any offense involving fraud connected with a case under title 11 (except a case under section 157 of this title), fraud in the sale of securities, or the felonious manufacture, importation, receiving, concealment, buying, selling, or otherwise dealing in a controlled substance or listed chemical (as defined in section 102 of the Controlled Substances Act), punishable under any law of the United States,

(E) any act which is indictable under the Currency and Foreign Transactions Reporting Act,

(F) any act which is indictable under the Immigration and Nationality Act, section 274 (bringing in and harboring certain aliens), section 277 (aiding or assisting certain aliens to enter the United States), or section 278 (importation of alien for immoral purpose) if the act indictable under such section of such Act was committed for the purpose of financial gain, or

(G) any act that is indictable under any provision listed in section 2332b(g)(5)(B).

Federal Crimes of Terrorism

18 U.S.C. 2332b(g)(5)(B)

(i) section 32 (destruction of aircraft or aircraft facilities), 37 (violence at international airports), 81 (arson within special maritime and territorial jurisdiction), 175 or 175b (biological weapons), 175c (variola virus), 229 (chemical weapons), subsection (a), (b), (c), or (d) of section 351 (congressional, cabinet, and Supreme Court assassination and kidnaping), 831 (nuclear materials), 832 (participation in nuclear and weapons of mass destruction threats to the United States) [FN1] 842(m) or (n) (plastic explosives), 844(f)(2) or (3) (arson and bombing of Government property risking or causing death), 844(i) (arson and bombing of property used in interstate commerce), 930(c) (killing or attempted killing during an attack on a Federal facility with a dangerous weapon), 956(a)(1) (conspiracy to murder, kidnap, or maim persons abroad), 1030(a)(1) (protection of computers), 1030(a)(5)(A)(i) resulting in damage as defined in 1030(a)(5)(B)(ii) through (v) (protection of computers), 1114 (killing or attempted killing of officers and employees of the United States), 1116 (murder or manslaughter of foreign officials, official guests, or internationally protected persons), 1203 (hostage taking), 1361 (government property or contracts), 1362 (destruction of communication lines, stations, or systems), 1363 (injury to buildings or property within special maritime and territorial jurisdiction of the United States), 1366(a) (destruction of an energy facility), 1751(a), (b), (c), or (d) (Presidential and Presidential staff assassination and kidnaping), 1992 (terrorist attacks and other acts of violence against railroad carriers and against mass transportation systems on land, on water, or through the air), 2155 (destruction of national defense materials, premises, or utilities), 2156 (national defense material, premises, or utilities), 2280 (violence against maritime navigation), 2281 (violence against maritime fixed platforms), 2332 (certain homicides and other violence against United States nationals occurring outside of the United States), 2332a (use of weapons of mass destruction), 2332b (acts of terrorism transcending national boundaries), 2332f (bombing of public places and facilities), 2332g (missile systems designed to destroy aircraft), 2332h (radiological dispersal devices), 2339 (harboring terrorists), 2339A (providing material support to terrorists), 2339B (providing material support to terrorist organizations), 2339C (financing of terrorism), 2339D (military-type training from a foreign terrorist organization), or 2340A (torture) of this title;

(ii) sections 92 (prohibitions governing atomic weapons) or 236 (sabotage of nuclear facilities or fuel) of the Atomic Energy Act of 1954 (42 U.S.C. 2122 or 2284);

(iii) section 46502 (aircraft piracy), the second sentence of section 46504 (assault on a flight crew with a dangerous weapon), section 46505(b)(3) or (c) (explosive or incendiary devices, or endangerment of human life by means of weapons, on aircraft), section 46506 if homicide or attempted homicide is involved (application of certain criminal laws to acts on aircraft), or section 60123(b) (destruction of interstate gas or hazardous liquid pipeline facility) of title 49; or

(iv) section 1010A of the Controlled Substances Import and Export Act (narco-terrorism).

18 U.S.C. 1992

(a) Whoever, in a circumstance described in subsection (c), knowingly and without lawful authority or permission—(1) wrecks, derails, sets fire to, or disables railroad on-track equipment or a mass transportation vehicle; . . . (4) sets fire to, undermines, makes unworkable, unusable, or hazardous to work on or use . . . in, upon, or near any—(A) tunnel, bridge, viaduct, trestle, track, electromagnetic guideway, signal, station, depot, warehouse, terminal, or any other way, structure, property, or appurtenance used in the operation of, or in support of the operation of, a railroad carrier, and with intent to, or knowing or having reason to know, such activity would likely, derail, disable, or wreck railroad on-track equipment; or (B) garage, terminal, structure, track, electromagnetic guideway, supply, or facility used in the operation of, or in support of the operation of, a mass transportation vehicle, and with intent to, or knowing or having reason to know, such activity would likely, derail, disable, or wreck a mass transportation vehicle used, operated, or employed by a mass transportation provider; (5) removes an appurtenance from, damages, or otherwise impairs the operation of a railroad signal system or mass transportation signal or dispatching system, including a train control system, centralized dispatching system, or highway-railroad grade crossing warning signal; (6) with intent to endanger the safety of any person, or with a reckless disregard for the safety of human life, interferes with, disables, or incapacitates any dispatcher, driver, captain, locomotive engineer, railroad conductor, or other person while the person is employed in dispatching, operating, controlling, or maintaining railroad on-track equipment or a mass transportation vehicle; (7) commits an act. . . with the intent to cause death or serious bodily injury to any person who is on property described in subparagraph (A) or (B) of paragraph (4); (8) surveils, photographs, videotapes, diagrams, or otherwise collects information with the intent to plan or assist in planning any of the acts described in paragraphs (1) through (6); (9) conveys false information, knowing the information to be false, concerning an attempt or alleged attempt to engage in a violation of this subsection; or (10) attempts, threatens, or conspires to engage in any violation of any of paragraphs (1) through (9), shall be fined under this title or imprisoned not more than 20 years, or both, and if the offense results in the death of any person, shall be imprisoned for any term of years or for life, or subject to death, except in the case of a violation of paragraph (8), (9), or (10).

(b) Aggravated offense.—Whoever commits an offense under subsection (a) of this section in a circumstance in which—(1) the railroad on-track equipment or mass transportation vehicle was carrying a passenger or employee at the time of the offense; (2) the railroad on-track equipment or mass transportation vehicle was carrying high-level radioactive waste or spent nuclear fuel at the time of the offense; or (3) the offense was committed with the intent to endanger the safety of any person, or with a reckless disregard for the safety of any person, and the railroad on-track equipment or mass transportation vehicle was carrying a hazardous material at the time of the offense that—(A) was required to be placarded under subpart F of part 172 of title 49, Code of Federal Regulations; and (B) is identified as class number 3, 4, 5, 6.1, or 8 and packing group I or packing group II, or class number 1, 2, or 7 under the hazardous materials table of section 172.101 of title 49, Code of Federal Regulations, shall be fined under this title or imprisoned for any term of years or life, or both, and if the offense resulted in the death of any person, the person may be sentenced to death.

(c) Circumstances required for offense.—A circumstance referred to in subsection (a) is any of the following: (1) Any of the conduct required for the offense is, or, in the case of an attempt, threat, or conspiracy to engage in conduct, the conduct required for the completed offense would be, engaged in, on, against, or affecting a mass transportation provider, or a railroad carrier engaged in interstate or foreign commerce. (2) Any person travels or communicates across a State line in order to commit the offense, or transports materials across a State line in aid of the commission of the offense.

(d) Definitions.—In this section . . . (7) the term 'mass transportation' has the meaning given to that term in section 5302(a)(7) of title 49, except that the term includes intercity bus transportation school bus, charter, and sightseeing transportation and passenger vessel as that term is defined in section 2101(22) of title 46, United States Code; (8) the term 'on-track equipment' means a carriage or other contrivance that runs on rails or electromagnetic guideways; (9) the term 'railroad on-track equipment' means a train, locomotive, tender, motor unit, freight or passenger car, or other on-track equipment used, operated, or employed by a railroad carrier; (10) the term 'railroad' has the meaning given to that term in chapter 201 of title 49; (11) the term 'railroad carrier' has the meaning given to that term in chapter 201 of title 49; (12) the term 'serious bodily injury' has the meaning given to that term in section 1365; (13) the term 'spent nuclear fuel' has the meaning given to that term in section 2(23) of the Nuclear Waste Policy Act of 1982 (42 U.S.C. 10101(23) . . .(16) the term 'vehicle' means any carriage or other contrivance used, or capable of being used, as a means of transportation on land, on water, or through the air.

CYBERTERRORISM: ANALYSIS, WARNING, AND LESSONS LEARNED

Commentary

By
Douglas C. Lovelace, Jr.

The final three documents presented in this volume provide assessments of the extent to which U.S. information systems are defended against the threat posed by cyber-terrorists. The first addresses extant approaches to analyzing cyber-attacks and identifies significant challenges yet to be overcome to protect the nation's information systems. The second discusses the lessons the Department of Homeland Security learned as a result of a simulation exercise conducted to assess the nation's cyber-attack capabilities, and what it had done or plans to do, having learned those lessons. The final document provides a useful case study of the defensive posture *vis-à-vis* cyber-attacks of the nation's largest public power company. The report offers important insights into the efficacy of extant cyber-defenses.

We caution the reader that the information these three reports provide is limited in three important ways, with respect to providing an assessment of the cyber-terror threat. First, the reports do not provide comprehensive coverage of the many issues the threat of cyberterrorism raises. However, they do present sufficient content to enable the reader to gain an overall appreciation of the threat and efforts taken and needed to counter and mitigate it. Second, the reports derive from unclassified information. Because much data and analysis concerning the cyberterrorism threat and programs to counter it are not available to the general public, the reports presented in this section do not necessarily provide all the texture needed for a full understanding of cyberterrorism and the actual threat it poses to U.S. national security. Third, the documents discuss only the defensive measures taken to counter the cyberterrorism threat. They do not describe any offensive computer network attack and retaliation measures that might exist. Again, that may be due mainly to information classification or sensitivity.

In the first document presented, *Cyber Analysis and Warning: DHS Faces Challenges in Establishing a Comprehensive National Capability*, the Government Accountability Office (GAO) identified key cyber-analysis and warning capability requirements, compared them to the United States Computer

Emergency Readiness Team's (US-CERT's) current capabilities in order to perform a gap analysis, and identified what actions should be taken to fill the gaps revealed. The key capabilities include detection of network anomalies, determining whether they are threats, providing timely warning, promulgating other useful threat and mitigation information, and responding to the threat. After identifying 15 key attributes associated with the capabilities, the report assesses the extent to which relevant attributes contribute to the efficacy of the US-CERT's capabilities. Using this methodology, the report's authors were able to expose capability deficiencies where the attributes were not present in sufficient measure to provide adequate capability. The result is identification of capability and capacity deficiencies that require attention.

The capability and capacity deficiencies identified include the lack of a baseline of the nation's critical network assets and operations, inadequate predictive analyses, lack of consistency in providing actionable or timely notifications, and operating without organizational stability and leadership within the department of homeland Security (DHS). The report concludes that until US-CERT addresses those deficiencies, it will not be able to perform its cyber-analysis and warning missions adequately. The report's authors make ten recommendations to the Secretary of Homeland Security, who accepted all but one: to ensure distinct and transparent lines of authority and responsibilities between its organizations, stating the Department had already addressed the issue adequately.

The report's recommendations are striking in that they suggest DHS has a long way to go before achieving satisfactory security of U.S. information systems from cyber-attack. They suggest an apparent lack of priority given to securing information systems over the past several years. The assessment of inadequate measures is consistent with the previously discussed waning of the threat perception since the September 11, 2001 attacks, notwithstanding the Estonian experience. Prudent renewed concern about the security of U.S. information systems makes this report a very important document, and we commend it for a very careful read.

Critical Infrastructure Protection: DHS Needs to Fully Address Lessons Learned from Its First Cyber Storm Exercise is a GOA report on the extent to which DHS has internalized and addressed the lessons it learned from its first cyber-attack simulation exercise. The exercise was designed to expose vulnerabilities to cyber-attack for the purpose of strengthening public and private incident response capabilities. In 2006, DHS inaugurated an exercise series named "Cyber Storm." The Department has conducted two such exercises, the first in 2006 and the second in 2008. The exercises seek to simulate multiple concurrent cyber-attacks involving federal, state and foreign government information systems, as well as those of private industry.

GAO's report identifies the lessons DHS learned from the 2006 Cyber Storm exercise, assesses what actions DHS has taken as a result of learning the lessons, and discusses views of key participants of the 2008 exercise.

The GAO report is fairly critical of the DHS. It found that DHS had identified eight significant lessons, but has not yet taken sufficient action to address them fully. The lessons include improving interagency coordination; better risk assessment and contingency planning; more effective determination of attacks; more complete integration of incidents across infrastructures; greater access to information; better coordination of responses; more effective strategic communications and public relations; improvement of processes, tools, and technology; and improvement of the exercise program itself. Additionally, following the 2006 exercise, DHS identified 66 activities that address one or more of the lessons and has completed most of them. Nonetheless, it has not completed some of the more important ones and has not been able to set a completion date for most of those. Consequently, the GAO report finds, DHS risks encountering many of the same lessons in future exercises, rather than moving beyond the lessons of the first exercise. Therefore, the repost suggests that DHS has not fully benefitted from the 2006 exercise and enhancements to security from cyber-threats that should have accrued have not.

GAO's conclusion that DHS's learning from the 2006 exercise is incomplete was supported by participants in the March 2008 Cyber Storm exercise. While they reported progress since the 2006 exercise, they also noted that many challenges remained in the areas of properly scoping the exercise, roles and responsibilities, public relations, communications, exercise infrastructure, handling of classified information, and the role of law enforcement during a cyber-attack. Notwithstanding the many specific criticisms leveled, the report's authors framed their recommendation in general: that the Secretary of Homeland Security direct the Assistant Secretary for Cybersecurity and Communications to ensure the scheduling and completion of the corrective actions addressing lessons learned during Cyber Storm I before conducting the next Cyber Storm Exercise.

This GAO report comes at a propitious time, given the renewed appreciation for the cyber-terrorist threat. Its presentation to the House of Representatives' Committee on Homeland Security's Subcommittee on Emerging Threats, Cybersecurity, and Science and Technology should add urgency to DHS' efforts to internalize and act on all the lessons it learned from the 2006 and 2008 exercises. The GAO report authors were arguably excessively harsh in their criticism, given that DHS is not only a relatively new and still developing department, but also is very large and disparate. Effecting significant change in an organization such as DHS often takes years, if not decades. The most important point is that DHS leadership sees the need for improvement and is committed to it.

The final document in this section, *Information Security: TVA Needs to Address Weaknesses in Control Systems and Networks*, reports on a GAO study conducted to determine whether the Tennessee Valley Authority (TVA) has implemented appropriate information security practices to protect its control systems. The study's purpose is extraordinarily important given that TVA is the nation's largest public power company and generates and distributes power in an area of about 80,000 square miles. GAO correctly noted that securing the control systems that regulate the nation's critical infrastructures is vital to ensuring U.S. economic security and public health and safety. To assess the extent to which TVA has secured its vast assets from cyber-attack, GAO examined the security of several TVA facilities; analyzed the agency's information security policies, plans, and procedures and interviewed Authority officials.

The GAO's assessment is a clarion call for remedial action. It concluded that significant security deficiencies exist in TVA's control systems and networks and that the deficiencies were multi-level and interactive; i.e., problems at one level or in one area could manifest themselves at other levels and in other areas. Deficiencies observed include the following: the intrusion detection system had limited capability, firewalls were inadequate or not used, key patches were lacking, and physical security at multiple locations did not sufficiently protect critical control systems. Additionally, the report notes that the TVA had not consistently implemented key activities such as systems inventory, risk assessment, system security planning, testing and monitoring, training, and tracking remedial actions. The report provides additional detail in each of the deficiency areas and provides astute insights into the challenges associated with protecting a significant part of the Nation's critical infrastructure from cyber-attack.

The GAO investigators were not completely sanguine about TVA's commitment to correcting the many deficiencies noted. The report states that although Authority officials said they planned to address the issues, they have not established timelines for completion of corrective actions in key deficiency areas. In addition, the report also notes ineffective prioritization of work, which suggests management issues. The report very soberly concludes that until TVA fully addresses the myriad security issues, it is vulnerable to cyberterrorism. That assessment is very significant, given that TVA is a longstanding, well established, and well funded organization. It begs the question that if TVA has not been able to satisfactorily attend to its cyber-security challenges, it is reasonable to expect that other components of the U.S. critical infrastructure have? If the TVA case study points to the state of cyber-security prevalent across the nation's key infrastructure, much work needs to be accomplished very quickly.

GAO offered TVA several recommendations. The report presents nineteen such recommendations and states that GAO is recommending 73 additional actions to address specific weaknesses in information security controls in a separate report designated "Limited Official Use Only." The recommendations GAO made, as a result of this study, appear considerably more specific than normally found in GAO reports. Perhaps that is in recognition of the urgency of the action required. The recommendations contained in the report herein presented, not to mention those made in the limited distribution report, are striking for two reasons. First, they are quite comprehensive, if not sweeping. They affect virtually every aspect of TVA's information system architecture. Second, many suggest actions that one would think an organization like TVA would be taking in the normal course of business. As suggested above, if the TVA experience is even close to being representative of other critical infrastructures, then greater concern over the cyber-terrorist threat than many currently perceive appears warranted.

DOCUMENT NO. 7

CYBER ANALYSIS AND WARNING: DHS FACES CHALLENGES IN ESTABLISHING A COMPREHENSIVE NATIONAL CAPABILITY

GAO Report
GAO-08-588

July 2008

What GAO Found

Cyber analysis and warning capabilities include (1) monitoring network activity to detect anomalies, (2) analyzing information and investigating anomalies to determine whether they are threats, (3) warning appropriate officials with timely and actionable threat and mitigation information, and (4) responding to the threat. GAO identified 15 key attributes associated with these capabilities, as shown in the following table:

Key Attributes of Cyber Analysis and Warning

Capability	Attribute
Monitoring	• Establish a baseline understanding of network assets and normal network traffic volume and flow • Assess risks to network assets • Obtain internal information on network operations via technical tools and user reports • Obtain external information on threats, vulnerabilities, and incidents • Detect anomalous activities
Analysis	• Verify that an anomaly is an incident (threat of attack or actual attack) • Investigate the incident to identify the type of cyber attack, estimate impact, and collect evidence • Identify possible actions to mitigate the impact of the incident • Integrate results into predictive analysis of broader implications or potential future attack

Capability	Attribute
Warning	• Develop attack and other notifications that are targeted and actionable • Provide notifications in a timely manner • Distribute notifications using appropriate communications methods
Response	• Contain and mitigate the incident • Recover from damages and remediate vulnerabilities • Evaluate actions and incorporate lessons learned

Source: GAO analysis.

While US-CERT's cyber analysis and warning capabilities include aspects of each of the key attributes, they do not fully incorporate all of them. For example, as part of its monitoring, US-CERT obtains information from numerous external information sources; however, it has not established a baseline of our nation's critical network assets and operations. In addition, while it investigates if identified anomalies constitute actual cyber threats or attacks as part of its analysis, it does not integrate its work into predictive analyses. Further, it provides warnings by developing and distributing a wide array of notifications; however, these notifications are not consistently actionable or timely.

US-CERT faces a number of newly identified and ongoing challenges that impede it from fully incorporating the key attributes and thus being able to coordinate the national efforts to prepare for, prevent, and respond to cyber threats. The newly identified challenge is creating warnings that are consistently actionable and timely. Ongoing challenges that GAO previously identified, and made recommendations to address, include employing predictive analysis and operating without organizational stability and leadership within DHS, including possible overlapping roles and responsibilities. Until US-CERT addresses these challenges and fully incorporates all key attributes, it will not have the full complement of cyber analysis and warning capabilities essential to effectively performing its national mission.

Abbreviations

CERT/CC	CERT Coordination Center
DHS	Department of Homeland Security
DOD	Department of Defense
HITRAC	Homeland Infrastructure Threat and Risk Analysis Center
HSPD	Homeland Security Presidential Directive
ISAC	information sharing and analysis center

NCRCG	National Cyber Response Coordination Group
NCSD	National Cyber Security Division
NIST	National Institute of Standards and Technology
OMB	Office of Management and Budget
US-CERT	United States Computer Emergency Readiness Team

United States Goverment Accountability Office
Washington, DC 2058

July 31, 2008

The Honorable James R. Langevin
Chairman
The Honorable Michael T. McCaul
Ranking Member
Subcommittee on Emerging Threats, Cybersecurity, and
Science and Technology
Committee on Homeland Security
House of Representatives

The rapid increase in computer connectivity has revolutionized the way that our government, our nation, and much of the world communicate and conduct business. While the benefits have been enormous, this widespread interconnectivity also poses significant risks to our nation's computer-reliant critical operations. Establishing analytical and warning capabilities is essential to thwarting computer-based, or cyber, threats and attacks. Cyber analysis and warning capabilities include (1) monitoring network activity to detect anomalies, (2) analyzing information and investigating anomalies to determine whether they are threats, (3) warning appropriate officials with timely and actionable threat and mitigation information, and (4) responding to the threat.

Federal law and policy direct the Department of Homeland Security (DHS) to establish such capabilities for our nation. To fulfill this requirement, the department established the United States Computer Emergency Readiness Team (US-CERT) to develop and implement these capabilities and, in doing so, coordinate the nation's efforts to prepare for, prevent, and respond to cyber threats and attacks.

Our objectives were to (1) identify key attributes of cyber analysis and warning capabilities, (2) compare these attributes with US-CERT's current analysis and warning capabilities to identify whether there are gaps, and (3) identify US-CERT's challenges to developing and implementing key attributes and a successful national cyber analysis and warning capability.

To identify key attributes, we identified and analyzed relevant laws, strategies, policies, reports, and studies; observed cyber analysis and warning operations at numerous entities; and interviewed responsible officials and experts from federal and nonfederal entities.[1] To determine US-CERT's current capabilities and related challenges, we analyzed DHS's policies, procedures, and program plans and interviewed relevant officials. Appendix I provides further details on our objectives, scope, and methodology.

We conducted this performance audit from June 2007 to July 2008 in accordance with generally accepted government auditing standards. Those standards require that we plan and perform the audit to obtain sufficient, appropriate evidence to provide a reasonable basis for our findings and conclusions based on our audit objectives. We believe that the evidence obtained provides a reasonable basis for our findings and conclusions based on our audit objectives.

Results in Brief

Cyber analysis and warning typically encompasses four key capabilities: monitoring, analysis, warning, and response. Monitoring system and communication networks includes activities to detect cyber threats, attacks, and vulnerabilities. Analysis involves taking the information gathered from monitoring and hypothesizing about what the threat or attack might be, investigating it, and identifying any impact and, if necessary, mitigation steps. Warning includes alerting recipients about potential or imminent, as well as ongoing, cyber threats or attacks. Response includes containing and recovering from cyber incidents that occur. Our research and past experience identified 15 key attributes associated with these cyber analysis and warning capabilities, as shown in the following table:

Table 1. Attributes of Cyber Analysis and Warning

Capability	Attribute
Monitoring	Establish a baseline understanding of network assets and normal network traffic volume and flow Assess risks to network assets Obtain internal information on network operations via technical tools and user reports Obtain external information on threats, vulnerabilities, and incidents Detect anomalous activities
Analysis	Verify that an anomaly is an incident (threat of attack or actual attack) Investigate the incident to identify the type of cyber attack, estimate impact, and collect evidence

[1] Nonfederal entities include state and local governments, private sector entities, and academic institutions.

Capability	Attribute
	Identify possible actions to mitigate the impact of the incident Integrate results into predictive analysis of broader implications or potential future attack
Warning	Develop attack and other notifications that are targeted and actionable Provide notifications in a timely manner Distribute notifications using appropriate communications methods
Response	Contain and mitigate the incident Recover from damages and remediate vulnerabilities Evaluate actions and incorporate lessons learned

Source: GAO analysis.

While US-CERT's cyber analysis and warning capabilities include aspects of each of the key attributes, they do not fully incorporate all of them. For example, as part of its monitoring, US-CERT obtains information from numerous external information sources; however, it has not established a comprehensive baseline of our nation's critical computer-reliant critical assets and network operations. In addition, while it investigates if identified anomalies constitute actual cyber threats or attacks as part of its analysis, the organization does not integrate its work into predictive analyses, nor does it have the analytical or technical resources to analyze multiple, simultaneous cyber incidents. The organization also provides warnings by developing and distributing a wide array of attack and other notifications; however, these notifications are not consistently actionable or timely—providing the right information to the right persons or groups as early as possible to give them time to take appropriate action. Further, while it responds to a limited number of affected entities in their efforts to contain and mitigate an attack, recover from damages, and remediate vulnerabilities, the organization does not possess the resources to handle multiple events across the nation.

US-CERT faces a number of newly identified and ongoing challenges that impede it from fully implementing the key attributes and in turn establishing cyber analysis and warning capabilities essential to coordinating the national effort to prepare for, prevent, and respond to cyber threats. The newly identified challenge is creating warnings that are actionable and timely—US-CERT does not consistently issue warning and other notifications that its customers find useful. Ongoing challenges that we previously identified and made recommendations to address are

- employing predictive cyber analysis—the organization has not established the ability to determine broader implications from ongoing network activity, predict or protect against future threats, or identify emerging attack methods;

- developing more trusted relationships to encourage information sharing—federal and nonfederal entities are reluctant to share information because US-CERT and these parties have yet to develop close working and trusted relationships that would allow the free flow of information;
- having sufficient analytical and technical capabilities—the organization has difficulty hiring and retaining adequately trained staff and acquiring supporting technology tools to handle a steadily increasing workload; and
- operating without organizational stability and leadership within DHS—the department has not provided the sustained leadership to make cyber analysis and warning a priority. This is due in part to frequent turnover in key management positions that currently also remain vacant. In addition, US-CERT's role as the central provider of cyber analysis and warning may be diminished by the creation of a new DHS center at a higher organizational level.

Until DHS addresses these challenges and fully incorporates all key attributes into its capabilities, it will not have the full complement of cyber analysis and warning capabilities essential to effectively performing its national mission.

Accordingly, we are making 10 recommendations to the Secretary of Homeland Security to improve DHS's cyber analysis and warning capabilities by implementing key cyber analysis and warning attributes and addressing the challenges, including

- developing close working and more trusted relationships with federal and nonfederal entities that would allow the free flow of information,
- expeditiously hiring sufficiently trained staff and acquiring supporting technology tools to handle the steadily increasing workload,
- ensuring consistent notifications that are actionable and timely,
- filling key management positions to provide organizational stability and leadership, and
- ensuring that there are distinct and transparent lines of authority and responsibility assigned to DHS organizations with cybersecurity roles and responsibilities.

In written comments on a draft of this report (see app. II), the department concurred with 9 of our 10 recommendations. It also described actions planned and under way to implement these recommendations. DHS took exception to 1 recommendation, stating that it had developed a concept-of-operations document that clearly defined roles and responsibilities for key DHS organizations. However, this document is still in draft, and the department has yet to establish a date for it to be finalized and implemented.

Background

Increasing computer interconnectivity—most notably growth in the use of the Internet—has revolutionized the way that our government, our nation, and much of the world communicate and conduct business. While the benefits have been enormous, they are accompanied by significant risks to the nation's computer systems and to the critical operations and infrastructures that those systems support.[2]

Cyber Threats and Incidents Adversely Affect the Nation's Critical Infrastructure

Different types of cyber threats from numerous sources may adversely affect computers, software, a network, an agency's operations, an industry, or the Internet itself. Cyber threats can be unintentional or intentional. Unintentional threats can be caused by software upgrades or maintenance procedures that inadvertently disrupt systems. Intentional threats include both targeted and untargeted attacks. A targeted attack occurs when a group or individual specifically attacks a cyber asset. An untargeted attack occurs when the intended target of the attack is uncertain, such as when a virus, worm, or malware is released on the Internet with no specific target.

Threats to the Nation's Critical Infrastructure Are Proliferating

There is increasing concern among both government officials and industry experts regarding the potential for a cyber attack on the national critical infrastructure, including the infrastructure's control systems. The Department of Defense (DOD) and the Federal Bureau of Investigation, among others, have identified multiple sources of threats to our nation's critical infrastructure, including foreign nation states engaged in information warfare, domestic criminals, hackers, virus writers, and disgruntled employees working within an organization. In addition, there is concern about the growing vulnerabilities to our nation as the design, manufacture, and service of

[2] Critical infrastructure is systems and assets, whether physical or virtual, so vital to the United States that their incapacity or destruction would have a debilitating impact on national security, national economic security, national public health or safety, or any combination of those matters. There are 18 critical infrastructure sectors: agriculture and food, banking and finance, chemical, commercial facilities, communications, critical manufacturing, dams, defense industrial base, emergency services, energy, government facilities, information technology, national monuments and icons, nuclear reactors, materials and waste, postal and shipping, public health and health care, transportation systems, and water.

information technology have moved overseas.[3] For example, according to media reports, technology has been shipped to the United States from foreign countries with viruses on the storage devices.[4] Further, U.S. authorities are concerned about the prospect of combined physical and cyber attacks, which could have devastating consequences. For example, a cyber attack could disable a security system in order to facilitate a physical attack. Table 2 lists sources of threats that have been identified by the U.S. intelligence community and others.

Table 2. Sources of Emerging Cybersecurity Threats

Threat	Description
Bot-network operators	Bot-network operators take over multiple systems in order to coordinate attacks and to distribute phishing schemes, spam, and malware attacks (See Table 3 for definitions). The services of these networks are sometimes made available on underground markets (e.g., purchasing a denial-of-service attack or servers to relay spam or phishing attacks).
Criminal groups	Criminal groups seek to attack systems for monetary gain. Specifically, organized crime groups are using spam, phishing, and spyware/malware to commit identity theft and online fraud. International corporate spies and organized crime organizations also pose a threat to the United States through their ability to conduct industrial espionage and large-scale monetary theft and to hire or develop hacker talent.
Foreign intelligence services	Foreign intelligence services use cyber tools as part of their information-gathering and espionage activities. In addition, several nations are aggressively working to develop information warfare doctrine, programs, and capabilities. Such capabilities enable a single entity to have a significant and serious impact by disrupting the supply, communications, and economic infrastructures that support military power—impacts that could affect the daily lives of U.S. citizens across the country.
Hackers	Hackers break into networks for the thrill of the challenge or for bragging rights in the hacker community. While gaining unauthorized access once required a fair amount of skill or computer knowledge, hackers can now download attack scripts and protocols from the Internet and launch them against victim sites. Thus, while attack tools have become more sophisticated, they have also become easier to use.

[3] Statement of the Director of National Intelligence before the Senate Select Committee on Intelligence, *Annual Threat Assessment of the Director of National Intelligence for the Senate Select Committee on Intelligence* (Feb. 5, 2008).

[4] Robert McMillan, "Seagate Ships Virus-Laden Hard Drives," InfoWorld (San Francisco, California: InfoWorld Media Group, Nov. 12, 2007), http://www.infoworld.com/ article/07/11/12/Seagate-ships-virus-laden-hard-drives_1.html (accessed Apr. 9, 2008).

Threat	Description
	According to the Central Intelligence Agency, the large majority of hackers do not have the requisite expertise to threaten difficult targets such as critical U.S. networks. Nevertheless, the worldwide population of hackers poses a relatively high threat of an isolated or brief disruption causing serious damage.
Insiders	The disgruntled organization insider is a principal source of computer crime. Insiders may not need a great deal of knowledge about computer intrusions because their knowledge of a target system often allows them to gain unrestricted access to cause damage to the system or to steal system data. The insider threat includes contractors hired by the organization as well as employees who accidentally introduce malware into systems.
Phishers	Individuals, or small groups, execute phishing schemes in an attempt to steal identities or information for monetary gain. Phishers may also use spam and spyware/malware to accomplish their objectives.
Spammers	Individuals or organizations distribute unsolicited e-mail with hidden or false information in order to sell products, conduct phishing schemes, distribute spyware/malware, or attack organizations (i.e., denial of service).
Spyware/malware authors	Individuals or organizations with malicious intent carry out attacks against users by producing and distributing spyware and malware. Several destructive computer viruses and worms have harmed files and hard drives, including the Melissa Macro Virus, the Explore.Zip worm, the CIH (Chernobyl) Virus, Nimda, Code Red, Slammer, and Blaster.
Terrorists	Terrorists seek to destroy, incapacitate, or exploit critical infrastructures in order to threaten national security, cause mass casualties, weaken the U.S. economy, and damage public morale and confidence. Terrorists may use phishing schemes or spyware/malware in order to generate funds or gather sensitive information.

Source: GAO analysis based on data from the Federal Bureau of Investigation, the Central Intelligence Agency, and the Software Engineering Institute's CERT® Coordination Center.

The nation's critical infrastructure operates in an environment of increasing and dynamic threats, and adversaries are becoming more agile and sophisticated. Terrorists, transnational criminals, and intelligence services use various cyber tools that can deny access, degrade the integrity of, intercept, or destroy data and jeopardize the security of the nation's critical infrastructure (see table 3).

Table 3. Types of Cyber Attacks

Type of Attack	Description
Denial of service	A method of attack from a single source that denies system access to legitimate users by overwhelming the target computer with messages and blocking legitimate traffic. It can prevent a system from being able to exchange data with other systems or use the Internet.
Distributed denial of service	A variant of the denial-of-service attack that uses a coordinated attack from a distributed system of computers rather than from a single source. It often makes use of worms to spread to multiple computers that can then attack the target.
Exploit tools	Publicly available and sophisticated tools that intruders of various skill levels can use to determine vulnerabilities and gain entry into targeted systems.
Logic bombs	A form of sabotage in which a programmer inserts code that causes the program to perform a destructive action when some triggering event occurs, such as terminating the programmer's employment.
Phishing	The creation and use of e-mails and Web sites—designed to look like those of well-known legitimate businesses, financial institutions, and government agencies—in order to deceive Internet users into disclosing their personal data, such as bank and financial account information and passwords. The phishers then use that information for criminal purposes, such as identity theft and fraud.
Sniffer	Synonymous with packet sniffer. A program that intercepts routed data and examines each packet in search of specified information, such as passwords transmitted in clear text.
Trojan horse	A computer program that conceals harmful code. A Trojan horse usually masquerades as a useful program that a user would wish to execute.
Virus	A program that infects computer files, usually executable programs, by inserting a copy of itself into the file. These copies are usually executed when the infected file is loaded into memory, allowing the virus to infect other files. Unlike a computer worm, a virus requires human involvement (usually unwitting) to propagate.
Vishing	A method of phishing based on voice-over-Internet Protocol technology and open-source call center software that have made it inexpensive for scammers to set up phony call centers and criminals to send e-mail or text messages to potential victims, saying there has been a security problem and they need to call their bank to reactivate a credit or debit card, or send text messages to cell phones, instructing potential victims to contact fake online banks to renew their accounts.

Type of Attack	Description
War driving	A method of gaining entry into wireless computer networks using a laptop, antennas, and a wireless network adaptor that involves patrolling locations to gain unauthorized access.
Worm	An independent computer program that reproduces by copying itself from one system to another across a network. Unlike computer viruses, worms do not require human involvement to propagate.
Zero-day exploit	A cyber threat taking advantage of a security vulnerability on the same day that the vulnerability becomes known to the general public and for which there are no available fixes.

Source: GAO analysis of data from GAO and industry reports.

Cyber Incidents Have Caused Serious Damage

The growing number of known vulnerabilities increases the potential number of attacks. By exploiting software vulnerabilities, hackers and others who spread malicious code can cause significant damage, ranging from defacing Web sites to taking control of entire systems and thereby being able to read, modify, or delete sensitive information; disrupt operations; launch attacks against other organizations' systems; or destroy systems. Reports of attacks involving critical infrastructure demonstrate that a serious attack could be devastating, as the following examples illustrate.

- In June 2003, the U.S. government issued a warning concerning a virus that specifically targeted financial institutions. Experts said the BugBear.b virus was programmed to determine whether a victim had used an e-mail address for any of the roughly 1,300 financial institutions listed in the virus's code. If a match was found, the software attempted to collect and document user input by logging keystrokes and then provide this information to a hacker, who could use it in attempts to break into the banks' networks.[5]
- In August 2006, two Los Angeles city employees hacked into computers controlling the city's traffic lights and disrupted signal lights at four intersections, causing substantial backups and delays. The attacks were launched prior to an anticipated labor protest by the employees.[6]
- In October 2006, a foreign hacker penetrated security at a water filtering plant in Harrisburg, Pennsylvania. The intruder planted malicious

[5] GAO, *Critical Infrastructure Protection: Department of Homeland Security Faces Challenges in Fulfilling Cybersecurity Responsibilities*, GAO-05-434 (Washington, D.C.: May 26, 2005).
[6] GAO, *Critical Infrastructure Protection: Multiple Efforts to Secure Control Systems Are Under Way, but Challenges Remain*, GAO-08-119T (Washington, D.C.: Oct. 17, 2007).

software that was capable of affecting the plant's water treatment operations.[7]

- In May 2007, Estonia was the reported target of a denial-of-service cyber attack with national consequences. The coordinated attack created mass outages of its government and commercial Web sites.[8]
- In March 2008, the Department of Defense reported that in 2007 computer networks operated by Defense, other federal agencies, and defense-related think tanks and contractors were targets of cyber warfare intrusion techniques. Although those responsible were not definitively substantiated, the attacks appeared to have originated in China.[9]

As these examples illustrate, attacks resulting in the incapacitation or destruction of the nation's critical infrastructures could have a debilitating impact on national and economic security and on public health and safety.

Federal Law and Policy Establish the Need for National Cyber Analysis and Warning

To protect the nation's critical computer-dependent infrastructures against cyber threats and attacks, federal law and policy have identified the need to enhance cybersecurity and establish cyber analytical and warning capabilities, which are sometimes referred to as "indications and warnings." The laws and policies include (1) the Homeland Security Act of 2002, (2) the National Strategy to Secure Cyberspace, (3) Homeland Security Presidential Directive 7, and (4) the National Response Framework. In addition, the President issued in January 2008 Homeland Security Presidential Directive 23, which, according to US-CERT officials, has provisions that affect cyber analysis and warning efforts of the federal government.

Homeland Security Act of 2002

The Homeland Security Act of 2002 established the Department of Homeland Security and gave it lead responsibility for preventing terrorist attacks in the United States, reducing the vulnerability of the United States to terrorist attacks, and minimizing the damage and assisting in recovery

[7] GAO-08-119T.

[8] Computer Emergency Response Team of Estonia, "Malicious Cyber Attacks Against Estonia Come from Abroad," April 29, 2007, and Remarks by Homeland Security Secretary Michael Chertoff to the 2008 RSA Conference, April 8, 2008.

[9] Office of the Secretary of Defense, *Annual Report to Congress: Military Power of the People's Republic of China 2008*.

from attacks that do occur.[10] The act assigned the department, among other things, a number of critical infrastructure protection responsibilities, including gathering of threat information, including cyber-related, from law enforcement, intelligence sources, and other agencies of the federal, state, and local governments and private sector entities to identify, assess, and understand threats; carrying out assessments of the vulnerabilities of key resources to determine the risks posed by attacks; and integrating information, analyses, and vulnerability assessments in order to identify priorities for protection. In addition, the department is responsible for disseminating, as appropriate, information that it analyzes—both within the department and to other federal, state, and local government agencies and private sector entities—to assist in the deterrence, prevention, preemption of, or response to terrorist acts.

National Strategy to Secure Cyberspace

The National Strategy to Secure Cyberspace proposes that a public/private architecture be provided for analyzing, warning, and managing incidents of national significance.[11] The strategy states that cyber analysis includes both (1) tactical analytical support during a cyber incident and (2) strategic analyses of threats. Tactical support involves providing current information on specific factors associated with incidents under investigation or specific identified vulnerabilities. Examples of tactical support include analysis of (1) a computer virus delivery mechanism to issue immediate guidance on ways to prevent or mitigate damage related to an imminent threat or (2) a specific computer intrusion or set of intrusions to determine the perpetrator, motive, and method of attack. Strategic analysis is predictive in that it looks beyond one specific incident to consider a broader set of incidents or implications that may indicate a potential future threat of national importance. For example, strategic analyses may identify long-term vulnerability and threat trends that provide advance warnings of increased risk, such as emerging attack methods. Strategic analyses are intended to provide policymakers with information that they can use to anticipate and prepare for attacks, thereby diminishing the damage from such attacks.

Homeland Security Presidential Directive 7

Homeland Security Presidential Directive 7 (HSPD 7) directs DHS to, among other things, serve as the focal point for securing cyberspace. This includes analysis, warning, information sharing, vulnerability reduction, mitigation,

[10] Homeland Security Act of 2002, Pub. L. 107-296 (Nov. 25, 2002).
[11] The White House, *The National Strategy to Secure Cyberspace* (Washington, D.C.: February 2003).

and recovery efforts for critical infrastructure information systems.[12] It also directs DHS to develop a national indications and warnings architecture for infrastructure protection and capabilities, including cyber, that will facilitate an understanding of baseline infrastructure operations, the identification of indicators and precursors to an attack, and create a surge capacity for detecting and analyzing patterns of potential attacks.

In May 2005, we reported that DHS has many cybersecurity-related roles and responsibilities, including developing and enhancing national cyber analysis and warning capabilities.[13] However, we found that DHS had not fully addressed all its cybersecurity-related responsibilities and that it faced challenges that impeded its ability to fulfill its responsibilities. These challenges included having organizational stability and authority, hiring employees, establishing information sharing and effective partnerships, and developing strategic analysis and warning. We made recommendations to the Secretary of Homeland Security to engage appropriate stakeholders to prioritize key cybersecurity responsibilities, develop a prioritized list of key activities to addressing underlying challenges, and identify performance measures and milestones for fulfilling its responsibilities and for addressing its challenges. We did not make new recommendations regarding cyber-related analysis and warning because our previous recommendations had not been fully implemented. Specifically, in 2001, we recommended that responsible executive branch officials and agencies establish a capability for strategic analysis of computer-based threats, including developing a methodology, acquiring expertise, and obtaining infrastructure data.[14]

National Response Framework

The National Response Framework, issued by DHS in January 2008, provides guidance to coordinate cyber incident response among federal entities and, upon request, state and local governments and private sector entities.[15] Specifically, the Cyber Incident Annex describes the framework for federal cyber incident response in the event of a cyber-related incident of national significance affecting the critical national processes. Further, the annex formalizes the National Cyber Response Coordination Group (NCRCG). As established under the preceding National Response Plan, the NCRCG continues to be cochaired by DHS's National Cyber Security Division (NCSD), the Department of Justice's Computer Crime and

[12] The White House, *Homeland Security Presidential Directive 7, Critical Infrastructure Identification, Prioritization, and Protection* (Washington, D.C.: Dec. 17, 2003).

[13] GAO-05-434.

[14] GAO, *Critical Infrastructure Protection: Significant Challenges in Developing National Capabilities*, GAO-01-323 (Washington, D.C.: Apr. 25, 2001).

[15] Department of Homeland Security, *National Response Framework* (Washington, D.C.: January 2008).

Intellectual Property Section, and the DOD. It is to bring together officials from all agencies that have responsibility for cybersecurity and the sector-specific agencies identified in HSPD 7. The group coordinates intergovernmental and public/private preparedness and response to and recovery from national-level cyber incidents and physical attacks that have significant cyber-related consequences. During and in anticipation of such an incident, the NCRCG's senior-level membership is responsible for providing subject matter expertise, recommendations, and strategic policy support and ensuring that the full range of federal capabilities is deployed in a coordinated and effective fashion.

Homeland Security Presidential Directive 23

In January 2008, the President issued HSPD 23—also referred to as National Security Presidential Directive 54 and the President's "Cyber Initiative"—to improve the federal government's cybersecurity efforts, including protecting against intrusion attempts and better anticipating future threats.[16] While the directive is a classified document, US-CERT officials stated that it includes steps to enhance cyber analysis related efforts, such as requirements that federal agencies implement a centralized monitoring tool and that the federal government reduce the number of connections to the Internet, referred to as Trusted Internet Connections.

DHS Established US-CERT to Provide National Cyber Analysis and Warning

To help protect the nation's information infrastructure, DHS established the US-CERT. It is currently positioned within the NCSD of DHS's Office of Cybersecurity and Communications. Figure 1 shows the position of these offices within DHS's organizational structure.

US-CERT is to serve as a focal point for the government's interaction with federal and nonfederal entities on a 24-hour-a-day, 7-day-a-week basis regarding cyber-related analysis, warning, information sharing, major incident response, and national-level recovery efforts.[17] It is charged with aggregating and disseminating cybersecurity information to improve warning of and response to incidents, increasing coordination of response information, reducing vulnerabilities, and enhancing prevention and protection. In addition, the organization is to collect incident reports from all federal agencies and assist agencies in their incident response efforts. It is also to accept incident reports when voluntarily submitted by other public and private entities and assist them in their response efforts, as requested.

[16] The White House, *National Security Presidential Directive 54/Homeland Security Presidential Directive 23* Washington, D.C.: Jan. 8, 2008).

[17] Nonfederal entities include state and local governments, private sector entities, and individuals.

Figure 1: Department of Homeland Security Organizational Chart

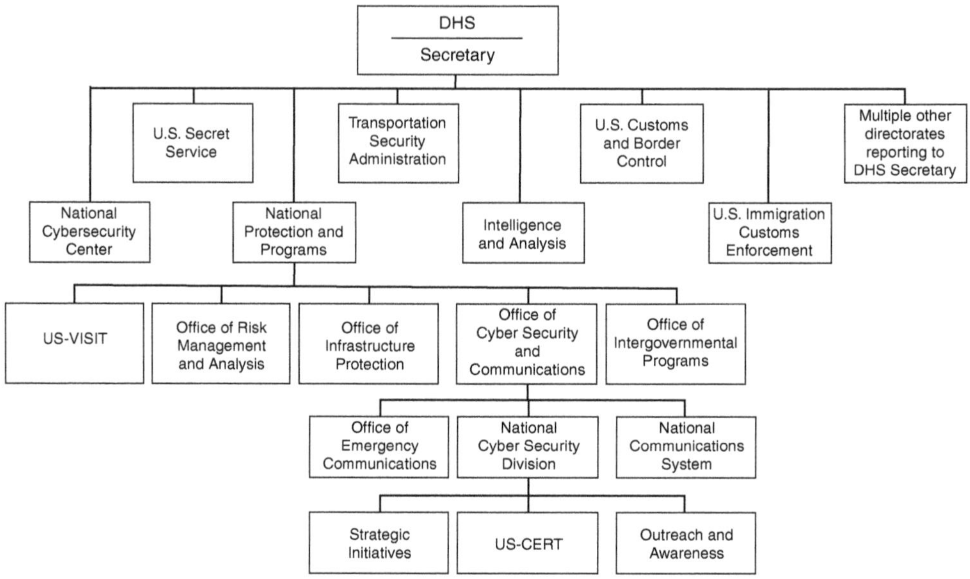

Source: GAO based on DHS data.

US-CERT is composed of five branches, as shown in figure 2: Operations, Situational Awareness, Law Enforcement and Intelligence, Future Operations, and Mission Support. Each branch has specific responsibilities

- The Operations branch is to receive and respond to incidents, disseminate reasoned and actionable cybersecurity information, and analyze various types of data to improve overall understanding of current or emerging cyber threats affecting the nation's critical infrastructure.
- The Situational Awareness branch is to identify, analyze, and comprehend broad network activity and to support incident handling and analysis of cybersecurity trends for federal agencies so that they may increase their own situational awareness and reduce cyber threats and vulnerabilities. As part of its responsibilities, the branch is responsible for managing the information garnered from the US-CERT Einstein program, which obtains network flow data from federal agencies, and analyzing the traffic patterns and behavior. This information is then combined with other relevant data to (1) detect potential deviations and identify how Internet activities are likely to affect federal agencies and (2) provide insight into the health of the Internet and into suspicious activities.
- The Law Enforcement and Intelligence branch is to facilitate information sharing and collaboration among law enforcement agencies,

Figure 2: US-CERT Organizational Structure

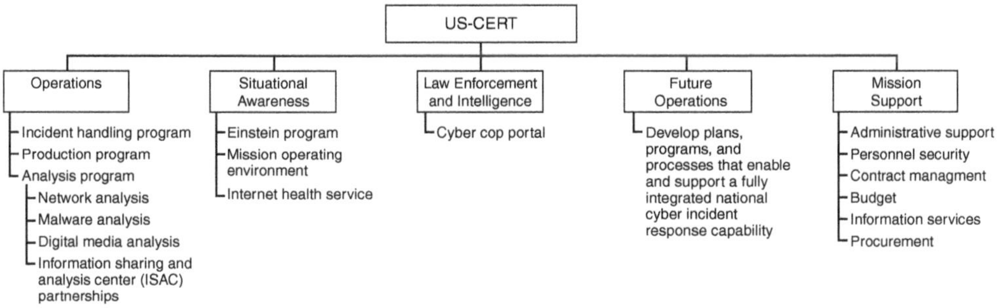

Source: GAO based on Dhs data.

the intelligence community, and US-CERT through the presence of liaisons from those organizations at US-CERT.

- The Future Operations branch was established in January 2007 to lead or participate in the development of related policies, protocols, procedures, and plans to support US-CERT's coordination of national response to cyber incidents.
- The Mission Support branch is to manage US-CERT's communications mechanisms, including reports, alerts, notices, and its public and classified Web site content.

Cyber Analysis and Warning Encompasses Four Key Capabilities

Our research and observations at federal and nonfederal entities show that cyber analysis and warning typically encompasses four key capabilities:

- **Monitoring**—detecting cyber threats, attacks, and vulnerabilities and establishing a baseline of system and communication network assets and normal traffic.
- **Analysis**—using the information or intelligence gathered from monitoring to hypothesize about what the threat might be, investigate it with technical and contextual expertise and identify the threat and its impact, and determine possible mitigation steps. Analysis may be initiated in reaction to a detected anomaly. This is a tactical approach intended to triage information during a cyber incident and help make decisions. It may also be predictive, proactively reviewing data collected during monitoring to look at cyber events and the network environment to find trends, patterns, or anomaly correlations that indicate more serious attacks or future threats.
- **Warning**—developing and issuing informal and formal notifications that alert recipients in advance of potential or imminent, as well as

ongoing, cyber threats or attacks. Warnings are intended to alert entities to the presence of cyber attack, help delineate the relevance and immediacy of cyber attacks, provide information on how to remediate vulnerabilities and mitigate incidents, or make overall statements about the health and welfare of the Internet.

- **Response**—taking actions to contain an incident, manage the protection of network operations, and recover from damages when vulnerabilities are revealed or when cyber incidents occur. In addition, response includes lessons learned and cyber threat data being documented and integrated back into the capabilities to improve overall cyber analysis and warning.

Through our consultations with experts, we found that the terminology may vary, but the functions of these capabilities are fairly consistent across cyber analysis and warning entities. Figure 3 depicts the basic process of cyber analysis and warning capabilities.

Typically, cyber analysis and warning is executed, or managed, from a central focal point known as an operation center or watch center. Such centers can serve a single organization or a number of organizations. Centers generally include physically and electronically connected multidisciplinary teams with access to a variety of communication and software tools. The teams are made up of specialized analysts, sometimes referred to as watch standers, with a combination of expertise in information security, intelligence, and cyber forensics. Teams may also include subject area experts with specialized expertise in certain critical infrastructure sectors, industries, or technologies. The centers operate tools that integrate data and facilitate analysis by the watch standers. The data come from a multitude of sources, including internal or external monitoring, human or signals intelligence, analytical results, warnings from other entities, and information collected from previous threat responses. Centers decide when and

Figure 3: A Simplified View of How Cyber Analysis and Warning Capabilities Are Executed

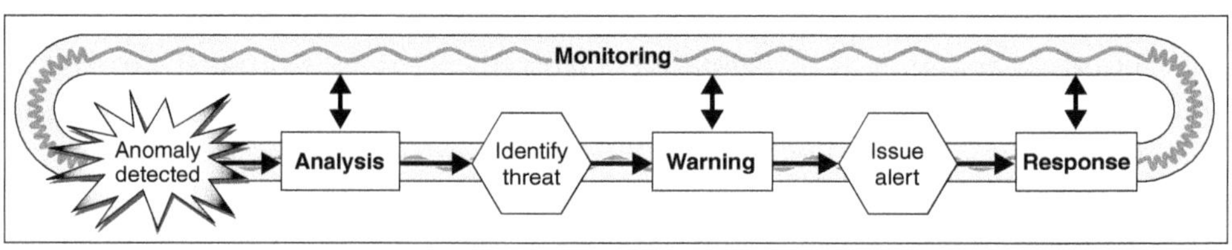

Source: GAO analysis.

how to issue formal and informal warnings that contribute to further analysis or provide information that aids in decisions about how to respond to an incident.

Depending on the size and organizational structure of an organization, the analysis and warning team may work with incident response teams during a cyber incident. The incident response team manages the decisions required for handling an incident using information discovered during monitoring, analysis, and warning. The team may also coordinate with those responsible for information security for the organization in order to assess risks, remediate vulnerabilities, and prepare for and respond to attacks.

Fifteen Key Attributes Essential to Establishing Cyber Analysis and Warning Capabilities

Our research and past experience at federal and nonfederal entities identified 15 key attributes associated with the cyber analysis and warning capabilities of monitoring, analysis, warning, and response. These attributes are displayed in table 4, which is followed by a detailed description by capability of each attribute.

Table 4. Key Attributes of the Cyber Analysis and Warning Capabilities

Capability	Attribute
Monitoring	Establish a baseline understanding of network assets and normal network traffic volume and flow Assess risks to network assets Obtain internal information on network operations via technical tools and user reports Obtain external information on threats, vulnerabilities, and incidents through various relationships, alerts, and other sources Detect anomalous activities
Analysis	Verify that an anomaly is an incident (threat of attack or actual attack) Investigate the incident to identify the type of cyber attack, estimate impact, and collect evidence Identify possible actions to mitigate the impact of the incident Integrate results into predictive analysis of broader implications or potential future attack
Warning	Develop attack and other notifications that are targeted and actionable Provide notifications in a timely manner Distribute notifications using appropriate communications methods
Response	Contain and mitigate the incident Recover from damages and remediate vulnerabilities Evaluate actions and incorporate lessons learned

Source: GAO analysis.

Monitoring

Monitoring provides the data used to understand one's operating environment and detect changes that indicate the presence of anomalies that may be cyber attacks. It encompasses five key attributes:

1. Establishing a baseline understanding of network assets and normal network traffic volume and flow

In order to detect unusual activity in network traffic or changes in an operating environment, organizations require knowledge of ordinary traffic and environmental conditions. This knowledge forms the baseline against which changes or anomalies can be detected, identified, and mitigated. A baseline is established through activities such as creating an accurate inventory of systems, prioritizing resources and assets, maintaining an understanding of the expected volume and nature of network traffic, and instituting operational procedures such as procedures for handling incidents. Without a baseline, it may be difficult to effectively detect threats or respond to a warning with the appropriate resources.

2. Assessing risks to network assets

Assessments should be conducted to determine what risks are posed by combinations of threats and vulnerabilities and inform the monitoring capability so that it is focused on the most critical assets. According to CERT® Coordination Center (CERT/CC) officials,[18] having a baseline knowledge of networks and systems and their associated risks in advance helps individual organizations understand what threats they may be susceptible to, what resources are at risk, and what the potential damage of an attack might be. Risks should be prioritized and mitigated until a reasonable acceptable level of risk is reached.

3. Obtain internal information on network operations via technical tools and user reports

Another key attribute is monitoring traffic on internal networks using (1) network and information security-related technology tools and (2) reports on network activity. As table 5 shows, various technologies can be used for internal network monitoring to help compile and identify patterns in network data. Each type of technology may detect anomalies that the other types of software cannot.

[18] The CERT Coordination Center is a center of Internet security expertise at the Software Engineering Institute, a federally funded research and development center operated by the Carnegie Mellon University. CERT Coordination Center is registered in the U.S. Patent and Trademark Office by Carnegie Mellon University.

Table 5. Common Types of Technology Used for Internal Monitoring

Technology	Function
Antivirus software	Provides protection against malicious code, such as viruses, worms, and Trojan horses.
Firewalls	Control access to and from a network or computer.
Intrusion detection systems	Detect inappropriate, incorrect, or anomalous activity on a network or computer system.
Intrusion prevention systems	Build on intrusion detection systems to detect attacks on a network and take action to prevent them from being successful.
Signature-based tools	Compare files or packets to a list of "signatures"—patterns of specific files or packets that have been identified as a threat. Each signature is the unique arrangement of zeros and ones that make up the file.
Security event correlation tools	Monitor and document actions on network devices and analyze the actions to determine if an attack is ongoing or has occurred. Enable an organization to determine if ongoing system activities are operating according to its security policy.
Scanners	Analyze computers or networks for security vulnerabilities.

Source: GAO.

These technologies can be used to examine data logs from networks on a 24-hour-a-day, 7-day-a-week schedule in an effort to identify (1) precursors and indicators of cyber threats or other anomalies and (2) the occurrence of known attacks. The data logged from these technologies are typically prepared using automated tools to help analysts observe or detect a single anomaly or to discover patterns in data over time. According to several federal and nonfederal entities, hands-on monitoring by trained analysts is essential because it can be difficult for automated tools to identify anomalies and incidents. For example, some automated signature-based tools focus on known threats and may not automatically recognize or alert analysts to new attack patterns or new threat delivery techniques. Other intrusion detection systems can produce large numbers of alerts indicating a problem when one does not exist (false positives); therefore, an analyst must look into anomalies more closely to see if detected intrusions are indications of a threat or simply an equipment malfunction.

4. Obtaining external information on threats, vulnerabilities, and incidents through various relationships, alerts, and other sources

External monitoring includes observing and receiving information that is either publicly or not publicly available for the purpose of maintaining environmental or situational awareness, detecting anomalies, and providing data for analysis, warning, and response. External sources of information include

- formal relationships, such as with and between critical infrastructure sector-related information sharing and analysis centers (ISAC);[19] federal agencies, including military, civilian, law enforcement, and intelligence agencies; international computer emergency response team organizations; the CERT/CC and vendors under contract for services;
- informal relationships established on a personal basis between analysts located at different operations centers;
- alerts issued by federal, state, and local governments;
- alerts issued by commercial external sources such as network security and antivirus software vendors;
- vulnerability databases, standards, and frameworks such as the National Vulnerability Database,[20] the Common Vulnerability and Exposures List,[21] Common Vulnerability Scoring System,[22] and the Open Vulnerability Assessment Language;[23]
- media outlets, such as television news and newspapers; and
- Web sites, such as law enforcement entities' sites, known hacker and criminal sites and chat rooms, and cooperative cyber analysis and warning services.[24]

---

[19] ISACs are to facilitate the private sector's participation in critical infrastructure protection efforts by serving as mechanisms for gathering and analyzing information and sharing it among the critical infrastructure sectors and between the private sector and government. ISACs have been established for many sectors, including financial services, electricity, information technology, research and education, the states, and telecommunications.

[20] According to the National Institute of Standards and Technology, the National Vulnerability Database is the U.S. government repository of standards-based vulnerability management data. These data enable automation of vulnerability management, security measurement, and compliance (e.g., to meet the requirements of the Federal Information Security Management Act). This database includes databases of security checklists, security-related software flaws, misconfigurations, product names, and impact metrics.

[21] According to MITRE, the Common Vulnerabilities and Exposures (CVE®) list is a dictionary of common names (i.e., CVE Identifiers) for publicly known information security vulnerabilities. CVE's common identifiers make it easier to share data across separate information security databases and tools, and provide a baseline for evaluating the coverage of an organization's security tools.

[22] According to NIST, the Common Vulnerability Scoring System (CVSS) is an open framework for communicating the characteristics and impacts of IT vulnerabilities. Specifically, CVSS provides a standard measurement system for industries, organizations, and governments that need accurate and consistent vulnerability impact scores.

[23] According to MITRE, Open Vulnerability and Assessment Language (OVAL™) is an international information security community standard to promote open and publicly available security content, and to standardize the transfer of this information across the entire spectrum of security tools and services.

[24] The SANS Internet Storm Center (ISC) is an example of a cooperative cyber analysis and warning center. The ISC provides free analysis and warning services for those who monitor the Web site. Participation is voluntary. In addition, the SANS Institute sponsors intrusion detection software that acts as a monitoring sensor for data collection from which threat information and data trends can be analyzed.

5. Detecting anomalous activities

Continuous monitoring occurs in order to detect significant changes from the baseline operations or the occurrence of an attack through an already known threat or vulnerability. It is ultimately the detection of an anomaly—observed internally or received from external information—and the recognition of its relevance that triggers analysis of the incident to begin.

Analysis

Analysis uses technical methods in combination with contextual expertise to hypothesize about the threat and associated risks concerning an anomaly and, if necessary, determine mitigation solutions. It encompasses four key attributes:

1. Verifying that an anomaly is an incident

Once an anomaly is detected, it should be verified whether it is a genuine cyber incident by determining that the data are from a trusted source and are accurate. For example, if the anomaly was identified by an internal sensor, analysts start by confirming that the sensor was working correctly and not indicating a false positive. If the anomaly was reported by an external source, analysts try to determine the trustworthiness of that source and begin to identify internal and external corroborating sources. Anomalies that are verified may require in-depth investigation and incident handling or more observation through monitoring.

2. Investigating the incident to identify the type of cyber attack, estimate impacts, and collect evidence

Once the anomaly is verified as a potential, impending, or occurring incident, analysts should combine information from multiple sources and/or perform investigative testing using available tools. Analysis often occurs through collaboration between analysts, the exchange of notifications and warnings, and the use of analytical research techniques. Analysts use these techniques to investigate the type of attack, its source (where it originates), its target (whom it affects), and the immediate risk to network assets and mission performance. In addition, these techniques are used to compile evidence for law enforcement. Techniques for investigation include

- comparing and correlating additional monitoring data available with the anomaly to determine what other internal and external entities are experiencing;
- comparing data about the anomaly with standardized databases to determine if the threats are known; and

- performing investigations, such as cyber forensic examinations,[25] reverse engineering, malware analysis, and isolating anomalies in a test environment such as a honeypot or a sandbox.[26]

3. Identifying possible actions to mitigate the impact of the incident

Analysis should culminate in identifying essential details about an anomaly such as what specific vulnerabilities are exploited or what impacts are expected for a specific incident. Steps should then be taken to identify alternative courses of action to mitigate the risks of the incident according to the severity of the exploit, available resources, and mission priorities. Such steps may include isolating the affected system to prevent further compromise, disabling the affected service that is being exploited, or blocking the connections providing the attacker a route into the network environment.[27] These courses of action may lead to more analysis or be used to support the warning capability.

4. Integrating results into predictive analysis of broader implications or potential future attacks

Information resulting from analysis of an individual incident should be used to determine any broader implications and predict and protect against future threats. This type of effort, or predictive analysis, should look beyond one specific incident to consider a broader set of incidents or implications that may indicate a potential threat of importance. For example, it may include detailed trend analysis of threats that have occurred over a certain period of time that is issued in public reports that discuss current trends, predict future incident activity, or emerging attack methods. However, according to many experts, this type of predictive analysis is complex and it is still difficult to predict future threats with current data.

Warning

Warnings are intended to alert entities to the presence of anomalies, help delineate the relevancy and immediacy of cyber attacks, provide information on how to remediate vulnerabilities and mitigate incidents, or make

[25] Computer forensics is the practice of gathering, retaining, and analyzing computer-related data for investigative purposes in a manner that maintains the integrity of the data.

[26] A honeypot is an intentionally underprotected computer host that is designed to collect data on suspicious activity. It generally has no authorized users other than its administrators. A sandbox is an isolated computer host used by analysts to let them observe cyber threats in order to gather data about how a specific threat might act. It is used to observe threats without endangering a live network and proprietary data.

[27] NIST, *Computer Security Incident Handling Guide: Recommendations of the National Institute of Standards and Technology*, Special Publication 800-61 Revision 1 (Gaithersburg, Maryland: March 2008). This guide was issued to assist organizations in establishing computer security incident response capabilities and in handling incidents efficiently and effectively.

overall statements about the health and welfare of the Internet. Warning includes three key attributes:

1. Developing notifications that are targeted and actionable

Warning messages should be targeted to the appropriate audience and provide details that are accurate, specific, and relevant enough to be acted upon. Developing actionable notifications requires providing the right incident information to the right person or group. If a single group is the only target of a threat, a warning directly to it may be more appropriate than a general public announcement. In addition, warnings are tailored to address technical or nontechnical recipients. Some warnings may be more appropriate for chief information officers, while other may include technical details for network administrators. Although notifications and warnings are delivered throughout incident handling, it is important to reach a balance between releasing actionable information and disclosing warnings too often, which can overwhelm the recipients and stretch limited resources. By addressing the specific audience, warnings avoid overwhelming recipients with extraneous or irrelevant information.

Also, recipients of notifications and warnings need to be able to use them to protect or defend their networks against cyber attacks. For example, many organizations have designated thresholds that determine how and when warnings are issued. To do so, the messages must include specific and accurate information about the incident as it relates to the recipient's monitoring, analysis, or response capabilities. An actionable warning may also include recommendations about how to respond to an incident. Federal and nonfederal entities also noted that sensitivity of information and privacy are key considerations when trying to develop an actionable warning. Warnings are sanitized or stripped of identifying or proprietary information in order to protect the privacy of individuals or entities involved in the incident. In addition, the federal government and its private sector partners must also adhere to procedures to make sure that they share useful information at the appropriate clearance level.

2. Providing notifications in a timely manner

Warnings are intended to give information to recipients as early as possible—preferably in advance of a cyber attack—to give them time to take appropriate action. In addition, the National Institute of Standards and Technology (NIST) provides guidance to federal agencies that describes when incidents are considered reportable and how long they may take to report them to US-CERT.[28] Similarly, several ISACs stated that they have procedures that determine when and how warnings are issued and when and how members should report incidents.

---

[28] NIST Special Pub. 800-61 Rev. 1.

3. Distributing notifications using the most appropriate communications methods

Once a warning is developed, it is important to determine the best method for getting that message out without overwhelming the public or incident handlers. Warnings can be provided both informally and formally. Informal warnings between colleagues with established trusted relationships can happen quickly and without significant regard to the organizational structure. Formal warnings, which are typically held to a higher standard of accuracy by recipients than informal warnings, come in many forms, such as e-mail bulletins, vulnerability alerts, Web postings, targeted warnings to a specific entity, or broad security notices to the general public. In addition to specific formal warnings, operations centers that perform analysis and warning for multiple organizations, such as the ISACs and commercial vendors, use level-based or color-coded alert systems on their Web sites to quickly notify members and the public of the general threat status of the infrastructure or Internet. Changing from one level or color to another indicates that the threat level is increasing or decreasing. These same organizations send alerts about threats and vulnerabilities to members only or may issue specific warnings to a single organization that has been identified through analysis as being targeted by a cyber threat.

Response

Response includes actions to contain an incident, manage the protection of network operations, and recover from damages when vulnerabilities are revealed or when cyber incidents occur. It encompasses three key attributes:

1. Containing and mitigating the incident

When an incident is identified, immediate steps should be taken to protect network assets. Decisions are made to control further impacts on the network and then eliminate the threat. These actions may include installing a software patch, blocking a port known to be used by a particular threat, or deploying other appropriate network resources. In the case of a serious threat, the decision may be to turn off the network gateway and temporarily isolate the network from the Internet, depending upon what assets are at risk. One industry expert noted that investigation may occur before any mitigation steps are taken in order to consider the necessity of law enforcement involvement. On the other hand, if little is known about a threat and it does not appear to endanger critical assets, a decision might be made to watch the threat emerge in a contained area to allow for further monitoring and analysis. Decisions to act or not are based on acceptable risks, available resources, and ability to remedy the known threat. In addition, decisions must be made in the context of the impact that actions will have on other related efforts, such as a law enforcement investigation.

2. Recovering from damage and remediating vulnerabilities

Once an incident is contained and mitigated, restoring damaged areas of the network to return it to its baseline becomes a priority. To understand the damage, a cyber damage or loss assessment may be conducted to identify, among other things, how the incident was discovered, what network(s) were affected, when the incident occurred, who attacked the network and by what methods, what was the intention of the attacker, what occurred during the attack, and what is the impact or severity of the incident. The recovery efforts may involve restoring or reinstalling computers, network devices, applications, or systems that have been compromised.

Taking action to remediate vulnerabilities in a network may also result from analysis and incident management. Entities work to discover and reduce the number of vulnerabilities in their computers, network devices, applications, or systems.

3. Evaluating actions and incorporating lessons learned

Entities should ensure that threat data, results, and lessons learned are evaluated and appropriately incorporated to improve the overall cyber analysis and warning capability. For example, teams can be used to simulate network threats by purposefully attacking a network in order to see how the network responds. From these simulations, an evaluation can be made about the response, and recommendations on how to improve can be developed. In addition, cyber simulations allow critical infrastructure organizations to prepare for threat scenarios and to test analysis, warning, and response capabilities. NIST guidance also states that holding lessons learned meetings after major incidents is helpful in improving security measures and the incident handling process itself.[29]

US-CERT's Capabilities Include Some but Not All Aspects of Key Attributes

US-CERT has established cyber analysis and warning capabilities that includee aspects of each of the key attributes. However, they do not fully incorporate all of them.

Monitoring Capability Includes Most but Not All Aspects of Key Attributes

US-CERT has established capabilities that include aspects of key attributes of monitoring. For example, it obtains internal network operation information via technical tools and Einstein; obtains external information on threats, vulnerabilities, and incidents; and detects anomalous activities based on the information it receives. However, its capabilities do not fully

[29] NIST Special Pub. 800-61, Rev. 1.

incorporate all of the key attributes of monitoring. For example, it has not established a baseline of our nation's critical infrastructure information systems. Table 6 shows our analysis of its monitoring capability.

Table 6. US-CERT Capabilities Includes Most but Not All Aspects of Monitoring

Attribute	Aspects Incorporated	Aspects not Incorporated
Establish a baseline understanding of network assets and normal network traffic volume and flow	The organization has a limited baseline understanding of network assets and normal network traffic volume through the 16 federal participants in its situational awareness tool, US-CERT Einstein. In addition, it receives additional network flow information through contracts with information security vendors.	It does not have a comprehensive national-level baseline across the nation's computer-reliant critical infrastructure, including the information systems of federal civilian and military entities, state and local governments, the private sector, and other entities. For example, under Einstein, the organization monitors 16 agencies, a practice that does not provide an overall view of federal network traffic. In addition, the tool's current capabilities are manually driven, thereby complicating and slowing the collection and compilation of data.
Assess risks to network assets	—	Though US-CERT is involved in cyber-related risk assessment efforts being performed by other DHS organizations and the private sector, it does not perform risk assessments.
Obtain internal information on network operations via technical tools and user reports	The organization obtains internal information using security tools and user reports regarding its presence on the Internet and its internal network operations.	Its ability to obtain real-time internal traffic information is reduced by Einstein's limitation of requiring manually intensive analysis.
Obtain external information on threats, vulnerabilities, and incidents.	US-CERT monitors a variety of external information sources, including network traffic data, incident reports, and threat reports from federal, state, local, and foreign governments and the private sector, such as the following: • federal agencies providing an enhanced view of their networks through participation in Einstein;	Its information does not encompass all critical infrastructure information networks. For example, by monitoring only 16 agencies, Einstein does not provide an overall view of federal network traffic. Also, the Department of Energy and DOD use their own similar situational awareness tools, but their data are not currently combined with Einstein's data to provide a more

Attribute	Aspects Incorporated	Aspects not Incorporated
	• various vendors providing Internet operational data; • the Homeland Infrastructure Threat and Risk Analysis Center (HITRAC),[a] law enforcement, and the intelligence community, providing threat information and other data; • federal agencies reporting information security incidents to the organization, as required by the Federal Information Security Management Act;[b] • nonfederal entities voluntarily reporting incidents, malware, and other information; • foreign governments providing information on cyber incidents; • CERT/CC providing vulnerability information; and • other analysis and warning entities, including the Financial Services-ISAC, Multistate ISAC, the Internet Storm Center, and information security vendors, sharing incident and other situational awareness information.	complete view of federal traffic. There are efforts under way to develop automated information exchanges between DOD's system and Einstein, but as of March 2008, this had not been finalized. Regarding nonfederal entities, the organization does not directly monitor any private sector networks, nor are nonfederal entities required to report to it incidents or anomalous activity. Typically, nonfederal entities, including the ISACs, that report incident and other data filter sensitive details from the data reported.
Detect anomalous activities.	The organization detects anomalies based on its monitoring of network traffic flow. Einstein provides network flow data from 16 agencies with the primary goal of looking for unique activity that may indicate a cyber attack or other undesirable activity.[c] According to US-CERT officials, Einstein provides the participating agencies a capability to compare their network traffic data with activity at other federal agencies and against law	The organization does not detect anomalies across the nation's computer-reliant critical infrastructure. For example, it does not directly monitor any private sector networks, nor are nonfederal entities required to report incidents or anomalous activity.

Attribute	Aspects Incorporated	Aspects not Incorporated
	enforcement and intelligence agencies' threat data to determine if they are the victim of serious attacks. In addition, it works with its various partners in the private sector as well as other federal, state, and local governments to determine the extent of abnormal behavior. For example, the organization receives limited information from certain computer security vendors regarding Internet traffic flow of their respective customer bases.	

Source: GAO analysis.

[a]HITRAC is a fusion center of intelligence analysts from DHS's Office of Intelligence and Analysis and subject matter experts from the National Protection and Programs Directorate working together to analyze threats, vulnerabilities, and risks to the 18 Critical Infrastructure/ Key Resource sectors of the United States. Additionally, HITRAC focuses solely on analyzing and identifying the threat aspect of cybersecurity incidents as they occur. HITRAC shares these threat data with numerous customers, including US-CERT.

[b]The Federal Information Security Management Act requires the operation of a central federal information security incident center. 44 U.S.C. 3546. The act also requires agencies to report incidents to the organization, in addition to law enforcement agencies, relevant offices of inspector general, and other designated entities. 44 U.S.C. 3544(b)(7).

[c]These data are analyzed for traffic patterns and behavior; this information can be combined with other relevant data to (1) detect potential deviations and identify how Internet activities are likely to affect federal agencies and (2) provide insight into the health of the Internet and suspicious activities.

As part of the President's Cyber Initiative, DHS has a lead role for several provisions that, if implemented appropriately, could address key monitoring deficiencies, such as not having a comprehensive national baseline and sufficient external information on threats, vulnerabilities, and incidents. According to testimony by the Under Secretary for the National Protection and Programs Directorate, the initiative makes the Einstein program mandatory across all federal agencies. In addition, DHS plans to enhance Einstein's capabilities to be a real-time intrusion detection and situational awareness system. Further, DHS, along with the Office of Management and Budget (OMB), is responsible for working with federal agencies to reduce the number of Trusted Internet Connections used by the federal government. According to DHS and OMB officials, these initiatives will enhance the ability of the US-CERT to monitor federal systems for cyber attacks and other threats. According to US-CERT officials, the reduction in

Trusted Internet Connections, along with the positioning of Einstein in front of those connections to the Internet, will help provide a governmentwide baseline and view of the traffic entering and leaving federal networks as well as access to the content of the traffic. In addition, according to the Assistant Secretary for Cybersecurity and Communications, the recently announced National Cybersecurity Center, which reports directly to the Secretary of Homeland Security, will be responsible for ensuring coordination among the cyber-related efforts across the federal government, including improving the sharing of incident and threat information. However, the efforts to use Einstein, reduce Internet connections, and implement the National Cybersecurity Center are in their early stages and have not yet been fully planned or implemented, so whether these efforts will fully address all five of the monitoring attributes is not known at this time.

Analysis Capability Does Not Fully Incorporate All Aspects of Key Attributes

US-CERT has established capabilities that include key attributes of analysis. For example, it verifies anomalies, performs investigations, and identifies possible courses of action. However, its capabilities do not fully incorporate other attributes because of technical and human resource constraints and the gaps in the monitoring capability. Table 8 shows our analysis of the organization's analysis capability.

Table 7. US-CERT Incorporates Some but Not All Aspects of Analysis

Attribute	Aspects Incorporated	Aspects not Incorporated
Verify that an anomaly is an incident (threat of attack or actual attack)	When an anomaly is detected or reported, US-CERT works directly with its various public and private sector partners to determine whether the anomaly is an incident. For example, it notifies federal agencies when it observes abnormal activities. In turn, federal agencies take the information provided and are to verify whether the activity constitutes a cybersecurity incident and if any support is required from US-CERT.	The lack of a robust monitoring capability negatively affects the organization's ability to verify and investigate anomalies and to identify threats. Specifically, although the Einstein flow data are collected in real time, the actual analysis is manually intensive and does not occur simultaneously or in real time. Another limiting factor of Einstein data is that the organization is unable to analyze the content of the potentially malicious traffic.

Attribute	Aspects Incorporated	Aspects not Incorporated
Investigate the incident to identify the type of cyber attack, estimate impacts, and collect evidence	The organization investigates incidents through network and malware analysis. For example, it correlates Einstein network traffic data with known vulnerabilities and threats to identify abnormal activity, and then it focuses on identifying emerging threats, ongoing trends, and intrusions that have already occurred. According to agency officials, through the implementation of Einstein, the amount of time needed to discover and understand a potential cyber attack and communicate it to agencies has been significantly reduced from 4 to 5 days to 4 to 5 hours. In addition, according to US-CERT officials, its malware analysis focuses on reverse engineering malicious code to determine how the code works, its effect on a network or system, and potentially who developed it. The organization receives the malware code from a variety of sources, including its own monitoring, anonymous submissions, and formal submissions from affected entities, such as federal agencies, Internet service providers, and other entities. For example, according to agency officials, they receive on average between 5,000 and 24,000 individual pieces of malware in a 24-hour period. Additionally as of April 2008, officials stated that the organization had conducted analysis on 1,520,022 samples of malware code during fiscal year 2008. To do this work, the organization has established a segregated facility, or malware laboratory, that provides a controlled environment to conduct detailed analysis on infected computer hardware and software. According to officials, its malware capability has provided value to federal and nonfederal partners because it can analyze the potential impact of malware with the known threat information received from its partners in the law enforcement and intelligence communities.	The number of incidents that can be analyzed at one time is limited.

Attribute	Aspects Incorporated	Aspects not Incorporated
Identify possible actions to mitigate the impact of the incident	US-CERT's analysts develop alternative actions for stopping or controlling the threat. These alternatives are based on risk, required resources, mission priorities, and existing network requirements and limitations. Its network analysts work with all US-CERT partners to identify possible courses of action and methods to respond to cyber incidents. For example, in January 2008, an analysis of malware discovered at a targeted federal agency led to the identification of three zero-day exploits and a subsequent alert issued to federal and nonfederal entities.	The organization's ability to develop possible actions to mitigate the identified threat is limited by its inability to engage other partners in analysis efforts because the information may be sensitive or classified.
Integrate results into predictive analysis of broader implications or potential future attack	According to NCSD officials, the organization is engaged in activities with other NCSD entities to develop more strategic views of the nation's critical cyber infrastructures.	The organization does not possess the capability to integrate its work into predictive analysis.

Source: GAO analysis.

As part of the Cyber Initiative, the organization has received additional resources to develop the next version of the Einstein situational awareness tool. According to US-CERT officials, this new version, referred to as Einstein 2.0, will provide real-time intrusion detection monitoring, a content analysis capability, and automated analysis functions that are currently manual. In addition, it has received authorization for an additional 30 government and 50 contractor employee full-time equivalents. According to US-CERT officials, they plan to fill the additional positions by leveraging graduates of the Scholarship for Service program, which provides cybersecurity-related scholarships to students willing to serve the federal government for a time commitment. However, these efforts are in their early stages and have not yet been fully planned or implemented. Consequently, whether these efforts will fully address all four of the analysis attributes is not known at this time.

Warning Capability Exhibits Some but Not All Characteristics of Key Attributes

The organization has established capabilities that include key attributes of warning. For example, it develops and distributes a number of attack and other notifications targeted to different audiences with varying frequency.

However, according to customers, these warning products are not consistently actionable and timely. Table 8 shows our analysis of the organization's warning capability. Tables 9 and 10 show types of warning products and the quantity of products issued during fiscal year 2007.

Table 8. US-CERT Exhibits Some but Not All Aspects of Warning

Attribute	Aspects Incorporated	Aspects not Incorporated
Develop attack and other notifications that are targeted and actionable	As tables 9 and 10 depict, the organization develops various attack and other notifications for a varied set of customers.	Officials from entities with robust cyber analysis and warning capabilities, such as the ISACs, DOD, and the Department of Energy, stated that the organization's notifications typically did not offer new or additional information beyond their own efforts.
Provide notifications in a timely manner	The organization is occasionally able to provide notifications to certain customers in a timely manner. For example, officials from organizations with limited cyber analysis and warning capabilities stated that certain US-CERT notifications, especially those warnings with For Official Use Only (FOUO) information, were extremely timely.	The organization is not consistently able to provide notifications in a timely manner. Its ability to disseminate timely notifications is hindered by a number of factors. First, as the national cyber analysis and warning organization, it must ensure a high level of accuracy in the products it releases. In order to avoid disseminating incomplete or inaccurate information, its warning products are subjected to a review process, which can prevent their rapid dissemination. Further, the sensitivity of information can be a hindrance. Specifically, highly sensitive information must be coordinated with other components as part of the review process, which can add days to the release time. Finally, dissemination efforts are limited by lack of performance measures that assess or provide feedback on the value of US-CERT products.
Distribute notifications using appropriate communications methods	As table 9 depicts, the organization distributes a wide array of attack and other "warning" products through various mechanisms to a diverse set of customers.	According to NSCD officials, the organization is refining its distribution lists and collaborating with various federal and nonfederal user groups to better ensure appropriate officials (those having the understanding and ability to appropriately respond) receive its notifications.

Source: GAO analysis.

As part of the Cyber Initiative, the enhancements to the Einstein program, as well as the reduction in the number of Trusted Internet Connections can lead to more complete data. According to US-CERT officials, the improved data will lead to an enhanced warning capability that could provide the ability to issue targeted and actionable alerts in advance of actual cyber attacks. However, these efforts are in their early stages and have not yet been fully planned or implemented; thus, it is not clear whether these efforts will fully address the three warning attributes.

Response Capability Satisfies Some but Not All Aspects of Key Attributes

US-CERT possesses a limited response capability to assist other entities in the containment, mitigation, and recovery from significant cyber incidents. For example, while it provides on-site assistance to various entities, its ability to provide response at the national level is hindered by limitations in the resources available and authority over affected entities. Table 11 shows our analysis of its response capability.

To improve the organization's response capability, US-CERT officials stated that they needed to perform internal exercises that test its national-level response capability more often than every 2 years, as is the case with the Cyber Storm exercise.[30] It plans to develop "tabletop" exercises to more frequently test its response capabilities. In addition, according to NCSD officials, they are working collaboratively with other federal and nonfederal working groups to improve their performance measures so that they can understand the value and use of their products and make continuous improvements. However, until they do so, it is not clear whether these efforts will lead to US-CERT fully addressing the three response attributes.

[30] Cyber Storm is a biennial national-level exercise to test the ability of federal and nonfederal stakeholders, including federal, state, and local agencies; private sector entities; and foreign governments, to respond to major cyber attacks. The last exercise, referred to as Cyber Storm II, was held in March 2008.

Table 9. US-CERT Warning Products, Fiscal Year 2007

US-CERT Products	Product Audience					
	White House	Federal Government	GFIRST[a]	Select International Partners[b]	ISACs[c]	General Public
Situational awareness report	●		●	●	●	
Federal information notice	●	●	●			
Critical infrastructure information notice	●			●	●	
Public trends and analysis report		●	●	●	●	●
Technical information paper	●	●	●	●	●	●
Cyber daily briefing			●		●	
Non-technical alerts						●
Technical alerts	●	●	●	●	●	●
Security bulletins	●	●	●	●	●	●
Security tips						●
Current activity	●	●	●	●	●	●
Vulnerability notes	●	●	●	●	●	●

Source: US-CERT.

[a]Government Forum of Incident Response and Security Teams (GFIRST) is a group of technical and tactical practitioners from government agency security response teams responsible for securing government information technology systems.

[b]Select international partners including Australia, Canada, New Zealand, and the United Kingdom.

[c]Information sharing and analysis center.

[d]Homeland Secure Data Network (HSDN) is a secure portal that provides the ability to share information at the Secret category level among other federal, state, and local government entities.

[e]DHS considers the Homeland Security Information Network (HSIN) to be its primary communication application for transmitting sensitive but unclassified information. According to DHS, this network is an encrypted, unclassified, Web-based communications application that serves as DHS's primary nationwide information-sharing and collaboration tool. It is intended to offer both real-time chat and instant messaging capability, as well as a document library that contains reports from multiple federal, state, and local sources.

[f]DHS established the National Cyber Alert System (NCAS) to deliver targeted, timely, and actionable information to the public on how to secure computer systems. Information provided by the alert system is designed to be understandable by all computer users, both technical and nontechnical.

[g]Really Simple Syndication (RSS) is a format for gathering and making available content from Web sites. RSS can be used to provide any kind of information that can be broken down into discrete items and put into RSS format, typically called an RSS feed. Software is available that can periodically check RSS feeds for changes, download new items, and make them available to the users.

Distribution Mechanism						Frequency					
US-CERT Web site	US-CERT HSDN Web site[d]	US-CERT HSIN Portal[e]	NCAS[f]	E-mail Distribution	RSS Feeds[g]	Daily	Weekly	Every other Week	Monthly	Quarterly	As Needed
	●	●							●		●
	●	●		●							●
	●	●		●							●
●	●	●								●	
●	●	●									●
		●		●		●					
●	●		●	●							●
●	●		●	●	●		●				●
●	●		●	●	●		●				
●			●	●	●			●			
●	●			●	●	●					●
●	●			●	●						●

Table 10. Quantity of US-CERT Warning Products, Fiscal Year 2007

Product	Quantity	Interval
Public trends and analysis reports	4	Quarterly
Vulnerability notes	353	As needed
Situational awareness reports (SAR)	83	As needed
Federal information notices (FIN)	7	As needed
Technical information papers (TIP)	8	As needed
Critical infrastructure information notices (CIIN)	9	As needed
Security bulletins	52	Weekly
Technical alerts	39	As needed
Nontechnical alerts	27	As needed
Current activity	260	As needed
Cyber daily briefings	356	Daily

Source: US-CERT.

Table 11. US-CERT Satisfies Some but Not All Aspects of Response

Attribute	Aspects Incorporated	Aspects not Incorporated
Contain and mitigate the incident	The organization assists entities in federal, state, and local governments as well as the private sector with the containment and mitigation of cybersecurity incidents as they occur, on a requested basis. According to agency officials, the US-CERT routinely deploys its two digital media analysis teams to perform on-site response to serious incidents. These teams have the capabilities and depth of knowledge to perform detailed analysis on compromised media (e.g., hard drives and thumb drives). For example, as of April 2008, the organization had provided on-site incident response eight times for fiscal year 2008, making about 30 visits to various federal agencies to address incidents dealing with unauthorized access, malware activity, as well as misconfigured network devices. Also, in November 2007, the organization deployed at least one response team to each of five different federal agencies over 5 consecutive days. In addition, the Law Enforcement and Intelligence branch works with organizations such as the Federal Bureau of Investigation and United States Secret Service to contain incidents on a global scale using established	Though the organization is responsible for responding to national-level incidents, it does not possess the authority to compel an agency or organization to take action.

Attribute	Aspects Incorporated	Aspects not Incorporated
	relationships with other nations. According to officials, the organization has also assisted at the international level, most recently deploying officials to Estonia to help its government improve its cybersecurity posture after suffering a major cyber attack. Further, DHS, in conjunction with DOD and the Department of Justice, formed the NCRCG to coordinate the federal response to cyber incidents of national significance. During a significant national incident, the NCRCG is to provide subject matter expertise, recommendations, and strategic policy support to the Secretary of Homeland Security. At the time of our review, the senior-level membership had coordinated and communicated about incidents; however, there had not been a cyber incident of national significance to activate these procedures.	
Recover from damages and remediate vulnerabilities	The organization routinely deploys its two digital media analysis teams to perform on-site response to serious incidents at federal agencies. According to agency officials, these teams focus on serious incidents, typically involving advanced threats, such as those propagated by nation states as well as advanced malware attacks.	To handle a cyber attack that affects multiple entities across the nation, officials stated that the organization would need at least three additional digital media analysis teams.
Evaluate actions and incorporate lessons learned	US-CERT has identified shortcomings in its processes, communications methods, and policies by conducting exercises that simulate a national-level incident. For example, once a digital media team has completed its on-site response assistance, it generates an after-action report that summarizes what steps were taken and any further suggested actions for the affected organization. In addition, during Cyber Storm II, which occurred in March 2008, the organization identified a number of issues for improvement that will be addressed in after-action reports and tracked to ensure changes occur.	While it measures certain items, such as the number and type of products it distributes, the organization has not established performance measures to determine the effectiveness of its efforts. According to US-CERT officials, other than an occasional statement of appreciation from other organizations, they do not know who benefits from their efforts or who uses their products.

Source: GAO analysis.

US-CERT Faces New and Ongoing Challenges to Fulfilling Its Mission

US-CERT faces a number of newly identified and ongoing challenges that impede it from fully implementing the key attributes and in turn establishing cyber analysis and warning capabilities essential to coordinating the national effort to prepare for, prevent, and respond to cyber threats. The new challenge is creating warnings that are actionable and timely—it does not consistently issue warning and other notifications that its customers find useful. In addition, US-CERT continues to face four challenges that we previously identified: (1) employing predictive cyber analysis, (2) developing more trusted relationships to encourage information sharing, (3) having sufficient analytical and technical capabilities, and (4) operating without organizational stability and leadership within DHS. Until DHS addresses these challenges and fully incorporates all key attributes into its capabilities, it will not have the full complement of cyber analysis and warning capabilities essential to effectively performing its national mission.

New Challenge Involves Creating Warnings That Are Actionable and Timely

Developing and disseminating cyber threat warnings to enable customers to effectively mitigate a threat in advance of an attack can be challenging for the US-CERT. According to the organization's Acting Deputy Director, it serves as the nation's cyber analysis and warning center and must ensure that its warnings are accurate. In addition, owners of classified or law enforcement information must review and agree to the release of related information. Therefore, the organization's products are subjected to a stringent review and revision process that could adversely affect the timeliness of its products—potentially adding days to the release if classified or law enforcement information must be removed from the product. For example, an official from a cybersecurity-focused organization at a university stated that the alerts from US-CERT generally arrive a day or two after they might have been helpful. An official from another private entity stated that the bureaucratic process US-CERT must follow prevents it from providing useful alerts in a timely manner and that as a result, it does not have the credibility to drive a reaction when an alert is finally issued. Another private sector official stated that, in some cases, the organization gets information on cyber incidents and attacks faster from media sources than US-CERT because its analysts need time to verify the reliability of the data they receive.

In addition, according to federal officials responsible for determining cyber-related threats, US-CERT, as well as other organizations with cybersecurity-related responsibilities, must also balance the need to develop and release warnings with the activities of other organizations, such as law enforcement and intelligence support, to identify and mitigate cyber threats. For example, the release of a warning to address a threat or attack may also alert the intruders that their methods have been discovered and cause them to change their methods prior to the completion of an investigation about their activities.

Further, when there is sensitive information to share, US-CERT officials stated that on numerous occasions, they were unable to share the details of threats to customers' networks because no one within the federal agency or nonfederal entity possessed a security clearance high enough to receive the information. In some organizations, the individuals who do possess security clearances are in the upper echelons of the organization and do not possess a cyber or information security background. As a result, they are not always able to accurately comprehend and relay the threat information to those who would actually handle the mitigation efforts. In September 2007, we reported that DHS lacked a rapid, efficient process for disseminating sensitive information to private industry owners and operators of critical infrastructures.[31] We recommended that DHS establish a rapid and secure process for sharing sensitive vulnerability information with critical infrastructure stakeholders, including vendors, owners, and operators; however, DHS has not yet fulfilled this recommendation.

To provide actionable information to its customers, the organization attempts to combine incident information with related cyber threat information to determine the seriousness of the attack. However, according to the Acting Director of US-CERT, its efforts are limited by other federal entities' abilities to determine specific cyber threats to the nation's critical infrastructure. One reason for the lack of cyber threat data is that the task is complex and difficult and there are no established, generally accepted methodologies for performing such analysis. In addition, such entities are hampered by the limited number of analysts dedicated to cyber threat identification. For example, in January 2008, the Director of HITRAC stated that only 5 percent of HITRAC's total number of analyst positions was focused on analyzing and identifying cyber threats to our nation's critical information infrastructure. According to the director, it had received approval to double the number of cyber-related analysts and was in the process of filling those positions. In addition, the director stated that HITRAC's primary focus is on identifying physical threats.

[31] GAO, *Critical Infrastructure Protection: Multiple Efforts to Secure Control Systems Are Under Way, but Challenges Remain*, GAO-07-1036 (Washington, D.C.: Sept. 10, 2007).

Ongoing Challenges Involve Establishing Predictive Analysis, Trusted Relationships, Analytical and Technical Capabilities, and a Stable Organization

US-CERT faces ongoing challenges that we identified in previous reports as impeding DHS's ability to fulfill its cyber critical infrastructure protection responsibilities.

Employing predictive cyber analysis—US-CERT has been unable to establish the solid foundation needed to perform predictive cyber analysis that would enable it to determine any broader implications from ongoing network activity, predict or protect against future threats, or identify emerging attack methods prior to an attack. Since 2001, we have identified the challenges associated with establishing strategic, predictive analysis and warning and have made recommendations that responsible executive branch officials and agencies establish such capabilities, including developing methodologies.[32] According to the Acting Director of US-CERT, it has not been able to establish such capabilities because there is not a generally accepted methodology for performing predictive cyber analysis and warning. In addition, officials from US-CERT and other federal and nonfederal entities with cyber analysis and warning capabilities stated that while they can determine the motivations for the various threat sources to use cyber attacks, it is a formidable task to foresee prior to attacks how those threats would actually conduct attacks and to establish indicators to recognize that such cyber attacks are about to occur. Also, the relative newness of the cyber analysis and warning discipline and immaturity of the related methodologies and tools add to the complexity.

Developing more trusted relationships to encourage information sharing—Implementing cyber analysis and warning capabilities, including all of the key attributes, requires that entities be willing and able to share information, including details about incidents, threats, vulnerabilities, and network operations. However, US-CERT continues to be challenged to develop relationships with external sources that would encourage information sharing. For example, nonfederal entities do not consistently fully disclose incident and other data—they filter sensitive details from the data reported, thus reducing its value to US-CERT. The lack of such relationships negatively affects the organization's cyber analysis and warning capability.

In 2005, we reported that entities within critical infrastructure sectors possess an inherent disincentive to share cybersecurity information with DHS.[33] Much of their concern was that the potential release of sensitive

[32] GAO-01-323.
[33] GAO-05-434.

information could increase the threat they face. In addition, when information was shared, it was not clear whether the information would be shared with other entities, such as other federal entities, state and local entities, law enforcement, or various regulators, or how it would be used or protected from disclosure. Alternatively, sector representatives expressed concerns that DHS was not effectively communicating information with them and had not matched private sector efforts to share valuable information with a corresponding level of trusted information sharing. We also identified information sharing in support of homeland security as a high-risk area in 2005, and we noted that establishing an effective two-way exchange of information to help detect, prevent, and mitigate potential terrorist attacks requires an extraordinary level of cooperation and perseverance among federal, state, and local governments and the private sector.[34]

Federal and nonfederal officials raised similar concerns about the ability to develop trusted relationships and share information with and between cyber analysis and warning entities, including US-CERT. For example, frequent staff turnover at NCSD and US-CERT hindered the ability to build trusted relationships with both public and private entities. Federal and nonfederal officials stated that reliance was placed on personal relationships to support sharing of sensitive information about cybersecurity and cyber incidents. However, according to the NCSD director, six senior staff members within the Office of Cybersecurity and Communications (the national focal point for addressing cybersecurity issues) were leaving for various reasons, affecting the ability to develop such relationships. In addition, private sector officials stated that their organizations continued to be hesitant to share information on vulnerabilities and threats because of the fear that such sharing might negatively affect their financial bottom line. For example, private sector officials stated that it was difficult to share unfiltered information with their respective infrastructure sector ISAC because a competitor operated the ISAC, thus negatively affecting the information received by US-CERT.

Having sufficient analytical and technical capabilities—Obtaining and retaining adequately trained cyber analysts and acquiring up-to-date technological tools to implement the analysis capability attributes is an ongoing challenge to US-CERT and other analysis and warning centers, hindering their ability to respond to increasingly fast, nimble, and sophisticated cyber attacks. As we have reported, NCSD has had difficulty hiring personnel to fill vacant positions.[35] We reported that once it found qualified candidates, some candidates decided not to apply or withdrew their applications because it took too long to be hired. This is still a concern because current

[34] GAO-05-207.
[35] GAO-05-434.

staff has limited organizational backup and, in some cases, performs multiple roles. In addition, a private sector official stated that it is not clear whether or not the government has the number of technical analysts necessary to perform analysis on large and complex data sets that are generated whether or not an incident is in progress or not.

Keeping cyber analysts trained and up to date on the latest cybersecurity tools and techniques can be difficult. For example, a DOD official representing one of its cyber analysis and warning centers stated that its analysts must develop their expertise on the job because there is no formal training program available that teaches them how to detect and perform analysis of an anomaly or intrusion. A private sector official stated that while analysts are often trained to use existing tools, their understanding of the key attributes of analysis is often limited, resulting in a solution too late to be helpful.

Analysts also need the appropriate technological tools to handle the volume, velocity, and variety of malicious data and activity they are faced with, according to federal officials. For example, although the Einstein flow data are collected in real time, the actual analysis is manually intensive and does not occur simultaneously or in real time. Another limiting factor of Einstein data is that US-CERT is unable to analyze the content of the potentially malicious traffic and must rely on the affected agency to perform any analysis of the content of the traffic. Thus both the reaction time to determine the intent of the anomalous activity and the necessary actions to address it are significantly slowed. In addition, officials from one private sector entity questioned if agencies can sufficiently protect their networks using the tools they are mandated to use.

As part of the efforts to address the President's Cyber Initiative, US-CERT recently received approval to fill 80 new positions—30 government and 50 contractor—and is attempting to fill these analytical positions by extending offers to candidates in the National Science Foundation's Scholarship for Service Program. However, these positions have yet to be completely filled with qualified candidates.

Operating without organizational stability and authority—We have identified challenges regarding DHS's organizational stability, leadership, and authority that affect US-CERT's ability to successfully perform its mission. In the past, we have reported that the lack of stable leadership has diminished NCSD's ability to maintain trusted relationships with its infrastructure partners and has hindered its ability to adequately plan and execute activities.[36] While DHS has taken steps to fill key positions, organizational

[36] GAO-05-434

instability among cybersecurity officials continues to affect NCSD and thus US-CERT. For example, at least six senior staff members were leaving DHS's Office of Cybersecurity and Communications, including the NCSD Director. Losing senior staff members in such large numbers has negatively affected the agency's long-term planning and hampered the ability of NCSD/US-CERT to establish trusted relationships with public and private entities and to build adequate functions to carry out its mission, including expanded cyber analysis and warning capabilities, according to the official.

Furthermore, when new senior leadership has joined DHS, NCSD/US-CERT's objectives were reassessed and redirected, thus affecting NCSD's ability to have a consistent long-term strategy, according to the former official. For example, senior officials wanted to broaden the role and focus of US-CERT by having it provide centralized network monitoring for the entire federal government on a 24-hour-a-day, 7-day-a-week basis. However, the Director of NCSD disagreed with this strategy, stating that each federal agency should have its own 24-hour-a-day, 7-day-a-week incident-handling capability (either in-house or contracted out) to respond to incidents affecting its own network. He viewed US-CERT as a fusion center that would provide analysis and warning for national-level incidents, support federal agency incident-handling capabilities during crisis situations, and offer a mechanism for federal agencies to coordinate with law enforcement.

The organization's future position in the government's efforts to establish a national-level cyber analysis and warning capability is uncertain. Specifically, Homeland Security Presidential Directive 23, which is classified, creates questions about US-CERT's future role as the focal point for national cyber analysis and warning. In addition, DHS established a new National Cybersecurity Center at a higher organizational level, which may diminish the Assistant Secretary of Cyber Security and Communications' authority as the focal point for the federal government's cybersecurity-related critical infrastructure protection efforts, and thus US-CERT's role as the central provider of cyber analysis and warning capabilities across federal and nonfederal critical infrastructure entities.

As stated above, we did not make new recommendations in 2005 regarding cyber analysis and warning because our previous recommendations had not yet been fully implemented. At the time, we did recommend that the Secretary of Homeland Security require NCSD to develop a prioritized list of key activities for addressing the underlying challenges related to information sharing, hiring staff with appropriate capabilities, and organizational stability and authority. In addition, we recommended that performance measures and milestones for performing activities to address these challenges be identified. However, since that time, DHS has not provided evidence that it has taken actions on these activities.

Conclusions

In seeking to counter the growing cyber threats to the nation's critical infrastructures, DHS has established a range of cyber analysis and warning capabilities, such as monitoring federal Internet traffic and the issuance of routine warnings to federal and nonfederal customers. However, while DHS has actions under way aimed at helping US-CERT better fulfill attributes identified as critical to demonstrating a capability, US-CERT still does not exhibit aspects of the attributes essential to having a truly national capability. It lacks a comprehensive baseline understanding of the nation's critical information infrastructure operations, does not monitor all critical infrastructure information systems, does not consistently provide actionable and timely warnings, and lacks the capacity to assist in mitigation and recovery in the event of multiple, simultaneous incidents of national significance.

Planned actions could help to mitigate deficiencies. For example, as part of the Cyber Initiative, US-CERT plans to enhance its Einstein situational awareness tool so that it has real-time intrusion detection monitoring, a content analysis capability, and automated analysis functions. By placing the tool in front of Trusted Internet Connections, officials expect to obtain a governmentwide baseline view of the traffic and content entering and leaving federal networks. US-CERT also plans to hire 80 additional cyber analysts and to increase the frequency of exercises that test its national-level response capability.

However, at this point, it is unclear whether these actions will help US-CERT—or whatever organizational structure is ultimately charged with coordinating national cyber analysis and warning efforts—achieve the objectives set forth in policy. DHS faces a number of challenges that impede its ability to achieve its objectives, including fostering trusted relationships with critical infrastructure sectors, hiring and retaining skilled cyber analysts, ensuring that US-CERT warning products provide useful information in advance of attacks, enhancing predictive analysis, and ensuring that any changes brought about by HSPD 23 are marked by well-defined and transparent lines of authority and responsibility. We identified most of these challenges in our prior reviews and made broad recommendations to address them. DHS's actions to address these challenges have not been adequate. Because of this, addressing these challenges is as critical as ever to overcome the growing and formidable threats against our nation's critical cyber infrastructure. If these challenges are not addressed, US-CERT will not be able to provide an effective national cyber analysis and warning capability.

Recommendations for Executive Action

We recommend that the Secretary of Homeland Security take four actions to fully establish a national cyber analysis and warning capability. Specifically, the Secretary should address deficiencies in each of the attributes identified for

- monitoring, including establish a comprehensive baseline understanding of the nation's critical information infrastructure and engage appropriate nonfederal stakeholders to support a national-level cyber monitoring capability;
- analysis, including expanding its capabilities to investigate incidents;
- warning, including ensuring consistent notifications that are targeted, actionable, and timely; and
- response, including ensuring that US-CERT provides assistance in the mitigation of and recovery from simultaneous severe incidents, including incidents of national significance.

We also recommend that the Secretary address the challenges that impede DHS from fully implementing the key attributes, including the following 6 items:

- engaging appropriate stakeholders in federal and nonfederal entities to determine ways to develop closer working and more trusted relationships;
- expeditiously hiring sufficiently trained cyber analysts and developing strategies for hiring and retaining highly qualified cyber analysts;
- identifying and acquiring technological tools to strengthen cyber analytical capabilities and handling the steadily increasing workload;
- developing predictive analysis capabilities by defining terminology, methodologies, and indicators, and engaging appropriate stakeholders in other federal and nonfederal entities;
- filling key management positions and developing strategies for hiring and retaining those officials; and
- ensuring that there are distinct and transparent lines of authority and responsibility assigned to DHS organizations with cybersecurity roles and responsibilities, including the Office of Cybersecurity and Communications and the National Cybersecurity Center.

Agency Comments and Our Evaluation

In written comments on a draft of this report (see app. II), signed by the Director of DHS's GAO/OIG Liaison Office, the department concurred with 9 of our 10 recommendations. It also described actions planned and under way to implement the 9 recommendations. In particular, the department said that to fully establish a cyber analysis and warning capability, it plans to continue expansion of the Einstein intrusion detection system and increase US-CERT's staffing. In addition, to address the challenges that impede DHS from fully implementing key cyber analysis and warning attributes, the department stated that it plans to continue to build new relationships and grow existing ones with stakeholders. Further, to strengthen its analysis and warning capability and develop its predictive analysis capability, the department cited, among other things, its planned implementation of an upgraded version of Einstein.

DHS took exception to our last recommendation, stating that the department had developed a concept-of-operations document that clearly defined roles and responsibilities for the National Cybersecurity Center and NCSD. However, this concept-of-operations document is still in draft, and the department could not provide a date for when the document would be finalized and implemented.

DHS also commented on the report's description of US-CERT as "the center." Specifically, DHS was concerned that referring to US-CERT as the center might lead to confusion with the department's newly established National Cybersecurity Center. DHS requested that we remove references to US-CERT as the center. We agree with this comment and have incorporated it in the report where appropriate.

In addition to its written response, the department provided technical comments that have been incorporated in the report where appropriate. We also incorporated technical comments provided by other entities involved in this review.

As agreed with your office, unless you publicly announce the contents of this report earlier, we plan no further distribution until 30 days from the report date. At that time, we will send copies of this report to interested congressional committees, the Secretary of Homeland Security, and other interested parties. We also will make copies available to others upon request. In addition, this report will be available at no charge on GAO's Web site at http://www.gao.gov.

If you or your staff have any questions about this report, please contact David Powner at (202) 512-9286, or pownerd@gao.gov, or Dr. Nabajyoti Barkakati at (202) 512-4499, or barkakatin@gao.gov. Contact points for our Offices of Congressional Relations and Public Affairs may be found on the last page of this report. Major contributors to this report are listed in appendix III.

David A. Powner Director,
Information Technology Management Issues

Dr. Nabajyoti Barkakati
Acting Chief Technologist

Appendix I: Objectives, Scope, and Methodology

Our objectives were to (1) identify key attributes of cyber analysis and warning capabilities, (2) compare these attributes with the United States Computer Emergency Readiness Team's (US-CERT) current analysis and warning capabilities to identify whether there are gaps, and (3) identify US-CERT's challenges to developing and implementing key attributes and a successful national cyber analysis and warning capability.

To identify key attributes of cyber analysis and warning capabilities, we identified entities based on our previous work related to cyber critical infrastructure protection, information security, and information sharing and analyzed relevant laws, strategies, and policies. In addition, we solicited suggestions from a variety of sources familiar with cyber analysis and warning organizations, including GAO's chief information technology officer and members of our Executive Council on Information Management and Technology, which is a group of executives with extensive experience in information technology management who advise us on major information management issues affecting federal agencies. On the basis of the entities identified, we selected those that were relevant and agreed to participate. We then gathered and analyzed policies, reports, and surveys; made site visits to observe the operation of cyber analysis and warning capabilities; conducted structured interviews; and received written responses to structured interview questions. These activities were performed, as appropriate, at the following entities:

- Department of Defense: Commander and Deputy Commander of the Joint Task Force—Global Network Operations and Director of the Defense Information Systems Agency; Commanding Officer, Navy Cyber Defense Operations Command; Chief Information Officer and Electronic Data Service officials of the Navy's Global Network Operations Center. We also toured the Joint Task Force's Global Network Operations Center; the Navy's Cyber Defense Operation Command Center; and the Navy Marine Corps Intranet Network's Operations Center, Computer Incident Response Team Laboratory, Request Management Center, and Enterprise Global Networks Operations Center.
- Department of Energy: the Associate Chief Information Officer for Cyber Security for the Department of Energy and other relevant officials, and the Chief Information Officer of the National Nuclear Security Administration and other relevant officials.
- Department of Homeland Security: the Director of the National Cyber Security Division, the Acting Director of the National Cyber Security Division, and the Acting Director of US-CERT.

- National Institute of Standards and Technology: the Director of the Information Technology Laboratory and officials from the Information Technology Laboratory's Computer Security Division.
- Private sector: Carnegie Mellon University's CERT® Coordination Center, Internet Storm Center, LUMETA, Microsoft, MITRE, National Association of State Chief Information Officers, SANS Institute, SRI International, and Symantec.
- Information sharing and analysis centers representing the following sectors: financial services, information technology, states, surface transportation, and research and education.
- Federal agencies in the intelligence community.

On the basis of the evidence gathered and our observations regarding each entity's capabilities and operations, we determined the key common attributes of cyber analysis and warning capabilities. To verify the attributes we identified, we solicited comments from each entity regarding the attributes identified and incorporated the comments as appropriate.

To determine US-CERT's current national analysis and warning capabilities and compare them with the attributes identified to determine whether there were any gaps, we gathered and analyzed a variety of US-CERT policies, procedures, and program plans to identify the organization's key activities related to cyber analysis and warning. We also observed US-CERT operations. In addition, we held interviews with key US-CERT officials, including the Director and Acting Director of the National Cyber Security Division, the Acting Director and Deputy Director of the US-CERT, and other relevant officials, to further clarify and confirm the key initiatives we identified through our analysis of the aforementioned documents. In addition, we interviewed the Director of Intelligence for the Department of Homeland Security's Homeland Infrastructure Threat and Risk Analysis Center to determine that organization's interaction with US-CERT and its role regarding identifying cyber threats. We also interviewed the Deputy Director of the Department of Homeland Security's National Cybersecurity Center to obtain information about its concept-of-operations document. We then compared those activities to the key attributes of cyber analysis and warning capabilities in order to determine US-CERT's ability to provide cyber analysis and warning and identify any related gaps.

To identify US-CERT's challenges to developing and implementing the key attributes and a successful national cyber analysis and warning capability, we gathered and analyzed relevant documents, such as past GAO reports and studies by various cybersecurity-related entities, and interviewed key federal and nonfederal officials regarding the challenges associated with cyber analysis and warning. On the basis of the information received and our knowledge of the issues, we determined the major challenges to developing and implementing the key attributes and a successful national cyber analysis and warning capability.

We performed this performance audit between June 2007 and July 2008 in the Washington, D.C., metropolitan area; Atlanta, Georgia; Bloomington, Indiana; Pittsburgh, Pennsylvania; and Norfolk, Virginia; in accordance with generally accepted government auditing standards. Those standards require that we plan and perform the audit to obtain sufficient, appropriate evidence to provide a reasonable basis for our findings and conclusions based on our audit objectives. We believe that the evidence obtained provides a reasonable basis for our findings and conclusions based on our audit objectives.

Appendix II: Comments from the Department of Homeland Security

U.S. Department of Homeland Security
Washington, DC 20528

US GAO

2008 JUL -3 PM 2:52

Homeland Security

July 2, 2008

Mr. David Powner
Director
Information Technology Management Issues
United States Government Accountability Office
441 G Street, N.W.
Washington, DC 20001

Dear Mr. Powner:

Re: Draft Report GAO-08-588, *Cyber Analysis and Warning: DHS Faces Challenges in Establishing a Comprehensive National Capability* (GAO Job Code 310851)

The Department of Homeland Security (DHS) appreciates the opportunity to review and comment on the subject draft report. We recognize that cyber threats are growing and are increasing in sophistication and accuracy. We also realize that as technology advances and our dependence on an interconnected cyberspace grows, the risks associated with cyber threats increase. The Department's National Protection and Programs Directorate (NPPD) National Cyber Security Division (NCSD) and its United States Computer Emergency Readiness Team (US-CERT)[1] are significantly changing and growing to address these cyber threats.

The federal government has undertaken a National Cybersecurity Initiative (NCI), which includes programs that strengthen US-CERT's capabilities for analyzing malicious activity, issuing warnings, and responding to incidents. With its newly expanded mission, budget and staff and a more customer-driven and outcome oriented culture, US-CERT will continue to increase its cyber analysis and warning capabilities. As US-CERT moves forward, the organization will work to address various recommendations set forth by GAO.

US-CERT is continually working to establish more effective outcome measures that will inform our program delivery and focus our resources on the most prevalent and highest risk issues. In addition to metrics analysis, US-CERT will continue to work with partners to determine how we can address the deficiencies identified by the GAO.

[1] Note: The Department requests that GAO use the acronym, "US-CERT," when referring to the United States Computer Emergency Readiness Team and remove any references to it as "the center." US-CERT is not classified or defined as a center by the Department or any other entity. The GAO's use of the term "the center" can be confusing because the report also refers to the National Cyber Security *Center* (NCSC), which is an organization separate from NCSD. The NCSC will not duplicate the roles and responsibilities of the participating organizations, such as US-CERT, but will support them and ensure coordination and shared cyber security situational awareness across these organizations.

www.dhs.gov

***GAO* <u>Recommendation 1:</u>** *We recommend that the Secretary of Homeland Security–to fully establish a national cyber analysis and warning capability–specifically address deficiencies in monitoring, including establish a comprehensive baseline understanding of the nation's critical information infrastructure and engage appropriate nonfederal stakeholders to support a national-level cyber monitoring capability.*

<u>Response:</u> US-CERT concurs with this recommendation. Under the NCI, US-CERT is expanding its initial EINSTEIN program, referred to as EINSTEIN 1. The expanded program, referred to as EINSTEIN 2, is a 24x7 intrusion detection system that gathers network flow data from federal agencies and analyzes traffic patterns and behaviors. To improve US-CERT's capability to maintain situational awareness, all federal executive agencies, in accordance with the Office of Management and Budget (OMB) November 20, 2007, Memorandum M-08-05, Implementation of Trusted Internet Connection, will be required to use EINSTEIN 2. This expanded use of EINSTEIN 2 enables the US-CERT to gain increased situational awareness from all the federal executive agencies and fulfill its mandate to act as a central point for computer network security of the federal enterprise.

US-CERT does not directly monitor malicious activity involving nonfederal networks. However, NPPD and US-CERT actively reach out to private sector partners via various mechanisms to develop a baseline understanding of the nation's critical information infrastructure. NPPD Protective Security Advisors (PSAs) within the Office of Infrastructure Protection are located in field offices across the country and regularly conduct site visits to assess vulnerabilities, including cyber vulnerabilities, at Critical Infrastructure/Key Resource (CIKR) facilities. Further, NCSD co-chairs the Cross Sector Cyber Security Working Group under the National Infrastructure Protection Plan (NIPP) Framework, which includes representatives from all CIKR sectors and provides a monthly venue for engagement, collaboration and information sharing on cyber security issues.

A specific example of how the Department identifies specific vulnerabilities in the Nation's critical information infrastructure is the AURORA scenario, which involves the protective control systems used in the Nation's electric power grid. As soon as DHS identified this vulnerability, a Tiger Team of subject matter experts from government and industry was convened to determine the scope, potential consequences of this vulnerability, and to develop a better system for guiding private industry efforts to secure control systems. DHS is currently working with its government and industry partners to closely monitor this vulnerability, asses the risk it poses, and take appropriate proactive measures.

***GAO* <u>Recommendation 2:</u>** *We recommend that the Secretary of Homeland Security–to fully establish a national cyber analysis and warning capability–specifically address deficiencies in analysis, including expanding its capabilities to investigate incidents.*

<u>Response:</u> We concur and are actively implementing improvements that will address the recommendation. Since January 2008, there has been an increase in funding of $115M in Fiscal Year 2008 for US-CERT. This funding includes salaries and benefits for 35 additional federal personnel and related costs, which will allow US-CERT to increase its cyber analysis and warning capabilities.

Much of the increased funding will be focused on developing and deploying EINSTEIN 2. EINSTEIN 2, like EINSTEIN 1, will continue to passively observe network traffic to and from participating federal executive agencies' networks. In addition, EINSTEIN 2 will alert when specific malicious network activity is detected and provide US-CERT with increased insight into the nature of that activity. Through EINSTEIN 2, US-CERT will be able to analyze malicious activity occurring across the federal IT networks resulting in improved computer network security situational awareness. This increase in situational awareness can then be shared with federal executive agencies in an effort to reduce and prevent computer network vulnerabilities.

EINSTEIN 2 adds to EINSTEIN 1 a network intrusion detection technology that will monitor for malicious activity in network traffic to and from participating federal executive agencies. EINSTEIN 2 will alert US-CERT when the system identifies malicious network traffic occurring in a federal executive agencies' network in response to specific predefined signatures. By scanning communications during transmission, EINSTEIN 2 identifies harmful communications that warrant analysis. A US-CERT analyst may then query that specific information in EINSTEIN 2 to analyze the potentially harmful network traffic identified by the alert.

EINSTEIN 2 is to augment -- not replace or reduce -- the current computer network security practices of participating federal executive agencies. Participating agencies will continue to operate their own intrusion detection and prevention systems, perform network monitoring, and use other information security technologies. EINSTEIN 2 enables US-CERT to correlate activity across the entire federal enterprise. With the enhanced correlation capability, US-CERT achieves increased situational awareness of federal executive agency computer networks which is required to perform the computer network security responsibilities assigned to DHS.

GAO Recommendation 3: *We recommend that the Secretary of Homeland Security–to fully establish a national cyber analysis and warning capability–specifically address deficiencies in warning, including ensuring consistent notifications that are targeted, actionable, and timely.*

Response: We concur with the recommendation. A key goal of US-CERT is to ensure that alerts—Critical Infrastructure Information Notices (CIINs) in particular—reach the appropriate stakeholders. US-CERT recognizes the importance of targeted information sharing and is working with NCSD's Outreach and Awareness Program and other cross sector working groups to increase awareness and communication channels.

The following communication channels are currently used for notification and activation in the event of a Cyber Incident:

- The National Cyber Alert System: This system provides an infrastructure, managed by US-CERT, for relaying timely and actionable computer security updates and warning information to all users.
- National Operations Center: This is the primary national-level hub for domestic incident management communications and operations.
- Homeland Security Information Network (HSIN) Critical Sector (CS): This communications network provides States and critical infrastructure owners and operators with real-time interactive connectivity to the National Operations Center (NOC) on a

Sensitive-but-Unclassified (SBU) level to all users. HSIN-CS is the NOC's primary suite of tools for information sharing, coordination, planning, mitigation, and response.

- US-CERT Portal: This secure collaboration tool enables private and public sectors to actively share information about cyber security vulnerabilities, exploits, and incidents in a trusted and secure environment among members.
- US-CERT Public Web Site: www.uscert.gov provides the primary means for US-CERT to convey information to the public at large. The site includes relevant information on cyber security issues, cyber activity, and vulnerability resources.
- Information Sharing and Analysis Centers (ISACs): Through secure websites and secure e-mail, information on infrastructure threats and vulnerabilities is provided to the members.

We do not agree with the report's repeated description of US-CERT's warnings and notifications as "not consistently actionable or timely (*i.e.*, providing the right information to the right person or group when needed)." We believe this statement inaccurately generalizes all US-CERT products. While US-CERT is charged with analyzing cyber threats and disseminating warning information, it relies on other stakeholders and entities such as ISACs, State, local, and tribal entities to review and maintain an accurate list of members who disseminate information to the correct personnel within their organization.[2]

GAO ***Recommendation 4:*** *We recommend that the Secretary of Homeland Security–to fully establish a national cyber analysis and warning capability–specifically address deficiencies in response, including ensuring that US-CERT provides assistance in the mitigation and recovery from simultaneous severe incidents, including incidents of national significance.*

Response: We concur and are actively implementing improvements for addressing the recommendation. While the Department is constantly enhancing its capabilities and currently increasing its budget and staffing, we do have recent examples of success in mitigating the effects of cyber incidents.

The GAO report mentioned the May 2007 denial-of-service cyber attack in Estonia; US-CERT successfully mitigated the effects of this attack. Bot-networks were flooding Estonia's IT systems with traffic, causing a denial of service for many of their government sites. US-CERT coordinated with its federal, international, and private sector partners to identify over 2,500 unique sources from 21 NATO countries participating in the attacking botnets on Estonia. The information was shared with military, intelligence, law enforcement, and US-CERT personnel from NATO member nations.

The GAO report also mentioned the Cyber Storm II exercise. The Cyber Storm II exercise, hosted by the Department of Homeland Security, helped participating organizations—public and private—prepare for, respond to, and mitigate cyber attacks that could affect their ability to

[2] With regard to targeted dissemination of US-CERT's vetted products [*e.g.*, Federal Information Notices (FINs), US-CERT CIINs issued via the Homeland Security Information Network – Critical Sectors (HSIN-CS) portal, and Situational Awareness Reports (SARs) US-CERT only vets the membership for the Government Forum of Incident Response and Security Teams (GFIRST)].

deliver critical services. This exercise is one of DHS's primary methods for enhancing crisis management and improving risk management across all participating organizations and highlights the interdependencies that exist between cyber and physical infrastructure. The exercise included elements of the private sector in the transportation, chemical, information technology, and communications sectors as well as federal agencies and departments and several international partners.

Also, EINSTEIN has proven successful in enhancing security within the federal government. Through the Department of Transportation's (DOT's) participation in the EINSTEIN program, US-CERT was able to quickly detect malicious activity and prevent it from infecting other government computers. In this case, a computer worm had infected an unsecured government computer in a U.S. Government agency. When the worm attempted to attack DOT's network, EINSTEIN detected the unusual traffic, and the subsequent US-CERT investigation uncovered the worm and worked with the affected departments and agencies to prevent its spread.

GAO <u>Recommendation 5:</u> *We recommend that the Secretary address the challenges that impede DHS from fully implementing the key attributes, including engaging appropriate stakeholders in federal and nonfederal entities to determine ways to develop closer working and more trusted relationships.*

<u>Response:</u> We concur and are actively implementing approaches for addressing the recommendation. Significant progress has been made in establishing or strengthening relationships with stakeholders, both internationally and domestically. The Department will continue to build new relationships and grow existing ones.

US-CERT coordinates information sharing and incident response activities with international partners to improve cyber incident response at the international level. US-CERT representatives participate in conferences to enhance international cyber coordination. US-CERT also meets individually with other countries' CERTs to discuss cyber incident mitigation and response strategies.

NCSD is committed to providing timely and actionable information on cyber incidents so that State cyber security responders can take appropriate action. Also, the information provided by State/local partners supplies important situational awareness for NCSD. There are channels in place that DHS uses to disseminate cyber information to State and local homeland security stakeholders.

- Government Forum of Incident Response and Security Teams (GFIRST): NCSD recently extended GFIRST membership to State and local governments. This is very significant as it links technical cyber experts in federal agencies with their counterparts in State/local governments and provides State/local governments access to tools and additional technical analysis. The GFIRST forum provides these technical experts with a collaborative space that will increase States' situational awareness of cyber incident response activity. US-CERT products and alerts are sent via the US-CERT-managed GFIRST portal.

- Multi-State Information Sharing and Analysis Center (MS-ISAC): The MS-ISAC membership is comprised of cyber officials from all States. NCSD provides funding to the MS-ISAC to assist with State/local coordination and information sharing on operational and other cyber security activities. NCSD provides a dedicated secure compartment within the US-CERT portal to enable collaboration among the State/local community and with NCSD/US-CERT. NCSD uses the Portal to both coordinate cyber awareness activities and initiatives, as well as disseminate critical cyber alerts and information. The MS-ISAC also maintains a distribution list of State and local points of contact, which allows NCSD to reach out to State/local decision makers regarding challenges, needs, and opportunities. In addition, NCSD participates in monthly calls with MS-ISAC membership and provides updates on Department activities and works with State/local representatives through established working groups that meet via monthly conference calls.

- Lessons Learned Information Sharing: NCSD has created a cyber security page on the LLIS.GOV site, which all homeland security personnel at the State and local level can access. NCSD populated this page with information regarding exercise after action reports, awareness materials, policies, plans, and other information on cyber security. States can post their best practices and materials here as well.

- Direct Contact: NCSD/US-CERT maintains positive relationships with numerous State points of contact and communicates/collaborates with them directly on a variety of topics.

GAO Recommendation 6: *We recommend that the Secretary address the challenges that impede DHS from fully implementing the key attributes, including expeditiously hiring sufficiently trained cyber analysts and developing strategies for hiring and retaining highly qualified cyber analysts.*

Response: We concur with the recommendation, and a strategy is already in place to address this need. DHS has recently entered into a contract to develop and implement a recruitment strategy to assist with cyber-related vacancies. NPPD has established an agreement with the Office of Personnel Management (OPM) to put a contracted human capital team in place to support the hiring requirement.

Vacancies are posted through a variety of internal and external mechanisms, including less traditional federal government venues, such as recruiting websites and various local newspapers. DHS and US-CERT participate in various career fairs and accepts referrals from other agencies and employees. Graduating students are also targeted through the Scholarship for Service program.

GAO Recommendation 7: *We recommend that the Secretary address the challenges that impede DHS from fully implementing the key attributes, including identifying and acquiring technological tools to strengthen cyber analytical capabilities and handling the steadily increasing workload.*

Response: We concur and are actively implementing approaches that address the recommendation. As described above, US-CERT is implementing an upgraded version of Einstein. Einstein 2 is an automated process for collecting, correlating, analyzing, and sharing computer security information across the Federal government so that Federal agencies are aware, in near real-time, of threats to infrastructure and can act swiftly to take corrective measures. It will incorporate network intrusion detection technology capable of alerting US-CERT to the presence of malicious or potentially harmful computer network activity in Federal executive agencies' network traffic.

In addition to implementing US-CERT's Einstein 2, DHS' Office of Science and Technology (S&T) and CS&C collaborate on cyber research and development (R&D) priorities to identify and develop technological tools to strengthen cyber analytical capabilities. Specifically, S&T created an Integrated Product Team (IPT) process to ensure proponents of R&D requirements, such as CS&C, are able to provide their requirements to S&T (i.e., existing capability shortfalls). A Research, Development, Test and Evaluation (RDT&E) program was established by S&T to address these requirements. CS&C developed a list of cyber security RDT&E requirements for the NCI which are in the process of being forwarded to S&T. These cyber related RDT&E requirements for critical infrastructures have been developed in a government-industry consensus process and are specified in the R&D portions of the Communications and IT Sector Specific Plans.

GAO Recommendation 8: *We recommend that the Secretary address the challenges that impede DHS from fully implementing the key attributes, including developing predictive analysis capabilities by defining terminology, methodologies, and indicators, and engaging appropriate stakeholders in other federal and nonfederal entities.*

Response: We concur and are actively implementing approaches that address the recommendation. EINSTEIN 2 uses anomaly-based detection methods to identify harmful or malicious computer network incidents. Anomaly-based detection, as defined in NIST Special Publication 800-94, is defined as "the process of comparing definitions of what activity is considered normal against observed events to identify significant deviations."

While an intrusion detection system uses a defined set of rules or filters that have been crafted to catch a specific, malicious event, the EINSTEIN 2 anomaly detection capability utilizes the network flow data and alerts to focus on the system's baseline of normal activity. As described above, behavior that varies from this standard is noted. Intrusion detection systems look for a misuse signature and anomaly detection looks for a strange event.

NCSD is also working with other Departmental and Interagency components to develop the strategic analysis of the Nation's critical cyber infrastructure, integrating all relevant and appropriate sources of information to support predictive analysis. NCSD is also seeking to engage stakeholders in other federal and nonfederal agencies to provide them with actionable information based on this predictive analysis.

GAO Recommendation 9: *We recommend that the Secretary address the challenges that impede DHS from fully implementing the key attributes, including filling key management positions and developing strategies for hiring and retaining those officials.*

Response: We concur with this recommendation. However, it is important to note that since the Exit Conference NCSD has filled several key management positions, including the positions of NCSD Director, US-CERT Director of Operations, and NCSD Chief of Staff. Further, DHS has recently entered into a contract to develop and implement a recruitment strategy to assist with cyber-related vacancies. NPPD has established an agreement with the Office of Personnel Management (OPM) to put a contracted human capital team in place to support the hiring requirement.

GAO ***<u>Recommendation 10:</u>*** *We recommend that the Secretary address the challenges that impede DHS from fully implementing the key attributes, including ensuring that there are distinct and transparent lines of authority and responsibility assigned to DHS organizations with cybersecurity roles and responsibilities, including the Office of Cyber Security and Communications and the National Cyber Security Center.*

<u>Response:</u> We do not concur with this recommendation. During the time period that GAO conducted their Cyber Analysis and Warning review, extensive interagency collaboration and coordination took place. This resulted in a NCSC Concept of Operations (CONOPS) with clearly defined roles and responsibilities for NCSC and NCSD. NCSC coordinates cyber security efforts and improves situational awareness and information sharing to support the entities defending government networks, such as US-CERT. US-CERT's ability to synthesize information and provide situational awareness will be enhanced through its work with the NCSC. The NCSC does not duplicate the roles and responsibilities of the participating organizations, such as US-CERT, but supports them in their mission and ensures coordination and shared cyber security situational awareness across these organizations.

Sincerely,

Jerald E. Levine
Jerald E. Levine
Director
Departmental GAO/OIG Liaison Office

Appendix III: GAO Contacts and Staff Acknowledgments

GAO Contacts

David A. Powner, (202) 512-9286 or pownerd@gao.gov
Dr. Nabajyoti Barkakati, (202) 512-4499 or barkakatin@gao.gov

Staff Acknowledgments

In addition to the persons named above, Neil Doherty, Michael Gilmore, Barbarol James, Kenneth A. Johnson, Kush K. Malhotra, Gary Mountjoy, Jennifer Stavros-Turner, and Amos Tevelow made key contributions to this report.

GAO's Mission

The Government Accountability Office, the audit, evaluation, and investigative arm of Congress, exists to support Congress in meeting its constitutional responsibilities and to help improve the performance and accountability of the federal government for the American people. GAO examines the use of public funds; evaluates federal programs and policies; and provides analyses, recommendations, and other assistance to help Congress make informed oversight, policy, and funding decisions. GAO's commitment to good government is reflected in its core values of accountability, integrity, and reliability.

Obtaining Copies of GAO Reports and Testimony

The fastest and easiest way to obtain copies of GAO documents at no cost is through GAO's Web site (www.gao.gov). Each weekday, GAO posts newly released reports, testimony, and correspondence on its Web site. To have GAO e-mail you a list of newly posted products every afternoon, go to www.gao.gov and select "E-mail Updates."

Order by Mail or Phone

The first copy of each printed report is free. Additional copies are $2 each. A check or money order should be made out to the Superintendent of Documents. GAO also accepts VISA and Mastercard. Orders for 100 or more copies mailed to a single address are discounted 25 percent. Orders should be sent to:

U.S. Government Accountability Office
441 G Street NW, Room LM
Washington, DC 20548

To order by Phone:	Voice:	(202) 512-6000
	TDD:	(202) 512-2537
	Fax:	(202) 512-6061

To Report Fraud, Waste, and Abuse in Federal Programs

Contact:

Web site: www.gao.gov/fraudnet/fraudnet.htm
E-mail: fraudnet@gao.gov
Automated answering system: (800) 424-5454 or (202) 512-7470

Congressional Relations

Ralph Dawn, Managing Director, dawnr@gao.gov, (202) 512-4400
U.S. Government Accountability Office, 441 G Street NW, Room 7125
Washington, DC 20548

Public Affairs

Chuck Young, Managing Director, youngc1@gao.gov, (202) 512-4800
U.S. Government Accountability Office, 441 G Street NW, Room 7149
Washington, DC 20548

DOCUMENT NO. 8

CRITICAL INFRASTRUCTURE PROTECTION: DHS NEEDS TO FULLY ADDRESS LESSONS LEARNED FROM ITS FIRST CYBER STORM EXERCISE

GAO Report
GAO-08-825

September 2008

What GAO Found

As a result of its first Cyber Storm exercise, in February 2006, DHS identified eight lessons that had significant impact across sectors, agencies, and exercise participants. These lessons involved improving (1) the interagency coordination groups; (2) contingency planning, risk assessment, and roles and responsibilities; (3) integration of incidents across infrastructures; (4) access to information; (5) coordination of response activities; (6) strategic communications and public relations; (7) processes, tools, and technology; and (8) the exercise program.

While DHS has demonstrated progress in addressing the lessons it learned from its first Cyber Storm exercise, more remains to be done to fully address the lessons. In the months following its first exercise, DHS identified 66 activities that address one or more of the lessons, including hosting meetings with key cyber response officials from foreign, federal, and state governments and private industry, and refining their operating procedures. To date, DHS has completed a majority of these activities (see table). However, key activities have not yet been completed. Specifically, DHS identified 16 activities as ongoing and 7 activities as planned for the future. Further, while DHS has identified completion dates for its planned activities, it has not identified completion dates for its ongoing activities. Until DHS schedules and completes its remaining activities, the agency risks conducting subsequent exercises that repeat the lessons learned during the first exercise.

Commenting on their experiences during the second Cyber Storm exercise, in March 2008, participants observed both progress and continued challenges in building a comprehensive national cyber response capability. Their observations addressed several key areas, including the value and scope of the exercise, roles and responsibilities, public relations, communications, the exercise infrastructure, and the handling of classified information. For example, many participants reported that their organizations found value in the exercise because it led them to update their contact lists and improve their response capabilities. Other participants, however, reported the need for clarifying the role of the law enforcement community during a cyber incident and for improving policies governing the handling of classified information so that key information can be shared. Many of the challenges identified during Cyber Storm II were similar to challenges identified during the first exercise.

Summary of Status of Activities

Status of DHS Activities	Number of Activities
Reported and validated as completed	42
Reported as completed, but not validated due to insufficient evidence	1
Reported as ongoing	16
Reported as planned for the future	7
Total	**66**

Source: GAO analysis of DHS data.

Abbreviations

DHS	Department of Homeland Security
ISAC	Information Sharing and Analysis Center
NCRCG	National Cyber Response Coordination Group
NCSD	National Cyber Security Division
US-CERT	United States Computer Emergency Readiness Team

United States Government Accountability Office
Washington, DC 20548

September 9, 2008

The Honorable Bennie G. Thompson
Chairman
Committee on Homeland Security
House of Representatives

The Honorable James R. Langevin
Chairman
Subcommittee on Emerging Threats, Cybersecurity, and Science and Technology
Committee on Homeland Security
House of Representatives

Since the early 1990s, increasing computer interconnectivity—most notably growth in the use of the Internet—has revolutionized the way that our government, our nation, and much of the world communicate and conduct business. While the benefits of this technology have been enormous, this widespread interconnectivity poses significant risks to the government's and our nation's computer systems and, more important, to the critical operations and infrastructures they support.

Federal policies establish the Department of Homeland Security (DHS) as the focal point for the security of cyberspace—including analysis, warning, information sharing, vulnerability reduction, mitigation, and recovery efforts for public and private critical infrastructure systems.[1] To accomplish this mission, DHS is to work with federal agencies, state and local governments, and the private sector. Federal policy also recognizes the importance of building public/private partnerships because the private sector owns a large percentage of the nation's critical infrastructure—including banking and financial institutions, telecommunications networks, and energy production and transmission facilities.

As part of DHS's cybersecurity responsibilities, the agency is required to coordinate cyber attack simulation exercises to strengthen public and private incident response capabilities. One major exercise program, called Cyber Storm, is a large-scale simulation of multiple concurrent cyber attacks involving the federal government, states, foreign governments, and private industry. To date, DHS has conducted Cyber Storm exercises in 2006 and 2008, and it is currently planning a third for 2010. Because of your interest in these exercises, we agreed to (1) identify the lessons that DHS

[1] The White House, *National Strategy to Secure Cyberspace* (Washington, D.C.: February 2003), and Homeland Security Presidential Directive 7: Critical Infrastructure Identification, Prioritization, and Protection (Dec. 17, 2003).

learned from the first Cyber Storm exercise, (2) assess DHS's efforts to address the lessons learned from this exercise, and (3) identify key participants' views of their experiences during the second Cyber Storm exercise.

To address these objectives, we reviewed relevant DHS documents, including the Cyber Storm I Exercise Report, a list of planned post-Cyber Storm activities, and artifacts showing actions taken to address activities. We attended the second Cyber Storm exercise, held in Washington, D.C., in March 2008. We also interviewed DHS officials responsible for planning the exercises as well as participants in the Cyber Storm exercises, including officials representing three federal agencies, three private industry sectors, and one representing state governments. In addition, this work builds on a body of work we have done over the last several years on the cyber aspects of critical infrastructure protection.[2]

We performed our work from January to September 2008 in accordance with generally accepted government auditing standards. Those standards require that we plan and perform the audit to obtain sufficient, appropriate evidence to provide a reasonable basis for our findings and conclusions based on our audit objectives. We believe that the evidence obtained provides a reasonable basis for our findings and conclusions based on our audit objectives. Additional details on our objectives, scope, and methodology are provided in appendix I.

Results in Brief

As a result of its first Cyber Storm exercise, in February 2006, DHS identified eight lessons that had significant impact across sectors, agencies, and exercise participants. These lessons involved improving (1) the interagency coordination groups; (2) contingency planning, risk assessment, and roles and responsibilities; (3) integration of incidents across infrastructures; (4) access to information; (5) coordination of response activities; (6) strategic communications and public relations; (7) processes, tools, and technology; and (8) the exercise program.

[2] GAO, *Critical Infrastructure Protection: Department of Homeland Security Faces Challenges in Fulfilling Cybersecurity Responsibilities*, GAO-05-434 (Washington, D.C.: May 26, 2005); *Critical Infrastructure Protection: Challenges in Addressing Cybersecurity*, GAO-05-827T (Washington, D.C.: July 19, 2005); *Internet Infrastructure: DHS Faces Challenges in Developing a Joint Public/Private Recovery Plan*, GAO-06-672 (Washington, D.C.: June 16, 2006); *Internet Infrastructure: Challenges in Developing a Public/Private Recovery Plan, GAO-06-863T* (Washington, D.C.: July 28, 2006); *Critical Infrastructure Protection: DHS Leadership Needed to Enhance Cybersecurity Elements*, GAO-06-1087T (Washington, D.C.: Sept. 13, 2006); *Critical Infrastructure Protection: Multiple Efforts to Secure Control Systems Are Under Way, but Challenges Remain*, GAO-07-1036 (Washington, D.C.: Sept. 10, 2007); *Critical Infrastructure Protection: Multiple Efforts to Secure Control Systems Are Under Way, but Challenges Remain*, GAO-08-119T (Washington, D.C.: Oct. 17, 2007); *Critical Infrastructure Protection: Sector-Specific Plans' Coverage of Key Cyber Security Elements Varies*, GAO-08-113 (Washington, D.C.: Oct. 31, 2007).

While DHS has demonstrated progress in addressing the lessons it learned from its first Cyber Storm exercise, more remains to be done to fully address the lessons. In the months following its first exercise, DHS identified 66 activities that address one or more of the lessons, including hosting meetings with key cyber response officials from foreign, federal, and state governments and private industry; refining operating procedures; and obtaining new tools and technologies to support incident response operations. Since that time, DHS has completed 42 of these activities.[3] However, key activities have not yet been completed. DHS identified 16 activities as ongoing and 7 as planned for the future. In addition, while DHS identified completion dates for its planned activities, it has not identified completion dates associated with activities that are reported as ongoing. For example, DHS reports that it has work under way to issue guidance to information sharing and analysis centers on public communications related to cybersecurity, but has not established a milestone for completing this activity. Until DHS schedules and completes its remaining activities, the agency risks conducting subsequent exercises that repeat the lessons learned during the first exercise.

Commenting on their experiences during the second Cyber Storm exercise in March 2008, participants observed both progress and continuing challenges in building a comprehensive national cyber response capability. Their observations addressed several key areas, including the value and scope of the exercise, roles and responsibilities, public relations, communications, the exercise infrastructure, and the handling of classified information. For example, many participants reported that their organizations found value in the exercise because it led them to update their contact lists and improve their response capabilities. Other participants, however, reported the need for clarifying the role of the law enforcement community during a cyber incident and for improving policies governing the handling of classified information so that key information can be shared. Many of the challenges noted during Cyber Storm II were similar to ones identified during the first exercise.

We are making a recommendation to the Secretary of Homeland Security to direct the Assistant Secretary for Cybersecurity and Communications to oversee the completion of corrective activities resulting from Cyber Storm I, many of which were reiterated during Cyber Storm II. DHS provided written comments on a draft of this report (see app. IV). In its comments, DHS concurred with our recommendation and reported that the department is working to complete applicable activities identified during the first Cyber Storm exercise. DHS officials also provided technical comments, which we have incorporated as appropriate.

[3] DHS reported that one other activity had been completed, but the department was unable to provide evidence demonstrating its completion.

Background

Critical infrastructures are physical or virtual systems and assets so vital to the nation that their incapacitation or destruction would have a debilitating impact on national security, national economic security, national public health or safety, or any combination of these matters. These systems and assets—such as the electric power grid, chemical plants, and water treatment facilities—are essential to the operations of the economy and the government. Recent terrorist attacks and threats have underscored the need to protect our nation's critical infrastructures. If vulnerabilities in these infrastructures are exploited, they could be disrupted or disabled, leading to physical damage, economic losses, and even loss of life.

The Federal Government Plays a Critical Role in Helping Secure Critical Infrastructures

Federal law and policies call for critical infrastructure protection activities to enhance the physical and cybersecurity of both public and private infrastructures that are essential to national security, economic well-being, and national public health and safety.[4] Federal policies identify 18 critical infrastructure sectors and designate certain federal agencies as lead points of contact for each (see table 1). Further, they assign these agencies responsibility for infrastructure protection activities in their assigned sectors and for coordination with other relevant federal agencies, state and local governments, and the private sector. In addition, federal policies establish DHS as the focal point for the security of cyberspace—including analysis, warning, information sharing, vulnerability reduction, mitigation, and recovery efforts for public and private critical infrastructure systems.

Table 1. Critical Infrastructure Sectors and Their Lead Agencies

Sector	Description	Lead Agency
Agriculture and food	Provides for the fundamental need for food. The infrastructure includes supply chains for feed and crop production, processing, and retail sales.	Department of Agriculture, Department of Health and Human Services, Food and Drug Administration [a]
Banking and finance	Provides the financial infrastructure of the nation. This sector consists of commercial banks, insurance companies, mutual funds, government-sponsored enterprises, pension funds, and other financial institutions that carry out transactions, including clearing and settlement.	Department of the Treasury

[4] The law and policies include the Homeland Security Act of 2002 (Pub. L. No. 107-296, Nov. 25, 2002); Homeland Security Presidential Directive 7: Critical Infrastructure Identification, Prioritization, and Protection (Dec. 17, 2003); and *The National Strategy to Secure Cyberspace* (February 2003).

Sector	Description	Lead Agency
Chemical	Transforms natural raw materials into commonly used products benefiting society's health, safety, and productivity. The chemical industry produces more than 70,000 products that are essential to automobiles, pharmaceuticals, food supply, electronics, water treatment, health, construction, and other necessities.	Department of Homeland Security
Commercial facilities	Includes prominent commercial centers, office buildings, sports stadiums, theme parks, and other sites where large numbers of people congregate to pursue business activities, conduct personal commercial transactions, or enjoy recreational pastimes.	Department of Homeland Security
Commercial nuclear reactors, materials, and waste	Includes 104 commercial nuclear reactors; research and test nuclear reactors; nuclear materials; and the transportation, storage, and disposal of nuclear materials and waste.	Department of Homeland Security
Dams	Comprises approximately 80,000 dam facilities, including larger and nationally symbolic dams that are major components of other critical infrastructures that provide electricity and water.	Department of Homeland Security
Defense industrial base	Supplies the military with the means to protect the nation by producing weapons, aircraft, and ships and providing essential services, including information technology and supply and maintenance.	Department of Defense
Drinking water and water treatment systems	Sanitizes the water supply through about 170,000 public water systems. These systems depend on reservoirs, dams, wells, treatment facilities, pumping stations, and transmission lines.	Environmental Protection Agency
Emergency services	Saves lives and property from accidents and disasters. This sector includes fire, rescue, emergency medical services, and law enforcement organizations.	Department of Homeland Security
Energy	Provides the electric power used by all sectors and the refining, storage, and distribution of oil and gas. This sector is divided into electricity and oil and natural gas.	Department of Energy

Sector	Description	Lead Agency
Government facilities	Includes the buildings owned and leased by the federal government for use by federal entities.	Department of Homeland Security
Information technology	Produces hardware, software, and services that enable other sectors to function.	Department of Homeland Security
National monuments and icons	Includes key assets that are symbolically identified with traditional American values and institutions or U.S. political and economic power.	Department of the Interior
Manufacturing	Includes key critical manufacturing operations based on highly integrated and interdependent supply chains. This sector provides metal, machinery, electrical equipment, appliances, components, and transportation equipment.	Department of Homeland Security
Postal and shipping	Delivers private and commercial letters, packages, and bulk assets. The United States Postal Service and other carriers provide the services of this sector.	Department of Homeland Security
Public health and health care	Mitigates the risk of disasters and attacks and also provides recovery assistance if an attack occurs. This sector consists of health departments, clinics, and hospitals.	Department of Health and Human Services
Tele-communications	Provides wired, wireless, and satellite communications to meet the needs of businesses and governments.	Department of Homeland Security
Transportation systems	Enables movement of people and assets that are vital to our economy, mobility, and security, using aviation, ships, rail, pipelines, highways, trucks, buses, and mass transit.	Department of Homeland Security

Source: GAO analysis of The National Infrastructure Protection Plan, Homeland Security Presidential Directive 7, and the National Strategy for Homeland Security.

[a]The Department of Agriculture is responsible for food (meat, poultry, and eggs) and agriculture; and the Department of Health and Human Services, Food and Drug Administration, is responsible for food other than meat, poultry, and egg products.

DHS Organization Is the Focal Point for National Cybersecurity Efforts

In June 2003, DHS created the National Cyber Security Division (NCSD), to serve as a national focal point for addressing cybersecurity issues and to coordinate the implementation of the National Strategy to Secure Cyberspace (the Cyberspace Strategy). Its mission is to secure cyberspace and America's cyber assets in cooperation with public, private, and international entities. NCSD reports to the Assistant Secretary for Cybersecurity and Communications.

A key component of NCSD, the U.S. Computer Emergency Readiness Team (US-CERT), is an operational organization responsible for analyzing and addressing cyber threats and vulnerabilities and disseminating cyber threat warning information. In the event of an Internet disruption, US-CERT facilitates coordination of recovery activities with the network and security operations centers of owners and operators of the Internet and with government incident response teams. We recently reported on US-CERT's challenges in establishing a comprehensive national cyber analysis and warning capability.[5]

NCSD also cochairs the National Cyber Response Coordination Group (NCRCG), which includes officials from the agencies that have a responsibility for cybersecurity as well as the lead agencies for different critical infrastructure sectors.[6] This group is the principal federal interagency mechanism for coordinating the response to and recovery from significant national cyber incidents. In the event of a major incident, NCRCG is responsible for providing subject matter expertise, recommendations, and strategic policy support to the Secretary of Homeland Security.

In addition, DHS recently announced that it is establishing a new National Cyber Security Center that is to report directly to the Secretary of Homeland Security. According to the Assistant Secretary for Cybersecurity and Communications, this center will be responsible for ensuring coordination among the cyber-related efforts across the federal government and improving situational awareness and information sharing to support the entities defending government networks, including US-CERT.

DHS Is Responsible for Conducting and Coordinating Cyber Exercises to Improve National Preparedness, Response, and Recovery Capabilities

Federal policies call for DHS to establish a national exercise program to improve the nation's ability to prevent, prepare for, respond to, and recover from terrorist attacks, major disasters, and other emergencies.[7] More specifically, the Cyberspace Strategy calls for DHS to conduct cybersecurity exercises to evaluate the impact of cyber attacks on governmentwide processes and to explore the use of such exercises to test coordination of public and private incident management, response, and recovery capabilities. Further,

[5] GAO, *Cyber Analysis and Warning: DHS Faces Challenges in Establishing a Comprehensive National Capability*, GAO-08-588 (Washington, D.C.: July 31, 2008).

[6] The Department of Justice's Computer Crime and Intellectual Property Section and the Department of Defense also cochair this group.

[7] Homeland Security Presidential Directive 8: National Preparedness (Dec. 17, 2003) and *The National Strategy to Secure Cyberspace* (February 2003).

in its National Infrastructure Protection Plan, DHS states that it will conduct national cyber exercises to improve cyber preparedness, response, coordination, and recovery capabilities.[8]

To address its cyber exercise responsibilities, DHS works with other federal agencies, state and city governments, regional coalitions, and international partners. DHS's role can range from providing cyber scenarios or expertise to local or regional exercises, cosponsoring exercises, or conducting its own large-scale cyber attack simulations (called Cyber Storm exercises). See table 2 for examples of recent and planned cyber exercises.

Table 2. Recent and Planned Cyber Exercises

Date	Exercise Name	Description	Participant(s)
September 2004	Blue Cascades II	Cosponsored by DHS and organized by members of the Pacific Northwest Economic Region. This exercise tested regional capabilities to deal with threats, interdependencies, and cascading impacts by simulating a series of attacks that disrupted infrastructures and organizations, including critical telecommunications and electricity assets.	Federal, state, and local governments and private industry
October 2004	Purple Crescent II	Sponsored by the Gulf Coast Regional Partnership for Infrastructure Security and funded by DHS. The exercise was designed to raise awareness of infrastructure interdependencies and identify how to improve regional preparedness by simulating cyber attacks on regional infrastructures as well as government and private organizations during an approaching hurricane.	Federal, state, and local governments; academic institutions; and private industry
April 2005	Top Officials-3	Sponsored by DHS, this exercise was to evaluate decision making by federal, state, and local governments by simulating terrorist threats and attacks involving chemicals, biological agents, and explosives.	Federal, state, local, and foreign governments and private industry

[8] Department of Homeland Security, *National Infrastructure Protection Plan* (Washington, D.C.: June 2006).

Date	Exercise Name	Description	Participant(s)
April 2005	Multi-State Information Sharing and Analysis Center's Tabletop Exercise	Cosponsored by DHS and the Multi-State Information Sharing and Analysis Center during the center's annual meeting. This tabletop exercise was designed to offer an opportunity for the state information technology participants to discuss their state policies and procedures and to prepare for the Cyber Storm I exercise.	State governments
February 2006	Cyber Storm I	Sponsored by DHS, Cyber Storm I was the first large-scale national cyber exercise to improve incident response and coordination capabilities by simulating multiple cyber incidents affecting the energy, information technology, telecommunications, and transportation critical infrastructure sectors.	Federal, state, and foreign governments and private industry
March 2006	Blue Cascades III	Cosponsored by DHS and organized by members of the Pacific Northwest Economic Region. This exercise was designed to focus on efforts to recover and restore services by simulating the impact of a major earthquake in the area.	Federal, state, local, and foreign governments and private industry
October 2006	Delaware Cyber Security Tabletop Exercise	Sponsored by the state of Delaware, with assistance from DHS. This exercise was designed to discuss the technical implications of a pandemic disaster scenario.	State government
December 2006	Cyber Tempest	Cosponsored by DHS and the New York State Office of Cyber Security and Critical Infrastructure Coordination. This exercise was designed to focus on regional stakeholders' procedures for response and coordination during emergencies.	State governments

Date	Exercise Name	Description	Participant(s)
April 2007	Multi-State Information Sharing and Analysis Center's Tabletop Exercise	Cosponsored by DHS and the Multi-State Information Sharing and Analysis Center during the center's annual meeting. This exercise was designed to offer an opportunity for the state information technology participants to discuss their state policies and procedures and to prepare for the Cyber Storm II exercise.	State governments
September 2007	ChicagoFIRST Exercise	Cosponsored by DHS and ChicagoFIRST, a nonprofit organization representing financial institutions. This exercise was designed to offer the city government an opportunity to collaborate with greater Chicago regional stakeholders.	Local/regional government
October 2007	Top Officials-4	Sponsored by DHS. This exercise was designed to test federal, state, territorial, and local response capabilities by simulating coordinated attacks using a radiological dispersal device.	Federal, state, local, and foreign governments and private industry
October 2007	Illinois Cyber Tabletop Exercise	Sponsored by the state of Illinois, with assistance from DHS. This exercise was designed to provide participants with an opportunity to discuss a cyber scenario affecting multiple state critical infrastructures, resulting in cascading effects across the state.	State government
October 2007	Delaware Cyber Security Tabletop Exercise	Sponsored by the state of Delaware, with assistance from DHS. The exercise was designed to discuss the increasing threat of financial and identify thefts with stakeholders.	State government
March 2008	Cyber Storm II	Sponsored by DHS, this exercise was to improve national incident response and coordination capabilities by simulating physical and cyber attacks against the transportation, information technology, and chemical critical infrastructure sectors.	Federal, state, and foreign governments and private industry

Date	Exercise Name	Description	Participant(s)
May 2008	Massachusetts Cyber Exercise	Cosponsored by DHS and the state of Massachusetts. This exercise was to examine processes, procedures, and the operational architecture of system operators, law enforcement officials, local/state government, and several private sector partners in response to specific cyber attack scenarios.	State and local governments
September 2008	ChicagoFIRST Exercise	Cosponsored by DHS and ChicagoFIRST. This exercise is planned to focus on the financial sector.	Private industry

Source: GAO analysis of DHS data.

DHS's Cyber Storm Exercises

DHS's Cyber Storm exercises are intended to examine national preparedness, response, coordination, and recovery efforts when faced with a large-scale cyber incident. Participants include federal and state agencies, private industry representatives, and selected foreign governments. DHS conducted Cyber Storm exercises in 2006 and 2008, and is planning to conduct a third exercise in 2010.

In February 2006, DHS conducted Cyber Storm I at a cost of about $3.7 million. The exercise simulated a large-scale attack affecting the energy and transportation infrastructures, using the telecommunications infrastructure as a medium for the attack. Participants included eight federal departments and three agencies, three states, and four foreign countries. The exercise also involved representatives from the private sector—including 11 information technology companies, 7 electric companies, 1 banking and finance company, and 2 airlines—and over 100 public and private agencies, associations, and corporations. DHS officials conducted the exercise primarily on a separate network to minimize the impact on "real world" information systems. The objectives of Cyber Storm I were to

- exercise interagency coordination by convening NCRCG and the Interagency Incident Management Group, a multi-agency team of federal executives responsible for providing strategic advice during nationally significant incidents;[9]

[9] The Interagency Incident Management Group was later reorganized and renamed the Crisis Action Team.

- exercise intergovernmental and intragovernmental coordination and incident response;
- identify policies and issues that hinder or support cybersecurity requirements;
- identify public/private interface communications and thresholds of coordination to improve cyber incident response and recovery, as well as identify critical information sharing paths and mechanisms;
- identify, improve, and promote public and private sector interaction in processes and procedures for communicating appropriate information to key stakeholders and the public;
- identify cyber and physical infrastructure interdependencies with real world economic and political impact;
- raise awareness of the economic and national security impacts associated with a significant cyber incident; and
- highlight available tools and technologies with analytical cyber incident response and recovery capabilities.

In March 2008, DHS conducted its second broad-scale exercise, called Cyber Storm II. The exercise cost about $6.4 million, and simulated a large-scale cyber attack affecting the communications, information technology, chemical, and transportation infrastructures. According to DHS, the exercise involved 18 federal agencies, 9 states, 10 information sharing and analysis centers, 5 foreign countries, and over 40 industry representatives from the private sector. The objectives of Cyber Storm II were to

- examine the capabilities of participating organizations to prepare for, protect from, and respond to the effects of cyber attacks;
- exercise senior leadership decision making and interagency coordination of incident responses in accordance with national-level policies and procedures;
- validate information sharing relationships and communication paths for the collection and dissemination of cyber incident situational awareness, response, and recovery information; and
- examine the means and processes to share sensitive and classified information across standard boundaries in safe and secure ways without compromising proprietary or national security interests.

DHS plans to issue a report on what it learned from Cyber Storm II by the end of 2008.

DHS Identified Eight Lessons during Cyber Storm 1

While Cyber Storm I participants reported that the exercise was valuable in that it helped them establish and improve interagency and public/private response relationships, DHS also identified eight lessons during the Cyber Storm I exercise that affected all participating sectors and agencies. These lessons involved improving (1) the interagency coordination groups; (2) contingency planning, risk assessment, and roles and responsibilities; (3) integration of incidents across infrastructures; (4) access to information; (5) coordination of response activities; (6) strategic communications and public relations; (7) processes, tools, and technology; and (8) the exercise program.

Interagency Coordination Groups

DHS reported that during the exercise, the two key interagency coordination groups—NCRCG and the Interagency Incident Management Group—were convened appropriately and that they worked well together. For example, the two groups coordinated to develop a refined awareness of the attack situation and to assess effects on the nation's critical infrastructure. However, the agency found that a broader understanding of how these groups operate would improve coordination, both within the government and with the private sector. Specifically, participants reported that

- greater collaboration could be achieved if the private sector was allowed interaction with NCRCG during major incidents,
- additional work was needed to determine how to effectively elevate the alert levels in response to cyber attacks or threats,
- NCRCG did not have enough technical experts on staff to fully leverage the large volume of incident information,
- communication procedures were needed to deliver key technical messages at a layman's level to organizations' public affairs groups in a timely manner, and
- an established information sharing process between NCRCG and allied nations would facilitate communication and help ensure a more effective response.

Contingency Planning, Risk Assessment, and Roles and Responsibilities

DHS found that formal contingency planning, risk assessment, and the definition of roles and responsibilities across the entire cyber community must continue to be solidified. It reported that in cases where procedures were clear and fully understood by participants, incident responses were timely and well coordinated. However, in cases where there were no previously established relationships and procedures for coordinating responses and assessing risks were not clear, participants had difficulty determining which organizations and people to contact. In addition, DHS found that contingency planning for backup or resilient communications was critical. The agency noted that during the exercise many participants relied heavily on communications systems that could be vulnerable to attack or failure.

Integration of Incidents across Infrastructures

According to DHS, the integration of multiple incidents across multiple infrastructures and between the public and private sectors remained a challenge. DHS reported that the cyber incident response community was generally effective in addressing single threats or attacks and, to some extent, in addressing multiple threats and attacks when these incidents were treated as individual and discrete events. However, participants were challenged when attempting to develop an integrated situational awareness and to understand the impact of multiple attacks across sectors. As the organization responsible for analyzing cyber threats and disseminating warnings, US-CERT had a lead role in forming an integrated situational awareness. However, during the exercise, US-CERT was inundated with information and questions from both the public and the private sectors. The US-CERT team found that the volume of information limited its ability to simultaneously provide situational awareness coordination and conduct technical analyses. Participants reported that a prioritization scheme is needed in order to rapidly assess cyber incidents, their sources, and their applicability to the broad-scale attack. In addition, DHS noted that there needs to be greater clarification of US-CERT's roles, responsibilities, and procedures.

Access to Information

While DHS reported that a continuous flow of information created a common framework for responding to the incidents, the majority of exercise participants reported difficulty in identifying accurate and up-to-date sources of information. For example, during the exercise, participants received multiple alerts on a single issue, which created confusion and made it more difficult to establish a single coordinated response. Participants observed that establishing a single point of contact for information would allow a common framework for responses, and noted that US-CERT is the correct agency to disseminate time sensitive and critical information to the appropriate organizations. In addition, while US-CERT provided significant information in the form of alerts and technical bulletins, participants stated that US-CERT's capabilities to post information in a timely, secure, and accurate manner needed to be further explored.

Coordination of Response Activities

DHS found that coordinating responses became more challenging as the number of cyber events increased, thus highlighting the importance of cooperation and communication. For example, during the exercise, participants noted the overwhelming effects that multiple, simultaneous, and coordinated attacks had on their response activities, which proved that the ability to accurately fuse information is crucial for responding appropriately to simultaneous attacks. Participants reported that clarifying roles and responsibilities across government, as well as the expectations between public and private sectors, is needed to coordinate preventive measures and responses to disruptions.

Strategic Communications and Public Relations

DHS reported that public messaging must be an integral part of plans for responding to a cyber incident in order to provide critical information to the response community and to empower the public to take appropriate actions. Exercise participants stated that publicly released information could undermine consumer confidence, and noted the importance of aligning both public and private sector public relations plans in order to have a coordinated approach during a crisis. In addition, DHS found that federal responses to cyber incidents must include public affairs teams to ensure that press releases and accurate situation updates are provided to partner organizations and media outlets.

Processes, Tools, and Technology

DHS reported that improved processes, tools, and training for analyzing and prioritizing the physical, economic, and national security impacts of cyber attack scenarios would enhance the quality, speed, and coordination of response. In particular, participants reported that exchanging and sharing classified information was a challenge and suggested that processes be developed to downgrade classified information so that it could be shared throughout the response community.

The Exercise Program

DHS reported that recurring exercises would strengthen participants' awareness of organizational cyber incident response, roles, policies, and procedures. Participants observed that ongoing training, discussions, and exercises are needed to build relationships among organizations and to strengthen the coordination of responses to cyber incidents. In addition, several participants in Cyber Storm I recommended the execution of smaller, more routine exercises.

DHS Has Demonstrated Progress in Addressing Lessons from Its First Cyber Storm Exercise, but More Remains to Be Done

While DHS has demonstrated progress in addressing the lessons it learned from its first Cyber Storm exercise, more remains to be done to fully address the lessons. Federal policy requires that DHS develop and maintain a system to collect, analyze, and disseminate lessons learned, best practices, and information from exercises, training events, and other sources.[10] In addition, DHS's homeland security exercise program guidance requires that, following an exercise, planners must identify a list of corrective actions and track their implementation.[11]

DHS has begun to fulfill these requirements. Specifically, DHS documented the lessons it learned during the first Cyber Storm exercise and identified 66 activities that address one or more of the lessons. These activities included hosting meetings with key cyber response officials from foreign, federal, and state governments and private industry; refining the procedures under which these entities operate; and participating in smaller cyber exercises to test these refined procedures (see app. II for a list of activities).

In addition, DHS has made progress in completing its planned activities, but more remains to be done. Of the 66 activities intended to address the lessons, 42 activities have been completed. These completed activities range from clarified procedures to improved technology for emergency responders, and they should improve communications and response activities during a significant cyber incident. DHS reported that another activity had been completed, but was unable to provide evidence demonstrating its completion. However, key activities needed to improve coordination and response during a significant cyber incident have not yet been completed. The remaining 23 activities include 16 activities that are ongoing and 7 activities that are planned for the future. While DHS has identified completion dates for its planned activities, it has not identified completion dates associated with activities that are reported as ongoing. For example, DHS reported that it has work under way to issue guidance to information sharing and analysis centers on public communications related to cybersecurity, but has not identified a milestone for completing this activity. Table 3 provides the number of activities in each of these categories.

[10] Homeland Security Presidential Directive 8: National Preparedness (Dec. 17, 2003).

[11] Department of Homeland Security, *Homeland Security Exercise and Evaluation Program* (Washington, D.C.: 2007).

Table 3. Summary of Status of Activities

Status of DHS Activities	Number of Activities
Reported and validated as completed	42
Reported as completed, but not validated due to insufficient evidence	1
Reported as ongoing	16
Reported as planned for the future	7
Total	**66**

Source: GAO analysis of DHS data.

Focusing on each of the eight lessons, DHS has completed selected activities within each lesson, but has more to do. The department's progress on each of the lessons learned during the first Cyber Storm exercise is discussed below. In reviewing this progress, it is important to note that because many of DHS's activities are intended to address more than one lesson, the sum of the activities supporting all eight lessons is higher than the net number of activities. Specifically, DHS listed 121 activities to address lessons 1 through 8, but 55 of these repeat a prior activity. A complete list of the activities supporting each lesson and their status are provided in appendix III.

- **Interagency coordination groups**—DHS identified 32 activities to address the need for improving the interagency coordination groups. Of these, 24 activities have been completed and 8 are ongoing or planned for the future. DHS completed activities such as researching and procuring situation awareness visualization and communication tools and conducting a tabletop exercise among NCRCG, the Homeland Security Operations Center, the Crisis Action Team, and US-CERT. Activities that still remain to be completed include establishing secure communications with all international partners and working with leadership to frame possible changes in rules for raising alert levels.
- **Contingency planning, risk assessment, and roles and responsibilities**—DHS identified 15 activities to address the need for improved contingency planning, risk assessment, and roles and responsibilities. Of these, 8 activities had been completed and 7 are ongoing or planned for the future. DHS completed activities such as researching secure cell phone capability for NCRCG members and procuring satellite phones. Activities that still remain to be completed include coordinating standard operating procedures and concepts of operations with

several information sharing and analysis centers and establishing a continuity-of-operations plan.

- **Integration of incidents across infrastructures**—DHS identified 16 activities to address the need for improved integration of incidents across infrastructures. Of these, 9 have been completed and 7 are ongoing or planned for the future. Completed activities include meeting with international participants to share capabilities and establish working relationships and researching alternatives to the Emergency Notification System. Activities that still remain to be completed include filling open spots at US-CERT to better address its mission and coordinating standard operating procedures with US-CERT and the information technology and communications information sharing and analysis centers.
- **Access to information**—DHS identified 15 activities to address the need for improved access to information. Of these, 8 activities have been completed and 7 are ongoing or planned for the future. DHS completed developing a contact list of key public and private sector subject matter experts and meeting with international participants to share capabilities and establish working relationships. Activities that still remain to be completed include identifying and organizing a private sector counterpart for NCRCG and establishing processes, procedures, and physical means to communicate securely with counterparts.
- **Coordination of response activities**—DHS identified 15 activities to address the need for improved coordination of response activities. Of these, 11 have been completed and 4 are ongoing or planned for the future. DHS completed activities such as significantly revising the NCRCG's standard operating procedures and refining situation report development and communication within those procedures. Activities that still remain to be completed include developing policies for handling classified information and educating the law enforcement community on the role and function of NCRCG.
- **Strategic communications and public relations plan**—DHS identified 5 activities to address the lesson that public messaging must be an integral part of contingency planning and incident response. Of these, 1 activity has been completed and 4 are ongoing or planned for the future. DHS completed efforts to establish a mechanism for communicating real world implications of cyber incidents to DHS Public Affairs and the Public Affairs Working Group. Activities that still remain to be completed include issuing guidance to information sharing and analysis centers on a set of policies for cybersecurity-related public communications and developing public affairs messaging coordination between public and private information technology organizations for normal and emergency operations.

- **Processes, tools, and technology**—DHS identified 12 activities to address the need for improved processes, tools, and technology. Of these, 8 activities have been completed and 4 are ongoing or planned for the future. Completed activities include developing a comprehensive set of cyber scenarios to support the exercises and clarifying interfaces and expectations at every level of NCRCG engagement. Activities that still remain to be completed include requesting that all federal computer emergency response teams obtain secure communications and developing policies for handling classified information.
- **Exercise program**—DHS identified 11 activities to address the need for improvements to the exercise program. Of these, 9 activities have been completed and 2 are ongoing or planned for the future. Completed activities include participating in a tabletop exercise and a full-scale exercise, and improving the communications infrastructure for the exercise. DHS has not yet completed activities including implementing a relational database consistent with industry standards in order to allow better correlation, analysis, and communication of incidents.

Until DHS schedules and completes its planned corrective activities, the agency risks wasting resources on subsequent exercises that repeat the lessons it learned in its first exercise.

Cyber Storm II Participants Observed Progress and Continued Challenges in Exercising the National Cyber Response Capability

Commenting on their experiences during Cyber Storm II, participants observed both progress and continued challenges in building a comprehensive national cyber response capability. Their observations addressed several key areas, including the value and scope of the exercise, roles and responsibilities, public relations, communications, the exercise infrastructure, and the handling of classified information.

Exercise value and scope—The participants we met with reported that their organization found value in participating in the exercise. For example, one agency official stated that the exercises were invaluable because they allowed the agency to update call lists and to practice how it would respond to cyber events. In addition, a participant stated that the exercise had a positive outcome for his organization and that the real benefit of the exercise was in sharing information.

However, participants agreed that smaller, more frequent exercises would be helpful in planning for cyber incidents. One agency official stated that the "doomsday" scenarios made it difficult to test agencies' responses to less dramatic cyber incidents. Another agency official reported that the sheer number of e-mail alerts received during the exercise was difficult to handle. Another participant suggested that DHS conduct exercises focusing on different infrastructure sectors during every quarterly meeting of NCRCG.

Roles and responsibilities—Cyber Storm II participants reported having a much better understanding of the various organizations' roles and whom to contact within those organizations during a cyber incident. For example, a participant noted that NCRCG has had time to stabilize over the 2 years since the first Cyber Storm exercise.

However, participants also reported that there is room for improvement in defining the roles and responsibilities of both NCRCG and the law enforcement community. Specifically, selected Information Sharing and Analysis Center (ISAC) members reported that there is still confusion in the private sector on NCRCG's role during a cyber incident. ISAC officials stated that it was unclear to the private sector what NCRCG is responsible for, what it means when the group is activated, and what this activation means to the private sector. In addition, Cyber Storm II participants reported the need for further clarification of the roles and responsibilities of the law enforcement community during a cyber incident. Specifically, law enforcement participants noted that other exercise participants may not have been properly reporting incidents to the law enforcement community, even though most scenarios involved criminal violations. They stated that not being appropriately involved in the exercise scenarios made it difficult to fully test investigative and legal processes.

Public relations—While participants generally agreed that media relations went well during the exercise, they also identified the need for further improvements. To address prior concerns, DHS included a public relations specialist in the NCRCG membership to help develop messages for NCRCG and other organizations involved in the exercise, and provided a technical specialist to the department's public affairs office to ensure cyber issues were described accurately. However, a private sector participant commented that there appeared to be minimal alignment of communications and public relations plans between the public and private sectors during the exercise.

Communications—Participants also reported a need for further improvement in communication between participants during the exercise. For example, a private sector participant cited a breakdown in communication where participants were not aware that the US-CERT alert level had been raised. Another participant reported that US-CERT did not resolve conflicting data before issuing information—even after this individual's ISAC contacted US-CERT. In another instance, a private sector participant reported not knowing how to contact US-CERT during the exercise. Another participant reported that there were instances where private sector players were sharing information with DHS, but the information appeared never to have made it to the decision makers.

Exercise infrastructure—Participants generally agreed that improvements to the exercise's infrastructure could be made. For example, several participants reported that DHS was not able to use an encrypted communications system it developed for the exercise because the technology failed. However, DHS reported that the technology did not fail, but rather that it turned off the technology because of security concerns. Participants also reported issues with receiving e-mails of the exercises, downloading the exercise directory, and accessing the exercise's Web page. Another participant stated that his organization did not have time to run some of the exercise scenarios due to technical issues it encountered during the exercise.

Classified information handling—Participants stated that there is a continuing challenge in accessing sensitive information on cyber threats and incidents, and that policies dealing with classified information need to be improved. For example, one private sector participant stated that it is not clear how information gets classified or what information is available to the private sector. An agency official stated that it has been a challenge to pull unclassified information out of classified information systems in order to share it. Other participants stated that they would like to see additional effort expended on sharing unclassified information on the government's public response portal—the Government Forum of Incident Response and Security Teams portal—which is available to federal agencies and to a limited number of local agencies and organizations. Participants noted that the portal is too open for truly secure communication but not open enough to share information between public and private sectors.

Many of the challenges that participants noted during Cyber Storm II were similar to challenges identified during the first Cyber Storm exercise. For example, comments regarding the need for better understanding of roles and responsibilities after Cyber Storm II were similar to comments made in four of the eight lessons resulting from Cyber Storm I. Also, both exercises resulted in comments calling for improvements to the exercise program and for better internal and external communications.

Conclusions

Both public and private sector participants in DHS's Cyber Storm exercises agreed that the exercises are valuable in helping them coordinate their responses to significant cyber incidents. After the completion of the first Cyber Storm exercise in February 2006, DHS identified 8 lessons and 66 activities to address these lessons, ranging from revising operating procedures to holding tabletop exercises to test and evaluate those revised procedures.

While DHS has made progress in completing over 60 percent of these activities, it has more to do to complete key activities—including those that are planned for the future as well as those identified as ongoing without a completion date. More recently, key federal, state, and private sector officials who participated in the second Cyber Storm exercise in March 2008 observed areas of progress as well as continued challenges—many similar to challenges identified during the first exercise. Until DHS schedules and completes its corrective activities, the agency risks wasting resources on subsequent exercises that repeat the lessons it learned in 2006.

Recommendation for Executive Action

Given the importance of continuously improving cyber exercises, we are making one recommendation to the Secretary of Homeland Security to direct the Assistant Secretary for Cybersecurity and Communications to ensure the scheduling and completion of the corrective actions addressing lessons learned during Cyber Storm I before conducting the next Cyber Storm Exercise.

Agency Comments and Our Evaluation

We received written comments on a draft of this report from DHS (see app. IV). In the department's response, the Director of the Departmental GAO/Office of Inspector General Liaison Office concurred with our recommendation and stated that DHS will continue to address actions related to Cyber Storm I findings. DHS also reported that after receiving the draft report, it has completed additional items, raising the percentage of corrective actions completed to over 70 percent. We did not modify the status of the activities identified in our report because DHS has not yet provided sufficient evidence to demonstrate that these activities have been completed.

In its comments, DHS also stated that end dates are not applicable for many of the remaining corrective actions because they are either dependent upon outside stakeholder actions or are ongoing or long-term activities that are being addressed incrementally over time. However, we found that most of the remaining activities are finite in nature and could be associated with a time frame. For example, it would be possible to establish time frames for issuing guidance to the information sharing and analysis centers on public communications, requesting that all computer emergency response teams have secure communications, and identifying international counterparts to NCRCG. Further, while we agree that some activities may involve other stakeholders or take more time, it is important for DHS to identify interim and final milestones for these activities so that they can monitor their progress. This approach is consistent with DHS's guidance for its exercise programs, which requires that each corrective action have a time frame for implementation.

DHS officials also provided technical comments, which we have incorporated as appropriate.

As agreed with your offices, unless you publicly announce the contents of the report earlier, we plan no further distribution until 30 days from the report date. At that time, we will send copies of this report to interested congressional committees, the Secretary of Homeland Security, the Director of the Office of Management and Budget, and other interested parties. In addition, this report will be available at no charge on GAO's Web site at http://www.gao.gov.

If you have any questions on matters discussed in this report, please contact me at (202) 512-9286 or pownerd@gao.gov. Contact points for our Offices of Congressional Relations and Public Affairs may be found on the last page of this report. GAO staff who made key contributions to this report are listed in appendix V.

David A. Powner
Director, Information Technology
Management Issues

Appendix I: Objectives, Scope, and Methodology

Our objectives were to (1) identify the lessons that the Department of Homeland Security (DHS) learned from the first Cyber Storm exercise, (2) assess DHS's efforts to implement lessons learned from this exercise, and (3) identify key participants' views of their experiences during the second Cyber Storm exercise.

To identify the lessons learned from DHS's cyber attack simulations, we reviewed the agency's Cyber Storm Exercise Report. We also interviewed agency officials to obtain clarification on this exercise and the lessons learned.

To assess DHS's efforts to address the lessons it learned from its exercise, we analyzed DHS's list of planned activities and the status of these activities. We analyzed documentation of the activities that were reported as completed, including concepts of operations and standard operating procedures for relevant organizations as well as evidence of additional staff hires and completion of tabletop exercises. We also visited the United States Computer Emergency Readiness Team (US-CERT) to observe network and technology changes that were made to address lessons identified during Cyber Storm I. We interviewed DHS officials from the National Cyber Security Division (NCSD) and US-CERT to obtain clarification on documentation and plans.

To identify key participants' views of their experiences during the second Cyber Storm exercise, we interviewed Cyber Storm planners, observers, and participants from federal agencies, state governments, and the private sector. Specifically, we interviewed representatives from the Departments of Transportation, Justice, and Energy because these organizations were identified by DHS as key participants in the Cyber Storm exercises—either as an organization that was subject to simulated cyber incidents or as an organization critical to the recovery from the incidents. We interviewed the Multi-State Information Sharing and Analysis Center (ISAC) because it was able to represent multiple state governments that participated in the exercises. We also interviewed private sector officials representing the Information Technology ISAC, the Electricity ISAC, and the chemical sector. We asked participants about the issues raised during Cyber Storm I and whether these were improved or remained as challenges during Cyber Storm II. After discussing both Cyber Storm exercises with these participants, we analyzed their observations for commonalities and organized them into broad categories. These observations are not intended to be generalized to other exercise participants.

We performed our work at the headquarters of the Departments of Homeland Security, Transportation, Energy, and Justice and in Washington, D.C.

In addition, we attended the Cyber Storm II exercise held in Washington, D.C., in March 2008. We performed our work from January 2008 to September 2008 in accordance with generally accepted government auditing standards. Those standards require that we plan and perform the audit to obtain sufficient, appropriate evidence to provide a reasonable basis for our findings and conclusions based on our audit objectives. We believe that the evidence obtained provides a reasonable basis for our findings and conclusions based on our audit objectives.

Appendix II: DHS Activities to Address Lessons from Cyber Storm I

DHS identified 66 activities to address lessons identified in Cyber Storm I. Almost half of these activities are intended to address multiple lessons. Table 4 shows the list of activities and which lessons they are intended to address.

Table 4. DHS's Planned Activities and the Lessons They Address

Activity Identification Number	DHS Activity	Lesson(s) Targeted by This Activity[a]
1.	Significantly revise standard operating procedures for the National Cyber Response Coordination Group (NCRCG)	1, 2, 3, 4, 5, 7, 8
2.	Refine definition of Cyber Incident of National Significance	1
3.	Conduct meeting with member agencies to ensure they understand the needed resources to support NCRCG during activation	1
4.	Establish in standard operating procedures a means of quickly and clearly communicating changes in NCRCG engagement status with interfacing organizations	1, 4
5.	Within standard operating procedures, refine situation reports and situation report development and communication procedures	1, 4, 5, 7, 8
6.	Research and procure appropriate situation awareness visualization and communication tools	1
7.	Request access to classified DHS networks in NCRCG's room	1, 4, 5, 7, 8
8.	Hold meeting among NCRCG, Homeland Security Operations Center, Interagency Advisory Council (now the Crisis Action Team), and US-CERT	1

Activity Identification Number	DHS Activity	Lesson(s) Targeted by This Activity[a]
9.	Conduct a tabletop exercise among NCRCG, the Homeland Security Operations Center, the Interagency Advisory Council (now the Crisis Action Team), and US-CERT	1
10.	Work with the Office of Public Affairs to ensure NCRCG receives situation reports	1
11.	Provide a liaison to an interfacing group from NCRCG	1
12.	During the meeting in June 2006 with international participants, discuss coordination with entities similar to NCRCG	1
13.	Clarify interfaces and expectation at every level of NCRCG engagement	1, 7
14.	Move triage capability into US-CERT main facility	1, 3, 5
15.	Create four new positions to ensure staffing and continuity in US-CERT through normal and emergency operations	1, 7
16.	Refine and prioritize use and purposes of key US-CERT communications portals to eliminate redundancy and streamline communication with subscribers and counterparts	1, 4
17.	Meet in June 2006 with all international participants to share capabilities and establish working relationships	1, 2, 3, 4
18.	Discuss an initial international participant tabletop exercise and additional follow-on exercise activities with international participants and policy representatives in order to build clear way ahead for Cyber Storm II in 2008	1, 3
19.	Coordinate support of DHS's Operations office as noted in its revised standard operation procedures	1, 3, 4, 5, 7
20.	Once refined standard operating procedures are established for NCRCG, US-CERT, National Operations Center, and Interagency Advisory Council (now the Crisis Action Team) organize and support the tabletop exercise to validate and refine interaction	1
21.	Support the development of a contact list of key public and private sector subject matter experts	1, 4, 5
22.	Once clear engagement thresholds are established, ensure that all interfacing organizations are aware of thresholds, levels of engagement, and implications of each	1

Activity Identification Number	DHS Activity	Lesson(s) Targeted by This Activity[a]
23.	Establish a mechanism for communicating real world implications of cyber incidents to DHS Public Affairs and the Public Affairs Working Group	1, 6
24.	Modify standard operating procedures to reflect any changes in Homeland Security Advisory System policy	1, 3
25.	Work to identify and contact NCRCG counterpart organizations within international partners	1, 2, 4
26.	Develop the capability to reach back to the private sector	1
27.	Move to develop public affairs messaging coordination among NCRCG, NCSD, the Information Technology Information Sharing and Analysis Center, and the Information Technology Sector Coordinating Council for both normal and emergency operations	1, 3, 6
28.	Engage in conversations with leadership to frame possible changes in rules for raising alert levels based on threats to cross-sector support structure	1, 3
29.	Establish processes, procedures, and physical means to communicate securely with NCRCG counterparts at a policy level	1, 2, 4
30.	Once Situation Awareness Toolset is established, arrange for appropriate centers to have it	1, 4
31.	In meeting with international participants, address coordination of standard operating procedures and concept of operations	1
32.	Work to establish secure communications with all international partners	1
33.	Procure Government Emergency Telecommunications Service cards for all NCRCG members	2
34.	Research secure cell phone capability for NCRCG members	2
35.	Work with a foreign computer emergency response team to cosponsor another foreign computer emergency response team into an intragovernmental incident response forum	2
36.	Install Critical Infrastructure Warning Information Network terminal in US-CERT	2
37.	Add redundant network support to US-CERT	2
38.	Procure 15 satellite phones	2

Activity Identification Number	DHS Activity	Lesson(s) Targeted by This Activity[a]
39.	Work to identify and organize a private sector counterpart for NCRCG with appropriate concepts of operations and standard operating procedures	2, 4, 5, 7
40.	Address public policy issues for industry incident response activities in cooperation with the industry and leadership	2
41.	Facilitate the development and implementation of cyber risk assessment methodologies across the information technology sector and in coordination with other sectors	2
42.	Coordinate standard operating procedures and concepts of operations with several ISACs	2, 3, 5
43.	Submit request for continuity-of-operations space and establish continuity-of-operations plan	2
44.	Research alternatives to the Emergency Notification System	3
45.	Add dedicated support staff person to focus on processes and procedures	3
46.	Establish better e-mail connection during exercise to avoid spam filtering of injects	3, 5
47.	Execute semiannual tabletop exercise with accompanying education workshops focused on high-risk scenarios and cyber risk assessment	3, 5, 7, 8
48.	Coordinate standard operating procedures with US-CERT and the Information Technology and Communication ISACs	3, 4
49.	Transfer ticket tracking system over to an industry standard relational database tracking system for better correlation, analysis, and communication of incidents	3, 8
50.	Fill open spots with qualified personnel to gain bandwidth necessary to better address all aspects of US-CERT mission	3, 8
51.	Continue to expand network of informal and semiformal relationships with cyber-related associations and interest groups	4
52.	Forward request to require all federal computer emergency response teams to have secure communications, up to at least Secret	4, 7
53.	Request additional NCRCG support staff to address planning, correlation, and communication requirements	5

Activity Identification Aumber	DHS Activity	Lesson(s) Targeted by This Activity[a]
54.	Plan for significant pre-Cyber Storm II intelligence and law enforcement buildup exercise segment	5
55.	Complete permanent home of US-CERT, allowing classified operations to occur on-site	5
56.	Work to educate law enforcement on role and function of the NCRCG and establish sharing of cyber issues	5, 7
57.	Work to expedite tear-line policies (policies for organizing official documents so that unclassified information can be easily separated from classified information and disseminated)	5, 7
58.	Advocate inclusion of cyber public affairs in all exercises where appropriate	6
59.	Issue guidance to ISACs on a set of policies for cybersecurity-related public communications	6
60.	Establish baseline of public messaging based on cyber probable scenarios to include best channels for message delivery	6
61.	Develop comprehensive set of cyber scenarios to support exercises and planning	7
62.	Develop reporting process in coordination with reporting entities	8
63.	Participate in Internet Disruption Working Group tabletop exercise	8
64.	Plan and support cyber aspects of Top Officials 4 exercise	8
65.	Plan and execute Cyber Storm II	8
66.	Coordinate and develop situation report reporting process with National Operations Center and NCRCG	8

Source: GAO analysis of DHS data.

[a] The lessons are

Lesson 1: Interagency Coordination Groups

Lesson 2: Contingency Planning, Risk Assessment, and Roles and Responsibilities

Lesson 3: Integration of Incidents across Infrastructures

Lesson 4: Access to Information

Lesson 5: Coordination of Response Activities

Lesson 6: Strategic Communications and Public Relations

Lesson 7: Processes, Tools, and Technology

Lesson 8: The Exercise Program

Appendix III: GAO Analysis of DHS Efforts to Address Lessons from Cyber Storm I

Figure 1 shows, for each lesson learned during Cyber Storm I, the status of the activity as reported by DHS and whether the status could be validated by GAO. The activities are identified by number in appendix II.

Figure 1: Activity Status, as of June 2008, by Lesson

	Activities																																
Lessons	1	2	3	4	5	6	7	8	9	10	11	12	13	14	15	16	17	18	19	20	21	22	23	24	25	26	27	28	29	30	31	32	33
Lesson 1: Interagency Coordination Groups	+	+	+	+	+	+	+	+	+	+	+	+	+	+	+	+	+	+	+	+	+	+	+	0	0	0	0	0	0	>	+	>	
Lesson 2: Contingency Planning, Risk Assessment, and Roles and Responsibilities	+																+								0				0				+
Lesson 3: Integration of Incidents across Infrastructures	+													+			+	+	+					0			0	0					
Lesson 4: Access to Information	+			+	+		+									+	+		+		+				0				0	>			
Lesson 5: Coordination of Response Activities	+				+		+							+					+		+												
Lesson 6: Strategic Communications and Public Relations Plan																							+				0						
Lesson 7: Processes, Tools, and Technology	+				+		+						+		+				+														
Lesson 8: The Exercise Program	+				+		+																										

Key:
+ - Completed and validated
± - Completed but not validated
0 - Ongoing
> - Planned for the future
A blank box indicates the activity is not applicable to the lesson

Source: GAO analysis of DHS data.

	Activities																																
Lessons	34	35	36	37	38	39	40	41	42	43	44	45	46	47	48	49	50	51	52	53	54	55	56	57	58	59	60	61	62	63	64	65	66
Lesson 1: Interagency Coordination Groups																																	
Lesson 2: Contingency Planning, Risk Assessment, and Roles and Responsibilities	+	+	+	+	+	0	0	0	>	>																							
Lesson 3: Integration of Incidents across Infrastructures									>		+	+	+	+	>	>	>																
Lesson 4: Access to Information						0									>			0	0														
Lesson 5: Coordination of Response Activities						0			>				+	+						±	+	+	0	0									
Lesson 6: Strategic Communications and Public Relations Plan																									0	0	0						
Lesson 7: Processes, Tools, and Technology						0								+					0				0	0				+					
Lesson 8: The Exercise Program														+		>	>												+	+	+	+	+

Key:

+ - Completed and validated

± - Completed but not validated

0 - Ongoing

> - Planned for the future

A blank box indicates the activity is not applicable to the lesson

Source: GAO analysis of DHS data.

Appendix IV: Comments from the Department of Homeland Security

U.S. Department of Homeland Security
Washington, DC 20528

Homeland Security

August 22, 2008

Mr. David Powner
Director
Information Technology Management Issues
United States Government Accountability Office
441 G Street, N.W.
Washington, DC 20548

Dear Mr. Powner:

Thank you for the opportunity to review and comment on the Government Accountability Office's (GAO's) draft report entitled *CRITICAL INFRASTRUCTURE PROTECTION: DHS Needs to Fully Address Lessons Learned from Its First Cyber Storm Exercise* (GAO-08-825). Technical comments have been provided under separate cover.

The Department of Homeland Security's (DHS's) efforts to develop and refine procedures for addressing and tracking corrective actions have benefited from this GAO engagement. DHS fully agrees with GAO assertions that continuous progress and validation of exercise findings is essential to improving our Nation's cyber security, preparedness posture, and ensuring the best use of resources.

GAO states in its draft report that DHS addressed and completed 43 of the 66 corrective actions. The remaining 23 corrective actions included 16 items labeled "ongoing" and 7 items labeled "planned for the future." DHS addressed and completed over 66 percent of the total corrective actions at the time the GAO's report was drafted. Since the release of GAO's draft report, DHS completed additional items, raising the percentage of corrective actions completed to over 70 percent. A full breakdown of recent actions undertaken and discussion of their status is enclosed as Appendix A.

Recommendation: *Given the importance of continuously improving cyber exercises, we are making one recommendation to the Secretary of Homeland Security to direct the Assistant Secretary for Cybersecurity and Communications to ensure the scheduling and completion of the corrective actions addressing lessons learned during Cyber Storm I before conducting the next Cyber Storm exercise.*

Response: DHS concurs with the draft GAO report's recommendation and will continue to address actions related to Cyber Storm I findings. Many of the remaining corrective actions, however, are inherently long-term or ongoing in nature. Some corrective actions are within DHS's direct power to manage or perform, while others require extensive coordination with stakeholders.

Fulfilling the report's recommendation that the Department take action to ensure these remaining corrective actions are scheduled and completed before executing the next Cyber Storm exercise is dependent on various factors. DHS suggests that the remaining corrective actions are either: (1) *long-term* activities and are being incrementally addressed over time; (2) dependent upon *outside*

www.dhs.gov

stakeholder action; or (3) *ongoing*, addressed in different capacities over time, and a specific "end date" does not apply.

DHS appreciates the thorough analysis and very constructive points raised by the GAO draft report. To best capitalize on this analysis and recommendation, DHS plans an enhanced emphasis on how corrective action categories are defined for purposes of planning and integration into future exercises. DHS is willing to work with GAO as these efforts go forward. Finally, we ask that GAO modify the report to reflect the additional items the National Cyber Security Division (NCSD) has completed since the draft report's release.

Thank you again for the opportunity to comment on this draft report and we look forward to working with you on future homeland security issues.

Sincerely,

Jerald E. Levine
Director
Departmental GAO/OIG Liaison Office

Enclosure

Appendix V: GAO Contact and Staff Acknowledgments

GAO Contact

David A. Powner, (202) 512-9286, or pownerd@gao.gov.

Staff Acknowledgments

In addition to the contact person named above, Colleen Phillips, Assistant Director; Neil Doherty; Nancy Glover; Jim MacAulay; Lee McCracken; and Jessica Waselkow made key contributions to this report.

GAO's Mission

The Government Accountability Office, the audit, evaluation, and investigative arm of Congress, exists to support Congress in meeting its constitutional responsibilities and to help improve the performance and accountability of the federal government for the American people. GAO examines the use of public funds; evaluates federal programs and policies; and provides analyses, recommendations, and other assistance to help Congress make informed oversight, policy, and funding decisions. GAO's commitment to good government is reflected in its core values of accountability, integrity, and reliability.

Obtaining Copies of GAO Reports and Testimony

The fastest and easiest way to obtain copies of GAO documents at no cost is through GAO's Web site (www.gao.gov). Each weekday, GAO posts newly released reports, testimony, and correspondence on its Web site. To have GAO e-mail you a list of newly posted products every afternoon, go to www.gao.gov and select "E-mail Updates."

Order by Mail or Phone

The first copy of each printed report is free. Additional copies are $2 each. A check or money order should be made out to the Superintendent of Documents. GAO also accepts VISA and Mastercard. Orders for 100 or more copies mailed to a single address are discounted 25 percent. Orders should be sent to:

U.S. Government Accountability Office
441 G Street NW, Room LM
Washington, DC 20548

To order by Phone:	Voice:	(202) 512-6000
	TDD:	(202) 512-2537
	Fax:	(202) 512-6061

To Report Fraud, Waste, and Abuse in Federal Programs

Contact:

Web site: www.gao.gov/fraudnet/fraudnet.htm
E-mail: fraudnet@gao.gov
Automated answering system: (800) 424-5454 or (202) 512-7470

Congressional Relations

Ralph Dawn, Managing Director, dawnr@gao.gov, (202) 512-4400

U.S. Government Accountability Office, 441 G Street NW, Room 7125 Washington, DC 20548

Public Affairs

Chuck Young, Managing Director, youngc1@gao.gov, (202) 512-4800 U.S. Government Accountability Office, 441 G Street NW, Room 7149 Washington, DC 20548

DOCUMENT NO. 9

INFORMATION SECURITY: TVA NEEDS TO ADDRESS WEAKNESSES IN CONTROL SYSTEMS AND NETWORKS

GAO Report
GAO-08-526

May 2008

What GAO Found

TVA has not fully implemented appropriate security practices to secure the control systems and networks used to operate its critical infrastructures. Both its corporate network infrastructure and control systems networks and devices were vulnerable to disruption. The corporate network was interconnected with control systems networks GAO reviewed, thereby increasing the risk that security weaknesses on the corporate network could affect those control systems networks. On TVA's corporate network, certain individual workstations lacked key software patches and had inadequate security settings, and numerous network infrastructure protocols and devices had limited or ineffective security configurations. In addition, the intrusion detection system had significant limitations. On control systems networks, firewalls reviewed were either inadequately configured or had been bypassed, passwords were not effectively implemented, logging of certain activity was limited, configuration management policies for control systems software were inconsistently implemented, and servers and workstations lacked key patches and effective virus protection. In addition, physical security at multiple locations did not sufficiently protect critical control systems. As a result, systems that operate TVA's critical infrastructures are at increased risk of unauthorized modification or disruption by both internal and external threats.

An underlying reason for these weaknesses is that TVA had not consistently implemented significant elements of its information security program.

Although TVA had developed and implemented program activities related to contingency planning and incident response, it had not consistently implemented key activities related to developing an inventory of systems, assessing risk, developing policies and procedures, developing security plans, testing and monitoring the effectiveness of controls, completing appropriate training, and identifying and tracking remedial actions. For example, the agency lacked a complete inventory of its control systems and had not categorized all of its control systems according to risk, thereby limiting assurance that these systems were adequately protected. Agency officials stated that they plan to complete these risk assessments and related activities but have not established a completion date. Key information security policies and procedures were also in draft or under revision. Additionally, the agency's patch management process lacked a way to effectively prioritize vulnerabilities. TVA had only completed one system security plan,and another plan was under development. The agency had also tested the effectiveness of its control systems' security using outdated federal guidance, and many control systems had not been tested for security. In addition, only 25 percent of relevant agency staff had completed required role-based security training in fiscal year 2007. Furthermore, while the agency had developed a process to track remedial actions for information security, this process had not been implemented for the majority of its control systems. Until TVA fully implements these security program activities, it risks a disruption of its operations as a result of a cyber incident, which could impact its customers.

Abbreviations

CIO	chief information officer
FERC	Federal Energy Regulatory Commission
FIPS	Federal Information Processing Standard
FISCAM	Federal Information System Controls Audit Manual
FISMA	Federal Information Security Management Act of 2002
NEI	Nuclear Energy Institute
NERC	North American Electric Reliability Corporation
NIST	National Institute of Standards and Technology
NRC	Nuclear Regulatory Commission
OMB	Office of Management and Budget
SCADA	supervisory control and data acquisition
SP	Special Publication
TVA	Tennessee Valley Authority
US-CERT	U.S. Computer Emergency Readiness Team
VPN	virtual private network

United States Government Accountability Office
Washington, DC 20548

May 21, 2008

Congressional Requesters

Securing the control systems that perform vital functions in the complex networks of digital information systems on which the nation's critical infrastructures rely is critical to ensuring our national and economic security and public health and safety. Control systems are computer-based systems used by critical infrastructure sectors and industries to monitor and control sensitive processes and physical functions such as electric power generation and its transmission, oil and gas refining, water treatment and its distribution, and transportation.

We have previously reported that critical infrastructure control systems face increasing risks due to cyber threats, system vulnerabilities, and the serious potential impact of attacks as demonstrated by reported incidents.[1] If control systems are not adequately secured, their system vulnerabilities could be exploited, and our critical infrastructures could be disrupted or disabled, possibly resulting in loss of life, physical damage, or economic losses.

The majority of our nation's critical infrastructures are owned by the private sector; however, the federal government owns and operates critical infrastructure facilities including those in energy, water treatment and distribution, and transportation. One such entity, the Tennessee Valley Authority (TVA)—a federal corporation and the nation's largest public power company—generates electricity using its 52 fossil, hydro, and nuclear facilities—all of which use control systems. As a wholly owned government corporation, TVA must comply with the Federal Information Security Management Act of 2002[2] (FISMA) by developing a risk-based information security program and implementing information security controls for its computer systems.

Our objective was to determine whether TVA has effectively implemented appropriate information security practices for the control systems used to operate its critical infrastructures. To accomplish this objective, we examined the security practices in place at six TVA facilities. In addition, we analyzed the agency's information security policies, plans, and procedures and interviewed agency officials who are responsible for overseeing TVA's control systems and their security. See appendix I for a complete description of our objective, scope, and methodology.

---

[1] GAO, *Critical Infrastructure Protection: Federal Efforts to Secure Control Systems Are Under Way, but Challenges Remain*, GAO-07-1036 (Washington, D.C.: Sept. 10, 2007).

[2] FISMA was enacted as title III, E-Government Act of 2002, Pub. L. No. 107-347 (Dec.17, 2002).

We conducted this performance audit from March 2007 to May 2008 in accordance with generally accepted government auditing standards. Those standards require that we plan and perform the audit to obtain sufficient, appropriate evidence to provide a reasonable basis for our findings and conclusions based on our audit objectives. We believe that the evidence obtained provides a reasonable basis for our findings and conclusions based on our audit objectives.

Results in Brief

TVA has not fully implemented appropriate security practices to protect the control systems used to operate its critical infrastructures. TVA's corporate network infrastructure and its control systems networks and devices at individual facilities and plants reviewed were vulnerable to disruption. For example, on the corporate network, one remote access system we reviewed that was used for the network was not securely configured, and individual workstations we reviewed lacked key patches and had inadequate security settings for key programs. Further, network infrastructure protocols and devices provided limited protections. In addition, the intrusion detection system[3] that TVA used had significant limitations on its ability to effectively monitor the network. For example, although a network intrusion detection system was deployed by TVA to monitor network traffic, it could not effectively monitor certain data for key computer assets. On control systems networks, firewalls[4] were bypassed or inadequately configured, passwords were not effectively implemented, logging of certain activity was limited, configuration management policies for control systems software were not consistently implemented, and servers and workstations lacked key patches and effective virus protection. In addition, physical security at multiple locations did not sufficiently protect critical control systems. Moreover, the interconnections between TVA's control system networks and its corporate network increase the risk that security weaknesses on the corporate network could affect control systems networks. Although TVA used multiple network segments to separate more sensitive equipment, such as control systems, from the corporate network, weaknesses in the separation of these network segments could allow an attacker who gained access to a less secure portion of the interconnected network, such as the corporate network, to compromise equipment in a more secure portion of the interconnected network. This could include

---

[3] An intrusion detection system detects inappropriate, incorrect, or anomalous activity that is aimed at disrupting the confidentiality, integrity, or availability of a protected network and its computer systems.

[4] A firewall is a hardware or software component that protects computers or networks from attacks by outside network users by blocking and checking all incoming traffic.

equipment that has access to control systems. As a result, TVA's control systems that operate its critical infrastructures are at increased risk of unauthorized modification or disruption by both internal and external threats.

An underlying reason for these weaknesses is that TVA had not consistently implemented significant elements of its information security program. Although TVA had developed and implemented program activities related to contingency planning and incident response, it had not consistently implemented key activities related to developing an inventory of systems, assessing risk, developing policies and procedures, developing security plans, testing and monitoring the effectiveness of controls, establishing sufficient training, and identifying and tracking remedial actions. For example, the agency lacked a complete and accurate inventory of its control systems and had included only two control systems on its federally required inventory of information systems. Of these two systems, TVA had only completed a security plan for one, while the plan for the other system was under development. The agency had also not categorized all of its control systems according to risk or magnitude of harm from compromise, leaving these systems at risk of harm due to inadequate security. Agency officials stated that they plan to complete these risk assessments and related activities but have not established a completion date for all facilities. Key information security policies and procedures were also in draft or under revision. TVA's patch management process also lacked a way to effectively prioritize vulnerabilities. In addition, only 25 percent of relevant TVA staff completed required role-based security training in fiscal year 2007. TVA also tested the effectiveness of its control systems' security using outdated federal guidance and did not test many control systems for security at all. Furthermore, while the agency had developed a process to track remedial actions for information security, this process had been implemented for only one of its control systems. Until TVA addresses the control systems security weaknesses we have identified, it risks a disruption of its operations as a result of a cyber incident, which could impact both TVA and its customers.

To help implement effective information security practices over its control systems, we are making 19 recommendations to the Chief Executive Officer of TVA to improve the implementation of TVA's agencywide information security program.

In a separate report designated "Limited Official Use Only,"[5] we are also making 73 recommendations to correct specific information security weaknesses.

[5] GAO, *Information Security: TVA Needs to Address Weaknesses in Control Systems and Networks*, GAO-08-459SU (Washington, D.C.: May 21, 2008).

In written comments on a draft of this report, the TVA Executive Vice President, Administrative Services, agreed on the importance of protecting critical infrastructures, concurred with all 19 recommendations in this report, and provided information on steps the agency was taking to implement the recommendations.

Background

Information security is a critical consideration for any organization that depends on information systems and computer networks to carry out its mission or business. It is especially important for government agencies, where maintaining the public's trust is essential. The dramatic expansion in computer interconnectivity and the rapid increase in the use of the Internet have changed the way our government, the nation, and much of the world communicate and conduct business. However, without proper safeguards, systems are unprotected from individuals and groups with malicious intent to intrude and use the access to obtain sensitive information, commit fraud, disrupt operations, or launch attacks against other computer systems and networks. This concern is well-founded for a number of reasons, including the increase in reports of security incidents, the ease of obtaining and using hacking tools, the steady advance in the sophistication and effectiveness of attack technology, and the dire warnings of new and more destructive attacks to come. Computer-supported federal operations are likewise at risk. Our previous reports and those of agency inspectors general describe persistent information security weaknesses that place a variety of federal operations at risk of disruption, fraud, and inappropriate disclosure. Thus, we have designated information security as a governmentwide high-risk area since 1997,[6] a designation that remains in effect.[7]

Control Systems Are Used in Critical Infrastructures, Including Those Operated by the Federal Government

We have specifically recognized the importance of information security related to critical infrastructures. Critical infrastructures are physical or virtual systems and assets so vital to the nation that their incapacitation or destruction would have a debilitating impact on national and economic security and on public health and safety. These systems and assets—such as the electric power grid, chemical plants, and water treatment facilities—are essential to the operations of the economy and the government. Recent

[6] GAO, *High-Risk Series: Information Management and Technology*, GAO/HR-97-9 (Washington, D.C.: February 1997).
[7] GAO, *High-Risk Series: An Update*, GAO-07-310 (Washington, D.C.: January 2007).

terrorist attacks and threats have underscored the need to protect these critical infrastructures. If their vulnerabilities are exploited, our nation's critical infrastructures could be disrupted or disabled, possibly causing loss of life, physical damage, and economic losses.

Although the majority of our nation's critical infrastructures are owned by the private sector, the federal government owns and operates key facilities that use control systems, including oil, gas, water, energy, and nuclear facilities. Control systems are used within these infrastructures to monitor and control sensitive processes and physical functions. Typically, control systems collect sensor measurements and operational data from the field, process and display this information, and relay control commands to local or remote equipment. Control systems perform functions that range from simple to complex. They can be used to simply monitor processes—for example, the environmental conditions in a small office building—or to manage the complex activities of a municipal water system or a nuclear power plant. In the electric power industry, control systems can be used to manage and control the generation, transmission, and distribution of electric power. For example, control systems can open and close circuit breakers and set thresholds for preventive shutdowns.

Control Systems: Types and Components

There are two primary types of control systems: distributed control systems and supervisory control and data acquisition (SCADA) systems. Distributed control systems typically are used within a single processing or generating plant or over a small geographic area and communicate using local area networks, while SCADA systems typically are used for large, geographically dispersed operations and rely on long-distance communication networks. In general, critical infrastructure sectors and industries depend on both types of control systems to fulfill their missions or conduct business. For example, a utility company that serves a large geographic area may use distributed control systems to manage power generation at each power plant and a SCADA system to manage power distribution to its customers.

A SCADA system is generally composed of these six components (see fig. 1): (1) operating equipment, which includes pumps, valves, conveyors, and substation breakers; (2) instruments, which sense conditions such as pH, temperature, pressure, power level, and flow rate; (3) local processors, which communicate with the site's instruments and operating equipment, collect instrument data, and identify alarm conditions; (4) short-range communication, which carries analog and discrete signals between the local processors and the instruments and operating equipment; (5) host computers, where a human operator can supervise the process, receive alarms,

Figure 1: Major Components of a SCADA System

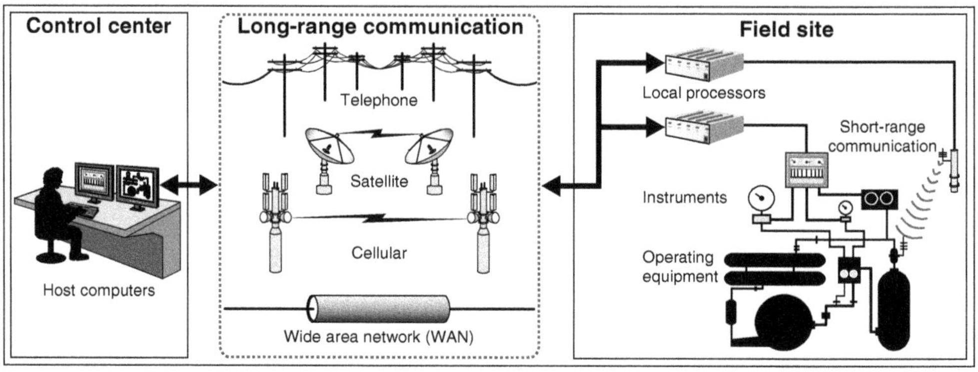

Source: GAO analysis of NIST guidance.

review data, and exercise control; and (6) long-range communication, which connects local processors and host computers using, for example, leased phone lines, satellite, and cellular packet data. A distributed control system is similar to a SCADA system but does not operate over a large geographic area or use long-range communications.

Control Systems for Critical Infrastructures Face Increasing Cyber Threats

We have previously reported that critical infrastructure control systems face increasing risks due to cyber threats, system vulnerabilities, and the potential impact of attacks as demonstrated by reported incidents.[8] Cyber threats can be intentional or unintentional, targeted or nontargeted, and can come from a variety of sources. The Federal Bureau of Investigation has identified multiple sources of threats to our nation's critical infrastructures, including foreign nation states engaged in information warfare, domestic criminals and hackers, and disgruntled employees working within an organization. Table 1 summarizes those groups or individuals that are considered to be key sources of threats to our nation's infrastructures.

Control systems are more vulnerable to cyber threats, including intentional attacks and unintended incidents, than in the past for several reasons, including their increasing standardization and their increased connectivity to other systems and the Internet. For example, in August 2006, two circulation pumps at Unit 3 of the Browns Ferry, Alabama, nuclear power plant

[8] See GAO-07-1036.

Table 1. Sources of Cyber Threats to Critical Infrastructures

Threat Source	Description
Criminal groups	There is an increased use of cyber intrusions by criminal groups that attack systems for monetary gain.
Foreign nation states	Foreign intelligence services use cyber tools as part of their information gathering and espionage activities. Also, several nations are aggressively working to develop information warfare doctrine, programs, and capabilities. Such capabilities enable a single entity to have a significant and serious impact by disrupting the supply, communications, and economic infrastructures that support military power—impacts that, according to the Director of the Central Intelligence Agency, can affect the daily lives of Americans across the country.[a]
Hackers	Hackers sometimes crack into networks for the thrill of the challenge or for bragging rights in the hacker community. While remote cracking once required a fair amount of skill or computer knowledge, hackers can now download attack scripts and protocols from the Internet and launch them against victim sites. Thus, attack tools have become more sophisticated and easier to use.
Hacktivists	Hacktivism refers to politically motivated attacks on publicly accessible Web pages or e-mail servers. These groups and individuals overload e-mail servers and hack into Web sites to send a political message.
Disgruntled insiders	The disgruntled insider, working from within an organization, is a principal source of computer crimes. Insiders may not need a great deal of knowledge about computer intrusions because their knowledge of a victim system often allows them to gain unrestricted access to cause damage to the system or to steal system data. The insider threat also includes contractor personnel.
Terrorists	Terrorists seek to destroy, incapacitate, or exploit critical infrastructures to threaten national security, cause mass casualties, weaken the U.S. economy, and damage public morale and confidence. However, terrorist adversaries of the United States are less developed in their computer network capabilities than other adversaries. Terrorists likely pose a limited cyber threat. The Central Intelligence Agency believes terrorists will stay focused on traditional attack methods, but it anticipates growing cyber threats as a more technically competent generation enters the ranks.

Source: Federal Bureau of Investigation, unless otherwise indicated.

[a]Prepared statement of George J. Tenet, Director of Central Intelligence, before the Senate Select Committee on Intelligence, February 2, 2000.

operated by TVA failed, forcing the unit to be shut down manually. The failure of the pumps was traced to an unintended incident involving excessive traffic on the control system network caused by the failure of another control system device.

Critical infrastructure owners face both technical and organizational challenges to securing control systems. Technical challenges—including control systems' limited processing capabilities, real-time operations, and design constraints—hinder an infrastructure owner's ability to implement traditional information technology (IT) security processes, such as strong user authentication and patch management. Organizational challenges include difficulty in developing a compelling business case for investing in control systems security and differing priorities of information security personnel and control systems engineers.

Disruptions to control systems can have a significant effect on utilities such as electricity and water. The following are selected examples of disruptions that we previously reported in GAO-07-1036:

Maroochy Shire sewage spill:

In the spring of 2000, a former employee of an Australian organization that developed manufacturing software applied for a job with the local government, but was rejected. Over a 2-month period, this individual reportedly used a radio transmitter on as many as 46 occasions to remotely break into the controls of a sewage treatment system, ultimately releasing about 264,000 gallons of raw sewage into nearby rivers and parks.

Davis-Besse power plant:

The Nuclear Regulatory Commission confirmed that in January 2003, the Microsoft SQL Server worm known as Slammer infected a computer network at the idled Davis-Besse nuclear power plant in Oak Harbor, Ohio, disabling a safety monitoring system for nearly 5 hours and the plant's process computer for about 6 hours.

Northeast power blackout:

In August 2003, failure of the alarm processor in the control system of FirstEnergy, an Ohio-based electric utility, prevented control room operators from having adequate awareness of critical changes to the electrical grid. This problem was compounded when the state estimating program at the Midwest Independent System Operator failed. When several key transmission lines in northern Ohio tripped due to contact with trees, they initiated a cascading failure of 508 generating units at 265 power plants across eight states and a Canadian province.

Taum Sauk Water Storage Dam failure:

In December 2005, the Taum Sauk Water Storage Dam, approximately 100 miles south of St. Louis, Missouri, suffered a catastrophic failure, releasing a billion gallons of water. According to the dam's operator, the incident may have occurred because the gauges at the dam read differently than the gauges at the dam's remote monitoring station.

Federal Regulations, Standards, and Guidance Establish Requirements to Secure Control Systems

To address the increasing threat to control systems governing critical infrastructures, both federal and private organizations have begun efforts to develop requirements, guidance, and best practices for securing control systems. For example, FISMA outlines a comprehensive, risk-based approach to securing federal information systems, which encompass control systems. Federal organizations, including the National Institute of Standards and Technology (NIST), the Federal Energy Regulatory Commission (FERC), and the Nuclear Regulatory Commission (NRC), have used a risk-based approach to develop guidance and standards to secure control systems. NIST guidance has been developed that currently applies to federal agencies; however, much FERC and NRC guidance and many standards have not been finalized. Once implemented, FERC and NRC standards will apply to both public and private organizations that operate covered critical infrastructures.

We have previously reported on the importance of using a risk-based approach for securing critical infrastructures, including control systems.[9] Risk management has received widespread support within and outside government as a tool that can help set priorities on how to protect critical infrastructures. While numerous and substantial gaps in security may exist, resources for closing these gaps are limited and must compete with other national priorities.

FISMA Established Requirements to Strengthen Information Security Practices at Federal Agencies

Recognizing the importance of securing federal agencies' information and systems, Congress enacted FISMA to strengthen the security of information and information systems within federal agencies, which include control systems.[10]

---

[9] See GAO, *Risk Management: Further Refinements Needed to Assess Risks and Prioritize Protective Measures at Ports and Other Critical Infrastructure*, GAO-06-91 (Washington, D.C.: Dec. 15, 2005).

[10] FISMA was enacted as title III, E-Government Act of 2002, Pub. L. No. 107-347 (Dec.17, 2002).

FISMA requires each agency to develop, document, and implement an agencywide information security program to provide security for the information and information systems that support the operations and assets of the agency, including those provided or managed by another agency, contractor, or other source. Specifically, this program is to include

- periodic assessments of the risk and magnitude of harm that could result from the unauthorized access, use, disclosure, disruption, modification, or destruction of information or information systems;
- risk-based policies and procedures that cost effectively reduce information security risks to an acceptable level and ensure that information security is addressed throughout the life cycle of each information system;
- subordinate plans for providing adequate information security for networks, facilities, and systems or groups of information systems;
- security awareness training for agency personnel, including contractors and other users of information systems that support the operations and assets of the agency;
- periodic testing and evaluation of the effectiveness of information security policies, procedures, and practices, performed with a frequency depending on risk, but no less than annually, and that includes testing of management, operational, and technical controls for every system identified in the agency's required inventory of major information systems;
- a process for planning, implementing, evaluating, and documenting remedial action to address any deficiencies in the information security policies, procedures, and practices of the agency;
- procedures for detecting, reporting, and responding to security incidents; and
- plans and procedures to ensure continuity of operations for information systems that support the operations and assets of the agency.

Furthermore, FISMA established a requirement that each agency develop, maintain, and annually update an inventory of major information systems (including major national security systems) operated by the agency or under its control. This inventory is to include an identification of the interfaces between each system and all other systems or networks, including those not operated by or under the control of the agency.

NIST Has Developed Standards and Guidance to Implement FISMA

FISMA also directs NIST to develop standards and guidelines for systems other than national security systems. As required by FISMA and based on the objectives of providing appropriate levels of information security, NIST developed

- standards for all agencies to categorize their information and information systems according to a range of risk levels,[11]
- guidelines recommending the types of information and information systems to be included in each category,[12] and
- minimum information security requirements for information and information systems in each category.[13]

NIST standards and guidelines establish a risk management framework that instructs agencies on providing an acceptable level of information security for all agency operations and assets and that guides the testing and evaluation of information security control effectiveness within an agencywide information security program. Recognizing the importance of documenting standards and guidelines as part of an agencywide information security program, NIST emphasizes that agencies must develop and promulgate formal, documented policies and procedures in order to ensure the effective implementation of security requirements.

NIST also collaborates with federal and industry stakeholders to develop standards, guidelines, checklists, and test methods to help secure federal information and information systems, including control systems. For example, NIST is currently developing guidance for federal agencies that own or operate control systems to comply with federal information system security standards and guidelines.[14] The guidance identifies issues and modifications to consider in applying information security standards and guidelines to control systems. In December 2007, NIST released an augmentation to Special Publication (SP) 800-53, *Recommended Security Controls for Federal Information Systems*, which provides a security control framework for control systems.[15] According to NIST officials, while most controls in SP 800-53 are applicable to control systems as written, several controls do require supplemental guidance and enhancements.

---

11 NIST, *Standards for Security Categorization of Federal Information and Information Systems*, FIPS 199 (Gaithersburg, Md.: February 2004).

12 NIST, *Volume 1: Guide for Mapping Types of Information and Information Systems to Security Categories*, SP 800-60 (Gaithersburg, Md.; June 2004) and NIST, *Volume II: Appendixes to Guide for Mapping Types of Information and Information Systems to Security Categories*, SP 800-60 (Gaithersburg, Md.: June 2004).

13 NIST, *Minimum Security Requirements for Federal Information and Information Systems*, FIPS 200 (Gaithersburg, Md.: March 2006).

14 See NIST, *Guide to Industrial Control Systems (ICS) Security: Supervisory Control and Data Acquisition (SCADA) Systems, Distributed Control Systems (DCS), and Other Control System Configurations Such As Programmable Logic Controllers (PLC)*, Draft SP 800-829, (Gaithersburg, Md.: September 2007).

15 NIST, *Recommended Security Controls for Federal Information System*, SP 800-53 Revision 2 (Gaithersburg, Md.: December 2007).

FERC Has Recently Approved Reliability Standards That Address Control Systems Security

Under the Energy Policy Act of 2005, FERC was authorized to (1) appoint an electricity reliability organization to develop and enforce mandatory electricity reliability standards, including cyber security, and (2) approve or remand each proposed standard. The commission may also direct the reliability organization to develop a new standard or modify approved standards. Both the commission and the reliability organization have the authority to enforce approved standards, investigate incidents, and impose penalties (up to $1 million a day) on noncompliant electricity asset owners or operators.

FERC has conducted several activities to begin implementing the requirements of the act. In July 2006, FERC certified the North American Electric Reliability Corporation (NERC) as the national electric reliability organization. In August 2003, prior to passage of the Energy Policy Act of 2005, NERC adopted Urgent Action 1200, a temporary, voluntary cyber security standard for the electric industry. Urgent Action 1200 directed electricity transmission and generation owners and operators to develop a cyber security policy, identify critical cyber assets, and establish controls for and monitor electronic and physical access to critical cyber assets. Urgent Action 1200 remained in effect on a voluntary basis until June 1, 2006, at which time NERC proposed eight critical infrastructure protection reliability standards to replace the Urgent Action 1200 standard.

In July 2007, FERC issued a notice of proposed rulemaking in which it proposed to approve eight critical infrastructure reliability standards, which included standards for control systems security. FERC also proposed to direct NERC to modify the areas of these standards that required improvement. In January 2008, after considering public comments on the notice of proposed rulemaking, FERC approved the reliability standards and the accompanying implementation plan. It also directed NERC to develop modifications to strengthen the standards and to monitor the development and implementation of the NIST standards to determine if they contain provisions that will protect the bulk-power system better than NERC's reliability standards. The organizations subject to the standards, including utilities like TVA, must be auditably compliant with the standards by 2010.

NRC Is Conducting A Rulemaking Process on Cyber Security, Including Control Systems

The NRC, which has regulatory authority over nuclear power plant safety and security, has conducted several activities related to enhancing the cyber security of control systems. In 2005, an industry task force led by the Nuclear Energy Institute (NEI) developed and released the *Cyber Security*

Program for Power Reactors (NEI 04-04) to provide nuclear power reactor licensees a means for developing and maintaining effective cyber security programs at their sites. In December 2005, the commission staff accepted the method outlined in NEI 04-04 for establishing and maintaining cyber security programs at nuclear power plants. TVA officials stated that the agency has begun a program to comply with NEI 04-04 guidelines and plans to complete implementation of corrective actions identified as a result of these guidelines over the next 3 years, consistent with planned plant outages and upgrade projects.

In January 2006, the commission issued a revision to Regulatory Guide 1.152, *Criteria for Use of Computers in Safety Systems of Nuclear Power Plants,* which provides cyber security-related guidance for the design of nuclear power plant safety systems. In April 2007, the commission finalized a rule that added "external cyber attack" to the events that power reactor licensees are required to prepare to defend against. In addition, the commission initiated a rulemaking process that provides cyber security requirements for digital computer and communication networks, including systems that are needed for plant safety, security, or emergency response. The public comment period for this rulemaking closed in March 2007. Commission officials stated that they estimate this rulemaking process will be completed in early 2009. Once the rulemaking process is completed and requirements for nuclear power plant cyber security programs are finalized, the commission is planning to conduct a range of oversight activities, including inspections at power plants. According to commission officials, all nuclear plant operators have committed to complete implementation of the NEI-04-04 program at their sites.

TVA Provides Power to the Southeastern United States

The TVA is a federal corporation and the nation's largest public power company. Its mission is to supply affordable, reliable power, support a thriving river system, and stimulate sustainable economic development in the public interest. In addition to generating and transmitting power, TVA also manages the nation's fifth-largest river system to minimize flood risk, maintain navigation, provide recreational opportunities, and protect water quality. TVA is governed by a nine-member Board of Directors that is led by the Chairman. Each board member is nominated by the President of the United States and confirmed by the Senate. The TVA Chief Executive Officer reports to the TVA Board of Directors.

TVA's power service area covers 80,000 square miles in the southeastern United States, an area that includes almost all of Tennessee and parts of Mississippi, Kentucky, Alabama, Georgia, North Carolina, and Virginia, and has a total population of about 8.7 million people (see fig. 2).

Figure 2: TVA's Seven State Service Area and Generating Facilities

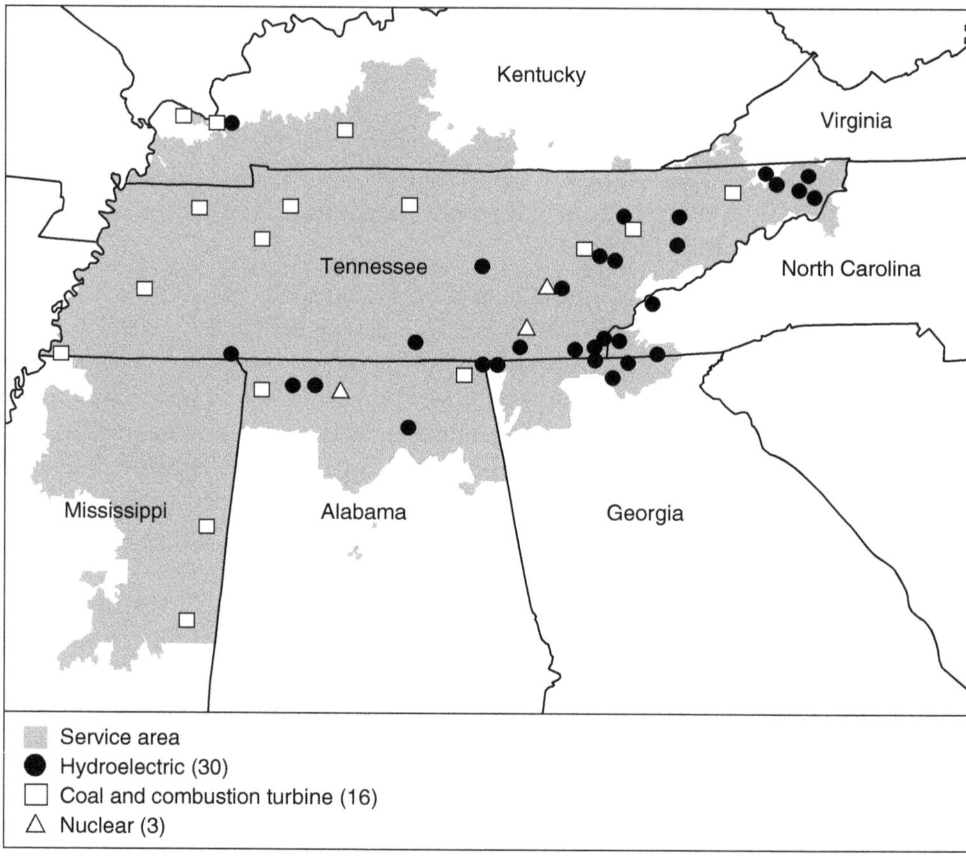

Source: GAO analysis of TVA data.

TVA operates 11 coal-fired fossil plants, 8 combustion turbine plants,[16] 3 nuclear plants, and a hydroelectric system that includes 29 hydroelectric dams and one pumped storage facility (see fig. 2 and fig. 3).[17] Fossil plants produce about 60 percent of TVA's power, nuclear plants about 30 percent, and the hydroelectric system about 10 percent. TVA also owns and operates one of the largest transmission systems in North America. TVA's transmission system moves electric power from the generating plants where it

[16] Three of the combustion turbine plants are located immediately adjacent to coal generation facilities.

[17] A pumped-storage plant uses two reservoirs, with one located at a much higher elevation than the other. During periods of low demand for electricity, such as nights and weekends, energy is stored by reversing the turbines and pumping water from the lower to the upper reservoir. The stored water can later be released to turn the turbines and generate electricity as it flows back into the lower reservoir.

Figure 3: Examples of TVA Generation Facilities

Source: TVA.
Note: Clockwise from upper left are coal, nuclear, and hydroelectric generation facilities.

is produced to distributors of TVA power and to industrial and federal customers across the region.

TVA provides power to three main customer groups: distributors, directly served customers, and off-system customers. There are 159 distributors—109 municipal utility companies and 50 cooperatives—that resell TVA power to consumers. These groups represent the base of TVA's business, accounting for 85 percent of their total revenue. Fifty-three large industrial customers and six federal installations buy TVA power directly. They represent 11 percent of TVA's total revenue. Twelve surrounding utilities buy power from TVA on the interchange market. Sales to these utilities represent 4 percent of TVA's total revenue.

Control systems are essential to TVA's operation. TVA uses control systems to both generate and deliver power. In generation, control systems are used within power plants to open and close valves, control equipment, monitor sensors, and ensure the safe and efficient operation of a generating unit. Many control systems networks connect with TVA's corporate network to transmit information about system status.

To deliver power, TVA monitors the status of its own and surrounding transmission facilities from two operations centers. Each center is staffed 24 hours a day and can serve as a backup for the other center. Control systems at these centers are used to open and close breakers and balance the transmission of power across the TVA network while accounting for changes in network capacity due to outages and changes in demand that occur continuously throughout the day. TVA's control systems range in capacity from simple systems with limited functionality located in one facility to complex, geographically dispersed systems with multiple functions. The ages of these control systems range from modern systems to systems dating back 20 or more years to the original construction of a facility.

As shown in table 2, TVA has designated certain senior managers to serve the key roles in information security designated by FISMA.

Responsibility for control systems security is distributed throughout TVA (see fig. 4). TVA's Information Services organization provides general guidance, assistance in FISMA compliance, and technical assistance in control systems security. The Information Services organization also manages the overall TVA corporate computer network that links facilities throughout

Table 2. Key TVA Information Security Responsibilities

FISMA Role	TVA Official	Key Responsibilities
Agency head	President and Chief Executive Officer	The agency head is responsible for the agencywide information security program. The agency head provides oversight for TVA's Information Security and Privacy Program and ensures that adequate resources are available to support the success of the program.
Inspector general	TVA Inspector General	The inspector general is responsible for promoting the efficiency, effectiveness, and integrity of TVA's Information Security and Privacy Program. This responsibility is accomplished, in part, by performing security audits, investigations, and inspections to evaluate compliance of the program with established federal laws, regulations, and accepted best practices. The Inspector General's responsibilities are also met by performing an annual, comprehensive review of TVA's Information Security and Privacy Program to include policies, procedures, and practices.
Chief information officer	Vice President, Information Services	The chief information officer (CIO) is responsible for the organization's information system planning, budgeting, investment, performance, and acquisition. As such, the CIO provides advice and assistance to senior agency officials in acquiring the most efficient and effective information system to fit the organization's enterprise architecture. The CIO is also responsible for managing TVA's Information Security and Privacy Program, both within TVA and with external business partners and other federal agencies and ensuring compliance with the program.

FISMA Role	TVA Official	Key Responsibilities
Senior agency information security officer	Senior Manager, Enterprise IT Security	The senior agency information security officer is responsible for carrying out the CIO information security responsibilities such as developing and maintaining TVA's Information Security and Privacy Program and ensuring compliance with the program. The officer plays a leading role in introducing an appropriate, structured methodology to help identify, evaluate, and minimize information security risks to an organization. The senior agency information security officer • serves as the CIO's principal point of contact for all matters relating to the security of TVA's systems and information resources; • develops, maintains, and enforces information security policies, procedures, and standards to ensure the confidentiality, integrity, and availability of TVA's information resources and to ensure compliance with federal laws and regulations and accepted best practices in information security and privacy; • facilitates the development of agency-level implementing procedures for security controls; • monitors, evaluates, and reports to the CIO on the status and adequacy of the Information Security and Privacy Program within TVA; and • provides oversight, guidance, and support to TVA's information security and privacy personnel.

Source: GAO analysis of TVA data.

the TVA service area and is connected to the Internet. As of February 2008, the Enterprise IT Security organization within Information Services was given specific responsibility for cyber security throughout the agency.

However, the control systems located within a plant are integrated with and managed as part of the generation equipment, safety and environmental systems, and other physical equipment located at that plant. This means that development, day-to-day maintenance and operation, and upgrades of control systems are handled by the business units responsible for the facilities where the systems are located. Specifically, nuclear systems are managed by the Nuclear Power Group; coal and combustion turbine control systems are managed by the Fossil Power Group; and hydroelectric facilities are managed by River Operations. Transmission control systems are managed by TVA's Transmission and Reliability Organization, located within its Power Systems Operations business unit.

The Transmission and Reliability Organization is highly dependent on control systems. To comply with NERC Urgent Action 1200, and in an effort to ensure its systems are secure, the Transmission and Reliability Organization

Figure 4: TVA Organizational Responsibilities for Control Systems

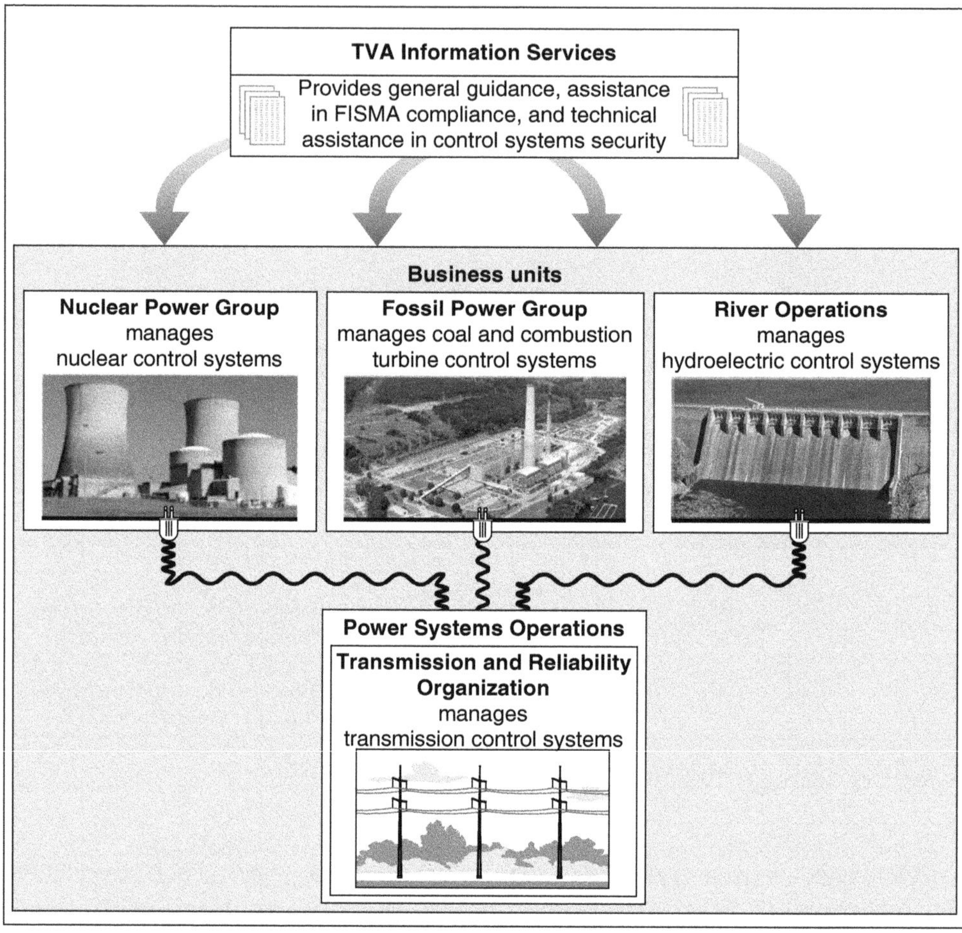

Source: GAO analysis of TVA data (text), TVA (photos).

has handled additional aspects of information security compared with other TVA organizations. For example, the organization manages portions of its own network infrastructure. It also has arranged for both internal and external security assessments in order to enhance the security of its control systems.

TVA Had Not Fully Implemented Appropriate Security Practices to Protect Its Critical Infrastructures

TVA had not fully implemented appropriate security practices to secure the control systems used to operate its critical infrastructures. Both the corporate network infrastructure and control systems networks and devices at individual facilities and plants were vulnerable to disruption. In addition, physical security controls at multiple locations did not sufficiently protect critical control systems. The interconnections between TVA's control system networks and its corporate network increase the risk that security weaknesses on the corporate network could affect control systems networks. For example, because of weaknesses in the separation of lower security network segments from higher security network segments on TVA networks, an attacker who gained access to a less secure portion of a network such as the corporate network could potentially compromise equipment in a more secure portion of the network, including equipment that has access to control systems. As a result, TVA's control systems that operate its critical infrastructures are at increased risk of unauthorized modification or disruption by both internal and external threats.

TVA Corporate Network Was Vulnerable to Disruption

The TVA corporate network infrastructure had multiple weaknesses that left it vulnerable to intentional or unintentional compromise of the confidentiality, integrity, and availability of the network and devices on the network. These weaknesses applied both at TVA headquarters and to the portions of the corporate network located at the individual facilities we reviewed. For example, one remote access system used for the network that we reviewed was not securely configured. Further, individual servers and workstations lacked key patches and were insecurely configured. In addition, the configuration of numerous network infrastructure protocols and devices provided limited or ineffective security protections. Moreover, the intrusion detection system that TVA used had significant limitations. As a result, TVA's control systems were at an increased risk of unauthorized access or disruption via access from the corporate network. Furthermore, weaknesses in the intrusion detection system could limit the ability of TVA to detect malicious or unintended events on its network.

TVA Remote Access Was Insecurely Configured

Remote access is any access to an organizational information system by a user (or an information system) that communicates through an external, nonorganization-controlled network (e.g., the Internet). NIST guidance states that information systems should establish a trusted communications path between remote users and an information system and that two-factor authentication should be part of an organization's remote access authentication requirements. Additionally, TVA policy requires that if remote access technology is used to connect to the network, it must be configured securely. One device used for remote access is a virtual private network (VPN).[18]

[18] A VPN is a private network that is maintained across a shared or public network, such as the Internet, by means of specialized security procedures. VPNs are intended to provide secure connections between remote clients, such as branch offices or traveling personnel, and a central office.

TVA did not configure a VPN system to include effective security mechanisms. This could allow an attacker who compromised a remote user's computer to remotely access the user's secure session to TVA, thereby increasing the risk that unauthorized users could gain access to TVA systems and sensitive information.

Individual Servers and Workstations Were Insecurely Configured

Federal and agency guidance call for effective patch management, firewall configuration, and application security settings. TVA has a patch management[19] policy that requires it to regularly monitor, identify, and remediate vulnerabilities to applications in its software inventory. NIST guidance also states that firewalls should be carefully configured to provide adequate protection. Furthermore, NIST guidance states that organizations should effectively configure security settings in key applications to the highest level possible.

However, almost all of the workstations and servers that we examined on the corporate network lacked key security patches or had inadequate security settings. Furthermore, TVA did not effectively implement host firewall controls on its laptops. In addition, inadequate security settings existed in key applications installed on laptops, servers, and workstations we examined. Consequently, TVA is at an increased risk that known vulnerabilities in these applications could allow an attacker to execute malicious code and gain control of or compromise a system.

Network Infrastructure Protocols and Devices Provided Limited or Ineffective Protections

Federal and agency guidance state that organizations should have strong passwords, identification and authentication, and network segmentation. National Security Agency guidance states that Windows passwords should be 12 or more characters long, include upper and lower case letters, numbers, and special characters, and not consist of dictionary words and has advised against the use of weak encryption. NIST guidance states that systems should uniquely identify and authenticate users with passwords or other authentication mechanisms or implement other compensating controls. NIST guidance also states that organizations should take steps to secure their e-mail systems. Finally, NIST guidance states that organizations should partition networks containing higher risk systems from lower risk systems and configure interfaces between those systems to manage risk.

---

[19] Patch management is a critical process used to help alleviate many of the challenges involved with securing computing systems from attack. It includes acquiring, testing, applying, and monitoring patches to a computer system.

However, the TVA corporate network used several protocols and devices that did not provide sufficient security controls. For example, certain network protocols and devices were not adequately protected by password or authentication controls or encryption. In addition, TVA had network services that spanned different security network segments. As a result, a malicious user could exploit these weaknesses to gain access to sensitive systems or to otherwise modify or disrupt network traffic.

Intrusion Detection System Had Significant Limitations

Even strong controls may not block all intrusions and misuse, but organizations can reduce the risks associated with such events if they take steps to promptly detect, report, and respond to them before significant damage is done. In addition, analyzing security events allows organizations to gain a better understanding of the threats to their information and the costs of their security-related problems. Such analyses can pinpoint vulnerabilities that need to be eliminated so that they will not be exploited again. NIST states that intrusion detection is the process of monitoring events occurring in a computer system or network and analyzing the events for signs of intrusion, which it defines as an attempt to compromise the confidentiality, integrity, or availability of a computer or network. NIST guidance prescribes network and host-based intrusion detection systems[20] as a means of protecting systems from the threats that come with increasing network connectivity.

TVA had limited ability to effectively monitor its network with its intrusion detection system. Although a network intrusion detection system was deployed by TVA to monitor network traffic, it could not effectively monitor key computer assets. As a result, there is an increased risk that unauthorized access to TVA's networks may not be detected and mitigated in a timely manner.

TVA Control System Networks and Devices Were Vulnerable to Disruption

TVA's control system networks and devices on these networks were vulnerable to disruption due to inadequate information security controls. Specifically, firewalls were either bypassed or inadequately configured, passwords were either weak or not used at all, logging of certain activity was limited, configuration management policies for control systems software were not consistently implemented, and servers and workstations lacked key patches and effective virus protection. The combination of these weaknesses with the weaknesses in the TVA corporate network identified in the previous section places TVA's control systems that operate its

[20] An intrusion detection system detects inappropriate, incorrect, or anomalous activity that is aimed at disrupting the confidentiality, availability, or integrity of a protected network and its computer systems.

critical infrastructures at increased risk of unauthorized modification or disruption by both internal and external threats.

Firewalls Were Either Bypassed or Inadequately Configured

A firewall is a hardware or software component that protects given computers or networks from attacks by blocking network traffic. NIST guidance states that firewalls should be configured to provide adequate protection for the organization's networks and that the transmitted information between interconnected systems should be controlled and regulated.

TVA had implemented firewalls to segment control systems networks from the corporate network at all facilities we reviewed with connections between these two networks. However, firewalls at three of six facilities reviewed were either bypassed or inadequately configured. As a result, the hosts on higher security control system networks were at increased risk of compromise or disruption from the other lower security networks.

Passwords or Other Compensating Controls Were Not Effectively Implemented

Passwords are used to establish the validity of a user's claimed identity by requesting some kind of information that is known only by the user—a process known as authentication. The combination of identification, using, for example, a unique user account, and authentication, using, for example, a password, provides the basis for establishing individual accountability and for controlling access to the system. In cases where passwords cannot be implemented because of technological limitations or other concerns, such as impact on emergency response, NIST states that an organization should document controls that have been put in place to compensate for this weakness. TVA policy requires authentication of users except where security requirements or limitations in the hardware or software preclude it. In addition, agency policy requires users to establish complex passwords.

TVA did not have effective passwords or other documented compensating controls governing control systems we reviewed. According to agency officials, in certain cases, passwords were not technologically possible to implement but in these cases, there were no documented compensating controls. Until the agency implements either effective password practices or documented compensating controls, it faces an increased risk of unauthorized access to its control systems.

Audit Controls Did Not Effectively Log Certain Activity on Control Systems

Determining what, when, and by whom specific actions are taken on a system is crucial to establishing individual accountability, monitoring compliance with security policies, and investigating security violations. Audit and monitoring involves the regular collection, review, and analysis of auditable events for indications of inappropriate or unusual activity and the appropriate investigation and reporting of such activity. Audit and monitoring can help security professionals routinely assess computer security, perform investigations during and after an attack, and even recognize an ongoing attack. Federal guidance states that organizations should develop formal audit policies and procedures. TVA guidance states that sufficient audit logs should be maintained that allow monitoring of key user activities.

While TVA had taken steps to establish audit logs for its transmission control centers, it had not established effective audit logs or compensating controls at other facilities we reviewed. According to agency officials, system limitations at these facilities have historically meant that multiple users shared a single account to access these control systems. Therefore, audit logs would not have served a useful purpose because activities could not be traced to a single user. Until TVA establishes detailed audit logs for its control systems at these facilities or compensating controls in cases where such logs are not feasible, it risks being unable to determine if malicious incidents are occurring and, after an event occurs, being able to determine who or what caused the incident.

Configuration Management Policies Were Not Consistently Implemented on TVA Control Systems

Federal guidance states that all applications and changes to those applications should go through a formal, documented process that identifies all changes to the baseline configuration. Also, procedures should ensure that no unauthorized software is installed. TVA has established configuration management policies and procedures for its information technology systems. Specifically, its policies define the roles and responsibilities of application owners and developers; require business units to implement procedural controls that define documentation and testing required for software changes; and establish procedures to ensure that all changes relating to infrastructure and applications be managed and controlled.

However, TVA did not consistently apply its configuration management policies and procedures to control systems. The transmission control system had a configuration management process, and the hardware at individual plants was governed by a configuration management process, including plant drawings that tracked individual pieces of equipment. However, there was no formal configuration management process for software that was part of the control systems at the hydroelectric and fossil facilities that we reviewed. As a result, increased risk exists that unapproved changes to control systems could be made.

Software Patches on Control Systems Were Not Current

Patch management, including up-to-date patch installation, helps to mitigate vulnerabilities associated with flaws in software code, which could be exploited to cause significant damage. According to NIST, agencies should identify, report, and correct their information system flaws. According to NIST, tracking patches allows organizations to identify which patches are installed on a system and provides confirmation that the appropriate patches have been applied. Moreover, TVA policy requires the agency to remediate these vulnerabilities in a timely manner.

TVA had not installed current versions of patches for key applications on computers on control systems networks. While TVA had an agencywide policy and procedure for patch management, these policies did not apply to individual plant-level control systems. According to the operators at two of the facilities we reviewed, they applied vendor-approved patches to control systems but did not track versions of patches on these machines. Failure to keep software patches up-to-date could allow unauthorized individuals to gain access to network resources or disrupt network operations.

Virus Protection Software Was Not Consistently Implemented

Virus and worm[21] protection for information systems is a serious challenge. Computer attack tools and techniques are becoming increasingly sophisticated; viruses are spreading faster as a result of the increasing connectivity of today's networks; commercial off-the-shelf products can be easily exploited for attack by their users; and there is no single solution such as firewalls or encryption to protect systems. To combat viruses and worms specifically, entities should keep antivirus programs up-to-date. According to NIST, agencies should implement malicious code protection that includes a capability for automatic updates so that virus definitions are kept up-to-date on servers, workstations, and mobile computing devices. Virus-scanning software should be provided at critical entry points, such as remote-access servers, and at each desktop system on the network.

Although TVA implemented antivirus software on its transmission control systems network, it did not consistently implement antivirus software on other control systems we reviewed. In one case, according to agency officials, the vendor that developed the control systems software would not support an antivirus application, and the agency did not have plans to require the vendor to address this weakness. In another case, antivirus software was implemented, but it was not up-to-date. In the event that

[21] A virus is a program that contains hidden code that usually performs some unwanted function as a side effect. A worm is a program that can run independently, can propagate a complete working version of itself onto other hosts on a network, and may consume computer resources destructively.

using antivirus software is infeasible on a control system, the agency must document the controls, such as training or physical security, that would compensate for this deficiency. TVA had not done this. According to agency officials, such documentation is under way for its hydroelectric facilities, but not for other facilities. As a result, there is increased risk that the integrity of these networks and devices could be compromised.

Physical Security Controls Did Not Effectively Limit Access to Sensitive Control Systems

Physical security controls are important for protecting computer facilities and resources from espionage, sabotage, damage, and theft. These controls restrict physical access to computer resources, usually by limiting access to the buildings and rooms in which the resources are housed and by periodically reviewing the access granted in order to ensure that access continues to be appropriate. TVA policy requires that appropriate physical and environmental controls be implemented to provide security commensurate with the level of risk and magnitude of harm that would result from loss, misuse, unauthorized access, or modification of information or information systems. Further, NIST policy requires that federal organizations implement a variety of physical security controls to protect information and industrial control systems and the facilities in which they are located.

TVA had taken steps to provide physical security for its control systems. For example, it had issued electronic badges to agency personnel and contractors to help control access to many of its sensitive and restricted areas. TVA had also established law enforcement liaisons that help ensure additional backup security and facilitate the accurate flow of timely security information between appropriate government agencies. In addition, the agency had implemented physical security training for its employees to help achieve greater security awareness and accountability. However, the agency had not effectively implemented physical security controls at various locations, as the following examples illustrate:

- Live network jacks connected to TVA's internal network at certain facilities we reviewed had not been adequately secured from access by the public.
- TVA did not adequately control or change its keys to industrial control rooms containing sensitive equipment at one facility we reviewed. For example, the agency could neither account for all keys issued at the facility, which relies on manual locks for the security of rooms containing sensitive computer and control equipment, nor could it determine when keys had last been changed.
- TVA did not have an effective visitor control program at one facility we reviewed. For example, the agency had not maintained a visitor

log describing visitors' names, organizations, purpose of visits, forms of identification, or the names of the persons visited.

- Physical security policies and plans were either in draft form or were nonexistent.
- Rooms containing sensitive IT equipment had not been adequately environmentally protected. For example, sufficient emergency lighting was not available outside the control room at one facility we reviewed, a server room at the facility had no smoke detection capability, a control room at the facility contained a kitchen (a potential fire and water hazard), and a communications room had batteries collocated with sensitive communications gear.
- TVA had not always ensured that access to sensitive computing and industrial control systems resources had been granted to only those who needed it to perform their jobs at one facility we reviewed. About 75 percent of those who were issued facility badges had access to a facility computer room, but the vast majority of these badgeholders did not need access to the room. While TVA officials stated that all of those with access had been through the background investigation and training process required for all employees at the facility, an underlying principle for secure computer systems and data recommended by NIST is that users should be granted only those access rights and permissions needed to perform their official duties.

As a consequence of weaknesses such as these, increased risk exists that sensitive computing resources and data could be inadvertently or deliberately misused or destroyed.

Cumulative Effect of Inconsistencies and Weaknesses in Layered Network Defense Placed Critical Infrastructure Control Systems at Risk

Federal guidance and best practices in information security call for the use of multiple layers of defense to secure information resources. These multiple layers include the use of protection mechanisms and key network control points such as firewalls, routers, and intrusion detection systems to segment and control access to networks. Higher risk networks and devices, such as critical infrastructure control systems, may require additional security controls and should be on networks that are separate from lower risk devices.

TVA had deployed a layered defense model to control access between and among the corporate and control systems networks. For example, in all cases we examined, control systems were located on networks that had been segmented from business computing resources. The agency had also deployed protection mechanisms such as firewalls, router access control lists, virtual local area networking, and physical security controls at multiple locations throughout its network. For example, TVA's transmission control organization used layered networks with increasing levels of security to separate critical control devices from the corporate network.

However, these mechanisms and information security controls had been inconsistently applied. As a result, the effectiveness of the multiple layers of defense was limited. For example, while the transmission control organization network restricted access to control systems using multiple firewalls at outer and inner network boundaries, some plant systems had significantly fewer levels of security to reach control systems that impacted the same facilities. In addition, specific weaknesses in security configurations on key systems further reduced the overall effectiveness of security controls. The cumulative effect of these individual weaknesses and the interconnectedness of TVA critical infrastructure control systems places these systems at risk of compromise or disruption from internal and external threats.

Information Security Management Program Was Not Consistently Implemented Across TVA's Critical Infrastructure

An underlying reason for TVA's information security control weaknesses is that it had not consistently implemented significant elements of its information security program. The effective implementation of an information security program includes implementing the key elements required under FISMA and the establishment of a continuing cycle of activity—which includes developing an inventory of systems, assessing risk, developing policies and procedures, developing security plans,[22] testing and monitoring the effectiveness of controls, identifying and tracking remedial actions, and establishing appropriate training. TVA had not consistently implemented key elements of these activities. As a result of not fully developing and implementing its information security program, an increased potential for disruption or compromise of its control systems exists.

Inventory of Systems Was Not Complete or Accurate

FISMA requires that each agency develop, maintain, and annually update an inventory of major information systems operated by the agency or that are under its control. A complete and accurate inventory of major information systems is a key element of managing the agency's information

[22] FISMA requires that agencywide information security programs include subordinate plans for providing adequate information security for networks, facilities, and systems or groups of information systems, as appropriate. These plans are commonly referred to as system security plans.

technology resources, including the security of those resources. The inventory can be used to track agency systems for purposes such as periodic security testing and evaluation, patch management, contingency planning, and identifying system interconnections. TVA requires that the senior agency information security officer maintain an authoritative inventory of general support systems, major applications, major information systems, and minor applications.

TVA did not have a complete and accurate inventory of its control systems. In its fiscal year 2007 FISMA submission, TVA included in its inventory of major applications the transmission and the hydro automation control systems. Although TVA stated that the plant control systems at its nuclear and fossil facilities were minor applications, these applications had not been included in TVA's inventory of minor applications or accounted for as part of a consolidated general support system. These systems are essential to automated operation of generation facilities. At the conclusion of our review, agency officials stated they had developed a plan to develop a more complete and accurate system inventory by September 2008. Until TVA has a complete and accurate inventory of its control systems, it cannot ensure that the appropriate security controls have been implemented to protect these systems.

TVA Had Not Assessed Risk for Almost All of Its Control Systems

FISMA mandates that agencies assess the risk and magnitude of harm that could result from the unauthorized access, use, disclosure disruption, modification, or destruction of their information and information systems. The Federal Information Processing Standard (FIPS) 199, *Standards for Security Categorization of Federal Information and Information Systems*, and related NIST guidance provide a common framework for categorizing systems according to risk. The framework establishes three levels of potential impact on organizational operation, assets, or individuals should a breach of security occur—high (severe or catastrophic), moderate (serious), and low (limited)—and it is used to determine the impact for each of the FISMA-specified security objectives of confidentiality, integrity, and availability. Once determined, security categories are to be used in conjunction with vulnerability and threat information in determining minimum security requirements for the system and in assessing the risk to an organization. Risk assessments help ensure that the greatest risks have been identified and addressed, increase the understanding of risk, and provide support for needed controls. Office of Management and Budget (OMB) Circular A-130, appendix III, prescribes that risk be assessed when significant changes are made to major systems and applications in an agency's inventory or at least every 3 years. Consistent with NIST guidance, TVA policy states that risk assessments should be updated to reflect the results of security tests and evaluations.

TVA had not completed assigning risk levels or assessing the risk of its control systems. While TVA categorized the transmission and hydro automation control systems as high-impact systems using FIPS 199, its nuclear division and fossil business unit, which include its coal and combustion turbine facilities, had not assigned risk levels to their control systems. Further, although TVA had performed a risk assessment for the transmission control system, the risk assessment did not include the risks associated with the newly identified vulnerabilities identified during the latest security test and evaluation. TVA had not completed risk assessments for the control systems at their nuclear, hydroelectric, coal, and combustion turbine facilities. According to TVA officials, the agency plans to complete risk assessments by May 2008 at the nuclear facility and June 2008 at the hydroelectric facility. For the fossil facility and all remaining control systems throughout TVA, agency officials stated that they would complete the security categorization of these systems by the end of September 2008. However, no date has been set for completion of risk assessments. Without assigned risk levels, TVA cannot make risk-based decisions on the security needs of their information and information systems. Moreover, until TVA assesses the risks of all its control systems, the agency cannot be assured that its control systems apply the appropriate level of controls to help prevent their unauthorized access, use, disclosure, disruption, modification, or destruction.

Security Policies Existed but Were Not Always Consistent and Did Not Clearly Define All Roles and Responsibilities

A key task in developing, documenting, and implementing an effective information security program is to establish and implement risk-based policies, procedures, and technical standards that cover security over an agency's computing environment. If properly implemented, policies and procedures can help to reduce the risk that could come from unauthorized access or disruption of services. Because security policies are the primary mechanism by which management communicates its views and requirements, it is important to document and implement them.

Several shortcomings existed in TVA's information security policies. First, the agency had not consistently applied information security policies to its control systems. Second, business unit security policies were not always consistent with overall agency information security policies. Third, cyber security responsibilities for interfaces between TVA's transmission control system and its fossil and hydroelectric generation units had not been documented. Fourth, TVA's patch management process was not in compliance with federal guidance. Finally, physical security standards for control system sites were in draft.

TVA Had Not Consistently Applied Information Security Policies to Control Systems

TVA had developed and documented policies, standards, and guidelines for information security; however, it had not consistently applied these policies to its control systems. Although neither FISMA nor TVA's agencywide IT security policy explicitly mentions control systems, our analysis of NIST guidance and the stated position of NIST officials is that the guidance does apply to industrial control systems, such as the systems that TVA uses to operate critical infrastructures. Furthermore, NIST has recently developed and released guidance to assist agencies in applying federal IT security requirements to control systems. As a result of not applying this guidance with the same level of rigor to its control systems, numerous shortfalls existed in TVA's information security management program for its control systems, including outdated risk assessments; incomplete system security categorizations, system security plans, and testing and evaluation activities; and an ineffective remediation process. TVA officials stated that they are in the process of applying current NIST criteria to their control systems and plan to complete this process by the end of fiscal year 2008. Until TVA consistently applies federal IT security policies to its control systems and addresses identified weaknesses, its control systems will remain at risk of compromise and disruption.

Business Unit Policies Were Not Consistent with Overall Agency Policy

While two TVA business units had developed IT security policies to address anticipated cyber security guidance from their respective industries, these policies were not always consistent with agencywide IT security policy. According to TVA policy, business units may establish their own IT security policies but must still comply with agencywide IT security policy. For example, TVA's Nuclear Power Group had developed a cyber security policy and the Power Systems Operations business unit had developed two cyber security policies—one business unit policy that was in draft, and one approved policy developed by and applicable to the unit's Transmission and Reliability Organization. These policies addressed many of the same issues as TVA's agencywide IT security policy, including establishing roles and responsibilities, access controls, configuration management, training, and emergency planning and response. However, the policies were not always consistent with the agencywide IT security policy. For example, although both the Nuclear Power Group and the Transmission and Reliability Organization policies had been developed to establish requirements for cyber security of plant systems, neither policy directed system security officers to implement minimum baseline security controls to protect the confidentiality, integrity, and availability of these systems, as is required by agency policy, nor did they establish a link or reference to agencywide IT security policy or federal IT security requirements. Although the Power System Operations cyber security policy reiterated requirements outlined by FISMA and the TVA IT security policy, this policy remained in draft. The existence of inconsistent policies at different levels of TVA could hinder its ability to apply IT security requirements consistently across the agency. Without developing and implementing consistent policies, procedures, and standards across all agency divisions and groups, TVA has less assurance that its systems controlling critical infrastructure are protected from unauthorized access and cyber threats.

Cyber Security Responsibilities for Interfaces with Transmission Organization Were Not Defined

NIST guidance states that organizations should authorize all connections from an information system to another information system through the use of system connection agreements.[23] Documentation should include security roles and responsibilities and any service level agreements, which should define the expectations of performance for each required security control, and remedy and response requirements for any identified instance of noncompliance.

The agreements established by TVA's Transmission and Reliability Organization with other TVA business units did not fully address information that should be included based on NIST guidance. For example, the control systems operated by the Transmission and Reliability Organization interface with power plant control systems operated by TVA's fossil and hydroelectric business units. Although the transmission organization had established agreements with the fossil and hydroelectric business units, these agreements made no mention of cyber security roles and responsibilities, performance expectations for security controls, and remedy and response requirements for noncompliance. TVA officials stated that the type of interface between the transmission control system and individual plant systems means that, in most cases, a cyber security incident on a plant control network would not impact the overall transmission control network. While the likelihood of direct transmission of malware such as a virus might be small, without clear documentation of information required in an intergroup agreement, TVA faces the risk that security controls may not be in place or work as intended at an individual plant, resulting in a situation where critical generation equipment may not be able to start, safely shut down, or otherwise be controlled by the transmission control system when necessary. This is particularly of concern because of the vari-

[23] NIST, *Guide for Developing Security Plans for Federal Information Systems*, SP 800-18 (Gaithersburg, Md.: February 2006).

ation in cyber security controls that we observed between the overall transmission control system and the individual plants. Without clear documentation of cyber security-related roles and responsibilities, TVA faces the risk that security controls may not be in place or work as intended.

Patch Management Policies Were Not in Compliance with NIST Guidance

NIST guidance states that federal agencies should create a comprehensive patch management process.[24] The process should include

- monitoring of security sources for vulnerability announcements;
- an accurate inventory of the organization's IT resources, using commercially available automated inventory management tools whenever possible;
- prioritization of the order in which the vulnerabilities are addressed with a focus on high-priority systems such as those essential for mission-critical operations; and
- automated deployment of patches to IT devices using enterprise patch management tools.

TVA had not fully implemented such a comprehensive process. It had a patch management process, including staff whose primary responsibility is to monitor security sources for vulnerability announcements. However, the agency lacked an accurate inventory of its IT resources produced using an automated management tool. For example, agency staff did not have timely access to version numbers and build numbers of software applications in the agency, although officials stated this information could be obtained manually. In addition, the agency's patch management policy did not apply to individual plant-level control systems or network infrastructure devices such as routers and switches.

Furthermore, TVA's written guidance on patch management provided only limited guidance on how to prioritize vulnerabilities. For example, the guidance did not refer to the criticality of IT resources. In addition, as previously noted, the agency had not categorized the impact of many of its control systems. The guidance also did not specify situations for which it was acceptable to upgrade or downgrade a vulnerability's priority from that given by industry standard sources such as the vendor or third-party patch tracking services. As a result, patches that were identified as critical, meaning they should be applied immediately to vulnerable systems, were not applied in a timely manner. For example, agency staff had reduced the

[24] NIST, *Creating a Patch and Vulnerability Management Program,* SP 800-40 (Gaithersburg, Md.: November 2005).

priority of three vulnerabilities identified as critical or important by the vendor or a patch tracking service and did not provide sufficient documentation of the basis for this decision. TVA also did not document many vulnerabilities on its systems. For a 15-month period, TVA documented its analysis of 351 reported vulnerabilities, while NIST's National Vulnerability Database[25] reported about 2,000 vulnerabilities rated as high or medium-risk for the types of systems in operation at TVA for the same time period. Finally, the agency lacked an automated tool to assess the deployment of many types of application patches. As a result, certain systems were missing patches more than 6 months past TVA deadlines for patching. Without a fully effective patch management process, TVA faces an increased risk that critical systems may remain vulnerable to known vulnerabilities and be open to compromise or disruption.

Physical Security Policies Remained in Draft

NIST guidance states that organizations should develop formal documented physical security policies and procedures to facilitate the implementation of physical and environmental protection controls. However, TVA's physical security standards for protection of its assets, including sensitive computer and industrial control equipment, as well as employees, contractors, visitors, and the general public, had been drafted but not approved by management. These standards are intended to provide clear and consistent physical security policy for all nonnuclear facilities. According to TVA Police officials, most sites budget for and implement their own physical security guidance and measures. Finalized physical security standards agencywide would provide consistent guidelines for facilities to make risk-based decisions on implementing these recommendations. Consequently, TVA has less assurance that control systems will be consistently and effectively protected from inadvertent or deliberate misuse including damage or destruction.

Security Plans for Most Control Systems Had Not Been Completed

The objective of system security planning is to improve the protection of IT resources. A system security plan provides a complete and up-to-date overview of the system's security requirements and describes the controls that are in place—or planned—to meet those requirements. FISMA requires that agency information security programs include subordinate plans for providing adequate information security for networks, facilities, and systems or groups of information systems, as appropriate. OMB Circular

[25] The National Vulnerability Database is the U.S. government repository of standards based vulnerability management data. This data enables automation of vulnerability management, security measurement, and compliance.

A-130 specifies that agencies develop and implement system security plans for major applications and for general support systems and that these plans address policies and procedures for providing management, operational, and technical controls. NIST guidance states that minor applications that are not connected to a general support system or major application should be described in a general support system plan that has either a common physical location or is supported by the same organization. Further, TVA policy states that minor applications should be briefly described in a general support system security plan. NIST guidance states that security plans should contain key information needed to select the appropriate security controls, such as the FIPS 199 category and the certification and accreditation status of the connected systems. Plans should also be updated to include the latest security test and evaluation and risk assessment results.

TVA had only developed a system security plan that covered two of the six facilities we reviewed, and this plan was incomplete and not up-to-date. The transmission control system security plan, which addressed systems at two transmission control centers, included many elements required by NIST, such as the description of the individuals responsible for security, and addressed management, operational, and technical controls. Although the plan listed interconnected systems, it did not completely address interconnectivity with other systems operated by other organizations. Specifically, it did not include essential information needed to select the appropriate security controls, such as the FIPS 199 category or the certification and accreditation status of the connected systems. Further, the plan was not updated to include the latest security test and evaluation or risk assessment results. According to agency officials, TVA is developing a system security plan for its hydroelectric automation control system as part of its certification and accreditation process. Agency officials stated that this plan will be completed by June 2008.

TVA nuclear and fossil facilities had not developed security plans for their control systems. Agency officials stated that they were planning to develop security plans and complete the certification and accreditation process for these control systems. The plan for the nuclear facility is scheduled to be completed by June 2008. For the fossil facility, TVA officials stated that they intend to complete a security plan and certification and accreditation activities based on the results of security categorizations that will be completed by September 2008. However, no time frame has been set for completion of the plan or accreditation. Until these activities are completed, TVA cannot ensure that the security requirements have been identified and that the appropriate controls will be in place to protect these critical control systems.

General Security Awareness Training Was Completed, but Training for Specific Roles Was Not Completed

FISMA mandates that federal employees and contractors who use agency information systems be provided with periodic training in information security awareness. FISMA also requires agencies to provide appropriate training on information security to personnel who have significant security responsibilities. This training, described in NIST guidance,[26] should inform personnel, including contractors and other users of information systems supporting the operations and assets of an agency, of information security risks associated with their activities and their roles and responsibilities to properly and effectively implement the practices that are designed to reduce these risks. Depending on an employee's specific security role, training could include specialized topics such as incident detection and response, physical security, or firewall configuration. TVA also has a policy that requires that all employees and others who have access to its corporate network to complete annual security awareness training. The policy requires that employees and contractors who do not complete the training within a set time frame have their network access suspended.

Although for fiscal year 2007 TVA reported that 98 percent of its employees and contractors completed its annual security awareness training, other shortfalls existed in TVA's training program. For example, the agency policy of suspending network access for employees who did not complete security awareness training did not apply to control system-specific networks, such as those at the nuclear, hydroelectric, and fossil facilities we reviewed. At these sites, there were no controls in place to enforce completion of the required training by employees using these control systems.

In addition, a substantial number of TVA employees who have significant security responsibilities did not complete role-based training in the last fiscal year, and the required training did not include specialized technical topics. In fiscal year 2007, TVA reported that only 25 percent of 197 applicable employees who had significant IT security responsibilities had completed role-based training, compared with 86 percent and 72 percent who reportedly received such training in fiscal years 2005 and 2006, respectively. According to agency officials, training had not been completed primarily due to a lack of staff to provide the training. Furthermore, the role-based training that was required was focused on management and procedural issues. TVA had technical security training available to its information security staff, which comprised approximately 14 of the 197 employees

[26] NIST, *Information Technology Security Training Requirements: A Role- and Performance-Based Model*, SP 800-16 (Gaithersburg, Md.: April 1998), and NIST, *Building an Information Technology Security Awareness and Training Program*, 800-50 (Gaithersburg, Md.: October 2003).

who needed role-based training, but this training was not required. For these 14 staff, TVA reported a 100 percent completion rate for the technical training. At the end of our review, agency officials provided a plan to improve the number of employees completing role-based training and to examine adding technical training to training requirements. The plan is to be completed by July 2008. Until this plan is fully implemented, security lapses are more likely to occur and could contribute to information security weaknesses at TVA.

TVA Did Not Adequately Test and Evaluate the Effectiveness of Security Practices

A key element of an information security program is ongoing testing and evaluation to ensure that systems are in compliance with policies and that the policies and controls are both appropriate and effective. Testing and evaluation demonstrates management's commitment to the security program, reminds employees of their roles and responsibilities, and identifies areas of noncompliance and ineffectiveness requiring remediation. Starting in fiscal year 2007, OMB required agencies to discontinue using SP 800-26 and to use NIST SP 800-53A for the assessment of security controls effectiveness when performing periodic security testing and evaluation of their information systems.[27] In addition, TVA policy requires all minor applications to be assigned to a general support system or major application that is tested and evaluated as part of the certification and accreditation process performed every 3 years.

TVA did not properly test and evaluate all of its control systems. Although TVA had performed annual self-assessments of the two control systems designated as major applications (transmission and hydro automation control systems) in fiscal year 2007, it did so using outdated NIST guidance contained in SP 800-26, rather than the current guidance in SP 800-53A. Of these two control systems, TVA performed a complete test and evaluation of the security controls on one of the systems—the transmission control system—within the last 3 years. Although TVA officials at the nuclear and fossil facilities considered their plant-level control systems to be minor applications, they were not part of any general support system. As a result, TVA did not appropriately identify, test, or evaluate the effectiveness of the security controls in place for the control systems at these facilities. Without appropriate tests and evaluations of all its control systems, the agency has limited assurance that policies and controls are appropriate and working as intended. Additionally, increased risk exists that undetected vulnerabilities could be exploited to allow unauthorized access to these critical systems.

[27] OMB, *FY 2006 Reporting Instructions for the Federal Information Security Management Act and Agency Privacy Management*, M-06-20 (Washington, D.C.: July 17, 2006).

Most Remedial Action Plans Had Not Been Developed

A remedial action plan is a key component described in FISMA. Such a plan assists agencies in identifying, assessing, prioritizing, and monitoring progress in correcting security weaknesses that are found in information systems. In its annual FISMA guidance to agencies, OMB requires agencies' remedial action plans, also known as plans of action and milestones, to include, at a minimum, the resources necessary to correct an identified weakness, the original scheduled completion date, the status of the weakness as completed or ongoing, and key milestones with completion dates.[28] According to TVA policy, the agency should document weaknesses found during security assessments and document any planned remedial actions to correct any deficiencies.

TVA did not always address known significant deficiencies in its remedial action plans. The agency had developed a plan of action and milestones for its transmission control system; however, it did not do so for the control systems at the fossil, hydroelectric, or nuclear facilities. In addition, while the agency tracks weaknesses identified by the TVA Inspector General for its transmission control system, it did not include these weaknesses in its plan of action and milestones. Until the agency implements an effective remediation process for all control systems, it will not have assurance that the proper resources will be applied to known vulnerabilities or that those vulnerabilities will be properly mitigated.

Incident Response Procedures Had Not Been Finalized

Even strong controls may not block all intrusions and misuse, but organizations can reduce the risks associated with such events if they take steps to promptly detect, report, and respond to them before significant damage is done. In addition, analyzing security incidents allows organizations to gain a better understanding of the threats to their information and the costs of their security-related problems. Such analyses can pinpoint vulnerabilities that need to be eliminated so that they will not be exploited again. Incident reports can be used to provide valuable input for risk assessments, can help in prioritizing security improvement efforts, and can illustrate risks and related trends for senior management. FISMA and NIST guidance require that agency information security programs include procedures for detecting, reporting, and responding to security incidents, including reporting them to the U.S. Computer Emergency Readiness Team (US-CERT). Furthermore, NIST guidance prescribes network and host-

[28] See OMB, *Reporting Instructions for the Federal Information Security Management Act and Updated Guidance on Quarterly IT Security Reporting*, M-03-19 (Washington, D.C.: Aug. 6, 2003) for OMB's 2003 FISMA reporting guidance.

based intrusion detection systems as a means of protecting systems from the threats that come with increasing network connectivity.

TVA had developed incident detection, response, and reporting procedures. However, while the TVA organization responsible for operating its transmission control center had approved incident response and reporting procedures, the agencywide incident response and reporting procedure remained in draft form, although it is currently being used by TVA information security personnel. According to agency officials, the procedure is being revised and finalized to align with incident reporting guidelines developed by US-CERT. Until TVA finalizes these procedures, it cannot be assured that facilities are prepared to respond to and report incidents in an effective manner.

Contingency Planning Activities Were Completed but Were Not Fully Documented

Contingency planning includes developing and testing plans and activities so that when unexpected events occur, critical operations can continue without disruption or can be promptly resumed and that critical and sensitive data are protected. If contingency planning controls are inadequate, even relatively minor interruptions can result in a loss of system function and expensive recovery efforts. For some TVA control systems, system interruptions or malfunctions could result in loss of power, injuries, or loss of life. Given these severe implications, it is critical that an entity have in place (1) procedures for protecting information systems and minimizing the risk of unplanned interruptions and (2) a plan to recover critical operations should interruptions occur. To determine whether recovery plans will work as intended, they should be tested periodically in disaster-simulation exercises. FISMA requires that each federal agency implement an information security program that includes plans and procedures to ensure continuity of operations for information systems that support the operation and assets of the agency.

TVA had taken steps to address contingency planning for physical incidents such as fire, explosion, and natural disasters, and for other events such as cyber incidents. At the facilities we reviewed, staff performed regular drills and tests to address physical contingencies. According to agency officials, in many cases, these same drills are applicable to cyber incidents that could have physical consequences. In addition, the agency had developed backup[29] procedures for key information resources, including those that support its control systems. In TVA's transmission control centers, written backup procedures existed; however, in the hydroelectric,

[29] Backup is the activity of copying files or databases so that they will be preserved in case of equipment failure or other catastrophe. Backup is usually a routine part of business operations.

coal, and gas turbine facilities we reviewed, the backup procedures were not documented. Until TVA consistently documents backup procedures across all of its facilities, it has limited assurance that all TVA facilities will be able to respond appropriately in the event of a physical or cyber incident.

Conclusions

TVA's power generation and transmission critical infrastructures are important to the economy of the southeastern United States and the safety, security, and welfare of millions of people. Control systems are essential to the operation of these infrastructures; however, multiple information security weaknesses existed in both the agency's corporate network and individual control systems networks and devices. As a result, although TVA had implemented multiple layers of information security controls to protect its critical infrastructures, such as segmenting control systems networks from the corporate network, in many cases, these layers were not as effective as intended. An underlying cause for these weaknesses is that the agency had not consistently implemented its information security program throughout the agency. If TVA does not take sufficient steps to secure its control systems and implement an information security program, it risks not being able to respond properly to a major disruption that is the result of an intended or unintended cyber incident, which could affect the agency's operations and its customers.

Recommendations for Executive Action

To improve the implementation of information security program activites for the control systems governing TVA's critical infrastructures, we are recommending that the Chief Executive Officer of TVA take the following 19 actions:

- Establish a formal, documented configuration management process for changes to software governing control systems at TVA hydroelectric and fossil facilities.
- Establish a patch management policy for all control systems.
- Establish a complete and accurate inventory of agency information systems that includes each TVA control system either as a major application, or as a minor application to a general support system.
- Categorize and assess the risk of all control systems.
- Update the transmission control system risk assessment to include the risk associated with vulnerabilities identified during security testing and evaluations and self-assessments.

- Revise TVA information security policies and procedures to specifically mention their applicability to control systems.
- Ensure that any division-level information security policies and procedures established to address industry regulations or guidance are consistent with, refer to, and are fully integrated with TVA corporate security policy and federal guidance.
- Revise the intergroup agreements between TVA's Transmission and Reliability Organization and its fossil and hydroelectric business units to explicitly define cyber security roles and responsibilities.
- Revise TVA patch management policy to clarify its applicability to control systems and network infrastructure devices, provide guidance to prioritize vulnerabilities based on criticality of IT resources, and define situations where it would be appropriate to upgrade or downgrade a vulnerability's priority from that given by industry standard sources.
- Finalize draft TVA physical security standards.
- Complete system security plans that cover all control systems in accordance with NIST guidance and include all information required by NIST in security plans, such as the FIPS 199 category and the certification and accreditation status of connected systems.
- Enforce a process to ensure that employees who do not complete required security awareness training cannot access control system-specific networks.
- Ensure that all designated employees complete role-based security training and that this training includes relevant technical topics.
- Develop and implement a TVA policy to ensure that periodic (at least annual) assessments of control effectiveness use NIST SP 800-53A for major applications and general support systems.
- Perform assessments of control effectiveness following the methodology in NIST SP 800-53A.
- Develop and implement remedial action plans for all control systems.
- Include the results of inspector general assessments in the remedial action plan for the transmission control system.
- Finalize the draft agencywide cyber incident response procedure.
- Document backup procedures at all control system facilities.

In a separate report designated "Limited Official Use Only,"[30] we are also making 73 recommendations to the Chief Executive Officer of TVA to address weaknesses in information security controls.

[30] GAO-08-459SU.

Agency Comments and Our Evaluation

In written comments on a draft of this report, the Executive Vice President of Administrative Services for TVA agreed on the importance of protecting critical infrastructures and described several actions TVA has taken to strengthen information security for control systems, such as centralizing responsibility for cyber security within the agency. The Executive Vice President concurred with all 19 recommendations in this report and provided information on steps the agency was taking to implement the recommendations. A copy of the agency's response is included in appendix II.

Additionally, in a meeting with GAO officials, TVA officials expressed concerns about the level of detail in this report. Based on that meeting and subsequent discussions with agency officials, we have modified the wording in this report to address the agency's concerns. The agency also provided technical comments that we have incorporated where appropriate.

We are sending copies of this report to OMB, the TVA Inspector General and other interested parties. We will also make copies available to others upon request. In addition, the report will be available at no charge on the GAO Web site at http:www.gao.gov.

If you have any questions on matters discussed in this report, please contact Gregory Wilshusen at (202) 512-6244 or Nabajyoti Barkakati (202) 512-4499, or by e-mail at wilshuseng@gao.gov and barkakatin@gao.gov. Contact points for our Offices of Congressional Relations and Public Affairs may be found on the last page of this report. GAO staff who made major contributions to this report are listed in appendix III.

Gregory C. Wilshusen
Director, Information Security Issues

Nabajyoti Barkakati
Acting Chief Technologist

List of Requesters

The Honorable Joseph I. Lieberman
Chairman
The Honorable Susan M. Collins
Ranking Member
Committee on Homeland Security and Governmental Affairs
United States Senate

The Honorable Jim Langevin
Chairman
The Honorable Michael T. McCaul
Ranking Member
Subcommittee on Emerging Threats, Cybersecurity, and
Science and Technology
Committee on Homeland Security
House of Representatives

The Honorable Sheila Jackson-Lee
Chairwoman
The Honorable Daniel E. Lungren
Ranking Member
Subcommittee on Transportation Security and Infrastructure Protection
Committee on Homeland Security
House of Representatives

Appendix I: Objective, Scope, and Methodology

The objective of our review was to determine if the Tennessee Valley Authority (TVA) has effectively implemented appropriate information security practices for the control systems used to operate its critical infrastructure. We conducted our review using our Federal Information System Controls Audit Manual,[31] a methodology for reviewing information system controls that affect the confidentiality, integrity, and availability of computerized data. We focused our work on the control systems located at six TVA facilities. These facilities were selected to provide a cross-section of the variety of control systems by type of generation facility (coal, combustion turbine, hydroelectric, and nuclear) and function (generation and transmission).

To evaluate the effectiveness of TVA's information security practices, we conducted tests and observations using federal guidance, checklists, and vendor best practices for information security. Where federal requirements or guidelines, including National Institute of Standards and Technology (NIST) guidance, were applicable, we used them to assess the extent to which TVA had complied with specific requirements. Specifically, we used NIST guidance for the security of federal information systems.[32] For example, we

- analyzed the password hashing implementation used for identification and authentication;
- evaluated and reviewed the complexity and expiration of passwords on servers to determine if strong password management was enforced;
- examined user and application system authorizations to determine whether they had more permissions than necessary to perform their assigned functions;
- analyzed system configurations to determine whether sensitive data were being encrypted;
- observed whether system security software was configured to log successful system changes;
- inspected key servers, workstations, and network infrastructure devices to determine whether critical patches had been installed or were up-to-date;

---

[31] GAO, *Federal Information System Controls Audit Manual*, GAO/AIMD-12.19.6 (Washington, D.C.: January 1999).

[32] See, for example, NIST, *Recommended Security Controls for Federal Information System*, SP 800-53, Revision 2 (Gaithersburg, Md.: December 2007).

- tested and observed physical access controls to determine if computer facilities and resources were being protected from espionage, sabotage, damage, and theft; and
- synthesized the information obtained about networks and applications to develop an accurate understanding of overall network and system architecture.

The Federal Information Security Management Act of 2002 (FISMA) establishes key elements of an effective agencywide information security program. We evaluated TVA's implementation of these key elements by

- reviewing TVA's system inventory to determine whether it contained an accurate and comprehensive list of control systems;
- analyzing risk assessments for key TVA systems to determine whether risks and threats were documented;
- examining security plans to determine if management, operational, and technical controls were in place or planned and whether these security plans were updated;
- analyzing TVA policies, procedures, practices, and standards to determine their effectiveness in providing guidance to personnel responsible for securing information and information systems;
- inspecting training records for personnel with significant responsibilities to determine if they received training commensurate with those responsibilities;
- analyzing test plans and test results for key TVA systems to determine whether management, operational, and technical controls were adequately tested at least annually and were based on risk;
- evaluating TVA's process to correct weaknesses and determining whether remedial action plans complied with federal guidance; and
- examining contingency plans for key TVA systems to determine whether those plans had been tested or updated.

To conduct our work, we reviewed and analyzed relevant documentation and held discussions with key security representatives, system administrators, and management officials to determine whether information system controls were in place, adequately designed, and operating effectively. We also reviewed previous reports issued by the TVA Inspector General's Office. We conducted this performance audit from March 2007 to April 2008 in accordance with generally accepted government auditing standards. Those standards require that we plan and perform the audit to obtain sufficient, appropriate evidence to provide a reasonable basis for our findings and conclusions based on our audit objectives. We believe that the evidence obtained provides a reasonable basis for our findings and conclusions based on our audit objectives.

Appendix II: Comments from the Tennessee Valley Authority

Tennessee Valley Authority, 400 West Summit Hill Drive, Knoxville, Tennessee 37902-1401

John E. Long, Jr.
Executive Vice President
Administrative Services

May 14, 2008

Mr. Gregory C. Wilshusen, Director
Information Security Issues
U.S. Government Accountability Office
441 G Street, NW
Washington, DC 20548

RE: Revised GAO Draft Public Report -- GAO-08-526 TVA Control Systems Security

Dear Mr. Wilshusen:

We appreciate the opportunity to provide the comments of the Tennessee Valley Authority (TVA) on the subject revised draft of GAO's Public report, which was transmitted to us by GAO on May 13, 2008. These comments replace those comments TVA provided on May 7, 2008, on an earlier draft of the Public report.

TVA agrees with the central premise that preserving the security of our nation's critical infrastructures is essential to ensuring national and economic security and protecting public health and safety.

As a result of the field work on this performance audit which commenced in October 2007, and was completed in February 2008, GAO is making 19 recommendations to TVA in its revised draft Public report. TVA was in the process of addressing 17 of the 19 recommendation areas when the field work on this performance audit began in October 2007, including an Office of the Inspector General/Science Applications International Corporation audit for IT Security Organizational Effectiveness, for which planning began in July 2007, and an agency-wide physical access control project which began in October 2005.

TVA also commenced a number of actions in other recommendation areas while the audit was ongoing. In July 2007, TVA established a new structure for its Information Services organization and by December 2007 had approved plans to centralize all responsibility for IT security in a single, corporate-level function. The implementation of this transition for IT security was completed on February 7, 2008, with the announcement by TVA's Chief Executive Officer of the centralization of TVA-wide cyber security policy, administration, and oversight in a new corporate-level Enterprise IT Security organization.

A specific example of steps being taken by TVA during this same time period was the enlistment of a third-party consultant to perform uninformed and informed penetration

Mr. Gregory C. Wilshusen
Page 2
May 14, 2008

testing of TVA's infrastructure to identify weaknesses and provide recommendations for remediation. As noted in the April 14, 2008 report to TVA from the third-party consultant, "the team was unable to gain access to any of the targeted Process Control Networks." During this testing, TVA did receive immediate alerts from our security perimeter monitoring service and also from some of our key internal monitoring systems. As a consequence of this testing, some weaknesses and areas were identified for improvement and enhancement to strengthen TVA's current defense-in-depth security posture. Remedial steps have already been taken to address those issues.

To memorialize the actions completed or already in process by TVA with respect to specific recommendation areas during the field audit period and to summarize TVA's ongoing action plans for all of the remaining GAO recommendations, please find enclosed Exhibit I, which addresses each of the 19 recommendations in the "Public" report.

We believe that our actions clearly demonstrate TVA's commitment to assuring the security of its critical infrastructures and related information and control systems.

As you are aware, TVA, GAO, and DHS representatives met on May 2 to discuss the certain changes that TVA had requested be made in the earlier version of the draft Public Report. In suggesting those changes, it was TVA's overarching concern that the public disclosure of certain references and examples would unintentionally encourage, and might actually facilitate, efforts by certain types of individuals to try to disrupt or sabotage TVA's critical infrastructure systems by specifically identifying TVA systems, applications, or areas.

Our review of the revised draft Public report provided to us on May 13 indicates that changes have been made by GAO which address TVA's most material concerns. TVA appreciates GAO's willingness to make those changes. If there are any questions, please contact Wayne R. Gildroy, Assistant General Counsel, at 865/632-7361.

Sincerely,

John E. Long, Jr.

John E. Long, Jr.

Enclosure

Exhibit 1

EXHIBIT I

TVA RESPONSES TO GAO RECOMMENDATIONS

PUBLIC REPORT

GAO Recommendations (Public Report)

1. Establish a formal, documented configuration management process for changes to software governing control systems at TVA's hydroelectric and fossil facilities.

   TVA Response: Management agrees. Fossil Power Group (FPG) process development was scheduled prior to GAO field work. Development began during audit and will be complete by July 31, 2008. Procedures for conventional hydro plants for River Operations (RO) are in progress and will be complete by June 30, 2008. Additionally Nuclear Power Group (NPG) has a formal, documented configuration management process in accordance with NRC requirements.

2. Establish a patch management policy for all control systems.

   TVA Response: Management agrees. TVA had a patch management policy in place for its corporate systems prior to the start of GAO's field work. This process was not consistently applied to control systems. As a result of TVA's centralization of all IT security as a corporate-level function on February 7, 2008, this policy has been extended to be agency-wide including control

Exhibit 1

systems. A cross organizational task team to evaluate the patch management process has been formed and objectives have been drafted. Appropriate actions will be implemented with a target completion date of December 31, 2008.

3. Establish a complete and accurate inventory of agency information systems as required by FISMA that includes each TVA control system either as a major application, or as a minor application to a general support system.

   TVA Response: Management agrees. There was a system inventory effort established prior to GAO field work. This effort is being enhanced and will be complete May 30, 2008. A process will be established for assuring the maintenance of a complete and accurate inventory by May 30, 2008. Categorizations for control systems will be completed by September 30, 2008.

4. Categorize and assess the risk of all control systems.

   TVA Response: Management agrees.

   TVA has an established standard set of security steps. This process, which TVA already had in place prior to GAO field work, was not consistently applied to control systems. With the TVA CEO's February 7, 2008, announcement of the TVA-wide cyber security policy, administration, and oversight centralizing in a new corporate-level Enterprise IT Security organization, TVA will be completing the security categorizations for all control systems by September 30, 2008. Major applications and General Support Systems (GSS) will have appropriate system security plans, risk assessments, and security test and evaluation steps developed with a targeted completion date of September 30, 2009.

5. Update the transmission control system risk assessment to include the risk associated with vulnerabilities identified during security testing and evaluations and self assessments.

   TVA Response: Management agrees. This was completed April 23, 2008.

Page 2 GAO-08-526 TVA Control Systems Security

Exhibit 1

6. Revise TVA information security policies and procedures to specifically mention their applicability to control systems.

   TVA Response: Management agrees. Communication Practice 1, Business Practice 29, and Computer Security and Privacy Incident Response policy / procedure were issued May 5, 2008.

7. Ensure that any division-level information security policies and procedures established to address industry regulations or guidance are consistent with, refer to, and are fully integrated with TVA corporate security policy and federal guidance.

   TVA Response: Management agrees. Power System Operations (PSO) procedures with references that were specifically mentioned in the report were issued May 2, 2008. Nuclear Power Group (NPG) procedures with references that were specifically mentioned in the report were issued April 30, 2008. Additionally, conventional hydro's are in progress and will be updated by June 30, 2008 and Raccoon Mountain by December 31, 2008.

8. Revise the intergroup agreements between TVA's Transmission and Reliability Organization and its fossil and hydroelectric business units to explicitly define cyber security roles and responsibilities.

   TVA Response: Management agrees. Information Services Enterprise IT Security has responsibility for agency-wide cyber security management and administration on all TVA cyber assets. Revisions to agreements are in progress. The Transmission Reliability Organization (TRO) will complete an interconnection service agreement (ISA) with FPG, RO, and NPG to define cyber security roles and responsibilities by June 30, 2008. The ISA documents will reference the intergroup agreements and will be added to the intergroup agreements on their next revision. TRO will follow EITS guidance to ensure alignment with TVA-wide governance.

9. Revise TVA patch management policy to clarify its applicability to control systems and network infrastructure devices; provide guidance to prioritize vulnerabilities based on criticality of IT resources; and define situations where it would be appropriate to

Page 3 GAO-08-526 TVA Control Systems Security

Exhibit 1

upgrade or downgrade a vulnerability's priority from that given by industry standard sources.

TVA Response: Management agrees. TVA had a patch management policy in place for its corporate systems prior to the start of GAO's field work. This process was not consistently applied to control systems. As a result of TVA's centralization of all IT security as a corporate-level function on February 7, 2008, this policy has been extended to be agency-wide including control systems. A cross organizational task team to evaluate the patch management process has been formed and objectives have been drafted. Appropriate actions will be implemented with a target completion date of December 31, 2008.

10. Finalize draft TVA physical security standards.

    TVA Response: Management agrees. TVA physical security standards will be issued May 9, 2008.

11. Complete system security plans that cover all control systems in accordance with NIST guidance and include all information required by NIST in security plans, such as the FIPS 199 category and the certification and accreditation status of connected systems.

    TVA Response: Management agrees.

    TVA has an established standard set of security steps. This process, which TVA already had in place prior to GAO field work, was not consistently applied to control systems. With the TVA CEO's February 7, 2008, announcement of the TVA-wide cyber security policy, administration, and oversight centralizing in a new corporate-level Enterprise IT Security organization, TVA will be completing the security categorizations for all control systems by September 30, 2008. Major applications and General Support Systems (GSS) will have appropriate system security plans, risk assessments, and security test and evaluation steps developed with a targeted completion date of September 30, 2009.

12. Enforce a process to ensure that employees who do not complete required security awareness training cannot access control system-specific networks.

Exhibit 1

TVA Response: Management agrees. A cross organizational task team to evaluate enforcement options has been formed and objectives have been drafted. Implementation of compensatory controls such as logs will be completed by September 30, 2008.

13. Ensure that all designated employees complete role-based security training and that this training includes relevant technical topics.

    TVA Response: Management agrees. An improvement plan has been developed and is in progress. This plan will be implemented by July 31, 2008. This plan was previously provided to the GAO audit team.

14. Develop and implement a TVA policy to ensure that periodic (at least annual) assessments of control effectiveness use NIST SP 800-53A for major applications and general support systems.

    TVA Response: Management agrees. IT Security Procedure - Security Test and Evaluation was issued on May 7, 2008.

15. Perform assessments of control effectiveness following the methodology in NIST SP 800-53A.

    TVA Response: Management agrees.

    TVA has an established standard set of security steps. This process, which TVA already had in place prior to GAO field work, was not consistently applied to control systems. With the TVA CEO's February 7, 2008, announcement of the TVA-wide cyber security policy, administration, and oversight centralizing in a new corporate-level Enterprise IT Security organization, TVA will be completing the security categorizations for all control systems by September 30, 2008. Major applications and General Support Systems (GSS) will have appropriate system security plans, risk assessments, and security test and evaluation steps developed with a targeted completion date of September 30, 2009.

16. Develop and implement remedial action plans for all control systems.

    TVA Response: Management agrees.

Exhibit 1

TVA has an established standard set of security steps. This process, which TVA already had in place prior to GAO field work, was not consistently applied to control systems. With the TVA CEO's February 7, 2008, announcement of the TVA-wide cyber security policy, administration, and oversight centralizing in a new corporate-level Enterprise IT Security organization, TVA will be completing the security categorizations for all control systems by September 30, 2008. Major applications and General Support Systems (GSS) will have appropriate system security plans, risk assessments, and security test and evaluation steps developed with a targeted completion date of September 30, 2009.

17. Include the results of inspector general assessments in the remedial action plan for the transmission control system.

    TVA Response: Management agrees. Results were added and closed out on the remedial action plan by TRO on April 25, 2008.

18. Finalize the draft agency-wide cyber incident response procedure.

    TVA Response: Management agrees. The Computer Security and Privacy Incident Response policy / procedure was issued May 5, 2008.

19. Document backup procedures at all control system facilities.

    TVA Response: Management agrees. RO procedures are in progress and will be completed by June 30, 2008 for conventional hydro. Raccoon Mountain will be completed by December 31, 2008. NPG to complete by September 30, 2008. FPG backup procedures will be complete by August 31, 2008.

Page 6 GAO-08-526 TVA Control Systems Security

Appendix III: GAO Contacts and Staff Acknowledgments

GAO Contacts

Gregory C. Wilshusen, (202) 512-6244, wilshuseng@gao.gov

Nabajyoti Barkakati, (202) 512-4499, barkakatin@gao.gov

Staff Acknowledgements

In addition to the individuals named above, Nancy DeFrancesco and Lon Chin, Assistant Directors; Angela Bell; Bruce Cain; Mark Canter; Heather Collins; West Coile; Kirk Daubenspeck; Neil Doherty; Vijay D'Souza; Nancy Glover; Sairah Ijaz; Myong Kim; Stephanie Lee; Lee McCracken; Duc Ngo; Sylvia Shanks; John Spence; and Chris Warweg made key contributions to this report.

GAO's Mission

The Government Accountability Office, the audit, evaluation, and investigative arm of Congress, exists to support Congress in meeting its constitutional responsibilities and to help improve the performance and accountability of the federal government for the American people. GAO examines the use of public funds; evaluates federal programs and policies; and provides analyses, recommendations, and other assistance to help Congress make informed oversight, policy, and funding decisions. GAO's commitment to good government is reflected in its core values of accountability, integrity, and reliability.

Obtaining Copies of GAO Reports and Testimony

The fastest and easiest way to obtain copies of GAO documents at no cost is through GAO's Web site (www.gao.gov). Each weekday, GAO posts newly released reports, testimony, and correspondence on its Web site. To have GAO e-mail you a list of newly posted products every afternoon, go to www.gao.gov and select "E-mail Updates."

Order by Mail or Phone

The first copy of each printed report is free. Additional copies are $2 each. A check or money order should be made out to the Superintendent of Documents. GAO also accepts VISA and Mastercard. Orders for 100 or more copies mailed to a single address are discounted 25 percent. Orders should be sent to:

U.S. Government Accountability Office
441 G Street NW, Room LM
Washington, DC 20548

To order by Phone:	Voice:	(202) 512-6000
	TDD:	(202) 512-2537
	Fax:	(202) 512-6061

To Report Fraud, Waste, and Abuse in Federal Programs

Contact:

Web site: www.gao.gov/fraudnet/fraudnet.htm
E-mail: fraudnet@gao.gov Automated answering system: (800) 424-5454 or (202) 512-7470

Congressional Relations

Ralph Dawn, Managing Director, dawnr@gao.gov, (202) 512-4400 U.S. Government Accountability Office, 441 G Street NW, Room 7125 Washington, DC 20548

Public Affairs

Chuck Young, Managing Director, youngc1@gao.gov , (202) 512-4800 U.S. Government Accountability Office, 441 G Street NW, Room 7149 Washington, DC 20548

SUBJECT INDEX

Department of Homeland Security

Energy Security

Government Accountability Office (GAO) Reports

Doc/Pg

Legislation – Federal

National Security – Threats to

Senate Homeland Security and Governmental Affairs Committee

www.ingramcontent.com/pod-product-compliance
Ingram Content Group UK Ltd.
Pitfield, Milton Keynes, MK11 3LW, UK
UKHW051047150926
475595UK00005B/167

9 780195 382983